Bridging Traditions

Demystifying Differences Between Sephardic and Ashkenazic Jews

מגיד
MAGGID OUPRESS

Haim Jachter

BRIDGING TRADITIONS

DEMYSTIFYING DIFFERENCES BETWEEN SEPHARDIC AND ASHKENAZIC JEWS

OU Press
Maggid Books

Bridging Traditions
Demystifying Differences Between Sephardic and Ashkenazic Jews

First Edition, 2021

OU Press
An imprint of the Orthodox Union
11 Broadway, New York, NY 10004
www.oupress.org

Maggid Books
An imprint of Koren Publishers Jerusalem Ltd.

POB 8531, New Milford, CT 06776-8531, USA
& POB 4044, Jerusalem 9104001, Israel
www.maggidbooks.com

Cover art: Baklava image: Newfabrika – Freepik.com

The publication of this book was made possible
through the generous support of *The Jewish Book Trust.*

ISBN 978-1-59264-574-9, *hardcover*

Printed and bound in the United States

In Loving Memory and Honor of

Albert Allen

אברהם בן סלחא ע"ה

Mr. Albert Allen was born in Cairo, Egypt, and was dedicated to supporting and furthering Jewish causes. A founding member and gabbai of the Sephardic Minyan of Englewood, NJ, he was also involved in many other Jewish organizations including Yeshiva University, Yeshiva of North Jersey, Congregation Ahavath Torah of Englewood, NJ, and the Jewish Outreach Network. His endeavors were conducted with warmth, wisdom and generosity. He is greatly missed by his family and all who came in contact with him.

Dedicated by

The Allen Family

Charles and Julie Fleischner

Scott and Kelly Lichtenstein

In Loving Memory and Honor of

Sandra D. Bodenheimer
רוחמה סיילה בת החבר בנימין

and as an expression of gratitude
to the Ribbono Shel Olam.

Dedicated by
The Bodenheimer and Shushan Family

In Loving Memory and Honor of

Harry I. Varon
חזקיה בן יצחק

Beverly R. Varon
רבקה בת רחל

Rachel Varon
רחל בת ריינה

Anne Israel
חנולה בת רבקה

Howard S. Altschul
הלל בן ישראל הלוי

Dedicated by
Heidi and Jack Varon

In Honor of

Congregation Shaarei Orah,
the Sephardic Congregation of Teaneck

An oasis of love for and dedication to Sephardic life that has brought great fulfillment and joy to countless individuals and families. May our beloved Kehillah continue to grow and flourish with Hashem's bountiful Berachot.

Dedicated by

The Allen Family

The Bodenheimer Family

The Varon Family

Rabbi Meir Gavriel Elbaz, Rabbi and Dayan of the Sephardic Congregation of Kew Gardens Hills, NY*

YESHIVA OHEL SIMCHA

SEPHARDIC CONGREGATION OF KEW GARDENS HILLS

MEIR GAVRIEL ELBAZ
RAV AND DAYAN

מאיר גבריאל אלבז
רב ואב"ד

בס"ד

יום חמישי לסדר "ושמתי פדת בין עמי ובין עמך", ר"ח שבט תשפ"א לפ"ק

מכתב ברכה

לכבוד ידיד נפשי כלבבי, ליש ולביא, רב רחומי ורב חביבי, צולל במים אדירים ונקיט מרגניתא בידיה, מר דיינא דנחית לעומקא דדינא, קולע אל המטרה ולא יחטיא, כבוד **הרה"ג מעו"מ רבי חיים ג'קטר נר"ו**, מרא דאתרא דק"ק שערי אורה בטיניק, ניו ג'רסי וראב"ד מקודש דאליזאביט.

באתי בשורות אלו להביע שמחתי וקורת רוחי לרגל יציאתו לאור העולם של ספרו החשוב ***"Bridging Traditions"*** שכולו מלא וגדוש דברי אלהים חיים, הליכות והלכות לבית ישראל, בפרט הבדלי מנהגי הספרדים ועדות המזרח מול אלו של אחינו האשכנזים, ה' עליהם יחיו. וכבר יצאו להרהמ"ח מוניטין בעולם כבר אוריין ובר אבהן, והוא מתעסק רבות במקצועות הקשות של התורה מתוך פלפולא חריפתא והבנה ישרה, כמה לא חלי ולא מרגיש גברא דמריה סייעיה.

וכמעשהו בראשונים כך מעשהו עתה, אסף כעמיר גורנה שיטות הראשונים והאחרונים אשר מפיהם אנו חיים בענייני מנהגי בני מזרח ומערב במעגל השנה מתובלים במקורות ונימוקים, דבר דבור על אופניו, לפי גדולי פוסקי ספרד דור אחר דור, ועל צבאם מרן רבינו יוסף קארו זצוק"ל ומשנהו כסף מרן פאר הדור, רבינו עובדיה יוסף זצוק"ל. ובפרט בזה הספר שנכתב בשפה האנגלית כך שרבים יאותו לאורו ויזכו ללמוד ולקיים דבר ה' זו הלכה. ומה גדול כח המנהג שהרי אמרו חז"ל (יבמות קב.) שלעתים, המנהג מבטל הלכה. ועוד כהנה וכהנה מצאנו בש"ס ופוסקים לעמוד על משמר מנהגי עם סגולה, עיין לדוגמא בשו"ת מהרי"ק (שרש ט') בענין דחיית איסור שבות מחמת המנהג עיי"ש.

לא נצרכה אלא לברכה שהרהמ"ח ירום ונשא וגבה מאד ויזכהו צורו שיאריך ימים על ממלכתו ושכל נטיעות שנוטעין ממנו יהיו כמותו, מתוך בריאות איתנה ונהורא מעליא, חפץ ה' בידו יצלח ועליו יציץ וזרח, אכי"ר.

החותם באהבה לכבוד התורה ולומדיה,

מאיר גבריאל אלבז

מאיר גבריאל אלבז

141-41 72ND AVENUE | FLUSHING, NY 11367
718.261.0101

*Editor's Note: The Michtevei Beracha are arranged in alphabetical order according to the English names of the authors.

Rabbi Menachem Genack, CEO of OU Kosher, General Editor of OU Press, and Rabbi of Congregation Shomrei Emunah, Englewood, NJ

Established 1898

Orthodox Union

Union of Orthodox Jewish Congregations of America • איחוד קהילות האורתודוקסים באמריקה

Eleven Broadway • New York, NY 10004-1303 • Tel: 212-563-4000 • Fax: 212-564-9058 • www.ou.org

לכבוד ידידי הרה"ג ר' חיים ג'קל שליט"א

רב דקהל שערי אורה בטינעק נו דזערזי

ראיתי את כתבי שכת"ר עומד להוציא על

ענין מנהג ספרד ועדות המזרח, ולקרוא

בראשונים ואחרונים בענין חילוקי המנהגים

בין מנהג ספרד ומנהג אשכנז, ונפתח ביריעה

רחבה ועמוקה, בלשון צח וברור באנגלית.

ועברתי על הרבה מהעניינים ונהניתי מאוד, והוא

בודאי יהיה לתועלת הרבים, שכל הספר נכתב בטוב

טעם ודעת והקדמות מאירים ובאורים

ויהי רצון שיזכה לברך על המוגמר ויפוצו מעינותיו

חוצה להגדיל תורה ולהאדירה, ורבים יהנו לאורו

בידידות וברכה,

בברכת התורה,

מנחם צבי גנק

ר"ח שבט תשע"ו

Rabbi Shmuel Khoshkerman, Rabbi of Congregation Ner Hamizrach of Atlanta, Georgia

בס"ד

שמואל כאשכראמן
רב דק"ק ספרדים
מחב"ס "מנחת שמואל"
על בעיות אקטואליות
אטלאנטא גא"

Rabbi Shmuel Khoshkeraman

1340 Holly Lane
Atlanta, GA 30329

Home Phone (404) 636-0468
Study (404) 315-9020
Fax (404) 315-8829

ב׳ תמוז תש״ע

הנה ראיתי חיבור נאה ויפה בשם Bridging Traditions אוצר הלכה ומנהג
לספרדים שחיבר ידי״נ הרה״ג רבי חיים ג׳יקטר שליט״א רב בק״ק
שערי תורה, בני ג׳רסי. והסתכלתי בו הרבה ומצאתי הספר שימושי
מאוד לכל אחד ואחד ולא ראיתי ספר כזה בשפה האנגלית שכולם
יכולים להשתמש בזה. והספר הוא לפי מנהג כל עדות הספרדים
והרה״ג הנ״ל השתדל מאוד להביא מקורות לכל המנהגים וההלכות
ובלתי ספק שהנוהגים בו ימצאו בתוכו תועלת גדול בהלכות ומנהגי
הספרדים בלשון קל וצח. ע״כ ראוי מאוד לשבח את כבוד הרב המחבר
שיחי׳ שהוא בכלל מזכי הרבים. ובפרט אך עשה לעצמו שילמדו וידעו
מהו המקור של הרבה מנהגים.
והנני מברך הרב המחבר שליט״א שיזכה לפרסם מעינותיו ברבים
ויזכה לשפע ברכה ונחת.

בברכה
לכבוד התורה ולומדיה
שמואל כאשכראמן

שמואל כאשכראמן
רב דק"ק הספרדים
אטלאנטא, גא'
Atlanta, Georgia
Rabbi S. Khoshkrman

Rabbi Mordechai Lebhar, Rosh Kollel of Los Angeles Intercommunity Kollel*

בס"ד

LINK
CONNECT TO THE REAL THING

Los Angeles Intercommunity Kollel

1453 S. Robertson Blvd • Los Angeles, CA 90035
(310) 470- 5465 • Fax: (310) 421-9136 • www.linkla.org

Dean
Rabbi Asher Brander

Rosh Kollel
Rabbi Mordechai Lebhar

Outreach Director
Rabbi Eli Stern

מכתב ברכה

In great joy, I received from my esteemed friend, Rabbi Haim Jachter *Shlit"a*, member of the Bet Din of Elizabeth, N.J. and Rabbi of Shaari Orah Congregation, his new book, Bridging Traditions. Rabbi Jachter certainly does not need any introduction in the world of halacha and definitely not from me, as his teachings are well-known and respected.

This book fulfills a critical niche in halachic literature in the very unique circumstances that we find ourselves in today. Sephardim are often uninformed in halachic practice, as their exposure to the overwhelming majority of practices is based on the Ashkenazi Poskim. It is thus a significant contribution to the English-speaking Sephardic community that Rabbi Jachter has compiled and elucidated the different halachic issues that are encountered on a day to day basis.

One of the primary misconceptions is that all Sephardim basically share identical customs. This claim obviously stems from a lack of knowledge. Just as it is understood that Hungarian and German Jews have different practices, the same is true for Sephardim. Jews from Middle Eastern countries (*Edut Hamizrach*) have a very different approach to halacha then Jews originating from Spain (and exiled to North Africa, Greece, Turkey) - *Sepharadim.* The common uniter is that all Sephardim follow the *Shulchan Aruch.* However, details may differ based on the degree of Kabbalistic influence, local established customs, and *klalei hapsak - all of which* may account for huge discrepancies in these areas. This book addresses these concerns, and the reader will find clarity in the explanations of the differences between the different *edo*t in this confusing but vital subject.

We thank Rabbi Jachter for bringing to the English readership a true masterpiece on a subject that begs for clarity and elucidation.

Mordechai Lebhar

Tammuz Yahe"l 5780

Los Angeles

*Editor's Note: Rabbi Lebhar's comments on *Bridging Traditions,* which accompanied his *Michtav Beracha,* can be found in Appendix A.

Contents

Bet Kenesset

Tefillin

Birkat Kohanim

Keri'at Hatorah

Berachot

B'rit Mila

Shabbat

Yom Tov

Yamim Nora'im

Sukkot

Pesaḥ

Shavuot

Ḥanukka and Purim

Lag B'Omer

Fast Days, Three Weeks, Nine Days, and Tisha B'Av

Yom HaAtzma'ut

Kashrut

Mezuza

Marriage

Avelut

Monetary Matters

Hilchot Nidda

Sephardic Jewry

Moroccan Jews

Yemenite Jews

Tributes

Acknowledgements

My Sephardic journey began with a summer spent in the HaTikva Quarter of Tel Aviv in 1984 as part of a group of students from Yeshiva University. We engaged in a wide variety of religious outreach activities to the community. During this impactful summer, I was exposed to a wide variety of Sephardic practices, including Yemenite, Syrian, and Iraqi synagogues.

My Sephardic friend Dr. David Serur continued to guide me in Sephardic practice and culture during our many years of *ḥavruta* learning of the *teshuvot* (responsa) of Rav Ovadia Yosef.

Learning Rav Ovadia Yosef's *sefarim* and hearing him speak when he visited Yeshiva University during my years of Rabbinic studies have been life transforming. Rav Ovadia has raised the bar of Torah knowledge in a unique and extraordinary manner. Meeting him in person in July 1993 was an overwhelming experience for me. His intense expression and words are deeply etched in my memory, and I am incredibly grateful for his written authorization to serve as a *get* (Jewish Divorce) administrator.

The major event in my Sephardic journey, however, was being chosen in 2000 to serve as the Rav of the fledgling Congregation Shaarei Orah, the Sephardic Congregation of Teaneck.

Every day is a learning experience at Shaarei Orah, and I am grateful for everything our beloved congregants have taught me. This book consists of some of the many *shiurim* I have delivered over the years at Shaarei Orah. I aspired to transmit much of the energy and excitement surrounding this learning to our readers.

Special mention must be made of Heidi and Jack Varon, who have served as pillars of the Shaarei Orah community for many years. Their steadfast kindness, dedication, and wisdom have built Shaarei Orah into a warm and vibrant congregation where Sephardic life flourishes in the midst of the Teaneck, New Jersey Jewish community. Heidi and Jack have been especially supportive of my writings over the years, and I thank them for their sponsoring the publication of this work. I am honored to dedicate this volume in memory of Heidi's father, Mr. Howard Altshul *z"l*, and Jack's parents, Mr. Harry and Mrs. Rachel Varon *z"l*.

Immediately after assuming the position at Shaarei Orah, I began to seek halachic guidance from my *bet din* colleague and friend Rav Shmuel Khoshkerman of Atlanta's Congregation Ner HaMizrach. Rav Shmuel, in his quiet manner, is a master of Sephardic Halacha and is wise beyond words in his leadership of his congregation, whose makeup is similar to that of Shaarei Orah. I am grateful that Rav Khoshkerman took from his precious time to review this work and add dozens of very important comments. He is truly one of the greatest Sephardic *Rabbanim* in North America.

I am also grateful for the many people whose insights and comments have immeasurably enriched this book. I wish to specifically thank Rav Mordechai Djavaheri and Rav Ike Sultan, two young members of the Kollel at Yeshiva University, for their many and varied insights, which greatly improved the quality of this work. These two young men are of great promise, and we look forward to them emerging as leaders of the Sephardic community in the decades to come *b'ezrat Hashem*. I also thank Rav Jonathan Cohen for his help regarding the chapters on Yemenite Jews.

Rav Ely Allen, with whom I have had the privilege and honor of sharing the Rabbinic position at Shaarei Orah, is also owed much gratitude. Rav Allen has been a constant source of support and encouragement. I am deeply honored that he chose to sponsor this work in memory of his father, Mr. Albert Allen *z"l*.

Dr. Saul Bodenheimer has also been a constant source of encouragement and support. I feel honored that he chose to sponsor this book in honor of his late wife, Mrs. Sandy Bodenheimer *z"l*.

I am grateful to Rabbi Moshe Kinderlehrer, the editor of our esteemed local newspaper *The Jewish Link*, for his unswerving support. He has graciously allotted me a weekly column to share the Torah learning at Shaarei Orah with the broader Jewish community. I also thank *Link* editors Mrs. Elizabeth Kratz and Mrs. Jill Kirsch for their devotion and dedication to publishing a high-quality "Sephardic Corner" column each week at the *Link*. Special mention must be made of the hundreds of readers of the column, who have unceasingly shared kind words of appreciation and encouragement. These columns form the backbone of this book.

The combination of OU Press and Koren Publishers represents the top tier of publications in the Orthodox community. Their meticulous attention to every detail and supreme devotion to excellence live up to their lofty reputations and have exceeded all expectations. It is a pleasure and honor to work with these fine organizations. OU Press under the leadership of Rav Menachem Genack has been involved in this project since the outset. A special debt of gratitude is owed to the OU Press staff, including Rav Simon Posner for shepherding this project from beginning to end, Rav Gad Buchbinder for his extraordinary talented editing, and Debra Bree for her invaluable assistance. Thanks are due as well to Meira Mintz for her editing work on early versions of the manuscript under the supervision of OU Press. The lofty vision of Matthew Miller at the helm of Koren Publishers continues to elevate and inspire the worldwide Orthodox community. It is an honor to work with him once again on this groundbreaking work.

I thank my wife Malca for providing a loving and happy environment in our home. She is the source of the happiness and joy of our home, where our children Bracha and Yisroel (and their son Shmuel David), Binyamin, Chaya Ziporah, Atara, and Hillel grow and flourish, with *Hashem*'s help. My *shiurim* and articles easily flow in abundance due to the joyful environment Malca has created in our home. The accolade Rabbi Akiva bestowed upon his wife, "*Sheli v'shelachem shela hi*," "My learning and your learning is all due to her," applies at least in equal measure to Malca.

May this work serve *l'ilui nishmat* my parents, Ben and Shirley Jachter *a"h*. Although they never had the opportunity to meet their daughter-in-law Malca and their grandchildren, I am certain that they would have been enormously pleased with their complete dedication to Torah and quality character.

May this work serve *l'ilui nishmat* my recently deceased father-in-law, Rav Shmuel Tokayer *zt"l* and a source of comfort and support to my dedicated mother-in-law, Mrs. Chana Tokayer. May *Hashem* extend her much *beracha,* support, and kindness.

Most of all, I thank *Hashem* for fulfilling my dreams to be blessed with a loving spouse and children and to spend a life immersed in holy projects. As a young man, I dreamed of leading a friendly and warm *kehilla,* teaching Torah to teenagers, contributing to *Am Yisrael* as a *dayan,* and publishing valued works of Torah. Thank you *Hashem* for transforming all of these aspirations into reality! Thank you *Hashem* for facilitating such a large and loyal readership, way beyond any dreams I harbored! "*Mah ashiv laHashem kol tagmulohi alai*" (*Tehillim* 116:12) – I am overwhelmed with the enormous gratitude that I owe our Creator.

May it be His Will to continue bestowing all these blessings for many decades to come.

Rabbi Haim Jachter
2 Tevet 5781
Teaneck, New Jersey

Introduction

How interesting! A neighbor related to me that as a youngster living in Brooklyn, New York, whenever he and his Ashkenazic friends visited a Sephardic synagogue for *tefilla,* their reaction was, "How interesting!" When his Sephardic friends would visit an Ashkenazic *shul,* the reaction was the same: "How interesting!"

It is my hope that readers from both Sephardic and Ashkenazic communities, as they delve into this work and begin to learn and grasp the basis for the practices of the various sections of our Jewish community, will react similarly and proclaim, "How interesting!"

Upon their first exposure to the wide and deep world of Sephardic *posekim,* many people comment about how deep Sephardic Halacha is. How deep are the great debates between Rav Ovadia Yosef and Rav Shalom Messas! How deep are the halachic insights of Rav Ben Tzion Abba Sha'ul, Rav Mordechai Eliyahu, and Rav Ḥayim David HaLevy! How fascinating is the wide variety of customs of the different sub-groupings of Sephardic Jews! This will be your reaction as well, as *Bridging Traditions* presents rich discussions regarding a broad range of common contemporary areas of interest spanning each of the four sections of the *Shulḥan Aruch,* with an eye to the practices of all of the Sephardic communities.

A book like *Bridging Traditions* was not necessary in the Jewish communities of yesteryear, when most Jews could live a lifetime without ever having met Jews of a different background. Ashkenazic and Sephardic Jews had limited interaction until the modern age. The Jew of pre-modern times could manage very well even if he was familiar only with the customs and practices of his specific community.

Nowadays, however, almost all observant families have (or will soon have) at least one couple in their family who are of mixed Sephardic and Ashkenazic heritage. Most Orthodox communities of significant size support both a Sephardic and Ashkenazic *minyan,* or even a full-fledged Sephardic *bet kenesset.* Jews of this generation must therefore be acquainted with the halachic practices and approaches of all Jewish communities.

As a result, I have devoted much attention in *Bridging Traditions* to clarifications as how Sephardic and Ashkenazic Jews should manage their halachic differences when they join together for various occasions. *Bridging Traditions* provides halachic guidance for visiting synagogues, hosting guests on Shabbat and Pesaḥ, roommates with varying practices, weddings, *sheva berachot, b'rit mila,* and much more. Both Sephardic and Ashkenazic readers will emerge from reading this book fortified with the knowledge of how to act appropriately in these situations.

The goal of *Bridging Traditions* is to broaden every Jew's perception of "we" to include all Jews. Every Jew should take special pride in the practices of his particular *shevet*/sub-group. At the same time, however, every Jew should also feel a sense of oneness and unity with all Jews. Readers of *Bridging Traditions* will emerge much more knowledgeable regarding the nuanced differences between the communities and will gain a solid "feel" and savvy regarding the broader perspectives and halachic approaches of the wide variety of Sephardic communities. It is my hope that readers will come away with a tangible feeling that we are *am eḥad* – one nation serving *Hashem,* with variations. The core of the halachic practice of all the Orthodox Jewish communities is identical.

I learned much of what is imparted in these pages over the past twenty years during my service as the Rav of Shaarei Orah, the Sephardic Congregation of Teaneck, and from my Sephardic mentor, Rav Shmuel Khoshkerman of Atlanta's Congregation Ner HaMizrach. Serving as the Rav of Shaarei Orah has been a life-altering experience for me and my family. We have been immeasurably enriched by the wonderful congregants and Torah learning at Shaarei Orah, and I am eager to share this excitement and rich learning with the readers of this work. I hope it will be a life-transforming experience for you as well as you emerge with your *Bridging Traditions*.

Tefilla

Chapter 1

Synagogue Conformity: An Exploration of *Lo Titgodedu*

Does Halacha require that everyone praying in one synagogue follow the same practices? At first glance, it seems that the answer is a resounding yes. However, as we shall see, the matter is not as simple as it first appears.

LO TITGODEDU – SOURCE, CHARACTER, AND SCOPE

The Torah forbids us to cut ourselves in mourning for the dead: "*Lo titgodedu*" (*Devarim* 14:1). *Ḥazal* in turn interpret the command of *lo titgodedu* as teaching, "*Lo ta'asu agudot agudot*" – do not split into different factions (*Yevamot* 13b).[1]

The *Aḥaronim* debate whether the prohibition to separate into different groups is a Biblical or Rabbinic prohibition. The Maharal (*Gur Aryeh, Devarim* 14:1) maintains that it is a Torah-level prohibition, whereas the Ḥida (Rav Yosef David Ḥayim Azulai) argues that it is a Rabbinic edict (*Sha'ar Yosef, Horiyot* 7b).

1. See *Shem MiShemu'el, Parashat Re'eh*, year 5675, for an explanation of the connection between the prohibition to cut oneself in mourning and the prohibition to separate into factions.

Significantly, Rav Moshe Feinstein (*Teshuvot Igrot Moshe, Oraḥ Ḥayim* 4:34) rules that it is a Torah-level prohibition. Rav Ovadia Yosef (*Teshuvot Yeḥaveh Da'at* 4:36), on the other hand, rules in accordance with the Ḥida that it is only a Rabbinic-level prohibition. Thus, it is not surprising that Rav Ovadia takes a more lenient approach to *lo titgodedu* than does Rav Moshe.

The *Rishonim* debate the reason for the prohibition to form different groups. Rashi (*Yevamot* 13b, s.v. *lo ta'asu* and *amina*) explains that when some Jews follow one law and other Jews follow another, it gives the appearance as though there are two Torahs. The Rambam (*Hilchot Avoda Zara* 12:14), in contrast, states that the reason behind this prohibition is to avoid creating conflict among Jews.

Rava and Abaye (*Yevamot* 14a) debate whether the prohibition applies to a situation of "*shetei batei din b'ir aḥat*," two Rabbinic courts in one city, with Rava adopting the lenient view and Abaye adopting the stricter view. Abaye demands halachic conformity from a Jewish community, whereas Rava does not. Rava finds it tolerable to have a Jewish community with more than one halachic authority.

Although the Rambam accepts the opinion of Abaye, the majority of *Rishonim* – including the Rif (*Yevamot* 3b) and the Rosh (*Yevamot* 1:9) – rule in accordance with Rava, following the general rule (*Bava Metzia* 22b) that we follow Rava's rulings except for six specific cases (of which this debate is not one).

Despite the lenient view of the *Rishonim*, however, it seems that one synagogue certainly constitutes a single *bet din*, and a uniform practice should therefore be observed in such a setting. This appears to be the ruling of the Rama (*Oraḥ Ḥayim* 493:3), who writes that disparate observances of the *sefirat ha'omer* mourning period within a single community constitute a violation of *lo titgodedu*.

EXCEPTIONS TO THE RULE – HOMOGENOUS VS. HETEROGENEOUS COMMUNITIES

Rav Moshe Feinstein (*Teshuvot Igrot Moshe, Oraḥ Ḥayim* 1:159) notes that in the United States, Jews from various parts of Europe are all gathered together, and they continue the halachic practices of their former communities. Subsequent generations continue the practices of their parents and grandparents. Thus, in the United States, most communities do not have one unified *minhag* regarding the observance of the mourning during the *sefirat ha'omer* period. According to Rav Moshe, one might argue that American Jewry constitutes a case of a massive "*shetei batei din b'ir aḥat.*"[2] Thus, those who uphold their divergent practices do not violate *lo titgodedu.*

However, in another context (*Teshuvot Igrot Moshe, Oraḥ Ḥayim* 4:34), Rav Moshe does not go as far as to make such a sweeping statement. In fact, he prohibits having two different practices in one *bet kenesset,* such as some people wearing *tefillin* on *Ḥol HaMoed* while others do not (as we discuss at length in chapter 40).

Rav Moshe Sternbuch (*Teshuvot V'Hanhagot* 1:44 and 637), however, presents an argument supporting divergent practices regarding the wearing of *tefillin* on *Ḥol HaMoed,* even in one synagogue. He writes that after the Holocaust, after centuries-old communities with distinct customs were destroyed and survivors gathered and formed new communities, an implicit understanding emerged that everyone would follow the practices of their families and former communities. Thus, Rav Sternbuch countenances divergent practices in such communities regarding wearing *tefillin* on *Ḥol HaMoed.*

This is indeed prevalent in many Ashkenazic synagogues, where it is also common to see unmarried young men of German-Jewish descent wearing a *tallit* before marriage, even though most of the unmarried men in the synagogue do not wear a *tallit.* In such communities, there is an implicit understanding that everyone follows the respective practices of their ancestors.

Rav Sternbuch explains that *lo titgodedu* does not apply to such a situation, since there is communal consent to the divergent practices. This fits with the Rambam's reasoning that it is prohibited to break into factions because of inevitable conflict. In a case of consent, it follows, there is no prohibition of *lo titgodedu.*[3]

According to Rav Sternbuch (and to a lesser extent Rav Moshe), we may distinguish between homogenous and heterogeneous communities. The prohibition of *lo titgodedu* applies only to a homogenous community.

2. In this responsum, Rav Moshe refers to the situation as not just two, but rather many *batei din* in one Jewish community.
3. It appears that we can make such an assertion only if we assume that *lo titgodedu* regarding divergent practices constitutes a Rabbinic prohibition.

Even in a heterogeneous synagogue, however, there may be a blend of conformity and diversity. While different practices are tolerated and accepted regarding certain specific practices, such as wearing *tefillin* on *Ḥol HaMoed* and a *tallit* for unmarried men, there may be an expectation of uniformity with regard to many, or even most, other matters, such as the *nusaḥ* of the *tefilla*.

RAV OVADIA YOSEF'S LIMITATIONS ON *LO TITGODEDU*

In his aforementioned responsum, Rav Ovadia Yosef notes some dramatic limitations on the prohibition of *lo titgodedu*. He argues (based on Radbaz's *Leshonot HaRambam* #11) that *lo titgodedu* does not apply to well-known disagreements, such as those between Bet Hillel and Bet Shamai. Rav Ovadia applies this distinction to the different practices among Sephardic and Ashkenazic Jews. Thus, he permits Sephardic students who are learning in a predominantly Ashkenazic yeshiva to shave and cut their hair between the seventeenth of Tammuz and the week during which Tisha B'Av falls, even though this is not permitted according to Ashkenazic custom.

Rav Ovadia argues that this difference in practice should not lead to great discord, since it is well-known that Sephardic Jews follow the *Shulḥan Aruch* regarding this issue while Ashkenazim follow the Rama (*Oraḥ Ḥayim* 551:3). The assertion that divergent Ashkenazic and Sephardic customs do not violate *lo titgodedu* is a recurring theme in Rav Ovadia's writings. (See, for example, *Teshuvot Yabia Omer* 4: *Even HaEzer* 13; 5: *Oraḥ Ḥayim* 37:4 and *Yoreh De'ah* 3; and 6: *Oraḥ Ḥayim* 10.)

Furthermore, Rav Ovadia accepts the view of Rav Mordechai Benet (*Teshuvot Parashat Mordechai, Oraḥ Ḥayim* 4), who rules that in the case of divergent practices that stem from ancient disputes, *lo titgodedu* does not apply even when both practices are observed simultaneously in the same *bet kenesset*. In other words, Rav Ovadia rules that we extend Rava's tolerance of *shetei batei din b'ir aḥat* to accepting two *batei din* even in one yeshiva and in one synagogue.

Rav Ovadia applied this approach in practice. Rav Shmuel Khoshkerman vividly recalls Rav Ovadia's visit to Baltimore's Yeshivas Ner Yisroel in the 1980s. Rav Khoshkerman was among a large group of young Jews who had escaped from Iran and were separated from their parents for many years; Ner Yisroel took in many of these students.[4] When Rav Ovadia was given the honor of the third *aliya* to the Torah, he recited the *berachot* in full accordance with Sephardic pronunciation and text.[5] In conformity with Sephardic practice, he even recited *Kaddish* after his *aliya* (unlike the Ashkenazic practice, in which the *ba'al korei* recites this *Kaddish*), once again in complete conformity with the Sephardic pronunciation and text.

Moreover, Rav Khoshkerman reports that the great Rosh Yeshiva of Ner Yisroel, Rav Yaakov Yitzḥak Ruderman, instructed the Sephardic students to follow all Sephardic customs while they prayed together in the yeshiva's (Nusaḥ Ashkenaz) *minyan*.

RAV MOSHE FEINSTEIN VS. RAV OVADIA YOSEF

When I reported Rav Ruderman's ruling to Rav Hershel Schachter, he reacted with surprise. Rav Schachter remarked that Rav Ruderman should have instructed the Sephardic Talmidim to make a separate *minyan*. He noted that this is what was done when Moroccan students began attending the Mirrer Yeshiva in the 2000s.

Rav Schachter follows the approach of Rav Moshe Feinstein (*Teshuvot Igrot Moshe, Oraḥ Ḥayim* 2:23), who rules that when praying in a synagogue whose *nusaḥ* differs from one's own, one should pray in conformity with the *tzibbur*'s *nusaḥ* with regard to the portions of *tefilla* that are ordinarily said out loud.[6]

Although Rav Moshe prohibits even praying *Pesukei D'Zimra* in accordance with one's own *nusaḥ* in such a case, as it may be said aloud, Rav Schachter permits it. He argues that since it is common to recite *Pesukei D'Zimra* quietly in Modern Orthodox synagogues, it is permissible to quietly recite this portion of *tefilla* in accordance with one's own *nusaḥ*.

Thus, Rav Schachter rules that an Ashkenazic Jew who prays in a Sephardic *bet kenesset* should use an Ashkenazic *siddur* and pray in accordance

---

4. Quite a number of these young Persian Jews who learned for many years at Ner Yisroel later emerged as significant Rabbinic leaders in the Sephardic community and beyond.
5. Indeed, Rav Yitzḥak Yosef rules that this is the proper practice for a Sephardic Jew who receives an *aliya* in an Ashkenazic *bet kenesset*; see Rav Yonatan Nacson, *MiMizraḥ UmiMa'arav*, p. 273.
6. Rav Mordechai Willig told me that he also subscribes to Rav Moshe's approach.

with Ashkenazic practice, except for the portions of *tefilla* that are said out loud, such as *Kaddish* and *Kedusha.*

Rav Schachter permits an Ashkenazic Jew visiting a Sephardic synagogue to use a Sephardic *siddur* and to pray in complete conformity with the Sephardic *tefilla* if he would otherwise find it confusing. I advise most Ashkenazic Jews to follow this in practice, because experience indicates that using an Ashkenazic *siddur* in a Sephardic synagogue leads to considerable confusion.[7]

In contrast to Rav Moshe and Rav Schachter, Rav Ovadia Yosef (*Teshuvot Yeḥaveh Da'at* 4:36) adopts a dramatically more narrow definition of *lo titgodedu.* He urges Sephardic Jews praying in an Ashkenazic congregation to completely adhere to Sephardic practice.[8] He even goes as far as to say that a Sephardic mourner should recite *Kaddish* in conformity with the Sephardic text even when praying in an Ashkenazic congregation (*Yalkut Yosef, Oraḥ Ḥayim* 56:25)![9]

RAV OVADIA'S EXCEPTIONS

Even Rav Ovadia, however, sets limits about deviating from the practices of one's host synagogue. For example, he rules that a Sephardic Jew should stand for *Kaddish* when praying with Ashkenazim (*Teshuvot Yeḥaveh Da'at* 3:4).[10] He also rules that a *kehilla* should adopt a uniform manner of performing the *na'anuim* of the *arba minim* on Sukkot (*Ḥazon Ovadia, Sukkot* 353). Finally, he urges one to wear *tefillin* on Tisha B'Av in the afternoon when visiting a congregation where this is the prevailing *minhag* (*Ḥazon Ovadia, Daled Ta'aniot,* p. 370 in the *bi'urim*).

Rav Ovadia does not establish a guiding principle as to when to permit or forbid deviation from a congregation's prevailing *minhag.* It seems,

7. An exception would be one who is exceptionally proficient in both Ashkenazic and Sephardic *nusaḥ.*
8. Rav Shalom Messas (*Teshuvot Shemesh U'Magen* 3: *Oraḥ Ḥayim* 24) concurs. Rav Shlomo Amar (*Teshuvot Shema Shlomo* 2:7) writes that this has emerged as the accepted practice among Sephardic Jews when visiting Ashkenazic synagogues.
9. We discuss this issue at length in chapter 11. Whenever we refer to *Yalkut Yosef* in this volume, we refer to the 5766 version of Rav Yitzḥak Yosef's *Yalkut Yosef, Kitzur Shulḥan Aruch* (unless otherwise noted).
10. Note that *Masechet Derech Eretz Rabba* (ch. 7) specifically instructs one to avoid standing among those who are seated or sitting among those who are standing.

however, that even Rav Ovadia frowns upon divergent practices that irritate congregants. In other words, Rav Ovadia permits different practices when there is perceived permission and consent. In a situation in which such consent is lacking and there is concern for strife and conflict, the concern for *lo titgodedu* emerges.

Put differently, the implicit consent for divergent practices that Rav Sternbuch argues exists in contemporary heterogeneous synagogue settings has its limits. It does not apply when the prevailing community finds the varying practice to be irritating. Having divergent practices regarding *na'anuim* in one *minyan*, for example, is understandably irritating, and the communal consent does not extend to this differing comportment.

Thus, *lo titgodedu* does not apply when there is consent to divergent practice. Absent such consent, however, *lo titgodedu* applies. A community's *posek* must determine which varying behaviors are acceptable and which the community finds offensive.

DIVERGENT SEPHARDIC PRACTICES IN A PAN-SEPHARDIC *BET KENESSET*

Rav Shmuel Koshkerman has repeatedly told me that Rav Ovadia's ruling applies to variant Sephardic practices in a pan-Sephardic synagogue (whose members consists of a diverse assembly of Sephardim from a variety of backgrounds), such as Shaarei Orah in Teaneck and Ner Mizrach in Atlanta (where Rav Khoshkerman serves as the Rav). Rav Baruch Gigi told me that this is standard practice in pan-Sephardic congregations in Israel as well.

Accordingly, in a pan-Sephardic synagogue, it is acceptable to have some following the Minhag Yerushalyim to stand for the *Kaddish* prior to *Barechu* on Friday evening while others follow the Moroccan custom to sit. Similarly, at *Minḥa* on a *ta'anit tzibur*, it is acceptable for some men to wear *tefillin* while others refrain from doing so (see Rav David Yosef, *Halacha Berura* 38:20).

This would not seem to apply, however, to a homogeneous Sephardic synagogue, a synagogue that practices a specific rite, such as a synagogue designated as a Moroccan, Syrian, Turkish, or Persian *bet kenesset*. Once again, we distinguish between a homogenous and heterogeneous community. As we cited above from Rav Sternbuch, in a heterogeneous community, there is consent for divergence in practice. Even in that case, however, there is room to draw limits on certain issues, especially those for which there is a consensus among the various Sephardic communities.[11]

CONCLUSION

When Rav Shlomo Amar visited Congregation Shaarei Orah in August 2017, I asked him whether we are mandated to maintain one uniform practice in a Sephardic *bet kenesset* or if divergent practices may be countenanced. He replied that it is preferable to maintain one *minhag,* but if the synagogue rabbi feels it is in the best interest of the congregation to tolerate divergent Sephardic practices, he may elect to do so. Thus, a synagogue may choose to define itself as homogenous or heterogeneous.

Returning to the question we posed at the beginning of this chapter as to whether the Halacha requires everyone praying in one synagogue to follow the same practices – the answer is that it depends on the character of the synagogue and the particular issue at hand. Sometimes, the *lo titgodedu* principle demands conformity, while at other times divergence is acceptable.

---

11. The universally accepted Sephardic practice to refrain from wearing *tefillin* on *Ḥol HaMoed* may be one such example.

Chapter 2

Kaddish – Sitting or Standing?

Before we embark on an analysis of a significant difference between Sephardic and Ashkenazic practice during *tefilla,* we must emphasize that the commonalities between these two groups are dramatically greater than their differences. *Tefilla* is an excellent case in point. Although the melodies and pronunciation differ quite notably, the content and structure of the Sephardic and Ashkenazic *siddurim* are essentially identical. The differences lie only in nuance.

One of the most – if not the most – prominent difference relates to whether to stand or sit for *Kaddish.* Sephardim sit for almost all *Kaddishim,* whereas the Ashkenazic custom is to stand.

THREE SOURCES FOR THE ASHKENAZIC PRACTICE TO STAND FOR *KADDISH*

The Rama (*Darchei Moshe,* end of *Oraḥ Ḥayim* 56) records the Ashkenazic custom to stand for *Kaddish.* He cites the Talmud Yerushalmi as the source for this practice. The Yerushalmi, in turn, cites the unlikely role model of Eglon, the king of Moav, who stood when Ehud ben Gera announced that he came bearing a message of *Hashem* to him (*Shofetim* 3:20). The Yerushalmi states that, following this example, we should stand for "*Amen yehei shemeh rabba,"* as well as any other *devarim shebekedusha* (special prayers that require a *minyan,* such as *Kedusha* and *Barechu*).

The *Maḥatzit HaShekel* (*Oraḥ Ḥayim* 56) notes that the Talmud Bavli (*Sanhedrin* 60a) echoes a similar theme. The *gemara* discusses how testimony is presented regarding the regrettable situation of a *megadef,* a blasphemer who has insulted *Hashem* by cursing Him. The *mishna* states that the most prominent of the witnesses stand when they state the name of *Hashem* that was cursed. The judges, in turn, stand and rip their clothes. The *gemara* states that the source for standing when *Hashem*'s name is mentioned is none other than Eglon, the king of Moav. If the non-Jewish King Eglon was respectful and stood when he heard the name of *Hashem,* the *gemara* argues, how much more so must we stand!

Rav Shlomo Kluger (*Teshuvot Shenot Ḥayim* 81) cites yet another source for the Ashkenazic practice to stand during *Kaddish*. He marshals Bilaam's instruction to Balak, "*Kum Balak u'shema,*" "Stand, Balak, and listen" (*Bemidbar* 23:18), Bilaam's response to Balak's inquiry as to what *Hashem* had stated. The *midrash* (*Bemidbar Rabba* 20:20) states that based on this, we are not permitted to sit when the words of *Hashem* are proclaimed.

THE SEPHARDIC PRACTICE TO SIT FOR *KADDISH*

In light of these three impressive sources – the Yerushalmi, the Bavli, and a *midrash* – it seems difficult to comprehend the Sephardic practice to sit for *Kaddish*.

In order to understand this, we must first note the profound impact the Ari z"l had on Sephardic practice (and on Ḥassidic practice as well). Those who are not well-versed in Sephardic practices assume that the Rambam and Rav Yosef Karo (reverently referred to by Sephardim as Maran, our master) are the two central and exclusive pillars of Sephardic Halacha. While the Rambam and Maran certainly are most important, however, the contribution of the Ari z"l is enormous as well.

Indeed, there are a number of practices regarding which nearly all Sephardim follow the Ari z"l instead of Maran, including the arrangement of the *seder* plate, the blowing of shofar during the silent *Amida* of *Mussaf* on Rosh Hashana, and the order of the *na'anuim* of the *arba minim* on Sukkot. To illustrate the esteem in which Sephardim hold the Ari z"l, consider the *bakasha* (plea) many Sephardic Jews recite before blowing the shofar: The one blowing the shofar asks *Hashem* to consider it as though everyone has in mind the proper *kavanot* (mystical intentions) of *teki'at* shofar of Moshe Rabbenu, Rabbi Shimon Bar Yoḥai, and Rav Yitzḥak Luria (the Ari z"l). It is breathtaking that the Ari z"l is included in the same grouping as Moshe Rabbenu and Rabbi Shimon bar Yoḥai!

With this perspective, we can understand how Sephardim follow the practice of the Ari z"l (reported by his eminent student Rav Ḥayim Vital, *Sha'ar HaKavanot, Derush HaKaddish,* p. 16) to sit during *Kaddish.*

Rav Ḥayim Vital testifies that the Ari z"l told him, shockingly, that the Yerushalmi cited by the Rama is not authentic! The *Magen Avraham,* a major Ashkenazic authority who was greatly influenced by the Ari z"l, explains the basis for this astounding claim. He notes that the *pasuk* in *Shofetim* records that Ehud used the name "*Elokim*" in communicating with Eglon, whereas the Yerushalmi cited by the Rama quotes the *pasuk* using the name of *Hashem.* In addition, the Yerushalmi presents the *pasuk* as saying that Ehud commanded Eglon to stand, whereas the *pasuk* really states that Eglon stood of his own accord. An authentic passage in the Yerushalmi, explains the *Magen Avraham,* would never misquote a *pasuk*!

EXPLAINING THE SEPHARDIC CUSTOM

The *Ḥatan Sofer* (vol. 2, p. 35) defends the Sephardic custom based on a *gemara* (*Berachot* 34b) regarding bowing during the silent *Amida.* The *gemara* states that an ordinary individual bows at the beginning and conclusion of the *berachot* of *Avot* and *Hoda'ah* (*Modim*), a *Kohen Gadol* does so at the beginning and end of each *beracha,* and a king must remain in the bowing position throughout the entire *Amida.* Rashi (ad loc.) explains that the greater one's stature, the more he must express humility. This is reflected in the king's unique requirement to write a *sefer Torah* and carry it with him wherever he goes (*Devarim* 17:19–20). The Torah states that this requirement is intended to prevent the king from becoming haughty and to avoid letting his power corrupt him.

Accordingly, the fact that Eglon stood when the message of *Hashem* was delivered does not conclusively prove that everyone must stand when *devarim shebekedusha* are recited. It could be that more humility and respect is expected from a king than from one who is not endowed with such great power.

The same argument can be made with regard to the proof from Balak. Furthermore, the Balak situation was entirely different since, as Rashi explains (*Bemidbar* 23:18), when Balak asked, "What did *Hashem* speak?" he was mocking Bilaam and *Hashem*. In response to the mockery, Bilaam demanded that Balak rise and listen to *Hashem*'s words.

Similarly, it is not necessary to extrapolate from the case of the *megadef* that we must stand for *devarim shebekedusha*. One could argue that standing in such a situation is necessary to compensate for the terrible degradation of *Hashem*'s name in the course of the *bet din*'s hearing of the testimony regarding the cursing of *Hashem*. Thus, there is no conclusive proof to the Ashkenazic practice to stand for *Kaddish*.

Indeed, five of the greatest Sephardic halachic authorities support the Sephardic custom to sit for *Kaddish* – the *Ḥida* (*Tov Ayin* 18:32), Rav Ḥayim Palagi (*Kaf HaḤayim* 13:7), Rav Yosef Ḥayim of Baghdad (*Ben Ish Ḥai, Parashat Vayeḥi*, year 1, #8), Rav Yaakov Ḥayim Sofer (*Kaf HaḤayim* 56:20) and Rav Ovadia Yosef (*Teshuvot Yeḥaveh Da'at* 3:4). The *Mishna Berura* (56:8), on the other hand, while acknowledging the validity of the other opinion, encourages standing for *Kaddish*, and this has become the accepted Ashkenazic practice.

THREE POSSIBLE EXCEPTIONS TO THE SEPHARDIC PRACTICE

There are three situations in which even most Sephardim stand for *Kaddish*. Even the Ari z"l would remain standing for *Kaddish* if he was already standing, such as for the *Kaddish* recited after the completion of the repetition of the *Amida*. Although the Ari z"l did not require standing for *Kaddish*, deliberately sitting during *Kaddish* is regarded as disrespectful.[1] Another exception is the practice of many Sephardic Jews to stand during the *Kaddish* recited before the beginning of *Arvit* on Friday night (Sephardim and those who follow Nusaḥ Sephard recite *Kaddish* before the *Barechu* of *Arvit*).[2] Rav Ḥayim Vital explains in his *siddur* that one should stand for this *Kaddish* because it is at this point that one accepts *tosefet Shabbat* (a

1. Rav Eli Mansour (http://www.dailyhalacha.com/m/halacha.aspx?id=1765) notes: "Unfortunately, many people rush to sit down before the *ḥazan* begins *Kaddish* so that they can remain seated during the *Kaddish*. This is improper. Since they were already standing, they should remain standing until at least the end of the response of '*yehei shemeh rabba*.'"
2. Moroccan Jews do not stand for this *Kaddish*, as noted by Rav Shalom Messas (*Teshuvot Shemesh U'Magen* 3: *Oraḥ Ḥayim* 78:2). Rav Mordechai Eliyahu (*Siddur*

part of the additional *neshama yetara* that is bestowed upon a person on the advent of Shabbat).

Finally, Rav Ovadia Yosef notes that it is proper for a Sephardi who is praying at an Ashkenazic *bet kenesset* to stand during *Kaddish*. In addition to conforming to *minhag hamakom* (as noted in Chapter 1 on *lo titgodedu*), it seems disrespectful to *Hashem* to exclude oneself from a *kehilla* that is standing in honor of *Hashem*. Conversely, it is appropriate for an Ashkenazi praying at a Sephardic synagogue to follow the custom of the *kehilla* to remain seated for *Kaddish*.

CONCLUSION

Rav Ovadia Yosef concludes about this matter, "*Nehara nehara u'fashteh*," a Talmudic phrase that means that rivers flow at different rates and in their usual places (*Ḥullin* 18b and 57a; see Rashi, ad loc.). Similarly, Jewish communities have slight variances in customs and they should maintain their respective customs.

Kol Eliyahu) agrees with Rav Ovadia regarding this point and instructs Sephardim to stand for this *Kaddish*.

Chapter 3

Ḥochma Bina VaDa'at or De'ah Bina V'Haskel?

It is utterly fascinating to see Jewish history come to life with a mere perusal of the range of *siddurim* in a Sephardic synagogue! It sends chills down my spine simply to see how Jewish history is not relegated, God forbid, to museums or university classes. Rather, it is part of a living and vibrant way of life, with an illustrious past and brilliant future.

Consider the example of the fourth *beracha* of the *Amida*, the prayer for wisdom. In this blessing, do we request, "*ḥochma bina vada'at*," or do we ask for "*de'ah bina v'haskel*"? An examination of the wide range of Sephardic *siddurim* found in a diverse Sephardic congregation – such as Congregation Shaarei Orah, the Sephardic Congregation of Teaneck – reveals that the text in Moroccan and Turkish *siddurim* is "*de'ah bina v'haskel*." In contrast, *siddurim* based on Minhag Yerushalayim and the rulings of Rav Ovadia Yosef, as well as the Syrian *siddurim*, have the text of "*ḥochma bina vada'at*."

ARGUMENTS FOR *DE'AH BINA V'HASKEL*

Compelling arguments may be made for the assertion that "*de'ah bina v'haskel*" represents the original text. The oldest *siddurim* – including the *siddurim* of Rav Amram Gaon and Rav Saadia Gaon, as well as that of the

Rambam – have this version. The work *Divrei Shalom V'Emet* (1:50) offers another compelling proof that this was the original text: On Motza'ei Shabbat, in the *Ata Ḥonantanu* addition to the fourth *beracha* of the *Amida,* all Sephardic *siddurim* include a request for "*mada v'haskel*" or "*mada bina v'haskel,*" and "*mada*" is clearly a variation of "*de'ah,*" not "*ḥochma.*"

ARGUMENTS FOR *ḤOCHMA BINA VADA'AT*

The work *Sha'arei Tefilla* (*Dinei Amida* #5) asserts that the formulation "*ḥochma bina vada'at*" is based on a *pasuk* describing how *Hashem* endowed Betzalel, the chief architect of the *Mishkan,* "*b'ḥochma uv'tevuna uv'da'at*" (*Shemot* 31:3).

The work *Sha'ar Kollel* (14:12) offers another basis for the formula of "*ḥochma bina vada'at,*" noting that the Talmud refers to the fourth *beracha* of the *Amida* as the *beracha* of *Ḥochma* (*Berachot* 33a), *Bina* (*Megilla* 17a), and *Ḥonen HaDa'at* (*Berachot* 33a).

The Kabbalists embraced the formulation of "*ḥochma bina vada'at,*" and it was this version that was incorporated in the Nusaḥ Sephard *siddurim* used by Ḥassidim and those of Ḥassidic ancestry. The most famous proponents of this version are the Ari z"l (*Sha'ar HaKavanot, Derush* 6), the *siddur* of Rav Shalom Sharabi (a great eighteenth century Yemenite Kabbalist who exerted great influence on many *siddurim*), and the *Kaf HaḤayim* of Rav Ḥaim Palagi (15:23).

EXPLAINING THE COMMUNITIES' CUSTOMS

Why is it that Moroccan and Turkish Jews adopted the version of "*de'ah bina v'haskel,*" whereas the Minhag Yerushalayim and Syrian Jews recite, "*ḥochma bina vada'at*"? The reason is that the version of "*de'ah bina v'haskel*" is championed in the classic and authoritative *siddur* of the Avudraham, a late *Rishon* who resided in Spain.

The Spanish expulsion of a large number of Jews who refused to convert to Christianity – referred to as the *megorashim* (expellees) – caused considerable halachic upheaval in the countries to which they relocated. Tension emerged as to which *minhagim* (customs) should be followed, the Spanish *minhagim* of the *megorashim* or the *minhagim* of the original Jewish residents (*toshavim*). In Turkey and much of Morocco, the customs that the *megorashim* brought from Spain emerged as the dominant *minhag.*

Based on the *siddur* of the Avudraham, it appears that the formulation of "*de'ah bina v'haskel*" was the practice in Spain. Thus, in Turkey and most of Morocco, "*de'ah bina v'haskel*" emerged as the prevalent custom. This text had far less impact in Syria and Eretz Yisrael, where the customs of the *megorashim* had less of an effect. Moreover, the teachings of the Ari z"l exerted greatest influence upon Sephardic Jews residing in Eretz Yisrael and its neighboring countries.[1]

Furthermore, "*de'ah bina v'haskel*" is the formulation that appears in the classic Livorno *siddurim*. From the seventeenth until the early twentieth century, Livorno (Leghorn, Italy) was the home of Sephardic prayer book publishers. Since the *siddurim* used in Morocco were printed in Livorno, Moroccan practice follows the Livorno tradition to recite "*de'ah bina v'haskel.*"

In contrast, beginning in the late nineteenth century, other Sephardic communities began using *siddurim* influenced by the Ari z"l, Rav Shalom Sharabi, and the *Ben Ish Ḥai*. These prayer books use the text of "*ḥochma bina vada'at.*" This explains the popularity of the formulation of "*ḥochma bina vada'at*" in many Sephardic communities.

Thus, we see the effect of historical circumstances on the development of Sephardic customs in different parts of the world.

---

1. In addition, it is notable that Moroccan practices are generally less inclined to be influenced by Kabbalistic considerations.

Chapter 4

Machnia Zedim or Machnia Minim

Although we are aware of differences between Ashkenazic and Sephardic *nusaḥ*, many are struck by the wide variety of Sephardic *siddurim* and the nuanced differences among them. A particularly striking example is found in the twelfth *beracha* of the *Amida*.

In the Moroccan, Syrian, and Turkish *siddurim*, the conclusion of this *beracha* is "*shover oyevim umachnia minim*." However, in the *siddurim* that follow the rulings of Rav Ovadia Yosef, the conclusion is "*shover oyevim umachnia zedim*." The Yemenite *siddur* also concludes in this manner.

SUPPORT FOR CONCLUDING WITH THE WORD *MINIM*

The former group opts to conclude with the word "*minim*" because this is the conclusion recommended by the *Ḥida* (*Sefer Kesher Gudal* 17:7). The reason for this is that one must conclude every blessing in a similar manner to the way in which it started (a principle referred to by *Ḥazal* as "*ḥatima me'en petiḥa*"; see *Pesaḥim* 104a). Thus, for example, the blessing of *Ata Kadosh* ends with the words "*haKel hakadosh*," and the blessing of *Refa'enu* ends with the words "*rofeh ḥolei amo Yisrael*." Accordingly, the blessing of *LaMinim V'LaMalshinim* (the Sepharadic version of the

Ashkenazic blessing of *V'Lamalshinim Al Tehi Tikva*) should end with the words "*shover oyevim umachnia minim.*"[1]

Rabbenu Yosef Ḥaim, the author of the *Ben Ish Ḥai*, writes in his *Sefer Ben Yehoyada* (*Berachot* 28a) that a limited proof may be brought from the fact that the author of this blessing was Shmuel HaKatan. The *Ben Ish Ḥai* suggests that Shmuel HaKatan hinted to his name in acronym form at the end of the blessing, as is common in liturgical poetry. The *shin, mem, vav*, and *alef* begin the words, "***Sh**over **o**yevim **u**machnia **m**inim*;" the *lamed* is found in the first word of the blessing, "***La**Minim.*"

SUPPORT FOR CONCLUDING WITH THE WORD *ZEDIM*

Rav Ovadia Yosef disputes this position,[2] arguing in part that it seems far-fetched to think that Shmuel HaKatan would have hinted his name in a text that is intended as a curse upon heretics. We may add that the Talmud Yerushalmi (*Sotah* 9:13) writes that Shmuel HaKatan was given this nickname due to his great humility – "*shemaktin et atzmo*," "because he made himself small." It is difficult to assume that such a humble man would encrypt his name in the *beracha* he composed.

However, the argument of the *Ḥida* still stands. Since one must always end the *beracha* in a text similar to its beginning, the text of "*umachnia minim*" seems to be a more appropriate ending to the blessing that begins "*Laminim velamalshinim.*"

Nevertheless, Rav Ovadia argues that the correct version is indeed "*shover oyevim umachnia zedim.*" He notes that Rav Ḥayim Palagi rules likewise (*Kaf HaḤayim* 15:31) and that this is the custom of the *Mekubalim* in the famous Kabbalistic Bet El Yeshiva in the Old City of Jerusalem.[3]

---

1. Rav Shalom Messas (*Teshuvot Shemesh U'Magen* 3:58:3) rules that the concluding word of this *beracha* should be "*minim*," in light of the fact that the *beracha* is referred to as *Birkat HaMinim* (Rif, *Berachot* 19b). It is notable that according to the Ashkenazi *nusaḥ*, the *beracha* begins with the word "*V'LaMalshinim*" and does not include the word "*LaMinim*."
2. Sources for this section are the arguments referenced in *Yalkut Yosef, Oraḥ Ḥayim* 124: *Nusḥa'ot HaTefilla* 56.
3. This is noted by Rav Amram Aburabiyah in his important work *Nahagu HaAm*, which records Minhag Yerushalayim. Rav Ovadia and Rav Yitzḥak Yosef write that the custom in Jerusalem "in years past" was to conclude with the word "*zedim*."

Rav Ovadia notes that "*umachnia zedim*" is the version quoted in the works of all of the early *Geonim*, such as the *siddurim* of Rav Sa'adia Gaon and Rav Amram Gaon, as well as in the *siddur* of the Rambam (printed at the end of *Sefer Ahava* of the *Mishneh Torah*). Rav Ovadia and his son Rav Yitzḥak cite a large number of *Rishonim* who concur.[4] Moreover, we find in the Talmud Yerushalmi (*Berachot* 4:3) that the proper ending is "*zedim*."[5]

Regarding the *Ḥida*'s point that "*umachnia zedim*" does not match the beginning of the blessing, we can answer that the concluding term "*zedim*" emphasizes that only the deliberate sinners are included in this curse. Thus, only the leading heretics are cursed – not their followers who are misled.[6]

CONCLUSION

Although the ruling of Rav Ovadia Yosef is to conclude with the word "*zedim*," a variety of practices persist. Rav Mordechai Lebhar (*Magen Avot, Oraḥ Ḥayim*, pp. 109–111), as his wont, vigorously defends this dominant practice among Moroccan Jews. He even cites a personal ruling he received from Rav Yosef Shalom Eliashiv that those whose custom is to conclude with the word *minim* should continue to do so, despite the fact that many *Rishonim* support the text that concludes "*zedim*." Rav Mordechai Eliyahu's *siddur* also concludes this *beracha* with "*minim*."

Regarding this fascinating dispute, one must conclude, "*Elu v'elu divrei Elokim ḥayim*." Both options are supported by great *Rabbanim* and have a rich basis to support them. At Congregation Shaarei Orah, the *ḥazan* follows the ruling of Rav Ovadia and concludes with the word "*zedim*."

---

4. Rav Ovadia and Rav Yitzḥak argue that had the Ḥida known about the many *Rishonim* who support the conclusion of "*zedim*," he would have retracted his position. Rav Mordechai Lebhar (*Magen Avot, Oraḥ Ḥayim*, pp. 109–111) counters that it seems unreasonable to make such a claim regarding the *Ḥida*, who, as is well known, made a great effort to be familiar with a very wide variety of *Rishonim* and *Aḥaronim*, especially with regard to the texts to which he was exposed as a result of his extensive travels throughout much of the world.
5. Rav Lebhar counters that the position of the more authoritative Talmud Bavli is not clear regarding the proper conclusion to this *beracha*.
6. This is similar to the statement of the Rambam (*Hilchot Mamrim* 3:1–4) limiting severe punishment to the founding generation of heretical movements, such as the *Tzedukim* and *Kara'im*.

Chapter 5

HaNoten LaYa'ef Ko'aḥ

The *beracha* of *HaNoten LaYa'ef Ko'aḥ* ("Who gives strength to the weak") does not appear in the *gemara*. As a result, Rav Yosef Karo, the preeminent Sephardic halachic authority, rules in the *Shulḥan Aruch* (*Oraḥ Ḥayim* 46:6) that this *beracha* should not be recited among the other *Birkot HaShaḥar*. The Rama, in contrast, records that the widespread custom among Ashkenazim is to recite this *beracha*, and the *Mishna Berura* (46:21) writes that the consensus among Ashkenazic authorities is that the *beracha* should include *Hashem*'s name.

Based on this, an Ashkenazic Rabbinic colleague of mine told his students that Sephardic Jews do not recite the *beracha* of *HaNoten LaYa'ef Ko'aḥ*. The rabbi then consulted me to make sure he was correct. He was shocked to learn that Sephardic Jews (with the exception of Yemenite Jews) do, in fact, recite this *beracha* – against the ruling of Rav Yosef Karo![1]

1. Although Rav Shalom Messas (*Teshuvot Shemesh U'Magen* 1:25) records that the custom in Morocco is to recite this *beracha* without mentioning *Hashem*'s name, Rav Mordechai Lebhar (*Magen Avot, Oraḥ Ḥayim* 46:6) notes that this was the custom only in the Moroccan city of Meknes. In the rest of Morocco, the custom was to recite this *beracha* including the name of *Hashem*. The custom of Amsterdam's Sephardic Jews is to omit the *beracha* of *HaNoten LaYa'ef Ko'aḥ*.

THE REASONING OF RAV YOSEF KARO

This *beracha* is mentioned by the *Tur* (*Oraḥ Ḥayim* 46), as well as a number of other *Rishonim*, including the *Semag* and *Maḥzor Vitry*. Rav Yosef Karo, in his *Bet Yosef* commentary on the *Tur* (s.v. *od beracha aḥat*), disagrees with the *Tur* and wonders how one could possibly use *Hashem*'s name in a *beracha* that is not recorded in the Talmud.[2] Therefore, *Maran* rules in the *Shulḥan Aruch* that one should not recite it.[3] Based on this, the Vilna Gaon and the *Pri Ḥadash* (Rav Ḥizkiya DaSilva, 1656-1695, a major Sephardic halachic authority) also did not recite the *beracha*.[4]

THE INFLUENCE OF THE ARI Z"L

On the other hand, the *Ḥida* (*Tuv Ayin* #7) cites a tradition from the Ari z"l that the *beracha* of *HaNoten LaYa'ef Koaḥ* should be recited, including the mentioning of *Hashem*'s name.[5] Accordingly, the *Ḥida* and the *Ben Ish Ḥai* (year 1, *Parashat Vayeshev* 9) ruled that the *beracha* should be recited with *Hashem*'s name. The *Ḥida* argued that had Rav Yosef Karo known that the Ari z"l ruled to say the *beracha*, he would have retracted his view. Even if Rav Karo would disagree, however, and thereby create an uncertainty with regard to the *halacha*, the *Ḥida* and the *Ben Ish Ḥai* maintain that the general principle of "*safek berachot l'hakel*" (in cases of doubt, we are lenient and do not recite a *beracha*) does not apply to instances in which the Ari z"l would say the *beracha*.[6]

---

2. The *Bi'ur HaGra* cites the Rosh (*Kiddushin* 1:41) as the source for the assertion that we may not recite a *beracha* that does not appear in the Talmud. Interestingly, however, the Rosh elsewhere (*Ketuvot* 1:15) rules that it is acceptable to recite a *beracha* that was instituted in the Geonic era. Rav Ovadia Yosef (*Teshuvot Yeḥaveh Da'at* 4:4) explains that the consensus view among Sephardic *posekim*, such as the *Ḥida* (*Kesher Gudal* 5:23) and the *Ben Ish Ḥai* (year 1, *Parashat Vayeshev* 10), is for women to recite the *beracha* of *She'Asani Kirtzono* without mentioning *Hashem*'s name because this *beracha* not only does not appear the Talmud, it is not even mentioned in the Geonic literature.
3. The *Bet Yosef* also notes that the Rambam does not mention this *beracha*. However, the Avudraham (in his commentary on the weekday *Shaḥarit*) mentions that there are a number of communities that recite this *beracha*, including *Hashem*'s name.
4. Based on the practice of the Gra, Rav Yosef Dov Soloveitchik did not recite this *beracha*; see *Nefesh HaRav*, p. 107.
5. The *Magen Avraham* (46:12) and *Ba'er Hetev* (*Oraḥ Ḥayim* 46:10) also cite the Ari z"l to this effect.
6. This assertion is even more remarkable in light of the *Ben Ish Ḥai*'s statement (year 1, *Parashat Nitzavim* 19) that one should omit a *beracha* in a case of doubt even in

SEPHARDIC PRACTICE

Rav Ovadia Yosef usually prefers to follow the pure halachic approach of *Maran* over the Kabbalistic bent of the Ari z"l, *Ḥida*, and *Ben Ish Ḥai*. Surprisingly, however, Rav Ovadia rules (*Teshuvot Yabia Omer* 2: *Oraḥ Ḥayim* 25:12–13) to say the *beracha*. However, he takes issue with the *Ḥida*'s assumption that Rav Karo would have agreed with the Ari z"l had he known of his opinion.[7] In the view of Rav Ovadia, the *beracha* should be recited because that is the accepted Sephardic *minhag*, as indicated by the fact that almost all Sephardic *siddurim* include the *beracha*. Rav Ovadia writes that the principle of *safek berachot l'hakel* does not apply when the common custom is to recite the *beracha*.

Rav Ovadia explains that the widespread custom and the fact that this *beracha* is presented by a variety of *Rishonim* indicates its ancient origin. He even suggests that the *Rishonim* who recorded this *beracha* had an alternative text of the *gemara* that included *HaNoten LaYa'ef Ko'aḥ*.

Rav Shmuel Khoshkerman observes how interesting it is that Sephardic Jews have accepted the *minhagim* of the Ari z"l with regard to *tefilla* even when it runs counter to the *Shulḥan Aruch*. The recitation of the *beracha* of *HaNoten LaYa'ef Ko'ah* is but one of many examples of this phenomenon.[8]

---

a situation in which Rav Yosef Karo rules that one should recite the *beracha*. This reflects the astoundingly great esteem in which the *Ben Ish Ḥai* held the Ari z"l.

7. Most interestingly, the *Kenesset HaGedola* (cited by *Magen Avraham* 46:12) writes that he has a tradition that Rav Yosef Karo retracted his view at the end of his life and agreed that the *beracha* should be recited.
8. Rav Ben Tzion Abba Sha'ul (introduction to *Teshuvot Ohr L'Tzion* 2:16), in his explanation of why, regarding *tefilla*, we follow the Ari z"l even when he disagrees with the *Shulḥan Aruch*, cites the *Ben Ish Ḥai*, who states (*Teshuvot Rav Pa'alim* 4:8), "The words of the Ari z"l are said with *ru'aḥ hakodesh* that he heard from Eliyahu HaNavi."

Chapter 6

Nefilat Apayim

Those not familiar with Sephardic practice are often shocked to discover that Sephardim do not perform *nefilat apayim,* the practice of leaning towards the ground during the recitation of *Taḥanun.*[1] This is particularly surprising given that this practice is mentioned by the Talmud (*Megilla* 22b) and the Rambam (*Hilchot Tefilla* 9:5)!

THE *ZOHAR*'S WARNING

It turns out that this practice has to do with the *mizmor Tehillim* recited by Sephardic Jews for *Taḥanun.*[2] The Rambam, in describing *nefilat apayim,* does not mention a specific *mizmor* to be recited in this context. The *siddurim* of both the Rambam and the *Geonim* present certain *teḥinot* (supplications) to be recited during *nefilat apayim.* The Ra'ah (*Ḥiddushim* to *Berachot* 31a) mentions *Tehillim* 51, which describes David HaMelech's *teshuva* after the sin he committed with Bat-Sheva, as a most appropriate choice, due to its content of *vidduy* and *teshuva.*

---

1. Yemenite Jews do perform *nefilat apayim,* as noted by Rav Zecharia Ben Shlomo (*Orot HaHalacha,* p. 191).
2. Our outline of the history of this development follows the outstanding presentation in the Koren edition of the Sephardic Sidddur.

Sephardic practice, however, does not follow the Ra'ah, but rather the recommendation of the *Zohar* (*Bemidbar* 120b) to recite *mizmor* 25. This *mizmor* is indeed most powerful and very appropriate for one who wishes to pour out his heart before *Hashem*. However, the *Zohar* makes a very significant caveat regarding the recitation of this *perek* in the context of *nefilat apayim*, insisting that when reciting this *mizmor*, one must be wholeheartedly committed to sacrifice his soul for the sake of *Hashem*. The *Zohar* issues a severe warning to one who recites this *mizmor* without proper *kavana* (intent). The *Zohar*'s warning is presented by the *Bet Yosef* in his commentary to the *Tur* (*Oraḥ Ḥayim* 131). It is for this reason, writes the *Magen Avraham* (131:5), that Ashkenazim do not recite *mizmor* 25, despite the *Zohar*'s preference for it.

The Sephardic practice stems from the *Ben Ish Ḥai*, a work that has had a profound impact on Sephardic Jews. He writes (year 1, *Parashat Ki Tisa* 13) that we are no longer capable of sustaining the level of intensity demanded by the *Zohar* for recitation of *mizmor* 25 while engaged in *nefilat apayim*. As a result, he records, the practice emerged in Baghdad for everyone – from the most learned to the most simple – to refrain from *nefilat apayim*.

The *Ben Ish Ḥai* records that he reached out to the legendary center of Sephardic Kabbalistic study in Jerusalem, Yeshivat Bet El (which exists to this very day in Jerusalem's Old City). The Rosh Yeshiva responded that they too refrained from *nefilat apayim* due to this concern. The *Ben Ish Ḥai* concludes with a strong recommendation for all Sephardic Jews to refrain from *nefilat apayim*.[3]

Although there was some opposition to this practice from the great Turkish authority Rav Ḥayim Palagi (*Kaf HaḤayim* 16:14), Rav Ovadia Yosef (*Teshuvot Yeḥaveh Da'at* 6:7) notes that the practice of all Sephardic Jews has emerged to follow the recommendation of the *Ben Ish Ḥai*.[4] He notes that the *gemara* (*Bava Metzia* 59b) recounts how Rabban Gamliel

---

3. Rav Mordechai Lebhar (*Magen Avot, Oraḥ Ḥayim* 131:1) explains that since we rule that *nefilat apayim* is discretionary (*Tur, Oraḥ Ḥayim* 131; *Taz, Oraḥ Ḥayim* 131:11), we have the option to refrain from performing *nefilat apayim* if we conclude that it is dangerous for us to do so.
4. Rav Lebhar documents that prior to the *Ben Ish Ḥai*, the widespread Sephardic practice was to perform *nefilat apayim*. He notes that there are some elderly Sephardic Jews who to this day perform *nefilat apayim*. He reports that Rav Eliyahu

died immediately after Rabbi Eliezer engaged in *nefilat apayim* and asked *Hashem* to punish Rabban Gamliel for excommunicating him in the wake of the *tanur shel Achnai* incident. Based on this tragic episode, we readily understand the enormous power of *nefilat apayim* and realize that it might be preferable to avoid wielding such power.

The development of this *minhag* demonstrates that not every Sephardic practice emerges from the Rambam. The Rambam is not known for his mystical leaning, but Sephardic Jews are certainly greatly influenced by *Kabbala*. Refraining from *nefilat apayim* is an example of the profound impact of *Kabbala* on Sephardic practice, in which the *Ben Ish Ḥai* played a major role. Rav Ovadia Yosef rolled back some of this impact, but not with regard to this matter.[5]

Thus, do not be surprised when you attend a weekday *tefilla* at a Sephardic *kehilla* and they recite *Taḥanun* without *nefilat apayim*. Those who are not Sephardim who are praying with a Sephardic *kehilla* should follow the practice of the *tzibbur* and refrain from *nefilat apayim*.

Sephardim who pray in an Ashkenazic *bet kenesset* typically refrain from *nefilat apayim*, since there is a danger in reciting *mizmor* 25 while doing *nefilat apayim*. Although this is a public deviation from the *tzibbur*'s practice, it is done passively; it is not an active deviation.[6]

VIDDUY DURING *TAḤANUN*

Another difference in practice between Sephardic and Ashkenazic Jews is that Sephardim recite the *Vidduy* before *Taḥanun*. Rav Ben Tzion Abba Sha'ul (*Teshuvot Ohr L'Tzion* 2:9:1) rules that when praying in an Ashkenazic *bet kenesset* in which this is not the practice, a Sephardic Jew should recite the *Vidduy* before *Taḥanun*, but refrain from gently knocking his heart, since this is a public and active deviation from the community's practice. Indeed, Rav Mordechai Djavaheri reports that Rav Zecharia Ben Shlomo performs the *Vidduy* in an unobtrusive manner (beneath his jacket) when praying with an Ashkenazic *minyan* at Yeshivat Shaalvim.

Abba Sha'ul told him that his illustrious father, Rav Ben Tzion Abba Sha'ul, would perform *nefilat apayim* (although he did not instruct others to follow his example).

5. *Yalkut Yosef, Oraḥ Ḥayim* 131:16.
6. See our full discussion of deviating from a synagogue's custom in Chapter 1 on *lo titgodedu*.

Rav Ike Sultan reports that Rav Hershel Schachter has repeatedly stated that reciting *Vidduy* when the Ashkenazic *tzibbur* is reciting *nefilat apayim* violates *lo titgodedu*. He advises reciting the *Vidduy* in the position of *nefilat apayim*. *Mizmor* 25 can be said sitting, when everyone else is sitting as well.

Rav Ovadia would disagree with this ruling and permit a Sephardic Jew to openly recite *Vidduy* (including gently striking the heart) in an Ashkenazic *minyan* (*Teshuvot Yabia Omer* 6: *Oraḥ Ḥayim* 10). Indeed, Rav Sultan reports that he witnessed Rav Shlomo Amar praying *Minḥa* in the Yeshiva University *bet midrash* next to Rav Schachter. When the Ashkenazic *minyan* performed *nefilat apayim*, Rav Amar said the *Vidduy* while standing and knocking on his chest in a public manner.

Chapter 7

Pronunciation of *Hashem*'s Name

As is well known, traditional Ashkenazic pronunciation of Hebrew differs from the Sephardic pronunciation.[1] As a result, Ashkenazim pronounce the name of *Hashem* as "*Ado-Noi*," whereas Sephardim pronounce it as "*Ado-Nai*."

You may have witnessed the following: An Ashkenazic Jew attending a Sephardic synagogue receives an *aliya* to the Torah. Wishing to respect the practice of the congregation, he utters the *berachot* using Sephardic pronunciation – with the exception of the vital name of *Hashem*.[2] What is the basis for this practice, and is it correct?

EXPLANATION OF THE PRACTICE

The source of this practice is none other than the great *Ḥazon Ish* (cited by Rav Binyamin Zilber, *Teshuvot Az Nidberu* 3:101). In a well-known ruling, the *Ḥazon Ish* stated that an Ashkenazic Jew who recites his prayers using

1. Note that the commonly spoken Sephardic accent today in Israel is less precise than the original Sephardic accent. The contemporary Sephardic accent, which is used in *tefilla* even by most Sephardic Jews, does not differentiate between a *tet* and a *taf*, a *kuf* and a *kaf degusha*, a *taf degusha* and a *taf refuya*, or between a *kamatz* and a *pataḥ*.
2. I have seen Yemenite Jews do this as well. Yemenite Jews pronounce a *kametz* in a manner similar to Ashkenazic Jews.

Sephardic pronunciation must still pronounce the *shem Hashem* in accordance with Ashkenazic tradition.

Rav Aharon Lichtenstein offered an explanation for the *Ḥazon Ish*'s approach.[3] He argued that it is based on the *Teshuvot HaRashba,* who rules that although *tefilla* may be recited in any language (*Sota* 32a), the holy name of *Hashem* may be recited only in Hebrew.

CRITIQUE OF THE *ḤAZON ISH*'S APPROACH

Rav Lichtenstein noted the peculiarity of this approach in that it adopts the stance that for an Ashkenazic Jew, any pronunciation other than his tradition's pronunciation has the status of a language other than Hebrew. Rav Lichtenstein noted that his colleague Rav Yehuda Amital reported that his wife's illustrious grandfather, Rav Isser Zalman Meltzer, disagreed with the *Ḥazon Ish.* Rav Meltzer maintained that an Ashkenazic Jew may pray using Sephardic pronunciation even when uttering the holy name of *Hashem.* Hebrew has many varieties of pronunciation, and any credible pronunciation of Hebrew practiced by a Jewish community enjoys the halachic status of Hebrew for all Jews.

Rav Ben Tzion Uziel (*Teshuvot Mishpitei Uziel, Oraḥ Ḥayim* 1) agrees with Rav Meltzer's approach, but Rav Avraham Yitzḥak Kook (*Kol Torah* [Av 5693] and in his letter of approbation to *Mishpitei Uziel*) famously disagrees. Rav Kook argues that each group of Jews must preserve its specific practices, traditions, and customs. He continues that one who changes his accent is considered like "one who recited [the *Shema*] and was not meticulous in enunciating the letters" (*Berachot* 15a); even though he fulfills his obligation *b'diavad* (post facto), he should not do so *lechatḥila* (initially). Rav Tzvi Pesaḥ Frank (*Teshuvot Har Tzvi, Oraḥ Ḥayim* 1:4) agrees that all Jews should retain their original pronunciation.

RAV OVADIA YOSEF'S APPROACH

Rav Ovadia Yosef (*Teshuvot Yabia Omer* 6: *Orah Ḥayim* 11) bolsters the approach that Rav Meltzer and Rav Uziel partially adopt (at least with regard to an Ashkenazic Jew praying with a Sephardic congregation). Rav Ovadia argues that the Sephardic pronunciation of Hebrew is the more authentic

3. In a *shiur* delivered at Yeshivat Har Etzion in June 1983.

version.[4] As proof, he quotes *piyutim* whose rhyme scheme fits only with Sephardic pronunciation.

For example, Rav Elazar HaKalir's *krovetz* (liturgical poem) for Tisha B'Av and Purim states, "*Hinei bati el bet madanai, azai dinai omera LaAdo-Nai.* Only the Sephardic pronunciation of *Hashem*'s name fits with the rhyme scheme in this *piyut.* Rav Ovadia notes that *Tosafot* (*Ḥagiga* 13a, s.v. *v'raglei haḥayot*) state that Rav Elazar HaKalir was none other than the Tanna Rabbi Elazar ben Rav Shimon Bar Yoḥai, which certainly boosts the authority of his *piyyutim.*

In addition, Rav Ovadia notes that the ancient *piyut Tzur Mishelo* also proves the authenticity of the Sephardic pronunciation. The chorus of this *piyut* is "*Tzur mishelo achalno barechu emunai, savanu v'hotarnu k'dvar Ado-Nai.*" Once again, only the Sephardic pronunciation of this *piyut* fits with the rhyme scheme.

Finally, Rashi (*Berachot* 47a, s.v. *ḥutafa*) describes the vowel beneath the letter *alef* in the word "*amen*" as pronounced as a *pataḥ*. Rav Yaakov Emden, in his comments to this Rashi, notes that Rashi fits perfectly with the Sephardic pronunciation, in which the *kametz* is pronounced in a manner quite similar to a *pataḥ*.

CONCLUSION

While the *Ḥazon Ish*'s approach is quite popular in certain circles, an Ashkenazic Jew who does not abide by this ruling has ample authority and support for his practice.[5] In fact, one should consider not following this approach

4. Rav Yosef's argument that those who lived in lands closer to Eretz Yisrael better preserved their traditions of Hebrew pronunciation is difficult. Jews of all groups made extraordinary efforts to preserve their respective traditions, as is evident from even a mere perusal of the great works of the *Rishonim* and *Aḥaronim* from the entire spectrum of Torah Jews. However, perhaps one could argue for the advantage of those who lived in proximity to Eretz Yisrael in that their every day language was Arabic, a Semitic language similar in many ways to Hebrew, which helped them preserve the original Hebrew pronunciation.
5. At the conclusion of his *teshuva,* Rav Ovadia quotes Rav Unterman, the Ashkenazic Chief Rabbi of Israel from 1964–1972, who ruled that Ashkenazim who have become accustomed to praying in the Sephardic accent should not be compelled to revert to the Ashkenazic pronunciation even in regard to the name of *Hashem.* That is how they were educated, and they are comfortable in this accent because it is widespread throughout the whole country. Rav Ovadia adds that it is preferable that Israeli

when praying in a Sephardic congregation, as it appears quite strange to most congregants and might not be in harmony with Hillel's teaching to not separate from the *tzibbur* (*Avot* 2:5).

Ashkenazim pray in the spoken Hebrew dialect, for in that way the youth will feel more of a sense of belonging to the synagogue and the prayer service.

Rav Eliezer Melamed (*Peninei Halacha, Tefilla* 8) argues that even if a person were to stand before a human king, he would speak in the accepted dialect, and he would not necessarily precisely pronounce the letters. Since the Halacha derives many of the laws regarding *tefilla* from the way in which an individual conducts himself when standing before a king, it is also appropriate to speak in the accepted dialect in prayer.

Rav Melamed quotes Rav Tzvi Yehuda Kook as noting that there are practices that are accepted by the community even though the *Ḥachamim* are not pleased with them. He also said that something positive emerged from the fact that Ashkenazic Jews accepted Sephardic pronunciation: members of different ethnic groups can pray together and unity is increased.

Chapter 8

The Attraction of *Morid HaTal*

In the *Shulḥan Aruch* (*Oraḥ Ḥayim* 114:3), Rav Yosef Karo indicates that the Sephardic liturgy includes the words "*morid hatal*" in the second *beracha* of the *Amida* during the summer months, in place of "*mashiv haruaḥ umorid hageshem.*" The Rama, however, record that Ashkenazic Jews do not insert "*morid hatal.*" In fact, the *Tur* (*Oraḥ Ḥayim* 114) already notes this disparity between Minhag Sepharad and Minhag Ashkenaz.

Why, then, has Nusaḥ Sephard, used by Ḥassidim, adopted the Sephardic practice in this regard? Moreover, why has inserting "*morid hatal*" become the accepted custom in nearly every Ashkenazic *bet keneset* in Israel?

BASIS FOR THE ASHKENAZIC PRACTICE

The *gemara* (*Ta'anit* 3a) clearly states that it is optional to insert "*morid hatal*" in the summer, since – unlike rain – dew does not cease to fall. Therefore, the *Ḥachamim* (Sages) did not obligate us to say "*morid hatal,*" but if one wishes to, he may say it.

The *Kaf HaḤayim* explains that the traditional Ashkenazic practice to omit "*morid hatal*" stems from the fact that dew always falls, and it is therefore reasonable to conclude that there is no need to request dew. *Tefilla* is, to a great extent, about generating a divine response to our *Tefilla*. Why pray for something that does not require us to activate its appearance?

A MAJOR ADVANTAGE OF THE SEPHARDIC PRACTICE

Tosafot (*Berachot* 29b, s.v. *ha d'idkar*) note a significant advantage to reciting "*morid hatal*": The Yerushalmi states that although one must repeat the *Amida* if he omitted "*mashiv haruaḥ umorid hageshem*" in its proper time, he need not do so if he said "*morid hatal*" instead. Tosafot note that there are those who say "*morid hatal*" year round so that they will never need to be concerned with having to repeat the *Amida* due to omitting "*mashiv haruaḥ*"; they are habituated to saying its "backup" throughout the year.[1]

These words of Tosafot are cited by the *Bet Yosef* (*Oraḥ Ḥayim* 114) and are echoed by the *Aruch HaShulḥan* (*Oraḥ Ḥayim* 114:9), who states, "How beautiful is the Sephardic practice to recite '*morid hatal*' year-round!" Indeed, I personally heard Rav Yosef Dov Soloveitchik explain his practice to recite "*morid hatal*" so that he would not have to worry about omitting "*mashiv haruaḥ*."[2]

The *Tur* (*Oraḥ Ḥayim* 117) adds that Sephardim pray for *tal*, even though it never ceases to fall, because the prayers are that the *tal* should be for a blessing, and not the opposite, Heaven forfend.[3] The *Bet Yosef* (*Oraḥ Ḥayim* 114) adds that Sephardim say "*morid hatal*" year round, since, as the *gemara* (*Ta'anit* 4a) notes, *tal* is desirable year round – unlike rain, which in Israel is a *siman kelala* (bad omen) after Nissan (*Ta'anit* 12b).

ḤASSIDIC PRACTICE

Why do Ḥassidim recite "*morid hatal*"? This practice may stem from the view of the *Magen Avraham* (*Oraḥ Ḥayim* 114:4), who thinks it a good idea

1. It seems that *Tosafot* refer to Ashkenazim, as the *Ba'alei HaTosafot* lived in France and Germany. Thus, there is precedent from the times of the *Tosafot* for Ashkenazim to recite "*morid hatal*."
2. The *Mesoret HaRav siddur* cites this as Rav Soloveitchik's practice as well, noting, that Rav Soloveitchik's practice is based on the view of the Vilna Gaon, discussed below.
3. The *gemara* (*Sukka* 37b and *Ḥagiga* 12b) mentions that certain dews can be "*ra'ot*," detrimental. For this reason, many Sephardic Jews respond, "*L'vracha*!" when the *ḥazan* recites "*morid hatal*" during the repetition of the *Amida*.

to pray for dew in order to prevent detrimental *tal* from falling.[4] Usually, however, the Ḥassidic Nusaḥ Sephard practices stem from a Kabbalistic perspective. Why might the *Kabbala* be enthused about *tal*?

One answer is indicated in the following teaching of Rav Eli Mansour:

> An important difference exists between rain and dew. Rain is formed by the evaporation of water on the earth. The vapor rises to the heavens and then returns to the earth in the form of rain. In other words, rain actually originates from the earth. As such, rain is symbolic of the phenomenon described in the *Zohar* as "*itaruta d'letata*," the awakening from down below. When we take the initiative of performing *mitzvot*, we "awaken" blessing from the heavens. Our initiative is like the water's evaporation, as our good deeds ascend to the heavens and then return to us in the form of divine blessing. Dew, by contrast, originates from the heavens, not from the earth. Thus, dew symbolizes "*itaruta d'le'ela*," the inspiration initiated from above.
>
> Just as dew descends from the heavens each and every night, without exception, similarly, God is willing to come and inspire us regardless of our past, regardless of how many times we have sinned and how many mistakes we have made.[5]

Perhaps the symbolism of *tal* is the powerful draw for Ḥassidim to recite "*morid hatal*."

MINHAG ERETZ YISRAEL

Why has the insertion of "*morid hatal*" emerged as the standard practice even among Ashkenazim in Eretz Yisrael? The answer stems from a comment of the Vilna Gaon (*Bi'ur HaGra, Oraḥ Ḥayim* 114:3, s.v. *v'anu*) on the Rama's statement that the Minhag Ashkenaz is to refrain from saying "*morid hatal*." The Vilna Gaon notes that while the Talmud Bavli (*Ta'anit* 3a, cited above) supports the Rama, the Talmud Yerushalmi seems to support the

4. Ḥassidic sources, in particular the *Shulḥan Aruch HaRav*, are enthusiastic followers of the *Magen Avraham* due to his proclivity for Kabbalistic teachings. The *Magen Avraham* frequently cites the practices and approaches of the Ari z"l, for example.
5. http://www.dailyhalacha.com/WeeklyParasha.asp?ParashaClipID=418.

Sephardic practice to say "*morid hatal.*" This is understood as the Vilna Gaon's endorsement of inserting "*morid hatal*" and an indication that this was his personal practice.

As in the case of the *minhagim* to not wear *tefillin* on *Ḥol HaMoed* and to recite *Hallel* at *Arvit* on the first night of Pesaḥ, whenever there is a convergence of Sephardic practice, Ḥassidic practice, and the view of the Vilna Gaon, a consensus view has emerged in Eretz Yisrael. This is due to the fact that as the Jewish community in Eretz Yisrael began to grow in the early nineteenth century, the community there consisted primarily of Sephardic Jews, Ḥassidic Jews, and the followers of the Vilna Gaon. Thus, since these three groups agree to recite "*morid hatal,*" it has developed that almost all communities in Eretz Yisrael do so.

CONCLUSION

The case of "*morid hatal*" is a rarity; it reflects a situation in which the Ashkenazic custom has changed considerably since the time of the Rama. Although Ashkenazic Jews in the Rama's time apparently did not insert "*morid hatal,*" over the course of the last two hundred and fifty years, many Ashkenazic Jews have been attracted to the power of these two words. Indeed, in an incredibly beautiful *nevu'a* (prophecy), Hoshe'a describes Hashem as declaring, "*Eheyeh k'tal l'Yisrael,*" "I will be like dew for the Jewish People" (*Hoshe'a* 14:6).

Chapter 9

Counting a *Katan* Towards a *Minyan* and *Zimun*

It was a Sunday morning soon after I was privileged to assume the position of Rav at Congregation Shaarei Orah, the Sephardic Congregation of Teaneck, in 2000. There were nine men and an eleven-year old boy present. Could we count the boy as part of the *minyan* if he were to hold a Torah or a *Ḥumash*?

BACKGROUND TO THE DEBATE

In a long and winding discussion, the *gemara* discusses the possibility of a *katan* participating in a *zimun*, the group of three or ten men "invited" to participate in *Birkat HaMazon*.

> Rabbi Yehoshua ben Levi said: Nine Jews and a slave join together [to form a *zimun* of ten]. [The *gemara* raises an objection:] There was an incident involving Rabbi Eliezer, who entered a synagogue and did not find [a quorum] of ten, and he liberated his slave and he completed [the quorum] of ten…
>
> Rabbi Yoḥanan said: A mature minor [i.e., one who is still a minor in terms of age, but displays signs of puberty] is included in a *zimun*…

> [The *gemara* concludes:] The *halacha* is not in accordance with any of these statements. Rather, the *halacha* is in accordance with this statement that Rav Naḥman said: A minor who knows to Whom one recites a blessing is included in a *zimun*.
>
> Abaye and Rava, when they were children, were seated before Rabba. Rabba said to them: To whom does one recite blessings? They said to him: To God, the All-Merciful. [Rabba asked them:] And where does the All-Merciful reside? Rava pointed to the ceiling. Abaye went outside and pointed toward the heavens. Rabba said to them: You will both become Sages. (*Berachot* 47b–48a)

THE DEBATE AMONG THE *RISHONIM*

The Rambam (*Hilchot Berachot* 5:7) rules in accordance with the straightforward reading of the *gemara*: The entire discussion is dismissed except for the view of Rav Naḥman, who permits counting a *katan* who is aware of the One we bless towards a *zimun*. The implication is that we count a *katan* as a third or tenth for a *zimun*, but not for a *minyan* (*Hilchot Tefilla* 8:4).

Rav Yosef Karo (*Shulḥan Aruch, Oraḥ Ḥayim* 199:10) rules in accordance with this opinion and is lenient regarding counting a *katan* towards a *zimun*. Although he notes that some are lenient regarding counting a *katan* as the tenth in a *minyan*, he writes that the great *posekim* have rejected this view (*Oraḥ Ḥayim* 55:4). The *Bi'ur Halacha* (55:4, s.v. *v'lo nirin divreihem*) explains that regarding *devarim shebekedusha*, the portions of *tefilla* that require a *minyan*, Rav Yosef Karo adopts a stricter approach.

The *Shulḥan Aruch* permits including a *katan* from the age of "*onat hape'utot*" as the third or tenth for a *zimun*. The *Ben Ish Ḥai* (year 1, *Parashat Koraḥ* 11) rules that this refers to the age of nine. However, Rav Ovadia Yosef (*Teshuvot Yeḥaveh Da'at* 4:13 and *Teshuvot Yabia Omer* 9: *Oraḥ Ḥayim* 91:8:3) rules that he is permitted to join from age six. The story regarding Rava and Abaye, which seems to be presented by the *gemara* in order to show an example of children who recognize *Hashem* and may be counted towards a *zimun*, seems to be fit more with a child the age of six, rather than with a child aged nine.

Unlike the Rambam, Rabbenu Tam (cited in *Tosafot, Berachot* 48a, s.v. *v'leit*) maintains that the *gemara* in its conclusion does not reject the option of counting a *katan* as the tenth in a *minyan*. Rabbenu Tam notes that the *gemara* equates *zimun* with *tefilla*. Thus, Rabbenu Tam surprisingly permits counting a *katan* as a third or tenth in a *zimun* and as a tenth in a *minyan*.

Tosafot cite the practice of some to count a *katan* as the tenth if he is holding a *Ḥumash*. Rabbenu Tam dismisses this practice as a "*minhag shetut*" (foolish practice), just as the *gemara* dismisses attempts to argue that an *aron* or Shabbat may be counted towards a *minyan*.

Tosafot go on to cite the Ri, who reports that Rabbenu Tam never relied on his view in practice. Based on a statement in the Talmud Yerushalmi, the Ri rejects the idea of counting a *katan* towards either a *minyan* or a *zimun*. The Rosh (*Berachot* 7:20) and the *Tur* (*Oraḥ Ḥayim* 55) rule in accordance with this view. Thus, the Rama rules that a *katan* cannot serve as either the third or the tenth in a *zimun*. He notes that this is the accepted practice among Ashkenazim and that Ashkenazim should not deviate from this *minhag*.

Interestingly, even though the Rama rules out the possibility of counting a *katan* as the tenth for a *zimun*, he countenances including a *katan* as the tenth in a *minyan* in a case of great need if he is holding a *Ḥumash* (*Oraḥ Ḥayim* 55:4). The Rama's reasoning may be that there is never truly a pressing need to conduct a *zimun*, as there is for a community to conduct a *minyan*. Although Rav Naḥman seems to permit counting a *katan* towards a *zimun* if he recognizes to Whom we recite *Birkat HaMazon*, Rav Naḥman may be understood as referring only to a *katan* who exhibits signs of physical maturity as well.

SEPHARDIC PRACTICE

Rav Ovadia Yosef (*Teshuvot Yabia Omer* 4: *Oraḥ Ḥayim* 9) strongly endorses the *Shulḥan Aruch*'s stringent view, as does Rav Shalom Messas (*Teshuvot Shemesh U'Magen* 4:17) and Rav Mordechai Eliyahu (*Siddur Kol Eliyahu*). Rav Ovadia adamantly rejects the possibility of counting a *katan* towards a *minyan* even in an extreme situation, such as when only nine men reside in a particular community and the only way to create a *minyan* is to include a minor. Rav Ovadia even rules that if one is present at a Sephardic *minyan* that is about to rely on the lenient view, he should walk out so that the group does not conduct a *minyan* that violates Halacha.

Thus, at Shaarei Orah, we never count a *katan* towards a *minyan* even if he is holding a *Ḥumash*.

THE ASHKENAZIC APPROACH

There is a rich and varied approach among Ashkenazic Jews as to whether we may rely on the view presented by the Rama. This question has never been fully resolved.

The *Mishna Berura* (55:24) cites the *Levush* and *Magen Avraham,* who disagree as to whether this constitutes a viable opinion that may be followed in case of pressing need. The *Mishna Berura* concludes that in our time, this approach is followed in extenuating circumstances, even though many *Aḥaronim* object. The *Aruch HaShulḥan* (*Oraḥ Ḥayim* 55:10), in contrast, maintains that this view may never be followed.

Among twentieth-century Ashkenazic *posekim,* Rav Yaakov Breisch (*Teshuvot Ḥelkat Yaakov* 28), Rav Moshe Feinstein (*Teshuvot Igrot Moshe, Oraḥ Ḥayim* 2:18), and Rav Yosef Dov Soloveitchik (cited by Rav Hershel Schachter; see Rav Aryeh Lebowitz, *Sefer HaKoneh Olamo* 1:293–294) permit relying on the lenient approach in case of great need.[1] Rav David Tzvi Hoffman (*Teshuvot Melamed L'Ho'il, Oraḥ Ḥayim* 4) and Rav Betzalel Stern (*Teshuvot B'Tzel HaḤochma* 4:33) object to relying upon the lenient approach.

Contemporary Ashkenazic *Rabbanim* continue to debate the issue. Rav Aharon Lichtenstein told me that in case of pressing need, one may rely on the lenient opinion. Rav Gedalia Schwartz, on the other hand, stated during a speech at a convention of the Rabbinical Council of America that the lenient view may not be followed even in case of great need if there are Jews who live in the area but unfortunately choose not to attend the *minyan.*

SEPHARDIC AND ASHKENAZIC JEWS WHO EAT TOGETHER

What should be done if one Ashkenazic Jew and one Sephardic Jew join together for a meal with a *katan*? Should the Sephardic or Ashkenazic practice be followed? Both Rav Mordechai Eliyahu and Rav Pinḥas Scheinberg (cited in *V'Zot HaBracha* 14:4) rule that the Sephardic standard should be followed and the *katan* should be permitted to join. They both reason that we may assume that the Ashkenazic Jew consents to facilitate a *zimun.* However, they agree that the Sephardic Jew should be the one who recites the *zimun,* and they caution that the Ashkenazic Jew who is responding should

1. Rav Moshe maintains that the *katan* must hold an actual *sefer Torah,* not a *Ḥumash.*

omit *Hashem's* name in the case of a mixed group of ten (including a *katan*) Ashkenazic and Sephardic Jews joining together for a meal.

CONCLUSION

Sephardic Jews never count a *katan* towards a *minyan,* but will count a child beginning from the age of six (as long as he recognizes *Hashem* and is capable of reciting *Birkat HaMazon*) as the third or tenth in a *zimun*. Ashkenazic Jews never count a *katan* towards a *zimun,* but some count a *katan* holding a *Ḥumash* as the tenth towards a *minyan* in a case of great need.

Chapter 10

Different Conclusions of Wednesday's *Shir Shel Yom*

The *Shir Shel Yom* (Psalm of the Day) recited at the conclusion of *Shaḥarit* is patterned after the *Shir Shel Yom* recited by the *Levi'im* in the *Bet HaMikdash* (*Talmud Yerushalmi, Ta'anit* 4:5). But if it is a simple replication, why is there a divergence between Sephardic and Ashkenazic traditions as to where we conclude the psalm recited on Wednesday? Both groups recite *Tehillim* 94, but Ashkenazim add the first three *pesukim* of the next *mizmor*, which begin with the words "*Lechu neranena laHashem.*"

A RAV SOLOVEITCHIK STORY

A story about Rav Yosef Dov Soloveitchik may give some perspective on this difference.

A student of Rav Soloveitchik was once with him on Shemini Atzeret. During a short break, the student engaged Rav Soloveitchik in conversation, asking for the basis of the practice of many Ḥassidim to abstain from eating their meals in the *sukka* on Shemini Atzeret (outside of Israel). This practice on its face runs counter to the conclusion of both the *gemara* (*Sukka* 47a) and *Shulḥan Aruch* (*Oraḥ Ḥayim* 668:1) that one should sit in the *sukka* on Shemini Atzeret but refrain from reciting the *beracha*.[1]

Rav Soloveitchik responded with his classic answer, with which many Torah scholars are familiar.[2] He noted the importance of the night of Shemini Atzeret, following the positive judgment that Kabbalists and Ḥassidim associate with the day of Hoshana Rabba. Just as celebrants of *sheva berachot* are exempt from sitting in the *sukka* when the *sukka* does not comfortably provide adequate room, one can argue that the large celebrations of Ḥassidim on Shemini Atzeret, when they are *mekabel penei rabbam* (greet their rabbi), would similarly provide an exemption.

Rav Soloveitchik, recounts the student, excitedly developed the parallel between the *ḥatan* with his entourage and Ḥassidim on Shemini Atzeret. He compared Shemini Atzeret to a wedding. Just as the bride circles the groom seven times (at an Ashkenazic wedding), we circle seven times during the *hakafot*. Rav Soloveitchik became enthralled, explaining how during the seven days of Sukkot we circle the *sefer Torah* during the *Hoshanot*, but on Shemini Atzeret we hold the Torah as we circle, and the middle of the circle is empty.[3] Explained Rav Soloveitchik, the empty space is *Hashem*. We are the *kalla* circling the groom, who is none other than *Hashem*!

The student, impressed with Rav Soloveitchik's rousing defense of the Ḥassidic practice, proceeded to ask, "Then why do we sit in the *sukka* on Shemini Atzeret?"

Rav Soloveitchik simply responded, "Because that is what is stated in the *gemara*!"

What emerges from this charming exchange is that while some practices have elaborate and even elegant explanations, at times our preference is for the simple and straightforward approach.

THE CONCLUSION TO WEDNESDAY'S *SHIR SHEL YOM*

The Ari z"l introduced the idea of adding the first three *pesukim* of *Tehillim* 95 to the conclusion of the *Shir Shel Yom* of Wednesday in order not to end the *Shir Shel Yom* with the difficult conclusion of *Tehillim* 94, "The Lord our God will destroy them." This is similar to our practice regarding the

1. Non-Ḥassidic Ashkenazic and all Sephardic Jews sit in the *sukka* on Shemini Atzeret.
2. It is recorded in *Reshimot Shiurim* of Rav Soloveitchik to *Sukka* 25b.
3. Ḥassidim conduct *hakafot* on Shemini Atzeret as well as Simḥat Torah.

conclusion of our reading of *Megillat Eicha*, the book of *Yeshayahu* (when reading the *haftara* for Rosh Ḥodesh that falls on Shabbat), and the book of *Malachi* (when reading the *haftara* for Shabbat HaGadol), when we repeat the positive penultimate *pesukim* of these *sefarim* instead of concluding with a negative *pasuk*.[4] Ḥassidim (*Minhagei Ḥabad, Yalkut Minhagim*, p. 161) provide an additional reason, explaining that one needs to make spiritual and physical preparations for Shabbat beginning on Wednesday.[5] For this reason, Ashkenazim add these three *pesukim*, which are said at the beginning of the Kabbalat Shabbat service.[6]

EXPLANATION OF THE SEPHARDIC PRACTICE

We may offer two reasons why Sephardic Jews did not adopt this practice. First, there is no concern for concluding with *puranut*, since Sephardic Jews add the positive plea, "*Hoshi'enu Hashem Elokenu*," after the *Shir Shel Yom*. In addition, many Sephardic Jews begin Kabalat Shabbat with *Mizmor L'David* (*Mizmor* 29) and not *Lechu Neranena* (*Mizmor* 95),[7] such that the first three *pesukim* of *Mizmor* 95 do not necessarily stir feelings of Shabbat in a Sephardic Jew and would not necessarily alert them to begin preparing for Shabbat.

However, a more basic explanation may be offered for the Sephardic practice. Simply put, the *Shir Shel Yom* is, as we plainly state, the *shir* that was recited in the *Bet HaMikdash*. Thus, Sephardim argue that we must adhere to the text used in the *Bet HaMikdash* for Wednesdays – *Mizmor* 94 – without making any additions.

---

4. The source for this practice is *Megillah* 31b. The same is done by Sephardic Jews when reading *Shir HaShirim* before Shabbat; the penultimate *pasuk* is reread after the completion of the *sefer* in order to conclude on a positive note.
5. *Siddurim* based on the rulings of the *Ben Ish Ḥai* include an instruction that one should accept the light of the upcoming Shabbat when reciting the *Shir Shel Yom* of Wednesday.
6. Another reason is offered based on *Ta'anit* 29a, which describes the scene at the time of the *Ḥurban*: "The *Levi'im* were about to end the *Shir Shel Yom* and had reached the *pasuk*, 'And God turned their evil against them, and due to their evil He cut them off,' when the enemy entered the *Bet HaMikdash* – before they could finish the *mizmor* and conclude with, 'May God cut them off.'" Based on this passage, one could understand why one would not want to conclude the *Shir Shel Yom* with a *pasuk* that served as the prelude to the *Ḥurban*.
7. This is Minhag Yerushalayim (the custom of Sephardic Jews who reside in Jerusalem) and the practice of Syrian Jews.

In other words, in contrast to the stirring explanations given for the Ashkenazic practice, we may explain the Sephardic practice by simply noting (similar to Rav Soloveitchik and his student) that we say only precisely what was said by the *Levi'im* in the *Bet HaMikdash* on Wednesday.

Chapter 11

V'Yatzmaḥ Purkaneh V'Karev Mishiḥeh

"N*ein*!" cried the *gabbai* (sexton) at the German-Jewish synagogue in Switzerland. A guest was leading the congregation in prayer and included the words, "*V'yatzmaḥ purkaneh v'karev mishiḥeh*" in the *Kaddish,* arousing the *gabbai*'s ire.

Ḥassidic Jews who pray Nusaḥ Sephard add these words, following in the footsteps of Sephardic Jews.[1] Adherents of Nusaḥ Ashkenaz, however, resisted this change to the traditional Ashkenazic *Kaddish*. Traditionally, these four words have typified the differences between traditional Nusaḥ Ashkenaz and Ḥassidic Nusaḥ Sephard. What is the basis of this divergence in practice?

1. Sephardic Jews, especially in Eretz Yisrael and its neighboring countries, embraced the teachings of the Ari z"l soon after they were publicized in the sixteenth century. The acceptance of the teachings of the Ari z"l among Ashkenazic Jews accelerated after the emergence of the Ba'al Shem Tov (the founder of Ḥassidut) and his students in the eighteenth century. This accounts for the great overlap between Ḥassidic and Sephardic practices.

AN ANCIENT DISPUTE

This disparity long predates the split between Nusaḥ Sephard and Nusaḥ Ashkenaz. The Rambam (in the *siddur* included at the end of his *Sefer Ahava*) and the *siddur* of Rav Sa'adia Gaon include the words "*V'yatzmaḥ purkaneh v'karev mishiḥeh*" in the *Kaddish*. Others ancient sources, however, including the *siddur* of Rav Amram Gaon and the *Maḥzor Vitri* (which reflects the school of Rashi and his disciples), do not include this phrase in the *Kaddish*.

A REJECTED SUGGESTION

Rav Yoel Bin Nun, an Israeli Bible scholar, suggests that this difference in practice reflects the Tannaitic dispute recorded on *Sanhedrin* 99a, where Hillel boldly states that King Ḥizkiyahu had the potential to be *Mashiaḥ*, but once he failed to realize his potential, a Messianic king will not rise.[2] Rashi (ad loc., s.v. *en lahem*) clarifies that Hillel certainly subscribes to the idea of a Messianic Era; he rejects only the notion that there will be a Messianic king during that era. The Israeli scholar suggested that those who say, "*V'yatzmaḥ purkaneh v'karev mishiḥeh,*" "And may He sprout salvation and **bring close His Messiah,**" believe that there will be a *Mashiaḥ* in addition to a Messianic era, whereas those who omit these words believe that there will be only a Messianic era, but no human *Mashiaḥ*.

This approach is untenable. The aforementioned *gemara* rejects Hillel's opinion outright, noting that the second Temple Era prophet Zecharia, who lived centuries after Ḥizkiyahu, prophesies about an individual Messiah who will be a "poor man riding on a donkey" (*Zecharia* 9:9).[3] Zecharia demonstrates that the promise of a Messianic king did not at all expire after the passing of Ḥizkiyahu. Hence, the Israeli scholar's explanation for Nusaḥ Ashkenaz's omission of "*V'yatzmaḥ purkaneh v'karev mishiḥeh*" must be summarily dismissed.

A POSSIBLE EXPLANATION

One advantage of the Sephardic and Nusaḥ Sephard approach of including "*V'yatzmaḥ purkaneh v'karev mishiḥeh*" is that these words present

2. This does not refer to the famous *Tanna* Hillel HaZaken, but rather, to the *Amora* Rav Hillel.
3. In fact, the *Ḥatam Sofer* (*Teshuvot, Yoreh De'ah* 356) goes as far as to say that after the *gemara* rejects Hillel's view, anyone who espouses this view is considered a heretic, since he denies a fundamental principle of Jewish belief.

the opportunity to express one's yearning for *Mashiaḥ*. As the Rambam writes (*Hilchot Melachim* 11:1), not only do we believe in *Mashiaḥ*, but we also yearn for his arrival. Accordingly, it is quite fitting that the Rambam incorporates "*V'yatzmaḥ purkaneh v'karev mishiḥeh*" in the *Kaddish* that he includes in his *siddur*.[4]

On the other hand, two objectives are accomplished by omitting these words. First, the omission of the mention of *Mashiaḥ* emphasizes the ultimate goal of the Messianic era, and even the Messianic king, as articulated by Yeshayahu: "*V'nisgav Hashem levado*" (*Yeshayahu* 2:11) – *Hashem* will reign over the world. Moreover, the Ashkenazic version of *Kaddish* emphasizes the pressing need for the arrival of the Messianic era and the Messianic king – in order to correct the enormous *ḥillul Hashem* that results from our status in exile. The *Kaddish* paraphrases the words of *Yeḥezkel* (38:23): "*V'hitgdalti v'hitkadashti l'einei goyim rabbim*," "I will be announced and sanctified before the eyes of many nations." Indeed, Yeḥezkel repeatedly teaches that it is *kiddush Hashem* that will propel the arrival of the Messianic Era (see, for example, *Yeḥezkel* 36:16-23 and 37:28). This is the emphasis of the *Kaddish* according to Nusaḥ Ashkenaz.

Whether or not one recites "*V'yatzmaḥ purkaneh v'karev mishiḥeh*" in *Kaddish*, we all firmly believe in both a Messianic era and a Messianic king. The question of whether to include these four words hinges on whether the *kiddush Hashem* leading to our ultimate dream that "His name alone will be exalted" is the dominant or exclusive focus of *Kaddish*.

CONCLUSION

It is well known that Rav Ovadia Yosef (*Yalkut Yosef, Oraḥ Ḥayim* 56:25) rules that a Sephardic Jew should recite, "*V'yatzmaḥ purkaneh v'karev mishiḥeh*," even when praying in an Ashkenazic *bet kenesset*, and many Sephardic Jews follow this practice. However, this ruling should not be followed in a situation in which it will lead to strife. In many *batei kenesset*, congregants

4. Interestingly, Sephardic Jews explicitly express the yearning for *Mashiaḥ* in other contexts of prayer as well. For example, some Sephardic *siddurim* include the word "*v'tzipinu*," "and we yearn," in the *beracha* of the *Amida* in which we pray for the coming of the *Mashiaḥ*: "*Ki l'yeshuatecha kivinu v'tzipinu kol hayom*," "We have constantly yearned and hoped for the salvation." Similarly, the Sephardic version of *Adon Olam* includes the line, "*B'mikdasho tagel nafshi, meshiḥenu yishlaḥ mehera*," "My soul will delight in the *Bet HaMikdash*; He will speedily send his *Mashiaḥ*."

will become upset if there is such a blatant deviation from the accepted communal practice. Indeed, Rav Ben Tzion Abba Sha'ul (*Teshuvot Ohr L'Tziyon* 2:5:11) rules that in such a situation, a Sephardic Jew should not say, "*V'yatzmaḥ purkaneh v'karev mishiḥeh.*"

As noted above (p. 7), Ashkenazim praying in a Sephardic *bet kenesset* should use the Sephardic *nusaḥ* when reciting *Kaddish,* as Rav Moshe Feinstein (*Teshuvot Igrot Moshe, Oraḥ Ḥayim* 2:23) forbids any public deviance from the community's practice.

Bet Kenesset

Chapter 12

Ashkenazic Single Men without a *Tallit* at a Sephardic Congregation

Most Ashkenazic men do not wear a *tallit* until marriage, whereas Sephardim begin wearing a *tallit* for prayer beginning at the age of *bar mitzva.* Sephardic practice follows straightforward reasoning: A *bar mitzva* is responsible for all *mitzvot,* so why should he wait until marriage in order to wear a *tallit* during *tefilla*? Should a Sephardic congregation require Ashkenazic single men who visit to wear a *tallit*?

JUSTIFYING THE ASHKENAZIC PRACTICE

The Maharil (*Derashot Maharil, Nisu'in*), a late *Rishon,* cites the custom for single men not to don a *tallit.* He relates this *minhag* to the juxtaposition in the Torah of the *mitzva* of *tzitzit* and marriage (*Devarim* 22:12–13). Important Ashkenazic authorities, including the *Mishna Berura* (17:10), have difficulty justifying this *minhag,* but Rav Eliezer Waldenberg (*Teshuvot Tzitz Eliezer* 20:8) endorses it. Rav Yekutiel Yehuda Halberstam (*Teshuvot Divrei Yatziv, Oraḥ Ḥayim* 44) justifies the practice as well, arguing that since *tzitzit* reflect the need to keep all *mitzvot* and a single man has not fulfilled the *mitzva* of getting married, withholding the *tallit* encourages him to marry as soon as possible.

Rav Daniel Mann of the Eretz Hemdah Institute offers another suggestion. He notes that the Radvaz (I, 343) writes that one should cover his head with a *tallit* during *tefilla* (see opinions cited in *Mishna Berura* 8:4); if this were not so, those who wear *tzitzit* would have no need to wear a *tallit*. The *Magen Avraham* (8:3), however, states that single men, and possibly married men who are not *talmidei ḥachamim*, should not cover their heads with a *tallit* (based on *Kiddushin* 29b and 8a), so as not to appear haughty. According to the assumptions of these *posekim*, it is not advisable for a single man to wear a *tallit*. This explains the common Ashkenazic *minhag*.[1]

This reasoning does not apply to Sephardic Jews, who permit single men to cover their heads with a *tallit* even before marriage (*Kaf HaḤayim, Oraḥ Ḥayim* 8:12).[2]

Rav Yosef Dov Soloveitchik told me that he believed that it is proper for single Ashkenazic men to wear a *tallit* before marriage. (Indeed, I vividly recall that his grandsons, Rav Moshe Lichtenstein and Rav Mayer Lichtenstein, wore a *tallit* during *tefilla* at Yeshivat Har Etzion before they married.) However, Rav Soloveitchik maintained that one should honor his father's custom if he did not wear a *tallit* before his wedding.[3]

THE ADVICE OF RAV SHLOMO MAIMON AND RAV BARUCH GIGI

When the venerable Rav Shlomo Maimon of Seattle visited Congregation Shaarei Orah in 2002, I asked him whether I should demand that single Ashkenazic visitors wear a *tallit* during *tefilla*. He replied that I should let them remain without a *tallit*. When Rav Baruch Gigi, Rosh Yeshiva of Yeshivat Har Etzion, visited Shaarei Orah in March 2018, he offered the same advice.

---

1. http://www.eretzhemdah.org/newsletterArticle.asp?lang=en&pageid=48&cat=7&newsletter=637&article=2358.
2. Rav Yaakov Hillel (*Teshuvot VaYashev HaYam* 1:5, p. 104) rules that unmarried Sephardic young men should not cover their heads with a *tallit* when praying with in an Ashkenazic synagogue. However, Rav Shmuel Khoshkerman told me that is not the common practice. Single Sephardic men often do place a *tallit* over their heads even when praying in an Ashkenazic *minyan*.
3. This conversation occurred in September 1985.

The halachic basis for this ruling (in addition to the pastoral aspect of not wanting to make another Jew feel uncomfortable) is the halachic concept of *shenei batei din b'ir echad* (*Yevamot* 14a). As we discussed at length in Chapter 1, although the prohibition of *lo titgodedu* (*Devarim* 14:1) is interpreted by *Ḥazal* as teaching "*Lo ta'asu agudot agudot*," not to separate into different groups, this does not apply when there are two Rabbinic courts in the city. This reasoning applies when the community includes people of different halachic backgrounds.[4] Thus, a Sephardic congregation can tolerate someone publicly observing a different practice, as long as it does not interfere with the proceeding of the *tefilla*. Sephardim today understand that unmarried Ashkenazic men are not comfortable wearing a *tallit*, and they thus consent to Ashkenazic visitors maintain a divergent practice in this regard.

CONCLUSION

Two respected Sephardic *Rabbanim* from significantly different backgrounds, Rav Maimon and Rav Gigi, agree that it is acceptable for a Sephardic congregation to allow Ashkenazic single men to sit in a Sephardic *bet kenesset* during *Shaḥarit* without wearing a *tallit*. Rav Ḥayim David HaLevy (*Teshuvot Aseh Lecha Rav* 8:12) permits this as well for an Ashkenazic young man who is not comfortable wearing a *tallit*.[5] He notes that this is the common practice in *batei kenesset* throughout Eretz Yisrael.[6]

Conversely, unmarried Sephardic men should wear a *tallit* when visiting Ashkenazic *batei kenesset*, as noted emphatically by Rav Eliyahu Bakshi Doron (*Teshuvot Binyan Av* 2:7:1). Rav Shlomo Zalman Auerbach

4. As we noted in Chapter 1 on *lo titgodedu*, Rav Ovadia Yosef (*Teshuvot Yeḥaveh Da'at* 4:36) follows the ruling of Rav Mordechai Benet (*Teshuvot Parashat Mordechai, Oraḥ Ḥayim* 4), who rules that *lo titgodedu* does not apply in the case of divergent practices that stem from ancient disputes, even when both practices are observed simultaneously in the same *bet kenesset*.
5. Rav Shmuel Khoshkerman (*Minḥat Shmuel* 2:213) concurs.
6. The fact that both Rav Ovadia Yosef (*Teshuvot Yeḥaveh Da'at* 3:6) and Rav Shalom Messas (*Teshuvot Shemesh U'Magen* 3: *Oraḥ Ḥayim* 24) rule that a Sephardic Jew should observe the Sephardic customs even while praying in an Ashkenazic *bet kenesset* indicates their agreement with the rulings of Rav Maimon and Rav Gigi permitting variant practices in one *bet kenesset* in the current "multi-cultural" climate among *Am Yisrael*. See Chapter 1 on synagogue conformity, where we discuss this issue at length.

(*Halichot Shlomo* 5:23) permits this as well. Rav Shmuel Khoshkerman adds that the distinctive all-white Sephardic *tallit* (*Ben Ish Ḥai,* year 1, *Parashat No'aḥ* 11) may be worn by Sephardic men even when visiting an Ashkenazic *bet kenesset.*

Chapter 13

The Special Spiritual Energy at Sephardic *Tefilla*

Many Ashkenazic Jews who visit Sephardic congregations comment that they are struck by the vitality and energy of Sephardic *tefilla*. There is no doubt that the Sephardic practice of having the *shaliaḥ tzibur* (prayer leader) read every word aloud has a major impact on creating this special feeling.[1] The interactive nature of Sephardic prayer also contributes to the experience of Sephardic *tefilla*.

EXAMPLES OF INTERACTION

Many of the examples of "prayer interaction" are well-known, such as the response "*l'vracha*" to the declarations of both "*mashiv haruaḥ umorid hageshem*" and "*morid hatal*," depending on the season. There are a considerable number of other examples, although not all of these responses are practiced by every Sephardic community.

Examples of responses include stating, "*alehem hashalom*" after mentioning "*Elokei Avraham, Elokei Yitzḥak, V'Elokei Yaakov*," responding,

1. Such positive energy is generated at an Ashkenazic *bet kenesset* by those congregants who pray loudly, in an appropriate manner, to motivate their fellow congregants.

"*b'karov*" after the *ḥazan* says, "*umatzmi'aḥ yeshu'a,*" saying, "*baruch ḥei olamim,*" after the leader says, "*v'chol haḥayim yoducha sela,*" and responding, "*amen*" to each section of the *Elokenu V'Elokei Avotenu* portion of the fourth *beracha* of the Shabbat and Yom Tov *Amida.*[2] There are other responses depending on the type of Sephardic congregation.

EXPLANATIONS FOR THE RESPONSES

There is a compelling explanation for many or even most of these responses. For example, the "*l'vracha*" response to the mention of rain and dew echoes the *mishna*'s account of the saga of Ḥoni the Circle Drawer's plea for rain (*Ta'anit* 19a). Ḥoni demanded "*gishmei beracha*" – not mere drizzle on the one hand or destructive flooding on the other.[3]

However, not every one of these responses requires explanation. As Rav Mordechai Lebhar explains, many of these responses are intended simply to help keep the congregation focused on the service.[4] Indeed, the *Shulḥan Aruch* (*Oraḥ Ḥayim* 124:4) rules that one must concentrate on the *berachot* of the *shali'aḥ tzibbur* in order to answer "*baruch hu uvaruch shemo*" and "*amen.*" If there are not nine people in the congregation concentrating on these *berachot*, the *Shulḥan Aruch* writes that the *ḥazan* may possibly be saying unnecessary *berachot*. Therefore, these responses are added so that the congregation will remain focused on the *tefilla*.

INCREASING THE ENERGY AND POSITIVE VIBE

I submit that there is an additional source for this Sephardic practice. The *gemara* (*Berachot* 45a) presents the *pasuk*, "*Gadlu laHashem iti uneromema shemo yaḥdav,*" "O magnify *Hashem* with me, and let us exalt His name together" (*Tehillim* 34:4), as the source for the *beracha* of *zimun*, the introduction to the *Birkat HaMazon* recited when at least three men eat bread together. The *gemara* presents the *pasuk*, "*Ki shem Hashem ekra*

2. Sephardic congregations that follow Rav Ovadia Yosef and Rav Mordechai Eliyahu's example and recite the *Mi SheBerach* prayer for the soldiers of the Israel Defense Forces similarly answer "*amen*" to each portion of the request section of this special *tefilla*.
3. In Chapter 44, we note that Ḥoni serves as a role model for Sephardic Jews in other contexts as well. For example, the Sephardic *Seliḥot* include a plea that just as *Hashem* answered Ḥoni, He should answer us.
4. Cited in *Darké Abotenou*, p. 116, notes 118 and 121.

havu godel l'Elokenu," "For I will proclaim the name of *Hashem;* you shall ascribe greatness unto our God" (ibid. 32:3), as an alternative source for this practice.

These *pesukim* articulate the idea of collaboratively praising *Hashem.* The members of the congregation are not competing with each other, but rather working together to honor *Hashem,* in the manner of the *malachim* (angels), who are described in our *tefillot* as "*notenim reshut zeh lazeh*" (based on *Yeshayahu* 6:3). The repetition of the *Amida* (the *Ḥazara*) should not be perceived as the exclusive effort of the *shaliaḥ tzibbur.* The frequent responses not only maintain the congregation's attention, but also their participation, so that the *Ḥazara* is a collective effort rather than the toil of just one individual. This serves to increase the energy at a Sephardic synagogue.

TO ENERGIZE AND ENLIVEN THE *AZARA*

There is another aspect to this Sephardic practice based on the *gemara*'s explanation of certain practices in the *Bet HaMikdash.* The *mishna* in *Yoma* states that there were four lotteries held in the Temple every day. The *gemara* (*Yoma* 24b) asks:

> Why did they [assemble all the priests together and] hold a lottery, and once again [gather them together to] hold another lottery [four times, when the priests could be gathered one time and all the necessary lotteries held at once]?
>
> Rabbi Yoḥanan said: It was done this way in order to create a commotion throughout the Temple courtyard [as the priests would converge from all over to assemble there], as it is stated: "We took sweet counsel together, in the House of God we walked with the throng" (*Tehillim* 55:15).

According to the *gemara,* the *pasuk* from *Tehillim* teaches that it is proper to stir up a commotion and excitement in the course of the services in the *Bet HaMikdash.*

Similarly, the *gemara* (*Yoma* 33b) records:

> Why does the priest remove the ashes [from five lamps of the *menora*] and then return and remove the ashes [from the remaining two lamps of the *menora,* rather than arrange all seven lamps

> at once]? In order to enliven those present in the entire Temple courtyard.

The responsive nature of Sephardic prayer, as we have described, is intended not only to maintain the attention of the congregation. The goal is also to create an exciting service, which in turn generates exhilaration during the service.[5]

CONCLUSION

It has often been noted that a much higher percentage of Sephardic Jews maintain loyalty to their heritage than Ashkenazic Jews, and one major reason is the vibrant and interactive character of Sephardic *tefilla* services. For example, many not yet fully observant Sephardic Jews of all ages (including teenagers) throng to *Seliḥot*, due to the enjoyable high energy and interactive nature of Sephardic *Seliḥot*.[6]

The more energetic Sephardic *tefilla*, while not quite as solemn as the Ashkenazic rite, is an attractive model of *tefilla* that has succeeded in maintaining a deep loyalty among most Sephardic Jews.[7] There are critical lessons for all Jews to derive from the Sephardic prayer experience.

---

5. I believe that the selling of *aliyot* – which is typical at Sephardic congregations, especially on Yamim Tovim and other special occasions – is also intended to enliven the service. Rav Ovadia's justification of this practice appears in *Teshuvot Yeḥaveh Da'at* 2:41.
6. Sephardic *Seliḥot* are also written in straightforward Hebrew that is much easier to understand than the Ashkenazic *Seliḥot*, which consist to a great extent of the cryptic poems of Rabbi Eliezer HaKalir.
7. Rav Shmuel Khoshkerman adds that another reason for the special power of Sephardic *tefilla* is that the *niggunim* (tunes) used at Sephardic congregations have not changed from generation to generation. For example, the tune for *Seliḥot* is the same basic tune used by all Sephardic Jews for hundreds of years.

Tefillin

Chapter 14

Rabbenu Tam's *Tefillin*

If one joins a typical Sephardic congregation for a weekday *Shaḥarit,* he will notice a number of the men place not only Rashi's *tefillin,* but also Rabbenu Tam's *tefillin.* This is a rather uncommon sight at non-Ḥassidic Ashkenazic *bet kenesset,* where even the rabbi most often will not don the *tefillin* of Rabbenu Tam. What lies behind this difference in practice?

RASHI VS. RABBENU TAM

Rashi and Rabbenu Tam dispute the order in which the last two *parshiyot* should be placed in the *tefillin.* Rashi (*Menaḥot* 34b, s.v. *v'hakorei*) maintains that the *parasha* of *Shema* should precede that of *V'haya im Shamo'a,* while Rabbenu Tam (cited in *Tosafot,* ibid., s.v. *v'hakorei*) holds that *V'haya im Shamo'a* should precede *Shema.* The following diagrams (from the website of Machon Ot) illustrate the difference between what is referred to as "Rashi's *tefillin*" and "Rabbenu Tam's *tefillin*":

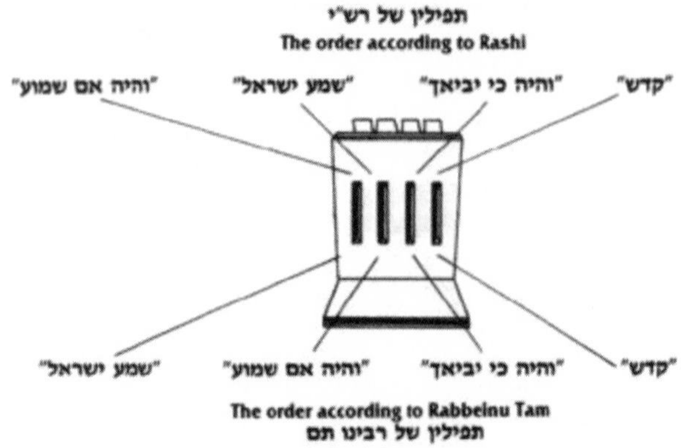

It is possible to distinguish between the *tefillin* of Rashi and Rabbenu Tam even without opening the *batim* (casing of the *tefillin*), as the *se'ar egel* (threads made of calves' hair) wrapped around the passage of *V'haya im Shamo'a* protrude outside of the *tefillin shel rosh*.

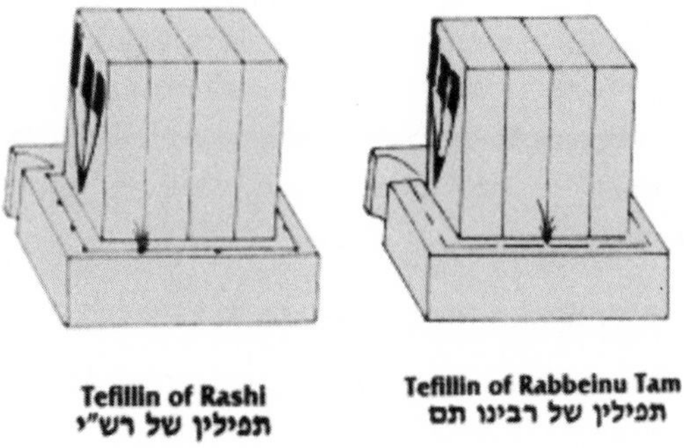

Rav Ovadia Yosef (*Teshuvot Yabia Omer* 1: *Oraḥ Ḥayim* 3) notes that many *Rishonim* side with Rashi and many *Rishonim* side with Rabbenu Tam. In fact, Rav Ovadia contends that the *Mechilta* and Talmud Yerushalmi already disputed this matter during the Talmudic era, centuries before the emergence of the debate between Rashi and Rabbenu Tam. Interestingly, in twentieth-century archaeological excavations of the Dead Sea area, both types of *tefillin* have been discovered (*Enyclopedia Judaica* 15:904). *Piskei Tosafot* (*Menaḥot* 92) already records, "In Naharde'a and Jerusalem, two pairs [of *tefillin*] were found, one in accordance with Rashi and the other in accordance with Rabbenu Tam."

The discovery that the Rashi-Rabbenu Tam debate already raged in earlier generations should not surprise us. The *gemara* frequently records disputes between the *Amora'im* and then notes that the *Tannaim* debated the same point in earlier generations.

The *Shulḥan Aruch* (*Oraḥ Ḥayim* 34:1) cites the Semag (positive command 22) and a number of other *Rishonim* who observe that the common practice is to follow the opinion of Rashi. Nevertheless, the *Shulḥan Aruch* (ibid. 34:2) writes that a God-fearing man should don both Rashi and Rabbenu Tam's *tefillin*.

Kabbalistic sources strongly support wearing both Rashi and Rabbenu Tam's *tefillin*. The *Ben Ish Ḥai* (*Parashat Vayera* 21), for example, famously writes, "The Ari z"l reports a tradition from Eliyahu HaNavi that both approaches are correct and both sets of *tefillin* should be worn. Both sets were worn from the days of Moshe Rabbenu until the Geonic era." He proceeds to quote the *Zohar*, which states that both pairs of *tefillin* are necessary.

Accordingly, in many Sephardic communities, it became common for men to wear both Rashi and Rabbenu Tam's *tefillin*, as noted by the *Ḥida* (*Birkei Yosef* 34). This is also common among Ḥassidic Jews. As we have noted elsewhere, the halachic practices of both Ḥassidic and (most) Sephardic Jews are significantly impacted by Kabbalistic considerations.

However, in non-Ḥassidic Ashkenazic circles, a different approach is taken, following the view of the Vilna Gaon. The Vilna Gaon was resolute in his endorsement of the opinion of Rashi regarding *tefillin* (*Bi'ur HaGra, Oraḥ Ḥayim* 34:1). In fact, when challenged as to why he did not don the *tefillin* of Rabbenu Tam, the Vilna Gaon famously replied, "If we wished to accommodate all opinions, we would have to wear sixty-four pairs of *tefillin*!" (*Ma'aseh Rav, Si'aḥ Eliyahu* 64). The *Mishna Berura* (34:4) cites the Vilna Gaon's ruling in accordance with Rashi without recording a dissenting opinion.

TRADITIONS NOT TO WEAR RABBENU TAM'S *TEFILLIN*

In the years that I served as one of the assistants to Rav Yosef Dov Soloveitchik, I had the privilege of assisting him in donning *tefillin*. Rav Soloveitchik wore only Rashi's version of *tefillin* and not that of Rabbenu Tam. This is hardly surprising, as Rav Soloveitchik was the scion of the line of Rav Ḥayim of Volozhin, the leading student of the Vilna Gaon, who shared his mentor's emphatic insistence on the correctness of Rashi's *tefillin*.

Similarly, Rav Moshe Feinstein did not wear Rabbenu Tam's *tefillin* until very late in life (1980), when the Lubavitcher Rebbe famously gifted him a specially made set of Rabbenu Tam's *tefillin* (*Teshuvot Igrot Moshe, Oraḥ Ḥayim* 4:9). Rav Aryeh Leibowitz relates that Rav Ḥayim Kanievsky does not wear Rabbenu Tam's *tefillin* (save for one time), even though his practice is to meticulously seek to satisfy every opinion in Halacha.

Other communities also have a tradition not to wear Rabbenu Tam's *tefillin*. Rav Shalom Messas (*Teshuvot Shemesh U'Magen* 3:5:4) reports that the Jews of Morocco did not have the custom to wear Rabbenu Tam's *tefillin*. *Darké Abotenou,* however, notes that today many Moroccan Jews have adopted the more popular Sephardic practice to wear both sets of *tefillin*.

The Baladi group of Yemenite Jews, who abide by the rulings of the Rambam, do not wear the *tefillin* of Rabbenu Tam, as the Rambam (*Hilchot Tefillin* 3:5) shares Rashi's view regarding the order of placement of the *parshiyot* in the *tefillin*.

Finally, the fact that the *Shulḥan Aruch* (*Oraḥ Ḥayim* 34:4) notes that only a person with a reputation of being exceptionally pious should wear Rabbenu Tam's *tefillin* in addition to that of Rashi convinces many to refrain from wearing Rabbenu Tam's *tefillin*.

IN SUPPORT OF WEARING RABBENU TAM'S *TEFILLIN*

On the other hand, the *Ben Ish Ḥai* and Rav Ovadia Yosef strongly advocate also wearing Rabbenu Tam's *tefillin*. The *Ben Ish Ḥai* promotes this practice largely due to Kabbalistic reasons; the *Kabbala* associates extraordinary value and *kedusha* with the *tefillin* of Rabbenu Tam. Rav Ovadia, in contrast, notes the many *Rishonim* who support the view of Rabbenu Tam.[1] The *gemara* comments (*Rosh Hashana* 17b) that one who has not worn *tefillin* ("*karkafta d'lo mana tefillin*") does not merit a share in *Olam HaBa*. This motivates Rav Ovadia and many others to encourage wearing Rabbenu Tam's *tefillin* due to the severe consequences for one who does not fulfill this very important *mitzva*.

1. Rav Ovadia similarly encourages observing Shabbat until it has ended in accordance with Rabbenu Tam's stricter view (72 minutes after sunset), since a very large group of *Rishonim* subscribe to this opinion.

However, there is a major difference between the view of the *Ben Ish Ḥai* and that of Rav Ovadia. The *Ben Ish Ḥai* vigorously advocates wearing Rashi and Rabbenu Tam's *tefillin* simultaneously, due to Kabbalistic reasons. He bases himself on the well-known *gemara* (*Eruvin* 95b) that states that there is room for two sets of *tefillin* on a man's body. This became the common practice among a large group of Sephardic Jews.

Rav Ovadia (*Teshuvot Yabia Omer* 1: *Oraḥ Ḥayim* 3), on the other hand, believes that it is best for even Sephardic Jews to wear the two pairs consecutively (with Rashi's being worn first, since fundamentally Rashi is the authoritative opinion) and not simultaneously.[2] Rav Ovadia writes that each pair of *tefillin* can be no wider than two centimeters each in order for both to be placed correctly on the arm and head, and this, he contends, is a difficult requirement for contemporary *soferim* to meet. Rav Ovadia argues that it is better to forego the Kabbalistic advantages of wearing the *tefillin* simultaneously and instead adopt the Ḥassidic practice of wearing the two pairs consecutively, in order to ensure that the *tefillin* are placed correctly on the arm and head.[3]

CONCLUSION

When Jerusalem Chief Rabbi Rav Shlomo Amar visited Shaarei Orah in the summer of 5777 (2017), he donned his Rabbenu Tam's *tefillin* after removing his Rashi's *tefillin*. I was surprised that even when traveling he brought his Rabbenu Tam *tefillin* along. Richard Schulz of Shaarei Orah reports that he saw Rav Ovadia Yosef do the same when he visited Manhattan's Congregation Shearith Israel. Clearly, it is proper for a Sephardic Jew to follow the example of the level of observance advocated by Rav Ovadia and the *Ben Ish Ḥai* whenever possible.[4]

---

2. Despite his great enthusiasm for Rabbenu Tam *tefillin*, *Yalkut Yosef* (*Oraḥ Ḥayim* 34:10) rules that if one by mistake first wore Rabbenu Tam *tefillin* and recited a *beracha* upon them, he should recite a *beracha* again when he wears Rashi *tefillin* afterwards. Thus, even Rav Ovadia maintains that the *halacha* is fundamentally in accord with Rashi's opinion.
3. Rav Mordechai Eliyahu (in his *Siddur Kol Eliyahu*), who typically follows the rulings of the *Ben Ish Ḥai*, encourages one to find sufficiently small *tefillin* that will allow one to wear both Rashi and Rabbenu Tam's *tefillin* simultaneously.
4. Rav Shmuel Khoshkerman reports that after he married while learning at Baltimore's Yeshiva Ner Yisrael, he wished to wear Rabbenu Tam's *tefillin* after he removed his

Rashi *tefillin*. He was told not to do so, since it would be considered *yohara* (arrogance) if he were to wear Rabbenu Tam's *tefillin* when Ner Yisrael's famed Rosh Yeshiva, Rav Yitzḥak Ruderman, did not don Rabbenu Tam's *tefillin*. Rav Khoshkerman notes that based on this reasoning, it is likely not proper for a Sephardic Jew to wear Rabbenu Tam's *tefillin* when praying in an Ashkenazic *bet kenesset* in which the rabbi does not wear Rabbenu Tam's *tefillin* (see, however, *Yalkut Yosef, Oraḥ Ḥayim* 34:8). Rav Khoshkerman is similarly concerned for *yohara* if a Sephardic Jew wears the two *tefillin* simultaneously in a congregation in which Rabbenu Tam's *tefillin* is worn only consecutively.

Chapter 15

Berachot on *Tefillin* at a Sephardic *Bet Kenesset*

How many *berachot* are recited upon donning *tefillin*? This is one of the differences between Sephardic and Ashkenazic practice whose roots go back at least to the time of the *Rishonim*. Rashi, the Rif, and the Rambam argue that under ordinary circumstances, only one *beracha* – "*l'haniaḥ tefillin*" – is recited. Rabbenu Tam and the Rosh, however, maintain that the *beracha* of "*l'haniaḥ tefillin*" is recited on the *tefillin shel yad* and the *beracha* of "*al mitzvat tefillin*" is recited upon placing the *tefillin shel rosh* on the head.

SEPHARDIC AND ASHKENAZIC RULINGS

Maran Rav Yosef Karo (*Shulḥan Aruch, Oraḥ Ḥayim* 25:5) rules in accordance with Rashi, the Rif, and the Rambam. The Rama, in turn, notes that the custom among Ashkenazic communities is to follow Rabbenu Tam and the Rosh. It is typical for Rav Karo to rule in accordance with the majority opinion among the Rif, Rambam, and the Rosh. It is also the norm for the Rama to rule in accordance with the commonly accepted practices among Ashkenazim. Not only was the Rama a great Torah scholar; he was also an alert observer of Jewish practice in his region.

Sephardim follow the view of the *Shulḥan Aruch* and recite one *beracha* on *tefillin*, whereas Ashkenazim follow the Rama and recite two *berachot*.

TALMUDIC SUPPORT FOR BOTH OPINIONS

The Ashkenazic practice draws solid support from the *gemara* in *Berachot* (60b), which presents the order of *berachot* to be recited upon awakening. The *gemara* specifically instructs that when placing the *tefillin* on the arm, the *beracha* of "*l'haniaḥ*" is recited, and when placing *tefillin* on the head, the *beracha* of "*al mitzvat tefillin*" is recited.

However, the *gemara* in *Menaḥot* (36a) serves as solid support for the Sephardic approach. This *gemara* states that if one does not talk between affixing the *tefillin shel yad* and the *shel rosh* (as is proper conduct), one recites only one *beracha*; only if one improperly interrupted with conversation is a second *beracha* ("*al mitzvat tefillin*") recited.

The *Rishonim* endeavor to interpret the text that does not fit smoothly into their respective approaches. Rashi, the Rif, and the Rambam interpret the *gemara* in *Berachot* to be discussing a situation in which one spoke between placing the *shel yad* and the *shel rosh*. Rabbenu Tam, on the other hand interprets the *gemara* in *Menaḥot* as referring only to the *shel rosh*; under ordinary circumstances, only one *beracha* is recited before placing the *shel rosh*, but if one spoke between placing the *shel yad* and the *shel rosh*, two *berachot* must be recited upon placing the *shel rosh* on the head.

BARUCH SHEM KEVOD MALCHUTO

Most interesting is the Rama's addition that Ashkenazim recite, "*Baruch shem kevod malchuto*" after saying, "*al mitzvat tefillin*" on the *shel rosh*. This phrase is uttered if one mistakenly made an unnecessary *beracha*. In this context, it is recited out of respect for the opinion of Rashi, the Rif, and the Rambam, who maintain that the *beracha* on the *shel rosh* is unnecessary.

This practice is interesting, given that if the Rama and Ashkenazic Jews were truly concerned for a *beracha l'vatala* (an unnecessary *beracha*), the *beracha* would have been omitted entirely. Indeed, the Rama does not recommend saying "*Baruch shem*" in any other situation in which Ashkenazic Jews recite a *beracha* that Sephardic Jews do not, such as the *beracha* on the recitation of *Ḥatzi Hallel* on Rosh Ḥodesh. One thus suspects that Kabbalistic concerns are at play regarding the recitation of "*Baruch shem*" after "*al mitzvat tefillin*."

In any event, the *Mishna Berura* (25:21) emphasizes that Ashkenazic Jews should not say *"Baruch shem"* until after the *tefillin shel rosh* is completely in place, so as not to create an unwarranted interruption.

AN ASHKENAZIC VISITOR TO A SEPHARDIC *BET KENESSET*

What should an Ashkenazic Jewish man do when visiting a Sephardic *bet kenesset* for *Shaḥarit* on a day on which *tefillin* are worn? Should he refrain from reciting *"al mitzvat tefillin"* on the *tefillin shel rosh* in deference to the practice of the *bet kenesset*? I posed this question to former Sephardic Chief Rabbi Rav Shlomo Amar during his visit to Congregation Shaarei Orah, the Sephardic Congregation of Teaneck, in August 2017. Rav Amar responded that the Ashkenazic Jew should recite the *beracha,* but he should do so in an inconspicuous manner so that he does not blatantly distinguish himself from the *tzibur* (community). Rav Amar suggested that he face the wall or cover his mouth while reciting the *beracha.*[1]

It is a wonderful experience for Ashkenazic Jews to visit a Sephardic *bet kenesset.* It is recommended, however, to be aware of Sephardic customs so that he shows respect to the community he is visiting while following one's personal practices.

1. According to Rav Hershel Schachter (personal conversation), the same does not apply to an Ashkenazic visitor to a Sephardic congregation that does not recite a *beracha* on *Ḥatzi Hallel* on Rosh Ḥodesh and the last days of Pesaḥ. In that case, one may recite the *beracha* normally to himself, as it is not obvious that he is reciting the *beracha;* it appears that he is simply reciting the *Hallel.*

Birkat Kohanim

Chapter 16

An Ashkenazic *Kohen* Visiting a Sephardic *Kehilla*

First-time Ashkenazic visitors to Sephardic synagogues often find it astonishing that Sephardic *Kohanim* conduct *Birkat Kohanim* (the *Kohanim*'s blessing to the congregation) every day, even outside of Eretz Yisrael. The truth is, however, that it is far more astonishing that Ashkenazic Jews refrain from daily *Birkat Kohanim* outside Eretz Yisrael!

The *mishna* (*Kiddushin* 1:9) sets forth the rule very clearly: "Any *mitzva* that is land-based (*teluya ba'aretz*) is practiced only in Eretz Yisrael; any *mitzva* that is not land-based applies both in Eretz Yisrael and in *Ḥutz LaAretz* (outside of Israel)." Since *Birkat Kohanim* (also referred to as "*nesiat kapayim*") is not a land-based *mitzva*, it is difficult to understand why Ashkenazim refrain from conducting the *Kohanim*'s blessing outside of Eretz Yisrael (except on Yom Tov and Yom Kippur). The Sephardic practice (strongly endorsed by Rav Yosef Karo in the *Bet Yosef*, end of *Oraḥ Ḥayim* 128) stems from what appears to be the straightforward reading of the *mishna* in *Kiddushin*.

EXPLAINING THE ASHKENAZIC CUSTOM

Ashkenazic authorities offer a variety of explanations for the Ashkenazic custom. The *Bet Yosef* cites the *Sefer HaAgur* (a late *Rishon*), who offers two explanations. One is that the *Kohanim* customarily immerse in a *mikveh* prior to blessing the congregation, and they find it difficult to immerse in a *mikveh* every day during the cold winter months. On Yom Tov, however, this is not a relevant concern, since the *gemara* (*Rosh Hashana* 16b) encourages purifying oneself before the three *Regalim*. The *Sefer HaAgur* adds that *bitul melacha*, detracting from fulfilling professional obligations, is another concern. *Ḥazal* were very sensitive to keeping people from their work-related responsibilities (see *Megilla* 21 and *Berachot* 45b, for example). Thus, for example, they limited the number of *aliyot* to the Torah on Mondays and Thursdays to three. Similarly, the *Sefer HaAgur* suggests, *Birkat Kohanim* is omitted because it leads to *bitul melacha*.

The *Sefer HaAgur* concludes that it is permitted to refrain from *Birkat Kohanim* for these reasons, since technically a *Kohen* does not violate his obligation to bless the nation unless he is summoned with the call, "*Kohanim*," to do so. Indeed, the Targum Onkelos translates the *pasuk*, "Instruct the children of Aharon that this is how to bless the children of Israel, say to them" (*Bemidbar* 6:23) as, "In this manner shall you bless *Bnei Yisrael* when they instruct you to do so" (see the *Torat Ḥayim* edition of Onkelos). Thus, the obligation for *Kohanim* to bless the Jewish People is triggered only by our summoning them to bless us. Since Ashkenazic Jews do not summon the *Kohanim* to bless the nation except for on Yom Tov, no obligation devolves upon the *Kohanim* to recite *Birkat Kohanim*.[1]

The Rama (*Oraḥ Ḥayim* 128:44) codifies the universal custom among Ashkenazic Jews to refrain from *nesiat kapayim* except during *Musaf* on Yamim Tovim. He justifies the practice by noting that *Kohanim* should be in a pleasant mood in order to bless the nation ("*tov lev hu yevarech*"). During the week and even on Shabbat, we are anxious about our livelihoods; even on Yom Tov, *Kohanim* are only in a proper frame of mind to bless during *Musaf*. The *Mishna Berura* (128:166) adds that there is also joy on Yom

1. Of course, this justification does not apply to an Ashkenazic Jew who prays in a Sephardic congregation that summons the *Kohanim* to bless the nation, as we will discuss below. On the other hand, *Yalkut Yosef* (*Oraḥ Ḥayim* 128:18) instructs Sephardic *Kohanim* not to deliberately leave an Ashkenazic service before the *shali'aḥ tzibur* reaches the appropriate place for *Birkat Kohanim*. *Yalkut Yosef* is not concerned that the *Kohen* fails to fulfill his obligation to bless the congregation in an Ashkenazic service; since Ashkenazim do not summon the *Kohanim* to bless, the obligation to bless is bypassed.

Kippur due to the forgiveness of our sins, and *Birkat Kohanim* is therefore conducted then as well. Indeed, the *mishna* (*Ta'anit* 4:8) and *gemara* (*Ta'anit* 30b) state that Yom Kippur is one of the two happiest days in the Jewish calendar due to the fact that it is a day of forgiveness.

A SURPRISING *MINHAG* WITH A HEAVENLY ENDORSEMENT

The *Aruch HaShulḥan* (*Oraḥ Ḥayim* 128:64) – written by Rav Yeḥiel Michel Epstein (1828–1908) and a pillar of Ashkenazic practice – expresses serious reservations about the Ashkenazic practice not to recite *Birkat Kohanim* every day outside of Israel:

> There is certainly no correct explanation of our custom to fail to fulfill the *mitzva* for *Kohanim* to bless the nation throughout the year. They [authorities] have written that this is a *minhag garu'a* (a custom with a weak basis), but what can we do? It is as if a *bat kol* (heavenly voice) has proclaimed that we should not perform *nesiat kapayim* year round. I have a tradition that two *gedolei hador* (leading Rabbinic authorities) in generations prior to ours, each one in his community, sought to institute the daily performance of *nesiat kapayim* in their communities, but when the time came to implement this plan, the plans went awry, and each great rabbi proclaimed that they understood that *Hashem* has decreed as such that we should not conduct daily *Birkat Kohanim*.[2]

The *Aruch HaShulḥan* typically champions the accepted practices of the Ashkenazic community, but he nonetheless refers to this practice as a *minhag garu'a*.

---

2. Rav Naftali Tzvi Yehudah Berlin (the Netziv) relates (*Teshuvot Meshiv Davar* 2:104): I recall hearing from my father-in-law, Rav Yitzḥak of Volozhin [the son of Rav Ḥayim of Volozhin, the leading student of the Vilna Gaon] that the Vilna Gaon decided to introduce daily *Birkat Kohanim* in his *bet midrash*. However, he was prevented from doing so from Heaven, since he was arrested during the terrible dispute that emerged in Vilna. Afterwards, my father-in-law's father, Rav Ḥayim of Volozhin, decided to begin daily recitation of *Birkat Kohanim* the next morning. That night, a huge fire erupted and burned half of the city, including the local *bet kenesset* (*lo alenu*). They saw this and understood that there is a secret mystical factor regarding the introduction of *Birkat Kohanim* in *Ḥutz LaAretz*.

This is not surprising in light of the fact that the aforementioned explanations for the Ashkenazic practice are not particularly compelling.[3]

ASHKENAZIC *KOHANIM* VISITING A SEPHARDIC CONGREGATION

It has clearly emerged as a non-negotiable custom that Ashkenazic congregations refrain from daily *nesiat kapayim* outside of Israel. However, what should an Ashkenazic *Kohen* do when he visits a Sephardic congregation? Does the Ashkenazic custom apply only to the community conducting *Birkat Kohanim*, or does it apply even to an individual Ashkenazic Jew visiting a different community? May he join the Sephardic *Kohanim* in the *mitzva* to bless the *Kohanim*, or should he leave the synagogue before the *shali'ah tzibur* summons the *Kohanim* to bless the nation, since the summons triggers the obligation?

A relevant story is told about Rav Shalom Schwadron, the famous twentieth-century *tzaddik* known as the Maggid of Yerushalayim, who was a *Kohen*. Rav Shalom often visited the New York area to deliver his *mussar* speeches. Whenever possible, the Maggid would make an effort to attend *Shaḥarit* at a Sephardic congregation where he would have the opportunity to perform *nesiat kapayim*.[4] Clearly, the holy Maggid maintained that the custom applies only to an Ashkenazic congregation and not to individual Ashkenazim.

This approach is very logical. The Ashkenazic custom is questionable, as noted by the *Aruch HaShulḥan*, and thus should not be applied in an expansive manner. Indeed, as Rav of Congregation Shaarei Orah, the Sephardic Congregation of Teaneck, I encourage visiting Ashkenazic *Kohanim* to seize the opportunity to fulfill a *mitzva* that they would otherwise miss and perform *nesiat kapayim* along with their Sephardic brothers. The Ashkenazic authority Rav Yitzhak Liebes (*Teshuvot Bet Avi* 3:4) supports this position as well, as does Rav Hershel Schachter (personal communication). Rav Shmuel Khoshkerman believes it has become the accepted practice for Ashkenazic *Kohanim* who visit Sephardic congregations to join in *Birkat Kohanim*.

---

3. It is for this reason that the Vilna Gaon and Rav Ḥayim of Volozhin were eager to change the Ashkenazic practice and recite *Birkat Kohanim* every day even outside Eretz Yisrael; see the previous note.
4. Rav Paysach Krohn, who was exceptionally close to the Maggid, verified this story in personal conversation.

THE JOY OF SERVING AS A *KOHEN*

A *Kohen* once commented to me that being a *Kohen* entails a life of *simḥa*. This is especially true of Sephardic *Kohanim*, who have the opportunity to bless the Jewish People on a daily basis even if they are not in Eretz Yisrael. Indeed, the Rambam (*Hilchot Tefilla* 15:12) concludes his presentation of the laws of *Birkat Kohanim* with a powerful statement: "A *Kohen* who does not bless is not blessed, and any *Kohen* who blesses is blessed, as it is written (*Bereshit* 12:3), 'I will bless those who will bless you.'"

Chapter 17

Who Begins *Birkat Kohanim*?

One might think that if the Rambam and *Shulḥan Aruch* rule in a specific manner, it should be obvious that all Sephardic Jews follow that practice – but this is not necessarily so. Sephardic Halacha is far too complex and nuanced to be reduced to such a simple formula. A prime example of this is found in the variety of Sephardic practices regarding whether the *Kohanim* or the *ḥazan* begins *Birkat Kohanim* by reciting the word, "*Yevarechecha*."

SHULḤAN ARUCH VS. RAMA

Universal practice among all Jews is for the *ḥazan* to prompt the *Kohanim* with the words of the *Birkat Kohanim*.[1] The simple explanation of this practice is that it helps the *Kohanim* stay on track and say the proper word

1. The *Bet Yosef* (*Oraḥ Ḥayim* 128, s.v. *v'ha d'amrinan*) insists that this is a custom and not a Torah requirement. The source of this *minhag*, the *Bet Yosef* explains, is that the Torah instructs (*Bemidbar* 6:23), "*emor lahem*"—to tell the *Kohanim* to bless. On a Torah level, "*emor lahem*" teaches that we prompt the *Kohanim* to bless through the pre-*Birkat Kohanim* announcement, "*Kohanim*," which triggers the obligation for the *Kohanim* to recite their *beracha*. The *minhag* is that, in addition, the *ḥazan* prompts the *Kohanim* with their blessing word by word.

(similar to the Ashkenazic practice for someone to prompt the shofar-blower with the note he is about to sound).

However, both the Rambam (*Hilchot Tefilla* 14:3)[2] and Rav Yosef Karo (*Shulḥan Aruch, Oraḥ Ḥayim* 128:13) rule that the *Kohanim* should declare the first word of *Birkat Kohanim*, "*Yevarechecha*," without waiting for the *ḥazan*'s prompt. The most straightforward explanation (as noted by the *Bet Yosef, Oraḥ Ḥayim* 128, s.v. *u'shaliaḥ tzibur*, and *Mishna Berura* 128:48) is that the *Kohanim* do not need to be kept on track for the first word. A second explanation of this approach is that it enables the *Kohanim* to begin the recitation of *Birkat Kohanim* as soon as possible after they finish reciting the *beracha*, "*l'varech et amo Yisrael b'ahava*."

The Rama notes that the Ran (*Megilla* 15b in the Rif's pages, s.v. *en haKohanim*) and the *Tur* (*Oraḥ Ḥayim* 128) disagree and rule that the *ḥazan* should prompt even the word "*Yevarechecha*." A beautiful mystical explanation for this opinion is presented by Rabbenu Beḥayei and Kli Yakar (*Bemidbar* 6:23):

> The *ḥazan* serves as an intermediary to trigger the flow of abundant heavenly blessings through the "divine pipeline." The blessings will first rest on the *Kohanim*, in order that they serve as a vessel filled with *Hashem*'s blessings. The *Kohanim* subsequently transfer this blessing to the congregation. The *Kohanim* act as a full vessel pouring out its content to an empty vessel. Were it not for the *ḥazan* prompting the *Kohanim*, the *Kohanim* would not be blessed and they would not be able to transfer the *beracha* to the assembled.

According to this approach, the *ḥazan* must prompt the *Kohanim* even with the word "*Yevarechecha*."

A STUNNING CHANGE IN PRACTICE

The Rama notes that the universal practice among Ashkenazic Jews is for the *ḥazan* to prompt the *Kohanim* with "*Yevarechecha*." This continues to be the unchallenged and universal practice among Ashkenazic Jews until today. The *Bet Yosef* (*Oraḥ Ḥayim* 128, s.v. *ushaliaḥ tzibur*), in turn, notes that the

2. As explained by the *Bet Yosef*.

practice throughout Eretz Yisrael and Egypt is for the *Kohanim* – and not the *ḥazan* – to begin "*Yevarechecha*."

This remained the accepted Sephardic practice until the *Ben Ish Ḥai* (year 1, *Parashat Tetzaveh* 1) made a revolution. He explains that those who say that the *ḥazan* begins "*Yevarechecha*" maintain that this is a requirement, but those who believe that the *Kohanim* begin "*Yevarechecha*" hold that it is permissible for them to begin "*Yevarechecha*" – not that it is required of them to do so. Thus, we may abandon this practice if there is a compelling reason. The *Ben Ish Ḥai* accepts the view that the *ḥazan* need not prompt the first word of *Birkat Kohanim*, as there is no concern for confusion. The *ḥazan*'s prompt is unnecessary – but it is permissible.[3]

The *Ben Ish Ḥai* notes that the *Kabbala* strongly supports the practice of the *ḥazan* prompting the *Kohanim* even with the word "*Yevarechecha*."[4] He adds that this is the practice of the celebrated Sephardic Kabbalistic Yeshivat Bet El (which exists to this day in the Old City of Jerusalem). The *Ben Ish Ḥai* writes:

> A number of years ago, *Hashem* helped me convince the community to change the practice in every *bet kenesset* in our city of Baghdad for the *ḥazan* to prompt the *Kohanim* even with the word "*Yevarechecha*." This is what should be done in every community.

The *Ben Ish Ḥai* notes a halachic advantage to adopting this practice: When the *Kohanim* initiate "*Yevarechecha*," they often begin before the *tzibur* has had a chance to answer "*amen*" to the *beracha* of "*l'varech et amo Yisrael b'ahava*," and this is inappropriate.

The *Kaf HaḤayim* (*Oraḥ Ḥayim* 128:82) endorses the *Ben Ish Ḥai*'s revolutionary approach. He notes that *Tosafot* (*Berachot* 34a, s.v. *lo ya'aneh*) seems to accept this view as well. In the wake of the rulings of the *Ben Ish Ḥai* and *Kaf HaḤayim*, many Sephardic communities changed their centuries-old practice to follow the Rambam and *Bet Yosef* and began to have the *ḥazan* prompt the *Kohanim* even with the word "*Yevarechecha*."

However, many Sephardic communities continued and continue to follow the ruling of the Rambam and the *Shulḥan Aruch*. Moroccan, Syrian,

---

3. As noted below, according to the second explanation of this approach – to minimize interruption between the *birkat hamitzva* and the recitation of *Birkat Kohanim* – it would seem to be a requirement that may not be abandoned.
4. As we have noted elsewhere, *Kabbala* exerted a profound influence on the *Ben Ish Ḥai*.

and Yemenite Jews are among the communities that retain the original practice. These communities seem to prefer the second explanation for the ruling of the Rambam and the *Shulḥan Aruch* – that we seek to minimize interruptions between the *birkat hamitzva* and the recitation of *Birkat Kohanim*. According to this approach, it is a requirement for the *Kohanim* to begin "*Yevarechecha*," and there is therefore no option of abandoning this practice.

RAV OVADIA YOSEF'S SURPRISING ENDORSEMENT OF THE BEN ISH ḤAI

One might expect Rav Ovadia Yosef to restore the original Sephardic practice. After all, in countless situations, Rav Ovadia overturns the ruling of the *Ben Ish Ḥai* in favor of "*haḥazarat atara l'yoshna*," restoring the crown to its original luster by following the ruling of *Maran* Rav Yosef Karo. For example, although many or even most Sephardic women followed the ruling of the *Ben Ish Ḥai* and *Kaf HaḤayim* to recite the *beracha* on Shabbat candles only after lighting, Rav Ovadia strongly advocates the return to the ruling of the Rambam and *Shulḥan Aruch* to recite the *beracha* before the lighting (as we discuss at length in Chapter 31).

Despite this expectation, however, in this case, Rav Ovadia strongly advocates following the ruling of the *Ben Ish Ḥai* and *Kaf HaḤayim*. In fact, he even records (*Teshuvot Yeḥaveh Da'at* 4:10; *Yalkut Yosef, Oraḥ Ḥayim* 128:42) that he convinced the *kehilla* he led while serving as the municipal rabbi of Tel Aviv to change their *minhag* to that of the *Ben Ish Ḥai* and *Kaf HaḤayim*.

Three reasons may be offered for why Rav Ovadia did not restore the ruling of the Rambam and *Shulḥan Aruch*. One reason may be that the practice of Yeshivat Bet El became the dominant practice in the synagogues of Yerushalayim, and Minhag Yerushalayim plays a major role in Rav Ovadia's rulings. A second reason is the halachic disadvantage of the *Kohanim* rushing to say "*Yevarechecha*" before the congregation responds "*amen*" to the *beracha*, as noted by the *Ben Ish Ḥai*.[5] Finally, the Rambam and Rav Karo permit the *Kohanim* to begin "*Yevarechecha*"; they do not insist that the *Kohanim* do so.

5. Congregation Shaarei Orah member Haim Tawil, a *Kohen* of Syrian background, reports that the Syrian *Rabbanim* often reiterate instructions to the *Kohanim* to pause and allow the *kahal* to respond "*amen*" before the *Kohanim* begin saying "*Yevarechecha*."

IF ONLY ONE KOHEN IS PRESENT

The Rambam and *Shulḥan Aruch* do not distinguish between a situation in which only one *Kohen* is present and when more than one *Kohen* is present, apparently indicating that they maintain that the *Kohen* begins "*Yevarechecha*" even if only one *Kohen* is present. This is the practice of Yemenite Jews until today.[6] *Teshuvot Pirḥei Kohanim* (*Oraḥ Ḥayim* 27, cited in *Yalkut Yosef*) notes that this is the custom of Algerian Jews as well.

However, both the *Kaf HaḤayim* and the *Yalkut Yosef* cite *Teshuvot Maharam Mintz* (#12), who rules that even the Rambam and *Shulḥan Aruch* would agree that if only one *Kohen* is present, the *ḥazan* should initiate "*Yevarechecha*." Only when more than one *Kohen* is present does the *ḥazan* declare, "*Kohanim*," thereby satisfying the requirement of "*emor lahem*" (that the *ḥazan*, on behalf of the community, initiates *Birkat Kohanim*). But when only one *Kohen* is present, the word "*Kohanim*" is not recited (*Sota* 38a). In the absence of this declaration beginning *Birkat Kohanim*, the *ḥazan* must say, "*Yevarechecha*." The *Kaf HaḤayim* concludes that the consensus of *Aḥaronim* concurs with the ruling of the Maharam Mintz (see, for example, *Mishna Berura* 128:47). *Yalkut Yosef* rules in accordance with this view as well.

CONCLUSION

The universal Ashkenazic practice is for the *ḥazan* to always prompt the *Kohanim* with the word "*Yevarechecha*." The original Sephardic practice was that the *Kohanim* always begin "*Yevarechecha*," and Yemenite Jews retain this practice in all circumstances. Syrian and Moroccan Jews retain this practice when there are two or more *Kohanim*. The *Ben Ish Ḥai*, *Kaf HaḤayim*, and Rav Ovadia Yosef advocate that even Sephardic Jews should always instruct the *ḥazan* to prompt the *Kohanim* with the word "*Yevarechecha*."[7]

---

6. Yemenite Jews maintain strong fidelity to the rulings of the Rambam and *Shulḥan Aruch*. This practice was reported to me by Congregation Shaarei Orah member Josh Hosseinoff, a *Kohen* who observed this practice in four different Yemenite *minyanim* in Israel.
7. It appears that these three major authorities do not distinguish between whether two or more *Kohanim* are present or if only one *Kohen* is present. They believe that the *ḥazan* should always prompt the *Kohen* with the word "*Yevarechecha*." Rav Shmuel Khoshkerman agrees to this interpretation and notes that this is the widely accepted practice in Sephardic congregations.

Keri'at HaTorah

Chapter 18

Standing or Sitting for *Keri'at HaTorah?*

In certain segments of the Ashkenazic Orthodox community, it is common practice to stand for *Keri'at HaTorah* (the public Torah reading). In Modern Orthodox synagogues, this is a result, in part, of the influence of Rav Yosef Dov Soloveitchik and Rav Aharon Lichtenstein, who were enthusiastic about the practice. They often stressed that standing for *Keri'at HaTorah* helps us experience the Torah reading as a recreation of the Divine Revelation at Har Sinai, at which time we stood (*Devarim* 4:11).[1] However, this is certainly not the practice at Sephardic synagogues.

SOURCES FOR THE DIFFERING PRACTICES

Sefer Neḥemia (8:4–5) presents the only incident of a public Torah reading recorded in *Tanach*:

> And Ezra the Scribe stood upon a wooden platform that they constructed for this purpose, and Matitya, Shema, Aniya, Uriya, Chilkiya, and Ma'aseya stood on his right side... And Ezra opened the

1. See, for example, *Shiurim L'Zecher Abba Mari Z"L* 2:210–211.

> scroll before the eyes of the entire nation, for he stood above the entire nation; and when he opened it, the entire nation stood.

The verse seemingly indicates that it is customary to stand when the Torah is read.

The ancient *siddur* of Rav Amram Gaon (2:25), however, explains that it is incorrect to interpret the verse to mean that "the entire nation stood" in a literal sense. Rather, "standing" in this context refers to being silent. This is indicated by the *gemara* in *Sota* (39a), where this verse is cited as the source of the law that immediately upon opening the *sefer Torah,* it is forbidden to speak even words of Halacha. Thus, Rav Amram Gaon convincingly demonstrates that there is no basis in the *Tanach* for the practice to stand during the reading of the Torah.

Nevertheless, the *Sefer HaAguda* (a *Rishon*) writes that despite the *gemara*'s interpretation of the word "standing" in the verse in *Neḥemia* to refer to being silent, a verse can never lose its *peshat* (straightforward) understanding entirely.[2] Thus, although *Ḥazal* derive from this *pasuk* that it is forbidden to speak during the time the Torah is read, we derive an additional law based on the straightforward understanding of the *pasuk* – that that one should stand during the Torah reading.

Most *Rishonim,* including the Rambam (*Teshuvot* #46), rule that there is no obligation to stand while the Torah is being read, and Rav Yosef Karo rules in accordance with the majority approach (*Shulḥan Aruch, Oraḥ Ḥayim* 146:4).[3] The *Mordechai* (*Shabbat* 222) records that the Maharam of Rothenburg stood during the Torah reading, and this custom is cited, in turn, by the Rama.

CONTEMPORARY PRACTICE

Some Ashkenazim observe the custom to stand for Torah reading, as noted by the Rama. Nevertheless, even those Ashkenazim who do follow this custom do so only as an added stringency and not the letter of the law, as implied by the language of the Rama.[4]

---

2. See *Shabbat* 63a.
3. In the *Bet Yosef* (*Oraḥ Ḥayim* 146), Rav Karo notes that the common practice is to sit for *Keri'at HaTorah.*
4. The Rama writes, "*Yesh maḥmirim v'omdim,*" "there are those who are stringent and stand." Had the Rama regarded this as a required practice, he would have written, "*Yesh ḥolkim v'omdim,*" "there are those who disagree and stand."

Such a custom does not exist among Sephardic Jews,[5] for even the Ari z"l would sit during the Torah reading (*Kaf HaḤayim, Oraḥ Ḥayim* 146:20). The *Kaf HaḤayim* notes that even very pious individuals and great Sephardic authorities behaved in this manner.[6] Indeed, Rav Ovadia Yosef would customarily sit during the Torah reading.[7]

CONCLUSION

Sephardic Jews sit during the Torah reading. Thus, even if an Ashkenazic guest is strict and his custom is to stand for *Keri'at HaTorah* when praying in an Ashkenazic synagogue, he should preferably sit for *Keri'at HaTorah* when visiting a Sephardic *bet kenesset*. However, if he wishes to stand, Rav David Yosef (*Halacha Berura* 7:141:3) permits him to do so. Similarly, Rav David Yosef rules that a Sephardic Jew who visits an Ashkenazic *bet kenesset* in which everyone stands for *Keri'at HaTorah* should preferably stand together with the congregation. However, if he wishes, he may remain seated.

5. Sephardic Jews do stand when their father, father-in-law, grandparent, or older brother is honored with an *aliya* to the Torah (*Kaf HaḤayim, Oraḥ Ḥayim* 141:35).
6. The *Kaf HaḤayim* writes that one does not stand even when responding, "*Baruch Hashem hamevorach l'olam va'ed.*"
7. As reported by his grandson, Rav Yaakov Sasson; see http://halachayomit.co.il/en/default.aspx?HalachaID=4451.

Chapter 19

B'Simana Tava on Simḥat Torah

Before beginning the reading of *Sefer Bereshit* on Simḥat Torah, many Sephardic Jews proclaim, "*B'simana tava*!" "In a good sign!" This *minhag* is recorded and endorsed by the venerated by Rav Yosef Ḥaim of Baghdad, the *Ben Ish Ḥai,* in his *Teshuvot Rav Pa'alim* (vol. 3, *Oraḥ Ḥayim* 42).

THE *BEN ISH ḤAI*'S DEFENSE

This seems like a beautiful way to begin *Sefer Bereshit.* Many have raised the problem, however, of a potential *hefsek,* an unwarranted interruption. If the *Ḥatan Bereshit* proclaims, "*B'simana tava*" after he recites his *beracha* and before the commencement of the Torah reading, this certainly appears to constitute a *hefsek.*

The *Ben Ish Ḥai* defends the practice in two manners. First, he argues that only a minimum of four words constitutes a *hefsek,* such as when one greets his Rav with the traditional salutation, "*Shalom alecha rabi umori.*" Second, "*B'simana tava*" is a form of *tefilla,* which the *Ben Ish Ḥai* contends is not a *hefsek.*

As precedent, the *Ben Ish Ḥai* cites a surprising ruling from the venerated work *Pe'at HaShulḥan* (*Hilchot Eretz Yisrael* 3). This highly respected and authoritative *sefer* reports that *shoḥetim* (ritual slaughterers) were compelled by the Moslem owners of animals to declare, "Allah Akbar!" after reciting the *beracha* on the *sheḥita,* so that the animal would be acceptable to Moslem purchasers.[1] The *Pe'at HaShulḥan* rules that this is acceptable, since it is less than four words.

The *Ateret Rosh* infers this conclusion from a *gemara* in *Berachot* (40a) that states that the words, "*Tol broch, tol broch*" do not constitute a *hefsek* between the recitation of a *beracha* and eating, due to their relevance to eating. The *gemara* deliberately repeats the term "*Tol broch,*" explains the *Ateret Rosh,* because less than four words certainly do not create a *hefsek* in any event; two words alone would not constitute a *hefsek* even if they were not connected to eating.[2]

RAV OVADIA YOSEF'S APPROACH

Rav Ovadia Yosef (*Teshuvot Yabia Omer* 10: *Oraḥ Ḥayim* 55:3:33), however, notes that the same *gemara* cited by the *Ateret Rosh* teaches that the two words "*gevil l'tori*" could potentially create a *hefsek,* even though it is only two words. Rav Ovadia cites quite a few *Rishonim* who indicate this as well, including the *Sefer HaEshkol* (p. 39), Meiri (*Magen Avot,* p. 16), and Ra'avya (112).

Moreover, Rav Ovadia cites many great *Aḥaronim* who rule that even one irrelevant word constitutes a *hefsek.* These include the *Mishna Berura* (*Be'ur Halacha* 25:9), *Ḥayei Adam* (5:11), *Peri Megadim* (*Oraḥ Ḥayim* 206:4), and *Tevu'ot Shor* (*Yoreh De'ah* 19:13).

Most importantly, Rav Ovadia notes that the *Shulḥan Aruch* (*Oraḥ Ḥayim* 167:6) seems to indicate that even saying the two words, "bring salt" could constitute a *hefsek* if it is not necessary. Thus, *Maran* Rav Yosef Karo seems to reject the position set forth by the *Ben Ish Ḥai* and the *Pe'at HaShulḥan*!

Finally, with regard to the *Ben Ish Ḥai's* argument that "*B'simana tava*" constitutes a relevant *tefilla,* Rav Ovadia is not comfortable with the insertion of a discretionary prayer between a *beracha* and the performance of the *mitzva.*[3]

---

1. Potential non-Jewish buyers of an animal's meat are essential, since there is a serious possibility that the animal will be discovered to be *terefa* and unfit for consumption by Jews.
2. Rav Mordechai Lebhar (*Magen Avot, Even HaEzer* 62:7) cites this ruling of the *Ben Ish Ḥai* to defend the practice of many Sephardic *ḥazanim* to add the word "*umatzliaḥ*" after completing the last of the *sheva berachot* under the *ḥuppa.*
3. Rav Ovadia refers to a discussion he presents in *Teshuvot Yabia Omer* (7: *Yoreh De'ah* 23:4) rejecting the idea of reciting *kaparot* between the *beracha* and the *shehita* of the chicken.

To top off his argument, Rav Ovadia cites Rav Ḥayim Palagi (*Mo'ed LeChol Ḥai* 85:25), a major nineteenth-century Sephardic authority, who considers the words "*B'simana tava*" to be a *hefsek*.

CONCLUSION

Rav Ovadia concludes his responsum on a dramatic note, saying that when he serves as a *shaliaḥ tzibur* to call up the *Ḥatan Bereshit,* he proclaims, "*B'simana tava*" before the *Ḥatan Bereshit* recites the *beracha,* thereby avoiding the issue of *hefsek*. Rav Ovadia's son, Rav Yitzḥak Yosef, codifies this approach in his *Yalkut Yosef,* and this is the practice at Congregation Shaarei Orah, the Sephardic Congregation of Teaneck. Rav Shmuel Khoshkerman observes that this has become a common practice in many Sephardic congregations. However, some Sephardic *kehillot* continue to declare, "*B'simana tava*" after the *Ḥatan Bereshit* recites the *beracha,* in accordance with the view of the *Ben Ish Ḥai.*[4]

4. This is the practice of Morrocan Jews. Rav Lebhar (*Magen Avot, Oraḥ Ḥayim* 669:1) bolsters this practice by noting that the Torah reader proclaims, "*B'simana tava,*" not the man who receives the *aliya*. Thus, concern that the words constitute a *hefsek* is considerably reduced, since the one reciting the *beracha* is not creating an interruption between the *beracha* and the Torah reading.

Chapter 20

Amen After the *Berachot* of the *Haftara*

One of my favorite things to do at Congregation Shaarei Orah, the Sephardic Congregation of Teaneck, is to examine the wide variety of Sephardic *siddurim* that line our bookshelves and discover the slightly nuanced differences in practice. One difference I discovered relates to the declaration of "*amen*" at the conclusion of the last *beracha* recited after the *haftara, Mekadesh HaShabbat. Siddurim* based on the rulings of Rav Ovadia Yosef, the Moroccan *siddur,*[1] and the Tunisian *siddur* "*Ish Matzli'aḥ*" instruct the reader to say "*amen*" at this point, whereas the Syrian, Turkish, Persian

1. At Shaarei Orah, we have the *Siddur Darchei Avot,* is a very popular *siddur* among Moroccan Jews. However, when Rav Baruch Gigi, Rosh Yeshiva of Yeshivat Har Etzion, visited Congregation Shaarei Orah in March 2018 and read the *haftara,* he did not say "*amen*" after the last *beracha.* He explained that this was what he recalled as the *minhag* in the Moroccan city of Meknes, in which he was raised. Similarly, Dr. Adam Ohayon, author of "*Darké Abotenou*: The Laws and Customs of the Jews of Morocco," informed me that this is also the custom in the Moroccan synagogue in which he prays in Toronto (Sephardic Kehila Centre, led by the respected Rav Amram Assayag). Rav David Banon, the prominent Moroccan *dayan* in Montreal, told me that the *minhag* in Casablanca was not to say "*amen*" after reciting "*mekadesh HaShabbat.*"

(Ghermezian), and Spanish-Portuguese (Minhag Amsterdam) *siddurim* do not include this instruction.[2]

This diversity in *siddurim* is reflected in practice at Shaarei Orah; some *haftara* readers say "*amen*" and others do not. What is the reason behind this divergence in practice?

A CLASSIC DIFFERENCE BETWEEN SEPHARDIC AND ASHKENAZIC JEWS

It all begins with a dispute as to how to interpret a passage in the *gemara* in *Berachot* (45b). The *gemara* presents two *beraitot* that contradict each other: One *beraita* praises those who answer "*amen*" to their own *berachot,* while the other criticizes those who do so. The *gemara* resolves this contradiction by saying that only regarding the *beracha* of *Boneh Yerushalayim* in *Birkat HaMazon* is it appropriate to answer "*amen*" to one's own *beracha.*

Tosafot (ad loc., s.v. *Boneh Yerushalayim*) and the Rama (*Oraḥ Ḥayim* 215:1) understand the *gemara* in a narrow sense, as referring specifically and exclusively to the *beracha* of *Boneh Yerushalayim*. Regarding this *beracha* in particular, there is a need to create a separation, distinguishing between the first three *berachot* of *Birkat HaMazon,* which originate in Torah law, and the fourth *beracha,* which is only a Rabbinic enactment. The Ashkenazic practice follows this view.

The Sephardic tradition, however, follows the view of the Rambam (*Hilchot Berachot* 1:16) and Rav Yosef Karo (*Shulḥan Aruch, Oraḥ Ḥayim* 215:1), who interpret the *gemara* broadly to refer to any *beracha* that resembles *Boneh Yerushalayim*. The Rambam and the *Shulḥan Aruch* understand that just as "*amen*" is recited by the reader after *Boneh Yerushalayim* since it is the last of the series of *berachot* (the first three blessings of *Birkat HaMazon,* which are of Biblical origin), "*amen*" is similarly recited after completing any series of *berachot*. For this reason, Sephardic Jews say "*amen*" after *Yishtabaḥ* (the concluding *beracha* of *Pesukei D'Zimra*), *Hashkivenu* (the last of the *berachot keri'at shema* of the evening), and *Sim Shalom* (the last of the *berachot* of the *Amida*).

APPLICATION TO THE *BERACHOT* OF THE *HAFTARA*

Accordingly, it would seem fairly obvious that Sephardim should say "*amen*" after completing the series of *berachot* recited after the *haftara* reading. Thus,

2. The new Artscroll Sephardic Siddur has this "*amen*" in parenthesis.

after finishing the last *beracha, Mekadesh HaShabbat,* the reader should say "*amen.*" In fact, the Ritva (*Hilchot Berachot* 6:5) explicitly states that after concluding *Mekadesh HaShabbat,* the reader should say "*amen,*" and Rav Ovadia Yosef (*Teshuvot Yeḥaveh Da'at* 2:23) and the *Ben Ish Ḥai* (year 1, *Parashat Masei* 14), the two greatest Sephardic authorities of the past 150 years, agree that "*amen*" should be recited after *Mekadesh HaShabbat.* The *Siddur Kol Eliyahu* of Rav Mordechai Eliyahu also includes "*amen*" after the concluding *beracha* of the *haftara.*

Why, then, do many Sephardic Jews omit "*amen*" after *Mekadesh HaShabbat*? The answer is that a number of prominent Sephardic authorities record that the *minhag* is not to say this "*amen.*" The *Kaf HaḤayim* (*Oraḥ Ḥayim* 215:1) notes that although there is a compelling reason for Sephardic Jews to say "*amen*" after completing *Mekadesh HaShabbat,* he has not seen anyone who does so. The *Ḥida* (*Birkei Yosef, Oraḥ Ḥayim* 215:1) similarly writes that only a few Sephardic Jews say "*amen*" after completing the *berachot* of the *haftara,* without explaining why the majority do not.

CONCLUSION

Rav Ovadia Yosef made an effort to educate and encourage Sephardic Jews to say "*amen*" after the *berachot* of the *haftara,* and Rav Mordechai Eliyahu joined him in this quest. They were successful in changing the practice among many Sephardim.

At Shaarei Orah, I have informed the congregation of this ruling of Rav Ovadia and Rav Mordechai Eliyahu a number of times. I always note that although some premier Sephardic authorities support those who do not say "*amen*" after *Mekadesh HaShabbat,* there appears to be no compelling evidence for this practice. If someone does not say "*amen*" after finishing the *berachot* on the *haftara,* we do not correct them. However, it is certainly preferable for Sephardim to say "*amen*" after concluding the *beracha* of *Mekadesh HaShabbat.*

Chapter 21

The *Haftara* of *Parashat Shemot*

It is always intriguing to analyze the different choices for the *haftara* among Sephardic and Ashkenazic Jews. One such example is the selection for *Parashat Shemot.* Due to its parallel with the *parasha,* Sephardic Jews read *Yirmiyahu* 1, the same *haftara* read by all Jews on the first Shabbat following Shiva Asar B'Tammuz. This chapter is the first of the *Telata D'Puranuta,* the three sad *haftarot* read during *Ben HaMetzarim,* the melancholy time between Shiva Asar B'Tammuz and Tisha B'Av. Ashkenazic Jews, however, do not read *Yirmiyahu* 1 as the *haftara* for *Parashat Shemot;* instead, they read portions of *Yeshayahu* 27–29.

EXPLAINING THE ASHKENAZIC PRACTICE

In both *Parashat Shemot* and *Yirmiyahu* 1, we read about two great *nevi'im,* Moshe Rabbenu and Yirmiyahu HaNavi, who were selected by *Hashem* to serve as prophetic messengers to *Am Yisrael.* Both prophets resist the choice to serve as *navi* but eventually relent. The obvious parallel seems to support the Sephardic choice of *haftara.*

Ashkenazic practice may be easily explained, however, by noting the enormous difference between the respective missions to which *Hashem* assigned the two prophets. Moshe Rabbenu was assigned to serve as the *navi* of the liberation of *Am Yisrael* from Mitzrayim, whereas Yirmiyahu was chosen to serve as the *navi* of the impending *ḥurban* (destruction) of the *Bet HaMikdash*! Thus, Ashkenazic tradition regards *Yirmiyahu* 1 as the perfect *haftara* for the first of the *Telata D'Puranuta*, but not for *Parashat Shemot.*

Ashkenazic practice might also emerge from the fundamental difference between the *nevu'a* of Moshe Rabbenu and the prophecies of all other *nevi'im*. Indeed, *Hashem* spells out to none other than Aharon and Miriam that Moshe Rabbenu is a *navi* in a class of his own and can never be compared to any other *navi* (*Bemidbar* 12). The Rambam devotes one principle of his thirteen principles of faith to belief in prophecy and a distinct principle of faith to belief in the unique *nevu'a* of Moshe Rabbenu. This might also detract from drawing a parallel between Moshe Rabbenu and Yirmiyahu HaNavi.[1]

EXPLAINING THE SEPHARDIC PRACTICE

A closer examination of the *haftara* clarifies the Sephardic practice. This passage tells us that Yirmiyahu was "set over the nations and over the kingdoms, to root out and to pull down, and to destroy and to overthrow; to build, and to plant" (*Yirmiyahu* 1:10).[2] In other words, Yirmiyahu's mission is not only to inform *Am Yisrael* of the impending *ḥurban,* but also to ready us for the subsequent rebuilding – "to build and to plant."

In fact, Yirmiyahu is the *navi* who presents the gripping scene of our mother Rachel crying for her children, refusing to be consoled until *Hashem* finally calms her with His promise that her children will return home (*Yirmiyahu* 31:16). It is Yirmiyahu HaNavi who informs us that we will enjoy an opportunity to return seventy years after the Babylonian exile (ch. 29).

Moreover, the closing of the *haftara* with the start of *Yirmiyahu* 2 reassures us that even in the exile, the relationship between *Hashem* and *Am Yisrael* prevails: "*Kodesh Yisrael laHashem,*" "The Jewish People are holy to *Hashem*"! Through Yirmiyahu, *Hashem* reminds us, "I remember for you the affection of your youth, the love of your espousals; how you went after Me in the wilderness, in a land that was not sown."

---

1. For an explanation of the Ashkenazic practice, see Rav Hayyim Angel, "A Study of Sephardic and Ashkenazic Liturgy", which may be accessed at https://www.jewishideas.org/article/study-sephardic-and-ashkenazic-liturgy-rabbi-hayyim-angel.
2. This and subsequent translations are based on the 1917 Jewish Publication Society translation.

Thus, there is indeed a proper parallel between Moshe Rabbenu's mission and that of Yirmiyahu. In fact, drawing this parallel reminds us that just as Moshe Rabbenu serves as the harbinger of redemption, Yirmiyahu plays that role as well. Highlighting this parallel reminds us that just as Yirmiyahu's prophecy of doom has been fulfilled, his prophecy of eventual redemption will also be fulfilled.[3]

CONCLUSION

Rav Yosef Dov Soloveitchik noted that the *berachot* for the *haftara* clearly indicate that the primary purpose of the *haftara* is to reinforce our belief in the eventual redemption of our people. In fact, it is the Sephardic practice to proclaim, "*Go'alenu Hashem Tzevakot shemo, Kedosh Yisrael*" ("*Hashem*, the Holy One of Israel, is our Redeemer") at the conclusion of every *haftara* reading.[4] Thus, Sephardic Jews connect the *hakdasha* (dedication) of Moshe Rabbenu and Yirmiyahu HaNavi as prophets, as the correlation reaffirms the future redemption of *Am Yisrael*. Sephardic Jews believe that the mission assignments of Moshe Rabbenu and Yirmiyahu HaNavi are simply perfect together as a *parasha* and *haftara* pairing.

3. This idea reflects Rabbi Akiva's immortal words (*Makkot* 24) uttered upon his witnessing a tell-tale sign of *ḥurban*, a fox scurrying along *Har HaBayit*.
4. For a justification of this practice, see *Teshuvot Yabia Omer* 1: *Oraḥ Ḥayim* 9.

Chapter 22

Hashem Imachem

Upon receiving an *aliya* to the Torah, many Sephardic Jews first declare, "*Hashem imachem*" ("May God be with you").[1] The congregation then responds, "*Yevarechecha Hashem*" ("May God bless you"), at which point the one receiving the *aliya* proceeds to recite the *beracha* over the Torah reading (*Kaf HaḤayim, Oraḥ Ḥayim* 139:35).

THE ORIGIN OF THE PRACTICE

The origin of this exchange is the story told in *Megillat Rut* of Boaz's arrival at his fields. He greets his workers with the wish, "*Hashem imachem,*" and

1. The actual name of *Hashem* is not said in the context. In general, Rav Ovadia Yosef (*Teshuvot Yabia Omer* 3: *Oraḥ Ḥayim* 14; *Teshuvot Yeḥaveh Da'at* 3:13) permits saying *Hashem*'s name even without completing a *pasuk*. However, when Rav Shlomo Amar visited Congregation Shaarei Orah in August 2017, he did not say *Hashem*'s name when he cited only a fragment of a *pasuk*. Rav Amar told me that this is his practice with regard to the name *Hashem*, but not regarding *Elokim*. Rav Daniel Raccah informed me that many Sephardic rabbis adopt a similar practice. Regardless, when saying "*Hashem imachem,*" *Hashem*'s name should not be uttered. The *Kaf HaḤayim* explains that this is because the *Zohar* (*Parashat Yitro*) objects to beginning a sentence with *Hashem*'s name. Rav Shmuel Khoshkerman told me that he heard quoted in the name of Rav Ovadia that if the *oleh* (person receiving the *aliya*) does say *Hashem*'s name, we need not correct him.

they respond, "*Yevarechecha Hashem*" (*Rut* 2:4). But why has it become customary to introduce the *beracha* over the Torah reading with this exchange?

To answer this question, we must consider why *Megillat Rut* found it necessary to add this brief account. Everything that appears in *Tanach* teaches a vital lesson relevant for each generation (*Megilla* 14a). What lesson is imparted by recording how Boaz greeted his workers and how they replied?

SNUBBING SNOBBERY

Ibn Ezra explains that this was simply a friendly greeting. While this may hardly seem to teach a profound lesson, indeed it does! This friendly exchange between the wealthy landowner Boaz and his workers demonstrates Boaz's abhorrence of pretentiousness and feeling superior to those in a lower socio-economic class. This led Boaz to connect with Rut despite the very wide economic gap between them, eventually leading to their marriage and the birth of a child who would be the grandfather of David HaMelech and the *Melech HaMashiaḥ*. All this is accomplished because Boaz snubbing snobbery!

It is important to convey this lesson specifically during *Keri'at HaTorah*. Unfortunately, some people view the Torah *aliyot* as an opportunity for social climbing, considering who receives the most and least prestigious *aliya*, etc. Perhaps the exchange of Boaz and his workers is recalled at this time to remind us to zealously avoid such destructive behavior, especially in connection with *Keri'at HaTorah*.[2]

PROMOTING RESPECT

The Malbim notes that *Ḥazal* (*Berachot* 54a and 63a) teach that Boaz, the *gadol hador* (leader of the generation; *Bava Batra* 91a), issued an edict that people should greet each other with *Hashem*'s name, despite the fact that it is generally forbidden to use *Hashem*'s name when exchanging friendly greetings. The era in which Boaz served as leader was a time of very poor behavior (*Bava Batra* 15b). Boaz instructed everyone to greet each other

2. Interestingly, Rav Ḥayim Palagi (*Sefer HaḤayim* 11:22) writes that the time of an *aliya* to the Torah is a time for humility, since the Torah strongly emphasizes the value of humility.

using *Hashem*'s name so that they would remind each other that *Hashem* was watching them.

Moreover, when people speak to each other with respect and honor, it changes the culture. Speaking with respect – beginning with the simple exchange of greetings and making others feel that they are worthy of having *Hashem*'s name associated with them – leads people to treat others with respect. The way one talks becomes the way one thinks and the way one acts.

Sephardic Jews accomplish this goal by regularly calling to mind Boaz's enactment. This reminds us of the vital lesson that *Hashem* watches each and every one of our actions. It also changes our lives for the better by reminding us to speak, think, and act respectfully.

A NEW EXPLANATION – ARE YOU OBSERVING THE TORAH?

Another lesson may also be derived from this exchange, as Dr. Yael Ziegler argues:

> The exchange between Boaz and his harvesters may not be a simple exchange of pleasantries. It is possible instead to read it as a conversation in which Boaz inquires about the reapers' adherence to Jewish law. In this reading, Boaz's inquiry, "Is God with you?" is an actual question directed to his workers: "Are you keeping the laws as you pick in my fields?" This reading is supported by the reapers' response to Boaz's query: "God shall bless you" [as reward for the fulfillment of those laws].[3]

When a man receives an *aliya*, he pledges allegiance to *Hashem* and His Torah. This is a perfect time for a brief spiritual checkup: Is *Hashem* with you? The *kehilla* responds that *Hashem* will indeed bless you if you always bear in mind that *Hashem* is with us.

CONCLUSION

By echoing Boaz's exchange with his workers, Sephardic Jews have the opportunity to vividly recall the vital lessons imparted by this conversation.

---

3. Dr. Yael Ziegler, *Ruth* (Jerusalem: Yeshivat Har Etzion and Maggid Books, 2015), pp. 197–198.

Spurning snobbery, recalling *Hashem*'s constant surveillance, and periodic examination as to whether we are living up to the Torah's ideals are all captured by reliving and maintaining Boaz's enactment to greet each other with *Hashem*'s name.

Berachot

Chapter 23

The *Beracha* on Matza

It comes as a shock to many Ashkenazic Jews, but the predominant Sephardic practice is to recite the *beracha* of *Mezonot* upon eating matza at times other than Pesaḥ. This follows the ruling of the *Ḥida* (*Maḥazik Beracha* 158:5), as confirmed by Rav Ovadia Yosef (*Teshuvot Yeḥaveh Da'at* 3:12), Rav Ben Tzion Abba Sha'ul (*Teshuvot Ohr L'Tzion* 3:9:4), and Rav Shalom Messas (*Teshuvot Shemesh U'Magen, Oraḥ Ḥayim* 1:34). When we examine the Halacha, however, this ruling does not appear as surprising.

CRACKERS AS *PAT HABA'AH B'KISNIN*

Halacha recognizes a category of food known as *pat haba'ah b'kisnin,* snack bread. The *Shulḥan Aruch* (*Oraḥ Ḥayim* 168:7) includes cake, pie, and crackers in this category. One recites the *beracha* of *Mezonot* on *pat haba'ah b'kisnin,* unless he is *kove'a seuda* – he makes a meal of that item. Since matza is essentially a cracker, Sephardim regard matza as *pat haba'ah b'kisnin,* upon which one recites *Mezonot.*

EXPLAINING THE ASHKENAZIC PRACTICE

Rav Eliezer Waldenberg (*Teshuvot Tzitz Eliezer* 11:19) explains the Ashkenazic practice to recite *HaMotzi* on matza year round, even if it is eaten as a snack. Among his reasons is that since one is accustomed to treating matza as bread on Pesaḥ, Ashkenazim regard it as bread throughout the year as well.

EXPLAINING THE SEPHARDIC PRACTICE

Indeed, why do Sephardic Jews recite *HaMotzi* on matza on Pesaḥ even when large amounts are not consumed? Why should Pesaḥ be different than all other times of the year? The answer is that matza is the "bread" for the duration of Pesaḥ. Thus, during this time, *HaMotzi* is recited upon it. Essentially, then, Sephardim and Ashkenazim debate whether the status of matza as bread during Pesaḥ spills over to the rest of the year.

Note that the unique status of matza on Pesaḥ is not generated by Pesaḥ per se. Rather, it is the unavailability of *ḥametz* that elevates matza to the *beracha* of *HaMotzi* at this time. Accordingly, Rav Ovadia rules (*Ḥazon Ovadia, Berachot*, p. 64) that on Motza'ei Pesaḥ, before people repurchase their *ḥametz*, the *beracha* on matza is still *HaMotzi*. Similarly, Rav Ben Tzion Abba Sha'ul (*Teshuvot Ohr L'Tzion* 3:9:4) rules that when the last day of Pesaḥ falls out on Friday, the *beracha* on matza for the Shabbat immediately following Pesaḥ is *HaMotzi*.

THE PREFERENCE TO BE STRICT

Ḥazon Ovadia (*Hilchot Berachot* 61–64) and *Yalkut Yosef* (*Oraḥ Ḥayim* 168:4) note, however, that according to the *Ḥida*, a God-fearing person should always eat matza in the course of a meal with real bread during the year, in order to avoid the halachic debate regarding whether the *beracha* on matza is *Mezonot* or *HaMotzi*. Rav David Yosef (*Orḥot Maran* 13:8) reports that this was the personal practice of Rav Ovadia, even though he maintained that the *beracha* on *matza* is essentially *Mezonot*.[1]

1. Rav David Yosef writes that he conferred about this matter with his father a few months before the latter's passing, since there were those who claimed that Rav Ovadia changed his mind and felt that even according to the *ikar hadin* (essential *halacha*), the *beracha* on matza is *HaMotzi*. Rav Ovadia responded that he remained committed to the view that the *beracha* on matza year-round is *Mezonot*; he simply maintained that it is preferable for a God-fearing individual to avoid the question by eating matza only during a bread meal.

SOFT MATZA

Rav Moshe HaLevy (*Birkat Hashem* 2:2:53) notes that even Sephardic Jews should recite *HaMotzi* and *Birkat HaMazon* on soft matza, which can hardly be described as a cracker, and thus is not considered *pat haba'ah b'kisnin.* He argues that the *beracha* on soft matza remains *HaMotzi* even if the soft matza eventually becomes as hard as a rock, since at first it was not at all cracker-like.

KEVIAT SEUDA

According to Sephardic *posekim* (*Kaf HaḤayim, Oraḥ Ḥayim* 168:45; Rav Ovadia Yosef, *Teshuvot Yeḥaveh Da'at* 3:12), *keviat seuda* on *pat haba'ah b'kisnin* entails consuming a very large amount of the food – preferably 216 grams (four *betzim*),[2] the equivalent of half a loaf of bread![3] Ashkenazim, in contrast, follow the view of the *Magen Avraham* (168:13) and *Mishna Berura* (168:24), who rule that all other foods in the meal combine with the *pat haba'ah b'kisnin* to establish it as a meal.

Nevertheless, *Yalkut Yosef* (*Oraḥ Ḥayim* 168:4) writes that during the year, Sephardim who wish to recite *HaMotzi* on matza when eaten as a meal can do so, even if they do not consume 216 grams. The *Yalkut Yosef* explains that this is because matza is something that people eat along with

2. The *Kaf HaḤayim* (*Oraḥ Ḥayim* 168:46) quotes a number of Sephardic *Aḥaronim,* including the *Ḥida* (*Birkei Yosef, Oraḥ Ḥayim* 168:4), who maintain that the Sephardic practice is to measure the *kezayit* and *betza* by weight. He writes that this is the common practice among halachic authorities even for measuring a *kezayit* of matza. Rav Ovadia Yosef (*Teshuvot Yeḥaveh Da'at* 1:16) and Rav Mordechai Eliyahu (*Teshuvot Ma'amar Mordechai* 11:96) agree.
3. Sephardic authorities (*Ben Ish Ḥai*, year 1, *Parashat Pinḥas* 19; *Kaf HaḤayim, Oraḥ Ḥayim* 168:45; *Teshuvot Shemesh U'Magen* 2, p. 318 in the addendum; *Ḥazon Ovadia, Berachot*, p. 56) recommend avoiding eating between three and four *betzim* (162 and 216 grams), as there is a *safek* as to whether three or four *betzim* constitute *keviat seuda.* This *safek* stems from a dispute between Rabbi Shimon and Rabbi Yoḥanan ben Beroka (*Eruvin* 82b) and continues to be disputed between Rashi (*Eruvin* 83a, s.v. *v'ḥatzi* and *ḥaser;* see *Tosafot* ad loc., s.v. *v'ḥatzi*) and the Rambam (*Hilchot Eruvin* 1:6). The *Shulḥan Aruch* (*Oraḥ Ḥayim* 368:3 and 612:4) cites both opinions, but the *Kaf HaḤayim* notes that the *Shulḥan Aruch* essentially rules in accordance with the Rambam's view that three *betzim* suffice. According to Sephardic authorities, *keviat seuda* takes into account only the amount of bread eaten; see *Ḥida, Birkei Yosef, Oraḥ Ḥayim* 168:6; *Teshuvot Yabia Omer* 10: *Orah Ḥayim* 18, as well as the other sources cited earlier in the note.

meal-type foods. Thus, it differs from other *pat haba'ah b'kisnin,* such as pie and cake, which are usually consumed as a dessert and are not typically eaten together with meal-type foods. Accordingly, matza can combine with other meal-type foods, such as salad and meat.[4]

4. Incidentally, this would seem to serve as an excellent justification for a Sephardic Jew to recite *HaMotzi* on egg *ḥalla,* even if he ate only one *kezayit* of it. Since egg *ḥalla* is typically eaten with meal-type foods and does not serve as dessert, it should combine with other foods to create *keviat seuda.* I find it surprising that this approach is not raised by the great Sephardic *posekim.* See our full discussion of this issue in the next chapter.

Chapter 24

The Question of Egg *Ḥalla*

An Ashkenazic woman called me in a bit of consternation. Why did her recent Sephardic guest request that her family be served water *ḥalla* and not egg *ḥalla* for the Shabbat meal?

I told her not to take it personally. The widespread *minhag* of the Sephardic community is to use only water *halla,* and not egg *halla,* for *leḥem mishneh* on Shabbat. This is due to the ruling of Rav Yosef Karo (*Shulḥan Aruch, Oraḥ Ḥayim* 168:7) to recite *Mezonot* – and not *HaMotzi* – on bread kneaded in fruit juice or eggs. The *Kaf HaḤayim* (*Oraḥ Ḥayim* 168:58), Rav Ovadia Yosef (*Teshuvot Yabia Omer* 10: *Oraḥ Ḥayim* 18), Rav Shalom Messas (*Teshuvot Shemesh U'Magen* 2: *Oraḥ Ḥayim* 1, addendum) and Rav Ben Tzion Abba Sha'ul (*Teshuvot Ohr L'Tzion* 2:12:4) instruct Sephardim to follow the ruling of Rav Yosef Karo.[1]

PAT HABA'AH B'KISNIN AND EGG *ḤALLA*

As noted in the previous chapter, Halacha recognizes a category of food known as *pat haba'ah b'kisnin,* snack bread. The *Shulḥan Aruch* (*Oraḥ Ḥayim* 168:7) includes cake, pie, and crackers in this category. One recites

1. Rav Abba Sha'ul recommends, however, for a God-fearing individual to eat egg *halla* only within a bread meal, to avoid the question as to whether its *beracha* is *Mezonot* or *HaMotzi.*

a *beracha* of *Mezonot* on snack bread unless he is *kove'a seuda,* making a meal of that item.

Although the Rama rules that one recites *HaMotzi* over sweetened bread – and this is the practice among Ashkenazim – the *Shulḥan Aruch* rules that dough baked with sweetening agents, such as honey and sugar, is considered cake and not bread if the sweet flavor is discernible, such as in the case of egg *ḥalla.* Such bread therefore requires the *beracha* of *Mezonot.* Accordingly, Rav Ovadia Yosef (*Ḥazon Ovadia, Berachot,* p. 55) rules that Sephardim may not recite *HaMotzi* over such bread and may not use it as the bread for Shabbat meals, as it does not have the halachic status of "bread." For the Shabbat meals, Sephardim must use only water *ḥalla* or other non-sweetened *ḥalla.* Sweetened *ḥalla* may be used only if the sweetening agents cannot be discerned.

A Sephardic Jew would recite *HaMotzi* on sweetened bread only if he were to eat the equivalent of 216 grams (four *betzim*) of that bread, as that is considered *keviat seuda.* According to Sephardic *posekim,* in order to be *kove'a seuda,* one must eat this amount of *ḥalla* itself; other foods eaten at the meal do not count toward this amount.[2]

A POSSIBLE LENIENCY FOR SEPHARDIC JEWS

There is a possible defense for those Sephardim who recite *HaMotzi* on egg *ḥalla* at Shabbat meals when they are guests of Ashkenazim who serve such bread. In the context of the laws of *terumot* and *ma'asrot,* the Rambam writes (*Hilchot Ma'aser* 3:1–3) that food eaten on Shabbat is never considered *arai,* a mere snack. Thus, although one may generally snack on Eretz Yisrael produce that is not yet fully processed (*gemar melacha*), such as fruit just picked from a tree, without first taking *terumot* and *ma'asrot,* this is not permissible on Shabbat and Yom Tov, since all eating on these holy days is considered *keva* and not *arai.*

The *Shibolei HaLeket* (cited by Rabbi Akiva Eiger, *Shulḥan Aruch, Oraḥ Ḥayim* 639:2) applies this rule beyond the laws of *terumot* and *ma'asrot* to the laws of Sukkot. The *Shibolei HaLeket* argues that although men are ordinarily permitted to snack outside of the *sukka,* this permission does not extend to Shabbat and Yom Tov. It is possible that this may be extended to

2. See the discussion of *keviat seuda* in the previous chapter.

all contexts on Shabbat, such that any snack bread eaten on Shabbat and Yom Tov should require *HaMotzi* and *Birkat HaMazon*.

This idea is suggested by *Teshuvot Maharaḥ Ohr Zarua* (71), but it is rejected by a variety of Sephardic *posekim*, such as *Teshuvot Ginat Veradim* (3:11) and the *Ḥida* (*Birkei Yosef, Oraḥ Ḥayim* 168:5).

However, in extenuating circumstances, such as when a Sephardic Jew visits an Ashkenazic family that serves egg *ḥallot*, perhaps he may rely on the view of the *Maharaḥ Ohr Zarua*. Indeed, the Radbaz (*Teshuvot* 1:489) relies on this approach to permit Sephardim to recite *HaMotzi* on egg matza when eating *seuda shelishit* on Erev Pesaḥ that falls on Shabbat. Rav Ovadia Yosef (*Teshuvot Yeḥaveh Da'at* 1:91), however, follows in the footsteps of the *Ḥida* (*Birkei Yosef, Oraḥ Ḥayim* 444), who rejects this approach and argues that Sephardim never regard less than 216 grams of *pat haba'ah b'kisnin* as *keviat seuda*.

Indeed, when Rav Shlomo Amar visited Congregation Shaarei Orah, the Sephardic Congregation of Teaneck, on Shabbat Naḥamu 5777, this idea was presented to Rav Amar, who summarily rejected it.[3] Rav Amar ruled that even when visiting an Ashkenazic family, a Sephardic Jew may not recite *HaMotzi* on egg *ḥalla*.

Rav Ovadia Yosef (*Teshuvot Yabia Omer* 10: *Oraḥ Ḥayim* 18) rules this way as well.[4] Interestingly, although Rav Ovadia often makes room for Sephardim and Ashkenazim to eat at each other's homes despite differences in halachic standards, such as regarding *ḥalak Bet Yosef* and *bishul akum*, on this issue he brooks no compromise. The *Teshuvot Avnei Yashfeh* (3:16) quotes Rav Ben Tzion Abba Sha'ul, who agrees that a Sephardic Jew who is a guest at an Ashkenazic home should recite *Mezonot* on egg *ḥalla*.

OTHER POSSIBLE AVENUES OF LENIENCY

Others, however, rule leniently. Rav Mordechai Eliyahu is cited as ruling that in case of difficulty, Sephardic Jews may recite *HaMotzi* and *Birkat HaMazon* even if they eat only one *kezayit* of sweet *ḥalla* (*VeZot HaBera-*

3. Rav Amar noted that the *halacha* does not follow the view of the *Shibolei HaLeket*, who forbids snacking outside of the *sukka* on Shabbat and Yom Tov (as noted by the *Yalkut Yosef, Kitzur Shulḥan Aruch, Oraḥ Ḥayim* 639:21).
4. Rav Yosef Shalom Eliashiv is also cited as ruling this way for Sephardic Jews.

cha 4:39).[5] Rav Shlomo Levy of Yeshivat Har Etzion agrees (*Kuntres Birkat HaPat*, p. 43).

This ruling is the result of a combination of considerations: (1) This definition of *pat haba'ah b'kisnin* is only one of three cited in the *Shulḥan Aruch* (*Oraḥ Ḥayim* 168:7), and it is possible that according to the other opinions, sweetened bread is defined as real bread. (2) According to the Rama's definition of *pat haba'ah b'kisnin*, the *beracha* on egg *ḥalla* is *HaMotzi*. (3) According to the *Bet Yosef* (*Oraḥ Ḥayim* 168, s.v *U'Mah sheperush Rabbenu b'pat*), since this sweet *ḥalla* is used regularly for a meal, the *beracha* should be *HaMotzi*.

Additionally, Rav Moshe HaLevy (*Birkat Hashem* 2:2:40) writes that one should make *HaMotzi* on sweet *ḥalla* if he eats a little more than a *betza* (two *kezetim*), unless the bread is made with a majority of sweeteners.[6] However, both Rav Ovadia and Rav Messas in their aforementioned *teshuvot* roundly reject Rav HaLevy's approach as running counter to the widely accepted Sephardic practice.

The lenient approach argues that the combination of these considerations creates a situation of *sefek sefeka* (multiple doubts), thus permitting recitation of *HaMotzi* and *Birkat HaMazon* in order to avoid an uncomfortable situation when a Sephardic Jew visits an Ashkenazic Jew for Shabbat. Rav Ovadia, however, argues that *sefek sefeka* is not relevant in this circumstance, since he maintains that we do not combine *sefekot* in order to recite a *beracha*.[7]

---

5. Rav Eliyahu prefers that Sephardic Jews consuming 162 grams of sweet bread, the equivalent of three *betzim*, in order to be *kove'a seuda*. This follows the view of the Rambam (essentially accepted by the *Shulḥan Aruch*) that three *betzim* is the necessary amount for *keviat seuda*; see the notes to the previous chapter.
6. Rav Moshe HaLevy was an up and coming late-twentieth century Sephardic *posek* who tragically died at a relatively young age. He wrote two well-received multi-volume works, *Menuḥat Ahava* on *Hilchot Shabbat* and *Birkat Hashem* on *Hilchot Berachot*.
7. The question of the propriety of reciting a *beracha* in a case of *sefek sefeka* is a hotly debated topic. The *Mishna Berura* appears to contradict himself regarding this issue (see *Mishna Berura* 215:20 and contrast *Sha'ar HaTziyun* 489:45). After a thorough review of this topic (in a footnote to *Teshuvot Yeḥaveh Da'at* 5:21), Rav Ovadia concludes that "after all has been heard on this matter, the majority of *Aḥaronim* agree that a *beracha* is not recited in case of *sefek sefeka*." Rav Ovadia rules this way even if there are multiple *sefekot* inclining one to recite the *beracha*.

CONCLUSION

It is difficult to permit a Sephardic Jew to recite *HaMotzi* and *Birkat HaMazon* on sweetened bread if he will not consume at least 162 grams (and preferably 216 grams) of it. Thus, whenever an Ashkenazic family invites a Sephardic family for a Shabbat or Yom Tov meal, they should be sure to serve water *ḥalla* so that the Sephardic guests will be able to recite *HaMotzi* and *Birkat HaMazon* without having to consume an extraordinarily large amount of egg *ḥalla*.

Chapter 25

Earliest Time for *Birkat HaLevana*

Non-Ḥassidic Asheknazic *kehillot* recite *Birkat HaLevana* ("*Kiddush Levana*," the blessing on the waxing moon) on Motza'ei Shabbat as long as three days have passed since the *molad* (the birth of the new moon). The practice among Sephardic Jews, however, differs.

THREE DAYS VS. SEVEN DAYS

The *Shulḥan Aruch* (*Oraḥ Ḥayim* 426:4) rules that one should not recite *Birkat HaLevana* until seven days have passed since the *molad.* This opinion is based on a classic kabbalistic work (cited in the *Bet Yosef*) called *Sha'arei Orah,* written by Rav Yosef Gikatilla. Although the Rama remains silent on this issue, the *Mishna Berura* (426:20) notes that most *Aḥaronim* (including the *Levush, Baḥ, Magen Avraham,* and *Taz*) disagree with the *Shulḥan Aruch* and permit reciting *Birkat HaLevana* after three days from the *molad* have passed. This is hardly surprising since most *Rishonim* (including Rashi, Rambam, the Semag, and Rabbenu Yonah) do not require waiting until the seventh day.

Most Sephardic Jews conform to the opinion of the *Shulḥan Aruch* (see *Teshuvot Yabia Omer* 6: *Oraḥ Ḥayim* 38:1 and *Teshuvot Yeḥaveh Da'at* 2:24, following in the footsteps of the *Ḥida, Moreh B'Etzba* 182, the *Ben Ish Hai,* year 2, *Parashat Vayikra* 23, and *Kaf HaḤayim, Oraḥ Ḥayim* 426:61).

Ḥassidic Jews adopt this approach as well, since it is rooted in the Kabbala. Non-Ḥassidic Ashkenazic Jews, on the other hand, recite *Birkat HaLevana* after three days from the *molad* have passed (*Aruch HaShulḥan* 426:13).

THE CONCEPTUAL BASIS FOR THE DEBATE

This question appears to reflect a classic debate as to which halachic principle enjoys precedence – *zerizim makdimim l'mitzvot,* the value of performing a *mitzva* at the earliest time possible, or *hiddur mitzva,* the importance of performing a *mitzva* in the most beautiful manner possible. For example, on Sukkot, is it preferable to take an ordinary *etrog* at the optimal, earliest possible time (sunrise) or to fulfill the *mitzva* with an extraordinarily beautiful *etrog* that one will have access to only later on in the day? (See *Teshuvot Shevut Yaakov* 1:34.)[1]

The Sephardic and Ḥassidic traditions seem to value *hiddur mitzva* over *zerizim makdimim l'mitzvot.* The *gemara* in *Shabbat* (133b) states that it is preferable to use a beautiful shofar, *lulav, sukka, tzitzit,* and *sefer Torah.* Similarly, reciting *Birkat HaLevana* on a "fuller" moon is a more *mehudar* way to perform the *mitzva,* as the moon is more beautiful when it is has reached half of its full size, and it is preferable to recite the *beracha* on a more beautiful moon (provided that it is recited before the latest time permitted by *halacha* for *Birkat HaLevana*). The non-Ḥassidic Ashkenazic tradition, in contrast, values *zerizim makdimim l'mitzvot* over *hiddur mitzva,* preferring to recite *Birkat HaLevana* as soon as three days have passed from the *molad.*

A THIN CLOUD COVERING OVER THE MOON

For a similar reason, the Sephardic custom is to delay *Birkat HaLevana* if the moon is covered by a thin cloud cover (*Ben Ish Ḥai* op. cit. and *Teshuvot Yabia Omer* 5: *Oraḥ Ḥayim* 24:2–7). Once again, Sephardic Jews attach greater priority to reciting *Birkat HaLevana* on a more aesthetically pleasing sight than reciting it as the earliest opportunity. Ashkenazic Jews, however, seize the opportunity to recite *Birkat HaLevana* even if there is a thin cloud

1. The *gemara* in *Rosh Hashana* 32b and *Yevamot* 39b seems to indicate a preference for *zerizim makdimim l'mitzvot* over *hiddur mitzva,* but *Sanhedrin* 12a seems to indicate that we do delay a *mitzva* in order to perform it in a more enhanced and beautiful manner. For further discussion of this issue, see *Terumat HaDeshen* 35, *Teshuvot Avodat HaGershuni* 12, and *Sedei Ḥemed* 2:7:1.

cover (*Mishna Berura* 426:3) due to their prioritizing the value of *zerizim makdimim l'mitzvot.*

THE MOROCCAN PRACTICE

Rav Shalom Messas (*Teshuvot Shemesh U'Magen* 3:55) records the practice of Moroccan Jews to wait until the seventh day from the *molad* except when there is an opportunity to recite *Birkat HaLevana* on a Motza'ei Shabbat.

The logic for this approach is compelling, as the *Shulḥan Aruch* (*Oraḥ Ḥayim* 426:2) records the preference to recite *Birkat HaLevana* specifically on Motza'ei Shabbat, when we have emerged from the sanctity of Shabbat and are wearing our best clothing. In many communities, there is a larger crowd reciting *Birkat HaLevana* on Motza'ei Shabbat as well. Thus, one achieves the objective of beautifying the recitation of *Birkat HaLevana* by reciting it on Motza'ei Shabbat even if it is recited before seven days from the *molad.*[2]

However, Rav Ḥaim David HaLevy (*Teshuvot Aseh Lecha Rav* 4:33) rules in accordance with the *Ḥida* that one should not recite *Birkat HaLevana* even on Motza'ei Shabbat unless seven days have passed. Rav HaLevy permitted the recitation of *Birkat HaLevana* on the seventh evening from the *molad,* even though seven full days have not passed. However, he noted that Minhag Yerushalayim is to wait until seven full days have passed (as noted in Rav Amram Aburabiah's *Netivei Am, Oraḥ Ḥayim* 426).

CONCLUSION

Rav Shmuel Khoshkerman reports that the general Sephardic custom is to be quite particular to recite *Birkat HaLevana* only after seven full days have passed since the *molad.* In fact, Rav Yitzḥak Yosef (in a responsum printed in Rav Yonatan Nacson, *MiMizraḥ UmiMa'arav,* p. 270) rules that it is preferable for a Sephardic Jew to recite *Birkat HaLevana* alone after the seven full days have passed from the *molad* than to recite it with a *minyan* three days after the *molad.*

However, in extenuating circumstances, Sephardic Jews may recite *Birkat HaLevana* before the seven days have passed. For example, Rav

2. Rav Mordechai Lebhar (*Magen Avot, Oraḥ Ḥayim* 426:4) argues that the *Shulḥan Aruch*'s preference to recite *Birkat HaLevana* on Motza'ei Shabbat applies even if it is recited earlier than the seventh day from the *molad.*

Zecharia Ben Shlomo (*Orot HaHalacha,* p. 670) urges Israeli soldiers to recite *Birkat HaLevana* at the earliest opportunity, as soon as three full days from the *molad* have passed, out of concern that unexpected needs and events may preclude the recitation of *Birkat HaLevana* by the soldiers at the optimal time. Similarly, Rav Pinḥas Zabichi, a leading student of Rav Ovadia Yosef, told us at Shaarei Orah that we may recite *Birkat HaLevana* earlier than the seven days if we are concerned that many people will miss its recitation if we wait until seven days have passed.

Chapter 26

Women Reciting a *Beracha* on *Mitzvot Aseh ShehaZeman Gerama*

All the *Rishonim* agree that women are exempt from performing most *mitzvot aseh shehazeman gerama* (positive time-bound *mitzvot*). They dispute, however, whether a woman may or should recite a *beracha* if she voluntarily performs such a *mitzva*.

Rabbenu Tam (cited by *Tosafot, Rosh Hashana* 33a, s.v. *ha*; *Kiddushin* 31a, s.v. *d'lo*) and the Rosh (*Rosh Hashana* 4:7) – the central sources of Ashkenazic practice – argue that women may recite a *beracha* if they choose to perform these *mitzvot*. In contrast, the Rambam (*Hilchot Tzitzit* 3:10; *Hilchot Sukkah V'Lulav* 6:13) – the major source of Sephardic practice – rules that they may not. This remains a hotly debated issue within the Sephardic community until today.

THE RAMBAM AND THE *SHULḤAN ARUCH*

The Rambam rules that women cannot recite a *beracha* on time-bound *mitzvot* because they cannot say, "*v'tzivanu*," "and commanded us," as they are exempt from these *mitzvot*. Rabbenu Tam, on the other hand, maintains that since "*v'tzivanu*" is in the plural, it refers to the Jewish People on a whole. Thus, a woman can thank God for commanding us to perform *mitzvot aseh shehazeman gerama*, since she is referring to the Jewish People as a community and not specifically to herself.

Not surprisingly, the preeminent Sephardic authority Rav Yosef Karo (*Shulḥan Aruch, Oraḥ Ḥayim* 589:6) rules in accordance with the Rambam, while the Rama follows Tosafot and the Rosh. Almost all Ashkenazic authorities rule in accordance with the Rama, and Ashkenazic women thus recite *berachot* on time-bound *mitzvot*. Rav Ovadia Yosef, however, vigorously argues that Sephardic women should follow the ruling of the *Shulḥan Aruch* to refrain from reciting a *beracha* in such circumstances.

Rav Ovadia reiterates that according to the Sephardic tradition, reciting an unnecessary *beracha* constitutes a Torah-level prohibition (see Rambam, *Teshuvot* 84; *Shulḥan Aruch, Oraḥ Ḥayim* 215:4). For this reason, Sephardic *posekim* very often invoke the rule of *safek berachot l'hakel* (commonly abbreviated as SaBaL), to avoid reciting a *beracha* in case of doubt. By contrast, Ashkenazic *posekim* (from *Tosafot, Rosh Hashana* 33a, s.v. *ha*, to the *Mishna Berura* 215:20) rule that reciting an unnecessary *beracha* is a Rabbinic prohibition. Thus, Ashkenazic *posekim* are not as zealous in their avoidance of a possible recitation of a *beracha she'eina tzericha* (unnecessary *beracha*).

RAV OVADIA VS. THE *ḤIDA*

Already in the eighteenth century, Rav Yonah Navon, the Rav of the *Ḥida*, noted that some Sephardic women who resided in Eretz Yisrael had begun to recite a *beracha* before performing *mitzvot aseh shehazman gerama*. Rav Navon objected to this practice, and the *Ḥida* (*Birkei Yosef, Oraḥ Ḥayim* 654) writes that the elders concurred with Rav Navon.

However, in a surprising move, the *Ḥida* himself approved of this practice (*Teshuvot Yosef Ometz* 82). The *Ḥida* argues that a very large number of *Rishonim* – including the Ramban (*Kiddushin* 31a, s.v. *l'man d'amar*), Rashba (*Teshuvot* 123), Ritva (*Kiddushin* 31a, s.v. *katvu*), and Ran (*Rosh Hashana* 9b in the pages of the Rif, s.v. *umikol makom*) – rule in accordance with *Tosafot*.[1] The *Ḥida* cites a colorful work known as the *Teshuvot Min HaShemayim*, whose author reports that a heavenly voice informed him in

1. Significantly, the Ramban, Rashba, Ritva, and Ran are *gedolei Sefarad*, Torah giants who resided in Spain.

a dream that women may recite a *beracha* on positive time-bound mitzvot. The *Ḥida* proceeds to argue that had Maran Rav Yosef Karo been aware of the *Teshuvot Min HaShemayim,* he certainly would have ruled in accordance with *Tosafot* and the majority of *Rishonim,* who permit women to recite a *beracha* on a *mitzvat aseh shehazeman gerama.*

Rav Ovadia Yosef notes that many Sephardic *Aḥaronim* followed the ruling of the *Ḥida.* Rav Ovadia, however, made every effort to restore the original Sephardic practice, in keeping with his well-known motto of "*haḥazarat atara l'yoshena,*" restoring the crown to its original glory. Rav Ovadia, along with his sons and students, have waged a decades-long battle for this ruling to be accepted, and it indeed has become fairly accepted in many Sephardic circles in recent years.

Already in the first volume of his *Teshuvot Yabia Omer,* Rav Ovadia devotes no less than four extended responsa (*Oraḥ Ḥayim* 39–42) to rejecting the approach of the *Ḥida.* Rav Ovadia notes that it is highly irregular to follow the rulings of *Teshuvot Min HaShemayim,* especially when it runs counter to the view of the Rambam and *Shulḥan Aruch.* Moreover, by citing a heavenly voice as support, this work violates the rule of "*lo bashamayim hi*" (articulated at the climax of the great *Tanur Shel Achnai* episode, *Bava Metzia* 59b), which teaches that *Hashem* has chosen to cede His authority to make halachic decisions to the Sages. Furthermore, the *gemara* states (*Sanhedrin* 30a; *Horiyot* 13b) that we do not attach halachic significance to that which is communicated in a dream.

In his many speaking engagements throughout the length and breadth of Eretz Yisrael and around the world, Rav Ovadia emphasized his ruling that women should not recite a *beracha* on *mitzvot aseh shehazeman gerama.* In his first volume of popular responsa (*Teshuvot Yeḥaveh Da'at* 1:68), Rav Ovadia again stressed this ruling. In later years, he reaffirmed this ruling (*Teshuvot Yabia Omer* 9: *Oraḥ Ḥayim* 23), arguing that the common practice among Sephardic women to recite a *beracha* is not legitimate, since it runs counter to the rulings of the Rambam and *Shulḥan Aruch* and was not initiated by great halachic authorities.[2]

2. In one responsum (*Teshuvot Yabia Omer* 9: *Oraḥ Ḥayim* 39), Rav Ovadia goes so far to say that a Sephardic Jew should not answer "*amen*" to an Ashkenazic woman who recites a *beracha* upon taking a *lulav* or performing any other *mitzvat aseh shehazeman gerama.*

THE DEBATE CONTINUES

Despite Rav Ovadia's vigorous stance, it is important to note that the *Ḥida*'s approach constituted the common practice in most Sephardic lands, even though it runs counter to the ruling of the Rambam and *Shulḥan Aruch*. This is documented by the classic compendium of Sephardic *minhagim* entitled *Keter Shem Tov* (7:82), which notes that in the mid-twentieth century, this was the *minhag* of the Jews of Eretz Yisrael,[3] Syria, Egypt, and Turkey.[4] *Teshuvot Rav Pe'alim* (1:12) notes that this was the custom in Bavel (Iraq) as well.[5] The *Kaf HaḤayim* (*Oraḥ Ḥayim* 589:23) also endorses the approach of the *Ḥida*. Accordingly, Rav Mordechai Lebhar (*Magen Avot, Oraḥ Ḥayim* 589:6) asserts that a woman who is certain that her mother recited *berachot* on *mitzvot aseh shehazeman gerama* is certainly entitled to continue her mother's *minhag*.[6]

---

3. Rav Amram Aburabiah (*Nahagu HaAm* 589), who is regarded as a great mid-twentieth century expert on the *minhagim* of Yerushalyim, writes that it is the accepted and widespread custom in Eretz Yisrael for Sephardic women to recite a *beracha* when taking the *lulav*.
4. *Ḥikrei Lev* (*Oraḥ Ḥayim* 10) records that the women in Turkey recited a *beracha* when taking the *lulav* on Sukkot. Indeed, Jack Varon of Congregation Shaarei Orah, who is of Turkish descent, vividly recalls that the women at the Turkish synagogue of Seattle, Sephardic Bikkur Holim, would recite a *beracha* on the *lulav*.
5. Rav Shmuel Khoshkerman reports that the custom of Persian women is to recite a *beracha* when taking the *lulav*.
6. Similarly, although Rav Shalom Messas (*Teshuvot Shemesh U'Magen* 2:55:4) prefers that a woman not recite *berachot* on *mitzvot aseh shehazeman gerama*, he rules that if a woman has a family custom to recite *berachot* on such *mitzvot*, she should maintain this practice. Rav Ḥaim David HaLevy (*Teshuvot Aseh Lecha Rav* 8:97) cites his Rav, Rav Ben Tzion Uziel, who concluded that Sephardic women whose custom is to recite a *beracha* on time-bound *mitzvot* are not reciting an unnecessary *beracha*. Rav HaLevy also records (ibid. 2:33), "I have seen with my own eyes great Sephardic rabbis of Jerusalem present the *lulav* to their wives, who then recited a *beracha*."

   I was once approached by a Sephardic Jew whose wife was raised as an Ashkenazic Jew and found it very difficult to adjust to refrain from reciting the *beracha* on the *lulav*. He asked if there was a way to permit her to recite the *beracha* on the *lulav*. I asked him where his family hailed from, and he responded that they were originally from Turkey. I excitedly informed him of the Turkish *minhag* and that his wife may follow that practice. However, the gentleman responded that his family's Torah observance had lapsed for fifty years and that he now follows Rav Ovadia Yosef's guidelines, as set forth in the *Yalkut Yosef*, in place of his lost family traditions. This exchange reflects a common unresolved tension within the Sephardic community – to follow the view

WOMEN RECITING THE *BERACHOT* ON *PESUKEI D'ZIMRA* AND *BIRKOT KERI'AT SHEMA*

Rav Ovadia (*Teshuvot Yabia Omer* 2: *Oraḥ Ḥayim* 6:10) takes his ruling to the next logical step and argues that Sephardic women may not recite the *berachot* of *Pesukei D'Zimra* and *keri'at Shema.* Since women are not obligated in these *mitzvot,* Rav Ovadia concludes that women should not recite the *berachot* for these *mitzvot.*

Notably, however, Rav Shalom Messas (*Teshuvot Shemesh U'Magen* 3: *Oraḥ Ḥayim* 63:5), Rav Mordechai Eliyahu (in his *Siddur Kol Eliyahu*), and Rav Ben Tzion Abba Sha'ul (*Teshuvot Ohr L'Tzion* 2:5:3 and 2:6:10) disagree. They argue that the ruling of the Rambam and the *Shulḥan Aruch* applies only to *birkot hamitzva,* in which the word "*v'tzivanu*" is used. It is only improper for women to recite such *berachot,* since they cannot describe themselves as being commanded. There is no reason, however, for women to omit the *berachot* on *mitzvot* such as *keri'at Shema,* in which the word "*v'tzivanu*" does not appear.

Rav Lebhar notes that the fact that no one before Rav Ovadia suggested that women should not recite these *berachot* is more than sufficient evidence that women may recite the *berachot* on *Pesukei D'Zimra* and *keri'at Shema.* Rav Lebhar also notes that there are many testimonials supporting the assertion that Sephardic women have customarily recited these *berachot.* Finally, the fact that the *Kaf HaḤayim* (*Oraḥ Ḥayim* 70:1) records that the custom is for women to recite the *berachot* of *Pesukei D'Zimra* and *keri'at Shema* motivates many to follow this ruling.

of Rav Ovadia Yosef or one's specific family traditions. These types of questions are especially acute for *ba'alei teshuva,* and there are, thank God, large numbers of Sephardic *ba'alei teshuva.*

Chapter 27

Responding *Baruch Hu UVaruch Shemo*

If you play close attention at a Sephardic *tefilla* service, you will notice that Sephardic Jews utter the response of "*Baruch Hu uvaruch shemo*" much more frequently than Ashkenazic Jews do. As indicated by Rav Moshe Feinstein (*Teshuvot Igrot Moshe, Oraḥ Ḥayim* 2:98), Ashkenazic Jews customarily say, "*Baruch Hu uvaruch shemo*" only in response to the *berachot* of the repetition of the *Amida*. Thus, for example, an Ashkenazic Jew reciting one of the *sheva berachot* at a wedding will not pause after saying *Hashem*'s name. However, at a Sephardic wedding, there most definitely is a pause to allow for the assembled to respond, "*Baruch Hu uvaruch shemo*" during the *sheva berachot*.

In fact, Sephardic Jews respond, "*Baruch Hu uvaruch shemo*" to the mention of the name of *Hashem* even when it is not said in the context of a traditionally formatted *beracha*. Thus, during *Birkat Kohanim*, Sephardic Jews respond, "*Baruch Hu uvaruch shemo*" each time the *Kohanim* say the name of *Hashem* (*Ben Ish Ḥai*, year 1, *Parashat Tetzaveh* 15; *Kaf HaḤayim, Oraḥ Ḥayim* 124:27; *Teshuvot Aseh Lecha Rav* 3:8; and *Teshuvot Yeḥaveh Da'at* 4:9, although Rav Ovadia instructs that this be recited under one's breath so as not to confuse the *ḥazan*). In Sephardic congregations that recite the *piyut "Hashem Shimacha Yareti"* during the *Yamim Nora'im,* the congregation responds, *"Baruch Hu uvaruch shemo"* after each time the *ḥazan* says the name of *Hashem.*

REASON FOR THE DIFFERENT PRACTICES

The response of *"Baruch Hu uvaruch shemo"* following *Hashem*'s name does not appear in the Talmud, but is rather based on a practice originated by the Rosh (as recorded by his son, the *Tur, Oraḥ Ḥayim* 124). In his translation of the *pasuk, "Ki shem Hashem ekra havu godel l'Elokenu"* (*Devarim* 32:3), Onkelos writes that Moshe Rabbenu intended, "When I mention *Hashem*'s name in prayer, give praise to *Hashem* our God." Accordingly, the Rosh would recite, *"Baruch Hu uvaruch shemo"* on any *beracha* he would hear in order to conform to the exhortation of the *pasuk.*

Maran Rav Yosef Karo codifies this practice in the *Shulḥan Aruch* (*Oraḥ Ḥayim* 124:5): "To every *beracha* one hears in any place, he responds, '*Baruch Hu uvaruch shemo.*'"

Rav Moshe Feinstein explains that since (in his opinion) responding, *"Baruch Hu uvaruch shemo"* is a *minhag* and is not obligatory, the times when it is said are fairly limited. This is in stark contrast to the response of *"amen"* to *berachot,* which constitutes a full-fledged Rabbinic obligation. By contrast, Sephardic Jews follow the straightforward reading of the *Shulḥan Aruch.*

WHEN ONE WISHES TO BE *YOTZEI* WITH A *BERACHA*

Despite the *Shulḥan Aruch*'s ruling regarding the response of *"Baruch Hu uvaruch shemo,"* the *Magen Avraham* (124:9) notes that if one hears a *beracha* while saying *Shema* and its *berachot,* or even if he is in the middle of *Pesukei D'Zimra,* he should not respond, *"Baruch Hu uvaruch shemo,"* as this would constitute a *hefsek* (an unwarranted interruption).

Similarly, *Teshuvot Devar Shmuel* (295) states:

> I have already pointed out to my peers that the aforementioned custom of the Rosh applies only to *berachot* that one is not obligated to recite. However, when the listener has in mind to fulfill his obligation by hearing the blessing and the one reciting the blessing likewise has in mind to include the listener, one may not interrupt in the middle of the blessing by declaring, *"Baruch Hu uvaruch shemo,"* for since one who listens is tantamount to one reciting the blessing on his own

> (*shome'a k'oneh*), by responding, "*Baruch Hu uvaruch shemo*" in the middle of the blessing, it is as if one is interrupting in the middle of the actual recitation of the blessing.

Ashkenazic *posekim* – beginning with the *Dagul MeRevava* (*Oraḥ Ḥayim* 124:5) and the *Shulḥan Aruch HaRav* (*Oraḥ Ḥayim* 124:2) and continuing with the *Mishna Berura* (124:21), *Aruch HaShulḥan* (*Oraḥ Ḥayim* 124:2 and 273:6), *Kitzur Shulḥan Aruch* (6:9), and Rav Moshe Feinstein (op cit.) – all rule in accordance with the *Teshuvot Devar Shmuel*. The *Shulḥan Aruch HaRav* and the *Ḥayei Adam* even raise the possibility that one who responds, "*Baruch Hu uvaruch shemo*" in such circumstances does not fulfill his obligation, and the *Aruch HaShulḥan* and Rav Moshe rule accordingly.

THE DEBATE BETWEEN RAV OVADIA YOSEF AND RAV SHALOM MESSAS

The scope of the Sephardic practice to respond, "*Baruch Hu uvaruch shemo*" to *Hashem*'s name in all *berachot* is a matter of intense debate between the two leading Sephardic authorities of the late twentieth century, Rav Ovadia Yosef (*Teshuvot Yeḥaveh Da'at* 4:9; *Teshuvot Yabia Omer* 8: *Oraḥ Ḥayim* 22:8) and Rav Shalom Messas (*Teshuvot Shemesh U'Magen* 2:34). Whereas Rav Ovadia adamantly insists that one should not respond, "*Baruch Hu uvaruch shemo*" to a *beracha* that is being said on one's behalf (such as *Kiddush, Havdala,* and the *berachot* on shofar and the *Megilla*), Rav Messas vehemently defends the view that "*Baruch Hu uvaruch shemo*" should be said even in such circumstances.

Rav Ovadia and Rav Messas had enormous respect and love for each other. Nonetheless, this dispute is one of the most vehement of their many debates.

Rav Ovadia notes that many Sephardic *posekim* subscribe to the ruling of the *Teshuvot Devar Shmuel*, including the *Ḥida* (*Birkei Yosef* 213:3), the *Kaf HaḤayim* (*Oraḥ Ḥayim* 124:26), and the *Sedei Ḥemed* (*Asifat Dinim, Ma'arechet Hefsek* 9).

Rav Ovadia, similar to the *Mishna Berura*, does not require one to repeat a *beracha* if one did say, "*Baruch hu uvaruch shemo*" in such a case, since some *posekim* (such as the *Ma'aseh Roke'aḥ, Hilchot Berachot* 1:11) endorse responding, "*Baruch Hu uvaruch shemo*" even to a *beracha* through which one fulfills his obligation. These *posekim* argue that when one fulfills his obligation when listening to the *beracha,* it is not as if he is actually reciting the *beracha* himself. This is clear from the fact that he responds, "*amen*" to the *beracha,* as one does not respond, "*amen*" to his own *beracha* except in limited circumstances. Accordingly, just as one responds "*amen*" even when he fulfills his obligation through *shome'a k'oneh,* he may respond, "*Baruch Hu uvaruch shemo*" to such a *beracha.*

Rav Ovadia reasons, as is common among Sephardic decisors, that the principle of *safek berachot l'hakel* (SaBaL) indicates that one should not recite a *beracha* in case of doubt. Rav Ovadia therefore does not go as far as to rule like the *Aruch HaShulḥan* and Rav Moshe that one does not fulfill his obligation to recite the *beracha* even *bedi'avad* (post-facto) if he responded, "*Baruch Hu uvaruch shemo.*" However, Rav Ovadia firmly insists that *lechatḥila,* one should refrain from saying, "*Baruch Hu uvaruch shemo,*" in accordance with what he believes is the majority of *posekim.* In case of doubt, Rav Ovadia argues, "*shev v'al ta'aseh adif*" – it is better to refrain from acting.

Rav Messas's response focuses on three points. The first relates to the view of the *Ḥida.* As Rav Ovadia notes, in *Birkei Yosef,* the *Ḥida* writes that he finds it difficult to decide which opinion is correct about this matter, and he therefore recommends refraining from responding, "*Baruch Hu uvaruch shemo*" to a *beracha* through which one seeks to fulfill his obligation, adding that one should not rebuke those who do respond. However, in his later work, *Teshuvot Yosef Ometz* (70:3), the *Ḥida* writes that the widespread custom among the learned and not so learned is to respond, "*Baruch Hu uvaruch shemo*" in such cases. Rav Messas interprets this as the *Ḥida*'s retraction from the stance he took in *Birkei Yosef.* Thus, Rav Messas understands the *Ḥida*'s final position as endorsing the common custom.

Rav Messas's second major argument is that the plain reading of the *Shulḥan Aruch* indicates that "*Baruch Hu uvaruch shemo*" is the appropriate response to **every** mention of *Hashem*'s name in **every** *beracha.* The *Shulḥan Aruch*'s language indeed leaves a broad and all-encompassing impression: "To every *beracha* that one hears in any place, he responds, '*Baruch Hu uvaruch shemo.*'" Rav Mordechai Eliyahu (*Teshuvot Ma'amar Mordechai* 2:4) draws the same conclusion from the *Shulḥan Aruch*'s language.

Rav Yosef, in turn, responds (*Teshuvot Yabia Omer* 8: *Oraḥ Ḥayim* 22:8) that the *Shulḥan Aruch*'s statement should be viewed in context. Since the context of his statement relates to the repetition of the *Amida,* Rav Ovadia insists that the *Shulḥan Aruch* is referring only to the *berachot* of the *Ḥazara.*

Rav Messas' third argument stems from *minhag*. He notes that the *Ḥida* already notes that the widespread custom is for one to respond, "*Baruch Hu uvaruch shemo*" even when one intends to fulfill his obligation with the *beracha*. He further notes that the major Sephardic authority Rav Ḥayim Palagi (*Ḥayim LaRosh*, p. 38) records that it was the *minhag* in the city of Izmir, Turkey and in all the neighboring areas to answer, "*Baruch Hu uvaruch shemo*" during *Kiddush* on Shabbat. Rav Palagi records that he instructed his family members to respond, "*Baruch Hu uvaruch shemo*" when he recited *Kiddush* for his family on Shabbat.

Finally, Rav Messas notes that Rav Amram Aburabiah (*Netivei Am* 167) records that the Minhag Yerushalayim is to respond, "*Baruch Hu uvaruch shemo*" to every *beracha*. Interestingly, Rav Eliezer Waldenburg (*Teshuvot Tzitz Eliezer* 11:10), who resided in Jerusalem, reports that he also has heard that this is the widespread custom of Sephardic Jews.

This last point is particularly powerful, since Minhag Yerushalayim is a major basis for the rulings of Rav Ovadia Yosef. Rav Yosef, however (in both *Yeḥaveh Da'at* and at greater length in *Yabia Omer*), vociferously responds that this custom was not instituted by great sages but is rather a folk custom lacking authority. Rav Ovadia notes that the classic sources that record Minhag Yerushalayim do not make mention of this specific practice.

CONCLUSION

Rav Ovadia writes that he made every effort to educate Sephardic Jews in his popular presentations (which attracted a very wide following) to refrain from responding, "*Baruch Hu uvaruch shemo*" when hearing a *beracha* through which one wishes to fulfill his obligation. Rav Messas, on the other hand, writes that he wishes to undo Rav Ovadia's teaching and "restore the crown to its glory"! Rav Messas believes that responding, "*Baruch Hu uvaruch shemo*" is essential for expressing and maintaining a proper reverence for *HaKadosh Baruch Hu*.

At Congregation Shaarei Orah, the Sephardic Congregation of Teaneck, our orientation is to follow the rulings of Rav Ovadia Yosef. Therefore, I announce prior to *Megilla* reading and shofar-blowing that Rav Ovadia urges refraining from responding, "*Baruch Hu uvaruch shemo*" to the *berachot* recited prior to performing these *mitzvot*. However, by noting that this is Rav Ovadia's ruling, we signal that others disagree, out of respect for the dissenting opinion.

The following story, told by Rav Mordechai Eliyahu (*Shiurei Kol Tzofayich, Parashat Kedoshim* 5763), demonstrates that responding, "*Baruch Hu uvaruch shemo*" to all *berachot* is a deeply rooted and unshakeable practice among Moroccan Jews:

> I was to perform the *ḥuppa* ceremony for the Baba Sali's daughter and his son-in-law, Rav Yehuda Yudayof. I instructed the *ḥatan* and *kalla* to answer, "*amen*" to the *beracha,* without answering, "*Baruch Hu uvaruch shemo.*" The Baba Sali *zt"l* tapped his cane on the ground and threatened to leave the wedding if "*Baruch Hu uvaruch shemo*" was not recited, because it was the *minhag* to recite it even for *berachot* that one is obligated to recite, such as *Kiddush.* Therefore, out of respect to the Baba Sali, I told the *ḥatan* to answer, "*Baruch Hu uvaruch shemo.*"

Rav Shmuel Khoshkerman concludes that although Moroccan Jews zealously respond, "*Baruch Hu uvaruch shemo*" even to a *birkat hamitzva* that they are about to fulfill, other Sephardic Jews are quite particular to refrain from responding, "*Baruch Hu uvaruch shemo*" in such situations.

B'rit Mila

Chapter 28

The *Beracha* of *L'Hachniso B'Vrito Shel Avraham Avinu*

It is well known that Ashkenazic and Sephardic practices sometimes differ from one another. As we have seen in other contexts, however, there is often significant debate regarding proper practice within the Sephardic community itself. One such example relates to the *beracha* recited by the father of the baby at a *b'rit mila*, "*l'hachniso b'vrito shel Avraham Avinu.*"

TWO *BERACHOT* AT A *B'RIT MILA*

The *gemara* in *Shabbat* (137b) establishes that two *berachot* are recited at a *b'rit mila*. The *mohel*, who performs the *b'rit*, recites the *beracha*, "*asher kideshanu... al hamila.*" The father of the baby recites, "*asher kideshanu... l'hachniso b'vrito shel Avraham Avinu*" (Who has commanded us to bring him into the covenant of our father Abraham). Those present respond, "Just as he entered the *b'rit*, so too should he enter into Torah, the *ḥuppa*, and good deeds."

The first *beracha* is undoubtedly a *birkat hamitzva*, a blessing recited upon performing a *mitzva*, and all *birkot hamitzva* are recited "*over l'asiyatan,*" immediately before their performance (*Pesaḥim* 7b). Thus, the first *beracha* is clearly recited before the *mohel* performs the *mila*. The *Rishonim* vigorously dispute, however, when the second *beracha* should be recited.

RASHBAM, RABBENU TAM, AND THE ROSH

The Rashbam (cited in *Tosafot, Shabbat* 137b, s.v. *avi haben*) champions the view that the father recites the *beracha* of "*l'hachniso*" before the cutting. He argues that the second *beracha* is also a *birkat hamitzva* and thus must also be recited "*over l'asiyatan*," before the *mohel* performs the *b'rit*.

The Rashbam notes that the *gemara* in *Pesaḥim* (7a) specifically states that a *bracha* that uses the liturgical formula "*l'*...," such as "*l'hadlik ner Ḥanukka*" or "*l'haniaḥ tefillin*," is recited before the *mitzva* is performed – before lighting the Ḥanukkah candles and before fastening the *tefillin* on the arm. Similarly, argues the Rashbam, the *beracha* of "*l'hachniso b'vrito shel Avraham Avinu*" should be recited before the act of the *mila*.

Traditionally, French Jews had recited the second *beracha* after the cutting. The Rashbam was so convinced of his view, however, that he advocated changing the practice of French Jewry regarding this matter. Moreover, he even emended the Talmudic text to concur with his view. The *gemara* states that the *mohel* cuts immediately after reciting his *beracha*, implying that the second *beracha* is recited after the cutting (recall that *mila* is performed very quickly). The Rashbam emended the text of the *gemara* to state that the father's *beracha* is recited **before** the *mohel* recites the *beracha* of "*al hamila*."

Rabbenu Tam vigorously opposed the approach of the Rashbam, his older brother. He restored the original practice of French Jewry and the traditional version of the Talmudic text, presenting a number of arguments to prove that the *beracha* of "*l'hachniso*" should be recited after the cutting (quoted in *Tosafot*, op. cit., and *Pesaḥim* 7a, s.v. *b'leva'er*).

One of Rabbenu Tam's arguments is based on the congregation's declaration, "Just as he entered the *b'rit*...," which is said in response to the father's recitation of the *beracha* of "*l'hachniso b'vrito shel Avraham Avinu*." The *gemara* indicates that we recite this response specifically after the *b'rit*, as the text is written in past tense, "Just as he **entered** the *b'rit*," implying that the *b'rit* has already occurred. Rabbenu Tam argues that just as the response to "*l'hachniso*" is said after the *b'rit*, the *beracha* itself is likewise recited after the *b'rit*.

The core of Rabbenu Tam's arguments is his belief that the *beracha* of "*l'hachniso*" is a *birkat hashevaḥ* (a blessing of praise to *Hashem*), rather than a *birkat hamitzva*, and there is therefore no requirement to recite this *beracha* before the *b'rit*.

The Rosh (*Shabbat* 19:10) offers a compromise approach that Ashkenazic and Moroccan Jews have accepted as normative practice, as reflected in the ruling of the *Shulḥan Aruch* (*Yoreh De'ah* 265:1). The Rosh maintains that if the father recites the *beracha* of "*l'hachniso*" in the middle of the *mila* process, he satisfies both the opinion of Rashbam and Rabbenu Tam. Since the *mitzva* of *mila* is not complete until the *mohel* performs *peri'a* (the removal of the entire foreskin), recitation of the *beracha* during the cutting is considered "*over l'asiyatan*." Since *mila* is typically performed very quickly, the father should hurry to recite "*l'hachniso*" immediately after the *mohel* finishes reciting the *beracha* of "*al hamila*."

THE BATTLE BETWEEN RAV OVADIA YOSEF AND RAV SHALOM MESSAS

In a rare deviation from the ruling of Rav Yosef Karo, Rav Ovadia Yosef rules that Sephardic Jews should recite the *beracha* of "*l'hachniso*" before the *b'rit*, in accordance with the view of the Rashbam and the other *Rishonim* who subscribe to his view.

Why does Rav Ovadia deviate from the ruling of the *Shulḥan Aruch* in this case? The answer is that Minhag Yerushalayim, as recorded in *Teshuvot Halachot Ketanot* (2:169) and the *Bet Leḥem Yehuda* (*Yoreh De'ah* 265:1), follows the ruling of the Rashbam.

The source of Minhag Yerushalayim is the *Teshuvot Maharam Alashkar* (#18), who notes that the Rif (*Teshuvot* #293) rules in accordance with the Rashbam that the *beracha* is recited before the *b'rit*. The Maharam Alashkar further notes that the Rambam's son Rabbenu Avraham testifies in a *teshuva* that his father also recited the *beracha* before the *mila*.

Rav Ovadia writes (*Teshuvot Yabia Omer* 7: *Yoreh De'ah* 21) that had Rav Yosef Karo been aware that both the Rif and the Rambam ruled like the Rashbam, he certainly would have ruled to recite the *beracha* before the *mila*, as Rav Karo usually rules in accordance with the predominant opinion among the Rif, Rambam, and Rosh. In this case, although the Rosh rules to recite the *beracha* between the *mila* and *peri'a*, the Rif and Rambam disagree.

It is far from obvious, however, that the Rambam and Rif concur with the view of the Rashbam. In the *Bet Yosef*, Rav Karo himself notes that the Rambam (*Hilchot Mila* 3:1) first lists the *beracha* of "*al hamila*" and only afterwards "*l'hachniso*," implying that the Rambam held that this *beracha* is recited after the *beracha* of "*al hamila*" – unlike the view of the Rashbam. The *Bet Yosef* draws the same implication from the words of the Rif (*Shabbat* 55b in the pages of the Rif).

Rav Shalom Messas (*Teshuvot Shemesh U'Magen* 2: *Yoreh De'ah* 25) argues with Rav Ovadia and asserts that the ruling of Rav Yosef Karo stands. Rav Messas writes that we cannot undo a ruling that appears in the *Shulḥan Aruch* based on newly discovered writings of the Rif and Rambam. Accordingly, Moroccan Jews maintain their custom to follow the ruling of the Rosh and *Shulḥan Aruch*, while Minhag Yerushalayim follows the approach of the Rashbam.

THE INFLUENCE OF SPAIN AND ITS LIMITS

The Rosh, who was originally from Ashkenaz, moved to Spain and exerted great influence there. Many of the *megorashim* (Jewish expellees) from Spain eventually settled in Morocco and Turkey, and the Spanish customs emerged as the dominant practice in these lands. It is therefore not surprising that Moroccan and Turkish Jews recite the *beracha* of "*l'hachniso*" between the *mila* and *peri'a*, following the view of the Rosh.

In Eretz Yisrael and Syria, the practices of the *toshavim* (residents who resided there before the arrival of the *megorashim*) remained dominant. Thus, the practice of Syrian Jews and the Minhag Yerushalyim to this day is to recite the *beracha* of "*l'hachniso*" before the *b'rit*.

CONCLUSION

At Congregation Shaarei Orah, the Sephardic Congregation of Teaneck, we usually follow the rulings of Rav Ovadia Yosef. However, since *mila* is performed after the *tefilla*, I permit each family to act in accordance with its custom, even if it differs from Minhag Yerushalayim.

Rav Shmuel Khoshkerman told me that he instructs Sephardic Jews to follow their family custom as to when to recite the *beracha* of "*l'hachniso b'vrito shel Avraham Avinu*." However, he instructs a Sephardic Jew who does not have a family custom regarding this matter to recite the *beracha* before the *b'rit*, in accordance with the ruling of Rav Ovadia.

Chapter 29

Shehehiyanu at a *B'rit Mila*

Upon attending a *b'rit mila* for a boy from a Sephardic family, Ashkenazic Jews outside of Israel may be taken by surprise when they hear the recitation of the *beracha* of *Sheheḥiyanu* at the *b'rit.*

The division between Sephardic and Ashkenazic Jews regarding this matter has its roots, as it often does, in a dispute between *Tosafot* and the Rambam. *Tosafot* (*Sukka* 46a, s.v. *ha'oseh*) rules that *Sheheḥiyanu* is not recited at a *b'rit,* drawing proof from the *gemara*'s omission of *Sheheḥiyanu* from the list of *berachot* for a *b'rit mila* (*Shabbat* 137b). The Rambam (*Hilchot Brachot* 11:9), in contrast, rules that *Sheheḥiyanu* is recited at a *b'rit mila.* He explains (*Teshuvot,* #141 in the Blau ed.) that the *gemara* did not mention the recitation of *Sheheḥiyanu* at a *b'rit mila* because it is obvious that it should be recited at this joyous occasion.

Accordingly, Sephardic Jews throughout the world recite *Sheheḥiyanu* at a *b'rit mila* (*Yalkut Yosef, Yoreh De'ah* 263:5:16), whereas Ashkenazic Jews outside of Eretz Yisrael do not, following the ruling of the *Shach* (*Yoreh De'ah* 265:17), who adopts the opinion of *Tosafot.*

THE VILNA GAON AND ASHKENAZIC PRACTICE IN ERETZ YISRAEL

The *Shulḥan Aruch* (*Yoreh De'ah* 265:7) notes that the practice in Eretz Yisrael is to recite the *beracha* of *Sheheḥiyanu* at a *b'rit mila,* and this is indeed the widespread custom in Eretz Yisrael today among both Sephardim and Ashkenazim. This is due to the fact that the Vilna Gaon (*Bi'ur HaGra* 265:36) strongly endorses the practice of reciting *Shehehiyanu* at a *b'rit.* A number of the Vilna Gaon's students were among the first Ashkenazic Jews to move to Eretz Yisrael in the mid-eighteenth century, and many of the Vilna Gaon's opinions have emerged as the accepted practice in Israel, shared by both Ashkenazic and Sephardic Jews. Thus, the ruling of the Vilna Gaon to recite *Shehehiyanu* at a *b'rit* became the accepted practice in Israel even among Ashkenazim.

The Vilna Gaon reviews and refutes each of the various arguments against reciting *Shehehiyanu* at a *b'rit.* He cites the argument that since a *b'rit* is not an event that occurs at regular intervals (such as the Yamim Tovim), *Shehehiyanu* should not be recited. The Vilna Gaon responds by noting that we recite *Shehehiyanu* at a *pidyon haben* even though it does not occur at regular intervals.

Another argument is that we are concerned that the child is a *nefel* (defective and unable to survive even thirty days of life), and it is inappropriate to recite *Shehehiyanu* on such a baby. The Vilna Gaon responds that the fact that we perform *mila* on Shabbat demonstrates that we are not concerned with the remote possibility that the child is so sickly that it cannot survive thirty days (see *Shabbat* 135b–136a).

The last argument is that since the baby is experiencing pain at the *mila,* it is inappropriate to recite *Shehehiyanu.* The Vilna Gaon responds by citing the *gemara*'s ruling (*Berachot* 59b) that if one hears the news of his father's death, Heaven forfend, he should recite both the *beracha* of *Baruch Dayan HaEmet* and *Shehehiyanu,* if his father left him an inheritance. This teaches that it is appropriate to recite *Shehehiyanu* even on a very sad occasion if it is tinged with an aspect of joy. Certainly, then, one should recite *Shehehiyanu* upon a very happy occasion even if it is tinged with a sad element.

CONCLUSION

Anyone who has experienced a *b'rit mila* at a Sephardic congregation has witnessed an exceedingly joyful experience, enhanced by the singing of *piyutim* celebrating, among other things, the presence of Eliyahu HaNavi at the *b'rit.* The *beracha* of *Shehehiyanu,* which expresses our overwhelming joy at having reached this milestone, is thus most fitting at a Sephardic *b'rit mila* anywhere in the world.

Chapter 30

Delayed *B'rit Mila* on Thursday or Friday

Everyone at Congregation Shaarei Orah, the Sephardic Congregation of Teaneck, was ecstatic. A first child had been born to one of our young couples, a beautiful little boy, and we all eagerly awaited the *b'rit mila*.

The baby, however, suffered from jaundice, and the *mohel* decided that the *b'rit* could not take place on the eighth day.[1] Moreover, the *mohel* determined that a seven-day wait was necessary after the boy had recovered from his jaundice. Finally, the seventh day wait was over on a Thursday, and the *kehilla* expected the *b'rit* to take place that day. Instead, it was delayed to Sunday! Why was the *b'rit mila* delayed yet again?

WITHIN THREE DAYS OF SHABBAT

The *gemara* in *Shabbat* (19a) prohibits embarking on a boat that will travel through Shabbat if the trip begins within three days of Shabbat. However, the *gemara* limits this restriction to trips taken for one's own needs (*devar hareshut*); one may set out for the sake of a *mitzva* even in the latter half of the week.

---

1. For further discussion regarding jaundice and *b'rit mila*, see my *Gray Matter*, vol. 4, pp. 163–165.

The *Rishonim* offer a number of explanations for the prohibition against beginning a trip too close to Shabbat.[2] The Rif (*Shabbat* 7b in the Rif's pages) explains that people generally need three days to adjust to sea travel. Thus, one who embarks within three days of Shabbat will probably experience an unpleasant Shabbat due to seasickness. The Rabbis therefore prohibited such trips in order to ensure that people properly enjoy Shabbat (*oneg Shabbat*).

The *Ba'al HaMa'or* (*Shabbat* 7a in the Rif's pages) claims that the three days immediately before Shabbat are considered "prior to Shabbat," such that one who embarks on a voyage within that period intentionally enters a situation that will require violating Shabbat in case of *piku'aḥ nefesh* (danger to life).[3]

The *Shulḥan Aruch* rules in accordance with the *gemara* and appears to codify both explanations (*Oraḥ Ḥayim* 248:2 and 248:4).

As noted, the *gemara* permits embarking on a trip during the latter half of a week "for the sake of a *mitzva*." Rabbenu Tam (cited approvingly by the *Tur, Oraḥ Ḥayim* 248) interprets this concept in an extraordinarily lenient manner, arguing that traveling for business purposes or to visit a friend is considered a *mitzva*; only a purely recreational trip would constitute a *devar hareshut*. The Rama (*Oraḥ Ḥayim* 248:4) accepts Rabbenu Tam's view.

The Steipler Gaon (*Kehilot Yaakov, Shabbat* 14) writes that the *gemara*'s prohibition is merely a Rabbinic enactment. The *Shulḥan Aruch HaRav* (*Oraḥ Ḥayim* 248:7) appears to agree with this view, and Rav Moshe Feinstein (*Teshuvot Igrot Moshe, Oraḥ Ḥayim* 1:127) and Rav Eliezer Waldenberg (*Teshuvot Tzitz Eliezer* 12:43:4) assert that most authorities indeed consider this prohibition to be Rabbinic in nature.[4]

DELAYED *B'RIT MILA*

When a *b'rit mila* takes place later than the eighth day of a boy's life (such as when a baby could not tolerate a *b'rit* on the eighth day due to health

2. In this chapter, we discuss only the two explanations that appear in the *Shulḥan Aruch*. For a summary and analysis of these and other opinions, see Ritva, *Shabbat* 19a, s.v. *tanu Rabbanan*.
3. In pre-modern times, travel was quite dangerous, making it likely that the crew would need to perform forbidden activities on Shabbat in order to ensure the passengers' safety.
4. Rav Hershel Schachter (*B'Ikvei HaTzon*, p. 153), however, offers an explanation for why he believes it to be a Biblical prohibition.

reasons, or in the case of a non-Jew who wishes to convert), the *Tashbetz* (1:21) forbids performing the *b'rit* on a Thursday. He notes that on the third day after a *b'rit mila* (including the day of the *b'rit* itself), the baby is presumed to be in tremendous pain (see *Bereshit* 34:25 and Rashbam, ad loc.). Thus, a baby who underwent a *b'rit mila* on Thursday may require medical treatment that will entail transgressing Shabbat (see *Shabbat* 86a), the third day if the *b'rit* is performed on Thursday.[5]

The *Tashbetz*'s view is cited as normative by Rav Yosef Karo in the *Bedek HaBayit* portion of his commentary to the *Tur* (*Yoreh De'ah* 262 and 266), as well as by the *Taz* (*Yoreh De'ah* 262:3). Significantly, Rav Yosef Karo does not cite the *Tashbetz* in the *Shulḥan Aruch*.

According to the *Taz*, this problem pertains if the delayed circumcision is performed on Friday as well, as the baby suffers pain every day through the third day.[6] The *Shach* (*Yoreh De'ah* 266:18) notes that although some *Rishonim* indeed assume that the baby suffers through the third day, the *Tashbetz* explicitly permits circumcising on Friday even when it is not the eighth day.

The *Shach* himself rejects even the *Tashbetz*'s position. He asserts that since circumcising constitutes a *mitzva*, one may perform it even when it may later require violating Shabbat to save a life, just as one may embark on a trip for the sake of a *mitzva* even during the latter half of the week. The *Ḥacham Tzvi* (*Teshuvot Nosafot* 14) and *Mishna Berura* (331:33) rule in accordance with the *Shach*.[7]

In defense of the *Tashbetz*, both the *Ḥida* (*Birkei Yosef, Oraḥ Ḥayim* 248) and *Ḥatam Sofer* (commentary to *Shabbat* 137a) argue that the *gemara*

---

5. Of course, these concerns do not apply when circumcising a baby on the eighth day of his life, as circumcision on the eighth day overrides Shabbat.
6. The *Taz* indicates concern for the baby's pain and suffering per se, not for the desecration of Shabbat that it might necessitate. Apparently, he understands the problem of circumcising close to Shabbat in the same manner that the Rif explains the prohibition against traveling before Shabbat—concern for causing unnecessary discomfort during Shabbat (see *Teshuvot Tzitz Eliezer* 12:43).
7. The *Ḥacham Tzvi*'s son, Rav Yaakov Emden (*She'elat Ya'avetz* 2:95), distinguishes between the delayed circumcision of a Jewish boy and the circumcision of a non-Jew who wishes to convert. Since a *mitzva* already exists to circumcise the Jewish child, Rav Emden agrees with the *Shach* that the *b'rit* should not be delayed. By contrast, the potential convert does not delay any *mitzva* by pushing off his *b'rit mila*, as he is not bound by *mitzvot* prior to the conversion process.

permits embarking on a trip on a Thursday or Friday only when the opportunity to fulfill the *mitzva* will not be available the following week. In a case of *b'rit mila,* they argue, the *mitzva* should be delayed until Sunday, since the *mitzva* can be fulfilled on Sunday just as well as on Thursday or Friday.

One could counter, however, that it is improper and possibly prohibited to delay a *b'rit,* even when it will not occur on the eighth day of the boy's life.

CURRENT PRACTICE

The *Magen Avraham* (331:9) notes that nowadays, we rarely need to violate Shabbat in order to save the life of a circumcised baby, and circumcising on Thursday should therefore undoubtedly be permitted. Indeed, common practice among Ashkenazic Jews is to circumcise on Thursday and Friday under all circumstances, as noted by the *Aruch HaShulḥan* (*Yoreh De'ah* 252:12). The *Aruch HaShulḥan* cites the absence of support for the *Tashbetz* among other *Rishonim* as evidence for the *Shach*'s critique of the *Tashbetz*'s view.

Rav Ovadia Yosef (*Teshuvot Yabia Omer* 5: *Yoreh De'ah* 23), however, rules that Sephardic Jews should not perform a delayed circumcision on Thursday or Friday unless their community has a custom to do so. Rav Ovadia writes that Sephardim should follow the *Tashbetz,* since his view is cited as authoritative by Rav Yosef Karo in the *Bedek HaBayit,* even though it is not presented in the *Shulḥan Aruch*. Rav Ovadia cites the custom to follow the *Tashbetz*'s ruling in a wide range of Sephardic communities, including Salonika, Turkey, Egypt, Aleppo, and Iraq. Moreover, major Sephardic *posekim* – such as the *Ḥida* (*Birkei Yosef, Yoreh De'ah* 262:2), *Ben Ish Ḥai* (*Teshuvot Rav Pe'alim* 4: *Yoreh De'ah* 28), and *Kaf HaḤayim* (*Oraḥ Ḥayim* 331:31) – rule in accordance with the *Tashbetz.*

Rav Shmuel Khoshkerman reports that the accepted custom among all Sephardic Jews has emerged to prohibit belated circumcisions on Thursday and Friday. Rav Mordechai Lebhar (*Magen Avot, Yoreh De'ah,* p. 161) confirms that this is the practice of Moroccan Jews.

Notably, Rav Ovadia (following the *Kaf HaḤayim*) limits his ruling to a case of performing a *mila* two days before Shabbat; this ruling does not apply to Yom Tov, which is not as strict as Shabbat. In addition, he does not believe that it is necessary to postpone to Sunday a *b'rit* for a boy born on Wednesday evening during *ben hashemashot* (the time between sunset and nightfall, the status of which is questionable). The *b'rit* is performed on Thursday in such a case.

CONCLUSION

The dispute about postponing a delayed *b'rit* from Thursday and Friday to Sunday involves a situation of competing values. On the one hand, there is the importance of performing the *b'rit* as soon as possible; on the other hand, we consider the need to preserve the integrity of Shabbat. Ashkenazic practice gives greater weight to performing a *b'rit* as soon as possible, whereas the Sephardic practice accords greater importance to taking precautions to avoid the need to violate Shabbat.

Shabbat

Chapter 31

The Timing of the *Beracha* on Shabbat Candle-Lighting

The various practices and approaches regarding when to recite the *beracha* on Shabbat candle-lighting reflect a variety of traditions of how to establish halachic practice.[1]

EXPLAINING THE ASHKENAZIC PRACTICE

The Ashkenazic tradition regarding Shabbat candle-lighting stems from the Rama's uncontested recording of the Ashkenazic practice to recite the *beracha* only after the candle-lighting (*Oraḥ Ḥayim* 263:5). The Rama, citing the Maharil, records that women first light candles, cover their eyes, and only then recite the *beracha* of "*l'hadlik ner shel Shabbat.*"

At first glance, the Ashkenazic practice appears to be quite odd. After all, the well-known rule is that a *birkat hamitzva* is always recited prior to performing a *mitzva*, "*over la'asiyatan*" (*Pesaḥim* 7b). Why should Shabbat candle-lighting be any different?

1. The *halacha* follows the opinion of Rabbenu Tam (see *Tosafot, Shabbat* 25b, s.v. *ḥova*) that a *beracha* is recited upon lighting Shabbat candles; see *Shulḥan Aruch, Oraḥ Ḥayim* 263:5 and *Mishna Berura* 263:22.

The logic for this approach is based on the ruling of the Behag, who maintains that once one lights Shabbat candles, she has accepted Shabbat automatically (cited in the Ran, *Shabbat* 10a in the Rif's pages, s.v. *u'mid'amrinan,* and in the *Shulḥan Aruch, Oraḥ Ḥayim* 263:10). The Rama notes that it is the accepted Ashkenazic practice that a woman automatically accepts Shabbat upon lighting the Shabbat candles. Moreover, the Behag may be understood as ruling that even reciting the *beracha* on Shabbat candle-lighting triggers the beginning of Shabbat.

The Ashkenazic practice is concerned for this strict version of the Behag's ruling. Accordingly, a woman first lights Shabbat candles and only afterwards recites the *beracha,* for once she recites the *beracha,* she can no longer light the candles; it is already Shabbat for her!

The reason that women cover their eyes after lighting the candles is that the Ashkenazic custom still attempts to accommodate the "*over la'asiyatan*" requirement of reciting the *beracha* prior to performing a *mitzva.* If we define the *mitzva* of Shabbat candle-lighting as benefiting from the light, one does not fulfill the *mitzva* until she uncovers her eyes. By reciting the *beracha* with her eyes covered, the woman recites the *beracha* before performing the *mitzva.*[2]

CANDLE-LIGHTING ON YOM TOV

Based on the logic outlined above, on Yom Tov – when one may light candles from a preexisting flame – an Ashkenazic woman should recite the beracha after striking a match and **before** candle-lighting. Indeed, the mother of the author of the Derisha famously asserted that the beracha should be recited before candle-lighting on Yom Tov (see Magen Avraham, Oraḥ Ḥayim 263:12).

2. This is similar to the Ashkenazic approach to the timing of the *beracha* recited by women upon immersion in the *mikveh.* The Ashkenazic tradition is for the woman to first immerse, then recite the *beracha,* and then immerse a second time (Rama, *Yoreh De'ah* 200:1; Shelah, cited in the *Ba'er Hetev* ad loc.). In this way, the woman satisfies the view that a *beracha* should be recited only after immersing (similar to the immersion of a convert, who cannot recite a *beracha* before he becomes a Jew through the immersion; see *Tosafot, Pesaḥim* 7b, s.v. *al hatevila*), while at the same time satisfying the *over l'asiyatan* requirement by immersing a second time after the *beracha.* For an in-depth analysis of this practice, see *Badei HaShulḥan, Hilchot Tevila,* 200, *Bi'urim,* s.v. *shel'aḥar tevila,* as well as our discussion of the issue in Chapter 89.

However, the *Magen Avraham* (263:12) rejects this approach, arguing that it would be too confusing for people to distinguish between Shabbat and Yom Tov in this regard. The *Magen Avraham* argues for the application of the famous rule of "*lo pelug Rabbanan*" (the rabbis made no exceptions and apply a rule even when its reason does not apply) to our situation.

The *Mishna Berura* (263:27) notes that many *Aḥaronim* reject the *Magen Avraham*'s approach and rule that on Yom Tov a woman should recite the *beracha* prior to lighting. These *posekim* include some of the greatest Ashkenazic authorities, such as Rav Yeḥezkel Landau (*Dagul Merevava, Oraḥ Ḥayim* 263:5), Rav Akiva Eiger, and the *Ḥayei Adam*. As evidence to this position, the *Dagul MeiRevava* notes that with regard to the lighting of Ḥanukka candles, everyone recites the *beracha* before the lighting; "*lo pelug Rabbanan*" is not applied. The *Aruch HaShulḥan* (*Oraḥ Ḥayim* 263:13) also endorses the approach made famous by the mother of the *Derisha*.

Even today, this dispute remains unresolved, with different Ashkenazic families adopting various approaches.

MEN LIGHTING SHABBAT CANDLES

In the circumstance of a man lighting Shabbat candles, the same dispute has emerged. The Rama (op. cit.) notes that only a woman is assumed to automatically accept Shabbat with her candle-lighting. Thus, it would seem reasonable to argue that a man should first recite the *beracha* and only then light. Moreover, perhaps the *Magen Avraham*'s "*lo pelug*" assertion applies only to a woman.

Although the *Be'ur Halacha* (263:5, s.v. *aḥar hahadlaka*) cites an opinion that the *Magen Avraham*'s "*lo pelug*" applies even to a man who lights Shabbat candles, he infers from both Rav Akiva Eiger and the *Ḥayei Adam* that a man should first recite the *beracha* and then light Shabbat candles. The *Aruch HaShulḥan* (op. cit.) rules in accordance with Rav Akiva Eiger and the *Ḥayei Adam* as well.

RAV OVADIA YOSEF'S UNDERSTANDING OF SEPHARDIC PRACTICE

Rav Yosef Karo does not present an explicit stance on this issue in the *Shulḥan Aruch*; he simply states, "*k'sheyadlik yevarech*," "when he lights, he should say the blessing" (*Oraḥ Ḥayim* 263:5). In fact, two major Sephardic *posekim*, the *Ben Ish Ḥai* (year 2, *Parashat Noaḥ* 8) and the *Kaf HaḤayim* (*Oraḥ Ḥayim* 263:34), support the practice recorded by the Rama of lighting first and only afterwards saying the *beracha*.[3] They even suggest kabbalistic considerations for adopting this practice.

However, Rav Ovadia Yosef (*Teshuvot Yabia Omer* 2: *Oraḥ Ḥayim* 16, 10:*Oraḥ Ḥayim* 21; *Teshuvot Yeḥaveh Da'at* 1:27, 2:33), adamantly argues that Sephardim should recite the *beracha* before lighting Shabbat candles. He infers that Rav Yosef Karo rules in accordance with the opinion articulated by the Rambam (*Hilchot Shabbat* 5:1) and most *Rishonim* – including the Ra'avya, Mordechai, and *Shibbolei HaLeket* – that Shabbat candle-lighting is no different than every other *mitzva*, such that the *beracha* should be recited before the *mitzva* is performed.

Rav Ovadia notes that the Ramban (cited in the Ran, *Shabbat* 10a in the Rif's pages, s.v. *u'mid'amrinan*, and in the *Shulḥan Aruch*, *Oraḥ Ḥayim* 263:10) and many other *Rishonim* disagree with the Behag and argue that one does not automatically accept Shabbat upon lighting Shabbat candles.[4] Rav Ovadia argues that the fact that Rav Karo first cites the Behag and then cites the Ramban demonstrates that Rav Karo accepts the opinion of the Ramban. In general, when the *Shulḥan Aruch* presents two opinions in the format of "there are those who say" followed by "and there are those who say," the second opinion is the one he endorses.

Moreover, Rav Ovadia notes, it is entirely possible that even the Behag would agree that one does not accept Shabbat by reciting the *beracha*. In fact, it is much more reasonable to assume that when one concludes the *beracha* with "*l'hadlik ner shel Shabbat*," "to light Shabbat candles," one is explicitly **not** accepting Shabbat, as he is declaring that he will be now be lighting Shabbat candles!

Rav Ovadia adds that there is a definite downside to reciting the *beracha* after the *mitzva* has been performed. He notes that the *Shach* (*Yoreh De'ah* 19:3) and many other *Aḥaronim* side with the Rambam (*Hilchot*

3. Rav Shmuel Khoshkerman told me that the practice of Iraqi and Persian women is to follow the *Ben Ish Ḥai*'s ruling to recite the *beracha* after candle-lighting.
4. These *Rishonim* include the Rashba (*Shabbat* 23b), Ritva (ad loc.), Ran (ad loc.), Meiri (ad loc.), Rosh (*Shabbat* 2:24), *Shibbolei HaLeket* (#59), and Rabbenu Yeruḥam and *Maggid Mishneh* (both cited by the *Bet Yosef*, *Oraḥ Ḥayim* 263).

Berachot 11:6), who rules that a *beracha* **may not** be recited after the *mitzva* has already been performed.[5]

Rav Ovadia and his family have made vigorous efforts to be "*maḥzir atara l'yoshena*," to restore the Sephardic crown to its former glory, encouraging Sephardic women to first recite the *beracha* and only then to light the Shabbat candles, even if this not their family custom.[6]

RAV SHALOM MESSAS AND THE MOROCCAN PRACTICE

However, many Sephardic *posekim* question Rav Ovadia's firm insistence that the *beracha* should be recited before the lighting. For example, the dean of Moroccan *posekim*, Rav Shalom Messas (*Teshuvot Shemesh U'Magen* 3: *Oraḥ Ḥayim* 71), writes that whenever a Moroccan woman poses the question to him, he instructs her to follow the old custom from Morocco to light and only afterwards recite the *beracha*. Rav Messas argues that the *Shulḥan Aruch* agrees that the *beracha* should be recited after the lighting, as his language of "*k'sheyadlik yevarech*" (*Oraḥ Ḥayim* 263:5) implies that the *beracha* is recited after the Shabbat candles are already lit.

Indeed, the Moroccan tradition is to follow the Rama whenever the *Shulḥan Aruch*'s view is not clear about the matter in question, and the question of when to recite a *beracha* on Shabbat candle-lighting is an example of such a situation. Thus, it is hardly surprising that the tradition in all Moroccan communities is for the women to recite the *beracha* after candle-lighting, in accordance with the Rama.

RAV BEN TZION ABBA SHA'UL AND RAV MORDECHAI ELIYAHU

Rav Ben Tzion Abba Sha'ul (*Teshuvot Ohr L'Tzion* 2:18:3) writes that those women whose practice is to first light and only afterwards recite the *beracha* should maintain their practice. If, however, a woman does not have a clear

---

5. The Rambam's ruling is unlike that of the *Ohr Zarua* (cited by the *Haghot Oshri*, *Ḥullin* 1:2) and *Sha'agat Aryeh* 26.
6. In general, Rav Ovadia has a very strong preference for reciting a *birkat hamitzva* before the *mitzva* is performed, *over la'asiyatan*. He adopts a similar approach in insisting that the *beracha* of "*l'hachniso b'vrito shel Avraham Avinu*" should be recited by the father before the *mila* (as we discussed in Chapter 28) and that a woman recite the *beracha* on immersion in the *mikveh* before she immerses (as we explain in Chapter 89).

family custom, he advocates reciting the *beracha* first.[7] Rav Eli Mansour reports that the great Syrian rabbinic leader Rav Baruch Ben-Ḥayim ruled that women should maintain the practice of their mothers to recite the *beracha* after the candle-lighting,[8] and Rav Mordechai Lebhar (*Magen Avot, Oraḥ Ḥayim* 263:5) cites Rav Mordechai Eliyahu as ruling that women should follow the venerated custom of Sephardic women to recite the *beracha* after candle-lighting.[9]

Rav Lebhar cites Rav Abba Sha'ul as saying that the *Shulḥan Aruch*'s ruling on the matter is unclear. As such, Rav Lebhar applies the *Ḥida*'s stance (*Teshuvot Ḥayim Sha'al* 2:21, s.v. *halo*) that Sephardic Jews are not bound by the *Shulḥan Aruch* when its ruling is not clear. Rav Lebhar adds that Rav Ovadia does not marshal any significant evidence that demonstrates that Sephardic women traditionally recited the *beracha* before lighting candles. Thus, Rav Lebhar argues that the well-established *minhag* for Sephardic women to recite the *beracha* after lighting candles should prevail.[10]

THE YEMENITE PRACTICE

Yemenite women customarily recite the *beracha* before lighting, since Yemenite practice is deeply impacted by the Rambam's rulings. Although there is considerable debate within the Yemenite community whether to regard the Rambam or *Shulḥan Aruch* as the prime halachic authority,[11] in a situation such as ours, where the *Shulḥan Aruch* is unclear, the default position for all Yemenites is to follow the opinion of the Rambam.

AN ONGOING DEBATE

Ashkenazic women should certainly recite the *beracha* only after lighting Shabbat candles, and Yemenite women should certainly recite the *beracha*

---

7. Rav Shmuel Khoshkerman told me that this is the approach he follows in practice. This approach is also adopted by Rav Eli Mansour (see the next footnote).
8. http://www.dailyhalacha.com/displayRead.asp?readID=2326.
9. Rav Eliyahu's ruling is hardly surprising, since he faithfully hews to the rulings of the *Ben Ish Ḥai*.
10. Rav Lebhar cites Rav Yosef Shalom Eliashiv and Rav Moshe Sternbuch, who rule that Sephardic women who have heeded Rav Ovadia's exhortation to recite the *beracha* before lighting should return to their original family custom. They even rule that such women do not require *hatarat nedarim*, since their deviation from their family tradition was done in error! Rav Lebhar notes, however, that Rav Mordechai Eliyahu requires *hatarat nedarim* in such a circumstance.
11. See Chapter 94 on the Yemenite halachic tradition.

before lighting Shabbat candles. However, no consensus has emerged in the general Sephardic community about this matter. Many Sephardic rabbis adopt the fierce resoluteness of Rav Ovadia's ruling, others follow the more conciliatory approach of Rav Ben Tzion Abba Sha'ul, and others insist that the older practice to recite the *beracha* only after candle-lighting should prevail.

This debate is an example of a much larger debate in the Sephardic community – whether to adhere to age-old Sephardic practices or to follow Rav Ovadia's rulings when he maintains that it is appropriate to veer from the accepted practices of recent generations.

It is important to note that Rav Abba Sha'ul rules that Sephardic women should undoubtedly recite the *beracha* before lighting on Erev Yom Tov, and it follows that a Sephardic man who lights should similarly recite the *beracha* before lighting the candles.

AN ASHKENAZIC WOMAN WHO MARRIES A SEPHARDIC MAN

The woman's role as the gatekeeper for Shabbat is reflected in the fact that Shabbat candle-lighting is considered a woman's *mitzva*. Thus, even though a woman generally adopts the customs of her husband upon their marriage, Rav Mordechai Willig (cited in *Gray Matter*, vol. 3, p. 135) and Rav Doniel Neustadt (*The Weekly Halachah Discussion*, vol. 1, pp.6-8, based on *Teshuvot Ya'avetz* 107) rule that when it comes to the order of lighting Shabbat candles and reciting its *beracha*, a woman should maintain the practices of her mother.

According to this approach, an Ashkenazic woman who marries a Sephardic man may maintain her mother's practice to first light Shabbat candles and only afterwards recite the *beracha*. It does not seem that Rav Ovadia Yosef adopts such an approach.

Chapter 32

A Guest Lighting Shabbat Candles

It was a very exciting Shabbat in March 2011 when Adina Bar Shalom, the distinguished daughter of Rav Ovadia Yosef, visited Congregation Shaarei Orah, the Sephardic Congregation of Teaneck. In addition to having the special pleasure and honor of hearing Rabbanit Bar Shalom speak, it was a privilege for the Jachter family to host her at our home. Not only did we have a very pleasant conversation and Torah discussions, but we also had the opportunity to see the practical application of the rulings of her father, Rav Ovadia Yosef. One of these areas relates to how a guest should light Shabbat candles at the home of his host.

SHULḤAN ARUCH VS. RAMA

Maran Rav Yosef Karo records in the *Bet Yosef* (*Oraḥ Ḥayim* 263):

> I have found in an Ashkenazic responsum [that of the Maharil] that if two individuals are eating together, each one should recite his own *beracha* on his Shabbat candles. Although the *Ohr Zarua* disagrees, nevertheless, some follow this custom, for any additional light in

> the house causes additional peace in the home, and this also causes additional joy in the house, since there is light in every corner.

Nevertheless, in the *Shulḥan Aruch* (*Oraḥ Ḥayim* 263:8), Rav Karo rules:

> If two individuals who are eating in the same place, some say that each one may recite a *beracha* upon lighting his own candles, and some disagree with this opinion. Thus, it is proper to take care regarding a situation of doubt regarding blessings, and only one of them should recite a blessing.

According to Rav Yosef Karo, one should not follow the Ashkenazic custom of each woman reciting her own *beracha* when several women are lighting in one place.[1] Rather, one person should recite a *beracha,* and the other women thereby fulfill their obligation to light Shabbat candles.

Based on this, a Sephardic daughter may not light Shabbat candles in addition to her mother's candles. If she wishes to light, she may do so only without reciting a *beracha,* following the rule of "*safek berachot l'hakel*" – a *beracha* is omitted in a situation of doubt. However, as noted by the Rama, according to the Ashkenazic custom, a guest may light additional candles and recite a blessing upon those candles, as Ashkenazim accept the ruling of the Maharil permitting a blessing on additional light.

RAV OVADIA YOSEF VS. RAV SHALOM MESSAS

Based on this, Rav Ovadia Yosef (*Teshuvot Yeḥaveh Da'at* 2:32) instructs single Sephardic women and girls not to recite a *beracha* on candle-lighting if they wish to light candles alongside their mother's lighting. He notes that traditionally, Sephardic girls never lit candles in addition to those of their mothers, but if a Sephardic girl wishes to follow the Lubavitcher Rebbe's

1. Rav Hershel Schachter often reiterates that even by Ashkenazic standards, additional candles are regarded as providing additional light only if the women are lighting on different sides of the room, not if many candles are lined up in one limited area (although many Ashkenazic women adopt a lenient approach to this issue). Rav Schachter also often expresses his view that the practice of many women to light tea lights together in hotel lobbies certainly constitutes a *beracha l'vatala* (an unnecessary *beracha*) even by Ashkenazic standards, since there is no added benefit from these candles.

exhortation for every woman in the home to light, she should certainly refrain from reciting a *beracha,* even if she lights in her own room.

In contrast to the ruling of Rav Ovadia, Rav Shalom Messas (*Teshuvot Shemesh U'Magen* 2:38), the great Moroccan halachic authority, rules that a guest or even a daughter is permitted recite a *beracha* on additional light, in accordance with the ruling of the Maharil and Rama, if they very much wish to do so. Rav Shalom notes that since Rav Karo did not oppose this ruling in an absolute fashion and only wrote that "it is proper to take care" regarding this matter, one may rely on the ruling of the Maharil. Rav Messas argues that it is certainly permissible for the guest or daughter to recite a *beracha* on candles they light in their own room.

Nevertheless, Rav Yitzḥak Yosef (*Yalkut Yosef, Oraḥ Hayim* 263:14) holds firm and rules that since Sephardic Jews have accepted the rulings of *Maran* Rav Yosef Karo, they should follow his opinion in this regard, especially since there is concern for a *beracha l'vatala,* an unnecessary *beracha.* Moroccan Jews, however, may follow the view of Rav Messas.

Nonetheless, Rav Yitzḥak Yosef adds that a guest should light Shabbat candles with a *beracha* in the designated room where she will be sleeping; it is as if the guest has rented the room in which she is staying, and she therefore has a halachic obligation to light Shabbat candles with a *beracha* in her separate quarters. However, she must take care to light candles that are large enough to remain lit until she returns to her room at night, in order that she can benefit from the light of the candles.[2]

CONCLUSION – RABBANIT BAR SHALOM'S AT THE JACHTER HOME

When we hosted Rabbanit Bar Shalom at our home, she was speaking that evening at a different synagogue, and it was thus impractical for her

2. Rav Yitzḥak Yosef adds that if it is not practical to light candles due to safety concerns, one may light an electric light with a *beracha.* He adds that he saw his father do this at hotels; Rav Ovadia would even light the bathroom light and recite the *beracha* in a hallway. Rav Yitzḥak Yosef notes that one may even use an LED light for this purpose (https://www.torahanytime.com/#/lectures?v=72808, Rav Yitzḥak Yosef, Motzaei Shabbat Vayigash 5779, min 35–38). Rav Hershel Schachter (https://www.yutorah.org/lectures/lecture.cfm/839951/Rabbi_Hershel_Schachter/Jewish_Heritage_Tour_of_Hungary_Part_10_of_10 minute 7, however, maintains that while one may light an incandescent bulb with a *beracha,* one may not light a fluorescent or neon bulb with a *beracha.*

to light candles in the room in which she was staying. Therefore, Rabbanit Bar Shalom (in addition to turning on the dim electric light in the closet of the room in which she was staying) lit candles alongside my wife Malca, without reciting a *beracha*. Instead, she asked my wife Malca to have her in mind when she recited the *beracha* on her candle-lighting. Rabbanit Bar Shalom answered, "*amen*," and then lit her candles.[3]

It was an honor to see Rav Ovadia's daughter following his rulings in practice. May we all merit having children who follow the halachic practices of their parents!

3. Rav Zecharia Ben-Shlomo (*Orot HaHalacha*, p. 302) notes that in a communal setting, when many wish to light Shabbat candles at the same venue, it is worthwhile to allow a Sephardic Jew to light first in order that she will be able to recite the *beracha*.

Chapter 33

Warming Food on Shabbat Sephardic-Style

Imagine the following scene: An Ashkenazic family is visiting a Sephardic family for Shabbat. On Shabbat morning, the Sephardic hostess removes chicken in sauce from the refrigerator and places it straight on the Shabbat tin (what Ashkenazic Jews refer to as a *blech*). The Ashkenazic family is shocked; they would never place cold food on the tin on Shabbat, even if it were solid and completely cooked! The Ashkenazim wonder if they are permitted to eat food that was reheated in this manner.

Luckily, they are able to consult their Rav, who informs them that their Sephardic hosts are simply following the approach of Rav Ovadia Yosef (*Teshuvot Yeḥaveh Da'at* 2:45).

ENO DERECH BISHUL

The *Shulḥan Aruch* (*Oraḥ Ḥayim* 253:5) rules that on Shabbat, one may place fully-cooked solid food on top of a pot filled with food cooking on the fire "because this is not the way of cooking," "*eno derech bishul.*" This permitted method of *haḥazara* (returning food to the fire) is referred to as "*kedera al gabei kedera.*" Since people do not cook food this way, this obviates any concern for *meḥzei k'mevashel,* the appearance of cooking. It does not appear like cooking, and the fact that one is reheating the food in this unusual manner demonstrates that he is not interested in stirring the coals (or adjusting the flame).

Ashkenazic authorities debate whether a non-adjustable hot-plate or warming table constitutes a permissible method for reheating food on Shabbat. Those who adopt the lenient approach argue that since people do not cook on a hot-plate or warming table, it is a permissible method to reheat food, similar to the *kedera al gabei kedera* method. Rav Mordechai Willig (*The Laws of Cooking and Warming Food on Shabbat,* pp. 145–148) rules leniently, whereas the *Shemirat Shabbat K'Hilchata* (1:25) rules strictly.

Rav Ovadia Yosef wholeheartedly endorses the lenient opinion, arguing that a non-adjustable hot-plate successfully avoids concern for adjusting the flame and the appearance of cooking. Moreover, he argues that even simply placing a tin over the fire successfully obviates these concerns. Ashkenazic authorities do not accept this last point, since the *Be'ur Halacha* (253:3, s.v. *v'yizaher*) rules in accordance with the *Peri Megadim,* who argues that *kedera al gabei kedeira* does not appear as cooking only if the bottom pot is filled with food. Rav Ovadia, on the other hand, follows the view of the *Maḥatzit HaShekel,* who permits *kedera al gabei kedera* even if the bottom pot does not contain food.

REHEATING A SOLID WITH MUCH LIQUID

The above discussion relates to reheating fully-cooked solid food. The Rama rules (*Oraḥ Ḥayim* 318:15) that one may not reheat a liquid that has completely cooled down, and according to the *Shulḥan Aruch,* a liquid may not be reheated if it has cooled down to a temperature of less than *yad soledet bo.*[1]

The question of reheating solid food that has some liquid in it has been debated by the *Aḥaronim* for centuries. Some *Aḥaronim* (the *Baḥ,* Vilna Gaon, and *Mishna Berura* 318:32, 104) maintain that a food must be

1. Rav Zecharia Ben-Shlomo (*Orot HaHalacha,* p. 335) notes that many Yemenite Jews follow the ruling of the Rambam (*Hilchot Shabbat* 22:8) that one may reheat a fully-cooked liquid even if it has completely cooled. Rav Eliezer Melamed (http://www.israelnationalnews.com/Articles/Article.aspx/23093) and the *Yalkut Yosef* (*Oraḥ Ḥayim* 253:11) note that it is permissible for all Jews to eat hot soup served at a home of a Yemenite Jew who follows this ancestral practice.

entirely free of liquid to qualify as a solid. This approach argues that there is no difference whether one is heating a small or large amount of liquid; just as heating the large amount of liquid is forbidden, as both the Rama and *Shulḥan Aruch* state, so too is heating a small amount of liquid in a solid food.

Other *Aḥaronim* (including the *Taz, Peri Megadim,* and the *Kaf HaḤayim, Oraḥ Ḥayim* 318:62) maintain that if the majority of a food is solid, it is classified as a solid. The logic of this approach is that the minority of liquid is "*batel,*" nullified to the majority of solid food.

Rav Yosef Adler cites the view of Rav Yosef Dov Soloveitchik as offering a practical guideline: If the food is eaten with a fork, it is a solid; if it is eaten with a spoon, it is a liquid. On the other hand, Rav Moshe Feinstein (*Teshuvot Igrot Moshe* 4:74:*Bishul*:7) rules in accordance with the strict view, except perhaps in a case of great need. Rav Shimon Eider (*Halachos of Shabbos,* p. 259, n. 114) presents a cogent defense of the lenient view based on an idea of Rav Tzvi Pesaḥ Frank. Most Ashkenazic Jews, however, follow the strict opinion of Rav Moshe.

Rav Ovadia follows the view of the *Minḥat Kohen,* who rules that one may follow the lenient approach and place cold, fully-cooked solid food that has some liquid in it on the tin on Shabbat morning. Two great contemporaries of Rav Ovadia, Rav Ben Tzion Abba Sha'ul (*Teshuvot Ohr L'Tzion* 2:30:13) and Rav Shalom Messas (*Teshuvot Tevu'ot Shemesh, Oraḥ Ḥayim* 66), strongly challenged Rav Ovadia's ruling. Nevertheless, Rav Ovadia stood firm, confirming his original position in his elder years without any reservation, especially since he marshals evidence that this is the Minhag Yerushalayim (*Teshuvot Yabia Omer* 7: *Oraḥ Ḥayim* 42:6; *Teshuvot Yabia Omer* 9: *Oraḥ Ḥayim* 108:169).

CONCLUSION

May Ashkenazim eat food on Shabbat that was reheated by Sephardic Jews in accordance with Rav Ovadia's ruling? The answer is an unequivocal yes. Although it is forbidden to benefit from work performed in a forbidden manner on Shabbat, this is only a Rabbinic prohibition. The *Mishna Berura* (318:2, citing the *Peri Megadim*) and *Yalkut Yosef* (*Oraḥ Ḥayim* 253:11) permit eating food cooked in accordance with a legitimate opinion that one does not follow, since we may rule leniently about Rabbinic matters. Thus, even though Ashkenazic Jews refrain from reheating food in this manner due to a possible violation of Halacha, once the food has been prepared, an Ashkenazic Jew may rely on the lenient view and enjoy the food. Accordingly, the Ashkenazic family in our hypothetical example may enjoy without reservations the food reheated by their Sephardic hosts, even if the Sephardim follow a more lenient approach than the Ashkenazim.

Chapter 34

Save the *Ḥamin*!

A number of congregants at Congregation Shaarei Orah, the Sephardic Congregation of Teaneck, have sent me concerned emails on a most pressing matter. Rav Eli Mansour (in his Daily Halacha series) has presented the rulings of Rav Yosef Karo (*Shulḥan Aruch, Oraḥ Ḥayim* 253:4) and Rav Ovadia Yosef (*Teshuvot Yeḥaveh Da'at* 4:22) unequivocally forbidding Sephardic Jews from placing hot water from an urn into *ḥamin/cholent* that is drying up on Shabbat![1] My congregants – committed, as all Orthodox Jews, to enjoying hot *ḥamin/cholent* – desperately need to know how to rescue their beloved Shabbat delicacy.[2]

SHULḤAN ARUCH VS. RAMA

Rav Yosef Karo's ruling (as he explains in his *Bet Yosef* commentary on the *Tur, Oraḥ Ḥayim* 253) is based on the view of Rabbenu Yona, who objects to those who set aside hot water before Shabbat to pour into *ḥamin* that dries up on Shabbat. Rabbenu Yona presents two reasons for his strict ruling. One concern is that the hot water may have cooled down to less than the temperature of *yad soledet bo* (hot to the touch, approximately 180°F in

1. http://www.dailyhalacha.com/displayRead.asp?readID=1632&txtSearch=halacha.
2. The Shabbat *cholent* is blessed by *Hashem* with especially savory taste (*Shabbat* 119a).

this context). If so, placing the hot water into the *ḥamin* would restore the water to a temperature hotter than *yad soledet bo,* thereby constituting a Torah-level violation of Shabbat. The second reason is that even if the water remains *yad soledet bo,* as soon as the water leaves the original utensil in which it was cooked (*k'li rishon*), it is viewed from a halachic lens as having cooled. Restoring the water to a *k'li rishon* would thus constitute an act of *bishul.*

Ashkenazim follow the ruling of the Rama, who does permit pouring hot water from an urn or kettle into drying *cholent.* This follows the view of the Ran, who rejects Rabbenu Yona's approach and argues that *en bishul aḥar bishul* – once an item (even a liquid) is cooked, reheating that item is not considered cooking. The Rama follows this opinion as long as the water has not completely cooled. Thus, even if the water is no longer *yad soledet bo,* it may be added to the drying *cholent* on Shabbat (*Oraḥ Ḥayim* 318:15).[3]

RAV SHALOM MESSAS – THE MOROCCAN PRACTICE

The great Moroccan authority Rav Shalom Messas (*Teshuvot Tevu'ot Shemesh, Oraḥ Ḥayim* 26) notes that although Moroccan Jews accept the rulings of Rav Yosef Karo, in this instance Moroccan Jews have an ancient custom to follow the lenient approach of the Ran. Rav Messas notes that Rav Yosef Karo writes in his introduction to the *Shulḥan Aruch* that his rulings are not intended to supersede established custom.

This is also not problematic for Yemenite Jews. Rav Zecharia Ben-Shlomo (*Orot HaHalacha,* p. 335) notes that many Yemenite Jews follow the ruling of the Rambam (*Hilchot Shabbat* 22:8) that one may reheat a fully-cooked liquid even if it is completely cooled. Thus, for Yemenites, there is no concern for reheating water that had been previously heated.

RAV OVADIA'S SUGGESTIONS

Rav Ovadia suggests that hot water may be poured into the *ḥamin/cholent* after it is removed from the cooking vessel on the fire (*k'li rishon*) and

---

3. Interestingly, Rav Yitzḥak Yosef (*Yalkut Yosef, Oraḥ Ḥayim* 318:72) forbids a Sephardic Jew to ask an Ashkenazic Jew to place hot water in the *ḥamin*: "Since it is forbidden for a Sephardic Jew to perform this activity, he may not ask an Ashkenazic Jew to perform it on his behalf." He similarly forbids a Sephardic Jew from asking an Ashkenazic Jew to reheat a liquid that has cooled to below *yad soledet bo* (180°F in this context) but has not cooled down completely, even though it is permissible for an Ashkenazic Jew to reheat a liquid in such circumstances (*Yalkut Yosef, Oraḥ Ḥayim* 318:59).

placed into a serving vessel (*k'li sheni*). In some situations, this may save the *ḥamin/cholent*. But what if this won't work?

Rav Shmuel Khoshkerman rules that one may be lenient if one brings the hot water urn and *ḥamin/cholent* as close as possible, to prevent the possibility of the water becoming cooler than *yad soledet bo* during the transfer of the boiling hot water from the urn to the food.

My congregants noted that this solution satisfies only the first concern of Rabbenu Yona, but not the second, and Rav Ovadia indeed insists that the *Shulḥan Aruch* rules in accordance with both of Rabbenu Yona's concerns. I noted, however, that the *Mishna Berura* (263:84) understands the *Shulḥan Aruch* to be concerned only with the temperature of the water dipping below *yad soledet bo*. If there is no other solution, I suggested that one may rely on the *Mishna Berura*'s understanding of the *Shulḥan Aruch* in order to preserve the centerpiece of the Shabbat *seuda*.

RAV MANSOUR'S SUGGESTIONS

Rav Mansour offers some practical suggestions regarding preemptive action to avoid this difficult situation:

> It is therefore advisable to take precautions before Shabbat to ensure that one's *cholent* will not dry out before lunchtime on Shabbat. One possibility is to keep the crockpot slightly elevated within the heating element, which has the effect of slowing the cooking process. Likewise, one who cooks *cholent* on a *blech* can place it off to the side, where there is less heat. The most advisable solution is to fill a cooking bag with water and place it inside the *cholent* pot before Shabbat, where it functions as a "reserve supply" of water. If one notices the *cholent* drying out, he can simply puncture the bag and allow the water to flow into the *cholent*. Since the water is already cooked inside the pot, it is permissible to allow the water out of the bag to mix with the *cholent*.

CONCLUSION

The best approach was offered by one of Shaarei Orah's congregants – make sure to add the proper amount of water when preparing the *ḥamin* on Erev Shabbat to avoid the need to rely on anything other than the straightforward rulings of *Maran* Rav Yosef Karo and Rav Ovadia!

Chapter 35

Clapping on Shabbat

At a recent Bar Mitzva celebration at a West Coast Sephardic congregation, a well-meaning and beloved visiting Ashkenazic rabbi began to lead the community in song, dance, and clapping. This caused an awkward moment, as Sephardic Jews refrain from clapping their hands to song on Shabbat and Yom Tov.

THE *MISHNA'S* PROHIBITION

The *mishna* in *Betza* (36b) includes clapping and dancing on Shabbat and Yom Tov on a fairly long list of *gezerot*, Rabbinic decrees forbidding certain actions to prevent the violation of a Torah violation on these holy days. The *gemara* explains that *Ḥazal* feared that if we were to clap hands and dance to song on Shabbat, we would come to play and eventually fix or tune a musical instrument, a violation of the *melacha* of *makeh bepatish*.

Many *Rishonim* codify this ruling, including the Rambam (*Hilchot Shabbat* 23:5) and the Rif, Rabbenu Ḥananel, Rosh, and Meiri (on *Betza* 36b). *Tosafot* (*Betza* 30a s.v. *Tenan*), however, maintain that this *gezera* no longer applies, as the people in their time were no longer proficient in tuning musical instruments.

Tosafot's approach is surprising. First, we remain, certainly in our times, capable of fixing and tuning musical instruments. Second, it is axiomatic that

Rabbinic decrees remain in effect even if the reason for their enactment no longer applies (*"davar shebeminyan tzarich minyan aḥer l'hatiro"*; *Betza* 5a).

Rav Yosef Karo, the primary Sephardic halachic authority, follows in the path of the majority of *Rishonim* in ruling that this decree remains in full effect in our times (*Shulḥan Aruch, Oraḥ Ḥayim* 339:3), whereas the Rama, the major Ashkenazic codifier, presents *Tosafot's* approach as normative, noting that the common practice of Ashkenazic communities is to follow the lenient approach of *Tosafot*. It is important to note that the *Mishna Berura* (339:10) is not enthusiastic about this Ashkenazic practice and prefers adopting a strict approach to this matter.

RAV OVADIA YOSEF VS. *ARUCH HASHULḤAN*

Not surprisingly, Rav Ovadia Yosef (*Teshuvot Yabia Omer* 3: *Oraḥ Ḥayim* 22; *Teshuvot Yeḥaveh Da'at* 2:57) vigorously endorses the ruling of the *Shulḥan Aruch*. Moreover, he even goes as far as to convince Ashkenazic Jews to refrain from clapping and dancing to song on Shabbat and Yom Tov.

Nonetheless, as noted by the *Aruch HaShulḥan* (*Oraḥ Ḥayim* 339:9), the Ashkenazic custom to be lenient has persisted. This is likely due to the fact that it is a bit counterintuitive to forbid clapping on Shabbat and Yom Tov lest one come to fix a musical instrument. Although the *Aruch HaShulḥan* rejects the justification offered by *Tosafot* and the Rama for this practice, he offers an interesting original defense, arguing that the *gezera* applies only to clapping and dancing to music that is being played. Clapping and dancing when music is not being played is not included in the *gezera* and is thus permitted on Shabbat and Yom Tov.

Although the *Aruch HaShulḥan*'s logic is compelling, Rav Ovadia notes that it lacks a solid basis in the *gemara*. Rav Ovadia is generally quite fond of the *Aruch HaShulḥan*'s approach to Halacha, and he quotes him frequently, but regarding this matter, Rav Ovadia believes that the ruling of the *Aruch HaShulḥan*'s view is not supported by proper evidence.

The great early twentieth-century Ḥassidic master, the Munkatcher Rebbe, attempted to defend the Ḥassidic practice to clap and dance to song on Shabbat and Yom Tov in his classic work *Teshuvot Minḥat Elazar* (1:29). He argues that the *gezera* never applied to a situation of *mitzva*, such as when Ḥassidim engage in singing in holy ecstasy.

Rav Ovadia handily dismisses this contention, however, noting that another great Ḥassidic Rebbe and Halachist – Rav Shneur Zalman of Liadi, the first Lubavitcher Rebbe – forbids clapping and dancing on Shabbat and Yom Tov even at a *mitzva* occasion, such as a rejoicing with a new bride and groom (*Shulḥan Aruch HaRav* 339:2).

CONCLUSION

Rav Ovadia concludes that one should gently urge any Jew who claps and dances to music on Shabbat and Yom Tov to refrain from doing so. However, Rav Yitzḥak Yosef (*Yalkut Yosef, Oraḥ Ḥayim* 339:5) limits this reproach to a Sephardic Jew who claps or dances to music on Shabbat and Yom Tov.

Even Rav Ovadia relents somewhat, permitting simply walking around in a circle while singing holy songs on Shabbat and Yom Tov, since this hardly qualifies as dancing (end of *Teshuvot Yeḥaveh Da'at* 2:57). Alumni of Yeshivat Har Etzion are fondly familiar with this approach, as our beloved Rav Aharon Lichtenstein similarly permitted only a shuffle around the hallway after the Friday night *tefilla* at the Yeshiva in joyously welcoming the holy day. Rav Shmuel Khoshkerman, however, is reluctant to permit even this sort of shuffle, since it may lead to confusion; if shuffling is permitted, people will think that full-fledged dancing is permissible as well.

Chapter 36

May a Sephardic Jew Rely on a Community *Eruv*?

A standard community *eruv* surrounds the area with *tzurot hapetaḥ* (doorframes), thereby rendering the area an enclosed area (*reshut hayaḥid*), in which it is permissible to carry on Shabbat. A *tzurat hapetaḥ* consists of a horizontal wire (or pole) that passes over the tops of two vertical poles, forming the shape of a doorway.

However, an area defined as a *reshut harabbim* (a public domain, in which it is forbidden to carry on a Biblical level) must be surrounded by a wall in order to render it a *reshut hayaḥid*. This affects the acceptability of many community *eruvin* according to Sephardic authorities, who define a *reshut harabbim* much more broadly than their Ashkenazic counterparts.

DOES A *RESHUT HARABBIM* REQUIRE 600,000 PEOPLE?

The precise definition of a *reshut harabbim* has been hotly debated since the time of the earliest *Rishonim*. The main point of contention is whether an area requires the presence of 600,000 people to attain the status of a *reshut harabbim*. If one does not accept this opinion, any street wider than 16 *amot* (approximately 26-28 feet) is regarded as a *reshut harabbim*, and a wall is required to render the area a *reshut hayaḥid*. Only if one accepts that the presence of 600,000 people is required to create a *reshut harabbim* is it possible to create a city *eruv* consisting of *tzurot hapetaḥ*.

RISHONIM

The Rambam (*Hilchot Shabbat* 14:1) does not mention that 600,000 people must be present in an area in order for it to be considered a *reshut harabbim*. Rashi (*Eruvin* 6a, s.v. *reshut harabbim*; *Eruvin* 59a, s.v. *ir*), however, maintains that a city that does not regularly have the presence of 600,000 people is not a *reshut harabbim*, as it has less population than the Jews' encampment in the desert. The practices and the activities of the encampment in the desert serve as the paradigm for forbidden activities on Shabbat (see *Shabbat* 73b–74a). Thus, only an area with a presence of 600,000 constitutes a *reshut harabbim* in which it is forbidden to carry on a Torah level. *Tosafot* (*Eruvin* 6a, s.v. *ketzad*) record that the Behag agrees with Rashi, whereas Rabbenu Tam finds Rashi's opinion problematic.

Accordingly, Rashi would permit the creation of an *eruv* consisting only of *tzurot hapetaḥ* around a city whose population is less than 600,000. The Rambam, on the other hand, would regard such an *eruv* as invalid, since the *eruv* encompasses streets that are wider than 16 *amot*.

THE *SHULḤAN ARUCH* AND ITS COMMENTARIES

The *Shulḥan Aruch* (*Oraḥ Ḥayim* 345:7) cites (and presumably accepts) the Rambam's opinion that an area may be defined as a *reshut harabbim* even in the absence of 600,000 people, although he does cite Rashi's lenient view as a second opinion. The Rama (*Oraḥ Ḥayim* 346:3) indicates that he accepts Rashi's requirement of 600,000 people.

Both the *Magen Avraham* (345:7) and the *Taz* (345:6) cite the *Masat Binyamin* (92) and the Maharshal (*Yam Shel Shlomo, Betza* 3:8), who rule in accordance with the stricter view that the presence of 600,000 people is not required to define a community as a *reshut harabbim*. However, the *Magen Avraham* and *Taz* themselves disagree with these authorities and write that the majority view follows that of Rashi, requiring 600,000 people.

The *Aruch HaShulḥan* (*Oraḥ Ḥayim* 345:17) writes that the *eruvin* in the Jewish towns of Eastern Europe were based on the acceptance of Rashi's leniency; otherwise, they could not have used *tzurot hapetaḥ* to create the community *eruv*. According to the *Aruch HaShulḥan*, the practice of most Ashkenazic Jews to rely upon such an *eruv* is acceptable.

THE OPINION OF RAV YOSEF KARO

Although *Maran* Rav Yosef Karo presents Rashi's lenient view merely as a second opinion in *Oraḥ Ḥayim* 345:7, his view is somewhat unclear, as he appears to contradict himself in *Oraḥ Ḥayim* 303:18, where he writes that no location today qualifies as a *reshut harabbim*. Presumably, the reason is that he requires the presence of 600,000 people to create a *reshut harabbim*.

Sephardic authorities throughout the generations have debated which view should be regarded as the opinion endorsed by Rav Karo. The *Ḥida* (*Birkei Yosef, Oraḥ Ḥayim* 345:2) regards the stricter opinion as the one accepted by Rav Karo, and thus the *halacha* for Sephardic Jews. However, the *Erech HaShulḥan* (*Oraḥ Ḥayim* 345:2) disagrees and argues that Rav Karo accepts Rashi's lenient opinion requiring the presence of 600,000 people in order to render the area a *reshut harabbim*.

This argument persists until this very day. Rav Shalom Messas (*Teshuvot Tevu'ot Shemesh* 1:65) rules that Rav Karo accepts the stricter opinion, while Rav Ovadia Yosef (*Teshuvot Yabia Omer* 9: *Oraḥ Ḥayim* 33) rules that Rav Karo accepts the more lenient view.

RAV OVADIA AND RAV MESSAS'S ENDORSEMENT OF AMERICAN COMMUNITY *ERUVIN*

Both Rav Ovadia (ibid.) and Rav Messas (*Teshuvot Shemesh U'Magen* 3: *Oraḥ Ḥayim* 84) urged the local rabbis to establish a community *eruv* in Deal, New Jersey. They both stated that their motivation derived from the fact that many Jews carried on Shabbat even though an *eruv* did not yet exist in the area, in a blatant breach of the laws of Shabbat.

Despite the fact that both Rav Ovadia and Rav Messas strongly encouraged the creation of this *eruv*, however, their respective approaches were significantly different. Rav Messas regarded the *eruv* as intended only for those who already carry without the *eruv*. He strongly encouraged others to refrain from relying on the *eruv*, since he fundamentally rules that the presence of 600,000 people is not required to create a *reshut harabbim*. Rav Ovadia adopted a more lenient view. While he writes that it is preferable to adopt the strict view and refrain from using a standard community *eruv*, he concludes that according to the baseline *halacha, tzurot hapetaḥ* suffice to render an area a *reshut hayaḥid*.

Rav Ovadia further notes that the *Kaf HaḤayim* (*Oraḥ Ḥayim* 345:37), who maintains that Sephardic Jews essentially do not rely on the lenient view requiring the presence of 600,000 people to constitute a *reshut harabbim*, writes that one may rely upon this lenient view if a supplementary lenient consideration exists. Rav Ovadia bolsters the lenient view requiring 600,000 people with the lenient consideration set forth by the *Ḥazon Ish* (*Oraḥ Ḥayim* 107:5–7) that the arrangement of buildings in modern cities creates a situation in which our cities constitute a *reshut hayaḥid* on a Torah level, rendering it permissible to create an *eruv* consisting only of *tzurot hapetaḥ* in the area. Rav Ovadia writes that with the *Ḥazon Ish*'s approach as an adjunct to the lenient view, "there certainly exists a great basis upon which to create an *eruv* consisting only of *tzurot hapetaḥ*."

LARGE CITY *ERUVIN*

Interestingly, Rav Ovadia records that he encouraged the creation of an *eruv* in Los Angeles, despite the fact that far more than 600,000 people reside in this city. Rav Ovadia is lenient even in this case, since he rules that people riding in cars, buses, and trains do not count towards the number 600,000. Rav Ovadia even endorsed the idea of an *eruv* in Flatbush, New York.[1] This approach would also justify the city-wide *eruv* of Jerusalem, despite the fact that its residents now exceed 600,000 people.

THE VIEW OF THE RAMBAM

An additional potentially challenging factor for Sephardic acceptance of community *eruvin* is the view of the Rambam (*Hilchot Shabbat* 16:16), who maintains that a *tzurat hapetaḥ* spanning more than ten *amot* is valid only if the majority of the *eruv* consists of wall. It is quite difficult to satisfy the Rambam's opinion in a typical community *eruv*. However, the *Shulḥan Aruch* (*Oraḥ Ḥayim* 362:10) presents the Rambam only as a secondary opinion, and the *Kaf HaḤayim* (362:91) rules that while it is preferable to abide by the Rambam's strict ruling, one may rely on the majority of *Rishonim* who disagree.

A SPECIAL SEPHARDIC *ERUV*

In a letter explaining his endorsement of the Sephardic Flatbush *eruv*, the legendary Syrian Jewish community leader Rav Sha'ul Kassin notes that

1. Rav Ovadia's endorsement appears in a letter archived at https://www.erub.org/c_services.

the Sephardic *eruv* consists of a majority of actual wall.[2] This is done to accommodate the opinion of the Rambam, the *tzurot hapetaḥ* represent only a minority of the *eruv* boundary.

Moreover, Rav Kassin notes that "doors" that could be opened and locked were posted throughout the area enclosed by the *eruv* (*daltot re'uyot l'nol*). When a *reshut harabbim* is periodically enclosed on all sides by doors, it ceases to be a *reshut harabbim* (*Shulḥan Aruch, Oraḥ Ḥayim* 364:2).[3] Rav Kassin assured that the doors of the *eruv* would indeed be locked periodically.

CONCLUSION

It is significant that Rav Ovadia Yosef does not say that a Sephardic Jew may rely only on a community *eruv* that consists mostly of walls and is surrounded by doors with the potential to expand. Indeed, as we noted above, the *Kaf HaḤayim* writes that one may rely on the majority of *Rishonim* who disagree with the Rambam.

Thus, it is clear from Rav Ovadia's writings that although it is preferable for a Sephardic Jew to refrain from using a communal *eruv* on Shabbat, he has significant basis upon which to rely on even in the case of a standard community *eruv*, without the enhancements made in the Flatbush *eruv*.[4]

---

2. See https://www.erub.org/c_services.
3. The classic example of this phenomenon is recorded in the *gemara* (*Eruvin* 22a), which states that "had Jerusalem's doors not been locked in the evenings, the city would have been considered a *reshut harabbim*."
4. In varying degrees, Rav Ovadia (*Teshuvot Yabia Omer* 9: *Oraḥ Ḥayim* 33), Rav Shalom Messas (*Teshuvot Shemesh U'Magen* 3: *Oraḥ Ḥayim* 84), Rav Mordechai Eliyahu (comments to Rav Zechariah Ben-Shlomo's *Orot HaHalacha*, p. 1236), and Rav Ben Tzion Abba Sha'ul (*Teshuvot Ohr L'Tzion* 2:23:12) permit relying on a community *eruv*. Rav Ben-Shlomo told me that it is generally accepted among Sephardic *posekim* that Sephardim are permitted to use a community *eruv*, but they all agree that it is preferable to avoid relying on a community *eruv* when possible.

Chapter 37

Eruv Standards According to Sephardic Measurements

As discussed in the previous chapter, it is much more difficult to create a community *eruv* based on Sephardic halachic standards, which may accept a stricter view of what constitutes a *reshut harabbim*. An additional issue relates to the size of an *amah* (cubit), the measurement of length used in discussion of creating *eruvin*. The size of an *amah* is vigorously debated among the *posekim*, and a significant difference exists between Sephardic and Ashkenazic traditions. Those building and maintaining *eruvin* should keep this in mind so that their *eruvin* satisfy both Sephardic and Ashkenazic traditions.

GAPS OF TEN *AMOT* AND WALLS OF TEN *TEFAḤIM*

The building of an *eruv* in the State of Israel, where we are at home and government authorities are supportive, is generally not very complicated.[1] Outside of Eretz Yisrael – as a practical matter and in order to take into account local sensibilities, especially in smaller Jewish communities – *eruvin*

1. See my essay, archived at https://www.jewishlinknj.com/features/31023-the-modi-in-eruv-and-the-jewish-state.

must be built in the least obtrusive manner possible. Every effort is made to use existing structures, such as utility poles (especially those with a wire running on top), very steep slopes, and fences. In such situations, gaps will often exist when seeking to continue the *eruv* from a fence to poles to steep slopes, etc. The Halacha tolerates a gap of up to ten *amot* in such circumstances (*Eruvin* 1:1; *Shulḥan Aruch, Oraḥ Ḥayim* 362:9; *Aruch HaShulḥan, Oraḥ Ḥayim* 362:30, 36 and 363:45).[2]

The length of an *amah* has ramifications for another aspect of *eruvin* as well. To be part of an *eruv*, a wall must be at least ten *tefaḥim* high (*Eruvin* 1:9; *Shulḥan Aruch, Oraḥ Ḥayim* 345:2), and there are six *tefaḥim* in an *amah*.

But how long is an *amah* in terms of feet and inches? (Or as a famous comedian once asked, "What's a cubit?!")

ḤAZON ISH, RAV MOSHE FEINSTEIN, AND RAV AVRAHAM ḤAYIM NA'EH

Twentieth-century *posekim* intensely debate the equivalent of an *amah* and *tefaḥ* in contemporary terms.[3] The three primary opinions are those of the *Ḥazon Ish*, Rav Moshe Feinstein, and Rav Avraham Ḥayim Na'eh. The *Ḥazon Ish* and Rav Na'eh were contemporaries who lived in Eretz Yisrael and engaged in vigorous debate about this topic from 5703 (1943) until 5713 (1953), the year in which both of these sages passed to the next world. Rav Moshe Feinstein issued his ruling on this issue in 1956 when he lived in the United States, independent of and without relating to the debate between the *Ḥazon Ish* and Rav Na'eh.

- According to Rav Moshe Feinstein (Teshuvot Igrot Moshe, Oraḥ Ḥayim 1:136), an amah is 21.25 inches (53.98 cm) and a tefaḥ is 3.54 inches (9 cm).[4]
- According to Rav Avraham Ḥayim Na'eh (*Shiurei Torah* 3:25), an *amah* is 18.9 inches (48 cm) and a *tefaḥ* is 3.15 inches (8 cm).

2. There is considerable debate as to whether we may tolerate a gap of ten *amot* between a *tzurat hapetaḥ* and a wall; see *Be'ur Halacha* 363:6, s.v. *tzarich*.
3. The very wide range of opinions on this matter is summarized in the *Encyclopedia Talmudit*, s.v. *amah*.
4. The *Aruch HaShulḥan*'s measurement of an *amah* (*Yoreh De'ah* 201:3 and 286:21) is almost identical to that of Rav Moshe, and the *Mishna Berura* (358:7) agrees (as explained at https://asif.co.il/download/kitvey-et/kol/kol-30/1–29.pdf).

- According to the *Ḥazon Ish* (*Oraḥ Ḥayim* 39), an *amah* is 24 inches (60.96 cm) and a *tefaḥ* is 4 inches (10.16 cm).

SEPHARDIC AND ASHKENAZIC APPROACHES

In Eretz Yisrael, the custom among Ashkenazic authorities is to apply the stringencies resulting from the views of both the *Ḥazon Ish* and Rav Avraham Ḥayim Na'eh.[5] Thus, they will require a fence that is part of an *eruv* to be 40 inches high (following the *Ḥazon Ish*'s measurement of a *tefaḥ*), but they will not permit a gap greater than 15 feet and 9 inches (following Rav Na'eh's measurement of an *amah*).

In the United States, Rav Hershel Schachter and Rav Mordechai Willig essentially follow Rav Moshe's ruling (*Teshuvot Igrot Moshe, Oraḥ Ḥayim* 1:136). Accordingly, they require a fence to be 36 inches high and permit a gap of up to 18 feet. *The Laws of an Eruv* (p. 264) reports that "many *posekim*" in the United States adopt a similar approach.

Sephardic practice, however, accords with the opinion of Rav Avraham Hayim Na'eh.[6] Rav Shalom Messas (*Yalkut Shemesh* 137–138) writes that the smaller *shiurim* of Rav Na'eh should be adopted.[7]

CREATING AN *ERUV* ACCEPTABLE FOR SEPHARDIC JEWS

There is no problem for Sephardim to rely on *eruvin* created by Ashkenazic *Rabbanim* in Eretz Yisrael, since they accommodate the opinion of Rav Na'eh when it results in a stringency. Thus, it is not surprising that in many contexts, the *Yalkut Yosef* permits reliance on the community *eruv* without any provisos

5. As reported in Rabbi Shlomo Francis and Rabbi Yonasan Glenner, *The Laws of an Eruv* (Israel Bookshop Publications: Lakewood, NJ, 2013), p. 264, and *Teḥumin* 32:413.
6. Rav Avraham Hadaya is cited by Rav Na'eh in the introduction to his *Shiur Mikveh* as clarifying the Sephardic tradition. In many contexts, the *Yalkut Yosef* rules that it is sufficient for *hadassim* and *aravot* to be three *tefaḥim* long according to the measurements of Rav Na'eh (see, for example, *Yalkut Yosef, Oraḥ Ḥayim* 650). Sephardim also maintain a smaller *shiur* for separating *ḥalla*, reciting a *beracha* if the dough contains a minimum of 3.5 pounds of flour (*Yalkut Yosef, Yoreh De'ah* 324:6), whereas Ashkenazim recite a *beracha* only on a minimum of 5 pounds. (*Ashkenazim* separate *ḥalla* without a *beracha* if the dough contains between 3 and 5 pounds of flour; see Rav Eliyahu Yosef Henkin, *Edut L'Yisrael*, p. 138.)
7. The Yemenite *posek* Rav Eli Kady reports that the Yemenite practice also conforms to the opinion of Rav Na'eh.

that the *eruv* conform to Sephardic standards (see, for example, *Yalkut Yosef, Oraḥ Ḥayim* 584; *Hanhagot Rosh Hashana* 2). Rav Ovadia Yosef considers it acceptable for Sephardim to rely on *eruvin* built according to Ashkenazic specifications without adjustments to accommodate Sephardim.[8]

However, this might not be true of *eruvin* created in the United States under the auspices of Ashkenazic *Rabbanim*, since many of the *eruvin* in the United States do not accommodate the stringent result of Rav Na'eh's measurements. It might therefore be improper for a Sephardic Jew to rely upon a community *eruv*, unless the *eruv* conforms to Rav Na'eh's measurements (i.e., gaps do not exceed 15 feet and 9 inches).

Any community that is blessed with a Sephardic *kehilla* should endeavor to comply with Rav Na'eh's measurements and ensure that gaps do not exceed 15 feet and 9 inches. As the *Rav HaMachshir* (supervising rabbi) of the Englewood *eruv* (which includes a significant Sephardic community), I ensure that the *eruv* conforms not only to Rav Moshe's measurements, but also those of Rav Avraham Ḥayim Na'eh. In my service on the *eruv* Rabbinic board of the Teaneck *eruv*, I similarly ensure that there are no gaps wider than 15 feet and 9 inches in the *eruv*.[9] When we had the honor of hosting Chief Rabbi Rav Shlomo Amar at Congregation Shaarei Orah in August 2017, he told me that he agrees that an *eruv* that services Sephardic Jews should insure that gaps not be wider than 15 feet and 9 inches.[10]

8. This point is also relevant regarding the issue of "*taḥuv*." Rav Yehuda Amital told me in 1990 that it is widely accepted in Israel to rely upon *taḥuv*, which refers to when the *eruv* wire is bolted through the pole instead of running above the pole (a common scenario in telephone poles in the United States). Although the *Kaf HaḤayim* (362:106) adopts the position of the *Peri Megadim* (*Mishbetzot Zahav* 363:19), who is unsure as to whether *taḥuv* is acceptable, the fact that the *Yalkut Yosef* accepts (as baseline Halacha) a typical community *eruv* indicates that he regards these *eruvin* as acceptable for Sephardim, despite their use of *taḥuv*. Indeed, Rav Zecharia Ben-Shlomo (*Orot HaHalacha*, p. 616) permits all Jews to rely on *taḥuv*. It is noteworthy that the standards Rav Ben-Shlomo presents for *eruv* construction are identical for all Jews.
9. Whenever possible, in the more than sixty community *eruvin* that I help supervise, every effort is made to conform to Rav Na'eh's *shiur* when it results in stringency.
10. Rav Ike Sultan reports, however, that Rav Zecharia Ben-Shlomo told him that in a case of great need, a Sephardic Jew may carry in an *eruv* that conforms to Rav Moshe Feinstein's *shiurim* (see *Orot HaHalacha*, p. 581). The basis of this ruling may be the convergence of two Rabbinic decrees (*trei d'Rabbanan*), as Rav Mordechai Willig argues (see below in the text). We may also suggest (based on the *Ḥazon Ish, Kuntres HaShiurim, Oraḥ Ḥayim* 39) that the *shiurim* of *amah* and *tefaḥ* are by

It is important to note that Ḥabad-affiliated Jews also follow the opinion of Rav Na'eh. Thus, if an *eruv* includes a Ḥabad community, it behooves the broader community leaders to ensure that there should be no gaps in the *eruv* wider than 15 feet and 9 inches.

It is also important to note that most Ashkenazim rely on Rav Na'eh's opinion in a lenient direction in the context of the size of *hadassim* used on Sukkot. Most of the *hadassim* sold in the United States conform to Rav Na'eh's opinion – they are *meshulash*, with all three leaves on the same level, on a majority of the rows of three *tefaḥim*, at least 9.45 inches – or those that conform to the *shiur* of the *Ḥazon Ish* (*meshulash* on at least 12 inches). Thus, many, if not most, of the members of many Orthodox synagogues nationwide rely on Rav Na'eh's view in a lenient direction regarding fulfillment of the Torah obligation to take *hadassim* on the first day of Sukkot. It seems logical that Rav Na'eh's opinion should thus be accommodated in a strict direction regarding community *eruvin*, even in a completely Ashkenazic community.[11]

Rav Mordechai Willig told me that he makes every effort to ensure that the Riverdale *eruv* (which he supervises) satisfies Rav Na'eh's opinion when it results in a stringency. However, Rav Willig defends those communities whose *eruvin* do not satisfy Rav Na'eh's opinion, but rather only that of Rav Moshe. He argues that since the situation involves two converging Rabbinic laws (*trei d'Rabbanan*), there is room to adopt the lenient approach. The prohibition to carry in an area that is suitable for an *eruv* consisting significantly of *tzurot hapetaḥ* (such as almost all city *eruvin* today) constitutes a Rabbinic prohibition, and the invalidity of a gap of more than ten *amot* when a majority of the side of the *eruv* is enclosed ("*omed meruba al haparutz*") also constitutes only a Rabbinic prohibition (Rav Ḥayim Ozer Grodzinsky, *Teshuvot Aḥiezer* 4:8; the *Ḥazon Ish*, op. cit. and *Oraḥ Ḥayim* 107:5–7; and Rav Moshe Feinstein, *Teshuvot Igrot Moshe, Oraḥ Ḥayim* 2:90).

---

definition flexible and vary from country to country. Thus, since America's greatest *posek*, Rav Moshe Feinstein, determined that in the United States an *amah* is 1.8 feet, that measurement is relevant even for Sephardic Jews.

11. Rav Zvi Sobolofsky told me that the community relies not upon Rav Na'eh's smaller *shiur*, but rather on the smaller *shiur* for a *tefaḥ* in the context of *hadassim* and *aravot* (as presented in *Sukka* 32b and *Shulḥan Aruch, Oraḥ Ḥayim* 650:5). The three *tefaḥim* required with respect to *hadassim* and *aravot* specifically, according to Rav Moshe Feinstein, are a bit smaller than what Rav Na'eh regards as the conventional three *tefaḥim*.

Chapter 38

A Sephardic Approach to the International Dateline

Since the time of the *Rishonim,* the location of the halachic dateline has been a subject of discussion among halachic authorities. The debate intensified in the mid-twentieth century and continues to rage unresolved until today.[1]

AN INTENSE THREE-WAY DEBATE

The three major opinions are those of the *Ḥazon Ish,* who believes that the dateline lies 90 degrees east of Jerusalem; Rav Yeḥiel Michel Tukachinsky, who argues that it lies 180 degrees from Jerusalem; and Rav Tzvi Pesaḥ Frank, who believes that Halacha accepts the international community's designation of 180 degrees from Greenwich, England as the dateline.

There are great ramifications that emerge from this major dispute. For example, Japan and New Zealand lie west of the International Dateline, but east of the dateline according to the *Ḥazon Ish.* Thus, in the *Ḥazon Ish*'s

---

1. For a full English-language discussion of this issue, see my essays on this topic archived at koltorah.org.

view, a Jew in Japan should observe Shabbat on what the international community regards as Sunday!

Hawaii, in turn, lies east of the International Dateline but west of the halachic dateline according to Rav Tukachinsky. According to this view, one should observe Shabbat in Hawaii on what the international community regards as Friday.

CONTEMPORARY ASHKENAZIC HALACHIC AUTHORITIES

Rav Hershel Schachter advises that one should make every effort to avoid spending Shabbat in countries that lie in the "*safek* (uncertain) zone," from the eastern Asian coast to the 180-degree line from Eretz Yisrael. These locations include Japan, Hawaii, American Samoa, and New Zealand. However, this view does not seem to be practical for many people today, as business travel to these countries has become commonplace. In fact, Rav Moshe Heinemann does not advocate such a stance even as an ideal.[2]

Furthermore, Rav Schachter views the *Ḥazon Ish*'s approach as constituting the majority view,[3] whereas Rav Heinemann does not present the *Ḥazon Ish* as the dominant view. Rav Elazar Meyer Teitz (Av Bet Din of Elizabeth, New Jersey) told me that he views the *Ḥazon Ish* as a *da'at yaḥid* (minority view) regarding this issue, noting that all of the great rabbis of Yerushalayim rejected the *Ḥazon Ish*'s opinion when they issued their response to the students of the Mirrer Yeshiva who found themselves in Japan in 1941 while escaping the Nazis.[4]

It is difficult to arrive at a definitive resolution of this debate, as all of the opinions present compelling arguments. Many contemporary Ashkenazic

---

2. Rav Heinemann's view is presented in an essay posted on the Star-K website: https://www.star-k.org/articles/kashrus-kurrents/493/a-travelers-guide-to-the-international-date line/.
3. Cited in Rav David Pahmer, "The International Date Line and Related Issues," *Journal of Halacha and Contemporary Society* XXI, p. 83.
4. Interestingly, Rav Herzog, the Ashkenazic Chief Rabbi at the time, instructed the *talmidim* to eat less than a *shiur* (the amount of food that would cause one to incur the punishment of *karet* on Yom Kippur) on the day on which Yom Kippur fell according to the opinion of the *Ḥazon Ish*, whereas the *Ḥazon Ish* told them to eat regular amounts on the day on which Yom Kippur fell according to the rabbis of Yerushalayim (cited in *Encyclopedia Talmudit* 22:680, n. 55).

posekim offer a variety of means to blend the opinions and arrive at a sort of compromise view between them.

Rav Ḥayim Kanievsky advises following the *Ḥazon Ish*'s view *me'ikar hadin* (essentially), but he recommends refraining from all *melacha* (work) when it is Shabbat according to Rav Tukachinsky.

Rav Mordechai Willig holds that *me'ikar hadin*, one should follow the view of Rav Tukachinsky, but avoid all *melacha* when it is Shabbat according to the *Ḥazon Ish*.

Rav Heinemann maintains that *me'ikar hadin*, one should follow the majority opinion,[5] but refrain from *melacha d'Oraita* (Torah-level prohibited activity) on Shabbat according to the minority opinion.[6]

A SEPHARDIC APPROACH IN THE ABSENCE OF A RULING FROM RAV OVADIA YOSEF

I often wondered how Sephardim should approach this issue, since – to the best of my knowledge – Rav Ovadia Yosef did not address this issue in any of his voluminous writings.[7]

Rav Shmuel Khoshkerman told me that Sephardic Jews essentially follow the ruling of Rav Tzvi Pesaḥ Frank to follow the practice of the local observant community.[8] According to Rav Khoshkermann, it is best to be strict for the opinions of the *Ḥazon Ish* (in Japan or New Zealand) and Rav Tukachinsky (in Hawaii), but those who wish to completely adhere to Rav

5. This essentially accepts Rav Frank's opinion as the determining factor. West of the International Dateline, Rav Tukachinsky combines with Rav Frank to constitute the majority opinion; east of the International Dateline, Rav Frank combines with the *Ḥazon Ish* to constitute the majority opinion.
6. The Star-K Kashrut certification agency posts a very helpful map that clearly delineates the areas of doubt; it may be accessed at https://www.star-k.org/articles/kashrus-kurrents/493/a-travelers-guide-to-the-international-date line/.
7. I heard that Rav Ben Tzion Abba Sha'ul adopted a position similar to that of Rav Schachter, that one should avoid Shabbat in any of the "*safek* zones," but as noted, this does not appear to be a practical option for many today.
8. As a young man, Rav Ovadia Yosef spent a great deal of time with Rav Frank. He remarked that he learned how to render halachic decisions from Rav Frank. Rav Khoshkerman further observes that a recurring theme in Rav Ovadia's writings is to follow the local *minhag*.

Frank's ruling have a legitimate source upon which to rely.[9] Rav Khoshkerman noted that he would issue this exact ruling to an Ashkenazic Jew as well.

When we had the privilege of hosting Rav Shlomo Amar at Congregation Shaarei Orah in Teaneck, New Jersey in August 2017, I asked him how he rules regarding the International Dateline. He responded that the he is inclined to the approach of Rav Tzvi Pesaḥ Frank because it has been accepted by many communities worldwide, thereby affirming the ruling of Rav Khoshkerman. Rav David Bannon, the prominent Moroccan *dayan* in Montreal, told me that he agrees with this approach as well.

CONCLUSION

Ideally, one should avoid the question of Shabbat and the International Dateline whenever possible. However, if necessary, Sephardic Jews may rely on the lenient opinion of Rav Tzvi Pesaḥ Frank that Halacha recognizes the International Dateline as the halachic dateline. Some Ashkenazic rabbis adopt a similar approach.

9. This approach of "*hamaḥmir tavo alav beracha vehamekil yesh lo al mah lismoch,*" "blessed is the one who is strict, but the lenient have a legitimate source upon what to rely," is also a recurring theme in Rav Ovadia's writings.

Yom Tov

Chapter 39

A *Beracha* on *Ḥatzi Hallel*

Both Ashkenazim and Sephardim recite *Ḥatzi Hallel* on Rosh Ḥodesh and the last six days of Pesaḥ, but whereas Ashkenazim recite a *beracha* on this *Hallel,* most Sephardim do not. What is the source of this divergent practice?

THE ORIGIN OF *ḤATZI HALLEL*

The *gemara* in *Arachin* (10) outlines eighteen days (twenty-one days for those who reside in the Diaspora) when we are mandated to recite *Hallel.* These are the eight days of Sukkot, the eight days of Ḥanukka, Shavuot, and the first day of Pesaḥ. The custom to recite *Hallel* on Rosh Ḥodesh and the last six days of Pesaḥ is recorded in the *gemara* (*Ta'anit* 28b), but it is a *minhag* and not mandated by law.

The *gemara* records that when the great Amoraic sage Rav first arrived in Babylonia from Eretz Yisrael, he was shocked to discover the locals reciting *Hallel* on Rosh Ḥodesh. He initially thought to stop them, but was satisfied when he saw that they were skipping portions of the *Hallel.* He concluded that this was the local custom and that it was entirely acceptable.

Eventually, the recitation of *Ḥatzi Hallel* on Rosh Ḥodesh and the last six days of Pesaḥ became the universally accepted practice (although there is some debate regarding the obligation of one who is not praying with a *minyan*; see Rambam, *Hilchot Ḥanukka* 3:7; Ra'avad, ad loc.).

THE DISPUTE BETWEEN THE RAMBAM AND RABBENU TAM

Despite the universal practice, the *Rishonim* debate whether a *beracha* should be recited on the recitation of *Ḥatzi Hallel.* The Rambam (*Hilchot Berachot* 11:16; *Hilchot Ḥanukka* 3:7) rules that one does not recite a *beracha* on *Ḥatzi Hallel,* because it is merely a *minhag.* The *Maḥzor Vitri* (a compilation of Rashi's practices and opinions compiled by his student, Rabbenu Simḥa) records that Rashi also holds that no *beracha* should be recited on *Ḥatzi Hallel.* Rabbenu Tam (cited in *Tosafot, Berachot* 14a, s.v. *yamim*), on the other hand, believes that one should recite a *beracha* on *Ḥatzi Hallel,* as he maintains that one recites a *beracha* on a *minhag.*

Both sides marshal proofs from the *gemara* to support their respective opinions. Rashi and Rambam can point to the *gemara* in *Sukka* (44b) that states that we do not recite a *beracha* when we beat the *arava* on the ground on Hoshana Rabba (*ḥibbut arava*) because it is only a *minhag* – in fact, a highly venerated custom that was initiated by the prophets (as we mention in our *tefillot* before we beat the *Hoshanot*). Rabbenu Tam, for his part, points to our practice to recite a *beracha* on the *mitzvot* that Jews outside of Eretz Yisrael perform on the second day of Yom Tov, even though we observe Yom Tov Sheni only as a custom now that we have a set calendar (see *Betza* 4b).

THE RULINGS OF THE *SHULḤAN ARUCH* AND RAMA

The Rama (*Oraḥ Ḥayim* 422:2) unequivocally rules in accordance with Rabbenu Tam, noting this is the accepted custom among Ashkenazic Jews. This remains the universal and uncontested practice among Ashkenazim to this day. The view of *Maran* Rav Yosef Karo, however, is not as straightforward. The *Shulḥan Aruch* presents two opinions: He first notes that some authorities (the Rif) hold that a *beracha* is recited on *Ḥatzi Hallel* when recited with the *tzibur.* He then proceeds to record that some authorities maintain ("*v'yesh omerim*") that a *beracha* is never recited on *Ḥatzi Hallel.* He adds that this is the opinion of the Rambam and the accepted practice of Eretz Yisrael and its neighboring countries (referring to Egypt and Syria).

Rav Zecharia Ben-Shlomo (*Orot HaHalacha*, p. 667) notes that – not surprisingly – the Yemenite custom is to follow the Rambam's opinion regarding this matter. Rav Ovadia Yosef and Rav Yitzḥak Yosef (*Yalkut Yosef, Oraḥ Ḥayim* 422:2) further insist that the *Shulḥan Aruch* rules in accordance with the Rambam. They note that the accepted rule is that when the *Shulḥan Aruch* presents two opinions as "*yesh omerim*" and "*yesh omerim*," he intends to rule in accordance with the second view cited.

Moroccan and Turkish Jews, however, rule in accordance with the first opinion cited by the *Shulḥan Aruch*. Rav Mordechai Lebhar (*Magen Avot, Oraḥ Ḥayim* 422) notes that the fact that the *Shulḥan Aruch* adds that the custom in Eretz Yisrael, Egypt, and Syria is not to recite a *beracha* indicates that this is not the universally accepted practice among Sephardic Jews. The *Shulḥan Aruch* clearly leaves room for an alternative practice among Sephardim who do not reside in these lands. Indeed, in the *Bet Yosef* (*Oraḥ Ḥayim* 422, s.v. *v'rabu bo*), Rav Yosef Karo notes that the custom in Spain was to recite a *beracha* on *Ḥatzi Hallel* on Rosh Ḥodesh.

Moreover, the Rosh (*Berachot* 2:5) rules that the custom is to recite the *beracha* of "*ligmor et haHallel*" on days when full *Hallel* is recited and the *beracha* of "*likro et haHallel*" on days when *Ḥatzi Hallel* is recited. This is done to signal to the *tzibur* when to say full *Hallel* and when to recite *Ḥatzi Hallel*. The Ran, *Maggid Mishneh* (cited by the *Bet Yosef, Oraḥ Ḥayim* 422), and Rivash (*Teshuvot* #111) record that this was the practice in Spain, which is not surprising considering that the Rosh exerted great influence in Spain after moving there. Moroccan and Turkish Jews follow this practice until this day. The aforementioned *Tosafot*, however, notes that there is no halachic requirement to make this distinction, and most Jews therefore never recite the *beracha* of "*ligmor et HaHallel*."

As we have noted elsewhere, it is not surprising to discover that Moroccan and Turkish Jews follow the Spanish practice to recite a *beracha* on *Ḥatzi Hallel*, since many of the *megorashim* (Jewish expellees) from Spain eventually settled in these two countries, and the customs of the *megorashim* eventually emerged as the dominant practice in these lands. The custom in Eretz Yisrael, Egypt, and Syria, in contrast, did not change, as in those countries, the practices of the *megorashim* did not overtake the practices of the *toshavim* (Jews who previously resided in those countries). Thus, Syrian Jews and the Sephardic Jews of Eretz Yisrael follow the view of the Rambam until today and do not recite a *beracha* on *Ḥatzi Hallel*.

CONCLUSION

It is most interesting that all three current practices regarding the *beracha* on *Ḥatzi Hallel* are already cited and vigorously debated in the aforementioned *Tosafot* – and all three opinions are very much alive today, with various communities following each of the opinions. At Congregation Shaarei Orah, the Sephardic Congregation of Teaneck, the *ḥazan* follows the *minhag* of Eretz Yisrael and the ruling of Rav Ovadia Yosef and does not recite a *beracha* on *Ḥatzi Hallel.*

Chapter 40

Tefillin on *Ḥol HaMo'ed*

It is probably one of the most famous divergent customs among Jews: Are *tefillin* worn on *Ḥol HaMo'ed*?

There are three prevalent customs regarding wearing *tefillin* during *Ḥol HaMo'ed*. Many do not wear *tefillin*, others wear *tefillin* and recite the *beracha* (albeit quietly), and others compromise and wear *tefillin* but do not recite the *beracha*. What is the basis for the variety of practices?

TEFILLIN ON SHABBAT AND YOM TOV

The *gemara* in *Menaḥot* (36) records a dispute regarding whether men should wear *tefillin* on Shabbat and Yom Tov, citing two *beraitot* that present reasons *tefillin* should not be worn on these days.

The first *beraita* cites a *pasuk* that states that one should wear *tefillin* "*miyamim yamima*" (*Shemot* 13:10). Literally, "*miyamim*" means "from among the days." The *beraita* explains that this means that on some days, we wear *tefillin*, while on others we do not. Shabbat and Yom Tov are days on which we do not wear *tefillin*.

The second *beraita* notes that in a number of contexts, the Torah states that *tefillin* serve as an *ot*, a sign. The *beraita* explains that one wears *tefillin* only on the days on which one requires an *ot*. One does not wear *tefillin* on Shabbat and Yom Tov, because those days themselves constitute *otot*.

THE ARGUMENT FOR NOT WEARING *TEFILLIN* ON *ḤOL HAMO'ED*

The Behag (cited by *Tosafot, Mo'ed Katan* 19a, s.v. *Rabbi Yosi*) rules that it is forbidden to wear *tefillin* on *Ḥol HaMo'ed,* just like on Yom Tov; *Ḥol HaMo'ed* also constitutes an *ot.* Many *Rishonim* agree with the Behag's assertion, including the Rambam (as interpreted by the *Kesef Mishna, Hilchot Yom Tov* 7:13), the Rashba (*Teshuvot* 1:690), and the Ri (cited by the *Hagahot Maimoniot, Hilchot Tefillin* 4:9).

Rav Yosef Dov Soloveitchik (*Shiurim L'Zecher Abba Mari Z"l* 1:118–120) further explains this opinion. He notes that there are four reflections of the *kedushat hayom* (sanctity of the day) of a Yom Tov: the *Korban Musaf,* the unique *mitzvot* of the day (such as the *mitzva* to eat in a *sukka* or to avoid *ḥametz*), the obligation on individuals to bring the *korbanot* of the Festivals (*Re'iya, Ḥagiga, Shalmei Simḥa*), and the prohibition to engage in *melacha* (forbidden labor). All four of these components pertain to *Ḥol HaMo'ed.* Although certain *melacha* is permitted on *Ḥol HaMo'ed,* the prohibition to perform *melacha* fundamentally applies; the Torah simply permits us to engage in certain *melachot* on *Ḥol HaMo'ed* (*Ḥagiga* 18a). Rav Soloveitchik cites the assertion of his grandfather, Rav Ḥayim Soloveitchik, that *Ḥol HaMo'ed* is as holy as any Yom Tov and enjoys the full status of a Yom Tov.

THE ARGUMENT FOR WEARING *TEFILLIN* ON *ḤOL HAMO'ED*

Many *Rishonim,* on the other hand, believe that one must wear *tefillin* on *Ḥol HaMo'ed.* These authorities include the Rosh (*Hilchot Tefillin* 16), *Ohr Zarua* (1:589), and the Maharam of Rothenberg (cited by the Mordechai). They argue that *Ḥol HaMo'ed* does not constitute an *ot,* since we are permitted to perform certain *melacha* on *Ḥol HaMo'ed.* This argument is particularly cogent according to the *Rishonim* who maintain that on a Torah level, all *melacha* is permitted on *Ḥol HaMo'ed* and the restrictions that exist with regard to performing *melacha* on *Ḥol HaMo'ed* were instituted by *Ḥazal.*

Moreover, these *Rishonim* argue that the Torah's language of "*miyamim*" excludes **only** Shabbat and Yom Tov, when the prohibition to engage in *melacha* profoundly distinguishes these days from all other days. One ramification of the permission to perform certain labor on *Ḥol HaMo'ed* is that the difference between *Ḥol HaMo'ed* and other days is not as pronounced.

As proof to their position, these *Rishonim* cite the fact that the *gemara* permits writing *tefillin* on *Ḥol HaMo'ed.* They argue that *Ḥazal* would not have permitted writing *tefillin* on *Ḥol HaMo'ed* had there been no use for the *tefillin* on *Ḥol HaMo'ed.* The *Rishonim* who maintain that *tefillin* are not worn on *Ḥol HaMo'ed* argue that this passage in the *gemara* represents the rejected opinion that maintain that one may wear *tefillin* on Shabbat and Yom Tov.

THE COMPROMISE VIEW – *TEFILLIN,* BUT NO *BERACHA*

Both sides of the argument are compelling. As a result, we already find *Rishonim* who advocate adopting a compromise view – to wear *tefillin,* but to refrain from reciting the *beracha.* The *Tur* (*Oraḥ Ḥayim* 31) notes that a number of *Rishonim* adopt this view due to the uncertainty, including the Ritva (*Eruvin* 96a), the *Semak* (153), and the Meiri (*Mo'ed Katan* 18b).

The advantage of this compromise is that one avoids possibly violating very serious transgressions. *Ḥazal* teach that failing to wear *tefillin* (*Rosh Hashana* 17a; *Tosafot,* ad loc., s.v. *karkafta*) and reciting an unnecessary *beracha* (*Berachot* 33a; *Shavuot* 39a) are grave violations of Torah Law. Wearing *tefillin* but omitting the *beracha* serves to avoid both of these serious concerns.

THE *SHULḤAN ARUCH* AND COMMENTARIES

In the *Bet Yosef* (*Oraḥ Ḥayim* 31, s.v. *v'holo*), Rav Yosef Karo notes that all Sephardic Jews refrain from wearing *tefillin* on *Ḥol HaMo'ed.* He cites at length from the *Midrash HaNe'elam* to *Shir HaShirim,* which presents a kabbalistic explanation for refraining from wearing *tefillin* on *Ḥol HaMo'ed.* In fact, the *Zohar Ḥadash* (*Shir HaShirim* 8a) strongly advocates refraining from wearing *tefillin* on *Ḥol HaMo'ed.*[1] Accordingly, Rav Yosef Karo rules in the *Shulḥan Aruch* (*Oraḥ Ḥayim* 31:2) that it is forbidden to wear *tefillin* on *Ḥol HaMo'ed.*

The Rama, however, records that the universally accepted practice among Ashkenazic Jews is to wear *tefillin* on *Ḥol HaMo'ed* and to recite the *berachot,* but the custom is to recite the *berachot* on *tefillin* quietly on *Ḥol HaMo'ed.* The *Mishna Berura* (31:8) writes that this is done to avoid conflict,

1. Note that many kabbalistic themes have been incorporated into the *halachot* of *tefillin.* See, for example, *Shulḥan Aruch, Oraḥ Ḥayim* 25:2, 25:11, and 25:13.

since the issue of reciting the *berachot* on *tefillin* is embroiled in controversy. There may be kabbalistic reasons for this practice as well.

Despite the Rama's ruling, the *Taz* (*Oraḥ Ḥayim* 31:2) encourages one to refrain from reciting the *berachot* on *tefillin* during *Ḥol HaMo'ed*, in deference to the authorities who forbid wearing *tefillin* on *Ḥol HaMo'ed*. Furthermore, the Vilna Gaon (*Bi'ur HaGra, Oraḥ Ḥayim* 31:2, s.v. *v'yesh omerim*) rules in accordance with the *Rishonim* who maintain that one should refrain from wearing *tefillin* on *Ḥol HaMo'ed*.

LATE CODIFIERS

The *Mishna Berura* (31:8) and the *Aruch HaShulḥan* (*Oraḥ Ḥayim* 31:4) accept the recommendation of the *Taz* to refrain from reciting the *berachot* when wearing *tefillin* during *Ḥol HaMo'ed*. The *Aruch HaShulḥan* concludes, however, that one should follow his *minhag* in this regard.

The *Aruch HaShulḥan* notes that "recently," a practice among some Ashkenazic Jews has developed to refrain from wearing *tefillin* on *Ḥol HaMo'ed*. He is referring to the practice of Ḥassidim. This was also the practice at the famed Volozhiner Yeshiva, as noted by Rav Yosef Dov Soloveitchik (*Shiurim L'Zecher Abba Mari Z"l*, p. 119). Rav Soloveitchik further records that Rav Ḥayim Soloveitchik did not wear *tefillin* on *Ḥol HaMo'ed*.

In Eretz Yisrael, the ruling of the Vilna Gaon to refrain from wearing *tefillin* on *Ḥol HaMo'ed* has been universally accepted. Indeed, one who publicly dons *tefillin* on *Ḥol HaMo'ed* in Eretz Yisrael is inviting a strong protest from his fellow worshippers.

CONCLUSION

The *Rishonim* and *Aḥaronim* debate whether one should wear *tefillin* on *Ḥol HaMo'ed*, and this debate has not been resolved; the various practices regarding this issue persist. This author heard from Rav Yosef Dov Soloveitchik that an Ashkenazic Jew should follow his father's practice in this regard.

All Sephardic Jews firmly maintain the practice to refrain from donning *tefillin* on *Ḥol HaMo'ed* (*Keter Shem Tov* 1:9), and a non-Ḥassidic Ashkenazic Jew who visits a Sephardic *bet kenesset* on *Ḥol HaMo'ed* therefore should not don his *tefillin*. Rav Hershel Schachter and Rav Mordechai Willig both subscribe to the approach of Rav Moshe Feinstein (*Teshuvot Igrot Moshe, Oraḥ Ḥayim* 4:34) to avoid behavior that blatantly runs counter to the prevailing practice of the synagogue in which one prays.

Conversely, Sephardic Jews should make every effort to avoid praying in an Ashkenazic *bet kenesset* on *Ḥol HaMo'ed* if the universal custom in that synagogue is to wear *tefillin* on *Ḥol HaMo'ed* (such as K'hal Adath Jeshurun, the Breuer's congregation in the Washington Heights section of Manhattan). If this is the only synagogue in the area, Rav Yitzḥak Yosef rules (*Yalkut Yosef, Hilchot Tefillin* 31, n. 7, based on *Teshuvot Yeḥaveh Da'at* 4:36) that a Sephardic Jew should nonetheless refrain from wearing *tefillin* in such a circumstance, as he believes that following the distinctions between Sephardic and Ashkenazic Jews does not violate the prohibition of *lo titgodedu* (as we discuss in Chapter 1).[2]

2. As we noted there, Rav Ovadia Yosef follows the ruling of Rav Mordechai Bennet (*Teshuvot Parashat Mordechai, Oraḥ Ḥayim* 4) that *lo titgodedu* does not apply with regard to divergent practices that stem from ancient disputes, even when both practices are observed simultaneously in the same *bet kenesset.*

Chapter 41

Visitors to Israel and Yom Tov Sheni

Until relatively recently, the question of how many days of Yom Tov a visitor to Eretz Yisrael should celebrate was not particularly pertinent. In our day, however, when it is quite common to visit Eretz Yisrael for Yom Tov, the question is quite common. Should a visitor observe two days of Yom Tov, as he does at home, one day of Yom Tov, like the residents of Eretz Yisrael, or a combination of the two?

MARAN RAV YOSEF KARO

Rav Yosef Karo (*Teshuvot Avkat Rochel* 26) rules that the *mishna*'s principle (*Pesaḥim* 50a–b) that a traveler must observe the restrictions of the community he left and the community to which he journeyed applies to Yom Tov Sheni. He also notes that this was the common practice among travelers to Eretz Yisrael, "who publicly gather to form *minyanim* to recite the Yom Tov prayers on Yom Tov Sheni."

Later Sephardic authorities confirm that this was the accepted practice in Eretz Yisrael (see *Teshuvot Halachot Ketanot* 4; *Birkei Yosef* 496:7). It is therefore not surprising that Rav Ovadia Yosef (*Teshuvot Yabia Omer* 6: *Oraḥ Ḥayim* 40; *Teshuvot Yeḥaveh Da'at* 1:26) rules that a visitor from the

Diaspora must observe two days of Yom Tov even in Eretz Yisrael. Most Ashkenazic authorities accept this opinion as well (see *Mishna Berura* 496:13; *Pe'at HaShulḥan* 2:15; *Aruch HaShulḥan, Oraḥ Ḥayim* 496:5; *Teshuvot Igrot Moshe, Oraḥ Ḥayim* 3:74 and 4:108).

THE *ḤACHAM TZVI*

Rav Tzvi Ashkenazi (*Teshuvot Ḥacham Tzvi* 167) disputes Rav Karo's ruling, however. He argues that the *mishna*'s rule of maintaining the restrictions of the place that one left does not apply to the observance of Yom Tov Sheni by visitors in Eretz Yisrael. He explains that Yom Tov Sheni differs from regular customs, which theoretically apply anywhere, because the practice of observing Yom Tov Sheni is geographically linked to the Diaspora. Usually, the **residents** of a particular community develop its customs; Yom Tov Sheni, in contrast, was instituted for the **physical area** of the Diaspora. When one is in Eretz Yisrael, he is in a place where Yom Tov Sheni has no meaning, regardless of where he normally resides. Only regarding other customs, which could theoretically exist even where they are not practiced, is it reasonable for someone who always did them in his own community to observe them while visiting elsewhere.[1] According to the *Ḥacham Tzvi*, a visitor in Israel is actually prohibited from observing Yom Tov Sheni, lest he violate the prohibition of *bal tosif* (adding to the Torah's precepts)!

Although the *Ḥacham Tzvi* is definitely the minority view on this issue, his position has attracted some support from other authorities (*Shulḥan Aruch HaRav* 496:11; *Teshuvot Sho'el U'Meshiv* 3:2:28). Lubavitcher Ḥassidim follow the ruling of the *Shulḥan Aruch HaRav* (authored by the first Lubavitcher Rebbe, Rav Shneur Zalman of Liadi) and observe only one day of Yom Tov when visiting Eretz Yisrael.

THE COMPROMISE APPROACH

Some Ashkenazic *posekim* are torn between the cogency of the *Ḥacham Tzvi*'s reasoning and the overwhelming majority of authorities, who side with Rav Yosef Karo, and they therefore adopt a compromise approach. In principle, they accept the view of the *Ḥacham Tzvi*, and thus rule that

---

1. According to this view, it follows that an Israeli visitor to the Diaspora should fully observe Yom Tov Sheni, as one's permanent place of residence is irrelevant.

tefillin should be worn and weekday prayers should be recited.[2] However, one should refrain from forbidden *melacha* on Yom Tov Sheni, in deference to the view of Rav Yosef Karo.

Rav Yeḥiel Michel Tukachinsky (*Ir HaKodesh V'HaMikdash* 19:11) records that Rav Shmuel Salant adopted such an approach. Similarly, Rav Aharon Lichtenstein recounted that when Rav Yosef Dov Soloveitchik was in Eretz Yisrael over Shavuot in 1935, he asked his eminent father, Rav Moshe Soloveitchik, what to do for Yom Tov Sheni, and Rav Moshe Soloveitchik replied that although he essentially concurred with the *Ḥacham Tzvi*'s view, one should nonetheless avoid doing *melacha* to accommodate the ruling of Rav Yosef Karo.[3]

SINGLE VISITORS TO ISRAEL – THE SEPHARDIC APPROACH

Rav Ovadia Yosef (*Teshuvot Yabia Omer* 6: *Oraḥ Ḥayim* 40; *Teshuvot Yeḥaveh Da'at* 1:26) cites and accepts the view of earlier Sephardic authorities, such as the *Ḥida* (*Teshuvot Ḥayim Sha'al* 55), to treat single yeshiva students of marriageable age as intending to permanently settle in Israel. He explains that a yeshiva student, even if he is not dating an Israeli at the time and expects to return to the Diaspora, theoretically could marry an Israeli and stay in Israel. A married man, on the other hand, must return to his family and job outside Israel. Presumably, the same logic applies to a single woman from Israel visiting Israel.

Rav Ovadia adds, however, that if a single man adamantly insists that he will not stay in Israel under any circumstances, such as if he feels that he cannot leave his parents, then he must observe two days of Yom Tov even in Israel.[4]

---

2. The second day of Pesaḥ and Sukkot is treated like *Ḥol HaMo'ed* for these purposes, such that one would follow his *minhag* regarding wearing *tefillin* on *Ḥol HaMo'ed*.
3. Rav Lichtenstein recounted this in a conversation with overseas students at Yeshivat Har Etzion in 1981.
4. Rav Ovadia adds that we should inform a young man who resolutely insists that he would not move to Israel against his parents' advice even for a perfect match that according to the Halacha, strictly speaking, in such circumstances he is not required to listen to his parents. If the young man relents, he would not be required to observe the second day of Yom Tov. We should note, however, that Rav Moshe Feinstein (*Teshuvot Igrot Moshe, Even HaEzer* 1:102) disagrees and believes that the *mitzva* to live in Israel does not override the *mitzva* to honor one's parents.

Moreover, Shaarei Orah member Isaac Dayan reports that he heard directly from Rav Ovadia in the mid-2000s that eighteen year old American Sephardim who are learning Torah in Israel for a year, who are completely financially dependent on their parents and are nearly certain to be returning to *Chutz La'Aretz* after the year, should observe two days of Yom Tov.[5]

However, Rav Shmuel Khoshkerman reports that the custom among Sephardic yeshiva students from abroad (who in general follow Rav Ovadia's rulings) is to observe only one day of Yom Tov during the time they are learning in Israel.

CONCLUSION

Sephardic visitors to Israel should observe two days of Yom Tov, in accordance with the ruling of *Maran* Rav Yosef Karo. Single Sephardim of marriageable age, however, need not observe the second day if they would be willing to move to Israel for an ideal marriage partner.

---

5. In a eulogy for Rav Ovadia delivered at Congregation Shaarei Orah, the Sephardic Congregation of Teaneck, in November 2013, noted Syrian rabbi Rav Eli Mansour cited an oral report of how Rav Ovadia responded to a single young man who insisted that he would under no circumstances move to Israel, even if offered an ideal *shidduch*. Rav Mansour reported that Rav Ovadia told the young man that his approach was unreasonable, and thus discounted. This report, however, runs counter to that which Rav Ovadia wrote in *Yeḥaveh Da'at* and *Yabia Omer*.

Chapter 42

Early Acceptance of the Second Day of Yom Tov

At Congregation Shaarei Orah, on the first day of Shavuot and on the seventh day of Pesaḥ, we pray *Arvit* early at the end of the first day of Yom Tov leading into the evening of Yom Tov Sheni.[1] This is clearly not the typical practice at Ashkenazic congregations, as Ashkenazic authorities rule that one may bring in Yom Tov Sheni early only in extenuating circumstances (see *Aruch HaShulḥan, Oraḥ Ḥayim* 668:6; *Yom Tov Sheni K'Hilchato*, p. 37, citing Rav Yosef Shalom Elyashiv). At Shaarei Orah, however, we follow the rulings of the venerable Rav Yosef Ḥayim of Baghdad, the *Ben Ish Ḥai*, who permits doing so.

A number of questions can be raised regarding this practice.

DOESN'T ACCEPTING YOM TOV SHENI EARLY DETRACT FROM YOM TOV RISHON?

Ḥazal (*Berachot* 27b) permit one to accept both Shabbat and Yom Tov before sunset. It is permissible to pray and recite *Kiddush* while it is still

1. Rav Ike Sultan reports that he has seen Syrian congregations in Deal, New Jersey do this as well. There are a variety of reasons that we cannot accept other Yamim Tovim early; these are beyond the scope of the present discussion.

light, as long as it is past *pelag haminḥa* (one and a quarter halachic hours prior to sunset or nightfall[2]).

The *Taz* (*Oraḥ Ḥayim* 489:10) objects to accepting Yom Tov Sheni early, however, since doing so detracts from the holiness of Yom Tov Rishon. Yom Tov Rishon is a Biblical requirement, whereas Yom Tov Sheni is only Rabbinic in origin; thus, it appears improper to reduce the holiness of the day by beginning Yom Tov Sheni early.

---

2. Rav Yitzḥak Yosef (torahanytime.com/#/lectures?v=81670, min. 37; see *Yalkut Yosef, Oraḥ Ḥayim* 263:45) argues that the calendars that calculate *pelag haminḥa* as 1.25 hours before *sheki'a* (astronomical sunset), in accordance with the view of the Vilna Gaon (*Oraḥ Ḥayim* 459:2, s.v. *v'shiur mil*), cause Sephardic Jews to recite *berachot l'vatala* (unnecessary *berachot*) when they pray *Arvit* immediately after *plag* according to this calculation. According to the ruling of the *Shulḥan Aruch* (*Oraḥ Ḥayim* 233:1, 263:4, in accordance with the understanding of the *Mishna Berura* 233:4 and 263:19) and the *Ben Ish Ḥai* (year 1, *Parashat Vayakhel* 8), *pelag haminḥa* is 1.25 hours before *tzet hakochavim* (nightfall). Although the difference between these two times is only about 20 minutes (13.5 *zemani'ot* minutes, according to the Sephardic standard; see *Yalkut Yosef, Oraḥ Ḥayim* 293), if a Sephardic Jew begins *Arvit* immediately after the Ashkenazic calculation of *pelag haminḥa,* he recites a *beracha l'vatala* according to Rav Yitzḥak Yosef.

Rav Yitzḥak Yosef's ruling is somewhat difficult, however, given that he essentially rules in accordance with the Vilna Gaon with regard to the calculation of the latest time for *keri'at Shema* (*Yalkut Yosef, Oraḥ Ḥayim* 58:3) and the ending time for Shabbat (*Yalkut Yosef, Oraḥ Ḥayim* 293). Even though this runs counter to the ruling of the *Shulḥan Aruch,* the custom even among Sephardic Jews is to follow the Vilna Gaon's approach regarding this matter. Why, then, may Sephardic Jews not follow the Vilna Gaon regarding the time of *pelag haminḥa,* even though it runs counter to the opinion of the *Shulḥan Aruch*? Indeed, the instructions of the acclaimed Koren Sephardic Siddur describe *pelag haminḥa* as 1.25 halachic hours before *shekia.*

Both Rav Ben Tzion Abba Sha'ul (*Teshuvot Ohr L'Tzion* 15:6) and Rav Mordechai Eliyahu (*Siddur Kol Eliyahu*) describe *pelag haminḥa* as 1.25 halachic hours before *tzet hakochavim.* Rav Abba Sha'ul and Rav Eliyahu follow the *Ben Ish Ḥai* in this regard, as they often do. However, the *Ben Ish Ḥai* calculates the halachic day from *alot hashaḥar* to *tzet hakochavim,* and it is therefore not surprising that he calculates *pelag haminḥa* as 1.25 halachic hours before *tzet.* Rav Yitzḥak Yosef, in contrast, calculates the day from *netz haḥama* to *shekiat haḥama,* and *pelag haminḥa* should thus be calculated as 1.25 halachic hours before *shekia.*

It is worth noting that Sephardic custom permits a *tzibur* to pray *Minḥa* after *pelag haminḥa* and *Arvit* before *shekia* even on the same day in case of need (*Ben Ish Ḥai,* year 1, *Parashat Vayakhel* 7; *Kaf HaḤayim, Oraḥ Ḥayim* 233:12; Rav Ben Tzion Abba Sha'ul, *Ohr L'Tzion* 15:6).

Most *Aḥaronim* reject the approach of the *Taz* (*Sha'ar HaTziyun* 668:11). The *Taz* maintains that accepting Shabbat or Yom Tov early transforms the day into the next halachic day, but most *posekim* believe that while one may expand the holiness of the Shabbat and Yom Tov to the day prior, this does not transform the prior day into a new calendric day. Thus, even after praying *Arvit* and reciting *Kiddush* early, the day fundamentally remains the first day of Yom Tov.

Some *Aḥaronim* are concerned that if one prays *Arvit* early, he will come to prepare on Yom Tov Rishon for Yom Tov Sheni. However, the *Ben Ish Ḥai* insists that this is a concern only for those who recite *Kiddush* after nightfall, as we shall explain.

LIGHTING CANDLES AND EATING EARLY

The *Ben Ish Ḥai* (*Teshuvot Rav Pe'alim* 4:23; *Ben Ish Ḥai*, year 1, *Parashat Bemidbar* 2) permits lighting candles while it is still light outside if *Kiddush* is also recited while it is still light. He writes that since one should see the candles while saying *Kiddush* – and some (especially the *Ḥachmei HaKabbala*) even say that this is absolutely necessary – lighting the candles is an immediate need, and not an issue of preparing from one day of Yom Tov for the next.

The *Ben Ish Ḥai* permits eating the Yom Tov meal while it is still light as well. The *gemara* obviously supports this point, since the meal must follow *Kiddush* immediately: "*En Kiddush ela b'makom seuda.*" The *Ben Ish Ḥai* even encouraged beginning Yom Tov Sheni early and eating while it is still light, since mosquitoes abounded at this time of year in Baghdad, and it was important to be sure that one would have sufficient light to ensure that he would not consume any of these bugs. Although this specific concern may not be relevant to the contemporary circumstance, the need for families to eat at a reasonable hour may also constitute sufficient need to begin the second day and its meal early.

If the meal may be eaten, one may obviously make all necessary preparations for the meal, such as setting the table and serving the food, on Yom Tov Rishon. This preparation may be done even before *pelag haminḥa* if a significant portion of the meal will be eaten before sunset. Although one may not prepare from the first day of Yom Tov for the other, since the meal is eaten before sunset, one is considered to be preparing for that which is needed on the first day.

Rav Shmuel Khoshkerman notes that although the *Ben Ish Ḥai* does not say so explicitly, it is implicit in his writings that one is even permitted to cook on Yom Tov Rishon before *pelag haminḥa* if a significant portion of the meal that one prepares will be eaten before sunset.

MOROCCAN AND ASHKENAZIC JEWS

Rav Mordechai Lebhar concludes that Moroccan Jews may rely on the ruling of the *Ben Ish Ḥai* if there is a compelling reason to do so. He writes that although this was not the practice in North Africa, in today's circumstances, a family's need to eat a reasonable hour may constitute a compelling reason to accept the second day of Yom Tov after *pelag haminha* of Yom Tov Rishon.

Rav Hershel Schachter rules that Ashkenazic Jews may also rely on the view of the *Ben Ish Ḥai*:[3]

> Those who have the custom to start the second day of Yom Tov early must be careful not to prepare on the first day for the second day (in order not to diminish the sanctity of the first day by preparing on it for the second day). Therefore, they should pray *Ma'ariv* of the second day immediately after *pelag*, make *Kiddush*, and eat, so that any preparation done on the first day will be utilized on the first day.[4]

However, Rav Shmuel Khoshkerman cautions that while we may rely on the ruling of the *Ben Ish Ḥai* regarding this matter, many disagree, as noted above, and that the custom in all *yeshivot* is to be strict about this matter.

CONCLUSION

Sephardic Jews have ample authority and basis upon which to rely in beginning Yom Tov Sheni early. Their Ashkenazic guests may join them on such occasions. Whether or not Ashkenazic Jews can begin Yom Tov Sheni early under ordinary circumstances, however, is subject to debate.

---

3. Rav Mordechai Willig, however, told me that he permits this only in case of great exceptional need.
4. This responsum was addressed to Rav Lawrence Rothwachs of Congregation Beth Aaron of Teaneck, New Jersey. Rav Schachter articulates this in his Piskei Corona #37 (archived at www.yutorah.org).

Yamim Nora'im

Chapter 43

Forty Days of *Seliḥot*

One of the most well-known differences between Sephardic *minhag* and Ashkenazic *minhag* relates to when the recitation of *Seliḥot* begins. The Sephardic practice is to recite *Seliḥot* beginning the day after Rosh Ḥodesh Elul. The Ashkenazic practice, in contrast, is to start saying *Seliḥot* from the Sunday before Rosh Hashana, unless Rosh Hashana falls out on Monday or Tuesday, in which case Ashkenazim begin *Seliḥot* two Sundays before Rosh Hashana. What is the basis for the differing practices?

GEONIM, RISHONIM, SHULḤAN ARUCH, AND RAMA

The practice of reciting *Seliḥot* is not mentioned in the Talmud.[1] The Rosh (*Rosh Hashana* 4:14) records that a number of *Geonim* had the *minhag* of

1. Rav Yosef Dov Soloveitchik explains that although the Talmud does not mention this practice, this does not necessarily mean that *Seliḥot* were not recited in the time of the Talmud. It is possible that the *Geonim* did not institute *Seliḥot,* but rather recorded a practice that was existence already since the Talmudic era. Rav Soloveitchik argues that the fact that the Rambam (*Hilchot Teshuva* 3:4) mentions that all Jews maintain this practice indicates that this was practiced from Talmudic times. The Rambam (in his introduction to his *Mishneh Torah*) mentions that only the Talmudic sages enjoy unquestioned authority (in contrast to the *Geonim*), since the Amoraic sages were accepted by all of Israel, whereas the *Geonim* were not. Rav Soloveitchik asserted that whenever the Rambam uses the term "all of Israel," the

reciting *Seliḥot* during the *Aseret Yemei Teshuva,* while others said them from Rosh Ḥodesh Elul because that is when Moshe Rabbenu was on Har Sinai receiving the second *luḥot* (see Rashi, *Devarim* 9:18). Although the Rambam (*Hilchot Teshuva* 3:4) follows the *minhag* of the *Geonim,* the *Shulḥan Aruch* (*Oraḥ Ḥayim* 581:1) writes that the Sephardic *minhag* is to say *Seliḥot* from Rosh Ḥodesh Elul. The Rama records that the Ashkenazic practice is to start saying *Seliḥot* from the Sunday before Rosh Hashana, unless Rosh Hashana falls on Monday or Tuesday.

THE CLASSIC EXPLANATIONS FOR THE ASHKENAZIC AND SEPHARDIC CUSTOMS

The *Mishna Berura* (581:6) explains that the reason for the Ashkenazic custom is that some had the custom to fast for ten days prior to Yom Kippur. However, since it is not permissible to fast on the two days of Rosh Hashana, Shabbat Shuva, and Erev Yom Kippur, to fulfill this custom, one begins *Seliḥot* four days prior to Rosh Hashana. The *Mishna Berura* offers another reason based on the *halacha* that four days are required to inspect a *korban* (sacrifice) for blemishes (*Pesaḥim* 96a). Since on Rosh Hashana we offer ourselves to *Hashem* as a metaphoric *korban,* we should "inspect" ourselves with the recitation of *Seliḥot* for a minimum of four days before Rosh Hashana.

The Vilna Gaon (*Bi'ur HaGra, Oraḥ Ḥayim* 581:1) notes an explanation presented by the Ran (*Rosh Hashana* 3a in the Rif's pages, s.v. *b'Rosh Hashana*): Although human beings were created on Rosh Hashana (according to the view of Rabbi Eliezer, cited in the *Pesikta, piska* 23), the world was created on the twenty-fifth of Elul. Therefore, Ashkenazim begin *Seliḥot* near this date.

The Vilna Gaon cites the Rosh's explanation of the Sephardic practice to begin reciting *Seliḥot* on the second day of Elul as a reenactment of Moshe Rabbenu's forty days of praying for forgiveness for the *ḥet ha'egel.* This is a most compelling reason, since Yom Kippur (as Rashi notes, *Devarim* 9:18) is the date upon which Moshe Rabbenu descended with the second *luḥot,* signaling that *Hashem* granted us atonement for this grievous sin.

---

practice to which he refers dates back to the Talmudic era, when all of Israel was concentrated in a relatively limited geographic area and consented to the authority of the Talmudic sages.

A NEW EXPLANATION FOR THE SEPHARDIC PRACTICE

I would suggest another reason for the Sephardic practice based on Yona's call to Nineveh, "In forty days Nineveh will be overturned" (*Yona* 3:4). Rashi (ad loc.) explains that the word overturned (*nehepachet*) has two potential meanings – it means that the city will either be destroyed or improved for the better. Yona is essentially communicating that if the residents of Nineveh do not change their ways, they will be destroyed.

I suggest that the Sephardic practice reflects this warning: Either we improve during the forty days between Rosh Ḥodesh Elul and Yom Kippur or *Hashem* will decree upon us an unpleasant future. Indeed, the Sephardic *Seliḥot* service begins by echoing the words of the captain of the ship upon which Yona sailed: "*Ben Adam, mah lecha nirdam*?!" (*Yona* 1:6). How can you be sleeping in the middle of a storm?! Wake up and cry out to your God! This liturgical poem also warns us, "*ufḥad me'asonim*," to fear catastrophes that might (Heaven forfend) strike if we do not improve. Thus, the Yona motif certainly fits with the themes of Sephardic *Seliḥot*.

WHY THE NUMBER FORTY?

Why is the number forty chosen as the amount of time for the people of Nineveh – and for us – to do *teshuva*? Perhaps it is because the number forty evokes thoughts of the forty days of destruction during the *Mabul* and the forty years in the *Midbar* when the older generation was eliminated. The number forty is associated with total destruction and elimination, regarding which we are forewarned to repent and avoid.

Rav Zvi Grumet argues that the number forty in Torah literature expresses an opportunity for rebirth:

> In the Bible, Moses is on the mountain for forty days and emerges as a man reborn with a radiant face. The spies enter the land as princes and forty days later return with the self-image of grasshoppers. The Israelite nation spends forty years in the desert and is transformed from a fractured nation of refugees into a unified nation of conquerors… In Rabbinic literature, there are forty minus one categories of prohibited (creative) work on Shabbat, a child is considered to be "alive" in the womb after forty days, and pregnancy lasts for forty weeks.[2]

2. *Genesis* (Jerusalem: Maggid Books, 2017), pp. 86–87.

We may add to this list that grape juice ferments into wine forty days after it is squeezed from the grape (*Eduyot* 6:1), and *bet din* administers "forty minus one" *malkot,* as they are intended to spur the emergence of a new personality after the traumatic experience. Similarly, the goal of *Seliḥot* is to emerge as a new and improved person by Yom Kippur.

CONCLUSION

The number forty conveys a similar message as the double-entendre word *nehepachet*: It can refer to utter destruction or rebirth. From Rosh Ḥodesh Elul until Yom Kippur, every Jew – like the people of Ninveh – is faced with the same stark choice as to which path we will choose – falling into the abyss or redeeming ourselves and restarting our lives.

Chapter 44

Ḥoni HaMa'agel: A Hero to Sephardic Jews

As noted in the previous chapter, Sephardic Jews recite *Seliḥot* beginning from the second day of Rosh Ḥodesh Elul for forty days, until Yom Kippur. Although the Sephardic *Selihot* differ significantly from the Ashkenazic version, the fundamental structure is identical. *Seliḥot* begin with *Ashrei* and *Ḥatzi Kaddish,* end with *Kaddish Titkabal,* and include *Vidduy* and *Taḥanun,* with the centerpiece being the recitation of the Thirteen *Middot* of *Raḥamim* (aspects of God's mercy).

ḤONI AS A ROLE MODEL IN SEPHARDIC *SELIḤOT*

For an Ashkenazic Jew, perhaps the most striking feature of the Sephardic *Seliḥot* is the appearance of Ḥoni HaMa'agel, Honi the circle-maker. Similar to the Ashkenazic liturgical passage "*Mi She'Anah*" (which is based on *Ta'anit* 2:4), Sephardic Jews recite a parallel Aramaic version appealing to *Hashem* to respond to our *tefillot* in the manner that He responded to a list of Biblical figures at critical junctures in their lives. At the end of the list, the Sephardic version pleas, "*D'anei l'Ḥoni anenan,*" "You Who answered Ḥoni should answer us." Ḥoni most decidedly does not appear in this list in the Ashkenazic version!

What lies behind this textual difference? This disparity stems from a dispute between Ḥoni and Rabbi Shimon ben Shetaḥ. The *mishna* (*Ta'anit* 3:8) relates that once during a severe drought, the Jews approached Ḥoni to beseech *Hashem* for rain. Ḥoni famously proceeded to draw a circle and declare to *Hashem* that he would not leave the circle until it rained. *Hashem* caused it to rain very lightly and then very strongly, but Ḥoni held fast and refused to leave the circle until *Hashem* sent "*gishmei beracha*," rain that would effectively alleviate the widespread suffering.

After *Hashem* finally responded to Ḥoni, Rabbi Shimon ben Shetaḥ declared that Ḥoni deserved to be excommunicated for the audacious manner in which he approached *Hashem*. Rabbi Shimon ben Shetaḥ declared that *Hashem* responded to Ḥoni just as a father heeds the pleas of his wayward son – simply because he is his son.

AVINU OR *MALKENU*?

In requesting that *Hashem* respond to their prayers in the same manner that He responded to Ḥoni, the Sephardic liturgy adopts Ḥoni's approach, whereas the Ashkenazic liturgy appears to follow the view of Rabbi Shimon ben Shetaḥ. Indeed, perhaps it can be said that Sephardim identify with Ḥoni precisely because they are comfortable relating to *Hashem* as a loving father.

All agree that *Hashem* is both are father and king, as both Ashkenazim and Sephardim express in the *Avinu Malkenu* prayer. The question is which aspect we emphasize: Sephardim stress the father element, whereas Ashkenazim, especially during the Yamim Nora'im, focus more on viewing *Hashem* as our King.

This distinction regarding the mention of Ḥoni during *Seliḥot* reflects the entire mood during the *tefillot* of Rosh Hashana and Yom Kippur. For those who have experienced both styles of Yamim Nora'im *tefillot*, it is most readily apparent the Ashkenazic version is far more solemn, while the Sephardic approach is much more buoyant and optimistic. When relating to Father, we are upbeat; when we relate to the King, we are most somber and serious.

THE CONCLUSION TO THE *HAFTARA* SELECTIONS FOR SHABBAT SHUVA

This difference in approach between Sephardic and Ashkenazic Jews in regards to the Yamim Nora'im may also explain the differing endings to the *haftara* of Shabbat Shuva, the Shabbat between Rosh Hashana and Yom Kippur.

On Shabbat Shuva, both groups begin the *haftara* with a selection from *Hoshe'a* 14 calling on the Jewish People to repent: "*Shuva Yisrael ad Hashem Elokecha*." The communities diverge, however, as to which selection supplements the reading from *Hoshe'a*. Ashkenazim read a selection from *Yoel* (Chapter 2) calling upon the Jews to assemble and engage in repentance that includes fasting and crying, as well as a portion from *Micha* (Chapter 7), which emphasizes the kindness of *Hashem* in His merciful acts of forgiveness. Sephardim, however, add only the selection from *Micha*. Unlike Ashkenazim, who also choose a prophetic reading that stresses solemnity and somberness, the Sephardic tradition focuses only on *Hashem*'s merciful and forgiving nature.

Once again, Ashkenazic practice places the stress on *Hashem* as our King, while the Sephardic approach accentuates *Hashem* as Father.

CONCLUSION

Perhaps the most important lesson to be gleaned from examining this issue is the profundity of both versions of the *tefilla*. The mere omission or inclusion of a short phrase marks a huge difference in approach regarding a most basic and fundamental issue. How beautifully rich and profound are our *tefillot*!

Chapter 45

Forgetting *HaMelech HaMishpat*

During the *Aseret Yemei Teshuva,* two changes are made to the *Amida*: The conclusion of the third *beracha, "HaKel hakadosh,"* is changed to, *"HaMelech hakadosh,"* and the conclusion of the eleventh *beracha, "Melech ohev tzedaka umishpat,"* is changed to, *"HaMelech hamishpat."* Many Jews learn at a very young age that if one forgot to make the latter change, he need not repeat the *Amida,* since in any event the word *"Melech"* was mentioned. This is in contrast to one who forgot to change the conclusion to *"HaMelech hakadosh,"* in which case he would have to repeat the *Amida.*

RAV OVADIA YOSEF'S APPROACH

This well-known ruling is based on the Rama (*Oraḥ Ḥayim* 118:1 and 582:1), the major halachic authority for Ashkenazic Jews. May Sephardic Jews rely on this ruling as well?

Rav Ovadia Yosef (*Teshuvot Yabia Omer* 2: *Oraḥ Ḥayim* 8–10; *Yeḥaveh Da'at* 1:57) responds emphatically in the negative and requires the repetition of the *Amida* if one did not say *"HaMelech hamishpat"* instead of *"HaMelech ohev tzedaka umishpat."* He lists the overwhelming majority of *Rishonim* who reject the Rama's approach, including the Rambam (*Hilchot Tefilla* 10:13), Rav Sa'adia Gaon (*siddur,* pp. 18 and 24), Rosh (*Berachot* 1:16), *Maḥzor Vitri* (#90 and #327), and Ritva (*Rosh Hashana* 34a). *Maran* Rav

Yosef Karo (*Shulḥan Aruch, Oraḥ Ḥayim* 118:1 and 582:1), in turn, rules in accordance with these many *Rishonim*.

Rav Ovadia cites Rabbenu Mano'aḥ (*Sefer HaMenuḥa*, p. 67), who notes that there is a world of difference between "*HaMelech hamishpat*," the King of justice, and "*Melech ohev tzedaka umishpat*," the King who loves when His creations act with justice and fairness. In fact, the *Talmidei Rabbenu Yona* (*Berachot* 6b in the Rif's pages, s.v. *v'asikna*) are the sole *Rishonim* who rule that "*Melech ohev tzedaka umishpat*" is an adequate substitution for "*HaMelech hamishpat*."

Rav Ovadia acknowledges that Ashkenazic *Aḥaronim*, such as the *Baḥ* (*Oraḥ Ḥayim* 582, s.v. *v'aviezri*) and *Magen Avraham* (118:1), support the Rama's approach, but he notes that the Sephardic *Aḥaronim* do not. Rav Ovadia presents a list of major Sephardic *posekim* who uphold the ruling of *Maran* Rav Yosef Karo, including the *Peri Ḥadash, Nehar Shalom, Ma'amar Mordechai, Ḥida*, Rav Ḥayim Palagi (*Moed L'Chol Ḥai* 13:28), and the *S'dei Ḥemed* (*Teshuvot Ohr Li* 29).[1]

THE *BEN ISH ḤAI*'S APPROACH AND RAV OVADIA'S RESPONSE

Given this background, it seems evident that a Sephardic Jew should follow the ruling of the *Shulḥan Aruch* in this instance, but the leading nineteenth-century Sephardic *posek*, the *Ben Ish Ḥai* (year 1, *Parashat Nitzavim* 19), does not subscribe to this approach. He argues that although the *Shulḥan Aruch* requires one who said, "*Melech ohev tzedaka umishpat*" to repeat the *Amida*, since the Rama does not require the repetition, this is a situation of *safek berachot*, uncertainty as to whether a *beracha* should be recited, in which case we rule that one should not recite the *beracha*.

The *Ben Ish Ḥai* therefore concludes that even a Sephardic Jew should not repeat the *Amida*, lest he recite an unnecessary *beracha*. The *Ben Ish Ḥai* insists that the rule of *safek berachot l'hakel* applies even when it runs counter to an explicit ruling of *Maran* Rav Yosef Karo! The *Kaf HaḤayim* (*Oraḥ Ḥayim* 582:2) rules in accordance with the *Ben Ish Ḥai*.

Rav Ovadia certainly considers the principle of *safek berachot l'hakel* in his ruling. In fact, it is a dominant theme in many of his rulings. However,

1. Rav Ovadia requires the repetition of the *Amida* even if one is in doubt as to whether he said, "*HaMelech hamishpat*" (*Teshuvot Yabia Omer* 7: *Oraḥ Ḥayim* 51).

he insists that it does not apply in this situation, since if one continues the *Amida* after saying "*Melech ohev tzedaka umishpat,*" he will be reciting an entire string of unnecessary *berachot* according to the majority of *Rishonim* and *Maran* Rav Yosef Karo.

Moreover, the rule of *safek berachot l'hakel* does not apply when there is a *minhag,* prevailing custom. Rav Ovadia presents a dramatic incident recounted by an eyewitness who was present when the *Ben Ish Ḥai* presented his ruling to his community. Upon hearing the *Ben Ish Ḥai*'s ruling, the *Av Bet Din* (chief justice) of the Baghdad Rabbinical court leaped to his feet and proclaimed that this ruling runs counter to the prevalent *minhag* in Baghdad! This story confirms the existence of a *minhag* to follow the ruling of *Maran* Rav Yosef Karo in this situation.

THE RULINGS OF RAV MESSAS AND RAV ELIYAHU

Rav Shalom Messas (cited in Rav Mordechai Lebhar, *Magen Avot* 582:1) disagrees with Rav Ovadia's ruling. Rav Lebhar notes that the *minhag* among Moroccan Jews follows the approach of the *Ben Ish Ḥai* and *Kaf HaḤayim,* thereby eliminating an important prong of Rav Ovadia's argument.

Rav Mordechai Eliyahu (in his *Siddur Kol Eliyahu*) also rules in accordance with the *Ben Ish Ḥai.* This is not surprising, since Rav Eliyahu is well-known for following in the footsteps of the *Ben Ish Ḥai.*

CONCLUSION

What many of us were taught as youngsters – that the *Amida* need not be repeated if one forgot to say "*HaMelech hamishpat*" during the *Aseret Yemei Teshuva* – is indeed true for Ashkenazim and Moroccan Jews. Yemenites should unquestionably follow the ruling of the Rambam and *Maran* Rav Yosef Karo and repeat the *Amida* if they omitted "*HaMelech hamishpat.*"[2]

For other Sephardic Jews, the matter remains unresolved, however. Rav Eli Mansour sets forth a reasonable approach: If one forgot "*HaMelech hamishpat,*" he should repeat the *Amida,* but stipulate that according to the view that he has already fulfilled his obligation of prayer (*Talmidei Rabbenu Yona,* Rama, *Ben Ish Ḥai,* Rav Messas, and Rav Eliyahu), the extra *Amida* should be regarded as a voluntary prayer.[3] Rav Ovadia Yosef (op. cit. and

---

2. As noted by Rav Zecharia Ben-Shlomo, *Orot HaHalacha,* p. 800.
3. http://www.dailyhalacha.com/Display.asp?ClipDate=9/25/2017.

Yalkut Yosef, Oraḥ Ḥayim 582:11) himself makes this suggestion. Rav Zecharia Ben-Shlomo (*Orot HaHalacha*, pp. 800–801), Rav Shmuel Khoskherman (personal communication), and Rav Yonatan Nacson (*MiMizrach U'MiMa'arav*, pp. 206–207) concur with this ruling as well.[4]

4. Accordingly, the comment of the Sephardic Artscroll Siddur (p. 1147, *halacha* 64) that most Sephardic communities follow the *Ben Ish Ḥai* regarding this question is highly questionable.

Chapter 46

Sephardic *Tekiat Shofar*

The *gemara* (*Rosh Hashana* 26a) states that the experience of *tekiat shofar* is comparable to that of the *Kohen Gadol* entering the *Kodesh HaKodashim* on Yom Kippur. Indeed, the rabbi often reminds his congregants that this is the moment we come closest to *Hashem* the entire year. Sephardic customs enhance and magnify the intense spirituality that envelopes the *bet kenesset* during *shofar* blowing.

ET SHA'AREI RATZON AND *MIZMOR* 47

The drama begins with the congregation singing a powerful and haunting *piyut* (with a matching haunting melody) invoking the intense drama of *akedat Yitzḥak*. The *piyut* is called *Et Sha'arei Ratzon*, and its refrain is "*oked v'hane'ekad v'hamizbe'aḥ*." It is most instructive to review this poem, as its content is provocative. An example:

ממאכלת יהמה מדברי

נא חדדה אבי ואת מאסרי

חזק ועת יקַד יקוד בבשרי

קח עמך הנשאר מאפרי

וֶאֱמֹר לשרה זה ליצחק ריח

Yitzḥak tells Avraham to sharpen the knife and tighten the ropes surrounding him... and take the remainder of his ashes, present them to his mother Sarah, and tell her that this is a fragrance of Yitzḥak!

The intensity is taken to the next level by reciting *Mizmor* 47 (*LaMenatze'aḥ L'Vnei Koraḥ Mizmor*) seven times. Congregants do not merely silently recite this *perek*; they chant it with a melodic tune, each time lead by a different community leader.

THE *TOKE'A'S* PLEA

The *toke'a* (*shofar*-blower) then utters a searing plea that his blowing should be acceptable to *Hashem*, incorporates by reference the proper *kavanot* (intentions) of Moshe Rabbenu, Rabbi Shimon bar Yoḥai, and Rabbi Yitzḥak Luria. The rabbi reminds the congregation to have *kavana* to fulfill this great *mitzva* before the *berachot* are recited.

To even further intensify the experience, it is customary for the *toke'a* to cover the *shofar* just before the *shofar*-blowing,[1] as he recites the *berachot* of "*l'shmo'a kol shofar*" and the *Sheheḥiyanu*.[2] The *toke'a* places the *shofar* underneath his *kouracha* (*tallit* bag) and leaves it covered until after he recites the *berachot*, when he is ready to begin blowing.

This practice commemorates the drama of *akedat Yitzḥak*. As Avraham Avinu constructed the altar upon which to offer his son, he feared that the *satan*, in his effort to disrupt the sacrifice, might throw a rock at Yitzḥak in order to inflict a wound that would render Yitzḥak blemished and unfit as an offering. Avraham Avinu therefore covered Yitzḥak to hide him from the *satan*. Sephardim commemorate Avraham Avinu's devotion by covering the *shofar* just before it is blown.

1. *Ben Ish Ḥai* (year 1, *Parashat Nitzavim* 15) and *Kaf HaḤayim* (*Oraḥ Ḥayim* 585:14).
2. Sephardic and Yemenite Jews recite *Sheheḥiyanu* before *teki'at shofar* only on the first day of Rosh Hashana. This matter is the subject of a dispute between Rav Yosef Karo and the Rama (*Shulḥan Aruch, Oraḥ Ḥayim* 601:3). Both Rav Ovadia Hadaya (*Teshuvot Yaskil Avdi* 4: *Oraḥ Ḥayim*: 31) and Rav Ovadia Yosef (*Teshuvot Yabia Omer* 1: *Oraḥ Ḥayim* 29:11) rule that a Sephardic Jew should not recite *Sheheḥiyanu* on the second day even if he blows *shofar* for an Ashkenazic congregation or individual.

TEKIAT SHOFAR

The *toke'a* blows a continuous flow of thirty *kolot* (blasts); no one calls out the name of the upcoming blast (*tekia, shevarim,* etc.).[3] The congregation sits during the first set of blasts, in keeping with the *gemara*'s description of this first set as "*tekiot demeyushav,*" blasts sounded while sitting (*Rosh Hashana* 16a). In keeping with the Ari z"l's recommendation (*Sha'ar HaKavanot, Inyan Rosh Hashana*), Sephardic Jews follow the *Aruch*'s ruling (cited by *Tosafot, Rosh Hashana* 33b, s.v. *shiur terua*) to blow thirty more sounds of the *shofar* to accompany and intensify the *Malchiot, Zichronot,* and *Shofarot* during the silent *Amida.*[4] Finally, *shofar*-blowing is topped off with the hundred and first blow of a *terua gedola* (not a *tekia gedola*), as instructed by the *Shulḥan Aruch* (*Oraḥ Ḥayim* 596:1), alerting us to carry the spiritual impact of the *shofar*-blowing throughout the day.[5]

CONCLUSION

A talented and devout *toke'a* makes the *shofar*-blowing into a peak event. Sephardic *tekiot,* with *Hashem*'s help, live up to the *gemara*'s description of the greatness of *tekiat shofar.* Devoted people practicing precious *minhagim* make *shofar*-blowing a truly magical moment.

---

3. This practice is mentioned by the Rama (*Oraḥ Ḥayim* 585:4) and not by the *Shulḥan Aruch.*
4. See Rav Ovadia Yosef, *Teshuvot Yeḥaveh Da'at* 2:75. This is done despite it running counter to the ruling of *Maran* Rav Yosef Karo (*Shulḥan Aruch, Oraḥ Ḥayim* 592:1).
5. For further explanations of this practice, see *Kaf HaḤayim* 596:1.

Chapter 47

Avinu Malkenu on Shabbat

Ashkenazic Jews are often shocked to discover that most Sephardic Jews recite the *tefilla* of *Avinu Malkenu* on Shabbat. In truth, this is not shocking at all, as it is the Rama (*Oraḥ Ḥayim* 584:1 and 602:1), the central halachic authority for Ashkenazic Jews, who presents the practice to omit *Avinu Malkenu* on Shabbat. In fact, there has been a range of opinions regarding this issue since the time of the *Rishonim*. The *Orḥot Ḥayim* (*Hilchot Rosh Hashana* 2) and the Rivash (*Teshuvot* 512) already cite differing customs among various communities about this matter.

RABBI AKIVA'S PRAYER

Avinu Malkenu is a particularly potent *tefilla*. Its source emerges from none other than Rabbi Akiva. When called upon to pray for rain during fast-day prayers amidst a severe drought, Rabbi Akiva proclaimed, "*Avinu Malkenu, ḥatanu lefanecha,*" and, "*Avinu Malkenu en lanu melech ela atah,*" and it began to rain immediately (*Ta'anit* 25b). When the rabbis saw the great efficacy of Rabbi Akiva's *tefilla*, they expanded it and designated it for recitation during the *Aseret Yemei Teshuva*.

THE ASHKENAZIC PRACTICE

Ashkenazim (as noted by the Rivash) and some Sephardim omit *Avinu Malkenu* on Shabbat – even on Yom Kippur – because one is not allowed to make requests on Shabbat (*Mishna Berura* 584:4). Although there are other passages that contain special requests (such as *Zachrenu L'Ḥayim* and *Mi Chamocha Av HaRaḥaman*) that are recited on Shabbat, since they are written in the plural, they are considered reflect a community need, and community requests may be presented to *Hashem* even on Shabbat and Yom Tov (see *Tosafot, Berachot* 34a, s.v. *emtza'iot*).

Although *Avinu Malkenu* is also written in plural and is part of our *tefilla* throughout the *Aseret Yemei Teshuva,* the fact that it originated as a special prayer for fast days is part of the reason that it is treated as a particularly poignant prayer that is inappropriate for Shabbat. The special prayers and supplications recited in times of distress are forbidden on Shabbat and Yom Tov except for cases of most severe and immediate trouble (*Shulḥan Aruch, Oraḥ Ḥayim* 576:12–13).

THE SEPHARDIC PRACTICE

The dominant Sephardic practice to recite *Avinu Malkenu* even on Shabbat is defended by none other than the Meiri (*Magen Avot* 24), who writes that although on Shabbat and Yom Tov we refrain from crying out to *Hashem* in most circumstances, the *Aseret Yemei Teshuva* are an exception. These ten days are designated for *teshuva* and added *tefillot,* and thus on Shabbat that falls during these days we cry out to *Hashem* with *Avinu Malkenu.*

Although the Rivash notes that there was a range of opinions in Spain – in some regions *Avinu Malkenu* was recited on Shabbat, and in others it was omitted – most Sephardim today do recite *Avinu Malkenu* on Shabbat. This is so despite the fact that the *Kisei Eliyahu* records that the custom in Jerusalem was to omit *Avinu Malkenu* on Shabbat.

Rav Ovadia Yosef (*Teshuvot Yeḥaveh Da'at* 1:54) explains the reason for the change. He relates that the first step was when the great kabbalist Rav Ḥayim Vital (*Sha'ar HaKavanot* 90a) revealed that his great master, the Ari z"l, would recite *Avinu Malkenu* on Shabbat. The next step was when this became practice in the legendary Sephardic Kabbalistic Yeshivat Bet El (which exists until this very day in the Jewish Quarter of Jerusalem's Old

City). Rav Ovadia writes that "slowly but surely, this emerged as the practice in most Sephardic congregations in Jerusalem," as is recorded in the major Sephardic halachic works the *Kaf HaḤayim* (*Oraḥ Ḥayim* 584:8) and Rav Amram Aburabiya's *Netivei Am* (584).

Rav Ovadia notes (following the Ari z"l) that on Shabbat, even Sephardim omit the lines "*Avinu Malkenu ḥatanu lefanecha*" and "*Avinu Malkenu meḥol uselaḥ l'chol pesha'enu*" and other mention of sins, since we do not wish to mention our shortcomings on Shabbat and Rosh Hashana.

MAKING REQUESTS TO *HASHEM* ON SHABBAT AND YOM TOV

Although the *Mishna Berura* notes the prohibition to make requests on Shabbat, Rav Ovadia notes that this is not absolute prohibition. In fact, the source of this prohibition, the Talmud Yerushalmi (*Shabbat* 15:3), already offers an exception, noting that we recite the requests that are incorporated into *Birkat HaMazon* even on Shabbat, since this is the standard text of *Birkat HaMazon*. *Tosafot* (*Berachot* 48b, s.v. *mathil*) cite this passage in the Yerushalmi as authoritative.

Rav Ovadia argues that this implies that the prohibition to plead to *Hashem* on Shabbat refers only to pleas and supplications composed by the individual himself. The prohibition does not apply to standard texts, such as the special supplications composed by the *Ḥida* for *Tashlich* and Simḥat Torah.

In general, Sephardic Jews limit the prohibition of supplications on Shabbat and Yom Tov, whereas Ashkenazic Jews view the prohibition as having a wider scope. For example, Ashkenazic *siddurim* instruct one to omit the special supplications respectively recited before saying the *Akeda*, *L'Olam Yehei Adam*, the *Korban Tamid*, and *Ezehu Mekoman* on Shabbat and Yom Tov. Sephardic congregations, in contrast, include these special supplications even on Shabbat and Yom Tov.

The debate as to whether one recites *Avinu Malkenu* on Shabbat reflects this broader debate as to the scope of the prohibition to recite special supplications to *Hashem* on Shabbat.

Although Ḥassidim have adopted the Sephardic practice with regard to many supplications recited on Shabbat and Yom Tov, Ḥassidim omit *Avinu Malkenu* on Shabbat in deference to the Rama's ruling.

CONCLUSION

Whichever practice is followed, the most important lesson we should derive from this to discussion is to cherish our recitation of *Avinu Malkenu*. It is a most potent weapon in our prayer arsenal, taught by the great and beloved Rabbi Akiva.

Sukkot

Chapter 48

Rain on the First Night of Sukkot

One year on Sukkot, it was raining heavily on the first night of the *ḥag*, and the [Ashkenazi] rabbi of a Sephardic synagogue in Brooklyn instructed his Sephardic (mostly Syrian) congregation to eat a *kezayit* of bread in the *sukka* despite the rain. This ruling is based on the Rama (*Oraḥ Ḥayim* 639:5), who follows the approach of the Rosh, Ran, and *Tur*. Since *Maran* Rav Yosef Karo is silent on the matter, the rabbi assumed that Sephardim follow the Rama in this case.

RAV OVADIA YOSEF'S RESPONSE

When someone brought this ruling to the attention of Rav Ovadia Yosef, however, he declared that the rabbi was in absolute error! Rav Ovadia explains his reasoning in *Teshuvot Yabia Omer* (9: *Oraḥ Ḥayim* 61). He notes that Rav Yosef Karo writes in his *Bet Yosef* commentary to the *Tur* that the Ran's ruling is rejected by the Rashba (*Teshuvot* 4:78). Whereas the Ran maintains that there is an absolute obligation to eat in the *sukka* on the first night of Sukkot, the Rashba holds that the exemption from eating in the *sukka* when it is raining applies in all circumstances.

Rav Ovadia notes that the Ra'avad (cited in the *Kol Bo, Hilchot Berachot* 55:4) and *Maggid Mishneh* (*Hilchot Sukka* 6:7) agree with the Rashba. Rav Yosef proceeds to cite the important authority the *Ma'amar*

Mordechai (639:6), who infers from the fact that the Rambam does not make a distinction between the first night and the rest of Sukkot regarding the rain exemption that the Rambam also agrees with Rashba. Most important, the *Ma'amar Mordechai* makes the same inference from *Maran* Rav Yosef Karo, who does not mention in the *Shulḥan Aruch* that one must eat in the *sukka* on the first evening even if it is raining.

Rav Ovadia bolsters his opinion exempting Sephardic Jews from eating in the *sukka* if it is raining even on the first night, based on the *mishna* (*Sukka* 2:9) that compares a situation of rain in the *sukka* to a servant who approaches his master to serve him and the master in turn pours the drink on the servant. In such a situation, reasons Rav Ovadia, "if the servant proceeds to try to serve the Master again, he certainly will anger Him even further, since he is acting against His will. Such a person is a *ḥasid shoteh*, a pious fool."

Rav Ovadia adds the factor of "*deracheha darchei no'am*," "the ways of the Torah are pleasant" (*Mishlei* 3:17). The *gemara* invokes this *pasuk* to prove that the Torah does not wish for us to act in an unpleasant manner. Based on this *pasuk*, for example, the *gemara* (*Sukka* 32b) rejects the possibility of using a stinging plant as one of the *arba minim* on Sukkot. Similarly, Rav Ovadia argues, requiring one to eat in the *sukka* while rain is pouring down is not in harmony with the "*deracheha darchei no'am*" principle.

Thus, Rav Ovadia firmly rules that Sephardim should not follow the ruling of the Rama in this situation. He cites as support the important Sephardic authorities the *Shulḥan Gevo'ah* (639:19) and the *Kaf HaḤayim* (*Oraḥ Ḥayim* 639:73), who assert that Rav Yosef Karo does not agree with Rama regarding this matter.

IN DEFENSE OF ADOPTING THE RAMA'S RULING

In defense of the rabbi from Brooklyn, we may cite two very prominent Sephardic authorities, the Radbaz (*Teshuvot* 5:2320) and Rav Ḥayim Palagi (*Mo'ed L'Chol Ḥai* 20:20), who subscribe to the Rama's approach. Nonetheless, Rav Ovadia holds firm that Sephardic Jews should follow the view of the Rashba, Ra'avad, *Maggid Mishneh*, and *Maran* Rav Yosef Karo that one is always exempt from the *sukka* if it rains, even on the first night of Sukkot.

Interestingly, Dr. Adam Ohayon and Ariel Picillo note (*Darké Abotenou* 2:153–154) that the Moroccan custom follows the ruling of the Rama.[1] This is not surprising, since the Moroccan practice, unlike that of Rav Ovadia, is to regard the Rama as authoritative if *Maran* Rav Yosef Karo does not explicitly disagree.

CONCLUSION

If the first night of Sukkot is very rainy, Ashkenazic and possibly Moroccan Jews should follow the protocol set forth by the Rama to eat a *kezayit* of bread in the *sukka* despite the rain. Other Sephardic Jews, however, should follow the ruling of Rav Ovadia Yosef and enjoy their Yom Tov meal inside their homes, without the men having to eat a *kezayit* in the *sukka* while it is pouring rain.

1. Rav Shmuel Khoshkerman reports, however, that he has seen many learned Moroccan Jews who do not follow this ruling of the Rama.

Chapter 49

Differences Between Sephardic and Ashkenazic *Na'anuim*

The *na'anuim* of the *arba minim* on Sukkot – the manner in which the four species are waved – present one example of a situation in which Ashkenazic Jews follow the ruling of Rav Yosef Karo as recorded in the *Shulḥan Aruch* while Sephardic Jews do not.

The *Shulḥan Aruch* (*Oraḥ Ḥayim* 651:9) rules that the *na'anuim* begin in front and then wind around clockwise (right, behind, left), concluding with up and down motions. Sephardim (and Ḥassidim), however, follow the practice of the Ari z"l, shaking to the south, then north, east, east in the upwards direction, east in a downward motion, and finally to the west (*Sha'ar HaKavanot, Inyan Netilat Lulav*; see *Kaf HaḤayim, Oraḥ Ḥayim* 651:49).

Furthermore, *Maran* Rav Yosef Karo writes that one performs the *na'anuim* simply by moving one's hands, and not his body. Although Ashkenazic Jews follow this practice, Sephardic Jews fully extend their arms, moving the four *minim* in a full motion back and forth, once again following the approach of the Ari z"l (*Kaf HaḤayim, Oraḥ Ḥayim* 651:48 and 93). Similarly, the *Kaf HaḤayim* (651:96) notes that the prevalent Sephardic practice in his area was to move one's entire body in the direction in which he is waving, and this appears to be the widespread practice among Sephardic Jews today.

Two other differences between Ashkenazic practice and Sephardic practice reflect differences between the rulings of *Maran* Rav Yosef Karo and the Rama. The Rama (*Oraḥ Ḥayim* 651:8), based on *Tosafot* (*Sukka* 37b, s.v. *b'Hodu*), records the Ashkenazic practice to shake the *arba minim* during *Hallel* not only during the recitation of "*Hodu laHashem ki tov ki l'olam ḥasdo*," but also when responding "*Hodu laHashem ki tov*" to the *shaliaḥ tzibur*'s recitation of "*Yomar na Yisrael*," etc. The Rambam (*Hilchot Lulav* 7:10), however, makes no mention of this, and Rav Yosef Karo similarly does not record such a practice, since Sephardic Jews do not respond with "*Hodu laHashem*" to the lines read by the *shaliaḥ tzibur*.

In addition, while the Rama (*Oraḥ Ḥayim* 651:9) defines the *na'anuim* as shaking the *lulav*, Rav Yosef Karo defines it simply as waving. This difference of opinion once again stems from a dispute between *Tosafot* and the Rambam. *Tosafot* (*Sukka* 37b, s.v. *k'dei*) mentions shaking in addition to the *gemara*'s mention of waving, while the Rambam (*Hilchot Lulav* 7:10) makes mention only of waving, but not of shaking.

There is an important ramification of this difference. While some Ashkenazic *posekim* express reservations about using a *lulav* whose tip is closed by brown bark (sometimes referred to as "*kora*"), since one is unable to shake such a *lulav*, this is not a concern for Sephardim. In fact, it is preferable for a Sephardic Jew to purchase such a *lulav*, since the sealing of the tip in this manner allows for the purchaser to assume that the tip of the *lulav* is intact (see *Shulḥan Aruch, Oraḥ Ḥayim* 645:3).[1]

1. It is reported that Rav Yitzhak Zev Soloveitchik (the Brisker Rav) would open up the *kora* around the *lulav* to ensure that it was truly closed and not held together by the *kora*. Both *Yalkut Yosef* (*Oraḥ Ḥayim* 645:15) and Rav Mordechai Lebhar (*Magen Avot, Oraḥ Ḥayim* 645:3) cite as authoritative the *S'dei Ḥemed*'s assertion (*Asifat Dinim, Ma'arachet Arba'at HaMinim* 3:1) that the Sephardic *minhag* is to choose such *lulavim* without removing the brownish bark from the leaves to ascertain that the top leaves are intact.

   As noted by Rav Lebhar (*Magen Avot, Oraḥ Ḥayim* 651:1), there are different practices among Sephardic Jews as to how to tie the *lulav*, *hadassim*, and *aravot* together. Moroccan Jews tie like non-Ḥassidic Ashkenazic Jews, placing the three *hadassim* on the right of the *lulav* and the two *aravot* on the left side. Other Sephardic Jews follow the Ari z"l's method of placing one *hadas* to the right of the *lulav*, a second

Finally, the *Yalkut Yosef* (*Oraḥ Ḥayim* 651:50) records the practice to wave the *lulav* only once when reciting the last *pasuk* of *Hodu* in *Hallel*, whereas Ashkenazic Jews wave both times the last *pasuk* of *Hodu* is recited.[2]

---

to the left of the *lulav*, and one in the middle of the *lulav*. One *arava* is placed to the right of the *lulav* and the second to the left of the *lulav*, according to this practice.

2. Rav Ovadia Yosef (*Ḥazon Ovadia, Sukkot*, p. 353) surprisingly rules that a Sephardic Jew visiting an Ashkenazic congregation on Sukkot should perform the *na'anuim* in accordance with Ashkenazic practice. The converse, when Ashkenazim visit a Sephardic congregation, should be true as well. This is a surprising ruling, since Rav Ovadia normally instructs Sephardic Jews to uphold their practices even when praying with Ashkenazim. It is even more surprising in light of the ruling of the *Aruch HaShulḥan* (*Oraḥ Ḥayim* 651:22), who permits divergent practices regarding the *na'anuim*, citing compelling evidence from the *mishna* (*Sukka* 3:8), which clearly states that Rabban Gamliel and Rabbi Yehoshua performed the *na'anuim* differently from the congregation in which they were present. See Chapter 1 regarding *lo titgodedu* for an explanation as to why regarding certain issues Rav Ovadia demands conformity and yet many other times does not.

Pesaḥ

Chapter 50

Kitniyot and Eating Out on Pesaḥ

Jewish communities throughout the world, and especially in Israel, have been blessed in recent decades to have Sephardim and Ashkenazim living in the same communities. *Baruch Hashem*, there is even a high percentage of marriages between Sephardim and Ashkenazim, leading to a variety of questions relating to variations in halachic practices. One such question relates to whether Ashkenazim may eat at the homes of Sephardic Jews on Pesaḥ.

This question primarily relates to the Ashkenazic *minhag* not to eat *kitniyot* (legumes) – including rice and corn – on Pesaḥ. This custom developed because *kitniyot* often grow near wheat or barley fields, and there was, therefore, concern that wheat kernels could be found among the legumes. In addition, *kitniyot* may, like wheat, be ground up and made into bread, which may likely lead to confusion. This *minhag* is recorded authoritative by the Rama (*Oraḥ Ḥayim* 453:1). Sephardim, however, did not accept this practice, and most Sephardim eat rice, corn, and the like on Pesaḥ.

RAV OVADIA YOSEF'S ARGUMENT

Rav Ovadia Yosef (*Teshuvot Yeḥaveh Da'at* 5:32) rules that an Ashkenazic Jew may eat non-*kitniyot* food at the home of a Sephardic Jew on Pesaḥ, even if the food was prepared in utensils that were used for *kitniyot*. Rav Ovadia bases his opinion on a similar ruling of the Rama (*Oraḥ Ḥayim* 453:1): "It is obvious that if *kitniyot* fell into food during Pesaḥ, it does not render the food forbidden *b'diavad* (post facto)." Accordingly, Rav Ovadia argues:

> It is clear that the food particles of *kitniyot* absorbed into pots in Sephardic homes that are released into non-*kitniyot* food do not forbid the food for Ashkenazim. Even if the utensils have been used within the past twenty-four hours [and thus emit a good taste], it is still permissible for Ashkenazim to eat from them, because there is surely more permissible food than there is *kitniyot* taste that emerges from the walls of the pot.

THREE PRECEDENTS

Rav Ovadia cites several interesting precedents for his ruling. The first is a responsum of the Rama (132:15) regarding those who are strict regarding the concern of *ḥadash* (the prohibition against eating grain sown after Pesaḥ) in the Diaspora.[1] The Rama writes that those who adopt the strict position regarding *ḥadash* may nonetheless eat food that absorbed flavor from the utensils of those who are lenient and permit *ḥadash*. The Rama reasons that in his community, even those who were strict treated *ḥadash* only as a possibly Rabbinic prohibition (as opposed to the many authorities who consider *ḥadash* to be an absolute Biblical prohibition even in the Diaspora). The Rama thus claims that the light nature of the *ḥadash* prohibition allows for eating food that may have absorbed its flavor from pots. The flavor of the *ḥadash* is nullified by the majority of non-*ḥadash* food (*batel b'rov*).

Rav Ovadia equates the case of *kitniyot* to the Rama's case of *ḥadash*. *Kitniyot* is also an unusually light prohibition for Ashkenazic Jews, and one may therefore be lenient regarding the flavor in pots used to cook *kitniyot*.

A second precedent cited by Rav Ovadia is a ruling of the Radbaz (*Teshuvot* 4:496) discussing whether those who do not rely on a particular *shoḥet* may eat food cooked by those who do rely on him. The Radbaz rules leniently, claiming that the *shoḥet* in question was probably acceptable.

1. Just as most observant Jews in the Diaspora today are lenient regarding *ḥadash*, most observant Ashkenazic Jews in pre-war Europe were lenient as well (see *Mishna Berura* 489:45). See Chapter 73 regarding the observance of the *ḥadash* prohibition in the Diaspora.

Thus, even those who do not rely on him for their meat can at least eat food cooked in utensils that absorbed the flavor of his meat. Again, writes Rav Ovadia, we see that when certain prohibitions are treated leniently, their flavor is permitted. *Kitniyot,* a mere custom of Ashkenazic Jewry, should also be treated this way.

Rav Ovadia's third precedent is an important ruling of the Rama (*Yoreh De'ah* 64:9) addressing a type of fat whose permissibility depended on varying customs among Ashkenazic communities of his time. The Rama permits members of the communities that abide by the strict view to eat food cooked in utensils of people in the lenient communities, reasoning that the lenient communities were following a legitimate ruling of their halachic authorities. Even one who was strict about the actual fat did not need to be strict about its flavor, because there is a valid opinion that permits the flavor.

Based on the above precedents, Rav Ovadia concludes that there are certain relatively light prohibitions regarding which flavor is nullified when mixed with permissible food, and he asserts that *kitniyot* is one such prohibition.

MORE SUPPORT FOR RAV OVADIA'S LENIENT APPROACH

The Rama (*Oraḥ Ḥayim* 453:1) writes that there need not be a sixty-to-one ratio of non-*kitniyot* to *kitniyot* in order to nullify any *kitniyot* that may have fallen into a pot of food (*batel b'shishim*). Rather, as long as a majority of non-*kitniyot* exists (*batel b'rov*), one has not violated the *minhag* of not eating *kitniyot.* Later authorities – including the *Eliah Rabba* (453:4), *Shulḥan Aruch HaRav* (*Oraḥ Ḥayim* 453:5), *Ḥok Yaakov* (453:5), *Ḥayei Adam* (127:1), and *Mishna Berura* (453:9) – appear to accept this view. The *Ḥok Yaakov* explains that although it appears from the *Terumat HaDeshen* that a sixty-to-one ratio is necessary to nullify *kitniyot,* the *halacha* follows the ruling of the Rama, who states only that a majority of the food must not be *kitniyot.*

The reason for this *halacha* is that refraining from *kitniyot* is merely a custom, and it is therefore not treated with the same severity as Biblical and Rabbinic laws. Since the aforementioned authorities rule that the non-*kitniyot* majority nullifies a minority of actual *kitniyot* food, undoubtedly they agree that non-*kitniyot* food cooked in a pot nullifies the flavor of *kitniyot* that emerges from the pot. The flavor of food should not be treated more stringently than the food itself. Indeed, the *Zera Emet* (3: *Oraḥ Ḥayim* 48) rules that the *minhag* to refrain from *kitniyot* does not include refraining from their flavor.

Rav Ovadia notes that all of these Ashkenazic authorities agree with his ruling, and it should therefore be permissible for an Ashkenazic Jew to eat non-*kitnityot* food cooked in a Sephardic Jew's dishes on Pesaḥ. Rav Shlomo Aviner (*Teshuvot She'elat Shlomo* 3:141) agrees with this ruling.

LIMITATIONS

When discussing pots in which *kitniyot* were cooked, however, the distinction between *l'chatḥila* (before the occurrence) and *b'diavad* (after the occurrence) must be stressed. The above-cited lenient rulings only permit a *b'diavad* situation, when food was already cooked in a pot that previously cooked *kitniyot*. However, Rav Ovadia (*Teshuvot Yeḥaveh Da'at* 1:9) and Rav Yehoshua Neuwirth (*Shemirat Shabbat K'Hilchata* 40:80) rule that an Ashkenazic Jew who must cook *kitniyot* on Pesaḥ (such as for a sick person) may not *l'chatḥila* cook non-*kitniyot* food for healthy Ashkenazic Jews in the same pot.

Moreover, Rav Efraim Greenblatt told this author that an Ashkenazic Jew who wishes to visit a Sephardic home on Pesaḥ should arrange for food that was not cooked in a pot that previously cooked *kitniyot*. His logic appears to be that this is a *l'chatḥila* situation, in which the nullification should not relied upon.[2]

Even regardless of the custom of *kitniyot*, some Ashkenazic Jews altogether avoid eating at other people's homes during Pesaḥ. Their concern

2. Similarly, Rav Ike Sultan, a student of Rav Hershel Schachter, writes: "I heard from Rav Schachter that it constitutes *bitul l'chatḥila* [deliberate nullification, which is forbidden] for an Ashkenazic Jew to visit a Sephardic Jew's house on Pesaḥ and eat on utensils that were used for *kitniyot*, even if the equipment has not been used in twenty-four hours. He did permit a brother to visit his sister who is married to a Sephardic Jew, since that is called *b'diavad*."

This question hinges upon a dispute between the Radbaz and the *Torat Ḥesed*. The Radbaz (*Teshuvot* 3:547) rules that purchasing food in which a non-Jew performed *bitul* is classified as *bitul l'chatḥila*. Although the *Torat Ḥesed* (*Oraḥ Ḥayim* 21) is lenient and Rav Schachter rules that the *halacha* essentially follows this opinion, Rav Schachter maintains that one should be strict. (Rav Sultan reports that this is also Rav Schachter's position regarding alcohol, such as whiskey or scotch, in which a small amount of non-kosher wine is blended and nullified). Concern for the strict opinion of the Radbaz seems to be the reason for Rav Greenblatt's ruling as well. Rav Ovadia (*Teshuvot Yabia Omer* 7: *Yoreh De'ah* 7) address this topic at some length and notes that this dispute has raged since the time of the *Rishonim*, concluding that we may be lenient regarding this matter.

is that different people observe divergent practices and customs regarding Pesaḥ, so the guests might not be permitted to eat from the food cooked in the utensils of their hosts. It is recounted that Rav Ḥayim Soloveitchik once visited the Ḥafetz Ḥayim on Pesaḥ, and the Ḥafetz Ḥayim, who was known for his warm hospitality, did not even offer his guest a cup of tea, due to this practice.[3] Apparently, this stringency was very common in many European circles.

CONCLUSION

Rav Ovadia Yosef rules that if an Ashkenazic Jew finds himself in a Sephardic Jew's home on Pesaḥ, he may eat food that was already cooked in pots that previously cooked *kitniyot*. However, an Ashkenazic Jew may not cook food for himself in utensils that were used to cook *kitniyot*. If an Ashkenazic Jew plans in advance to visit a Sephardic Jew on Pesaḥ, Rav Ovadia permits the Sephardic Jew to cook in his own pots for the visitor, whereas Rav Efraim Greenblatt requires alternate arrangements. Many Ashkenazic Jews follow this practice.

3. I heard this story from Rav Elazar Meyer Teitz, who heard it from Rav Michel Feinstein.

Chapter 51

Matza Ashira: Serving Egg Matza to Ashkenazim

A Sephardic Jew is hosting his Ashkenazic friend on Pesaḥ, and he wonders if he is permitted to serve his guest egg matza. Although Sephardic Jews consume egg matza on Pesaḥ, Ashkenazic Jews do not, save for exceptional circumstances, such as for a sick or elderly person. May the Sephardic host serve this product to his Ashkenazic guest, who appears robust and healthy?

THE EGG MATZA DEBATE

The debate regarding the status of egg matza is based on the question of how to resolve an apparent contradiction between two Talmudic passages. On the one hand, the *gemara* (*Pesaḥim* 35b) states that flour that is kneaded with fruit juice cannot become *ḥametz*. On the other hand, the *gemara* (ibid. 36a) states, "On Pesaḥ, one should not knead dough with wine, oil, or honey." Rashi (ad loc., s.v. *en lashin*) explains that this is forbidden "because it becomes *ḥametz* quickly" and it is difficult to ensure that it has not become *ḥametz*. Thus, one *gemara* expresses concern that dough mixed with fruit juice will become *ḥametz*, whereas another *gemara* states that dough kneaded with fruit juice cannot become *ḥametz*!

The *Rishonim* resolve this apparent contradiction in two ways. Rashi (ibid.) explains the *gemara* to mean that dough kneaded with fruit juice cannot become *ḥametz gamur* (full-fledged *ḥametz*); it does, however, become *ḥametz nuksheh* (partial *ḥametz*). Rashi explains that one is not punished with *karet* (excision) for eating *ḥametz nuksheh,* but one is nevertheless forbidden to eat *ḥametz nuksheh* on Pesaḥ.

Rabbenu Tam (cited in *Tosafot, Pesaḥim* 35b, s.v. *umei perot*) disagrees with Rashi. Rabbenu Tam interprets the *gemara* on 35b as teaching that fruit juice cannot create *ḥametz* at any level when mixed with dough. He explains that the *gemara* on 36a speaks of fruit juice mixed with water that one kneads with dough. The mixture of water with fruit juice greatly accelerates the process of *ḥimutz* (leavening). It is therefore difficult to ensure that it will not become *ḥametz,* and it thus must be avoided on Pesaḥ.

The Rambam (*Hilchot Ḥametz U'Matza* 5:2) adopts the same approach as Rabbenu Tam, ruling that a mixture of pure fruit juice and flour cannot become *ḥametz*: "Even if one lets the mixture rise the entire day until the dough becomes swollen, it is permissible to eat it, because fruit juice does not ferment; rather, it merely decays (*masriḥin*)." The Rambam adds that this applies only if no water has been added to the fruit juice.

The Ra'avad (ad loc.), however, cautions that some authorities disagree with the Rambam and assert that fruit juice mixed with dough becomes *ḥametz nuksheh*. The *Maggid Mishneh* (ad loc.) responds that the majority of the *Geonim* and *Rishonim* agree with the approach of the Rambam and reject Rashi's view. The *Maggid Mishneh* asserts that the Rambam and Rabbenu Tam are correct, and he records that common practice follows their lenient ruling. The *Rishonim* who side with Rabbenu Tam and the Rambam include the Rosh, Ramban, Rashba, Ran, Meiri, Ra'avya, Ri, Rabbenu Simḥa, *Ohr Zarua,* and Roke'aḥ.

ASHKENAZIC AND SEPHARDIC PRACTICE

Rav Yosef Karo (*Shulḥan Aruch, Oraḥ Ḥayim* 462:1–4) rules in accordance with the lenient ruling of the Rambam and Rabbenu Tam. The Rama presents a compromise approach to this issue, writing that Ashkenazim refrain from eating matza that was kneaded with fruit juice unless they are elderly or sick. The Vilna Gaon (*Bi'ur HaGra* 462:4, s.v. *ub'medinot*) explains that *l'chatḥila* (ab initio), Ashkenazim seek to accommodate Rashi's stringent view, and they are also concerned that water might have unknowingly been added to the fruit juice.

The *Aruch HaShulḥan* (*Oraḥ Ḥayim* 462:5) condemns those Ashkenazim who fail to abide by the stringent custom. However, Sephardim – as noted by two great Sephardic authorities, the *Peri Ḥadash* (*Oraḥ Ḥayim* 462) and the *Ḥida* (*Birkei Yosef* 462:7) – follow Rav Yosef Karo's codification of the majority view of the *Rishonim*.

Rav Ovadia Yosef (*Teshuvot Yeḥaveh Da'at* 1:10) writes that Ashkenazim are permitted to give matza that was kneaded with fruit juice to children. Although the Rama does not specifically mention children as an exception to the prohibition, elsewhere (*Oraḥ Ḥayim* 276:1, 328:17) he writes that children are considered to have the status of sick individuals. Twentieth-century authorities dispute until what age a child has this status (see *Nishmat Avraham* 1:197), with opinions ranging from age 3 to age 9. Dr. Abraham S. Abraham (ibid.) may be correct in suggesting that it is more appropriate to assess the health and maturity of the individual child, rather than assign a specific age for all children. A proof to this is the fact that the Rama does not mention a specific age.[1]

LIFNEI IVER CONSIDERATIONS

Providing a forbidden item violates the Torah prohibition of "*lifnei iver lo titen michshol*," placing a stumbling block before the blind (*Vayikra* 19:14). Accordingly, Rav Ovadia Yosef rules (*Teshuvot Yeḥaveh Da'at* 1:10) that it is forbidden for Sephardim to serve egg matza to Ashkenazim on Pesaḥ, even though Sephardim regard egg matza as permissible.

A precedent for this approach is found in the *mishna* (*Yevamot* 1:4) that states that men and women from the families of Bet Hillel and Bet Shammai used to marry each other, despite the fact that Bet Hillel and Bet

1. Rav Ike Sultan reports that Rav Hershel Schachter does not permit giving egg matza to children under normal circumstances. Rav Schachter argues that the Rama does not consider even very young children to be chronically ill. A child is regarded as a *ḥoleh she'en bo sakana* (an ill individual) only if he needs something for his health and otherwise would not function normally, which might even entail something as simple as being grumpy and not playing as usual. Rav Ovadia disagrees and considers every young child to be a chronic *ḥoleh she'en bo sakana* with regard to egg matza and in other areas of Halacha (such as the time necessary for a young child to wait between meat and milk).

Shammai had different standards regarding *mamzerut*. They were not concerned that a prospective mate was a *mamzer* because they informed each other if a prospective mate would be considered a *mamzer* according to the other's standards. Accordingly, the Rama (*Yoreh De'ah* 119:7) teaches that a host must inform his guest that a food item is forbidden to the guest by his standards, even though the host abides by the lenient standard.

Thus, Rav Ovadia rules (*Teshuvot Yeḥaveh Da'at* 4:53) that one may not serve products whose *kashrut* depends on the *Heter Mechira* (the sale of Israeli farmland to a non-Jew to avoid *shemitta* restrictions) if his guests do not subscribe to the *Heter Mechira*. Similarly, one should not serve milk that was not Rabbinically supervised to someone who subscribes to the strict opinion regarding *ḥalav Yisrael*.

Rav Ovadia notes that one who does not obey these rulings violates the prohibition of *lifnei iver*. Rashi (*Vayikra* 19:14) explains that the *pasuk* prohibits offering someone bad advice, and presenting someone with an item that is forbidden to him by his standards falls into the category of giving bad advice. This is similar to the *Minḥat Ḥinuch*'s assertion (*mitzva* 232) that one violates a Torah prohibition of *lifnei iver* if he facilitates the violation of a Rabbinic prohibition through his bad advice.

Hence, *kashrut* organizations print on the boxes of egg matza that Ashkenazim are forbidden to eat this product unless they are old or infirm, and bakery owners must prominently display signs that indicate which products are forbidden to Ashkenazim.[2]

CONCLUSION

The strength and vitality of *Klal Yisrael* rests upon respecting and revering the diverse halachic practices of the various segments of the Jewish community. Thus, a Sephardic Jew should not serve egg matza to an Ashkenazic Jew under ordinary circumstances.

2. What should one do if he sees an Ashkenazic Jew purchase egg matza on Pesaḥ? Rav Ovadia rules that one may attribute (*toleh*) the purchase of egg matza to a permitted purpose, such as feeding it to a sick or older individual. A precedent may be found in the *mishna* (*Shevi'it* 5:8) that teaches that one may sell an ox in the *shemitta* year to a farmer who is lax in his observance of *shemitta*. The *mishna* permits one to be *toleh* that the farmer is purchasing the ox for a permitted purpose, such as for slaughtering.

Chapter 52

Soft Matza for Sephardim and for Ashkenazim

Soft matza – which is very different from the typical Ashkenazic cracker-like matza – is popular among Yemenite and many Sephardic Jews on Pesaḥ. May Ashkenazim eat soft matza on Pesaḥ? Although my beloved Rav, Rav Hershel Schachter, rules that it is permissible for Ashkenazic Jews to use soft matza on Pesaḥ,[1] Rav Shlomo Zalman Auerbach did not agree (*Halichot Shlomo* 9, p. 281, n. 80; *Mikra'ei Kodesh* [Harari], *Halichot Leil HaSeder*, p. 286).

Many people have asked me if Ashkenazic Jews may rely on Rav Schachter's ruling. Below is the evolution of my thoughts on this matter.

THE RAMA'S RULING

I was initially very surprised to hear of Rav Schachter's ruling. After all, the Rama (*Oraḥ Ḥayim* 460:4) writes that matza should be made only as "*rekikin*," which seems to imply that they should be thin *matzot*, like the ubiquitous cracker- like matza with which we are familiar.

1. Rav Shlomo Aviner (*Teshuvot She'elat Shlomo* 4:111) rules in accordance with Rav Schachter.

EVIDENCE FOR RAV SCHACHTER'S APPROACH

However, this is not the entire story. The *Ba'er Hetev* (*Oraḥ Ḥayim* 460:8) comments on this Rama that "the custom is to make matza the thickness of a *tefaḥ* (a handbreadth, approximately 3–4 inches)." Moreover, the *Mishna Berura* (486:3) writes of soft and sponge-like matza without expressing any reservations whatsoever regarding its acceptability for Pesaḥ. This seems to constitute incontrovertible evidence to Rav Schachter's ruling! The fact that the *Shulḥan Aruch HaRav* (486:2) and *Aruch HaShulḥan* (*Oraḥ Ḥayim* 460:2) make similar statements provides further compelling evidence.

PRACTICAL CONCERNS REGARDING SOFT MATZA

My enthusiasm, however, was greatly diminished after reading an article by written by my friends Dr. Ari Greenspan and Rav Dr. Ari Zivotofsky:

> With the way that soft matza is made today, there is a very real concern of *ḥametz*. We have visited many matza factories, and in some of the soft matza bakeries, we saw what appears to us to be not fully baked dough, as opposed to fully baked soft bread. The *Shulḥan Aruch HaRav* (460:10) says that thick *matzot* are kosher – in theory. But one must inspect them carefully to ascertain that they are truly baked through the entire thickness. His admonition should be taken very seriously. Note that soft matza is often made much faster than hard matza..... Concern relates to the degree to which the interior of the matza is baked.
>
> It is disconcerting that the modern soft *matzot* are baked mimicking the process used for Ashkenazi *matzot* during the last 150 years. However, the ovens of soft matza were different years ago, and certainly not as hot as modern matza ovens, where a hand matza is often baked within 30 seconds. Such hot furnaces will quickly heat the outside of the thick matza, making it look well-baked, but not yet baking the inside. Removing it from the oven will yield a soft matza looking well-done outside, yet possibly *ḥametz* on the inside. This is not a new concern; the *Ḥatam Sofer* reported (*Teshuvot, Oraḥ Ḥayim* 121) that thick matza does not bake well. Soft is not what should be looked for; rather, fully-baked is required.[2]

---

2. "The Halachic Acceptability of Soft Matzah," *Journal of Halacha and Contemporary Society* (Spring 2014), pp. 115–116.

RAV ASHER WEISS' RESERVATIONS

Rav Asher Weiss similarly writes (*Haggada Minḥat Asher*, 5764, *siman* 15, p. 322) that although the basic *halacha* is that soft matza is permissible, he is concerned that we are not experts in making them soft and thick and guarding from becoming *ḥametz*. He suggests that it is possible that this is the concern that led to Ashkenazic *matzot* being so thin and hard. Furthermore, Rav Weiss writes that he is wary of innovation, and such matters fall under the rubric of "do not forsake the Torah of your mother" (*Mishlei* 1:8). Certainly on Pesaḥ, it is worthwhile to accept stringencies. Rav Dov Lior and Rav Yaakov Ariel agree with this conclusion.[3]

CONCLUSION

Despite the abundant love and respect I have for Rav Schachter, the practical concerns in this case appear to outweigh the persuasive theoretical support Rav Schachter draws from the *Mishna Berura, Shulḥan Aruch HaRav,* and *Aruch HaShulḥan.* In light of the fact that all Jews, and especially Ashkenazim, have adopted many stringencies regarding Pesaḥ, I am very hesitant to permit soft matza for Ashkenazim.

Rav Shlomo Zalman Auerbach, Rav Asher Weiss, Rav Lior, and Rav Ariel are not in general inclined to stringency and do not hesitate to issue a lenient ruling if it is appropriate to do so. The fact that all these prominent *posekim* express concern regarding soft matza gives one serious pause and motivates refraining from recommending soft matza to Ashkenazic Jews.

A possible exception would be if the soft matza were to be created in strict conformity to the Sephardic and Yemenite traditions and properly supervised by Torah scholars with the requisite knowledge, expertise, and experience to make sure that there is not even a remote chance of the soft matza being *ḥametz.*[4]

---

3. See https://www.yeshiva.org.il/ask/35098 and https://www.yeshiva.org.il/ask/46075.

4. Rav Shmuel Khoshkerman shares the concern for *ḥimutz*. He therefore does not permit soft matza for Sephardic Jews unless there is a high grade *hashgaḥa* ensuring that there is no *ḥimutz* concern.
   Rav Ovadia Yosef was comfortable with using soft matza at the *seder*, as noted by his grandson, Rav Yaakov Sasson (http://halachayomit.co.il/he/default.

aspx?HalachaID=4975), and the Badatz Bet Yosef *kashrut* agency, founded by Rav Ovadia, gives *hashgaḥa* on soft matza for Pesaḥ use. In fact, Rav Sasson wrote to me that Rav Ovadia himself ate soft *matzot* on Pesaḥ. He explains that the Sephardic tradition has been to use soft *matza* for Pesaḥ and it is acceptable even *lamehadrin* (for those who seek the highest *kashrut* standards) if it is baked in proper accordance with Halacha. Rav Mordechai Eliyahu is cited by his son Rav Shmuel as also permitting soft *matzot* for Pesaḥ.

Chapter 53

Glass Utensils

Among the other halachic differences between Ashkenazic and Sephardic practice on Pesaḥ that we have outlined in previous chapters, there is a discrepancy between the two communities regarding whether the same glass utensils may be used both for Pesaḥ and year round. There might also be a difference between Ashkenazim and Sephardim as to whether a glass utensil may be used for both milk and meat. We will survey the many opinions regarding these issues, emphasize the difference between Sephardim and Ashkenazim in this regard, and attempt to outline the halachic consensus.[1]

SHULḤAN ARUCH VS. RAMA

Rav Yosef Karo (*Shulḥan Aruch, Oraḥ Ḥayim* 451:26) rules that a glass utensil does not absorb taste, even if hot food was placed in it. A glass utensil used year round may therefore be used on Pesaḥ as well, with no need to *kasher* it (make it halachically permissible through the application of heat).

The fact that Rav Karo's lenient ruling appears specifically in the context of the laws of Pesaḥ is especially significant, in light of the overall

1. For a fuller review of the background in the *gemara* and *Rishonim* regarding this issue, see https://www.koltorah.org/halachah/kashering-glass-by-rabbi-chaim-jachter.

tendency of halachic decisors to rule more stringently regarding Pesaḥ issues than in other halachic contexts. The *Peri Ḥadash*, a premier Sephardic authority, echoes Rav Karo's view and writes: "It is correct, and this is our accepted practice." The *S'dei Ḥemed* (5:29) and Rav Ovadia Yosef (*Teshuvot Yeḥaveh Da'at* 1:6) write that common practice among Sephardim is to follow Rav Karo's ruling even if hot food was placed in a glass utensil and even for Pesaḥ use.[2] *Darké Abotenou* (2:11) confirms that this is also the practice of Moroccan, Tunisian, and Algerian Jews.[3]

The Rama, however, comments on the *Shulḥan Aruch*'s ruling: "There are those who are strict and maintain that glass utensils may not even be koshered, and this is the custom in Germany and the [Eastern European] lands." The Vilna Gaon (*Bi'ur HaGra, Oraḥ Ḥayim* 451:50), *Mishna Berura* (451:154), and *Aruch HaShulḥan* (*Oraḥ Ḥayim* 451:50) explain that the Rama is following the opinion of the *Rishonim* who rule that glass utensils have the status of earthenware in this context; it is impossible to *kasher* them.

However, Rav Ovadia Yosef (*Teshuvot Yabia Omer* 4: *Yoreh De'ah* 5:31; *Teshuvot Yeḥaveh Da'at* 1:6) adopts the approach of Rav Yaakov Emden (*Mor U'Ketzia* 451), who explains that the Rama follows the opinion of the Ra'ah cited by the Ritva – that in principle, glass, like metal, may be koshered, but in practice we forbid doing so due to the fact glass is delicate and we possibly may not *kasher* it properly. For example, to prevent damage to the utensil, we may not heat the water sufficiently or we may not cover the entire utensil with boiling water. The Ra'ah therefore rules

2. Rav Shlomo Kluger (*Teshuvot Tuv Taam V'Da'at* 3:2:25) and Maharam Shick (*Teshuvot Yoreh De'ah* 141) write that Rav Karo's ruling does not apply if a glass utensil absorbed *ḥametz* via fire, but both the *S'dei Ḥemed* and Rav Ovadia Yosef reject this interpretation of Rav Karo's ruling.
3. The *Yalkut Yosef* (*Oraḥ Ḥayim* 451:39) notes that some Sephardic communities outside of Israel (such as Iraqi Jews) adopt a strict approach with regard to use of glass on Pesaḥ. Mr. Jack Varon of Congregation Shaarei Orah, the Sephardic Congregation of Teaneck, confirms that this is the custom of the Turkish Jewish community in Seattle, Washington. The *Yalkut Yosef* rules that when such Jews move to Israel, they may follow the ruling of Rav Karo, the *Mara D'Atra* (halachic authority) of *Eretz Yisrael*. One wonders what Rav Ovadia would rule regarding whether Iraqi Jews who moved to Israel but later moved to North America should resume the strict practice their grandparents observed in Iraq.

that we may not *kasher* glass, lest we believe we have koshered it properly, when in fact we have not.[4]

OTHER PROHIBITIONS

The Rama records his stringent ruling concerning glass in the context of the laws of Pesaḥ, and some *Aḥaronim* (*Kenesset HaGedola, Yoreh De'ah* 121; *Kehal Yehuda, Yoreh De'ah* 121; *Zera Emet* 2: *Yoreh De'ah* 43) maintain that this is because the Rama's ruling applies exclusively to Pesaḥ. These authorities point out that halachic authorities generally rule more stringently on Pesaḥ issues relative to most other areas of Halacha. They also believe that this distinction may be inferred from the Rama's comments elsewhere. In the laws of non-kosher wine (*Yoreh De'ah* 135:8), the *Shulḥan Aruch* rules that glass utensils used for storing non-Jewish wine may be used to store kosher wine (after suitable cleaning), with no need for *kashering*, and the Rama makes no comment. These authorities interpret the Rama's silence as signaling agreement with the ruling that glass is not considered to absorb taste in halachic contexts other than that of Pesaḥ.

The *Magen Avraham* (451:49) disagrees. He writes that Rama's silence in the context of the laws of wine should be understood as the exception, rather than the rule, since drinking non-Jewish wine is one of the relatively less stringent Rabbinic prohibitions. Thus, in regard to *kashrut* issues other than those of wine, the Rama would rule that glass utensils cannot be koshered. This also appears to be the opinion of *Taz* (*Oraḥ Ḥayim* 87:2).

The *Aruch HaShulḥan* (*Oraḥ Ḥayim* 451:50) distinguishes, in the context of *Hilchot Pesaḥ*, between utensils that have absorbed hot food and those that have absorbed only cold. The *Aruch HaShulḥan* rules leniently regarding "cold absorption" in the case of glass, even regarding Pesaḥ. According to this approach, one could argue that the Rama did not comment on the *Shulḥan Aruch*'s ruling in the laws of wine because the *Shulḥan Aruch* was not discussing glass that absorbed hot non-kosher food. However, the *Mishna Berura* (451:156) rules regarding Pesaḥ that one may not *kasher* glass even if it absorbed only cold non-kosher food, except for exceptional circumstances.

---

4. Rav Ovadia follows the approach of Rav Yehuda Leib Graubart (*Teshuvot Ḥavalim B'Ni'imim* 4:6) in his ruling for Ashkenazim.

CONTEMPORARY *POSEKIM*

It is generally accepted that Sephardim follow Rav Karo's ruling that glass does not absorb taste from even hot food, and it thus need not be koshered even for use on Pesaḥ. Similarly, it is generally accepted that Ashkenazim do not *kasher* glass for Pesaḥ, save perhaps for exceptional circumstances. However, there is an active debate regarding whether one may *kasher* glass utensils for use other than for Pesaḥ.

Rav Eliezer Waldenberg (*Teshuvot Tzitz Eliezer* 9:26) cites Rav Yehudah Leib Zirelson, who maintains that the accepted Ashkenazic practice is never to permit glass utensils to be koshered. This is also the opinion of Rav Shmuel Wosner (*Teshuvot Shevet HaLevi, Yoreh De'ah* 1:43). On the other hand, Rav Aharon Felder (*Ohalei Yeshurun*, p. 87 n. 82) cites Rav Moshe Feinstein, who accepts the opinion that glass utensils do not absorb even hot foods and need not be koshered for non-Pesaḥ use. The *Yalkut Yosef* (*Oraḥ Ḥayim* 451:39) concurs and applies this ruling for Ashkenazic Jews.

Many Ashkenazic authorities adopt a compromise position regarding non-Pesaḥ use. They rule that glass absorbs taste from hot foods, but that it may be koshered. Proponents of this view include Rav Waldenberg (*Teshuvot Tzitz Eliezer* 6:21), Rav Ovadia Yosef (*Teshuvot Yeḥaveh Da'at* 1:6, regarding Ashkenazim), Rav Yeḥiel Yaakov Weinberg (*Teshuvot Seredei Esh* 2:36), and Rav Asher Weiss (*Teshuvot Minḥat Yitzḥak* 1:86). This approach is a compromise between the opinions that rule that glass may not be koshered and those who rule that glass need not be koshered because it does not absorb taste.

Rav Menachem Genack, Rabbinic Administrator of the Kashrut Division of the Union of Orthodox Jewish Congregations of America, reports[5] that the OU inquired of Rav Moshe Feinstein whether one may wash glass utensils in a non-kosher dishwasher, and Rav Feinstein ruled that one is permitted to do so, reflecting his view that glass is considered nonporous in non-Pesaḥ contexts.[6]

5. Rav Genack mentioned this in a Shiur he delivered at Yeshiva University in 1988.
6. When the OU posed this question to Rav Yosef Dov Soloveitchik, however, Rav Soloveitchik ruled that it is forbidden to do so. Rav Genack related this at a lecture for rabbinical students at Yeshiva University in 1989.
   A similar question may be raised regarding whether one may wash dairy glass utensils in a meat dishwasher and vice versa.

Rav Hershel Schachter rules that glass may be koshered, but he requires it to be koshered three times, in accordance with the opinion of the *Ba'al HaIttur* (*Sha'ar Hechsher HaBasar*) that earthenware may be rendered kosher by placing it in boiling water three times.[7] In addition, one should not use glass utensils for both meat and milk if either type of food is hot.[8]

Accordingly, it appears that the majority of the outstanding contemporary authorities rule for Ashkenazic Jews that glass is not considered to be porous, like earthenware, and it may be koshered for non-Pesaḥ use.

PYREX AND DURALEX UTENSILS

Rav Waldenberg (*Teshuvot Tzitz Eliezer* 9:26) and Rav Ovadia Yosef (*Teshuvot Yabia Omer* 4: *Yoreh De'ah* 41; *Teshuvot Yeḥaveh Da'at* 1:6) adopt opposing views regarding Pyrex and Duralex utensils, which are "glass-like." Rav Ovadia permits Sephardic Jews to use these products for both meat and milk after merely cleaning the items between uses. Rav Waldenberg, however, believes that the *Shulḥan Aruch*'s lenient ruling regarding glass does not apply to Pyrex and Duralex dishes, since these materials differ significantly from conventional glass. We may not extend the *Shulḥan Aruch*'s ruling to other materials, despite their great similarity to conventional glass.

On the other hand, Rav Waldenberg accepts the Ra'ah's interpretation of the Rama's strict ruling, maintaining that glass can be koshered in theory but not in practice. Accordingly, he rules that the Rama's strict ruling is limited to conventional glass, which may break when placed in exceedingly hot water. Since Pyrex and Duralex are designed to withstand heat and boiling water, the Rama's reasoning would permit utensils made of these materials to be koshered even for Pesaḥ.[9] Recall, however, that the Vilna

7. Although the *Ba'al HaIttur*'s opinion is not accepted as normative halachic practice, it is used as a consideration in rendering halachic opinions; see *Aruch HaShulḥan, Yoreh De'ah* 121:26–27; *Teshuvot Melamed LeHo'il* 2:52; and *Teshuvot Igrot Moshe* 3:26–29. Accordingly, Rav Schachter wishes to use the opinion of the *Ba'al HaIttur* as a consideration ("*s'nif l'hakel*") to rule that one may *kasher* glass.
8. Halacha's standard for determining whether something is hot is whether it is *yad soledet bo*, the temperature at which one's hand withdraws immediately for fear of being burned. Contemporary equivalents range from 110°F to 120°F; see Rav Shlomo Zalman Auerbach, *Teshuvot Minḥat Shlomo* 91:8, and Rav Shimon Eider, *Halachos of Shabbos*, p.243 n.19.
9. Rav Yitzḥak Weisz (*Teshuvot Minḥat Yitzḥak* 1:86) also permits Pyrex and Duralex to be koshered for non-Pesaḥ use, but he does not permit their use without kashering.

Gaon, *Mishna Berura*, and *Aruch HaShulḥan* disagree with this interpretation of the Rama, and would therefore not accept this conclusion.

Interestingly, at the conclusion of his responsum, Rav Waldenberg cites Rav Zvi Pesaḥ Frank's ruling that Pyrex may be koshered even for Pesaḥ if it is koshered three times.[10]

Although Rav Waldenberg maintains that Pyrex and Duralex can be koshered, both he and Rav Ovadia would agree that Ashkenazim should not use Pyrex and Duralex utensils for both meat and milk, since most Ashkenazic authorities maintain that glass does absorb taste, and we do not have reason to view Pyrex and Duralex as exceptional.[11]

CORELLE DISHES

The Star-K *kashrut* agency – reflecting the views of its halachic authority, Rav Moshe Heinemann – rules that Corelle has the status of glass.[12] This opens the possibility for Sephardic Jews to use Corelle dishes for both meat and milk. However, Rav Shmuel Khoshkerman feels that even Sephardim must be concerned for the possibility that Corelle has the status of *klei ḥeres* (earthenware), and thus it should not be used for both milk and meat. This also means that *hagala* (kashering via hot water) may not be performed on

10. Notably, Rav Waldenberg does not write that Rav Frank limits his ruling to instances of great need. Although Rav Waldenberg does not present Rav Frank's reasoning, we may suggest that it is based in a combination of four considerations: 1) The authorities who rule that glass is nonporous; 2) Rav Ovadia's reasoning regarding Pyrex; 3) the opinion of the Ra'ah; and 4) the opinion of the *Ba'al HaIttur* regarding kashering earthenware.
11. Rav Aharon Felder (*Ohalei Yeshurun* 1:73–74) cites Rav Moshe Feinstein as ruling that Pyrex and Duralex share the same halachic status as glass and therefore essentially need not be koshered if they came into contact with hot non-kosher food. However, Rav Felder rules that the same Pyrex and Duralex dishes may not be used for both meat and milk. He also recommends not using Pyrex and Duralex dishes for twenty-four hours after they contact non-kosher food.
12. The OU seems to hold this position as well; see https://oukosher.org/blog/kosher-professionals/lo-basi-ella-lorer-glass. The CRC, however, appears to treat Corelle as *safek ḥeres* and *safek zechuchit* (glass); see http://www.crcweb.org/Tevillas%20Keilim%20and%20Hechsher%20Keilim%20(2017–Jan).pdf.

    In an e-mail correspondence, Rav Mordechai Lebhar writes that the research varies regarding the glass content of Corelle, making this question a challenging one to resolve. A representative of the Orthodox Union wrote to me that "Corelle dishes and bowls are made of glass. However, Corelle mugs are ceramic."

these dishes. On the other hand, since the issue remains uncertain, *tevilat keilim* without a *beracha* is required for such *keilim.*[13]

Rav Moshe Feinstein is cited by his renowned *talmid* Rav Aharon Felder as adopting the position that Corelle is regarded as *safek ḥeres* and *safek zechuchit,* uncertain as to whether it is earthenware or glass (*Ohalei Yeshurun* 1:87). Rav Moshe is also cited as ruling that Corelle may be rendered kosher in case of great need if it has not been used for a minimum of twenty-four hours. In such a case, only a Rabbinic prohibition is involved, and in case of great need one may invoke the principle of *safek d'Rabbanan l'hakel.*

CONCLUSION

Most Sephardic Jews follow the ruling of the *Shulḥan Aruch* that glass utensils do not absorb taste. They follow this ruling even regarding Pesaḥ, and according to Rav Ovadia Yosef, regarding Pyrex and Duralex utensils as well, and they therefore may use the same glass utensils on Pesaḥ as during the year. Ashkenazic Jews, however, do not *kasher* glass utensils for Pesaḥ. The consensus view permits Ashkenazic Jews to *kasher* glass utensils for non-Pesaḥ use.[14] Ashkenazim may *kasher* Pyrex and Duralex for non-Pesaḥ use and may *kasher* such products even for Pesaḥ use if it is done three times, in accordance with the ruling of Rav Tzvi Pesaḥ Frank.

Sephardic Jews who host Ashkenazic Jews for Pesaḥ should not serve Ashkenazic Jews on glass utensils that were used for hot *ḥametz.* Rav Mordechai Djavaheri reports, however, that Rav Hershel Schachter ruled for his family that on occasions other than Pesaḥ, they may serve Ashkenazic Jews on *eno ben yomo* (not used within twenty-four hours) glass dishes used for both milk and meat.[15]

13. See, however, the *Halacha Yomit* written by Rav Ovadia's grandson Rav Yaakov Sasson, who writes that Corelle does have the same status as glass: http://halachayomit.co.il/en/default.aspx?HalachaID=4337.
14. There are various practices among Ashkenazic Jews as to whether they use the same glass drinking glasses (never used for hot drinks) for both meat and milk.
15. The same would apply to Pyrex and Duralex.

Chapter 54

Sephardic Jews Hosting Ashkenazim on Pesaḥ: A Summary

In the course of the last four chapters, we have outlined a number of concerns that an Ashkenazic Jew would have upon eating at a Sephardic home on Pesaḥ. We have concluded that the Sephardic host should refrain from serving Ashkenazic guests *kitniyot* (and possibly avoid food cooked in *kitniyot* dishes), egg matza, and soft matza, and he should not prepare or serve his Ashkenazic guest Pesaḥ food on glass that once was used for *ḥametz.*

There are two more significant discrepancies between Sephardic and Ashkenazic standards that, while relatively rare in application, are worth bearing in mind when hosting members of the different community.

The first issue regards methodology of *kashering.* In general, one *kashers* a utensil using a method that parallels its use. For example, a pot used for cooking liquids is rendered kosher through *hagala,* immersion in boiling water, whereas a roasting pan used on a fire requires a more intense form of *kashering* – *libun,* heating until glowing. What if a pan is used mostly for liquids and only occasionally for roasting over a fire?

According to the *Shulḥan Aruch* (*Oraḥ Ḥayim* 451:6), one must evaluate how the item is usually used. If it is usually used for liquids, *hagala* is sufficient, even though the utensil is occasionally used directly with fire. The Rama, however, requires *libun* even if the item was used over fire only once. The same dispute relates to vessels that are used mostly for cold foods but occasionally for hot foods. The *Shulḥan Aruch* requires that such a utensil merely be rinsed in cold water, whereas the Rama requires *hagala*.

Ashkenazim are forbidden from eating in a home in which the vessels have not been koshered according to the Rama's standards. A Sephardic Jew hosting Ashkenazim for Pesaḥ should bear this in mind and make sure to *kasher* his home in accordance with the stricter Ashkenazic standard in this regard, or refrain from preparing or serving Ashkenazim food using utensils that were koshered according to the more lenient Sephardic standard.

The second issue relates to the applicability of the principle of *noten ta'am l'fgam* on Pesaḥ. During the year, kosher food cooked in a non-kosher vessel that has not been used in twenty-four hours (*eno ben yomo*) may be eaten, since the taste emitted by the utensil is rancid and inedible – *noten ta'am l'fgam*. The *Rishonim* debate whether this *halacha* applies to food cooked on Pesaḥ in a pot that was previously used for *ḥametz*. The *Shulḥan Aruch* is lenient, but the Rama is stringent (*Oraḥ Ḥayim* 447:10). Thus, a Sephardic host should not serve an Ashkenazic guest food that was accidentally cooked on Pesaḥ in an *eno ben yomo* year-round utensil.

Chapter 55

Hallel During *Arvit* of the First Night of Pesaḥ

The practice of reciting *Hallel* in the *bet kenesset* after *Arvit* on the first night of Pesaḥ (and the second night for those outside of Eretz Yisrael) is a halachic rarity. The Rama (*Oraḥ Ḥayim* 487:4) records the widespread Ashkenazic *minhag* of not reciting *Hallel* in the *bet kenesset,* yet many Ashkenazic *batei kenesset* no longer follow this practice, but instead recite the *Hallel,* following the Sephardic practice. In order to understand this change, we must trace the *minhag* from its source until current developments.

SHULḤAN ARUCH VS. RAMA

Maran Rav Yosef Karo records the practice to recite *Hallel b'tzibur* (with the community in the *bet kenesset*) with a *beracha* on the first night of Pesaḥ (as well as the second night in the Diaspora). The almost universal Sephardic practice is to recite this *Hallel* with a *beracha,* as noted by Rav Ovadia Yosef (*Teshuvot Yeḥaveh Da'at* 5:34).[1] The Rama, however, insists that the Ashkenazic practice is not to say *Hallel* in the synagogue "at all."

1. Many Yemenite Jews do not recite a *beracha* when reciting this *Hallel,* since the Rambam makes no mention of this *Hallel,* as noted below.

The practice of reciting *Hallel* in the *bet kenesset* on the first night of Pesaḥ has an impressive pedigree. Its sources are the *Talmud Yerushalmi* (*Sukka* 4:5), *Tosefta* (*Sukka* 3:2), and *Masechet Soferim* (20:9). Why, then, does the Rama object to this practice? The answer is that the Talmud Bavli, the most authoritative Talmudic source, makes no mention of this practice! In fact, the Rambam makes no mention of this practice either. Thus, although there is a strong basis for reciting *Hallel* in the *bet kenesset* on the first night of Pesaḥ, there is also a strong basis for not reciting it at that time.

THE REASON FOR THE CHANGE IN PRACTICE OF MANY ASHKENAZIC CONGREGATIONS

The first major chink in the armor of the Ashkenazic custom resulted from the Ari z"l's enthusiastic endorsement of reciting *Hallel* on the first night of Pesaḥ, in great measure due to its great significance according to the Kabbala (as cited in the *Ba'er Hetev, Oraḥ Ḥayim* 487:9). This practice was subsequently adopted by Ḥassidim who pray Nusaḥ Sephard (as noted by the *Mishna Berura* 487:16), which is heavily influenced by the views of the Ari z"l.

The second major step was the Vilna Gaon's endorsement of the ruling of the *Shulḥan Aruch* (*Bi'ur HaGra, Oraḥ Ḥayim* 671:7) to recite a *beracha* on the *Hallel* recited in the *bet kenesset* on the first night of Pesaḥ. This view was adopted by Rav Ḥayim Soloveitchik (who often followed in the footsteps of the Vilna Gaon), as reported by his grandson, Rav Yosef Dov Soloveitchik (*Shiurim L'Zecher Abba Mari Z"l* 1:3). Rav Ḥayim brought evidence for the practice from a *pasuk* in *Yeshayahu* (30:29 with Rashi): "*Hashir yihyeh lachem k'lel hitkadesh ḥag,*" "You will ring out in song as on the first evening of the festival," which indicates that *Hallel* is recited on the first night of Pesaḥ.[2]

2. *Yeshayahu* 30 describes the *navi*'s prediction of the failure of the Assyrian siege of Yerushalayim (described at length in *Melachim II* 18 and 19). *Ḥazal* (cited by Rashi, *Melachim II* 20:1, s.v. *ḥala Ḥizkiya*, and Radak, *Melachim II* 19:35, s.v. *vayehi balayla hahu*) assert that the great catastrophe that befell the Assyrians occurred on the first night of Pesaḥ. Yeshayahu promises that the Jewish People will ring out in song in response to their salvation, "*k'lel hitkadesh ḥag.*" This clearly presumes that *Hallel* is recited on the night of Pesaḥ, and it also seems that Yeshayahu refers to a communal recitation of *Hallel*—note that the word "*lachem*" is in the plural—and not the *Hallel* recited at a family's *seder*.

Rav Yosef Dov Soloveitchik, in turn, instructed his Rabbinical students at Yeshiva University to introduce the recital of *Hallel* on the first night of Pesaḥ in their synagogues, if it was possible for them to do so (as reported by Rav Hershel Schachter, *Nefesh HaRav* [5754], pp. 183–184). Rav Soloveitchik's students often followed through on this recommendation. For example, Rav Yosef Adler has guided Congregation Rinat Yisrael in Teaneck, New Jersey to follow this practice. Indeed, Rav Soloveitchik's call has motivated dozens of congregations throughout North America to adopt the practice of reciting this *Hallel*.

Similarly, the *Yalkut Yosef* (*Oraḥ Ḥayim* 487:6) writes: "Even in those communities that have not yet adopted the practice to recite *Hallel* at *Arvit* on the first night of Pesaḥ, it is worthy and proper for them to accept this precious practice." Indeed, many Ashkenazim happily embrace this practice, since intuitively it feels proper to mark the first night of Pesaḥ with a unique outburst of song and gratitude to *Hashem*.

In Eretz Yisrael, it has become accepted for almost all congregations to recite *Hallel* in the *bet kenesset* on the first night of Pesaḥ. As we have noted in other contexts, whenever the practice of Sephardic Jews, Ḥassidic Jews, and the Vilna Gaon converges, this has emerged as the almost universally accepted practice in Israel, as at the time when the Jewish community in Eretz Yisrael began growing in the early nineteenth century, the three major groups of Jews there were Sephardim, Ḥassidim, and followers of the Vilna Gaon.[3] These three groups were in the right place at the right time to set the halachic tone for the great influx of Jews who arrived over the course of the following two centuries.

CONCLUSION

It is the universal Sephardic practice to recite *Hallel* in the *bet kenesset* on the first night of Pesaḥ. Although the Rama objected to this practice, most Ashkenazic Jews today have adopted the Sephardic practice due to the influence of the Ari z"l, the Vilna Ga'on, Rav Ḥayim Soloveitchik, Rav Yosef Dov Soloveitchik, and the *minhag* of Eretz Yisrael. With Israel emerging as the place of residence of the majority of world Jewry, it seems that the

3. See our discussions of the nearly universal practice in Israel to refrain from wearing *tefillin* on *Ḥol HaMo'ed* and the accepted practice in Israel to recite *morid hatal* from Pesaḥ to Sukkot.

halachic practices accepted there will continue to impact Jews throughout the world, leaving those who do not recite *Hallel* in the synagogue on the first night of Pesaḥ as a distinct minority. This is an interesting case, in which the Ashkenazic community has, for the most part, gradually adopted the Sephardic custom!

WOMEN AND THE *HALLEL* OF THE FIRST NIGHT OF PESAḤ

Rav Ovadia Yosef (op. cit.) surprisingly rules that women are also obligated to recite the *Hallel* of the night of Pesaḥ with a *beracha,* even if they do not attend services in the synagogue. This ruling is surprising for many reasons, including the fact that Rav Ovadia ruled that women should not recite a *beracha* on a variety of occasions, including on positive time-bound *mitzvot* such as *lulav* and *sukka.*[4]

Rav Ovadia assumes that the *Hallel* recited in the *bet kenesset* on the first night of Pesaḥ is an expression of thanksgiving for *yetziat Mitzrayim.* As such, since women were also part of the miracle ("*af hen hayu b'oto hanes*"), they are also included in the obligation to recite *Hallel* on the first night of Pesaḥ, even if they are not present in the *bet kenesset.*

Common practice, however, does not appear to accord with Rav Ovadia's ruling. Rav Moshe Sternbuch (*Mo'adim U'Zemanim* 7:179) explicitly disagrees, writing that this *Hallel* is meant to be recited only in the *bet kenesset.* The Vilna Gaon (*Oraḥ Ḥayim* 487:4, 671:7) unambiguously states that this *Hallel* is reserved for the *bet kenesset,* comparing it to the special lighting of the Ḥanukka candles in the synagogue.

Rav Ovadia marshals an impressive list of *posekim* who maintain that the *Hallel* on the first night of Pesaḥ should be recited even if the individual has not attended *bet kenesset.* These include the *Ḥida* (*Birkei Yosef, Oraḥ Ḥayim* 487:8), Rav Yeḥezkel Landau (as cited in *Teshuvot Teshuvah Me'Ahava* 1:90), and Rav Ḥayim Palagi (*Ruaḥ Ḥayim* 487:4).

However, at least two significant Sephardic *posekim,* Rav Yehudah Ayash (*Teshuvot Bet Yehuda* 2:33) and Rav Yosef Yedid HaLevi (*Teshuvot Yemei Yosef* 2: *Oraḥ Ḥayim* 23), disagree and limit the recital of this *Hallel* to a communal recitation in the synagogue. Indeed, the language of the *Shulḥan Aruch* – referring to "*Hallel b'tzibur,*" with the community – seems

4. See our discussion of this topic in Chapter 26.

to support this view. Thus, since women do not typically pray in the *bet kenesset* on the *seder* night, it seems that they should not recite this *Hallel.* Rav Shmuel Khoshkerman reports that many Sephardic women do not recite *Hallel* on the first night of Pesaḥ apart from that which is recited as part of the Haggada.

Rav Ovadia, as is typical of Sephardic *posekim,* liberally applies the principle of *safek berachot l'hakel,* that one does not recite a *beracha* in case of doubt. This application is so common, in fact, that Sephardic authorities use an acronym – *Saba"l* – to express it. Although Rav Ovadia and many other Sephardic *posekim* maintain that *Saba"l* does not apply when there is a *minhag* to recite a particular *beracha,* in our case there does not seem to be such a *minhag* for women to recite this *beracha* – or, for that matter, the *Hallel* altogether. For this reason, Rav Mordechai Lebhar (*Teshuvot Magen Avot* 7) rules that women should not recite a *beracha* upon reciting *Hallel* on the first night of Pesaḥ.

Based on the above, it seems reasonable to conclude that although a woman who wishes to rely on Rav Ovadia's ruling has a right to do so, women who wish to refrain from reciting the *beracha* or the *Hallel* altogether have the right to do so as well. As Rav Ovadia states many times in his *teshuvot,* whenever there is a doubt as to the proper course of action, one should determine the common practice and act accordingly (see, for example, *Berachot* 45a).

A similar approach may be adopted regarding a Sephardic Jew who prays in an Ashkenazic *bet kenesset* on the first evening of Pesaḥ. Rav Yitzḥak Yosef (*Yalkut Yosef, Mo'adim,* p. 382) rules that in such a situation, the Sephardic Jew should recite *Hallel* with a *beracha* by himself, either after the conclusion of *tefilla* at the *bet kenesset* or as soon as he arrives home after the *tefilla.* However, since many *Aḥaronim* rule that this *Hallel* is recited only by a *tzibur* in a *bet kenesset,* the Sephardic Jew in such a case should omit the *beracha* in deference to this view.

Chapter 56

Yehalelucha at the *Seder*

The Sephardic tradition is to recite the paragraph of *Yehalelucha* after *Nishmat* at the end of the *seder*, whereas the Ashkenazic tradition is to recite *Yehalelucha* after completing *Hallel HaMitzri* (the regular holiday *Hallel*). Although this does not seem to be an argument of much consequence, this dispute actually reflects a debate concerning a fundamental question regarding our relationship with *Hashem*.

THE TALMUDIC BACKGROUND

The *mishna* (*Pesaḥim* 10:7) states: "On the fourth cup, we recite *Hallel* and *Birkat HaShir* (the blessing of song)." While the meaning of *Hallel* is clear, the term "*Birkat HaShir*" is difficult to decipher. The *gemara* (*Pesaḥim* 118a) proceeds to outline a dispute between Rav Yehuda and Rabbi Yoḥanan regarding what *Birkat HaShir* refers to. Rav Yehuda argues that it refers to the paragraph of *Yehalelucha*, whereas Rabbi Yoḥanan argues that it refers to *Nishmat Kol Ḥai*.[1]

---

1. It should be obvious that *Hallel* is concluded with its usual conclusion of *Yehalelucha*. Why would the *mishna* need to inform us of this, according to Rav Yehuda? *Tosafot* (ad loc., s.v. *mai Birkat HaShir*) explain that it may come to teach that all agree that the *Hallel* recited at the *seder* concludes with a *beracha*, as some communities did not conclude any recitation of *Hallel* with a *beracha* (as noted in *Sukka* 3:11). Alternatively, *Tosafot* explain, the *mishna* teaches us that even *Hallel* recited at night concludes

Rav Shmuel Goldin (*Unlocking the Haggadah*, pp. 194–196) explains that Rav Yehuda and Rabbi Yoḥanan are debating a most fundamental question. The *Yehalelucha* conclusion of *Hallel* is a confident expression of our ability to properly praise *Hashem*. *Nishmat Kol Ḥai*, in contrast, expresses the opposite idea – that we are unable to adequately praise *Hashem*. Rav Yehuda and Rabbi Yoḥanan thus debate how we are to conclude the *seder* – with *Yehalelucha*, a confident assertion of our closeness to *Hashem* and our ability to adequately praise Him, or with *Nishmat*, a humbling recognition of the unbridgeable gap between us and *Hashem*, to the extent that all of our praises of Him fall short.

RISHONIM, SHULḤAN ARUCH, AND COMMENTARIES

The *Rishonim* debate which opinion is followed in practice. The Rambam (*Hilchot Ḥametz U'Matza* 8:10) follows the view of Rav Yehuda that *Hallel* is recited, concluding with *Yehalelucha*. At the other end of the spectrum, Rabbenu Ḥayim Kohen (cited in *Tosafot, Pesaḥim* 118a, s.v. *Rabbi Yoḥanan*) rules in accordance with Rabbi Yoḥanan that only *Nishmat* is recited after *Hallel*. The Rashbam (ad loc., s.v. *v'Rabbi Yoḥanan*) and *Tosafot* (op. cit.) rule that *Hallel* is recited concluding with both *Yehalelucha* and *Nishmat Kol Ḥai*. The *Shulḥan Aruch* (*Oraḥ Ḥayim* 480:1) rules in accordance with this view.[2]

Rav Goldin explains that we follow both opinions because we subscribe to a paradoxical view as to whether we are close or distant to *Hashem*. The Torah view is that both are true. Therefore, it is most appropriate for us to close the *seder* with the recitation of both *Yehalelucha* and *Nishmat*.

Rav Goldin further notes that this paradox is expressed in our twice and sometimes thrice-daily invocation of Yeshayahu's (6:3) description of *Hashem* as "*Kadosh, Kadosh, Kadosh*," holy and apart from us,[3] on the one

---

with *Yehalelucha*; one might have thought the dark night is an inappropriate time to make the confident assertion of *Yehalelucha*. Tosafot (ad loc., s.v. *Rabbi Yoḥanan*) explain that *Nishmat* is referred to as *Birkat HaShir* because it is recited on Shabbat at the conclusion of *Pesukei D'Zimra*. I would add that referring to *Nishmat* in this manner fits perfectly with the Sephardic custom to sing the entire poem of *Nishmat* (see *Ben Ish Ḥai*, year 2, *Parashat Toledot* 3).

2. *Hallel HaGadol* (*Tehillim* 136) is recited between *Hallel* and *Nishmat*, in accordance with Rabbi Tarfon's ruling (cited in a *beraita* in *Pesaḥim* 118a).
3. Rashi (*Vayikra* 19:2) equates *kedusha* with separation.

hand. On the other hand, *"melo chol ha'aretz kevodo"* – His Presence fills the world and He is most accessible to us.

This paradox is similarly expressed in each and every *beracha*. We begin each *beracha* with daring familiarity with *Hashem*, by addressing Him in the second person – *"Atah."* We then immediately shift into the third person – *"Elokenu Melech ha'olam"* – denoting that *Hashem* is distant from us.[4]

THE DISPUTE BETWEEN SEPHARDIM AND ASHKENAZIM REGARDING *YEHALELUCHA*

Although both Ashkenazim and Sephardim recite *Yehalelucha* and *Nishmat Kol Ḥai* after *Hallel* at the *seder*, Sephardim recite *Yehalelucha* only after *Nishmat*, whereas non-Ḥassidic Ashkenazic practice is to recite it immediately after *Hallel*, before *Nishmat*. (Ḥassidim have embraced the Sephardic approach.)

I would suggest that the question of the placement of *Yehalelucha* reflects a Sephardic/Ashkenazic divide we posited in Chapter 46. All agree that *Hashem* is both close to us, like a Father, and distant from us, like a King, as expressed in the *Avinu Malkenu* prayer, but Sephardim stress the Father element, whereas Ashkenazim focus more on *Hashem* as our King. Thus, Sephardim conclude the *seder* with *Yehalelucha*, as we wish to end the *seder* by expressing our closeness with *Hashem*. Ashkenazim, in contrast, end with *Nishmat Kol Ḥai*, since the emphasis should be on *Hashem* as King, who retains a respectful distance from us.

CONCLUSION

Although we have mined a magnificent nugget from a seemingly minor dispute between the Sephardic and Ashkenazic liturgy regarding the precise

---

4. The Torah rejected binary thinking millennia before the Western world caught up to this sophisticated way of thinking. The Torah teaches that life is not always a choice between this and that, but not both. Sometimes, the Torah teaches, both perspectives are true even if the result is a paradox. Thus, *Hashem* can be both close and distant from us.

   An interesting example of the Torah's rejection of binary thinking is the dual nature of the Jewish calendar. Whereas the Western world hews to a purely solar calendar and Moslems follow a purely lunar calendar, we follow a dual calendar that is both lunar and solar. Similarly, the Ritva (*Yoma* 47b) characterizes the time period between sunset (*shekia*) and nightfall (*tzet hakochavim*) as being both day and night simultaneously, and *Ḥazal* teach that both versions of the *luḥot* were communicated by *Hashem* simultaneously.

order of the conclusion of the *seder,* we should not overlook the fact that the Sephardic and Ashkenazic *Haggadot* are nearly identical. Differences are few and far between. The dispute regarding the placement of *Yehalelucha* and other variations, such as whether to recite a *beracha* on the second and fourth cups,[5] and whether to say the *mishna*'s text of "*Ḥayav adam l'rot et atzmo k'ilu hu yatza miMitzrayim*" (*Pesaḥim* 116b) or the Rambam's version (*Hilchot Ḥametz U'Matza* 7:6) of "*Ḥayav adam l'harot atzmo,*" are among the very minor and nuanced differences.

5. The *Shulḥan Aruch* and Rama dispute this question (*Oraḥ Ḥayim* 474). Sephardic Jews follow the ruling of Rav Karo that no *beracha* is recited on the second and fourth *kosot,* whereas Ashkenazic Jews follow the ruling of the Rama that a *beracha* should be recited on these *kosot.*

Shavuot

Chapter 57

Early Start to the First Night of Shavuot

It is well-known that Sephardim read each word of the *tefilla* aloud (except for the silent *Amida*) and that Sephardic *tefilla* usually takes longer than the Ashkenazic version as a result. Ashkenazic Jews are thus accustomed to seeing Sephardic Jews return late on Shabbat and Yom Tov evenings. However, Ashkenazic Jews often react with shock when they see their Sephardic brethren returning home early from *Arvit* on Shavuot eve.

THE ASHKENAZIC PRACTICE

Ashkenazim are accustomed to wait until *tzet hakochavim* (nightfall) before beginning *Arvit* on Shavuot, in accordance with the ruling of the *Mishna Berura* (494:1). The Torah requires us to count seven complete weeks ("*sheva shabbatot temimot*") between Pesaḥ and Shavuot; beginning *Arvit* early on Shavuot would impinge on the "*temimot*" nature of the count, since Shavuot would then begin before the forty-ninth day of the *omer* is complete.

Why, then, does Congregation Shaarei Orah, the Sephardic Congregation of Teaneck, begin *Arvit* on Shavuot eve considerably earlier than nightfall?

THE SEPHARDIC PRACTICE

Although the *Mishna Berura* requires waiting until *tzet hakochavim* to pray *Arvit* on Shavuot, the *Aruch HaShulḥan* (*Oraḥ Ḥayim* 494:3) requires only that we postpone *Kiddush* until nightfall. The iconic Sephardic work *Ben Ish Ḥai* (year 1, *Parashat Bemidbar* 2) adopts this approach as well. There is, in fact, a halachic advantage of this modified approach, as by praying *Arvit* early, one accepts Shavuot early and fulfills the *mitzva* of *tosefet Yom Tov*, accepting Yom Tov early. Delaying *Kiddush* until *tzet hakochavim* suffices to satisfy the *temimot* requirement.

Rav Ovadia Yosef (*Teshuvot Yeḥaveh Da'at* 6:30) cites Rav David Zvi Hoffman's further modification of the requirement to wait (*Teshuvot Melamed L'Ho'il, Oraḥ Ḥayim* 108). Rav Hoffman notes that since the majority of *Rishonim* maintain that in the unfortunate absence of the *Bet HaMikdash, sefirat ha'omer* is only a Rabbinic obligation, it is sufficient to wait until *sheki'a* (sunset) to begin *Kiddush* in a case of need.

Furthermore, Rav Ovadia challenges the requirement to wait even until *sheki'a* due to the requirement of *temimot*. The *gemara* (*Menaḥot* 66a) interprets *temimot* as teaching that the *omer* should be counted at night in order for the complete day to be counted. The Behag, a very important tenth-century Geonic halachic work, interprets *temimot* differently, as disqualifying those who missed one day of counting the *omer*. *Tosafot* (ad loc., s.v. *zecher l'Mikdash*) express surprise that the Behag interprets *temimot* in a manner that appears contrary to the *gemara*. Although the Behag's opinion is accepted to a certain extent, this is due to the preeminent status of the Behag as one of the *Geonim*, whose teachings are assumed to be rooted in oral traditions dating back to the Talmudic era. The much later interpretation of *temimot* as precluding ushering in Shavuot early is not nearly as authoritative. After all, halachic interpretation of *Tanach* is reserved for the *gemara*, and at most may be extended to the Geonic period.

Finally, Rav Ovadia cites a well-known comment of *Tosafot* and the Rosh on a *mishna* in *Pesaḥim* (10:1). The *mishna* notes that one should not begin eating on Erev Pesaḥ until nightfall, since the *Korban Pesaḥ* must be eaten only at night. *Tosafot* (*Pesaḥim* 99b, s.v. *ad*) and the Rosh (*Pesaḥim* 10:2) note that Pesaḥ is the sole exception to the rule that permits and even requires us to begin Shabbat and Yom Tov early.

Based on his arguments, Rav Ovadia rules that it is best for Sephardim to wait until *tzet hakochavim* to begin *Kiddush* on Shavuot eve, and if this is difficult, one should wait until *shekia*. If even this proves difficult, one may recite *Kiddush* even before *shekia*.

CONCLUSION

In light of these rulings, at Shaarei Orah, we conclude *Arvit* on Shavuot considerably earlier than *sheki'a*. Each family, in turn, decides if it is able to wait until *shekia* or *tzeit hakochavim* to recite *Kiddush*. Rav Eli Mansour cites the practice of Syrian Jewish leader Rav Baruch Ben-Ḥayim, who would recite *Arvit* and *Kiddush* before *tzet hakochavim* on the night of Shavuot, explaining that he wanted to ensure that the children remain awake to participate in the Yom Tov celebration.[1]

Rav Khoshkerman reports that many Sephardic Jews adopt a compromise approach. They recite *Arvit* after *shekia* and recite *Kiddush* twenty minutes after *sheki'a,* which is the time of *tzet haKochavim* according to Sephardic Halacha.

1. http://www.mishnaberura.com/Default.asp?PageIndex=11&ChelekID=5&SeifID=253&Version=Short.

Chapter 58

Standing or Sitting for the *Aseret HaDibrot*?

The Rambam adopts a very strong stance against those who stand for the *Aseret HaDibrot* (*Teshuvot HaRambam* 263 [Blau ed.]). Therefore, when we reach the *aliya* that includes the *Aseret HaDibrot* (Ten Commandments), I remind the congregation that many Sephardim remain seated for all public Torah-reading, including the reading of the *Aseret HaDibrot.*

THE STATUS OF THE *ASERET HADIBROT*

The *Aseret HaDibrot* undoubtedly constitute a cornerstone of Torah, as they express the essential messages of Torah. The *mitzvot* contained in the *Aseret HaDibrot* teach respect for *Hashem,* for others, and ultimately for ourselves. It is therefore not surprising that the *mishna* (*Tamid* 5:1) records that the *Aseret HaDibrot* were recited each day in the *Bet HaMikdash.*

The *gemara* (*Berachot* 12a), however, records that *Ḥazal* chose not to incorporate the *Aseret HaDibrot* in the daily *tefilla* due to concern for misinterpretation. A deviant sect of Judaism aggressively preached the heretical idea that **only** the *Aseret HaDibrot* constitute the revealed word of *Hashem. Ḥazal* rejected the idea of reciting the *Aseret HaDibrot* in our daily *tefilla* lest the deviant sect cite this practice as evidence for their heretical belief.

The Rambam similarly argues against standing only for the reading of the *Aseret HaDibrot*, as doing so strengthens the claim of those who maintain that only this portion of the Torah was revealed by *Hashem*. The Maharikash (*Teshuvot Ohalei Yaakov* 33) confirms this ruling of the Rambam.[1]

IN DEFENSE OF THE CUSTOM TO STAND

Nevertheless, some Sephardic authorities, such as the *Ḥida* (*Tov Ayin* 11), defended those who stand for the *Aseret HaDibrot*. The *Ḥida* argues that since we read the entire Torah, we clearly celebrate each word of the Torah as the word of God. We stand for the *Aseret HaDibrot* only in order to reenact the revelation at Har Sinai when, the Torah records, we all stood (*Shemot* 19:17).

Teshuvot Devar Shemuel (276) also defends the practice of those who stand for the *Aseret HaDibrot*. He argues that since it is well-known that the congregation stands as a reenactment of our experience at Har Sinai, the heretics' arguments will not be heeded.

Rav Yehuda Ayash (*Mateh Yehuda* 1:6) also defends the practice to stand for the *Aseret HaDibrot*, arguing that *Ḥazal* merely forbid the reading of the *Aseret HaDibrot* when it was not instituted to be read. However, once it was decreed to read the Torah on Shabbat and Yom Tov (including the *Aseret HaDibrot*), *Ḥazal* did not decree which posture we must assume when we discharge our obligation to read them.

RAV OVADIA YOSEF VS. RAV SHALOM MESSAS

Rav Ovadia Yosef (*Teshuvot Yeḥaveh Da'at* 1:29, 6:8) insists that had the *Ḥida*, the *Devar Shmuel*, and the *Mateh Yehuda* been aware of the Rambam's responsum, they never would have defended those who act against the Rambam's ruling. Rav Ovadia therefore maintains that Sephardim must sit during the reading of the *Aseret HaDibrot* in deference to the view of the Rambam.[2]

---

1. Not surprisingly, Yemenite Jews, who typically hew close to the Rambam's rulings, do not stand when the *Aseret HaDibrot* are read from the Torah.
2. According to Rav Ovadia, there is only one exception—if one's father or Rav receives the *aliya* in which the *Aseret HaDibrot* is read, as Sephardic custom is for children and *talmidim* to stand for their father or Rav during their *aliya*. In such a case, Rav Ovadia writes, the children and *talmidim* should rise as their father or Rav comes for his *aliya*, to clarify that they are standing in honor of their father or Rav and not in order to accord special status to the *Aseret HaDibrot*.

Rav Shalom Messas (*Teshuvot Shemesh U'Magen* 1:57, 3:55:3), however, defends the Moroccan *minhag* to stand for the *Aseret HaDibrot*. He argues that the age-old practice among many groups of Jews has been to stand when the *Aseret HaDibrot* are read from the Torah, indicating that the Rambam's ruling has not been accepted by the entirety of the Jewish People.

CONCLUSION

While we have deep appreciation for the *Aseret HaDibrot*, ultimately we love each and every detail in the Torah and treat each *pasuk* with equal reverence. Just as a responsible parent loves each child equally, Rav Ovadia Yosef strongly rules in accordance with the Rambam that Jews should love each part of the Torah equally, with no special preferences for one section over another.

Those who stand during the reading of the *Aseret HaDibrot* feel that their *minhag* is justified and does not imply a lack of reverence for other portions of the Torah.

Ḥanukka and Purim

Chapter 59

Yeshiva and University Students Lighting Ḥanukka Candles

The *gemara* (*Shabbat* 21b) states that the *mitzva* of lighting Ḥanukka candles can be fulfilled on three levels: The basic *mitzva* is to light one candle per household; the *mehadrin* (those who seek to fulfill the *mitzva* on a higher level) light one candle per family member; and the *mehadrin min hamehadrin* (those who seek to fulfill the *mitzva* on an even higher level) light one candle on the first night, two on the second, etc. Our practice is for everyone to follow the *mehadrin min hamehadrin* practice under ordinary conditions.

There is a well-known debate among the *Rishonim*, however, as to how to properly fulfill this highest level of Ḥanukka lighting.

According to *Tosafot* (*Shabbat* 21b, s.v. *v'hamehadrin*), the *mehadrin min hamehadrin* add one candle per night, but must light only one *ḥanukkia* per household. *Tosafot* explain that lighting more than one *ḥanukkia* per household would make it difficult for onlookers to determine how many candles are being lit for that day.

However, according to the Rambam (*Hilchot Ḥanukka* 4:1), the *mehadrin min hamehadrin* light one *ḥanukkia* per household member and add a candle to each *ḥanukkia* every night, such that if there are ten members in the household, ten candles would be lit in total on the first night, twenty the following night, etc. This highest level is obviously adding on to the level before it, in which a candle is lit for each member of the household.

SHULḤAN ARUCH VS. RAMA

Rav Yosef Karo (*Bet Yosef, Oraḥ Ḥayim* 671) cites this debate and writes that the custom is to follow *Tosafot*'s view and light only one *ḥanukkia* per household, adding a candle every night. This is how he rules in the *Shulḥan Aruch* (*Oraḥ Ḥayim* 671:2) as well, while the Rama (in a variation on the Rambam) rules that each member of the household should light his own *ḥanukkia*.

The *Taz* (*Oraḥ Ḥayim* 671:1) famously notes that this is a rare instance in which Sephardim follow *Tosafot*, while Ashkenazim follow the Rama's variation of the Rambam. Indeed, the practice of lighting only one Ḥanukka lamp has resonated deeply with Sephardic Jews and has become an iconic hallmark in Sephardic families.

Interestingly, Yemenite Jews also follow the ruling of Rav Yosef Karo, despite the strong inclination of Yemenite Jews to follow the rulings of the Rambam.[1] Teachers should be sensitive to Sephardic and Yemenite students and be alert to this difference in practice.[2]

RAV OVADIA YOSEF VS. RAV SHALOM MESSAS

Rav Ovadia Yosef (*Teshuvot Yeḥaveh Da'at* 6:43) applies the Sephardic practice even to *yeshiva* or university students who reside in an apartment or dormitory. Rav Ovadia writes that they should not light their own Ḥanukka candles, as they should rely on their parents' lighting. Indeed, reciting a *beracha* in such an instance would be a *beracha l'vatala* (a blessing uttered in vain). He insists that Sephardic students do not have the option to "opt out" of their parents' lighting and recite a *beracha* (based on *Shulḥan Aruch, Oraḥ Ḥayim* 677:3).[3]

By contrast, the great Moroccan authority Rav Shalom Messas (*Teshuvot Tevu'ot Shemesh, Oraḥ Ḥayim* 7; *Teshuvot Shemesh U'Magen* 2:3) disagrees and permits those in such a situation to opt out of their parents'

1. As noted by Rav Zecharia Ben-Shlomo, *Orot HaHalacha*, p. 886.
2. According to the *Sha'arei Teshuva* (671) and *Kaf HaḤayim* (*Oraḥ Ḥayim* 671:7), an Ashkenazic visitor to a Sephardic home may light his own candles without violating the prohibition of *lo titgodedu*.
3. An exception would be if the students are located in a place where no other Jews reside.

lighting and recite a *beracha* on their own lighting.[4] Moroccan Jews are encouraged to follow the ruling of Rav Messas, especially since students might not feel like they are experiencing Ḥanukka if they do not light their own *ḥanukkia* in such circumstances. Although Sephardic Jews are accustomed to relying on their parents' lighting, they might not feel a part of their parents' lighting if they are living at a distance.[5]

CONCLUSION

I recommend to Sephardic students who live in out-of-town dormitories (and are not of Moroccan descent) to light their own Ḥanukka lights but omit the *beracha*, out of respect for the view of Rav Ovadia. The *Yalkut Yosef* (*Oraḥ Ḥayim* 677:4) supports this approach.

There is one scenario in which Rav Ovadia permits students to recite a *beracha* on their own lighting: Students who live in a time zone to the east of their parents may recite a *beracha*, since their parents have not yet kindled Ḥanukka lights. For example, American youngsters learning in an Israeli *yeshiva* may light their own Ḥanukka lights and recite a *beracha* (*Yalkut Yosef, Oraḥ Ḥayim* 677:5).[6]

---

4. In response to Rav Messas' dissent, Rav Ovadia reports that he presented the issue to his venerable teacher, Rav Ezra Attia, who wholeheartedly endorsed Rav Ovadia's ruling.
5. Videoconferencing their parents' lighting can help alleviate this concern.
6. Rav Ben Tzion Abba Sha'ul (*Kovetz Zichron Yehuda, Sefer Zikaron*, vol. 1, pp. 106–107; see *Teshuvot Ohr L'Tzion*, vol 4, p. 281) rules that *yeshiva* students whose parents live outside of Israel in a different time zone should light and recite a *beracha* at the *yeshiva*; otherwise, they do not fulfill their obligation. Rav Ovadia writes (*Ḥazon Ovadia, Ḥanukka*, p. 150) that in such circumstances, the student can either light with a *beracha* or fulfill the *mitzva* with his parents' lighting. Rav Shlomo Zalman Auerbach (*Halichot Shlomo*, ch. 14, n. 22) also rules that a Sephardic student whose parents live outside of Israel in a different time zone can fulfill his obligation with the lighting of his parents.

   Rav Ike Sultan notes that if a student attends an institution that does not permit Ḥanukka candle-lighting in the dormitory room, there is an additional reason for him not to recite the *beracha* and to rely upon his parent's lighting, as it is highly questionable if the student fulfills his obligation by lighting in the institution's dining hall. (This is the subject of a great debate between Rav Moshe Feinstein and Rav Aharon Kotler, as cited by Rav Shimon Eider, *Halachos of Chanukah*, p. 37. It is also disputed by Rav Yitzḥak Yosef, *Yalkut Yosef, Ḥanukka* 5773, pp. 488, 495, and Rav David Yosef, *Torat HaMo'adim, Ḥanukka* 2:5, p. 49.)

Rav Shmuel Khoshkerman reports that Rav Ovadia ruled that the Persian *talmidim* learning in Baltimore's Ner Yisroel Yeshiva could rely on their parents' Ḥanukka lighting in Iran.[7] This is quite a bold ruling, considering that it is still daytime in Baltimore when it is the time for lighting candles in Iran! Indeed, in such a situation, Rav Moshe Feinstein rules that one does not fulfill the *mitzva* of Ḥanukka lighting through his family's lighting (as reported by Rav Aharon Felder, *Mo'adei Yeshurun*, p. 21).

7. Rav Khoshkerman reports that Rav Ovadia also offered the option of fulfilling the *mitzva* through the candle-lighting performed in the *yeshiva* at *Arvit* (as stated in *Teshuvot Yeḥaveh Da'at* 6:43).

Chapter 60

Birkat Kohanim in Ḥanukka *Keriat HaTorah*

Fascinating! Sephardic Jews begin the Torah reading on the first day of Ḥanukka with *Birkat Kohanim*! Equally fascinating is the fact that Ashkenazim do not include *Birkat Kohanim* in the Ḥanukka Torah reading. This discrepancy in practice seems to reflect a fundamental difference in approach to the role of the *Kohanim* in the Ḥanukka miracle.

BACKGROUND

The *mishna* (*Megilla* 30b) states that the *Parashat HaNesi'im* – the description of the donations of each *shevet*'s head for the *ḥanukkat hamizbe'aḥ* (dedication of the altar) in the *Mishkan*, recorded in *Parashat Naso* – serves as the Torah reading for Ḥanukka. Rashi explains that this is because the *Nesi'im* participated in a *ḥanukkat hamizbe'aḥ*, just as happened during the time of Ḥanukka. The *Tur* (*Oraḥ Ḥayim* 684) cites the *Pesikta*, which states that the *Mishkan* was dedicated on none other than the 25th of Kislev, making the parallel complete.

No mention is made in the *mishna* or *gemara* of reading the *Birkat Kohanim* as part of the Ḥanukka Torah reading, but the Rambam (*Hilchot Tefilla* 13:17) does record this practice. The *Tur* (op. cit.) explains that the

Rambam includes *Birkat Kohanim* because the miracle was accomplished by *Kohanim* – the Maccabees. The *Tur* notes that there are places where the Rambam's view is followed and other places where it is not.

Maran Rav Yosef Karo (*Shulḥan Aruch, Oraḥ Ḥayim* 684:1) rules in accordance with the Rambam, and Sephardic Jews include *Birkat Kohanim* in the Ḥanukka Torah reading, but the Rama notes that the Ashkenazic custom is not to incorporate *Birkat Kohanim* into the Ḥanukka Torah reading.

RAMBAM VS. RAMBAN

I suggest that this divergence in customs depends on the evaluation of the *Kohanim*'s participation in the Ḥanukka miracle. Ashkenazic practice seems to follow the view of the Ramban (*Bereishit* 49:10), who famously condemns the Ḥashmona'im for seizing the kingship. The Ramban insists that this was a violation of Yaakov Avinu's will that "*lo yasur shevet meYehuda*," that the kingship should remain exclusively in the hands of *Shevet Yehuda*. Ashkenazic practice is not inclined to celebrate the role of the *Kohanim* in the Ḥanukka miracle, due to the wrong course of action they took to assume the monarchy.

The Rambam, however, seems to be consistent with his approach to the *Kohanim*'s role in the Ḥanukka miracle. In his presentation of the events of Ḥanukka, the Rambam writes (*Hilchot Ḥanukka* 3:1), "*V'he'emidu melech min hakohanim*," "they appointed a king from among the *Kohanim*." There is not a hint of criticism emanating from the Rambam's words regarding this appointment. Moreover, the fact that *Kohanim* were appointed as kings appears to constitute a source of celebration for the Rambam, not a point to be criticized.[1]

Rav Yosef Dov Soloveitchik (cited in *Harerei Kedem* 1:272) understands that the Rambam does not subscribe to the Ramban's view regarding this matter. Rav Soloveitchik explains that appointing *Kohanim* as kings in the circumstances of Ḥanukka is a point to be celebrated, since the essence of the struggle against the Greeks related to the latter's desecration of the *Bet HaMikdash*. The fact that *Kohanim* were appointed as kings in the wake of the ouster of the Greeks is a cause for celebration, because it facilitates the *Kohanim*'s fulfillment of their role as guardians of the special holiness of the *Bet HaMikdash*.

1. The Rambam also does not raise an issue regarding the Hasmonean rule in his discussion of the eternal role of the Davidic dynasty (*Hilchot Melachim* 1:7–9).

Indeed, the Rambam (*Hilchot Bet HaBeḥira* 8:3) specifically notes that the *shemira* (guarding) of the *Bet HaMikdash* from the inside is a specific responsibility of the *Kohanim*. Rav Soloveitchik cites his grandfather, Rav Ḥayim Soloveitchik, who points out that the *navi* Zecharia indicates this as well, as he instructs the *Kohen Gadol*, "*v'gam tishmor et ḥatzerai*," "and you must also guard the sanctity of My courtyard" (*Zecharia* 3:7, included in the *haftara* reading for Shabbat Ḥanukka).

Rav Soloveitchik concludes that the *haftara* choice for Shabbat Ḥanukka supports the Rambam's approach. He notes that the *haftara* could have easily have been limited to Zecharia's vision of the *menora* attached to tubes bringing oil to its lamps and two olive trees to provide a continuous supply of fuel. This would indeed seem to be the portion of the *haftara* that is most relevant to Ḥanukka. Yet, we also read about the effort to help Yehoshua *Kohen Gadol* better serve in his role of guarding the holiness of the *Mikdash*. Thus, we see that the role of *Kohanim* guarding the sanctity of the *Mikdash* constitutes a major theme of Ḥanukka.[2]

Accordingly, it is most appropriate to incorporate *Birkat Kohanim* into the Ḥanukka Torah reading, especially since if this is not done, no mention will be made of the *Kohanim* until the very end of the Torah reading of the eighth day (as *Shevet Levi* did not directly participate in the *ḥanukkat hamizbe'aḥ* of the *Mishkan*).

The Ramban might respond that the role of the *Kohanim* should be limited to the *Mikdash* and separated from any political role, but the Rambam would reply that the best way to ensure the preservation of the *Kedusha* of the *Bet HaMikdash* is by assuming political power. Thus, a fundamental dispute has emerged between the Ramban and Rambam as to the separation of religious leadership and political leadership. The Ramban seems to endorse such as separation, while the Rambam does not.

---

2. Alternatively, the Rambam might adopt the approach of the Ran regarding the Ḥashmona'im assuming the role of kings. The Ran (*Derashot HaRan, derush* 7) argues with the Ramban regarding the status of the Hasmonean kings, based on the fact that their rule did not constitute a true *malchut*. A king must rule independently; any king who is subject to another political power is not considered to be a true *melech*. The Ḥashmona'im were subject to foreign authority, and therefore did not count as kings that were not from the tribe of Yehuda. The Ran argues that there was no requirement to have a king from Yehuda in such circumstances, as an authentic *malchut* did not exist at that time.

CONCLUSION

"*Minhag avotenu Torah hi*" – Jewish customs constitutes Torah. This is a mantra repeated by many *Rishonim* and *Aḥaronim*.[3] Traditionally, it is understood as teaching the importance to respect *minhagim* as an integral part of Torah. Rav Soloveitchik, however, took this a step further and understood it as teaching that just as we plumb the depths of Torah to explain its deeper meanings, so too we must properly explore the basis and meaning behind our *minhagim*.

Our exploration of the divergent *minhagim* as to whether to include *Birkat Kohanim* in the Ḥanukka Torah reading is an example of the abundant rewards that emerge from exploring our *minhagim*. Rather than a simple divergence of ritual observance, the practices reveal a fundamental dispute as to whether we should celebrate or denigrate the Ḥashmona'im's ascension to kingship after the defeat of the Syrian Greeks at the time of Ḥanukka. This, is turn, reflects a fundamental debate as to whether it is best for religious leadership to steer clear of political leadership. How rich is the study of our *minhagim*!

3. One very significant example is the Rosh, *Rosh Hashana* 4:14.

Chapter 61

Where the Rambam Lives (Especially on Purim)!

Many *kehillot* pride themselves on their devotion to study of the Rambam. Sephardic congregations, in addition to enjoying Rambam study, live the Rambam, as Sephardic Halacha is profoundly impacted by the Rambam's rulings.[1]

THE RAMBAM'S IMPACT ON SEPHARDIC PURIM

Purim is a time when many Rambam-based rulings are practiced in Sephardic congregations.

For example, *yeshiva* students delight in analyzing the dispute between the Rambam (*Hilchot Megilla* 1:3) and *Tosafot* (*Megilla* 4a, s.v.

1. An interesting question is which came first: Does Sephardic practice derive from the Rambam's rulings, or were the Rambam's rulings impacted to a great extent by Sephardic practice? It is reasonable to surmise that both of these options are partially correct.

Sephardic Jews regard Rav Yosef Karo's *Shulḥan Aruch* as their authoritative work. The Rambam is cited by the *Shulḥan Aruch* no less than 10,139 times! The next most quoted *Rishonim* in the *Shulḥan Aruch* are the Rosh, at 8,075 times, and the Rif, at 3,715 times.

ḥayav adam) as to whether *Sheheḥiyanu* is recited upon reading *Megillat Esther* on Purim morning. The Rambam did not recite this *beracha,* since *Sheheḥiyanu* was already recited before the night *Megilla* reading. *Tosafot,* in contrast, endeavor to demonstrate that the primary *Megilla* reading is the one conducted during the day, and *Sheheḥiyanu* should be said before the primary fulfillment of the *mitzva.* Not surprisingly, the *Shulḥan Aruch* (*Oraḥ Ḥayim* 692:1) rules in accordance with the Rambam and the Rama rules in accordance with *Tosafot.*

When I first attended a daytime *Megilla* reading at Congregation Shaarei Orah in 2000 – and, of course, *Sheheḥiyanu* was omitted – shivers ran up and down my spine. The Rambam's opinion regarding *Sheheḥiyanu,* which I enjoyed learning and teaching for many years, came to life! The Rambam's opinion is not simply a museum piece or mere foil for *Tosafot*'s opinion. It is alive and thriving in Sephardic congregations!

Another interesting difference between Sephardic and Ashkenazic practice relates to the reading of textual variants of *Megillat Esther*. There is a historical alternate tradition among Ashkenazim as to the correct text of *Esther* 8:11 ("*l'hashmid v'laharog ul'abed*" or the alternate tradition of "*l'hashmid l'harog ul'abed*") and 9:2 ("*v'ish lo amad l'fnehem*" or the alternate tradition of "*v'ish lo amad b'fnehem*"). To satisfy both traditions, readers following the Ashkenazic tradition generally read these words both possible ways.

Sephardim, on the other hand, read only the dominant tradition. Sephardic practice is supported by the Aleppo Codex, the oldest extant text of *Tanach,* which was endorsed as most authoritative by the Rambam (*Hilchot Sefer Torah* 8:4). Although the *Megillat Esther* portion of the Aleppo Codex is not available (it is housed in the Israel Museum in Jerusalem), one may derive from elsewhere in the text of the extant Aleppo Codex that the dominant tradition is the correct one.[2]

A third Purim example is the Torah reading of Purim morning. The *gemara* (*Megilla* 21b) establishes the rule that a minimum of ten *pesukim* is required for every Torah reading. *Tosafot* (ad loc., s.v. *en poḥatin*) notes that the Torah reading of Purim morning, recounting Amalek's attack on *B'nei Yisrael,* includes only nine *pesukim* and is an exception to the *gemara*'s rule. The Rambam (*Hilchot Tefilla* 12:3), on the other hand, in codifying the

2. See http://www.daat.ac.il/daat/kitveyet/taleley/kriot-2.htm.

gemara's ten-*pesukim* rule, makes no exception. Once again, not surprisingly, the *Shulḥan Aruch* (*Oraḥ Ḥayim* 693:4) rules in accordance with the implication of the Rambam, while the Rama rules in accordance with *Tosafot*'s approach. Thus, Sephardic practice is to repeat the last *pasuk* of the Purim morning Torah reading so that the requirement for 10 *pesukim* is satisfied.

CONCLUSION

Rambam-admirers among our Ashkenazic brethren are encouraged to visit Sephardic congregations on Purim and witness the teachings of their beloved Rambam come alive. On Purim, it is at Sephardic Congregations that the Rambam lives!

Chapter 62

My Favorite Sephardic Purim Practice: The King Could Not Sleep

The Rama (*Oraḥ Ḥayim* 690:17) records that when *Megillat Esther* is read in public on Purim, it is customary for the congregation to recite aloud four *pesukim* of *geula* (2:5, 8:15, 8:16, 10:3), which are then repeated by the reader. Although the practice of the *kahal* reading aloud certain *pesukim* from the *Tanach* is not mentioned in the Talmud, it is mentioned in prominent sources from the Geonic era, in the *siddurim* of both Rav Saadia Gaon and Rav Amram Gaon.[1]

In Sephardic synagogues, the congregation reads an additional *pasuk* aloud: "*Balayla hahu nadeda shenat hamelech,*" "On that night, the king could not sleep" (6:1) (*Ben Ish Ḥai*, year 1, *Parashat Tetzaveh* 7; *Yalkut Yosef, Oraḥ Ḥayim* 690:27). Although the *minhag* for the *kahal* to read this *pasuk* aloud

1. Rav Yosef Dov Soloveitchik stated (in a *shiur* delivered at Yeshiva University in 1985) that even though a practice is not recorded in the Talmud, it does not mean that it was not practiced during the time of the Talmud. The *Geonim* may have simply recorded an ancient practice that was followed during the time of the Talmud that for some reason was not actually recorded in the Talmud.

is not mentioned in the *Geonim* or *Rishonim*, it is nevertheless a most powerful custom – in fact, it is my favorite Purim custom!

I recall how struck by the poignancy of this tradition when I encountered it at Congregation Shaarei Orah, the Sephardic Congregation of Teaneck, for the first time. Of course, this practice reflects the interpretation of the *gemara* (*Megilla* 15b) that the king who could not sleep refers not only to Aḥashverosh, but more importantly, to *Hashem*!

Indeed, this *pasuk* constitutes the turning point of *Megillat Esther*. Before this *pasuk*, Haman was "riding high." He encountered no significant resistance to his plan to exterminate the Jewish People. The King/king's inability to sleep was the first in a string of events that led to Haman's defeat and demise. It was at this point that we begin to discern Divine intervention on our behalf to save us from Haman's evil decree.

A crucial goal of *Megilla* reading is to discern *Hashem*'s subtle role in saving the Jews from Haman. Interestingly, the *gemara* (*Megilla* 14a) describes the *Megilla* reading as a form of *Hallel*. The *Megilla* is not a direct praise of *Hashem*, especially since His holy name is not mentioned in the *Megilla*. It is, however, a subtle praise of *Hashem*, which the reader is challenged to notice.

Reading aloud the *pasuk* of "*Balayla hahu nadeda shenat hamelech*" is certainly a most effective way of noticing and proclaiming *Hashem*'s subtle hand manipulating the events that unfolded in the *Megilla*. It is as if we are announcing the celebrated *pasuk* in *Shir HaShirim* (2:9), "*Hinei zeh omed aḥar kotlenu, mashgiaḥ min haḥalonot, metzitz min haḥarakim*," "Behold, here He is standing behind the wall, watching from the windows, peering through the latticework."

This might be the reason the Rambam requires us to have *kavana* (intent) to fulfill the *mitzva* of *Megilla* reading (*Hilchot Megilla* 2:5), even though he makes no such demand for other *mitzvot*, such as eating matza (*Hilchot Ḥametz U'Matza* 6:3). This idea also fits with the Rambam's explanation (*Hilchot Ḥanukka* 3:6) that the *Megilla* serves as *Hallel*, and for that reason we do not recite *Hallel* on Purim. In order to transform and elevate the *Megilla* reading into *Hallel*, we must have *kavana*.

It is interesting that we recite the *beracha* of "*she'asa nissim la'avotenu*," "who performed miracles on behalf of our ancestors," on both Ḥanukka and Purim. It is understandable that we recite this *beracha* on Ḥanukka, when an obvious miracle occurred; the oil for the *menora* lasted for eight days when there was only sufficient oil for one day. On Purim, however, what miracle occurred? The answer is that the *Megilla* is replete with subtle miracles; we simply need to be alert to notice them. By reciting "*she'asa nissim*" before reading the *Megilla,* we are declaring that hidden miracles abound in *Megillat Esther*.

The Sephardic practice of reading the *pasuk* of "*Balayla hahu nadeda shenat hamelech*" similarly goes a very long way to highlight and alert us to the subtle behind-the-scenes role of *Hashem* in the *Megilla*. It reminds us to use our Jewish eyes and Jewish hearts to notice *Hashem* in the *Megilla,* and thereby come to recognize how His presence permeates each and every one of our days.

Lag B'Omer

Chapter 63

Haircut Day

For many Jews, Lag B'Omer is the day we've all been waiting for! Finally, men can shave and take a haircut! Why, then, do my Sephardic male neighbors wait until the next day, the thirty-fourth day in the *omer* to have their hair cut?[1]

DAY 33 VS. DAY 34

The difference in practice is due to differing rulings of *Maran* Rav Yosef Karo and the Rama. Rav Karo rules (*Shulḥan Aruch, Oraḥ Ḥayim* 493:2) that haircuts are permitted only on the thirty-fourth day of the *omer*, whereas the Rama permits taking a haircut on Lag B'Omer itself. Rav Ovadia Yosef insists that Sephardic Jews adhere to the ruling of *Maran* and refrain from weddings and haircutting until the thirty-fourth of the *omer* (*Teshuvot Yabia Omer* 3: *Oraḥ Ḥayim* 26; *Teshuvot Yeḥaveh Da'at* 4:32), and Rav Ovadia Hadaya (*Teshuvot Yaskil Avdi* 6: *Oraḥ Ḥayim* 6) arrives at the same conclusion.

---

1. Sephardic women are permitted to cut their hair during the *omer* (*Yalkut Yosef, Oraḥ Ḥayim* 493:18). They are permitted to do so even during *sheloshim* after the death of a relative (*Shulḥan Aruch, Yoreh De'ah* 390:5).

The *Mishna Berura* (493:8, citing the Vilna Gaon) explains that the dispute hinges upon a debate as to the date of the last death among Rabbi Akiva's twenty-four thousand *talmidim.*

The variety in customs is presented in the *Sefer HaManhig,* a classic twelfth century compilation of the halachic practices of France, Provence, and Spain, which records: "There is a *minhag* in France and Provence to begin marrying from Lag B'Omer and onwards." This is the basis of the Ashkenazic practice. The *Manhig* continues:

> And I heard in the name of Rav Zeraḥia of Gerona, who found an old manuscript from Sepharad [that notes that the students of Rabbi Akiva] died "from Pesaḥ until *P'ros HaAtzeret.*" What is *P'ros*? Half of a month – fifteen days before Shavuot.[2] This is Lag Ba'Omer.

Since fifteen days before Shavuot is the thirty-fourth day of the *omer, Maran* Rav Yosef Karo rules that one should continue practicing *minhagei avelut* through the morning of the thirty-fourth day.

THE PRACTICE OF THE ARI Z"L

The *Sha'arei Teshuva* (493:8) cites the Ari z"l, who advances a much different approach. The Ari z"l views the entire *omer* period as a period of judgment and as a type of "*Ḥol HaMo'ed*" between the festivals of Pesaḥ and Shavuot.[3] He therefore holds that one may not cut his hair or shave throughout the entire *omer* period, until Erev Shavuot. The *Yalkut Yosef* (493:16), however, rules that only those special individuals who always follow kabbalistic practices adopt this practice. Most Sephardic Jews take haircuts beginning from the thirty-fourth day of the *omer.*[4]

2. The phrase "*P'ros HaAtzeret*" appears in the *mishna* (*Shekalim* 3:1; *Bechorot* 9:5) and means fifteen days before Shavuot.
3. A similar idea is expressed by the Ramban in his commentary to the Torah (*Vayikra* 23:36).
4. The practice of some Ashkenazic Jews (especially German Jews) to refrain from haircutting from Rosh Ḥodesh Iyar until three days before Shavuot is recorded by the Rama but is not practiced by Sephardic Jews. This practice stems from combining mourning for the death of Rabbi Akiva's students with mourning for the Jews slaughtered in Germany during the Crusades. This practice did not reach Sephardic Jewry, since this tragic event did not transpire in Sephardic lands.

MOROCCAN JEWS

Rav Mordechai Lebhar (*Magen Avot, Oraḥ Ḥayim* 493) records that many Jews from North Africa take haircuts on Lag B'Omer, despite this being contrary to the ruling of the *Shulḥan Aruch.* Rav Lebhar defends this practice in part based on a comment of the great Sephardic *posek* the *Peri Ḥadash* (*Oraḥ Ḥayim* 493:2). The *Peri Ḥadash* notes the incongruity of refraining from *Taḥanun* and celebrating on Lag B'Omer on the one hand and continuing to mourn the loss of Rabbi Akiva's students until the thirty-fourth day of the *omer* on the other.

It is notable that only the Rama, and not *Maran* Rav Yosef Karo, records that *Taḥanun* is omitted due to the celebration that occurs on Lag B'Omer. One could argue that once Sephardic Jews adopted the kabbalistic practice to celebrate Lag B'Omer, they terminate the mourning for Rabbi Akiva's *talmidim* on that date as well.[5] This would be one of a number of kabbalistic practices that Sephardic Jews have embraced despite their being contrary to the ruling of the *Shulḥan Auch.*[6]

Rav Ovadia Yosef might respond that the two matters are not related to one another. The mourning for Rabbi Akiva's *talmidim* continues until the thirty-fourth of the *omer,* while the celebration of the great contributions of Rabbi Shimon Bar Yoḥai occurs on the thirty-third day of the *omer.*[7]

The historical circumstances also explain why Ashkenazic Jews recite *Av HaRaḥamim* before *Musaf,* while Sephardic Jews do not; this prayer mourns the tragic losses experienced by French and German Jewry during the Crusades. Similarly, on Tisha B'Av, Sephardic Jews do not recite *Kinot* relating to the Crusades. In turn, there are *Kinot* in the Sephardic liturgy that mourn the Spanish Inquisition, which, not surprisingly, are not recited by Ashkenazic Jews.

5. Similarly, Rav Moshe Feinstein (*Teshuvot Igrot Moshe, Oraḥ Ḥayim* 1:159) presumes that Sephardic Jews cut their hair on Lag B'Omer based on the celebrations in which Sephardic engage on Lag B'Omer.
6. Another example is Sephardic enthusiastic embrace of the *kaparot* custom of Erev Yom Kippur. Compare the *Shulḥan Aruch*'s rejection of *kaparot* (*Oraḥ Ḥayim* 605:1) with the embrace of this practice by the Ari z"l (cited in *Ba'er Hetev* 605:1). The *Yalkut Yosef* (*Oraḥ Ḥayim* 605) devotes a full discussion of the *halachot* surrounding *kaparot,* fully endorsing the practice.
7. Not coincidentally, Rabbi Shimon Bar Yohai was one of the five students taught by Rabbi Akiva after the last of his original 24,000 *talmidim* perished (*Yevamot* 62b).

CONCLUSION

As usual, the practices regarding the date on which haircutting is permitted are diverse. At Shaarei Orah, I advise men to wait until the thirty-fourth day of the *omer* to take a haircut, except if they originate from North Africa. I advise men whose family stems from North Africa to consult their parents as to their family custom.

Fast Days, Three Weeks, Nine Days, and Tisha B'Av

Chapter 64

The Three Weeks and Nine Days Sephardic-Style

Ashkenazim often initially react with shock. Why did my Sephardic neighbor get a haircut in the middle of the Three Weeks?! And why are they doing their laundry and bathing during the nine days?! Don't they know the Halacha?!

SHULḤAN ARUCH VS. RAMA

These practices do, indeed, run counter to the ruling of the Rama (*Oraḥ Ḥayim* 551:3). Rav Yosef Karo, however, is far more lenient than the Rama regarding mourning during the three week period between Shiva Asar B'Tamuz and Tisha B'Av and during the nine days between Rosh Ḥodesh Av and Tisha B'Av.

In fact, upon close examination of the original *halacha* as presented in the *mishnah* and *gemara* of the last *perek* of *Ta'anit* (as well as the fifth chapter of the Rambam's *Hilchot Ta'aniot*), one discovers that Sephardim actually hew closely to the original *halacha*: Haircutting and laundry are forbidden only during the *shavua sheḥal bo Tisha B'Av*, the week in which Tisha B'Av is observed. Ashkenazic custom has expanded the prohibitions of bathing and laundry to the entire Nine Days and haircutting to the entire Three Weeks.

Sephardim are even more lenient in a year in which Tisha B'Av falls on Shabbat but is observed on Sunday. *Maran* Rav Yosef Karo (*Shulḥan Aruch, Oraḥ Ḥayim* 551:4) cites two approaches in the *Rishonim* as to whether the entire week before Tisha B'Av in such a year is regarded as the *shavua sheḥal bo*. The primary opinion, as explained by Rav Ovadia Yosef (*Teshuvot Yeḥaveh Da'at* 3:39) and Rav Yitzḥak Yosef (*Yalkut Yosef, Oraḥ Ḥayim* 551:10), does not regard the week before Tisha B'Av that falls on Shabbat as the *shavua sheḥal bo*. Thus, bathing, haircutting, and laundry are permitted this entire week for Sephardic Jews.

EXPLAINING THE SEPHARDIC APPROACH

The question is why Sephardim have not adopted a stricter approach to the mourning of the Three Weeks and Nine Days. A standard answer is that Sephardic Halacha tends to be more conservative than Ashkenazic Halacha. The Rambam was much more of a "strict constructionist" than the *Ba'alei HaTosafot*, and Ashkenazic practice is more open to expanding stringencies than Sephardic practice. For example, those who have studied *Hilchot Sheḥita* are familiar with the myriad *ḥumrot* (stringencies) adopted by the Ashkenazic authorities regarding *sheḥita*, which are far more restrictive than the rules presented in *Masechet Ḥullin*.

Menahem Besthof of Congregation Shaarei Orah, the Sephardic Congregation of Teaneck, offers an additional explanation for why Sephardic practice tends towards a lenient observance of the Three Weeks and Nine Days. He notes that these periods of mourning are intended to ease us into the mourning of Tisha B'Av. Menahem argues that in a certain sense, such preparation is inappropriate, since we are bidden to hope and yearn for the *Mashiaḥ*'s arrival each and every day. Why should we prepare for Tisha B'Av if we are not certain that Tisha B'Av will be observed as a mournful day this year? Perhaps it is for this reason that Sephardim observe a much more minimal mourning during the Three Weeks and Nine Days.

Often, awareness of Sephardic practices helps Ashkenazic Jews understand their own. Observing one's Sephardic neighbors adopting a more lenient approach to the Three Weeks and Nine Days offers a precious insight into the Ashkenazic halachic tradition, as we have outlined.[1]

CONCLUSION

In the final analysis, all Jews share Menahem Besthof's hope that our observance of the Three Weeks and Nine Days should be for naught and that this Tisha B'Av should be one of rejoicing over the arrival of the *Mashiaḥ* and rebuilding the *Bet HaMikdash*.

1. In a most interesting ruling, Rav Yonatan Nacson (*MiMizraḥ U'MiMa'arav*, p. 189) writes: "If an Ashkenazi has only freshly laundered or new clothing after Rosh Ḥodesh Av [but before the *shavua sheḥal bo*], he may give his clothing to a Sephardi to wear.... and the Ashkenazi may then wear the clothing." This is logical, since the Sephardic Jew may wear laundered clothes at this time and the Ashkenazic Jew may subsequently wear the clothes, since they are no longer freshly laundered. Rav Mordechai Willig told me he agrees with this ruling, especially since Ashkenazim are forbidden to wear freshly laundered clothing at this time due to custom, not Biblical or Rabbinic law. Rav Zvi Sobolofsky stated (in a *shiur* delivered in Bergenfield, New Jersey) that he also agrees with this ruling.

Chapter 65

Anenu on a *Ta'anit Tzibur*

The *gemara* (*Ta'anit* 13b) teaches that on a *ta'anit tzibur* (public fast day), both the individual and the *shaliaḥ tzibur* (prayer leader) should insert a special prayer, *Anenu*, in the *Amida*.

When is *Anenu* inserted? The Talmud Yerushalmi (*Ta'anit* 2:2) records that *Anenu* should be recited during all three prayers of the fast day: *Arvit, Shaḥarit,* and *Minḥa*:

> Rav Yanai ben Rabbi Yishmael said in the name of Rav Shimon Lakish: Even an individual who decrees upon himself a fast must mention *me'en hame'ora* (the nature of the occasion). And where should he mention it? Rav Zeira said in the name of Rav Huna: He says it like the night of Shabbat and its day...

Similarly, the Talmud Bavli (*Shabbat* 24a) implies that one should insert *Anenu* in each prayer, including *Arvit.* Based on these sources, most *Rishonim* (*Teshuvot HaGeonim Sha'arei Teshuva* 77; Rif, *Ta'anit* 4a; Ran and Ramban on Rif; Ritva, *Shabbat* 24a; *Teshuvot HaRashba* 1:142, 387) rule this way, at least in theory. The Rambam (*Hilchot Tefilla* 2:14) indicates that he also maintains that *Anenu* should be recited during each of the *tefillot* of the *Ta'anit,* including *Arvit.*

The *Ba'al Ha-Ma'or* (*Ta'anit* 3a in the Rif's pages) disagrees, ruling that *Anenu* should not be recited at night. The text of *Anenu* reads, "*Anenu b'yom tzom ta'anitenu*," "Answer us on the day of our fasting." Accordingly, the *Ba'al HaMa'or* insists that "at a time during which one may eat, one should not insert *Anenu* into the evening prayer." Indeed, the Rashba, in his discussion of this opinion, asks, "How can one insert *Anenu* in the evening prayer while one's belly is still full?!"

The Ran, however, explains that according to the Rif, the fast fundamentally – although not practically – begins at night. Once one no longer intends to eat, the fast begins. Therefore, if one were to awaken in the middle of the night, one would not be permitted to eat.

Seemingly, these *Rishonim* disagree as to the nature of *Anenu*. While the *Ba'al Ha-Ma'or* views *Anenu* as a *tefilla* recited as part of one's fast, the Rif and Ran view *Anenu* as, in the language of the *gemara*, "*hazkarat me'en hame'ora*," an expression of the nature of the day, which technically begins at night.

Rashi (*Shabbat* 24a, s.v. *Arvit*) supports the position that *Anenu* should be recited three times. However, he proceeds to cite the opinion of the *Geonim*, who record that they were not accustomed to saying *Anenu* at night, nor even during the morning, lest a person not finish his fast, in which case he would retroactively have lied in his prayers. The Rashba (*Teshuvot* 1:142) explains that the Geonic position does not argue with the *Yerushalmi* cited above, but rather reflects the weakness and inability to fast that has overcome some of the Jewish People.

The Ritva (*Shabbat* 24, s.v. *v'im*) and *Tosafot* (*Ta'anit* 11b, s.v. *lan*) reject this concern. They explain that even if one felt weak later in the day and ate, that is considered to be an *ones* (a situation beyond one's control), and we do not consider his earlier prayer to be dishonest.

These *Rishonim* report, however, that the custom in France was for only the *shaliaḥ tzibur* to insert *Anenu* in the morning. They note that this practice does not seem to conform to either the *gemara* or to the *Geonim*! The Ritva explains that "it is inconceivable that there isn't at least one in the community who is fasting, so the *shali'aḥ tzibbur* may recite it," but an individual should not recite it until *Minḥa*. One would not be regarded as a *shakran* (liar) if he were compelled to break his fast after praying *Minḥa* (even *Minḥa Gedola*), since he had at least completed half a day of fasting.

THE *SHULḤAN ARUCH* AND RAMA

Maran Rav Yosef Karo (*Shulḥan Aruch, Oraḥ Ḥayim* 565:3) writes:

> Some say that an individual should not insert *Anenu* except during *Minḥa,* lest he is afflicted by *bulmus* [a condition for which he must eat] and he turns out to have lied in his prayer. However, the *shali'aḥ tzibur* should recite it during *Shaḥarit* when he prays aloud, as some members of the community must be fasting. On the four [public] fast days, even an individual recites it in **all of his prayers,** as even if he were to be afflicted by a *bulmus* and would eat, it is still appropriate to say "*Anenu b'yom ta'anitenu,*" since *Ḥazal* established it as a day to fast.

The words "all of his prayers" indicate that Rav Yosef Karo maintains that *Anenu* should be recited even at *Arvit* on fast days during which one may eat at night, before the fast begins (as explained by the Vilna Gaon 565:3, s.v. *b'chol tefilotav; Ma'amar Mordechai* 565:6).

The Rama, however, adds: "It is customary in our communities to recite *Anenu* only at *Minḥa,* except for the *shaliaḥ tzibur,* who inserts it during the morning repetition." The universally accepted practice of Ashkenazic Jews is to follow the practice cited by the Rama to not recite *Anenu* until *Minḥa.*

THE CURRENT PRACTICE IN SEPHARDIC COMMUNITIES

Surprisingly, most Sephardic communities do not recite *Anenu* at *Arvit* on a *ta'anit tzibur* when it is permitted to eat the night before the fast, in accordance with the opinion of the *Ba'al Ha-Ma'or.* This is a rare departure from the ruling of *Maran* Rav Yosef Karo. However, even these communities do insert *Anenu* during *Shaḥarit.* Rav Ovadia Yosef (*Teshuvot Yabia Omer* 1: *Yoreh De'ah* 21; *Teshuvot Yeḥaveh Da'at* 3:41) endorses this practice, citing as precedent a number of great Sephardic authorities (*Shulḥan Gavo'a* 565:2; *Ma'amar Mordechai* 557:3–4; and *Kaf HaḤayim* 557:5). This is the view followed by the *ḥazan* at Shaarei Orah, the Sephardic Congregation of Teaneck.[1]

---

1. This is also the ruling of Rav Mordechai Eliyahu, as presented in his *Siddur Kol Eliyahu.*

Why did the Sephardic community abandon the ruling of the *Shulḥan Aruch,* which is supported by the clear majority of *Rishonim,* in favor of the ruling of the *Ba'al HaMa'or,* which is a decidedly minority view and is not even cited in the *Shulḥan Aruch*? Indeed, Rav Ovadia Yosef characterizes the practice of the Sephardic communities that do recite *Anenu* at night (such as the Yemenite[2] and Moroccan communities[3]) as "certainly a correct custom." On Tisha B'Av, Rav Ovadia Yosef writes that all Sephardim recite *Anenu* at *Arvit.*

Rav Yitzḥak Yosef (*Yalkut Yosef, Mo'adim* 5:536) writes that the appeal of the *Ba'al HaMa'or*'s view is that it is a "middle of the road position" between Rashi, who holds that *Anenu* should be said only at *Minḥa,* and the many *Rishonim* who say it should be recited even at night.

Rav Yosef Dov Soloveitchik (*Shiurim L'Zecher Abba Mari Z"l* 1:84–85) delighted in discussing the conceptual elegance of reciting *Anenu* at *Arvit* before a fast, since the night before a fast such as Shiva Asar B'Tamuz is defined as part of the "*Yom Ta'anit*" even though the Halacha permits eating and drinking at that time. However, for most Jews, the idea of reciting *Anenu* at a time when it is permitted to eat is counterintuitive to the point of appearing unreasonable. This is the reason, I submit, that most Sephardic communities do not recite *Anenu* at *Arvit.*

THE MOROCCAN PRACTICE

Although Rav Mordechai Lebhar records that the Moroccan custom is to recite *Anenu* at *Arvit* even when it is permitted to eat, four knowledgeable Shaarei Orah members of Moroccan descent insist that they never heard of such a practice. Interestingly, these four men lived in a variety of Moroccan Jewish bastions – Morocco, Israel, Paris, and Montreal – yet none of these gentlemen were aware of this Moroccan practice. I posed this quandary to Dr. Adam Ohayon, co-author of *Darké Abotenou,* an excellent compendium of Moroccan customs. He responded that he also never heard of this practice until he began the research for his *sefer*!

Thus, even though in the authoritative works on Moroccan *minhagim* – such as Rav Yitzḥak Hazan's *Teshuvot Yehaveh Da'at* (1: *Oraḥ*

2. As recorded by Rav Zecharia Ben-Shlomo, *Orot HaHalacha,* p. 737. It is hardly surprising that this is the Yemenite custom in light of the fact that they are following the ruling of the Rambam and *Shulḥan Aruch* in this regard.
3. As noted by Rav Mordechai Lebhar, *Magen Avot, Oraḥ Ḥayim* 565:3.

Ḥayim 21), Rav Yosef Messas' *Otzar HaMichtavim* (2:38), and Rav David Ovadia's *Nahagu HaAm* (*Ta'anit* 1) – report that the Moroccan custom is to recite *Anenu* at *Arvit*, this practice did not reach all of the Moroccan Jewish community. The reason might be the exceedingly counter-intuitive nature of reciting *Anenu* at a time that it is permitted to eat, as noted above.

However, the prominent *dayan* in Montreal Rav David Banon told me that in Casablanca, the custom was to say *Anenu* even at *Arvit*. In fact, he even recalls the *ḥazan* making an announcement reminding the congregation to say *Anenu* at night. This was done in the presence of none other than Rav Shalom Messas. However, Rav Banon noted that there are some Moroccan Jews who do not say *Anenu* at night.[4]

4. Rav Betsalel Levy, the Av Bet Din of Paris, told me that the practice in his Moroccan community of Marrakech was not to recite *Anenu* at *Arvit* on a *ta'anit tzibur*. He acknowledged that there are varying practices in the Moroccan community regarding this issue.

Chapter 66

Naḥem at Every *Tefilla*

Ashkenazim are so accustomed to reciting the paragraph of *Naḥem* only at *Minḥa* of Tisha B'Av that they are shocked to discover that Yemenite[1] and many Sephardic Jews recite *Naḥem* at each of the *tefillot* on Tisha B'Av. In fact, Rav Ovadia Yosef (*Teshuvot Yeḥaveh Da'at* 1:44) presents no fewer than four compelling reason to include *Naḥem* at *Arvit* and *Shaḥarit* as well as *Minḥa* on Tisha B'Av.

FOUR COMPELLING REASONS TO SAY *NAḤEM* AT EVERY *TEFILLA*

Rav Ovadia begins by citing the *Talmud Yerushalmi* (*Berachot* 4:3), which describes reciting *Naḥem* as "*me'en hame'ora*," the appropriate *tefilla* for the occasion. Both the Rosh (*Ta'anit* 4:34) and the *Orḥot Ḥayim* (*Hilchot Tisha B'Av* 16) note that the *Yerushalmi*'s usage of this term implies that *Naḥem* is appropriate for each and every *tefilla* of the day, just as *Ya'aleh V'Yavo* is appropriate for all of the *tefillot* of Rosh Ḥodesh and *Ḥol HaMo'ed*.

A second compelling reason is the fact that the ancient and authoritative *siddur* of Rav Amram Gaon (2:132a) records the practice to recite *Naḥem* at every *tefilla* of Tisha B'Av. The fact that Rav Amram Gaon records

1. As reported by Rav Zecharia Ben-Shlomo, *Orot HaHalacha*, p. 776.

this practice teaches that there is a very old tradition to say *Naḥem* at every *tefilla* and that it likely represents the original practice instituted by *Ḥazal.*

The third reason is that *Maran* Rav Yosef Karo simply states in the *Shulḥan Aruch* (*Oraḥ Ḥayim* 557:1) that *Naḥem* is recited on Tisha B'Av. The fact that he does not limit *Naḥem* to *Minḥa* leads both the *Peri Ḥadash* and the *Ḥida* (*Birkei Yosef* 557:1) to interpret the *Shulḥan Aruch* as ruling that *Naḥem* is recited at every *tefilla.* The *Leḥem Mishneh* (*Hilchot Ta'aniot* 5:10) makes the same inference from the Rambam (*Hilchot Tefilla* 2:14), who mentions that *Naḥem* is recited on Tisha B'Av and does not distinguish between *Minḥa* and the other *tefillot* of the day.

Finally, the fact the Minhag Yerushalayim is to recite *Naḥem* at each of the *tefillot* clinches the point for Rav Ovadia. The fact that this is the practice in Jerusalem is noted by the aforementioned *Peri Ḥadash* and *Ḥida.*

THE ASHKENAZIC PRACTICE AND THE PRACTICE OF MANY SEPHARDIC JEWS

The Rama (557:1), however, notes that the accepted practice of Ashkenazic Jews is to recite *Naḥem* only at *Minḥa,* and this remains the uncontested Ashkenazic practice until today. The Rama explains that since the *gemara* (*Ta'anit* 29a) states that the *Bet HaMikdash* was set on fire towards the end of Tisha B'Av, this is the appropriate time to pray for the *neḥama,* the comforting of Tzion.

The Vilna Gaon (*Bi'ur HaGra* 555:2) explains that at the time of *Minḥa,* the heavenly judgment for the destruction was pronounced, making it the appropriate time for condolence. The Ritva (*Teshuvot* 63) adds that until *Minḥa,* the Jewish People are like someone who lost a close relative and has not yet buried him. After *Minḥa,* however, we are likened to one who has just buried a deceased relative, making it the proper time for condolence. The *Birkei Yosef* (559:7) adds in the name of the Ari z"l that it is at the time of *Minḥa* that *Mashiaḥ* will be born.

While we understand why Ashkenazim recite *Naḥem* only at *Minḥa,* why do many Sephardic Jews – including Sephardic Jews who hail from Iraq, North African, Persia, and Syria – follow the ruling of the Rama and not that of Rav Yosef Karo, who indicates in the *Shulḥan Aruch* that *Naḥem* should be recited at all of the *tefillot*? Many Sephardic Jews were influenced by the *Ben Ish Ḥai* (year 1, *Parashat Devarim* 7), who indicates that *Naḥem* is recited only at *Minḥa* of Tisha B'Av.

Rav Mordechai Lebhar (*Magen Avot, Oraḥ Ḥayim* 557) defends the North African practice. He notes that both the Avudraham (p. 257) and Rav Karo in his *Bet Yosef* commentary to the *Tur* (*Oraḥ Ḥayim* 557) write that the *minhag* is to recite *Naḥem* only at *Minḥa*. Rav Lebhar notes that Rav Karo famously writes in his introduction to the *Shulḥan Aruch* that he does not intend to override preexisting *minhagim*. Thus, Rav Lebhar concludes that since the custom of certain communities to recite *Naḥem* only at *Minḥa* precedes the composition of the *Shulḥan Aruch*, Rav Karo would agree that in such a case, his ruling in the *Shulḥan Aruch* should not be followed by those communities.[2]

CONCLUSION

Accordingly, North African Jews maintain their ancient custom to recite *Naḥem* only at *Minḥa*, while most Sephardic Jews adhere to the ruling of the *Shulḥan Aruch* and Minhag Yerushalayim to say *Naḥem* at all *tefillot* of Tisha B'Av. At Congregation Shaarei Orah, the Sephardic Congregation of Teaneck, the *ḥazan* follows Minhag Yerushalayim and the ruling of Rav Ovadia to recite *Naḥem* at each *tefilla* on Tisha B'Av.

2. Interestingly, Rav Lebhar notes that the Avudraham records the practice of Rav Sa'adia Gaon to recite *Naḥem* only at *Minḥa*. This would demonstrate that the dispute as to when to recite *Naḥem* is quite ancient—Rav Amram Gaon vs. Rav Sa'adia Gaon. However, Rav Ovadia Yosef challenges this point, noting that in the extant editions of the *siddur* of Rav Sa'adia Gaon (p. 319), it appears that he does not limit the recital of *Naḥem* to *Minḥa*. According to Rav Ovadia, the unchallenged view of the *Geonim* is to recite *Naḥem* at each of the *tefillot* of Tisha B'Av.

Chapter 67

Haftara at *Minḥa* of a *Ta'anit Tzibur*

This could be an awkward moment... The *gabbai* at an Ashkenazic *bet kenesset* calls a Sephardic Jew up for *Shelishi* at *Minḥa* on a *ta'anit* (fast day). This *oleh* not only receives an *aliya*, but also reads the *haftara*. This seems like a highly regarded honor, but it poses a serious dilemma for the Sephardic Jew. After all, it is the Rama (*Oraḥ Ḥayim* 566:1) who records the practice to read the beautiful *haftara* of "*Dirshu Hashem B'Himatze'o*" (*Yeshayahu* 55:6–56:8) on fast days, not *Maran* Rav Yosef Karo. Sephardic Jews do not recite a *haftara* at *Minḥa* on a *ta'anit* (with two notable exceptions).

May the Sephardic Jew accept the *aliya* and recite the *haftara*, with all of its *berachot*? Perhaps it is forbidden for him to accept this *aliya*, since by his standards it is regarded as an unnecessary utterance of a *beracha* (*beracha l'vatala*).

THE BACKGROUND

The *gemara* in *Megilla* (30b–32a) outlines the Torah and *haftara* readings for the various occasions in Jewish life. The only *haftara* reading specified for *ta'aniot* is the *haftara* selection for *Shaḥarit* of Tisha B'Av morning. Similarly, the Rambam mentions a *haftara* reading for Tisha B'Av only at *Shaḥarit*.

In addition, the *mishna* mentions a special Torah reading for *Shaḥarit* and *Minḥa* on a fast day – the passage of the *berachot* and *kelalot* (blessings and curses) in *Parashat Beḥukotai*. The Rambam and *Tosafot* (*Megilla* 31b, s.v. *Rosh Ḥodesh*), however, codify the ruling of *Masechet Soferim* (17:7), which states that instead we read Moshe Rabbenu's prayer for forgiveness after the *ḥet ha'egel* (*Shemot* 32 and 34). Ashkenazic and Sephardic Jews follow this practice (*Shulḥan Aruch, Oraḥ Ḥayim* 566:1).

Masechet Soferim (17:6) notes varying practices regarding the *haftara* for *Minḥa* on a *Ta'anit*, writing that some advocate the recitation of "*Dirshu Hashem*," while others do not. *Masechet Soferim* notes that the dominant practice is to recite this *haftara*, but the varying practices persist. The *Bet Yosef* (*Oraḥ Ḥayim* 575) records that Sephardic Jews follow the practice of the Rambam and the Avudraham to refrain from reciting a *haftara* for *Minḥa* on a *ta'anit* (except for Tisha B'Av, as discussed below).

THE RESOLUTION

In order to respond to our Sephardic Jew's dilemma, we must first understand the reason for the Sephardic practice. The *Bet Yosef* (ibid.) explains that the concern is *toraḥ hatzibur* (imposing an improper burden on the community). This is a well-founded concern, as the *mishna* (*Megilla* 21a) articulates the principle that a *haftara* is not recited on a work day for this reason. Rashi explains that reading a *haftara* on such a day is too burdensome for the community when they are pressured to rush to work. Since fast days are work days, it is inappropriate to read a *haftara* on such a day.

Based on this ruling, Rav Ovadia Hadaya (*Teshuvot Yaskil Avdi* 6:9), a leading mid-twentieth century Sephardic *posek*, permits a Sephardic Jew to read the fast day *haftara* at an Ashkenazic congregation. He reasons that there is no concern for *toraḥ hatzibur* if the community will in any event be reciting the *haftara*. Although Rav Hadaya forbids a Sephardic or Yemenite Jew who blows the shofar at an Ashkenazic *bet kenesset* to recite *Sheheḥiyanu* on the second day of Rosh Hashana, since this would constitute a *beracha l'vatala* according to Sephardic and Yemenite practice (*Shulḥan Aruch, Oraḥ Ḥayim* 601:3),[1] in this case, there is no fundamental objection to the recital of the *berachot* on the *haftara*. The only concern is one of *toraḥ hatzibur*.

1. See Rav Zecharia Ben-Shlomo, *Orot HaHalacha*, p. 811, regarding the Yemenite practice.

Similarly, although Rav Ovadia Yosef (*Teshuvot Yabia Omer* 1: *Oraḥ Ḥayim* 29; *Teshuvot Yeḥaveh Da'at* 4:31) forbids a Sephardic Jew who is serving as a *ḥazan* at an Ashkenazic *minyan* to recite the *beracha* on *Hallel* on Rosh Ḥodesh (see *Shulḥan Aruch, Oraḥ Ḥayim* 422:2), he endorses this ruling of Rav Hadaya (*Hazon Ovadia, Arba Ta'aniot*, p. 103; *Yalkut Yosef, Mo'adim*, p. 566). However, he advises trying to avoid receiving the *aliya* when possible.

TWO POSSIBLE EXCEPTIONS – TISHA B'AV AND TZOM GEDALIA

Many Sephardic Jews do read a *haftara* at *Minḥa* of Tisha B'Av, as noted by Rav Ovadia (*Teshuvot Yeḥaveh Da'at* 5:40).[2] Although this runs counter to the rulings of the Rambam and the *Shulḥan Aruch*, it follows the practice of Rav David Avudraham, who composed a most authoritative work on the *siddur*, a fact acknowledged by the *Bet Yosef* (*Oraḥ Ḥayim* 425). Moreover, the logic for this approach is compelling, as there is no concern for *toraḥ hatzibbur* on Tisha B'Av, since work is discouraged on this day (*Shulḥan Aruch, Oraḥ Ḥayim* 696:1). Indeed, *Ḥazal* already mandated a *haftara* for the morning of Tisha B'Av.

Rav Ovadia notes that this practice is also the Minhag Yerushalayim (as noted by *Teshuvot Sadeh HaAretz* 3: *Oraḥ Ḥayim* 28), and the *Bet Yosef* (op. cit.) writes that the practice of Sephardic Jews is to recite a *haftara* at *Minḥa* of Tisha B'Av. However, unlike Ashkenazic practice, which adopts "*Dirshu Hashem*" as the selection for this *haftara*, Sephardic Jews read "*Shuva Yisrael*" (*Hoshe'a* 14).

Interestingly, Moroccan Jews recite the *haftara* of "*Dirshu Hashem B'Himatze'o*" at *Minḥa* of Tzom Gedalia as well. This is the only time of the year that they recite this *haftara*. This practice is in accordance with the ruling of *Maran* Rav Yosef Karo as stated in the *Shulḥan Aruch* (*Oraḥ Ḥayim* 428:8), based on *Tosafot* (op. cit.). As the *Mishna Berura* (428:24) notes, the logic of this practice is compelling, since *Ḥazal* teach (*Rosh Hashana* 18a) that "*Dirshu Hashem B'Himatze'o*" (seek *Hashem* when He is present) refers to the period of the *Aseret Yemei Teshuva*.

2. Many Yemenite Jews do not recite this *haftara*, as noted by Rav Zechariah Ben-Shlomo, *Orot HaHalacha*, p. 779, hewing strictly to the rulings of the Rambam and *Shulḥan Aruch*.

Nonetheless, Minhag Yerushalayim – recorded by the *Ḥida* (*Teshuvot Hayim Sha'al* 2:38:91), the *Kaf HaḤayim* (428:47), and Rav Ovadia Yosef (op. cit.) – does not subscribe to this practice. The Minhag Yerushalayim accords with the *Bet Yosef*'s report that Sephardic Jews recite a *haftara* at *Minḥa* of a *ta'anit* only on Tisha B'Av. In addition, this practice fits with the *mishna* in *Megilla* that teaches that a *haftara* is not recited on a work day due to concern for *toraḥ hatzibur*.

CONCLUSION

At Congregation Shaarei Orah, the Sephardic Congregation of Teaneck, we follow the *Bet Yosef*'s recording that Sephardic Jews recite a *haftara* at *Minḥa* only on Tisha B'Av, when we recite the selection of "*Shuva Yisrael*" from *Hoshe'a*.

Chapter 68

Tefillin at *Shaḥarit* of Tisha B'Av

As I have noted repeatedly, Congregation Shaarei Orah, the Sephardic Congregation of Teaneck, generally follows the rulings of Rav Ovadia Yosef and the Minhag Yerushalayim, the custom of Jerusalem's Sephardic congregations. Why, then, do the men at Shaarei Orah not wear *tefillin* at *Shaḥarit* of Tisha B'Av? After all, Rav Ovadia (*Teshuvot Yeḥaveh Da'at* 2:67; *Yalkut Yosef, Oraḥ Ḥayim* 555) endorses the practice to wear *tefillin* at *Shaḥarit* on Tisha B'Av, and he insists, with considerable support, that this constitutes the Minhag Yerushalayim!

BACKGROUND IN THE *RISHONIM*

The question of wearing *tefillin* on Tisha B'Av is not addressed in the Talmud. However, the *Rishonim* address this issue at some length. Most *Rishonim* – including *Tosafot* (*Mo'ed Katan* 21a, s.v *mishelishi v'elach* and *mikan v'elach*), Rosh (*Ta'anit* 4:37), Ramban (*Torat HaAdam*, p. 55a [Warsaw 1841 ed.]), Ran (*Ta'anit* 10a in the Rif's pages), and the Rashba (*Teshuvot* 5:214) citing Rav Hai Gaon – rule that a man is obligated to wear *tefillin* on Tisha B'Av. The Rambam (*Hilchot Ta'aniot* 5:11) records that a small number of sages do not put on *tefillin shel rosh* on Tisha B'Av, which implies that he maintains that the consensus view is that there is an obligation of *tefillin* on Tisha B'Av (as noted by the *Maggid Misneh*, ad loc.).

The general rule established by the *gemara* (*Ta'anit* 30a) is that everything that applies to a mourner during *shiva* applies on Tisha B'Av. A mourner does not wear *tefillin* on the first day of mourning but does on subsequent days (*Shulḥan Aruch, Yoreh De'ah* 388:1). These *Rishonim* thus seek to prove that Tisha B'Av is more similar to the subsequent days of mourning, when a mourner does wear *tefillin*. For example, they note that it is permitted, technically speaking, to work on Tisha B'Av, whereas working is strictly forbidden under all circumstances during the first three days of *shiva*.

However, the Semag (Rabbinic positive commandment 3, *Hilchot Tisha B'Av*) and *Roke'aḥ* (310) rule that one should not wear *tefillin* on Tisha B'Av. This also seems to be the opinion of the Maharam of Rothenburg (*Hilchot Semaḥot Me'Et Rabbenu Meir ben Rabbenu Baruch MiRothenburg* 68), although the *Hagahot Maimoniyot* (*Hilchot Ta'aniyot* 5:11:3) testifies that he witnessed the Maharam donning *tefillin* in the afternoon.

THE PRACTICE TO WEAR *TEFILLIN* ONLY AT *MINḤA* ON TISHA B'AV

Not surprisingly, *Maran* Rav Yosef Karo (*Shulḥan Aruch, Oraḥ Ḥayim* 38:6), following the dominant view among the *Rishonim*, rules that men are obligated to wear *tefillin* on Tisha B'Av. The *Shulhan Aruch* later records (*Oraḥ Ḥayim* 555:1), however, that the common custom is what appears to be a middle position between the aforementioned *Rishonim*: One does not put on *tefillin* on Tisha B'Av in the morning, but rather does so for the *Minḥa* service. This represents the standard practice among Ashkenazic Jews.

What is the reason for this compromise custom? The *Magen Avraham* (555:1) explains that *tefillin* expresses the "glory" (*pe'er*) of our people (*Sukka* 25a), and on Tisha B'Av our glory was taken away. However, he offers no explanation for the difference between the morning and the afternoon. The *Mishna Berura* (555:3) explains that since men are obligated to wear *tefillin* on Tisha B'Av, they do so in the afternoon, since in the afternoon we are more lenient regarding some of the customs of mourning (such as sitting on the floor) because the Temple had already started burning in the afternoon. This means that the heavenly judgment was issued and executed, making it time for us to be consoled.

THE PRACTICE OF MANY SEPHARDIC JEWS TO WEAR *TEFILLIN* AT *SHAḤARIT* ON TISHA B'AV

Surprisingly, a significant group of Sephardic Jews wear *tefillin* even at *Shaḥarit* of Tisha B'Av, against the custom presented by *Maran* Rav Yosef Karo. They are influenced by the practice of two great kabbalists, the Ari z"l (cited in the *Ba'er Hetev* 555:1) and Rav Shalom Sharaby (cited by the *Kaf HaḤayim* 555:3). In fact, the *Kaf HaḤayim* notes that this is the practice of the great Sephardic Kabbalistic Yeshivat Bet El, located in Jerusalem's Old City, and he notes that this practice has spilled over to some more conventional Sephardic synagogues in Jerusalem. Rav Ovadia Yosef insists that this has emerged as the dominant custom in Sephardic Jerusalem and represents "*haḥzarat atara l'yoshena*," restoration of the crown to its glory, since this Jerusalem custom is an ancient one.

The *Ben Ish Ḥai* (year 1, *Parashat Devarim* 25) adopts a compromise view of sorts, advocating that one don *tefillin* at home, read *keriat Shema* while wearing the *tefillin*, and then attend *Shaḥarit* at synagogue without wearing *tefillin*. Rav Ovadia Yosef, however, encourages wearing *tefillin* during *Shaḥarit* in the *bet kenesset* and removing them prior to the recitation of the *Kinot*.

THE PRACTICE OF MANY SEPHARDIC COMMUNITIES

Despite the rulings of these iconic Sephardic halachic authorities, many Sephardic communities – most prominently, Moroccan and Turkish Jews – refrain from wearing *tefillin* on Tisha B'Av until *Minḥa*, in accordance with the custom recorded by Rav Yosef Karo. Rav Shalom Messas (*Teshuvot Shemesh U'Magen* 2:6–7) writes at length and insists that only those immersed in kabbalistic study should wear *tefillin* even in private at *Shaḥarit* on Tisha B'Av. Others should follow the practice recorded by *Maran* Rav Yosef Karo to wait until *Minḥa* to don *tefillin*.[1]

---

1. Rav Eliyahu Mansour insists that Sephardic Jews either wear *tefillin* at home or at the *bet kenesset* during the morning of Tisha B'Av (http://www.dailyhalacha.com/m/halacha.aspx?id=1249). However, it is clear from both the *Kaf HaḤayim* and Rav Ovadia Yosef that this is not the universal practice accepted by all Sephardim. Indeed, Rav Mordechai Eliyahu (*Siddur Kol Eliyahu*) presents the norm as *tefillin* worn only at *Minḥa*, with the exception of Minhag Yerushalayim to wear *tefillin* at *Shaḥarit* in the *bet kenesset*. Rav Yonatan Nacson (*Sefer MiMizraḥ U'MiMa'arav*, p. 191) writes that the general custom outside Jerusalem is not to wear *tefillin* at *Shaḥarit* of Tisha B'Av.

Rav Messas further endeavors to demonstrate that the practice of wearing *tefillin* at *Shaḥarit* on Tisha B'Av does not, in fact, constitute the dominant practice among Jerusalem's Sephardic congregations. He also forcefully argues that the *ḥurban Bet HaMikdash* should not be ignored in Jerusalem, of all places, by wearing *tefillin* at *Shaḥarit* of Tisha B'Av.

CONCLUSION

Even Rav Ovadia Yosef concludes that those congregations that refrain from wearing *tefillin* during *Shaḥarit* on Tisha B'Av, in accordance with the ruling of the *Shulḥan Aruch*, should maintain their custom. In keeping with this conclusion, the men of Shaarei Orah do not don *tefillin* on the morning of Tisha B'Av.[2]

2. Rav Ovadia (*Ḥazon Ovadia, Arba Ta'aniyot*, p. 370 in the *bi'urim*) rules that if someone who wears *tefilin* at *Shaḥarit* on Tisha B'Av visits a synagogue where the congregants do not wear *tefillin* at *Shaḥarit* but wear them at *Minḥa*, he must wear *tefillin* at *Minḥa* in order not to deviate from the practice of the community in which he finds himself. Rav Ben Zion Abba Sha'ul (*Teshuvot Ohr L'Tziyon* 3:29:22) adopts the same position and even goes further, counseling that one should avoid a synagogue whose congregants follow two different practices in this regard.

Yom HaAtzma'ut

Chapter 69

Sephardic Rabbinical Approaches to Zionism

Rav Baruch Gigi, the Rosh Yeshiva of Yeshivat Har Etzion (Israel's largest *Yeshivat Hesder*), served as scholar-in-residence at Congregation Shaarei Orah, the Sephardic Congregation of Teaneck, on Shabbat *Parashat Vayikra* 5778. One of Rav Gigi's outstanding presentations was a fascinating *shiur* on the topic of Sephardic Rabbinic approaches to Zionism.

THE ANTI-ZIONISM OF THE SATMAR RAV

Rav Gigi began by presenting the anti-Zionist approach of the Satmar Rav. This approach is rooted in the *gemara* (*Ketuvot* 111a), which states that *Hashem* imposed a *shevua* (oath) upon us that we would not take Eretz Yisrael by force ("*shelo ya'alu Yisrael b'ḥoma*").

Rav Meir Simḥa of Dvinsk (the famed author of the *Meshech Ḥochma* and the *Ohr Same'aḥ*) reacted to the League of Nations' ratification of the Balfour Declaration, which granted the Jews a national home in Eretz Yisrael, with three words: "*Sar paḥad hashevua*" – the concern for the oath not to take Eretz Yisrael by force no longer applies, since permission was granted by the international community. The *Avnei Nezer* (*Teshuvot, Yoreh De'ah* 456) agreed with this assessment.[1]

In contrast, the Satmar Rav insisted that the oath remained in effect even when permission for Jews to reside in and eventually govern part of the land was granted by the League of Nations and the United Nations. The Satmar Rav regarded the political pressure placed on the League of Nations and United Nations delegates by Zionist leaders as constituting returning to Eretz Yisrael by force.

This represents a fundamental opposition to Zionism, not simply a feeling of unease with cooperating with non-observant Jews. Rav Gigi argues that such fundamental opposition to Zionism is virtually non-existent among leading Sephardic rabbis.

RAV YEHUDA ALKALAI

Rav Yehuda Alkalai, a great Sephardic Rav from Serbia, is counted among the founders of modern Zionism. His work espousing large scale Jewish settlement in Eretz Yisrael, *Minḥat Yehuda,* predated Theodore Herzl. Moreover, in his *Goral LaHashem,* Rav Alkalai presented a detailed plan for the reestablishment of the Jewish State in Eretz Yisrael, which is said to have greatly influenced Herzl's extremely influential work, *The Jewish State.*

Rav Alkalai argues that natural redemption precedes the supernatural redemption. He refers to this as the Mashiaḥ ben Yosef preceding the Mashiaḥ ben David. A central and well-known idea of Rav Alkalai (that appears in *Minḥat Yehuda*) elaborates on the statement of Rav Eliezer (*Sanhedrin* 97b, codified by the Rambam, *Hilchot Teshuva* 7:5): "*En Yisrael nigalin ela beteshuva,*" "The Jewish People will not be redeemed without *teshuva.*" Rav Alkalai distinguishes between *teshuva* of the individual and *teshuva* of the community. The individual must repent in the most straightforward manner; he must correct any lapses in his Torah observance. In contrast, national *teshuva* refers to our nation returning to Eretz Yisrael. Rav Alkalai proves this point from the etymology of the word *teshuva,* which means to return to one's original place of residence, as in the *pasuk,* "*Uteshuvato haRamata ki sham beto*" (*Shemuel I* 7:17).

---

1. Rav Gigi noted that the Maharsha on the *gemara* in *Ketuvot* clearly supports the approach of the *Meshech Ḥochma* and *Avnei Nezer.* The Maharsha explains that Neḥemia was permitted to rebuild the walls of Yerushalayim (*Neḥemia,* chs. 1–9) because he had permission from the Persian emperor Artaxerxes.

After Rav Alkalai made *aliya* in 1874, he moved to Jerusalem, where he engaged in major debates with the rabbis of the Yishuv HaYashan, the traditional Jewish community in Jerusalem, which opposed activist settlement in Eretz Yisrael.

SUPPORT FOR ZIONISM AMONG GREAT MOROCCAN *RABBANIM*

The great Moroccan *Rabbanim*, ranging from Rav Shalom Messas to the famous Baba Sali, were enthusiastic supporters of Zionism. Indeed, Rav Gigi recalled from the years in which he was raised in Morocco that there was widespread support and enthusiasm for Zionism in all circles. Rav Shalom Messas maintained that one should recite *Hallel* on Yom HaAtzma'ut with a *beracha*. However, out of respect to the ruling of Rav Ovadia Yosef, he ruled that *Hallel* should be recited without a *beracha* (*Teshuvot Shemesh U'Magen* 3:63:6).

The Baba Sali asserted that the State of Israel was created in the merit of the poem composed by his son, the Baba Meir, called "*Degel Yisrael Herima*," "The flag of Israel has been raised." When the Baba Sali was told that secular Jews were building the State of Israel, he replied by citing the *tefilla* of *Naḥem*, which we recite on Tisha B'Av: "*Ki Atah b'esh hitzata, uva'esh Atah atid l'vnota*" – with fire Yerushalayim was destroyed and with fire it will be rebuilt. He explained that just as Jerusalem was destroyed by the fire of *avoda zara*, it will sadly be rebuilt by *avoda zara*.

Israeli agents for *aliya* were well received in Morocco. Rav Yitzchak Abuḥatzeira, the Chief Rabbi of Ramle, is remembered for allowing his house to serve as a place of transition for Jews making *aliya*. Although there was great debate in Moroccan communities about the Alliance schools, which brought secular studies to Sephardic communities, the debates related to the fact that these schools influenced their students to abandon Torah ways; they had nothing to do with Zionism.

Finally, Rav Amram Aburbeh was a noted Moroccan Rav who was an enthusiastic supporter of Zionism and predicted Israel's massive victory in the Six Day War with *Hashem*'s help, months before his passing in 1966.

RAV OVADIA YOSEF

Rav Ovadia Yosef recited a *MiSheberach* for the soldiers of *Tzahal* each time the *Heichal* was opened to remove the Torah on Shabbat morning. Rav Ovadia expresses his strong support for the State of Israel in one of his *teshuvot*

(*Yabia Omer* 11: *Ḥoshen Mishpat* 22), where he explains his position permitting the exchange of Israeli land for peace. Members of Kenesset from the Shas party, which was guided by Rav Ovadia, are permitted to serve as cabinet ministers in the Israeli government, unlike the Ashkenazic Ḥaredi members of Kenesset, who join the governing coalition but are forbidden by their Rabbinic leaders to serve as cabinet ministers. The *Yalkut Yosef* – written by Rav Ovadia's son, Rav Yitzḥak Yosef – is replete with instructions for Israeli soldiers, something that is (sadly) anathema in many Ashkenazic circles.

A contrast between Rav Ovadia's reaction to the great Entebbe rescue in 1976 with that of the Satmar Rav is most instructive. Whereas the Satmar Rav reacted with condemnation (based on the *mishna* in *Gittin* 45a),[2] Rav Ovadia reacted with the utmost enthusiasm (*Yabia Omer* 10: *Ḥoshen Mishpat* 7; *Yeḥaveh Da'at* 2:25).

Rav Ovadia rules (*Yeḥaveh Da'at* 5:63) that one must fully comply with Israeli tax regulations. In this responsum, Rav Ovadia even endorses Rav Kook's ruling that a government accepted by the Jewish People in Eretz Yisrael enjoys the status of a *melech* in certain regards.

SEPHARDIC RABBINICAL OPPOSITION TO ZIONISM

Rav Gigi noted that there were Sephardic *Rabbanim* who opposed Zionism and even issued proclamations to refrain from voting in Israeli elections. He observed, however, that their opposition was not rooted in a fundamental opposition to Zionism, but rather stemmed from disapproval of nonobservant members of the Israeli government and the improper pressure placed on Sephardic *olim* to enroll their children in secular public schools, which encouraged the abandonment of a Torah lifestyle.

RAV HALEVY, RAV UZIEL, AND RAV HADAYA

Rav Gigi concluded by noting two great Sephardic rabbis who were enthusiastic supporters of the State of Israel and Religious Zionism, Rav Ḥayim David HaLevy and Chief Rabbi Ben Tzion Meir Ḥai Uziel.

Rav Ḥayim David HaLevy, who for many years served as the Sephardic Chief Rabbi of Tel Aviv, makes his support for Religious Zionism clear in his works, such as his *Teshuvot Asei Lecha Rav*. His *Kitzur Shulḥan*

2. As cited in the weekly newspaper that serves as the organ of the Satmar community, *Der Yid*, Aug. 20, 1976.

Aruch Mekor Ḥayim has served for decades as the basic halachic work taught in Religious Zionist schools.

Rav Ben Tzion Meir Ḥai Uziel served as the first Sephardic Chief Rabbi of the State of Israel and composed, together with Chief Rabbi Yitzḥak Herzog and Shai Agnon, the *Tefillah L'Shlom HaMedina*. Rav Uziel wrote: "A great and miraculous merit has been revealed in this generation, to fulfill the words of the *nevi'im* to establish a Jewish State in Eretz Yisrael." Rav Uziel proceeded to implore all Jews "to return to full Torah observance and to guard the people and State of Israel."

We should add that Rav Ovadia Hadaya, a major Sephardic mid-twentieth century halachic authority, describes the establishment of the State of Israel as "*teḥilat hageula*," the beginning of our redemption (*Teshuvot Yaskil Avdi* 6:10). He describes the miracles of Israel's War of Independence as comparable to the miracles of Ḥanukka and the splitting of the Red Sea. Although he believes that a *beracha* should not be said on *Hallel* recited on Yom HaAtzma'ut, his enthusiasm for Medinat Yisrael is presented unambiguously.

CONCLUSION

Support for Zionism is quite strong among Sephardim, even in Ḥaredi circles.[3] Fundamental opposition to the State of Israel, such as was voiced by the Satmar Rav, is virtually unheard of in the Sephardic community.[4] Thus, I was not surprised to hear that Rav Eli Mansour, a Sephardic Ḥaredi leader in Brooklyn, strongly encouraged his followers to attend the AIPAC policy conference in Washington in 2018.[5]

---

3. It is striking that the Artscroll Sephardic *Siddur* includes Rav Ovadia's version of the prayer for Israeli soldiers, whereas the Ashkenazic version of the Artscroll *Siddur* does not include this prayer.
4. Numerous Sephardic rabbis have told me that Zionism for Sephardic Jews did not have the secular political overtones that were pervasive in the Ashkenazic community. Rather, for Sephardic Jews, Zionism is an expression of love for Eretz Yisrael, and thus fundamental opposition to Zionism among Sephardic Jews is uncommon.
5. I was also delighted to see that Rav Mansour writes (http://www.dailyhalacha.com/displayRead.asp?readID=2949): "Special preference should be given to the *etrogim* of Eretz Yisrael. Rav Yeḥiel Michel Epstein (*Aruch HaShulḥan, Oraḥ Ḥayim* 648) elaborates on the importance of using an *etrog* grown in Eretz Yisrael when such an *etrog* is available. He writes that it would be a grave affront to our land if one has the option of using an *etrog* from Eretz Yisrael but chooses instead to use an *etrog* grown outside the land."

Chapter 70

Hallel on Yom HaAtzma'ut

Is it appropriate to recite *Hallel* on Yom HaAtzma'ut, which commemorates the declaration of the establishment of the modern State of Israel? Rav Ovadia Yosef's *teshuva* (*Yabia Omer* 6: *Oraḥ Ḥayim* 41) is an invaluable resource for both sides of the debate on this issue and serves as the basis for much of this chapter.

One might argue that it is best to be "safe" and refrain from reciting *Hallel* in this case of doubt, but refraining from *Hallel* is not necessarily the best option. After all, the *gemara* (*Sanhedrin* 94a) strongly reprimands King Ḥizkiyahu for failing to recite *Hallel* upon the miraculous defeat of Sanḥerev, the king of Assyria. In fact, the *gemara* states that Ḥizkiyahu was a serious candidate to be the *Mashiaḥ*, but he was rejected because of his failure to recite *Hallel*.

On the other hand, reciting *Hallel* is also not necessarily the best option, as *Hallel* is reserved for special occasions; the *gemara* (*Shabbat* 118b) condemns those who recite *Hallel* every day and describes one who does not reserve *Hallel* for special occasions as a blasphemer. Accordingly, one must take a stand on this issue, either to recite *Hallel* or not to recite *Hallel* on Yom HaAtzma'ut.

THE ḤANUKKA PRECEDENT

In discussing the source of the obligation to recite *Hallel*, the *gemara* (*Pesaḥim* 117a) cites the Sages who stated, "The prophets instituted the recitation of *Hallel* at various times of the year and whenever Jews are redeemed from dire straits." Rashi (ad loc., s.v. *v'al*) adds that the *Hallel* of Ḥanukka is an example of reciting *Hallel* in celebration of redemption from a crisis.

The Meiri (ad loc.) clarifies that if a miracle happens to an individual or to a community of Jews, that individual or community may establish the day of redemption as a day for reciting *Hallel*, but without a *beracha*. Only if the miracle occurred to all Jews, such as the case of Ḥanukka, may we recite *Hallel* with a *beracha*.

The Rambam and *Shulḥan Aruch* do not codify this *gemara*. The *Magen Avraham* (686:4) and *Mishna Berura* (686:8), however, write that a community is authorized to declare a "Purim" celebration for all generations on a day that a miracle occurred. The *Ḥayei Adam* (155:41) recounts at length how he instituted a "Purim" for his family and future descendants for a miracle that occurred to his family.

The *posekim* debate whether the declaration of Medinat Yisrael constitutes a miracle for the entire Jewish community. Some argue that the restoration of the *Bet HaMikdash* constitutes redemption for the entire Jewish nation, but restoration of Jewish sovereignty over a portion of Eretz Yisrael redeems only the Jews who reside in Eretz Yisrael. On the other hand, Rav Ovadia Hadaya (*Teshuvot Yaskil Avdi* 6: *Oraḥ Ḥayim* 10) notes that the fact that the State of Israel serves as a safe haven for persecuted Jews worldwide constitutes redemption for all Jews. The fifth day of Iyar is appropriate to celebrate since it is the day that Jews were redeemed from the terrible predicament of having no refuge to which to flee in times of persecution.

AN OPEN MIRACLE?

The Maharatz Ḥayes (*Shabbat* 21b) asserts that we recite *Hallel* on Ḥanukka only because a *nes nigleh* (an obvious miracle) occurred on those days. He notes that the *gemara*, in explaining why we celebrate Ḥanukka, mentions the miracle of the oil but does not mention the military victory of the Hasmoneans. Accordingly, some argue that *Hallel* is inappropriate for Yom HaAtzma'ut, since no blatant miracle occurred during the establishment of the State of Israel and its War of Independence. Although they acknowledge that many subtle miracles occurred,[1] they argue that no obvious miracle occurred, comparable to one day's supply of oil lasting eight days.

One may respond to this argument that the *Al HaNissim* prayer presents the military victory of the Maccabees as the primary reason for celebrating Ḥanukka. The Rambam (*Hilchot Ḥanukka* 3:1–3) writes that we celebrate Ḥanukka for a variety of reasons, including not only the miracles of the oil and the military victory, but also that Jewish sovereignty was restored over Eretz Yisrael for more than two hundred years.

Moreover, when the *gemara* in *Megilla* (14a) questions why we do not recite *Hallel* on Purim, it does not offer the absence of an open miracle in the Purim story as one of the answers. In fact, a characterizing feature of *Megillat Esther* is that its miracles were subtle, but we are able to sense from the progression of events in the *Megilla* that *Hashem* quietly orchestrated them. According to many, this is why *Hashem*'s name does not appear in the *Megilla*. Similarly, one who studies the history of the State of Israel with a discerning eye readily perceives the guiding hand of the Creator tilting the events in our favor.[2]

Two anecdotes from Israel's War of Independence illustrate this point. Rav Dr. Mordechai Cohen of Yeshiva University relates that his father, while in the midst of a critical battle while fighting in Israel's War of Independence, was issued an astounding order by his commanding officer – to use fewer bullets due to severe ammunition shortages. Notwithstanding this, the side of the fighting that was forced to shoot fewer bullets emerged as the victor!

Rav Yehuda Amital, the founding Rosh Yeshiva of Yeshivat Har Etzion, recalled that when he enlisted to join the army, he was assigned the rank of an officer. They told him that since he presumably knew how to shoot a gun, he was qualified to serve as an officer!

These stories typify the desperate situation that we faced in the War of Independence. We emerged victorious only because of *Hashem*'s guiding hand. Many claim that this constitutes sufficient reason to recite *Hallel* on Yom HaAtzma'ut.

---

1. As is apparent from reading the detailed account of this war in Benny Morris' monumental work, *1948*.
2. See the extensive discussion in my *Reason to Believe: Rational Explanations of Orthodox Jewish Thought*, pp. 115–175.

Rav Amital stated many times that even if one does not believe it is appropriate to recite *Hallel* on Yom HaAtzmaut, he should find some other vehicle for expressing thanks to *Hashem* for granting us Medinat Yisrael. Some suggest reciting the *V'Hi SheAmda* section of the Pesaḥ *Haggada* to express gratitude to *Hashem* for Medinat Yisrael. Indeed, Medinat Yisrael has served for the past seventy years as *Hashem*'s instrument to save us from the oppressors who arise in our generation.

SUCCESSES AND FAILURES OF MEDINAT YISRAEL

Many note that while we are grateful to *Hashem* for giving us Medinat Yisrael, we must acknowledge its shortcomings – both physical and spiritual. Rav Ovadia Hadaya (*Teshuvot Yaskil Avdi, Oraḥ Ḥayim op. cit.*) rules that *Hallel* should not be recited on Yom HaAtzma'ut because of the unstable security situation in Israel. Instead, he suggests reciting the chapters of *Hallel* (omitting the *beracha*) after the completion of the *tefilla*. Rav Ovadia Yosef relates that Rav Zvi Pesaḥ Frank did not recite *Hallel* on Yom HaAtzma'ut in his *bet midrash* because of the security problems and the spiritual shortcomings of the nation.

Moreover, the *Ḥazon Ish* (*Letters* 97) writes that it is inappropriate for this generation, with all of its spiritual flaws, to institute new practices. The *Ḥazon Ish* wrote this in connection with establishing Yom HaSho'ah, and his reasoning also applies to instituting the recitation of *Hallel* on Yom HaAtzma'ut.

Nevertheless, many authorities endorse reciting *Hallel* on Yom HaAtzma'ut. *Teshuvot Kol Mevaser* (21) and *Teshuvot Netzer Mata'ai* (36) rule that *Hallel* may be recited with a *beracha*, while other authorities believe that it should be recited without a *beracha*. These authorities include Rav Ahron Soloveichik (*Gesher*, Yeshiva University, 1969) and Rav Yitzḥak Herzog (cited in *Teshuvot Yabia Omer* 6: *Oraḥ Ḥayim* 42).

Rav Ovadia Yosef notes that although we are profoundly disappointed with the overall spiritual level in Israel, we should appreciate the incredible growth of Torah study and observance in many sectors of the population. He writes that Israel has become the world Torah center. We might add that since the passing of Rav Moshe Feinstein and Rav Yosef Dov Soloveitchik in the latter part of the last century, there has been a dramatic increase in the referral of very serious halachic questions to the great halachic authorities in Israel for adjudication.

CONCLUSION

It is difficult to arrive at a definitive conclusion regarding whether one should recite *Hallel* with a *beracha* on Yom HaAtzma'ut. For this reason, many of those who recite *Hallel* on Yom HaAtzmaut omit the *beracha,* a possibility that is mentioned in the comment of the Meiri cited above. Moreover, the practice of reciting *Hallel* without a *beracha* is familiar to the many Sephardic Jews who follow the opinion of the Rambam (*Hilchot Ḥanukka* 3:7) and the *Shulḥan Aruch* (*Oraḥ Ḥayim* 422:2) to recite *Hallel* without a *beracha* on Rosh Ḥodesh and the last six days of Pesaḥ.

Far from being a "cop-out," the approach of reciting *Hallel* without a *beracha* is an expression of recognition of both the greatness and shortcomings of Medinat Yisrael. We are full of joy that Medinat Yisrael exists, but we do not ignore its shortcomings.

Although Rav Ovadia is not enthralled with the idea of reciting *Hallel* on Yom HaAtzama'ut,[3] at Congregation Shaarei Orah, the Sephardic Congregation of Teaneck, we follow in the footsteps of the great Rav Shalom Messas, who believed in reciting *Hallel* on Yom HaAtzmaut even with a *beracha* but who ruled that it should be recited without a *beracha* out of deference to Rav Ovadia.[4]

We hope, in the words of Rav Ovadia Hadaya, that in merit of the *Hallel* we recite on Yom HaAtzma'ut in gratitude for *Hashem* bringing us the beginning of the *geula,* He will bring us the full *geula.* As Rav Hadaya concludes, "Even if we omit the *beracha,* the acknowledgment and gratitude we express to *Hashem* will be accepted with great favor, and we will thereby merit an expeditious salvation and complete redemption."

3. Rav Shmuel Khoshkerman reports that Rav Ovadia himself did not recite *Hallel* on Yom HaAtzma'ut.
4. We also omit *Taḥanun,* in accordance with the instructions in the *siddur* of Rav Mordechai Eliyahu.

Kashrut

Chapter 71

Sephardic *Bishul Akum* Standards

In July 2013, Congregation Shaarei Orah celebrated the marriage of Rav Yaakov Douek to Sari Gabbay. Yaakov and Sari had married in Israel and had come to the United States to celebrate with the Douek family and friends in the local area. Rav Yaakov's father Ezra, a founding member of Congregation Shaarei Orah, is a professional caterer, and he prepared a festive meal replete with grilled steaks.

As I arrived at the event, I discovered that there was an intense discussion underway regarding the proper manner of preparing the food. Ezra had turned on the fire with which his non-Jewish workers would cook the steaks, in order to obviate the prohibition of *bishul Akum*, the Rabbinic prohibition to eat food cooked by a non-Jew. But Ezra's cousin, Rav Ben Zion Gabbay, who served for years as a senior *kashrut* specialist working for Rav Ovadia Yosef, objected to this means of food preparation.

Rav Gabbay argued that Sephardim require that the steaks must be placed on the fire by a Jew in order to obviate the issue of *bishul Akum*. Merely turning on the fire is insufficient, he argued. After insisting on following the Sephardic practice, and after Ezra agreed to his request, Rav Gabbay proceeded to place the steaks on the fire himself.

Upon learning of this intense discussion, I was quite surprised (as was Ezra). After all, Rav Ovadia Yosef (*Teshuvot Yeḥaveh Da'at* 5:54) presents what seems to be a cogently reasoned responsum explaining why Sephardic Jews can rely on the Ashkenazic standard of merely turning on the fire in order to obviate the problem of *bishul Akum*. Although Rav Ovadia concludes, "*hamaḥmir tavo alav beracha*," that it is preferable to be strict, he gives Sephardim the right to be lenient. If Ezra had every right to rely on merely turning on the fire, why did Rav Gabbay insist on placing the food on the fire?

There are three disputes regarding the prohibition of *bishul Akum* that are relevant to this discussion.

DEBATE #1 – TURNING ON THE FIRE

The *gemara* in *Avoda Zara* (38b) rules that if a Jew played a significant role in the cooking of the food, the *bishul Akum* decree does not apply. The *Rishonim* debate how far we may extend this leniency. Rav Yosef Karo (*Shulḥan Aruch, Yoreh De'ah* 113:7) rules in accordance with the Rashba (*Torat HaBayit*, end of *bayit* 3), Ran (*Avoda Zara* 38a), and Rivash (*Teshuvot* 514) that if a Jew merely turned on the flame but did not participate at all in the cooking process, the *bishul Akum* prohibition still applies. The Rama, however, adopts the view of the Ra'avan (*Avoda Zara* 303) and the Mordechai (*Avoda Zara*, ch. 2) and rules that even if the Jew merely turned on the fire, this avoids the *bishul Akum* prohibition.

DEBATE #2 – A NON-JEW COOKING IN A JEW'S HOME

Tosafot (*Avoda Zara* 38a. s.v. *ela*) cites two opinions regarding whether the *bishul Akum* prohibition applies when a non-Jew cooks the food in a Jew's home. Rabbenu Avraham ben David rules that the prohibition does not apply in this case, because the reasons for the prohibition do not apply. Only when the non-Jew prepares the food in his own home is the concern for intermarriage relevant. Rabbenu Tam rejects this view, stating that we do not find that *Ḥazal* made such a distinction. According to both Sephardic and Ashkenazic standards, the *halacha* follows the view of Rabbenu Tam (*Yoreh De'ah* 113:1).

DEBATE #3 – NON-JEWISH EMPLOYEES OF A JEW

Some *Rishonim* and *Aḥaronim* rule that the *bishul Akum* decree does not apply to food cooked by a non-Jew employed by the Jew. They reason that there is a concern for intermarriage only in a relationship of peers. The

Rama (*Yoreh De'ah* 113:4) rules that one may rely on these lenient views *b'diavad* (i.e. if the food was already cooked, one may rely on the lenient opinions and eat the food). However, the *Shach* (113:7), *Aruch HaShulḥan* (*Yoreh De'ah* 113:4), and *Ḥelkat Binyamin* (113:40 and *Bi'urim*, s.v. *ub'diavad yesh lismoch*) express serious reservations about relying on the lenient opinions even *b'diavad*.

The *Shulḥan Aruch* first cites the lenient view and then cites the stricter view. Rav Ovadia Yosef writes in many places that in such a situation, *Maran* Rav Karo considers the second opinion the primary one. Thus, the *Shulḥan Aruch* rules that the *bishul Akum* restriction applies even to food cooked by a non-Jewish employee.

THE RULING OF RAV OVADIA YOSEF

Rav Ovadia Yosef (*Teshuvot Yeḥaveh Da'at* 5:54, published in 1983) notes that Israeli restaurants and hotels whose *kashrut* supervision is provided by Israel's Chief Rabbinate follow the lenient Ashkenazic standard. He observes that Sephardic Jews regularly patronize these establishments, yet no one raises an objection to the fact that this practice runs counter to the view of the *Shulḥan Aruch*, to which Sephardic Jews subscribe.

Rav Ovadia, in turn, develops a halachic justification of this practice. He notes that it is a situation of *s'fek s'feka*, a double doubt, in which one can be lenient. One doubt is that turning on the fire may suffice to eliminate concern for *bishul Akum*. The second doubt is that the prohibition may not apply when the food is prepared in a Jewish home.[1] There is even a third *safek*: Perhaps the prohibition does not apply if the non-Jew is an employee.

Rav Ovadia concludes that since *bishul Akum* is a Rabbinic restriction, one may rely on the combination of these three considerations: A non-Jewish employee may cook food for a Jew in the latter's home if the Jew turns on the fire. Rav Ovadia concludes by stating that nevertheless, "*hamaḥmir tavo alav beracha*."

CRITIQUE OF RAV OVADIA'S RULING

Two leading Sephardic halachic authorities, Rav Ben Tzion Abba Sha'ul and Rav Shalom Messas, strongly reject Rav Ovadia's lenient ruling. Rav Messas

1. It would thus appear that Rav Ovadia's lenient ruling applies only if the food establishment is owned by a Jew.

(*Teshuvot Shemesh U'Magen* 2: *Yoreh De'ah* 11) notes that the *Shulḥan Aruch* rules stringently regarding each prong of Rav Ovadia's *s'fek s'feka*. Citing the premier Sephardic authority Rav Yosef Ḥayim of Baghdad (the *Ben Ish Ḥai, Teshuvot Rav Pe'alim* 2: *Yoreh De'ah* 7 and 3: *Yoreh De'ah* 9), Rav Messas insists that it is not legitimate for Sephardic Jews to rely on a *s'fek s'feka* when both its sides run counter to rulings of *Maran* Rav Yosef Karo.

Thus, since the *Shulḥan Aruch* forbids food cooked by a non-Jew if the Jew only lit the fire, food cooked by a non-Jew in a Jewish home, and food cooked by a non-Jewish employee, Rav Messas disqualifies Rav Ovadia's *s'fek s'feka*; all of its sides run counter to Rav Yosef Karo's explicit rulings.

Rav Messas adds that a close reading of the *Shulḥan Aruch* reveals that Rav Yosef Karo does not accept Rav Ovadia's approach. The *Shulḥan Aruch* forbids food cooked by a non-Jewish employee, and he does not qualify this by saying that it is permissible if a Jew lit the fire. Conversely, the *Shulḥan Aruch* does not write that a Jew lighting the fire is sufficient if the non-Jew cooks the food in a Jew's home and serves as an employee of that Jew. Accordingly, Rav Messas utterly rejects the view of Rav Ovadia.

Rav Abba Sha'ul (*Teshuvot Ohr L'Tzion* 2, introduction section 2) argues that even if one maintains that a Sephardic Jew may, in fact, rely on a *s'fek s'feka* when both prongs run counter to the ruling of *Maran* Rav Yosef Karo, this applies only if *Maran* does not completely dismiss the opinion. In the case at hand, since *Maran* in his *Bet Yosef* commentary to the *Tur* (*Yoreh De'ah* 113, s.v. *v'lo asru*) does not even cite the opinion that permits *bishul Akum* if a Jew lights the fire, it cannot be used as a prong in a *s'fek s'feka*. The fact that Rav Karo does not record the opinion demonstrates that he utterly rejects it, and its use as a component of a halachic decision is therefore not legitimate for Sephardic Jews.

RAV OVADIA YOSEF AND RAV YITZḤAK YOSEF RESPOND

Rav Ovadia (*Teshuvot Yabia Omer* 9: *Yoreh De'ah* 6; printed in 2002) vigorously defends his opinion against the critiques of Rav Messas and Rav Abba Sha'ul. He cites numerous sources (most prominently, the *Ḥida, Maḥazik Beracha* 52:5) to uphold the validity of a *s'fek s'feka* even if both prongs run counter to a ruling of Rav Yosef Karo. He even cites a responsum of Rav Messas (*Teshuvot Shemesh U'Magen, Oraḥ Ḥayim* 29) in which Rav Messas himself relies on a *s'fek s'feka* whose prongs both run counter to the view of *Maran*. Rav Ovadia concludes that even if the question of whether such a *s'fek s'feka* is permitted remains subject to dispute, one may be lenient regarding a Rabbinic prohibition such as *bishul Akum*.

Regarding Rav Abba Sha'ul's objection, Rav Ovadia writes, "How can one say that all of the great Ashkenazic authorities who permit are as if they do not exist? God forbid that we articulate such an approach!" Rav Ovadia maintains that although Sephardic Jews do not follow the rulings of the Rama, the Rama's views can nevertheless be taken into consideration for a *s'fek s'feka*, since one cannot simply dismiss his opinion.

One can, however, detect a bit of a softening of Rav Ovadia's position from that which he articulated in 1983 in *Teshuvot Yeḥaveh Da'at*. In *Yeḥaveh Da'at*, he writes, "There is a wide space for even Sephardic Jews to be lenient regarding this matter." In *Yabia Omer*, by contrast, he concludes, "One should not admonish one who adopts the lenient approach, since he has a basis upon which to rely."

The *Yabia Omer* approach is reflected by Rav Yitzḥak Yosef in the year 2000 edition of *Yalkut Yosef*, where he writes, "Sephardim should *l'chatḥila* adopt the strict position, but those who are lenient in public venues have a basis upon which to rely." However, in the 2006 edition of *Yalkut Yosef*, Rav Yitzḥak Yosef tilts even more towards strongly to the stricter view:

> Sephardim should *l'chatḥila* adopt the strict approach to this issue and ask the *mashgiaḥ* (*kashrut* supervisor) to place the pot on the oven for the food he is ordering. However, one who is lenient in a situation of large-scale food preparation has basis upon which to rely... Every *kashrut* agency should *l'chatḥila* take care that Jews should place the food on the fire, since many of the patrons of their establishments are Sephardic Jews who follow the rulings of Rav Yosef Karo.

Thus, we understand that while Ezra Douek and I were acting in accordance with Rav Ovadia's earlier *teshuva*, in which he seems to reserve adopting the strict approach to an elite group of Jews who are extra cautious in their Torah observance, Rav Gabbay was more or less hewing to the newer approach of Rav Yitzḥak that encourages all Sephardic Jews to follow the stricter standard.

Interestingly, the *Yalkut Yosef* adds an intriguing argument to bolster the lenient approach. He presents the possibility that the prohibition of *bishul Akum* applies only when the non-Jew prepares food for an individual, and not when he does so for a large group. One could argue that sharing food with an individual builds a relationship, whereas cooking for a large group does not. Thus, in the latter setting, the reason for the *bishul Akum* edict does not apply; there is no concern of bonding with a non-Jew when the food is cooked for a large group.

The advantage of this approach is that it does not clearly run counter to a ruling of *Maran* Rav Karo. Thus, Sephardic Jews may unquestionably utilize this opinion as a prong in a *s'fek s'feka*. Despite the cogency of this argument, however, Rav Yitzḥak Yosef steadfastly encourages Sephardic Jews to adopt the stricter approach.

CONCLUSION

Rav Yitzḥak Yosef's approach is significantly less enthusiastic than the original approach articulated by his father in *Teshuvot Yeḥaveh Da'at*. The compelling criticism expressed by Rav Messas and Rav Abba Sha'ul likely restrained Rav Yitzḥak Yosef's wholehearted endorsement of Rav Ovadia's opinion on this matter.

Today, many Sephardic Jews ask the *mashgiaḥ* at restaurants to place the pot in which their food is prepared on the fire, in accordance with the ruling of the *Shulḥan Aruch*. What was only a few decades ago a nearly totally forgotten and neglected *halacha* has once again returned to the consciousness of the Sephardic community and beyond, in keeping with Rav Ovadia's oft-repeated agenda of *haḥazarat atara l'yoshena*, restoring the Sephardic crown to its glory. However, since adherence to the strict approach to this issue is quite difficult at times, it is comforting for a Sephardic Jew to know that he can rely on a lenient approach developed by two of the leading Sephardic lights of our times, Rav Ovadia Yosef and Rav Yitzḥak Yosef.

Rav Shmuel Khoshkerman told me that many Sephardic Jews today are strict about this matter, but that in case of need one may rely on Rav Ovadia's lenient approach that appears in *Teshuvot Yeḥaveh Da'at*.

Accordingly, Ezra Douek was certainly in his halachic prerogative to rely simply on turning on the fire to obviate *bishul Akum*. Rav Gabbay, however, did have a point in reminding us of the higher standard set by the *Shulḥan Aruch*, to which many Sephardic Jews today adhere.

Chapter 72

Ḥalak Bet Yosef

An important lesson in Jewish unity may be gleaned from Rav Ovadia Yosef's approach to the issue of *ḥalak* ("*glatt* kosher") meat. On the one hand, Rav Ovadia was insistent that Sephardic Jews should make every effort to purchase meat that is *ḥalak* by Sephardic standards (*Teshuvot Yabia Omer* 5: *Yoreh De'ah* 3; *Teshuvot Yeḥaveh Da'at* 3:56). On the other hand, he developed an approach that allowed for Sephardic Jews to adopt the lenient approach in case of great need.

THE DEFINITION OF *ḤALAK*

One of the blemishes that render an animal forbidden for consumption as a *terefa* are *sirchot,* adhesions that cross the lung from side to side and resemble scabs. If there are *sirchot* on the lungs, this is a sign that there was once a hole in that area that was later sealed by this *sircha.* Certain *sirchot* raise questions regarding whether the animal can be rendered kosher.

Maran Rav Yosef Karo follows the *Teshuvot HaRashba* (304) and rules strictly in the *Shulḥan Aruch* (*Yoreh De'ah* 39:10). He writes that whenever *sirchot* are forbidden, there is no difference if the *sircha* is as thin as a strand of hair or if it is thick and strong. Rav Karo is opposed to the practice of rubbing the *sircha* to see if it falls off, under the assumption that this provides room for leniency.

The Rama (*Yoreh De'ah* 39:13), however, rules as follows:

> Some permit mashing *sirchot* and rubbing them; they claim that an actual *sircha* [that is forbidden and not merely mucus] cannot be disconnected even if one rubs it all day long. Thus, if it is indeed removed after being mashed, we rule leniently and assume it to be mucus and not a *sircha*. Although this is a great leniency, this is already the established custom in these countries; one need not protest this custom, for they have upon whom to rely.

One of the most basic rulings that Rav Ovadia Yosef instituted for Sephardic Jewry all over the world was not to purchase meat unless it was truly "*ḥalak*" (smooth) or "*glatt*" according to Rav Yosef Karo's standards ("*ḥalak Bet Yosef*"). He explained that according to the majority of the *posekim*, including *Maran* Rav Yosef Karo, this issue borders on a possible Torah prohibition of consuming non-kosher food.

Ḥalak Bet Yosef standards are stricter than the Ashkenazic standards for *glatt* kosher meat. Ashkenazic Jews regard meat as *glatt* kosher if one or two negligible and easily removable *sirchot* are found on the lung, whereas this does not meet the standard of *ḥalak Bet Yosef*. Rav Ovadia championed adopting the *ḥalak Bet Yosef* standard as another example of *haḥazarat atara l'yoshena*, restoring the Sephardic crown to its original glory.

Rav Ḥaim David HaLevy (*Teshuvot Aseh Lecha Rav* 6:51) similarly adopts a strict standard regarding *ḥalak Bet Yosef*. He even advises a Sephardic soldier in the Israel Defense Forces to refrain from eating meat served in the army unless it is *ḥalak*.[1]

A SEPHARDIC GUEST AT AN ASHKENAZIC HOME

Despite Rav Ovadia's firm stance regarding *ḥalak Bet Yosef*, he champions a lenient approach for a Sephardic Jew visiting an Ashkenazic friend or relative when obtaining meat that is *ḥalak Bet Yosef* is not a realistic option. In such a case, Rav Ovadia permits eating the meat as long as it is *glatt* kosher by Ashkenazic standards.

1. Rav Zecharia Ben-Shlomo (*Orot HaHalacha*, p. 1049) notes that already for many years the Israeli Army Rabbinate provides canned meat that is *ḥalak* by the Sephardic standard for a soldier who requests it.

Rav Ovadia cites the *Devar Shmuel* (320), who rules that one may rule leniently in such a situation due to a *s'fek s'feka*, a double doubt. (One may generally rely on a *s'fek s'feka* even regarding a Torah-level prohibition). One *safek* is whether the meat satisfies the *Bet Yosef* standard, since meat labeled as *glatt* by Ashkenazic standards might be *ḥalak* even according to *Maran.*[2] A second *safek* is that perhaps Rama and those who support him are correct. Thus, meat that is acceptable only for Ashkenazim is viewed as possibly acceptable for Sephardic Jews.

Rav Ovadia devotes considerable effort to defending and bolstering the approach of the *Devar Shmuel.* Rav Ovadia did not veer from this ruling throughout his life, and it is codified by his son, Rav Yitzḥak Yosef, in the *Yalkut Yosef* (*Yoreh De'ah* 35–48:4–7).

A JEWISH UNITY LESSON

In a number of other contexts, Rav Ovadia facilitates Sephardic and Ashkenazic Jews eating each other's food even when their halachic standards differ. Examples include permitting Sephardic Jews to eat food that meets only the more lenient *bishul Akum* standard (*Teshuvot Yeḥaveh Da'at* 5:54) and permitting Ashkenazim to eat at a Sephardic home on Pesaḥ despite the fact that Sephardim eat *kitniyot* (*Teshuvot Yeḥaveh Da'at* 5:32).[3] Similarly, in the aforementioned responsum in *Teshuvot Yabia Omer*, Rav Ovadia disagrees with the view of Rav Kook (*Igrot HaRa'ayah* 611) and permits Ashkenazim to eat animals slaughtered according to Sephardic standards, even though Ashkenazim follow the Rama, who adopted many *ḥumrot* (stringencies) in regard to *sheḥita.*[4]

---

2. Rav Shmuel Khoshkerman told me that his research reveals that much of the kosher meat marketed in the United States today is *ḥalak* by Sephardic standards, even though it is labeled merely as *glatt*. Thus, the *safek* that meat in the United States labeled as *glatt* may actually be *ḥalak* as well is quite a viable and legitimate prong of a *s'fek s'feka*. On the other hand, based on information presented by Rav Aryeh Leibowitz (https://www.yutorah.org/sidebar/lecture.cfm/917990/rabbi-aryeh-leibowitz/rabbanut-mehadrin-or-bedatz-an-introduction-to-kashrus-in-israel/), meat that is not labeled as *ḥalak* in Israel is highly unlikely to meet *ḥalak* standards. Thus, the *s'fek s'feka* presented by Rav Ovadia might not apply to such meat.
3. Both of these examples are discussed at length in Chapters 50 and 71.
4. Rav Ovadia may have had Rashi to *Devarim* 33:19 (s.v. *amim har yikra'u*) in mind, as Rashi describes *Am Yisrael* as a people with "one God and one food."

As much as Rav Ovadia championed restoring Sephardic greatness and Sephardic fidelity to the rulings of *Maran* Rav Yosef Karo, Rav Ovadia viewed the unity of *Am Yisrael* to be of great importance. Although each group of Jews can and should take pride in the practices and customs of their particular "tribe," we must always bear in mind we are *am eḥad,* one nation.[5]

5. See Rav Mordechai Lebhar, *Magen Avot, Yoreh De'ah* 39, for a detailed presentation of the more lenient Moroccan approach to the issue of adhesions to the lung (relative to that presented by Rav Ovadia). Yemenite tradition regarding this matter is presented by Rav Eliezer Melamed as follows (http://www.israelnationalnews.com/Articles/Article.aspx/23093):

According to Sephardic *minhag,* when a *sircha* is found on the lungs of an animal, the animal is *tref,* and therefore it is obligatory to eat *ḥalak,* namely, animals found not to have *sirchot* on their lungs. However, the Yemenite tradition was to be lenient and check the *sirchot* by means of peeling with a knife and examination by emerging in water to see if there is an aperture, in accordance with the specification for kosher meat.

Chapter 73

Ḥadash in Ḥutz LaAretz

The Torah (*Vayikra* 23:14) prohibits eating *ḥadash*, grain that takes root after the sixteenth of Nissan until the subsequent sixteenth day of Nissan has passed. There is considerable debate as to whether it takes three or fourteen days for grain to take root (see *Shach, Yoreh De'ah* 293:2; *Nekudot HaKesef* ad. loc). Thus, we may not eat grain that was planted after the fourth day of Nissan 5779 until the sixteenth day of Nissan 5780. This prohibition applies to the *ḥameshet minei dagan* (five species of grain): wheat, barley, rye, oats, and spelt. When the *Bet HaMikdash* functions, *ḥadash* is rendered permissible when the *Korban HaOmer* is offered on the sixteenth day of Nissan. In the regrettable absence of the *Bet HaMikdash*, we must wait until the end of the sixteenth day of Nissan to consume this grain, which is then labeled "*yashan*." Outside of Israel, we must wait one more day.

In Israel, observant Jews scrupulously abide by this prohibition.[1] However, the majority of observant Ashkenazic Jews who reside outside of Israel have followed a lenient approach towards this issue for many centuries. What is the basis of this lenient practice?

1. The strict approach to *ḥadash* is adopted even by the most basic level of *kashrut* standards required by Israel's State Rabbinate.

DOES *ḤADASH* APPLY IN *ḤUTZ LAARETZ*?

The Torah mentions that the *ḥadash* prohibition applies "in all your dwelling places," which seems to imply that the prohibition applies throughout the world. Nevertheless, the *Tanna'im* debate whether the *ḥadash* prohibition applies only in Israel or in the Diaspora as well (*Kiddushin* 1:9). According to Rabbi Elazar, *ḥadash* applies even outside of Eretz Yisrael. The *Tanna Kama* of the *mishna*, however, argues that this prohibition applies only in Eretz Yisrael. The latter opinion interprets the phrase "in all your dwelling places" as teaching that the prohibition applies to grain that grew in Eretz Yisrael even if it is exported from Eretz Yisrael (see *Yerushalmi Kiddushin* 1:8); the *ḥadash* prohibition does not apply to grain grown in *Ḥutz LaAretz*.

Most *Rishonim* rule in accordance with Rabbi Elazar in light of the uncontested statement of the *mishna* (*Orla* 3:9) that "*ḥadash* is Biblically prohibited in every place." These *Rishonim* include the Rambam (*Hilchot Ma'achalot Assurot* 10:2), Rif (*Kiddushin* 15a), Rosh (*Kiddushin* 1:62), and *Tur* (*Oraḥ Ḥayim* 489). The *Shulḥan Aruch* (*Oraḥ Ḥayim* 489:10; *Yoreh De'ah* 293:2) rules in accordance with this opinion.

The *Aruch HaShulḥan* (*Yoreh De'ah* 293:5) notes that some *Rishonim* maintain that *ḥadash* outside of Eretz Yisrael is only Rabbinically forbidden. These *Rishonim* include the *Ohr Zarua* (328), Rabbenu Baruch (author of the *Sefer HaTeruma*, cited in *Teshuvot HaRosh* 2:1), Ra'avan (as understood by *Teshuvot Mishkenot Yaakov* 64), and the Maharil. This view draws support from a *mishna* in *Menaḥot* (8:1), which states that the barley used for the *Korban HaOmer* must have grown in Eretz Yisrael. The *gemara* (*Menaḥot* 84a) implies that if one maintains that the barley used for the *Korban HaOmer* cannot be from *Ḥutz LaAretz*, he must believe that the prohibition to eat *ḥadash* in *Ḥutz LaAretz* is only Rabbinic in nature.

The *Ohr Zarua* notes how difficult it was to observe the prohibition of *ḥadash* in the area in which he resided (thirteenth-century Germany and France). He concludes that since it is a situation of great difficulty (*sha'at hadeḥak*), we may rely on the *mishna* in *Menaḥot* that seems to imply that *ḥadash* is forbidden only Rabbinically. Since we do not know whether the grain took root before the sixteenth of Nissan or after the sixteenth of Nissan, we can rely on the celebrated rule that one may be lenient in case of doubt when dealing with a Rabbinically prohibited matter (*safek d'Rabbanan l'kula*).

Interestingly, *Tosafot* (*Kiddushin* 36b, s.v. *kol mitzva*) writes that if one is unsure if barley is *ḥadash*, he may eat it, as one may assume that the barley has emerged from the majority of barley, which is planted before Pesaḥ. This is an application of the Talmudic principle of "*kol d'parish me'ruba parish*," whatever emerges, emerges from the majority.

Note that *Tosafot*'s lenient approach is relevant only when most of the grain has taken root before the sixteenth of Nissan. Moreover, *Tosafot* obviously did not subscribe to the *Ohr Zarua*'s approach to the *ḥadash* issue.

The *Taz* (*Yoreh De'ah* 293:4) also notes the difficulty in observing *ḥadash* in his area (seventeenth-century Poland), and he defends the lenient practice of the Jews of his area. The *Taz* notes that the *gemara* does not definitively conclude that the *halacha* follows the view of Rabbi Elazar. Accordingly, in a case of *sha'at hadeḥak*, we may rely on the opinion of the *Tanna Kama* that *ḥadash* does not apply in *Ḥutz LaAretz*.

The *Shach* (*Nekudot HaKesef, Yoreh De'ah* 293:4) sharply dissents, however. He argues that the aforementioned *mishna* in *Orla* unambiguously concludes that the *halacha* follows Rabbi Elazar. The Vilna Gaon (*Bi'ur HaGra, Yoreh De'ah* 293:2) concurs with the *Shach*.

ḤADASH OBSERVANCE IN LANDS DISTANT FROM ERETZ YISRAEL

Rabbenu Baruch (a *Rishon*) argues that *ḥadash* outside of Eretz Yisrael is forbidden only Rabbinically. He further agrees that the Rabbinic decree to observe *ḥadash* outside of Eretz Yisrael applies only in those lands that are close to Eretz Yisrael, such as Egypt. He notes that when *Ḥazal* instituted that *terumot* and *ma'aserot* be separated in *Ḥutz LaAretz*, they imposed this rule only in the lands that are close to Eretz Yisrael (see Rambam, *Hilchot Terumot* 1:1).

The *Magen Avraham* (489:17) and the *Aruch HaShulḥan* (*Yoreh De'ah* 293:20–21) conclude that this is the most convincing defense of the prevalent practice to be lenient regarding *ḥadash*. Nonetheless, the *Magen Avraham* counsels that a scrupulous individual should try to avoid relying on this very lenient approach. Furthermore, the Vilna Gaon (*Bi'ur HaGra, Yoreh De'ah* 293:2) vigorously rejects this leniency.

THE RAMA'S APPROACH AND RABBI AKIVA EIGER'S CRITIQUE

The Rama (*Yoreh De'ah* 293:3) presents an interesting, albeit puzzling, approach to this issue. He writes that one may be lenient regarding *ḥadash* if a *s'fek s'feka* (double doubt) is applicable: One doubt is if the grain took root before the most recent sixteenth of Nissan. The second doubt is that perhaps the grain is from a previous year. This approach appears difficult, as noted by Rabbi Akiva Eiger in his glosses to the *Shulḥan Aruch* (ad loc.). It seems that this is not a legitimate *s'fek s'feka*, since this is simply one doubt: Did the grain take root before the sixteenth of Nissan or not?[2]

THE LENIENT APPROACH OF THE *BAḤ*

The *Baḥ* (*Yoreh De'ah* 293, s.v. *ketiv v'leḥem*) notes that in his area of residence (sixteenth-century Poland), almost everyone (including great rabbis) was lenient regarding the *ḥadash* issue. In their defense, the *Baḥ* cites a number of lesser-known *Rishonim* who assert that *ḥadash* does not apply if the grain grows in a field owned by a non-Jew. He further cites the *gemara* in *Rosh Hashana* (13a), which states that one may not offer the *Korban HaOmer* from barley that grew in a field owned by a non-Jew, and compares it to the *gemara* in *Menaḥot* (84a), which states that *ḥadash* does not apply to grain that is not suitable to be used for the *Korban HaOmer*. Accordingly, the *Baḥ* concludes that *ḥadash* does not apply to grain that grew in a field owned by a non-Jew because that grain is not suitable for the *Korban HaOmer*.

This celebrated approach of the *Baḥ* elicited much criticism. The *Shach* (*Yoreh De'ah* 293:6), *Taz* (293:2), and the Vilna Gaon (*Bi'ur HaGra* 293:2) vigorously reject this approach. Indeed, *Tosafot* (*Kiddushin* 36b, s.v. *kol*) specifically state that the *Talmud Yerushalmi* indicates that *ḥadash* applies to grain grown in a field that is owned by non-Jews. Moreover, the *Shulḥan Aruch* (*Yoreh De'ah* 293:2) rules that *ḥadash* applies to grain grown in a field owned by non-Jews. Nevertheless, *Teshuvot Mishkenot Yaakov* (64) writes at length in defense of the *Baḥ* from his many eminent critics.

THE VIEWS OF THE *AḤARONIM*

Many *Aḥaronim* (cited by *Pitḥei Teshuva, Yoreh De'ah* 293:1; *Encyclopedia Talmudit* 12:628, n. 84) wrote at great length to defend the lenient practice of the overwhelming majority of observant Jews.

The *Aruch HaShulḥan* (*Yoreh De'ah* 293:18) describes how it was nearly impossible to follow the strict approach in his area (nineteenth-century Russia). He notes that very few people follow the strict approach.

2. In halachic parlance, this is referred to as a *safek mishem eḥad*.

He attempts to defend the lenient approach and concludes, "All the Jewish People are free from sin."

Interestingly, many Ḥassidim abide by the lenient approach to *ḥadash*. Indeed, there is a legend that the Ba'al Shem Tov heard a heavenly voice declaring that the *halacha* follows the *Baḥ*.

The *Mishna Berura* (489:45) notes that most observant Ashkenazic Jews adopt the lenient approach to the *ḥadash* issue. He writes that although one should not criticize one who follows the lenient approach, a halachically scrupulous individual should adhere to the *ḥadash* restrictions as best as he can. In the *Bi'ur Halacha* (489:10, s.v. *af*), the *Ḥafetz Ḥayim* laments the fact that some people adopt an "all or nothing" attitude towards *ḥadash*. He writes that even if one cannot observe the strict approach to *ḥadash* at all times at the highest level of observance, that does not mean that he should not observe it at all. One should do his best to observe the strict approach to *ḥadash* as often as possible.

SEPHARDIC APPROACHES

Rav Ovadia Yosef (*Yalkut Yosef, Yoreh De'ah* 293) rules that *Maran* Rav Yosef Karo adopts the strict approach to *ḥadash* – that the prohibition applies even in *Ḥutz LaAretz* and even to grain grown by a non-Jew. The *Yalkut Yosef* concludes that Sephardic Jews should adopt the strict approach with regards to *ḥadash*, in accordance with the ruling of Rav Karo.[3]

Rav Shmuel Khoshkerman told me that he does not understand why Rav Ovadia adopts such a strong stance in rejecting the Rama's *s'fek s'feka* approach. After all, Rav Khoshkerman argues, Rav Ovadia is renowned for his liberal usage and application of *s'fek s'feka*. For example, in cases of great need, Rav Ovadia permits Sephardic Jews to eat meat that is *glatt* by Ashkenazic standards, but not *ḥalak* by Sephardic standards, based on a *s'fek s'feka*; perhaps the Ashkenazic standard is correct, and perhaps the particular portion of meat meets the Sephardic standard (*Teshuvot Yabia Omer* 5: *Yoreh De'ah* 3).[4] Why, then, can't we assert a variation on the Rama's *s'fek s'feka* that perhaps the *Baḥ* (or one of the other lenient approaches to

---

3. The *Yalkut Yosef* (*Yoreh De'ah* 293:26) goes as far as ruling that a Sephardic Jew should not be *yotzei* with an Ashkenazic Jew's *beracha* of *HaMotzi* recited on bread that is permitted only according to the lenient standard regarding *ḥadash*.
4. We discussed this issue at length in Chapter 72.

ḥadash) is correct and perhaps the grain one is consuming is *yashan*?[5] In fact, Rav Khoshkerman notes that the *Kaf HaḤayim* (*Oraḥ Ḥayim* 499:110) cites and endorses this defense of those who adopt a lenient approach to *ḥadash* (although he strongly encourages one to follow the strict opinion whenever possible).[6]

I presented Rav Khoshkerman's thoughts to Rav Shlomo Amar when he visited Congregation Shaarei Orah on Shabbat Naḥamu 5777. Rav Amar defended Rav Ovadia's ruling, citing the *Shach* (*Yoreh De'ah* 110, *kelalei s'fek s'feka* 35) that when it is possible to determine the facts (*efshar l'varer*), the situation is not considered one of *safek*. Accordingly, since it can be readily determined whether a product is *ḥadash* or not based on a product's production date, as stamped on the item, the Rama's *s'fek s'feka* is no longer relevant. Thus, Rav Amar reinforces Rav Ovadia's strict stance regarding *ḥadash*.

When informed of Rav Amar's response, Rav Khoshkerman countered that in his investigation of the facts, it emerged that the production date only informs consumers when the product was made, not whether the item was made from grain that is *yashan*. Although some disagree and insist that the situation is one of *efshar l'varer* based on the food production date stamp, this is subject to dispute among leading North American *Rabbanim* (Rav Moshe Heinemann and Rav Shlomo Miller), and it is impossible to determine who is correct. Thus, the matter remains a *safek*, and the Rama's *s'fek s'feka* remains in effect even for Sephardic Jews in case of great need.[7]

---

5. Although the *Shulḥan Aruch* rules against both prongs of this *s'fek s'feka*, in the context of *bishul Akum*, Rav Ovadia similarly advances a *s'fek s'feka* in which both prongs run counter to the rulings of Rav Karo (as we discussed at length in Chapter 71).
6. The *Nehar Mitzrayim* (*Hilchot Ḥadash* 5), an important compendium of the practices of Egyptian Jewry, adopts a similar approach. He believes that there is a prohibition of *ḥadash* only regarding food that is discernably made with *ḥadash* grain. If there is doubt as to whether the grain is *ḥadash*, one may be lenient and rely on the *s'fek s'feka* of the Rama. Why does the *Nehar Mitzrayim* rule that Sephardic Jews may rely on the *s'fek s'feka* of the Rama if the *Shulḥan Aruch* disagrees? Rav David Bassous (*Jewish Law Meets Modern Challenges* 2:131) explains that Rav Karo cites this *s'fek s'feka* in the *Bet Yosef* (*Yoreh De'ah* 102) and does not reject it, indicating his consent to the *s'fek s'feka*. It is, however, significant that Rav Karo does not cite this *s'fek s'feka* in the portions of the *Shulḥan Aruch* that focus specifically on *ḥadash*.
7. Rav Ben Tzion Abba Sha'ul (*Teshuvot Ohr L'Tzion* 1:*Yoreh De'ah* 15) adopts a similar approach when certified *yashan* products are not available. As noted below, the

Moreover, Rav Mordechai Lebhar (*Teshuvot Magen Avot* 15) notes that most wheat in North America is winter wheat that is planted in the late fall or early winter and is harvested in the late spring or early summer. Since winter wheat is planted before Pesaḥ and is harvested after Pesaḥ, it is always *yashan*. He interviewed farmers from North Dakota (the location where most spring wheats are planted), who noted that they try to plant spring wheat approximately on March 17. Thus, in many years, most of the spring wheat will take root at least three days before Pesaḥ, rendering it *yashan*.[8] According to this approach, there is room for even a Sephardic Jew to follow the lenient opinion, since the majority of wheat in North America is *yashan*.

Indeed, the *Yalkut Yosef* (*Yoreh De'ah* 293:28) writes:

> The *Aḥaronim* dispute whether one may rely on the majority of flour, which is not *ḥadash*. The *halacha* is that one may rely on the majority (*rov*) regarding *ḥadash*. However, it is proper to be strict and investigate the situation and try to the extent possible to determine as to whether the product is *ḥadash*.

In contrast to the situation regarding wheat, however, the OU Kashrut department reports:

> In the United States, most barley and oats are *ḥadash*, since they do not take root prior to Pesaḥ. Canadian oats are also *ḥadash*, and a significant amount is imported into the United States. Domestic rye is always *yashan*; however, rye bread can be *ḥadash*, since it is primarily composed of spring wheat.[9]

Yalkut Yosef (*Yoreh De'ah* 293:28) also rules leniently in case of a legitimate doubt as to whether a product is *ḥadash*, if the matter was investigated to the extent that it is possible to do so.

8. In some years, the aforementioned debate as to whether it takes three or fourteen days for grain to take root may make the difference as to whether the majority of that year's spring wheat is *yashan*.
9. https://oukosher.org/blog/consumer-kosher/yoshon/.

CONCLUSION

It is most certainly preferable for a Sephardic Jew to adopt the stricter approach to *ḥadash*. While still challenging, it is far easier to adhere to the stricter opinion in the United States today as compared to the difficulties encountered by prior generations. However, there are viable arguments to justify Sephardic Jews adopting the lenient approach to *ḥadash*. Rav David Bassous (*Jewish Law Meets Modern Challenges* 2:139) concludes his discussion of this matter by asserting:

The prevailing custom of American Sephardic communities is to rely on the popular *kashrut* authorities' lenient ruling.[10] However, certainly in places where *yashan* is available with no incurred inconvenience, it would be proper for Sephardim to be strict in this regard.

10. We should note, however, that many Sephardic communities (especially large ones) currently make a significant effort to facilitate community-wide adherence to the stricter standard, which complies with the rulings of Rav Yosef Karo.

Chapter 74

Cheese, Milk, and Fish

Bagels, cream cheese, and lox are a favorite treat for many Jews, and practically ubiquitous at a *seudat b'rit mila*. Why, then, do many Sephardic Jews refrain from this delicious delicacy, as well as all mixtures of milk and fish (perhaps with the exception of butter)?

The *gemara* (*Pesaḥim* 76b) instructs us not to eat fish and meat together, as this is considered dangerous; this is why we rinse our mouths with water and some "abrasive" food, such as bread, between fish and meat served at a Shabbat meal. However, in no less than three places (*Pesaḥim* 42a, 76b; *Ḥullin* 111b, as explained in *Teshuvot Yeḥaveh Da'at* 6:48), the *gemara* indicates that it is permissible to eat fish together with milk. Why do Sephardim refrain from something that the *gemara* clearly indicates is permissible?

BET YOSEF VS. *DARKEI MOSHE*

The answer is that Rav Yosef Karo notes in his *Bet Yosef* commentary to the *Tur* (*Yoreh De'ah* 87, s.v. *dagim*) that it is dangerous to eat milk and fish together. Rav Moshe Isserles (the Rama), however, notes in his *Darkei Moshe* commentary to the *Tur* (*Yoreh De'ah* 87:4) that he has not seen anyone follow this practice.

The *Shach* (*Yoreh De'ah* 87:5) also notes that the Ashkenazic practice permits eating milk with fish.[1] For this reason Ashkenazim (with the exception of Ḥabad and some other Ḥassidic groups) enjoy bagels and cream cheese with lox, as well as other fish and milk mixtures. Many Sephardim, however, heed the concern that *Maran* Rav Yosef Karo expresses in the *Bet Yosef*.

THE VIEW OF THE *ḤIDA*

Not all Sephardim adhere to *Maran*'s warning. The *Ḥida* (*Maḥazik Beracha* 87:4) observes that Rav Yosef Karo does not present this rule in the *Shulḥan Aruch*. In both *Yoreh De'ah* 116 and *Oraḥ Ḥayim* 173, he instructs to avoid eating meat and fish together, but he makes no mention of the refraining from fish and milk. Two other premier Sephardic authorities, the *Peri Ḥadash* (*Yoreh De'ah* 87:6 and 116:3) and *Shulḥan Gavo'ah* (*Yoreh De'ah* 87:11), also subscribe to the lenient approach.

The *Ḥida* even agrees with the *Taz*'s bold assertion (*Yoreh De'ah* 87:3) that the remark recorded in the *Bet Yosef* is a *ta'ut sofer*, a scribal error. *Maran* Rav Yosef Karo, the *Ḥida* argues, originally must have written in the *Bet Yosef* to avoid meat and fish due to the danger, but a scribe erroneously copied milk and fish.

Rav Shalom Messas (*Teshuvot Shemesh U'Magen* 4: *Yoreh De'ah* 12), follows the approach of the *Ḥida*.[2] Moreover, he notes that contemporary medical experts do not regard consuming fish and milk together to be dangerous.[3]

Nonetheless, Rav Ovadia Yosef (*Teshuvot Yeḥaveh Da'at* 6:48) notes that many Sephardic communities customarily refrain from eating fish and dairy together. He notes that the *Ben Ish Ḥai* (year 2, *Parashat Beha'alotecha* 15), an exceedingly popular work that has had enormously influence on Sephardic practice, urges readers to refrain from combining fish and milk.[4]

---

1. This is confirmed by the *Aruch HaShulḥan*, *Yoreh De'ah* 87:15.
2. Despite this ruling from the eminent Rav Messas, Rav Mordechai Lebhar (*Magen Avot*, *Oraḥ Ḥayim* 173:2; *Yoreh De'ah* 87:3) notes that there is a variety of practices among Moroccan Jews regarding this matter.
3. With regard to mixtures of meat and fish, contemporary medical opinon is not taken in consideration, since its danger is mentioned explicitly in the Gemara.
4. The *Ben Ish Ḥai* also records a difference of opinion regarding if this danger applies to butter and fish. He concludes with a strict ruling regarding this issue. Rav Ovadia, however, notes that many *Aḥaronim* are lenient regarding butter and fish and

Thus, Rav Ovadia concludes, it is unlikely that the *Ben Ish Ḥai* regarded the relevant passage in the *Bet Yosef* as a scribal error. Accordingly, Rav Ovadia rules that it is best for Sephardic Jews to avoid mixing fish and milk.

Rav Eli Mansour, a leading Rav in the Syrian Jewish community, rules as follows:

> As for the final *halacha,* those who act leniently in this regard certainly have authorities on whom to rely. However, in light of the stringent position taken by Ḥacham Ovadia Yosef, whose rulings we generally follow, and given that this was the practice of our forebears in Halab (Aleppo, Syria), it would seem preferable to avoid eating fish together with milk or other dairy products.[5]

Rav Shmuel Khoshkerman similarly wrote to me that many Sephardic Jews are lenient, but it is preferable to be strict.

CONCLUSION

So don't be surprised at the next Sephardic *b'rit mila* you attend that bagels, cream cheese and lox are not served... This is, after all, in accordance with the strict approach of the *Ben Ish Ḥai* and Rav Ovadia. On the other hand, do not be surprised to see Sephardic Jews who do mix fish and milk products, in accordance with the lenient rulings of the *Peri Ḥadash, Ḥida, Shulḥan Gavo'ah,* and Rav Shalom Messas.

---

concludes that those who whose custom is to be lenient in this regard may continue to do so.

5. http://www.dailyhalacha.com/displayRead.asp?readID=770.

Chapter 75

Nat bar Nat

The *gemara* in *Ḥullin* (111b) records a dispute between Rav and Shmuel regarding a case in which hot fish was placed on a plate that had previously held hot meat, thereby causing meat "taste particles" to be absorbed into the plate. The *Amora'im* debate whether it is permissible to subsequently eat the fish with dairy. Rav rules that it is forbidden to do so, but Shmuel rules that it is permissible.

Rav maintains that it is forbidden because the fish absorbed meat taste from the plate. Shmuel, on the other hand, holds it is permissible because the fish is two steps removed from the meat; first, the meat was absorbed in the plate, and then the meat taste in the plate was transferred to the fish. The connection between the fish and the meat is too remote to create a prohibited mixture of meat and dairy if dairy is subsequently introduced into this fish. This situation is referred to by the Talmud as "*noten ta'am bar noten ta'am*" (abbreviated *nat bar nat*), which literally means "the transfer of taste the son of the transfer of taste."

After citing a number of incidents that support the view of Shmuel, the *gemara* concludes that the *halacha* follows his lenient view.

THE SCOPE OF THE *NAT BAR NAT* LENIENCY

The *Rishonim* debate the scope of the applicability of the rule of *nat bar nat.* The Rivan (cited in *Tosafot, Ḥullin* 111b, s.v. *hilchata*) cites the opinion of his illustrious father-in-law, Rashi, who limits the applicability of the *nat bar nat* leniency. He relates that Rashi maintained that only fish placed on a meat plate is considered *nat bar nat,* since only a small amount of meat taste is absorbed into the fish. However, if fish is actually cooked in a meat pot, the fish is not neutral (pareve) even according to Shmuel. This is because the fish has absorbed a great deal of meat taste from the meat pot. The Rivan relates that when he asked Rashi if an egg that was cooked in a dairy pot could be cooked with meat, Rashi replied in the negative.

Tosafot, however, notes that a different impression is gleaned from Rashi's commentary (*Ḥullin* 111b, s.v. *nat bar nat*). Rashi explains that the fish attains the status of being "meaty" only if it is cooked with actual meat. This clearly implies that if the fish is merely cooked in a meat pot, the fish remains pareve. Indeed, Rashi's grandson, Rabbenu Tam, and his great-grandson, the Ri, both maintain that the *nat bar nat* rule applies even in a case of cooking; even if the neutral item was cooked in a meat or dairy pot, the cooked item remains neutral (see *Haga'ot Oshri, Ḥullin* 8:29).

SEPHARDIC VS. ASHKENAZIC PRACTICE

Maran Rav Yosef Karo (*Bet Yosef, Yoreh De'ah* 95, s.v. *dagim*) cites many *Rishonim* (including the Rashba, Ran, and Ravya) who subscribe to the most lenient opinion – that neutral food cooked or even roasted in a meat or dairy pot is still considered neutral. Similarly, in the *Shulḥan Aruch* (*Yoreh De'ah* 95:2), Rav Karo rules that the *nat bar nat* leniency applies even to neutral food cooked or roasted in a meat or dairy pot. The Rama thereupon notes that the Ashkenazic practice is to be concerned with the strict opinion *l'chatḥila.* This means that, for instance, Ashkenazim should not eat a neutral item cooked in a meat pot with dairy foods. If, however, the neutral food happened to have been mixed with dairy food (i.e. *b'diavad*), the Ashkenazic practice is to follow the lenient view.

The Sephardic practice regarding this issue is dramatically more lenient than the Ashkenazic practice. In fact, Rav Ovadia Yosef (*Yalkut Yosef, Yoreh De'ah* 95:6) and Rav Shlomo Amar (*Teshuvot Shema Shlomo* 2:*Yoreh De'ah* 4, 6), permit Sephardim to cook a neutral item in a meat pot even if one intends to eat the neutral item with milk and even if the meat pot had been used for meat within the previous twenty-four hours (or vice versa, regarding cooking a neutral item in a milk pot for use with meat).

Rav Shalom Messas (*Teshuvot Shemesh U'Magen* 1:8, 2:42–43, and 3:1), however, rules that even according to Rav Yosef Karo, one may not cook a neutral item in a meat pot that has been used within twenty-four hours if one intends to eat the neutral item with milk. He believes (following the *Shach, Yoreh De'ah* 95:3) that the *Shulḥan Aruch* differs with the Rama only regarding a neutral item that was cooked in a meat pot with the intention of using it with only meat or neutral foods; in such a case, one may later decide to eat the neutral item with milk.

Rav Amar and Rav Messas engaged in an intense debate about this issue, with repeated letters back and forth defending their respective positions. Although Rav Amar retreated somewhat and acknowledged that it is preferable to adopt Rav Messas' opinion, Rav Yitzḥak Yosef (*Yalkut Yosef, Yoreh De'ah* 92–96:6) remains firmly supportive of his father's lenient view, noting that *Maran* Rav Karo explicitly supports this view in his *Bedek HaBayit.*

CONCLUSION

At Congregation Shaarei Orah, the Sephardic Congregation of Teaneck, I recommend that Moroccan Jews follow the stricter ruling of Rav Shalom Messas. Other Sephardic Jews, however, may follow Rav Ovadia's lenient approach. Thus, the issue of dairy or meat equipment is a non-issue for many Sephardic Jews.

Chapter 76

Dishwashers for Meat and Milk

Many Ashkenazic *posekim* forbid using one dishwasher for both meat and milk utensils (Rav Feivel Cohen, *Badei HaShulḥan* 95:77; Rav Binyamin Forst, *The Laws of Kashrus*, p. 261; Rav Yisrael Rozen, *Teḥumin* 11:130–136). Rav Yosef Adler reports that Rav Yosef Dov Soloveitchik also forbade using one dishwasher to clean both milk and meat utensils.

Moreover, it is fair to say that it is accepted in Ashkenazic families not to wash both milk and meat utensils in the same dishwasher. Although Rav Moshe Feinstein wrote no less than seven *teshuvot* permitting the use of a dishwasher for both meat and milk,[1] the fact that he required switching racks when switching from meat to milk (and vice versa) makes it quite inconvenient to use one dishwasher for both.

The premier Sephardic *posekim* Rav Ovadia Yosef and Rav Yitzḥak Yosef, on the other hand, permit using one dishwasher for both meat and milk (*Yalkut Yosef, Otzar Dinim L'Isha*, p. 618; *Yalkut Yosef, Issur V'Heter* 3:485; *Teshuvot Yabia Omer* 10: *Yoreh De'ah* 4). They even (essentially) permit simultaneous washing of both meat and milk in the same dishwasher!

1. For example, *Teshuvot Igrot Moshe, Oraḥ Ḥayim* 1:104; *Yoreh De'ah* 2:28–29, 3:10.

Even Rav Eli Mansour, who often rules strictly, essentially endorses Rav Ovadia's ruling on this matter, though he expresses preference to be strict.[2]

However, Rav Shlomo Amar told a group of Shaarei Orah congregants (during his visit to our congregation on Shabbat Naḥamu 5777) that he believes that a dishwasher should not be used for both milk and meat unless one *kashers* the dishwashers between uses of the different types.[3] Although Rav Amar typically follows the halachic path of Rav Ovadia Yosef, regarding this issue he is not comfortable doing so. Similarly, the great late twentieth-century Sephardic *posek* Rav Mordechai Eliyahu is cited as forbidding use of one dishwasher for both meat and milk (*Mitbaḥ KaHalacha*, p. 160).

We learn from these rulings that this issue is not necessarily a debate that runs along classic differences between Sephardic and Ashkenazic Jews. In order to explain Rav Amar's approach, we must first examine Rav Ovadia's reasoning.

RAV OVADIA'S REASONING

In his *teshuva* (*Teshuvot Yabia Omer* 10: *Yoreh De'ah* 4), Rav Ovadia first describes how a dishwasher works. One normally removes large residue or food particles from the dish before inserting into the dishwasher. After putting the dishes in the unit, one adds a cleansing agent into a designated compartment inside the machine. The process then begins. First, the dishes are rinsed with cold water. After the cold cycle completes, the water is warmed and the cleaning agent is released. The hot water mixes with the cleaning agent, and together they wash the dishes. Following this process, the water shuts off and a heating element is turned on to dry the dishes. Once dry, the process is complete.

Rav Ovadia argues that the dishwasher is perfectly analogous to a case addressed by *Maran* Rav Yosef Karo (*Shulḥan Aruch, Yoreh De'ah* 95:4). He describes a situation in which people wanted to use giant pots normally used for dairy cooking for the purpose of cleaning various tableware and cookware, including meat dishes. Rav Karo rules that it would be permissible to use this giant dairy pot to clean meat dishes so long as a distasting agent, such as *efer* (ashes) or soap, is added. Such an agent would

2. https://www.dailyhalacha.com/displayRead.asp?readID=810.
3. Sephardic *posekim* permit *kashering* utensils from meat to milk and vice versa (*Teshuvot Yabia Omer* 3: *Yoreh De'ah* 4 and 4:*Yoreh De'ah* 5).

render the milk in the walls of the pot *pagum* (unsavory, unfit, spoiled), thus allowing the insertion of a meat vessel for cleansing. This leniency applies even if the meat pot is dipped in the giant milk pot together with boiling hot water.

Rav Ovadia defends the *Shulḥan Aruch*'s ruling from its critics, including the *Shach* (*Yoreh De'ah* 95:21) and *Taz* (*Yoreh De'ah* 95:15), and demonstrates that this ruling is accepted in practice. Indeed, both the *Ḥochmat Adam* (48:15) and the *Aruch HaShulḥan* (*Yoreh De'ah* 95:24) accept the *Shulḥan Aruch*'s opinion.

Rav Ovadia applies the *Shulḥan Aruch*'s reasoning regarding the giant milk pot to permit simultaneous washing of meat dishes and dairy dishes in a dishwasher. The soap deposited into the designated compartment, when released together with the hot water, renders any food particles in the dishwasher as *pagum*. Therefore, Rav Ovadia concludes, not only is it permissible to use the same dishwasher for both meat and dairy dishes, but it is also permissible for one dishwasher to be used to wash dairy and meat dishes simultaneously.[4]

CONCERNS WITH RAV OVADIA'S RULING

Rav Ovadia's ruling seems to be convincing and even airtight. After all, the analogy between a dishwasher and the giant pot discussed in the *Shulḥan Aruch* seems perfect. Rav Ovadia cites those who disagree with his ruling and responds to their objections. Indeed, any objection can be rebutted by citing the precedent of the *Shulḥan Aruch*'s giant pot.

Rav Feivel Cohen and Rav Yisrael Rozen, for example, raise concern about food particles that remain in the dishwasher's filter. They argue that these food particles remain edible and that these particles are absorbed into utensils of the opposite type, rendering them thereby a non-kosher mixture of meat and milk.

However, the *Shulḥan Aruch* was not concerned with this issue, since the ashes added to the giant pot render the food particles inedible. Similarly, Rav Ovadia argues that the detergent used in dishwashers, which is at least as caustic as the ashes mentioned in the *Shulḥan Aruch*, also renders inedible any food particles remaining in the dishwasher's filter.

4. Rav Ovadia and Rav Yitzḥak both prefer that the dishwasher be used to wash meat and milk items consecutively, instead of simultaneously.

Why, then, is Rav Amar not comfortable with Rav Ovadia's ruling? There is one major chink in the armor of Rav Ovadia's ruling. Rav Forst raises the very serious concern that "in the very beginning of the washing cycle, hot water may start spraying before it has been rendered *pagum* by the detergents." Rav Menahem Genack, Chief Executive Officer of OU Kosher, expresses a similar concern in his *shiurim* to Yeshiva University *semicha* students.

Rav Yosef's description of the operation of a dishwasher shows that he assumed that the water released before the detergent is introduced is cold. However, this is not always the case. Indeed, if one simultaneously washes milk and meat utensils in the same dishwasher in which hot water is released before the detergent, not only are all the utensils rendered non-kosher, but one also runs afoul of the Torah-level prohibition to cook milk and meat together![5] Even if one washes meat and milk utensils consecutively in such a dishwasher, one renders the dishwasher itself a forbidden mixture of milk and meat, since its walls absorb both meat and milk taste particles.

CONCLUSION

Although Rav Ovadia Yosef wrote a very persuasive responsum permitting washing meat and milk dishes in one dishwasher, this ruling presumes that hot water is introduced only after the detergent has been released into the dishwasher. This assumption does not apply to all dishwashers, however. Indeed, Rav Shmuel Khoshkerman told me that Rav Ovadia's *teshuva* does

---

5. According to https://www.explainthatstuff.com/dishwashers.html, the water in a dishwasher is heated to a level that hands cannot usually touch, 86–140°F, so halachic cooking could certainly happen here; *yad soledet bo* is between 110–120° F. After the water spins around the dishwasher, the soap or detergent tablet is dropped into the already hot water: "Sometime during the wash cycle, usually a while after the machine first switches on, the dispenser flips open, dropping or dripping the detergent into the hot water bath in the bottom of the machine. After the water has bounced off your plates, it falls back to the bottom of the machine, where it is heated and pumped around the circuit again. After it flips out of the automatic dispenser on the door, the dishwasher tablet falls into the bottom of the machine and dissolves in the hot water there."

   The article explains that this applies only to dishwashers that are hooked up to a cold water supply; in some cases, the dishwashers are hooked up to hot water supply, in which case hot water is immediately pumped into the dishwasher. This clearly shows that regarding today's dishwashers (at least those commonly used in the United States), we can no longer allow simultaneously washing of meat and milk utensils.

not apply to today's dishwashers, due to concern that hot water is released into the dishwasher before the detergent is released.[6]

While one could try to determine that the dishwasher one purchases releases the water only after the detergent is introduced, this could lead to confusion and complications. If some dishwashers carry with them serious halachic concerns, it is sensible (at least in the United States) to adopt a policy of not permitting the simultaneous use of any dishwasher for both meat and milk. Rav Amar's atypical veering from Rav Ovadia's ruling may stem from concern that permitting the use of some dishwashers could lead to serious halachic violations.

In practice, it seems safest for Sephardic Jews to follow Rav Amar's advice and wash milk and meat in the same dishwasher only if one *kashers* the dishwasher between uses of the opposite type by running it through an empty cycle while filled with detergent. However, a compelling argument can be made permitting Sephardic Jews to use the same dishwasher for meat and milk if washed consecutively and not simultaneously.[7] Indeed, Rav Zecharia Ben-Shlomo (*Orot HaHalacha*, p. 1010) permits consecutive washing of meat and milk utensils in one dishwasher in certain circumstances.

---

6. I asked Rav Khoshkerman if one is permitted to eat at a home that still relies on Rav Ovadia's leniency and simultaneously washes meat and milk utensils in the dishwasher. He replied that he did not know how to respond. Rav Hershel Schachter agreed (personal communication) that this is a serious problem unless one is convinced of the opinion of Rav Moshe Feinstein (cited by Rav Aharon Felder, *Ohalei Yeshurun*, p. 72) that the dishwasher contains sixty times the amount of water to nullify the meat and milk particles. This presumption is subject to considerable debate, as noted in Rav Rozen's aforementioned article.

   Rav Khoshkerman told me that if the dishes were thoroughly mixed with soap before being placed in the dishwasher, it would be permissible to run the cycle with the meat and milk dishes simultaneously in the same dishwasher. However, Rav Khoshkerman believes that this is not a practical protocol for the community, because in order to be effective, the soap must be thoroughly applied to all the dishes placed in the dishwasher, something that requires significant effort and attention and is likely not to be done properly (except for particularly meticulous individuals). A non-Jewish or non-observant cleaning person could certainly not be entrusted (due to lack of halachic credibility, *ne'emanut*) to do this properly.
7. Once the initial full cycle runs, the dishes experience the entire wash cycle, so the hot water with soap/detergent has already rendered any particles *pagum*. The next wash should thus be ready for a run of the opposite type without a *kashering* run in between.

Mezuza

Chapter 77

Sephardic and Ashkenazic Roommates

The *gemara* in *Menaḥot* (33b) teaches that a *mezuza* may not be placed "in the manner of carpenters." There are two ways in which to understand this statement: Rashi (ad loc., s.v. *avida*) explains that this forbids placing *mezuzot* horizontally, whereas Rabbenu Tam (cited in *Tosafot,* ad loc., s.v. *ha*) believes that it forbids placing them vertically.

The non-Moroccan Sephardic tradition follows Rashi's vertical orientation (*Shulḥan Aruch, Yoreh De'ah* 289:6; *Yalkut Yosef, Kitzur Shulḥan Aruch, Yoreh De'ah* 285:5). However, Ashkenazic and most Moroccan Jews (as noted by Rav Mordechai Lebhar, *Magen Avot, Yoreh De'ah* 289:6) follow the recommendation of the *Tur* (*Yoreh De'ah* 289) and customarily attempt to satisfy two opinions, placing their *mezuzot* on a slant (see Rama, *Yoreh De'ah* 289:6).[1]

1. Yemenite tradition, not surprisingly, follows the ruling of the Rambam (as explained by the Radbaz, *Teshuvot* 3:530) and *Shulḥan Aruch* to place the *mezuzot* vertically (Rav Zecharia Ben-Shlomo, *Orot HaHalacha*, p. 1141).

RAV YITZḤAK YOSEF'S RULING

How should roommates of different Jewish backgrounds place the *mezuza* in their shared living space? Rav Yitzḥak Yosef (as recorded by Rav Yonatan Nacson, *MiMizraḥ U'MiMa'arav*, p. 270) rules that even if there is only one Sephardic Jew in the group, the *mezuzot* should be affixed vertically, without a slant. His reason presumably is that the vertical placement is acceptable even to Ashkenazic Jews, whereas the slanted approach is not acceptable for Sephardic Jews. Evidence that the vertical placement is acceptable for Ashkenazim is the fact that the Rama writes that "those who are particular" (*medakdekin*) place their *mezuzot* on a slant. This indicates that the Rama fundamentally accepts the ruling of Rashi that the *mezuza* should be placed in a vertical position.

The Vilna Gaon, in fact, explicitly states that Ashkenazic Jews fundamentally accept Rashi's approach (*Bi'ur HaGra, Yoreh De'ah* 289:14). For this reason, if there is insufficient room on the doorway to place the *mezuza* on a slant, Ashkenazic Jews place the *mezuza* vertically, as noted by the *Pitḥei Teshuva* (*Yoreh De'ah* 289:14).

Most interestingly, I witnessed Rav Yosef's ruling in practice. My family had the privilege of renting an apartment at 36 Jabotinsky Street in the Talbiah/Komemiyut section of Yerushalayim in August 2012. I was delighted to learn while there that Rav Ovadia Yosef and his family had at one point resided in the apartment just above the apartment that we rented. I distinctly recall that the *mezuza* for the common area was etched in the wall in a vertical position, in accordance with the ruling of Rashi and the *Shulḥan Aruch* – despite the fact that the Talbiah/Komemiyut area in general and this building in particular are predominantly Ashkenazic! Thus, I am a witness that Rav Yitzḥak Yosef seems to have adopted his ruling from that his father's practice in their home at 36 Jabotinsky.

AN ALTERNATIVE RULING

There is room to disagree with this ruling, however. One may argue that it is acceptable for Sephardic Jews to place the *mezuza* on a slant. The Vilna Gaon (*op. cit.*) notes that the logic of placing the *mezuza* on a slant is that it satisfies both the opinions of Rashi and Rabbenu Tam. Rashi objects to the *mezuza* being on its side and Rabbenu Tam objects to its being upright. Thus, placing the *mezuza* on a slant avoids the objections of both approaches.

Indeed, this is the reason, as noted by Rav Lebhar, that Moroccan Jews follow the Rama's recommendation. Had they understood that the *Shulḥan Aruch* objects to having a *mezuza* on a slant, they would not follow the Rama's recommendation.

If this is the case, then the identity of the majority of the roommates should determine the position of the *mezuza*. This is similar to a ruling of the *Ḥatam Sofer* (*Teshuvot Ḥatam Sofer, Ḥoshen Mishpat* 188, in the addendum). The *Ḥatam Sofer* was approached by members of a town in which two communities, one Sephardic and one Ashkenazic, had formerly functioned. A pogrom had caused most of the Jews to leave, and since the remaining populace could not sustain two separate *minyanim*, the two groups now had to combine into one functioning synagogue. The *Ḥatam Sofer* ruled that they should choose which of the two synagogues would continue to function based on the identity of the majority of the remaining Jewish residents, and then all should follow the *minhagim* of that synagogue. Rav Ovadia Yosef (*Teshuvot Yabia Omer* 6: *Oraḥ Ḥayim* 10) cites numerous authorities who concur with the *Ḥatam Sofer*'s ruling. Rav Yosef Shalom Eliashiv (*Kovetz Teshuvot* 1:12) also endorses this ruling of the *Ḥatam Sofer*.

However, the language of the *Shulḥan Aruch* – "It must be placed vertically" – would seem to support Rav Yitzḥak's understanding that the *Shulḥan Aruch* specifically requires the *mezuza* to be placed vertically. In addition, the Vilna Gaon supports the view of Rashi and the *Shulḥan Aruch* by noting our practice to have the *parshiot* in *tefillin* stand upright; *parshiot* on a slant are not acceptable. This explains why non-Moroccan Sephardic Jews specifically place their *mezuzot* vertically.[2] Thus, our question is a difficult one to resolve.

CONCLUSION

It is most interesting that Ashkenazic *Ba'alei Mussar* (masters of ethical teachings) note that the Ashkenazic practice to maintain the *mezuza* on a slant to accommodate both the opinions of both Rashi and Rabbenu Tam teaches a major lesson in *shalom bayit*. It teaches people of different temperaments

2. Rav Ḥayim Kanievsky is cited (Rav Aharon Zakkai, *HaMezuza V'Hilchoteha*, p. 92) as also ruling that a *mezuza* placed on a slant is not acceptable for Sephardic Jews. Indeed, the Ra'avya (*Menaḥot* 228) writes that a *mezuza* that is slanted is unacceptable.

to find a manner to accommodate the needs of both parties. This is a vital lesson in particular for people sharing a living space.

I posed the question of how roommates should place the *mezuza* in this situation to Rav Mordechai Willig, who wisely responded that whichever way one resolves this issue, it should be done in a manner that maintains *shalom bayit,* peace and harmony among the roommates. With good will on the part of all the roommates and consultation with a mutually trusted Rav, the issue can and should be resolved to the satisfaction of all the roommates. The placement of the *mezuza* on the door, which many see as communicating the central message of *shalom bayit,* should certainly serve to promote, and not detract, from harmonious living among house and apartment mates.[3]

3. In practice, both Rav Schachter (personal communication) and Rav Willig (personal communication) agree with Rav Yitzḥak's ruling that the *mezuza* should be kept straight even if only one roommate is a non-Moroccan Sephardic Jew.

Marriage

Chapter 78

The Sephardic *Ketuba*

During the glorious Shabbat Naḥamu 5777 when Rav Shlomo Amar joined us at Congregation Shaarei Orah, I had the opportunity to discuss a wide variety of halachic issues with him. Among the issues we discussed was the necessity of a Sephardic couple using the Sephardic text for their *ketuba*.

OMITTING THE WORD *MID'ORAITA*

Since the time of the *Rishonim*, Ashkenazic Jews have incorporated the word "*mid'oraita*" in their *ketubot* in describing the base amount (*ikar ketuba*) due to the bride (if it is her first marriage) – "*d'ḥazi lichi mid'oraita*" (that the Torah entitles you to). Ashkenazic *Rishonim*, such as *Tosafot* (*Ketubot* 10a, s.v. *amar Rav Naḥman*) and the Rosh (*Ketubot* 1:19), struggled to explain this phenomenon in light of the *gemara*'s explicit statement (*Yevamot* 89a; *Ketubot* 10a, 11a) that according to the majority Tannaitic opinion, the *ketuba* is a Rabbinic enactment designed and intended to prevent impulsive divorce. Rabbenu Tam explains that Ashkenazim follow the opinion of Rabban Shimon ben Gamliel, who argues that the *ketuba* is of Torah origin (*Ketubot* 110b). The Rosh explains that the phrase "*d'ḥazi lichi mid'oraita*" refers to the value of the coins to be used in case of collection of the *ketuba*; it is teaching that the payment must be made in higher value coins (i.e. *kesef*

Tzuri and not *kesef medina*) used in payment of Torah-level obligations (such as *pidyon haben*).

Rav Ovadia Yosef (*Teshuvot Yabia Omer* 3: *Even HaEzer* 12) and Rav Shalom Messas (*Teshuvot Shemesh U'Magen* 3: *Even HaEzer* 61) argue that the word "*mid'oraita*" should not be included in a *ketuba* for a Sephardic couple. Rav Ovadia insists that no matter what the explanation for its inclusion, the Sephardic *Rishonim*, such as the Ramban, did not include this word in the *ketuba*.[1]

Accordingly, some believe that as long as the word "*mid'oraita*" is not included in the text, the remainder of the Ashkenazic *ketuba* is acceptable for Sephardic Jews. There are also significant differences in the spellings of names and transliteration of foreign words, such as the location of the wedding (if it occurs outside of Israel). In addition, the Sephardic custom is for the *ḥatan* to sign the *ketuba* as a supplement to the witnesses.

THREE ADDITIONAL DIFFERENCES

I presented this perspective to Rav Amar, who strongly disagreed. He noted three additional reasons that a full Sephardic text of the *ketuba* is necessary for a Sephardic couple.

First, the Sephardic text includes towards the beginning of the *ketuba* the phrase "*anan sahadi*," "we are witnesses," a phrase that does not appear in the Ashkenazic version. Rav Amar notes that the Sephardic text is much more reasonable, as the witnesses are the "voice" of the *ketuba*, which is essentially their account having witnessed the groom accept with a *kinyan* the obligations set forth in the *ketuba*. In order to indicate this, the *ketuba* should state "*anan sahadi*" towards the outset of the document.

A second advantage of the Sephardic *ketuba* is that the set amount mentioned in the Ashkenazic *ketuba* for the *tosefet ketuba* (added amount of the *ketuba*) and *nedunya* (bridal dowry) for a first marriage is two hundred *zekukim kesef*, and there is an extraordinarily wide range of opinions regarding the contemporary equivalents of this monetary sum.[2] By con-

1. Rav Mordechai Lebhar (*Magen Avot, Even HaEzer* 66:6) argues that *b'diavad* (after the fact), a Sephardic *ketuba* is not rendered *pasul* if it includes the word "*mid'oraita*." Indeed, one textual version of the *ketuba* that appears in the Rambam's *Hilchot Yibum V'Ḥalitza* (4:33) includes the word "*mid'oraita*."
2. Rav Yonah Reiss summarizes the views in an article archived at http://www.jlaw.com/Articles/KETUBAH.pdf.

trast, Sephardic *ketubot* do not have set amounts for the *tosefet ketuba* and *nedunya*. Instead, each couple decides the amount using a realistic amount appropriate for them.

I noted the prevalent problem of exaggerated amounts and heated arguments that emerge regarding the designated amount, but Rav Amar responded that among the responsibilities of the officiating rabbi is to guide the couple as to a reasonable amount. He noted that Rav Ovadia typically would advise Israeli couples to use the amount of $52,000. (The Hebrew word *ben* (son) is the numerical equivalent of fifty-two.)[3]

A third reason for Sephardim to use a Sephardic *ketuba* results from the fact that the *Ḥerem D'Rabbenu Gershom,* the tenth-century ban on polygamy, is not binding on Sephardim. Rav Ovadia Yosef (*Teshuvot Yabia Omer* 5: *Even HaEzer* 1) notes that either Sephardim never accepted the *ḥerem* or have accepted the opinion (presented as authoritative in the *Shulḥan Aruch, Even HaEzer* 1:10) that the *ḥerem* expired at the end of the fifth millennium from Creation (i.e. 1240 C.E.). Instead, Sephardim commit themselves through a "*shevu'a ḥamura*" (solemn oath) that is recorded in the *ketuba* not to marry more than one wife unless a proper *bet din* grants permission to do so.[4] Accordingly, if a Sephardic couple utilizes an Ashkenazic text of the *ketuba,* the husband has failed to accept upon himself the prohibition of polygamy!

---

3. Rav Ike Sultan reports that for his wedding, his *mesader kiddushin,* Rav Hershel Schachter, recommended writing $100,000 in Rav Sultan's Sephardic *ketuba.*
4. The *Yalkut Yosef* (*Ḥuppa V'Kiddushin* 9:24) writes that some assert this has been the Sephardic custom since the time of the Rambam. This custom is also presented by many *Rishonim* and early *Aḥaronim,* such as the Radbaz (4:292), Mabit (2:7), and Maharit (1:60 and 1:118). The *Yalkut Yosef* records that this was the custom among all of the Sephardic *gedolim* of this generation and the previous one, such as Rav Ben Tzion Abba Sha'ul and Rav Yehuda Tzadka. Rav Shlomo Amar (*Teshuvot Shema Shlomo* 5:20) also defends and upholds this custom. However, Rav Amar writes that even if this oath is not included in the *ketuba* of a Sephardic husband, the husband is obligated to uphold its terms due to *minhag hamedina* (common custom) and *dina d'malchuta* (civil law).

   Although Rav Meir Mazouz (*Ohr Torah,* Shevat 5750) raises serious concerns regarding including this *shevu'a* in the contemporary setting, Rav Ben Zion Abba Sha'ul (in a responsum printed in *Teshuvot Kol Eliyahu, Even HaEzer* 1) dismisses those concerns. For a summary of this debate and a suggested compromise to limit the oath to prohibit bigamy, see Rav Mordechai Lebhar, *Magen Avot, Even HaEzer* 1:11.

CONCLUSION

Accordingly, Rav Amar insists that Sephardic Jews should use the Sephardic *ketuba* text, rather than merely omitting the word "*mid'oraita*" from the Ashkenazic text. However, *Rabbanim* outside of Israel have found it difficult to find an appropriate text for Sephardic Jews who are not part of either the Moroccan or Syrian communities.

This problem has been solved by Rav Eliyahu Bar Shalom, the Chief Rabbi of Bat Yam and an expert in the *halachot* of the *ketuba* (and author of the respected work *Mishpat HaKetuba*). He sent me a version acceptable for all Sephardic Jews that is adapted for use in the United States and meets the specifications set forth by Rav Amar. I recommend its widespread use by Sephardic rabbis in the United States.

Chapter 79

The Great Sephardic *Yiḥud* Controversy

According to Sephardic tradition since the time of the Radbaz (*Teshuvot* 1:45 and 931), a Sephardic *ḥatan* and *kalla* do not retire to the *yiḥud* room for a few minutes after the *ḥuppa*. Virtually all of the greatest Sephardic authorities of the prior generation – including Rav Ezra Attia (*Teshuvot Alei Ezra, Ḥiddushei Halacha* section, p. 83), Rav Ovadia Hadaya (*Teshuvot Yaskil Avdi* 7: *Even HaEzer* 10), Rav Ovadia Yosef (*Teshuvot Yeḥaveh Da'at* 5:62), Rav Ben Tzion Abba Sha'ul (cited by Rav Yitzḥak Yosef, *Teḥumin* 31:255), Rav Mordechai Eliyahu (*Teshuvot Ma'amar Mordechai* 2: *Even HaEzer* 6), Rav Hayim David HaLevy (*Teshuvot Asei Lecha Rav* 4:55), and Rav Shalom Messas (*Teshuvot Shemesh U'Magen* 1: *Even HaEzer* 4 and 3: *Even HaEzer* 34) – agree that Sephardim should continue to follow their age-old tradition to defer *yiḥud* until after the wedding.

ARGUMENTS OF RAV YITZḤAK YOSEF

Rav Yitzḥak Yosef, the son of Rav Ovadia and the current Sephardic Chief Rabbi of Israel, champions the traditional Sephardic approach in an essay printed in *Teḥumin* (vol. 31). Among his arguments is that the *ḥatan* and *kalla* locking themselves in the *ḥeder yiḥud* after the *ḥuppa* is unseemly (*mecho'ar*). Moreover, he argues that since *yiḥud* completes the process of *nissu'in* (the second portion of the marriage ceremony) according to the Rambam (*Hilchot Ishut* 10:1), *Tur* (*Even HaEzer* 61), and *Shulḥan Aruch* (*Even HaEzer* 61:1), the couple is married after *yiḥud*, and the *kalla* should therefore be required to cover her hair. Customarily, however, a *kalla* does not cover her hair during the wedding celebration.

There are, however, possible arguments against this view. For example, the *berachot* of *nissu'in* are recited at the *ḥuppa*. Delaying *yiḥud* for hours after the *Birchot HaNissu'in* are recited appears highly irregular. Rav Yitzḥak counters that these *berachot* are blessings of praise to *Hashem*, such that the process need not be completed soon after their recitation (unlike the case of *berachot* recited over a *mitzva*).

Another questionable element of Rav Yitzḥak's argument is that the *berachot* at the end of the wedding *seuda* seem out of place if *yiḥud* has not been completed. Rav Yitzḥak counters that in this regard, Sephardim abide by the *Rishonim* who consider the *ḥatan* covering the *kalla* with his *tallit* as the completion of *nissu'in*.[1]

RESPONSE OF RAV SHLOMO LEVY

In response to Rav Yitzḥak's article, Rav Shlomo Levy, the highly respected Rosh Kollel of Yeshivat Har Etzion (and son-in-law of the eminent Rav Ḥayim David HaLevy, the late Sephardic Chief Rabbi of Tel Aviv) penned a respectful rebuttal in *Teḥumin* (vol. 32).[2] Rav Levy defends what he presents as the current trend of Sephardic couples retiring to the *yiḥud* room after the *ḥuppa*, noting the difficulties in Rav Yitzḥak's arguments.

Moreover, Rav Levy offers a compelling reason to change the age-old Sephardic practice. In the contemporary setting, Sephardic couples will most often wish to honor some Ashkenazic guests with the recitation of one of the *sheva berachot*, but Ashkenazic practice does not accept such a large break between the *berachot* of *nissu'in* and the completion of *nissu'in*, as defended by Rav Yitzhak. If *yiḥud* is delayed until the *ḥatan* and *kalla* go

---

1. This is customarily done at Sephardic and German Jewish weddings.
2. I vividly recall Rav Levy from my years of learning at Yeshivat Har Etzion in 1981–1983. Rav Levy made a deep impression on me and my friends as a profoundly spiritual Rav who also was a Yeshivat Hesder hero of the Yom Kippur War.

home after the wedding, an Ashkenazic guest should not recite one of the *berachot* under the *ḥuppa*.[3]

This did not pose a problem in prior generations, when Sephardim and Ashkenazim were hardly as integrated as they are today. A change in the practice regarding the timing of *yiḥud* would enable Ashkenazim to recite *sheva berachot* at a Sephardic wedding.

In addition to Rav Levy's point, we should note that Rav Mordechai Willig cogently argues that the obligation for the *kalla* to cover her hair applies only after the wedding is consummated. He notes that the *halachot* of hair-covering are derived from the *sota* (*Ketubot* 72a), and the rules of *sota*, in turn, apply only if the husband and wife had previously consummated their marriage (*Sota* 24b). Thus, the married woman's obligation to cover her hair applies only after the marriage is consummated, not after *yiḥud* alone.[4]

CONCLUSION – A SUGGESTED COMPROMISE

Rav Yitzḥak Yosef describes how strongly his father, Rav Ovadia, felt about this issue.[5] On the other hand, many *kallot* (especially Ashkenazic women)

---

3. Rav Hershel Schachter (personal communication) told me that he would not recite one of the *sheva berachot* if *yiḥud* were not to occur immediately after the *ḥuppa*. See his *B'Ikvei HaTzon* 39:3 for further discussion. Indeed, Rav Schachter is fond of quoting the Maharil's statement that "*meritzin et haḥatan v'hakalla l'ḥeder hayiḥud miyad l'aḥar shevirat hakos*," that the *ḥatan* and *kalla* should proceed expeditiously to the *yiḥud* room immediately after the breaking of the glass under the *ḥuppa*. Rav Schachter notes, however, that Rav Ovadia responds to this point in *Teshuvot Yabia Omer* 5: *Even HaEzer* 8.
4. This is the reported opinion of Rav Moshe Feinstein as well. Rav Aryeh Leibowitz of Yeshiva University reports that he heard this confirmed by Rav Aharon Felder, a longtime *talmid* of Rav Moshe, and Rav Moshe Snow, another longtime *talmid*, confirms this as well. Rav Ben Tzion Abba Sha'ul (*Hilchot Shidduchim V'Ḥatuna, Amudei Shesh, Ketubot* 2a) and Rav Shlomo Zalman Auerbach (*Shalmei Simḥa*, p. 343), however, disagree and rule that hair-covering is required as soon as the *Kiddushin* occurs.

   Rav Willig does insist that the *kalla* should cover her hair slightly with the bridal headband throughout the wedding, in keeping with the description in the *mishna* (*Ketubot* 2:1) of the "bride with her headband" (*hinuma b'rosha*).
5. Rav Mordechai Eliyahu (as stated in his *Siddur Kol Eliyahu*), however, rules that if the couple wishes to conduct a *ḥeder yiḥud* after the *ḥuppa*, we should not prevent them from doing so.

and their families very much want to conduct a *yiḥud* after the *ḥuppa*. This can sometimes lead to conflict when planning a wedding.

Some have suggested a compromise to resolve such conflicts: Conduct a "*yiḥud*," but in a manner not defined as *yiḥud* according to Halacha. This involves leaving the door unlocked and not designating *eidim* to stand outside the *yiḥud* room. In fact, this was done at the wedding of Rav Shmuel Khosherman's son, who married an Ashkenazic woman. Rav Yonatan Nacson (*MiMizrach U'MiMa'arav*, p. 248) endorses this idea as well.[6] This option seems to be becoming increasingly popular, especially at weddings between Sephardic and Ashkenazic families.

6. See, however, Rav Yitzḥak Yosef (*Teshuvot HaRishon L'Tzion* 2:*Even HaEzer* 9) and Rav Meir Mazouz (*Mekor Ne'eman* 2, p. 183), who object to this compromise. On the other hand, Rav Mordechai Djavaheri (*Birkat Rivka*, p. 71) records a report that Rav Ovadia Yosef endorsed this compromise and even served as the extra person in the *yiḥud* room at his granddaughter's wedding!

Chapter 80

Sephardic Standards for *Sheva Berachot*

It was a great *simḥa* when Congregation Shaarei Orah's Joshua Schulz married Rachel Lina (Lini) Sassen in Israel in June 2017. The young couple returned to the US for *sheva berachot* in New Jersey, concluding with a *seuda shelishit* at Shaarei Orah, providing an opportunity to examine the Sephardic practices with regard to *sheva berachot.*

PANIM ḤADASHOT

When *sheva berachot* are recited after a meal during the week after a wedding, *panim ḥadashot* – literally, new faces, meaning people who have not yet participated in the wedding celebrations – must be present. Ashkenazic Jews follow the view of the Ran (*Ketuvot* 3a in the Rif's pages, s.v. *v'haTannaim*), who maintains that one adult male suffices for *panim ḥadashot* (see *Aruch HaShulḥan, Even HaEzer* 62:24; *Bet Shmuel* 62:7; *Ḥelkat Meḥokek* 62:9; *Pitḥei Teshuva, Even HaEzer* 62:14). However, both the *Ben Ish Ḥai* (year 1, *Parashat Shofetim* 15) and Rav Ovadia Yosef (*Teshuvot Yabia Omer* 3: *Even HaEzer* 11) insist that Sephardic practice follows the Rambam (cited by his son in *Teshuvot Rav Avraham ben HaRambam* 86), who requires two *panim ḥadashot*, as indicated by the use of the plural.[1]

Moreover, while Ashkenazic Jews follow the Rama (*Even HaEzer* 62:8) that Shabbat is regarded as *panim ḥadashot* even regarding *seuda shelishit* – such that no new guest is required on Shabbat at all – Sephardim follow the ruling of the *Shulḥan Aruch* that actual *panim ḥadashot* are required at *seuda shelishit* (as noted by Rav Ovadia, *op. cit.*).

I was delighted to note that both requirements were met at the *seuda shelishit* held in honor of Lini and Joshua's marriage – two new guests were present for *seuda shelishit.*

SHEVA BERACHOT OUTSIDE THE *BET ḤATAN*

There would seem to be a problem with conducting *sheva berachot* at Shaarei Orah, however. The *gemara* (*Sukka* 25b) states that *simḥa* occurs only at the marital residence, and *Tosafot* (ad loc., s.v. *en*) note that this teaches that *sheva berachot* may be recited only at the marital residence of the *ḥatan* and *kalla*, the *bet ḥatan*. Accordingly, Rav Ovadia Yosef insists (*Yalkut Yosef, Even HaEzer* 17:6–7; *Ḥazon Ovadia* 1:48) that *sheva berachot* celebrations take place only at the *bet ḥatan*.[2] Rav Ben Tzion Abba Sha'ul (*Teshuvot Ohr L'Tzion* 2:14) and Rav Mordechai Eliyahu (*Teshuvot Ma'amar Mordechai* 2:*Even HaEzer* 6) agree with Rav Ovadia.[3]

1. Rav Mordechai Lebhar (*Magen Avot, Even HaEzer* 62:7) records the Moroccan practice that one new adult male suffices for *panim ḥadashot*. It is not surprising that divergent practices have emerged among Sephardic Jews regarding this matter, since the *Shulḥan Aruch* does not take an explicit stand regarding this issue.
2. In a memorable passage, Rav Shalom Messas records (*Teshuvot Shemesh U'Magen* 3:EH 24): "Many times I was invited to *sheva berachot* that the Rishon L'Tziyon Rav Ovadia Yosef made for his sons and grandsons. There were very large crowds, replete with exceptionally great glory and many *Rabbanim* attending. The *simḥa* was enormous and intense, with original Torah thoughts and *zemirot* sung in honor of the *ḥatan* and *kalla*. With all this, the Rishon L'Tziyon did not recite the *sheva berachot*, except for the *berachot* of *Bore Pri HaGefen* and *Asher Bara*!"
3. In Rav Mordechai Eliyahu's *Siddur Kol Eliyahu*, he writes: "Some are lenient that in such circumstances [when *sheva berachot* celebrations are not held at the *bet ḥatan*] the *berachot* be recited by Ashkenazic guests who follow the *Taz* (*Even HaEzer* 62:7) that the *sheva berachot* may be recited even outside the marital residence." Rav Ike Sultan reports that he heard the same from Rav Shlomo Amar. An additional option is to give the *berachot* to guests who are followers of Rav Messas or any of the other *posekim* who support his approach to this issue.

However, many Sephardic Jews have not accepted this ruling. The marital residence is usually quite a small space and inadequate for hosting a *sheva berachot* celebration. Moreover, the marital residence is often hardly in order and ready to host a series of parties immediately after the wedding.

Thus, it is accepted among many Sephardic Jews that the conditions have changed since the time of the *gemara*, and *sheva berachot* may therefore be recited even outside of the *bet ḥatan*. In the current circumstances, one could argue that the new couple does not have a primary residence in regards to *sheva berachot*. Rather, wherever they go for a celebratory meal made in their honor is considered to be their *bet ḥatan*.[4]

This ruling is supported at considerable length by Rav Shalom Messas (*Teshuvot Shemesh U'Magen* 3: *Even HaEzer* 24–26), Rav Ḥayim David HaLevy (*Teshuvot Aseh Lecha Rav* 5:38–39), Rav Yaakov Hillel (*Teshuvot VaYashev HaYam* 2:21), and Rav Moshe HaLevy (in an essay published in *Ohr Torah* 5771 and *Birkat Hashem* 4:355 and 5:69).[5] Rav Mordechai Lebhar (*Magen Avot, Even HaEzer* 62:10) notes that the *Ben Ish Ḥai* (*op. cit.*) presents many *halachot* regarding *sheva berachot*, but does not mention that they may take place only at the marital residence.[6]

---

4. Support for this approach may be drawn from the Rosh (*Sukka* 2:8).
5. Rav Moshe HaLevy was an up and coming great late twentieth century Sephardic *posek* who tragically died at a relatively young age. He wrote two very well-received multi-volume works, *Menuḥat Ahava* on *Hilchot Shabbat* and *Birkat Hashem* on *Hilchot Berachot*.
6. Rav Mordechai Djavaheri argues that this is not a compelling proof, since during the time of the *Ben Ish Ḥai*, weddings and *sheva berachot* routinely took place at the home of the *ḥatan*'s parents. The *Ben Ish Ḥai* did not have to address a reality that did not exist during his era.

   Rav Eli Mansour rules in accordance with Rav Ovadia (http://www.dailyhalacha.com/m/halacha.aspx?id=977):

   Our *halacha* for the Sephardic community, according to Rav Ovadia Yosef, is to follow the opinion of *Maran*. In a place outside of the couple's home, only the two *berachot* should be made. This was also the opinion of Rav Ovadia's Rabbi, Rav Ezra Attia *z"l*. It is also the opinion our great Rabbi, the late Rav Baruch Ben Ḥayim *z"l*. The procedure would be to give the cup of wine to one of the individuals who ate bread and participated in the *Birkat HaMazon*. He would say the *Borei Peri HaGefen* and then the *beracha* of *Asher Bara Sasson V'Simcha*. He then drinks from the cup and gives it to the bride and groom to drink from it as well.

   My sister-in-law, Mrs. Esther Tokayer (neé Najar), who serves as the long-time assistant principal at Magen David High School in Brooklyn, New York, reports that

SHEVA BRACHOT AFTER *SHEKIA* ON THE SEVENTH DAY

We were all ready for the couple's *sheva berachot* when I realized that it might be too late to recite the *sheva berachot*! Lini and Joshua were married the previous Sunday before *shekia* (sunset), and that Sunday therefore counted as the first day of *sheva berachot*. Since *shekia* following Shabbat had already passed, it seemed that we could no longer recite *sheva berachot*! Although the *Ḥida* (*Maḥazik Beracha, Oraḥ Ḥayim, Kuntres Aḥaron* 131) permits the recitation of *sheva berachot* for the entire week (i.e. until 168 hours after the *huppa* have elapsed), Rav Ovadia (*Teshuvot Yabia Omer* 5: *Even HaEzer* 7:2) notes that the consensus rejects this approach.

However, I was delighted to discover that Rav Ovadia (ibid.) and Rav Yitzḥak Yosef (*Yalkut Yosef, Sova Semaḥot* 1:113) permit recitation of *sheva berachot* in such circumstances before *tzet hakochavim* (nightfall).[7] They note that the time between *shekia* and *tzet*, referred to as *ben hashemashot*, is regarded as *safek yom safek layla*, uncertain as to its identity as either day or night (*Shabbat* 34b). Moreover, it is possible that we follow Rabbenu Tam's view that the halachic day continues until 58.5 minutes after astronomical sunset.[8] Accordingly, we may recite *sheva berachot* on the seventh day after the *ḥuppa* during the time period of *ben hashemashot*.

In the case of Lini and Joshua's *sheva berachot*, we may add as a third *safek* the opinion of the *Ḥida* that *sheva berachot* may be recited a full seven days after the *ḥuppa*.

---

this is the accepted and widespread custom in the Syrian Jewish communities of Brooklyn, New York and Deal, New Jersey.

For further discussion of this issue, see https://www.yutorah.org/lectures/lecture.cfm/905536/mordechai-djavaheri/beit-chattanim-sheva-berachot-at-restaurants-catering-halls-celebrating-away-from-home/.

7. Rav Moshe Feintein (cited in *Ohalei Yeshurun* 1:25) and Rav Yaakov Kaminetzky (*Emet L'Yaakov, Even HaEzer* 62:29) concur with this lenient ruling. However, Rav Yosef Shalom Elyashiv (cited in *Mishnat HaGri"s*, p. 69), *Shemirat Shabbat K'Hilchata* (59:18), Rav Herschel Schachter, and Rav Mordechai Willig disagree and do not permit *sheva berachot* to be recited after *shekia* of the seventh day after the wedding.
8. Rav Ovadia and Rav Yitzḥak often take Rabbenu Tam's opinion regarding the calculation of the day into account. For example, the *Yalkut Yosef* (*Oraḥ Ḥayim* 624:9) strongly urges waiting to recite *Havdala* at the end of Yom Kippur until the day is over according to Rabbenu Tam's standards (72 minutes after *sheki'a*).

DRINKING BEFORE *HAVDALA*

One last halachic hurdle had to be overcome. Once *Birkat HaMazon* of *seuda shelishit* is recited, we are not permitted to eat until after *Havdala*. How could we drink from the *kosot* of the *sheva berachot* after *Birkat HaMazon*?! While there is wide discussion and a variety of opinions on the matter,[9] Rav Ovadia (*Teshuvot Yabia Omer op. cit.* and 8: *Oraḥ Ḥayim* 33) permits drinking the *kosot* even before *Havdala*. Moreover, Sephardic *posekim* always permit drinking the wine over which *Birkat HaMazon* was recited at *seuda shelishit*.[10]

CONCLUSION

There is no greater joy than witnessing the blossoming of a young congregant from a boy into a very capable young man who is deeply committed to Torah and who is marrying a wonderful *kalla* who shares his values. What a joy it was to have the privilege of reciting the concluding *sheva berachot* for Joshua and Lini at one of the *ḥatan*'s spiritual foundations, Congregation Shaarei Orah, the Sephardic Congregation of Teaneck!

---

9. See *Teshuvot Igrot Moshe* (*Oraḥ Ḥayim* 4:69), *Teshuvot Minḥat Yitzḥak* (3:113), and *Teshuvot Tzitz Eliezer* (10:45).
10. See *Kaf HaḤayim, Oraḥ Ḥayim* 299:19; *Yalkut Yosef, Orah Hayim* 291:21. Ashkenazic practice, however, does not permit drinking the wine from the *kos* of *Birkat HaMazon* unless one routinely recites *Birkat HaMazon* on a *kos* of wine (*Mishna Berura* 299:14; *Aruch HaShulḥan, Oraḥ Ḥayim* 299:9).

Chapter 81

One Cup or Two for *Sheva Berachot*?

A hallmark of Sephardic Halacha is adherence to the rulings of Rav Yosef Karo, the author of the *Bet Yosef* and *Shulḥan Aruch*. Thus, one would expect Sephardic practice to be a uniform and unvarying adherence to the rulings of Rav Yosef Karo. However, this is far from the case, as there is considerable variation in Sephardic practice. The question of whether Sephardic Jews use one or two *kosot* (goblets) at a *sheva berachot* is a good example of the development of varying Sephardic traditions and practices.

EN OSIN MITZVOT ḤAVILOT ḤAVILOT

The *gemara* in *Pesaḥim* (102b) teaches that two *kosot* are utilized in the odd case that *Birkat HaMazon* and *Kiddush* are recited consecutively. One *kos*, the *gemara* explains, may not be used for both *mitzvot*, since this is seen as degrading the *mitzvot*. The *gemara* calls this "bundling *mitzvot* together" ("*en osin mitzvot ḥavilot ḥavilot*"). Were we to use one *kos* for both *Birkat HaMazon* and *Kiddush*, we would be trying to kill the proverbial two birds with one stone, which makes it appear as if we (God forbid) regard the *mitzvot* as a burden.

However, the *gemara* notes that we do use one *kos* on a Motza'ei Shabbat heading into a Yom Tov. On such occasions, we follow the opinion of Rava to recite "YaKNHaZ" – *Yayin, Kiddush, Ner, Havdala,* and *Zeman* (*Borei Pri HaGefen, Kiddush, Borei Me'orei HaEsh,* and *Sheheḥiyanu*). The *gemara* wonders why this does not violate the rule of *en osin mitzvot ḥavilot ḥavilot.*

The *gemara* answers that the YaKNHaZ situation differs, since *Kiddush* and *Havdala* are fundamentally "one matter," whereas *Birkat HaMazon* and *Kiddush* are two different matters. This idea fits perfectly with the Rambam's understanding of *Havdala* (*Hilchot Shabbat* 29:1). The Rambam views *Havdala* as the flipside of *Kiddush,* as the *mitzva* of "*Zachor et yom haShabat l'kadesho*" ("Remember the Shabbat day to make it holy"; *Shemot* 20:8) teaches us to mark the unique stature of Shabbat both at its beginning and end. Accordingly, *Kiddush* and *Havdala* truly are "one matter." They are essentially the same *mitzva* – to designate a specific time interval as holy – and therefore may share one *kos.*

THE VIEWS CITED BY *TOSAFOT*

Tosafot (ad loc., s.v. *she'en*) present two opinions as to whether *sheva berachot* after a meal during a new couple's seven celebratory days (*shivat yemei hamishteh*) requires one *kos* or two *kosot.* Some require two separate *kosot* so as not to violate the rule of *en osin mitzvot ḥavilot ḥavilot* by using the same *kos* for *Birkat HaMazon* and the six special *berachot* blessing the *ḥatan* and *kalla.* According to this approach, the *Borei Peri HaGefen* and the six special *berachot* are not viewed as "one matter," and thus two *kosot* are required.

However, *Tosafot* continue and cite the opinion of Rabbenu Meshulam, who argues that one *kos* suffices. Rabbenu Meshulem believes that this does not run afoul of *en osin mitzvot ḥavilot ḥavilot,* since *Borei Peri HaGefen* and the six special *berachot* are, in fact, "one matter," as we do not recite the added six *berachot* without first reciting *Birkat HaMazon* on a *kos.*

Tosafot conclude by noting that under the *ḥuppa,* two separate *kosot* are customarily used for the *berachot* on *erusin* and the *berachot* on *nissu'in. Eirusin* and *nissu'in* are two separate matters. Although it is now customary to conduct these two components of a Jewish wedding at the same occasion, that most certainly was not always the case. Thus, since fundamentally the two components of the wedding need not occur at the same time, *erusin* and *nissu'in* are considered two independent matters.

Tosafot add that even today, when we perform *erusin* and *nisu'in* at the same occasion, we customarily read the *ketuba* between these two parts of the ceremony in order to deliberately create a *hefsek* (interruption) to distinguish between the two. Thus, even today, *erusin* and *nissu'in* remain two distinct matters, requiring two separate *kosot*. One gets the impression from *Tosafot* that even Rabbenu Meshulam would agree with this point.

THE RULING OF THE *SHULḤAN ARUCH*

Rav Yosef Karo (*Shulḥan Aruch, Even HaEzer* 62:9) presents both opinions cited in *Tosafot* as "*yesh omerim*," "there are those who say," with the opinion of Rabbenu Meshulam, who argues that one *kos* suffices, as the second opinion. The conventional understanding of the *Shulḥan Aruch* is that when Rav Karo presents both opinions as *yesh omerim*, the intention is to follow the second opinion.

In this case, Rav Karo makes his preference for the second opinion quite clear, as he notes that the *minhag* (custom) has spread to follow the second opinion.

Indeed, the *Tur* (*Even HaEzer* 62) notes that the custom among Spanish Jews is to recite *sheva berachot* on only one *kos*. Rav Karo was born in Spain, but due to the Expulsion in 1492, at the age of four he left for Turkey with his family. As an adult, he made *aliya* to Eretz Yisrael and settled in Tzfat.

The Rama notes that the custom among Ashkenazic Jews is to require two *kosot* for *sheva berachot*. This remains the uncontested and undisputed Ashkenazic practice until this day.

MINHAG YERUSHALAYIM – *ḤIDA* AND RAV OVADIA YOSEF

Surprisingly, Sephardic Jews who follow Minhag Yerushalayim use two *kosot* for *sheva berachot*. Why do these Sephardic Jews not follow the ruling of Rav Yosef Karo, as they most often do?

The change happened as a result of the influence of an eighteenth-century Sephardic authority of great stature, the *Ḥida*. The *Ḥida* (*Teshuvot Ḥayim Sha'al* 2:35:2) observes that the widespread custom in both Eretz Yisrael and Egypt is to use two *kosot* for *sheva berachot* at *Birkat HaMazon*. The *Ḥida* even makes the startling assertion that upon arriving in Eretz Yisrael, Rav Yosef Karo was so preoccupied with his Torah writings and rabbinic duties that he did not realize that the *minhag* in Eretz Yisrael was to use two *kosot*![1]

Rav Ovadia Yosef (*Teshuvot Yabia Omer* 9: *Even HaEzer* 22) suggests that the *minhag* in Eretz Yisrael changed between the fifteenth century, when Rav Karo lived, to the eighteenth century, when the *Ḥida* lived. Rav Ovadia notes that there are other cases in which the *minhag* changed from the time of the *Bet Yosef* to the time of the *Ḥida*.[2]

Rav Ovadia surmises that the reason for the change in the *minhag* is to satisfy the stricter opinions that require two *kosot*. He notes that Rabbenu Tam, the Rosh, the Ramban, and the Mordechai – all authorities of high prominence – demand two *kosot* to be used for *sheva berachot*.

We might add that even though Rav Karo rules that one *kos* suffices, he does not forbid satisfying the stricter view and using two *kosot*. Thus, the changed *minhag* among Sephardic Jews in Eretz Yisrael does not run counter to the ruling of Rav Karo; it simply seeks to satisfy a higher standard.

In any event, Rav Yosef records a plethora of later Sephardic authorities who note that the practice in Jerusalem and all of Eretz Yisrael is to use two *kosot* for *Birkat HaMazon*. Rav Ovadia, in turn, adds his full endorsement of this practice despite its deviation from the ruling of Rav Karo. He writes that the "*oseh ḥadashot ba'al milḥamot*," one who introduces a new practice, causes fights and friction, and this must be avoided.

THE NORTH AFRICAN CUSTOM

Rav Shalom Messas (*Teshuvot Shemesh U'Magen* 2: *Yoreh De'ah* 29), however, notes that North African Jews until this day maintain the custom recorded by Rav Karo to use only one *kos* for *Birkat HaMazon*. This is not surprising, since many – if not most – North African Jews descend from the refugees from the Spanish Expulsion.[3]

---

1. I understand the *Ḥida* to mean that Rav Yosef Karo was so accustomed to the custom of Spanish Jews with whom he was raised in Turkey that he did not notice the different practice of Jews in Eretz Yisrael.
2. One should not err and argue that the Sephardic Jews in Eretz Yisrael were influenced by the practice of their Ashkenazic brethren. Ashkenazic Jews did not live in Eretz Yisrael in significant numbers until the mid-eighteenth century, when the followers of the Ba'al Shem Tov and the followers of the Vilna Gaon began to settle the land.
3. The *ketuba* used by many Moroccan Jews until this day notes that it follows the custom of the Jews expelled from Castille.

Rav Messas adds a further defense to the opinion of Rabbenu Meshulam to use one *kos*, noting that today we recite *Birkat HaMazon* on a *kos* only when we recite *sheva berachot*. Now more than ever, argues Rav Shalom, are the *Borei Peri HaGefen* on the *kos* for *Birkat HaMazon* and the other six special *berachot* for the *ḥatan* and *kalla* considered "one matter," for which one *kos* suffices.

Moreover, Rav Messas (*Teshuvot Shemesh U'Magen* 4:87) fires back at Rav Ovadia, arguing that North African Jews who use one *kos* for *sheva berachot* are hardly "*oseh ḥadashot*," since their custom dates back to the custom practiced at the time of Rav Yosef Karo and even earlier, during the days of the *Tur* (1270–1340).

CONCLUSION

Among the highlights of twentieth-century Sephardic halachic literature are the rich debates between Rav Ovadia and Rav Messas. The dispute under discussion is one of dozens of these beautiful debates that emerge from time to time due to the divergence in practice between North African and other Sephardic Jews.

Sephardic practice is not monolithic, despite Sephardic allegiance to the rulings of Rav Yosef Karo. The divergence emerges as to how to interpret and implement Rav Yosef Karo's rulings. *Vive la difference*, and may we honor and respect both sides of this most interesting debate!

Chapter 82

A *Kohen* Marrying the Daughter of a Jewish Woman and a Non-Jewish Man

One of the topics that I had the opportunity to discuss with Rav Shlomo Amar during his exciting visit to Congregation Shaarei Orah in Teaneck in 5777 relates to an important ruling issued by Rav Amar while he served as a *dayan* on the Israeli Supreme Rabbinic Court of Appeals.

The question in that case related to whether a *Kohen* may marry a Jewish woman whose father is non-Jewish. In the specific instance, the district *bet din* of Rehovot ruled strictly, but Rav Amar, while sitting the State of Israel Supreme Rabbinic Court of Appeals, overturned this decision and ruled leniently due to a special circumstance.

THE CHILD OF A JEWISH WOMAN AND A NON-JEWISH MAN

The *gemara* (*Yevamot* 45b) presents that established Halacha regards the child of a non-Jewish man and a Jewish woman as Jewish and legitimate. No mention is made of the daughter's possible ineligibility to marry a *Kohen*.

The *Rishonim* debate how to interpret the *gemara*'s silence regarding the daughter's disqualification to marry a *Kohen*. The Rambam (*Hilchot Issurei Bi'ah* 15:3) permits the daughter to marry a *Kohen*, the Rosh (*Yevamot* 4:30) forbids her to marry a *Kohen*, and the Rif (*Yevamot* 15a) is uncertain about the matter. The Ramban (*Yevamot* 45a) is similarly uncertain, but he adds that if a *Kohen* does marry such a woman, we do not require that they divorce.

The *Shulḥan Aruch* (*Even HaEzer* 4:5 and 7:17) rules that the daughter may not marry a *Kohen*, in accordance with the view of the Rosh. However, the two premier commentaries to the *Even HaEzer* section of the *Shulḥan Aruch*, the *Bet Shmuel* (4:2 and 7:39) and the *Ḥelkat Meḥokek* (7:26), rule in accordance with the Ramban that if the couple is already married, we do not require that they divorce.

AḤARONIM

The *Aḥaronim* debate whether the strict opinions maintain that it is a Biblical prohibition or a Rabbinic prohibition for a *Kohen* to marry such a woman. The *Mishneh LaMelech* (*Hilchot Issurei Bi'ah* 17:7) and *Sha'ar HaMelech* (*Hilchot Issurei Biah* 15:3) believe that it is a Biblical prohibition. On the other hand, the *Ḥelkat Meḥokek* (*op. cit.*), Rabbi Akiva Eiger (*Teshuvot Rabbi Akiva Eiger* 91), the Maharshal (*Teshuvot Maharshal* 17), the *Bet Meir* (4:5), and the Rama MiPano (*Teshuvot Rama MiPano* 124) rule that the prohibition is Rabbinic in nature.

Among twentieth-century authorities, Rav Moshe Feinstein (*Teshuvot Igrot Moshe, Even HaEzer* 1:5) rules that it is a Biblical prohibition, while Rav Ovadia Yosef (*Teshuvot Yabia Omer* 7: *Even HaEzer* 9) and Rav Shalom Messas (*Teshuvot Shemesh U'Magen* 3: *Even HaEzer* 58) rule that it is a Rabbinic prohibition.

This debate carries serious ramifications, as it impacts whether one should be lenient or strict regarding the implementation of this *halacha*. The opinion that it is only a Rabbinic prohibition fits well with the fact that we do not compel the couple to separate if already married. Since it is only a Rabbinic prohibition, we do not impose the severe hardship of separating a couple that is already married.

CIVIL MARRIAGE

Another ramification of this dispute is the debate that rages between Rav Moshe Feinstein and Rav Messas as to whether a rabbi may officiate at a wedding of a *Kohen* to a Jewish woman whose father is non-Jewish if the couple already had been married civilly and had been living together for an extended period of time. Rav Moshe (op cit.) forbids a rabbi to conduct such a ceremony, whereas Rav Messas permits it.

This question depends on what circumstances allow the couple to remain together based on the Ramban's ruling. Rav Moshe's approach is based on the fact that the overwhelming consensus of Rabbinic opinions regards a couple that is married in a civil ceremony as unmarried according to Halacha. Since the couple is not halachically married, the Ramban's ruling does not apply, and Rav Moshe forbids a rabbi to conduct a ceremony that will facilitate a sinful marriage.[1]

Rav Messas, on the other hand, believes that since only a Rabbinic prohibition is involved, Halacha does not require the husband and wife to separate, since it is difficult for them to do so. He understands the Ramban's ruling as permitting the couple to remain together if it is difficult to separate. Rav Messas goes as far as to permit a rabbi to officiate at the wedding if the couple is already living together, even if they have not married civilly.[2] Rav Ovadia Yosef (*Teshuvot Yabia Omer* 10: *Even HaEzer* 10:14; see also *Teshuvot Yabia Omer* 11: *Even HaEzer* 34) later in life upheld a ruling from Rav Messas in a similar case.

Rav Shlomo Amar (*Teshuvot Shema Shlomo* 5: *Even HaEzer* 8) rules in accordance with the view of Rav Messas and Rav Ovadia. In fact, he is willing to consider extending this permissive ruling even if the couple is only engaged (*Melechet Shlomo* 1:45).[3] He is cautious, however, and refrains from

1. Rav Yonah Reiss, the *Av Bet Din* of the Chicago Rabbinical Council, told a conference of Orthodox Jewish educators in August 2007 that the Rabbinic courts in the United States are most likely to follow the ruling of Rav Moshe Feinstein, since Rav Feinstein's rulings, especially with regard to marital issues, are regarded by North American rabbis to be of the highest authority.
2. In a significant ruling, a leading *dayan*, Rav Eliyahu Ariel Edri (a student of Rav Shalom Messas) states that a daughter of such a marriage is permitted to marry a *Kohen* (and is not considered a *ḥalala*). Similarly, the son born of such a marriage is regarded as a full-fledged *Kohen* (and is not a *ḥalal*). This ruling was issued when Rav Edri was a member of the Rabbinic Court of Ashkelon (17 Sivan 5771) and is cited by Rav Ratzon Arussy in *Teḥumin* 38, p. 191. However, many Ashkenazic *posekim* disagree. See, for example, *Teshuvot Minḥat Yitzḥak* 2:132, who rules that a son of such a marriage is regarded as a *safek ḥalal*.
3. During his visit to Congregation Shaarei Orah, Rav Amar gave me a most precious gift—an inscribed copy of *Melechet Shlomo*, his most recent collection of *teshuvot*

issuing permission to marry in his role as Jerusalem's Chief Rabbi. He writes that a *bet din* must carefully investigate the situation and explore whether it is appropriate to apply his lenient approach to this specific circumstance.[4]

THE REHOVOT *BET DIN* VS. THE APPEALS *BET DIN*

In 2006, a *Kohen* wished to marry a Jewish woman whose father was not Jewish. The couple had been living together for approximately one and a half years. The district *bet din* of Rehovot denied the couple a marriage license, in accordance with the ruling of Rav Moshe Feinstein. Rav Amar, however, sitting on the Supreme Rabbinic Court of Appeals, overturned the ruling and permitted the couple to marry.

In response to this ruling, Rav J. David Bleich (*Tradition*, Summer 2007) wrote that the ruling of the Court of Appeals "strikes this writer as an abuse of appellate power," since it ruled simply that the rulings of Rav Messas and Rav Amar should be followed instead of that of Rav Moshe. Rav Bleich wrote that Halacha "bars exercise of purely subjective discretion in choosing one set of precedents over another" as considerations for a higher authority to reverse a decision of a lower authority.

In defense of Rav Amar's ruling, Rav Aviyam Levinson surmised that the couple in this case was presumably Sephardic. Hence, there was no compelling reason for them to abandon the rulings of the leading contemporary Sephardic rabbis in favor of that of Rav Moshe.

I asked Rav Amar if Rav Levinson's assumption was correct, and he confirmed that the husband in this case was indeed a Sephardic Jew. He added that it is most appropriate for a *bet din* to issue rulings for a Sephardic Jew in accordance with the rulings of the leading Sephardic Rabbinic authorities, such as Rav Ovadia and Rav Messas. Rav Amar explained that he maintains the highest level of respect for Rav Moshe Feinstein, but most

---

on marriage topics, in which this *teshuva* appears. Rav Ovadia raised this possibility as well in his responsum that appears in *Teshuvot Yabia Omer,* although in that case there was an additional factor permitting the marriage.

4. One would imagine that the *bet din* would investigate if the couple knew way in advance of their halachically questionable situation and became engaged simply to create a situation wherein the rabbis would feel compelled to rule leniently. Such an approach disrespects Halacha, and a lenient ruling in such a case constitutes a breach of the integrity of the halachic system. Performing a wedding in such a situation cannot be sanctioned.

Aharonim disagree with his view and rule that only a Rabbinic prohibition is at stake in the case of a *Kohen* marrying a Jewish woman whose father is not Jewish.

CONCLUSION

Although this is not a classic halachic divide between Sephardic and Ashkenazic *posekim,* the issue of a *Kohen* marrying a Jewish woman who has a non-Jewish father has emerged (at least in the Israeli Rabbinic courts) as a question that for the most part splits along the lines of Sephardic and Ashkenazic *dayanim.*[5]

However, the pressure to issue a lenient ruling in the situations described emerges from widespread ignorance of the Halacha that initially prohibits such marriages. It is the responsibility of learned Jews to help spread awareness of this Halacha. Although there is a need to be sensitive to the plight of a couple that finds itself in a situation described here, our responsibility and obligation to uphold our holy tradition forbids us to eviscerate a ruling of the *Shulhan Aruch. Kohanim* and Jewish women whose fathers are not Jewish should be made aware that they should not date each other.

May *Hashem* bless those who help spread the word and add a special *beracha* to one to whom this is relevant and who refrains from entering into a relationship that the Halacha does not initially permit. May *Hashem* help them find partner with whom they will have a successful and satisfying life.

5. Rav Ratzon Arussy documents this at length in his essay printed in *Tehumin* 38, pp. 186–195.

Chapter 83

Rav Ovadia Yosef's Ruling Confirming the Status of Ethiopian Jews

The most impactful and bold ruling of Rav Ovadia Yosef is arguably his ruling in which he forcefully asserts that the Jews of Ethiopia are indeed Jews in the fullest sense, without requiring *giyur l'ḥumra* (conversion done as a stringency). There are more than 150,000 Ethiopian Jews who currently reside in Israel as a direct consequence of Rav Ovadia's 1973 ruling, in his capacity of Chief Rabbi of the State of Israel, confirming their status as Jews. Rav Ovadia's ruling enabled these Jews to obtain automatic Israeli citizenship under Israel's Law of Return, which guarantees Israeli citizenship to any Jew who requests sanctuary in the Jewish state.

Some people very mistakenly think that Rav Ovadia issued this ruling without basis in Jewish law. They are under the misconception that Rav Ovadia invoked his Rabbinic authority to make an exception to Halacha due to the special circumstances at hand. Nothing could be further from the truth, however.

No rabbi has the authority to issue a ruling contrary to Jewish law. If a rabbi does so, his ruling enjoys no validity. Indeed, halachic authorities present their decisions in writing to enable colleagues and students to understand their ruling and subject it to scrutiny. No rabbi gets a free pass. For example, every *teshuva* penned by Rav Moshe Feinstein has been carefully reviewed and very often disputed. The same rigorous review has occurred with Rav Ovadia's rulings.

EXPLAINING RAV OVADIA'S RULING

Rav Ovadia's reasoning regarding the status of Ethiopian Jews is presented in *Teshuvot Yabia Omer* (8: *Even HaEzer* 11). He bases his ruling on the precedents set by two major sixteenth-century halachic authorities, the Radbaz (*Teshuvot* 4:219) and his eminent student the Maharikash (*Yoreh De'ah* 158), who accepted the members of the Ethiopian Jewish community as Jews. Rav Ovadia forcefully writes that once the Radbaz and the Maharikash, two pillars of Halacha, accepted the Ethiopian Jews' tradition of descent from the tribe of Dan, our generation enjoys no right to question this ruling.

RAV OVADIA'S REBUTTALS OF OPPOSING ARGUMENTS

Rav Ovadia cites the former Ashkenazic Chief Rabbi Yitzḥak Herzog (in a 1954 letter to the Jewish Agency), who questioned this ruling based on the views of anthropologists who express doubts regarding the Jewish identity of Ethiopian Jews. Rav Ovadia roundly rejects this view, noting that once a *ḥazaka* (halachic presumption) has been established of Jewish identity, we enjoy no right to disturb that *ḥazaka* based on sources extraneous to the halachic process. Elsewhere (*Teshuvot Yabia Omer* 10: *Yoreh De'ah* 24), Rav Ovadia argues that whenever there is a clash between the view of scientists and traditional Halacha, the Halacha unquestionably prevails.

After I presented Rav Ovadia's ruling to a particular audience, a gentleman asked me why I felt comfortable with Rav Ovadia's ruling, in light of the fact that so many great *Rabbanim*, such as Rav Moshe Feinstein (*Teshuvot Igrot Moshe, Yoreh De'ah* 4:41)[1] and Rav Eliezer Waldenberg (*Teshuvot Tzitz Eliezer* 12:66), disagree. I responded that Rav Ovadia was unusually adamant about this ruling. Indeed, upon scrutiny Rav Ovadia's reasoning appears to be unassailable.

Rav Ovadia persuasively and passionately writes, "*Mi hu zeh v'ezeh hu*" – who in the current generation has the audacity and gall to dispute,

1. In addition to appearing in the *Igrot Moshe*, this *teshuva* was also published in *Teḥumin* 12.

question, and impugn a ruling of the Radbaz and Maharikash? Rav Moshe expresses concern that the Radbaz did not adequately research the origins of the Ethiopian Jewish community. Rav Ovadia responds that he cannot fathom how anyone can call into question the competence of the Radbaz, who was recognized as a great halachic authority even in his time (fifteenth-century), which was a *dor de'ah,* a very learned generation that boasted luminaries such as Rav Yosef Karo and the thriving and pulsating Torah center of Tzefat.

Rav Waldenberg questions the viability of the *ḥezkat kashrut* of the Ethiopian Jewish community, since 500 years have passed since the Radbaz and Maharikash issued their rulings. Rav Ovadia dismisses this concern as well, noting that Ethiopian Jews zealously guarded their Jewish identity throughout the generations, even going to the extreme of requiring community members who spoke to gentiles to immerse in a river.

Rav Ovadia cites the 1988 decision of the respected Israeli Chief Rabbinate Rabbinic Council, which reconfirms the rulings of the prior Israeli Chief Rabbis (other than Rav Ovadia) who required a *giyur l'ḥumra* for Ethiopian Jews. This ruling confirms the rulings of the Radbaz and Maharikash, but notes that due to the thousands of years of disconnection from the rest of *Am Yisrael,* some doubt lingers, and thus a *giyur l'ḥumra* is required.

Rav Ovadia expresses astonishment at this ruling. He cannot understand how they cast aspersions on that which the Radbaz and Maharikash accepted. If the Rabbaz and Maharikash did not express such concern, it is the height of impudence for much later generations to deviate from their ruling.

CONCLUSION

The status of those Ethiopian Jews who have not undergone a *giyur l'ḥumra* remains a hotly debated issue. While the Ashkenazic Haredi community seems not to have accepted Rav Ovadia's ruling,[2] many segments of the Orthodox community do accept it. Rav Shlomo Aviner, for example, permitted his student who is a *Kohen* to marry an Ethiopian Jewish woman who

2. See https://www.jpost.com/International/Boycott-called-after-winery-fires-Ethiopian-staff-for-doubting-Jewishness-560910.

had apparently undergone a *giyur l'ḥumra,* despite the fact that a *Kohen* is not permitted to marry a convert.[3]

At first glance, it appears peculiar to follow Rav Ovadia's ruling when the consensus of halachic authority runs counter to his view. However, Rav Ovadia's ruling seems exceedingly convincing. Although, most often, "*yaḥid v'rabbim halacha k'rabbim*" – the Halacha usually follows the majority opinion – there are some rare situations in which the minority opinion is followed. Rav Ovadia's ruling regarding Ethiopian Jews is so convincing that he has won the support of much of the Orthodox community for this ruling.

The power of Rav Ovadia's pen is certainly mightier than the proverbial sword, especially since it was used to advance noble causes, such as the integrity of the majestic Ethiopian Jewish community, who sacrificed so much for so long to preserve their Jewish identity and connection to Zion.

3. http://www.ravaviner.com/2013/10/ha-gaon-ha-rav-ovadiah-yosef-ztzl.html.

Chapter 84

Rabbinical Council of America Prenuptial Agreement for Sephardic Jews

The Beth Din of America (BDA) and Rabbinical Council of America (RCA) prenuptial agreement is undoubtedly gaining in popularity and usage. It is has become accepted as a standard part of the wedding preparation for brides and grooms in many segments of the Orthodox community. In 2015, the Beth Din of America reported over 2,000 downloads of the prenuptial agreement from its website in one year alone.

In 2006, the Rabbinical Council of America even issued a resolution declaring that rabbis should not officiate a wedding if a proper prenuptial agreement has not been executed. As a very active practicing *mesader gittin* (*get* administrator) for more than twenty-six years, during which time I have served over 3,000 couples, I most wholeheartedly support this resolution. I have seen much suffering resulting from the failure to sign the BDA/RCA prenuptial and overwhelming success on the part of those who sign it.[1]

1. I offer a fuller explanation and defense of the agreement in *Gray Matter,* vol. 1, pp. 8–16, and vol. 4, pp. 245–250.

My wife Malca and I proudly signed the BDA/RCA prenuptial agreement before our wedding in 1995, and our daughter Bracha and son-in-law Yisroel Perton happily signed the BDA/RCA prenuptial agreement a few weeks before their wedding in 2018.

SEPHARDIC SUPPORT

Is the BDA/RCA agreement appropriate for usage by Sephardic Jews? The answer is a resounding yes. First of all, Rav Ovadia Yosef endorsed the RCA prenuptial agreement in writing.[2] Rav Ovadia is among a number of great *Rabbanim* who endorsed the agreement (including Rav Zalman Neḥemia Goldberg, Rav Hershel Schachter, Rav Gedalia Schwartz, Rav Elazar Meyer Teitz,[3] Rav Asher Weiss, and Rav Mordechai Willig).

Moreover, the first seeds of the BDA/RCA agreement were planted in Morocco many decades ago. This fascinating history is recorded by the great Rav Shalom Messas, widely regarded as the leading *posek* among Moroccan Jews. In *Teshuvot Tevuot Shemesh* (*Even HaEzer* 66) and *Teshuvot Shemesh U'Magen* (1: *Even HaEzer* 11–12; 2: *Even HaEzer* 36), Rav Messas records that in 1952, the Moroccan rabbinate instituted a prenuptial agreement to avoid problems of *agunot*. In 1984, this came to the attention of Rav Gilbert Klaperman, then president of the RCA, and he invited Rav Messas to address a convention of the members of the RCA about the prenuptial agreement.

So began the road to the eventual adoption of the prenuptial by the RCA, crowned with the approbations of the many aforementioned *gedolim*.

POSSIBLE OBJECTIONS

Rav Mordechai Lebhar (*Magen Avot, Even HaEzer* 134) voices criticism of the BDA/RCA agreement based on the criticisms offered against the original Moroccan prenuptial. Rav Lebhar documents the well-established Moroccan rabbinic court practice to avoid administering a *get* if there is any concern that the husband is giving the *get* due to a penalty. This practice emerged due to concern for the ruling of the *Teshuvot HaRashba* (4:40, cited

2. http://theprenup.org/pdf/Original_Prenup_Endorsement.pdf. Theprenup.org is a website maintained by the Beth Din of America. The endorsements of the other authorities mentioned here can also be found on the website.
3. Personal communication.

in the *Bet Yosef, Even HaEzer* 134) that disqualifies a *get* conducted due to a financial penalty. Thus, Rav Lebhar writes that the BDA/RCA agreement should be avoided due to concern for creating such a penalty.

Indeed, the Moroccan agreement, as presented by Rav Messas, constructs the husband's obligation as a penalty to give the *get*. For example, Rav Messas describes the Moroccan prenuptial agreement as a penalty (conclusion of *Teshuvot Shemesh U'Magen* 2: *Even HaEzer* 36). The Moroccan prenuptial describes the husband paying spousal support until a *get* is given, thereby creating specific linkage between the obligation and the *get*. Rav Messas concedes that the Moroccan prenuptial does not satisfy the view of the Rashba, but instead relies on the majority of *Rishonim*, who disagree. Rav Messas understands the *Shulḥan Aruch* and Rama as ruling in accordance with the many *Rishonim* who disagree with the Rashba.

However, the BDA/RCA agreement was specifically formulated by the Jerusalem Bet Din's Rav Zalman Neḥemia Goldberg and Rav Mordechai Willig of the RCA/BDA to avoid this concern and satisfy the view of the Rashba. In the RCA/BDA prenuptial agreement, the husband agrees to pay $150 per day to support his wife in case they do not maintain domestic residence. This obligation remains in effect for the duration of the halachic marriage. The document, following the guidance of Rav Goldberg, carefully avoids linking the husband's support obligation to his giving a *get*, in order to avoid the payment's being construed as a penalty for not giving a *get*.

Rav Asher Weiss notes that the RCA/BDA agreement differs from the situation that the Rashba addresses in two ways. First, the support obligation in the agreement is not a penalty, but rather a reasonable sum necessary to support the wife in an average manner.[4] Moreover, there is no direct linkage between the support obligation and a *get*, as the husband's financial obligations are a result of the marriage and are not a punishment for withholding a *get*. Linkage between the obligation and the *get* is the critical issue.[5]

---

4. Rav Mordechai Willig, the *Segan Av Bet Din* of the BDA, has for many years resisted pressure to increase the $150 amount specifically due to concern that the document should be constructed as a support agreement and not as a penalty for not delivering the *get*.
5. This point is explained in *Aruch HaShulḥan, Even HaEzer* 134:25, and *Teshuvot Igrot Moshe, Even HaEzer* 1:137 and 4:106 (according to Rav Zalman Nehemia Goldberg's explanation of the concluding paragraph, as told to me).

Indeed, the BDA/RCA agreement emulates the divorce agreement formulated by the famed Rav Yaakov of Lissa to provide financial motivation for giving a *get* without constituting coercion (*Torat Gittin* 134:4, s.v. *kenasot*, cited in *Pitḥei Teshuva, Even HaEzer* 134:9). In that agreement, the husband waives his halachic right to his wife's earnings (*ma'aseh yadayim*) while maintaining his obligation to support her. The man is thus motivated to give a *get* in order to release himself from his financial obligation to his estranged wife, but this does not constitute coercion because the husband's financial obligations are a result of the marriage and are not a punishment for withholding a *get*. Therefore, he gives a *get* due to dissatisfaction with his marriage, not because of financial penalty. Concerns of invalidating a *get* according to the Rashba arise only when a financial penalty is linked directly to the *get*.

CONCLUSION

The RCA prenuptial agreement is unquestionably suitable for Sephardic couples, as it carries the explicit imprimatur of Rav Ovadia Yosef. It certainly satisfies and even exceeds the criteria established by Rav Shalom Messas. Although Rav Ovadia and Rav Shalom vigorously disagreed about many areas of Halacha, regarding the BDA/RCA prenuptial agreement, these two Sephardic giants are in full agreement in their support. The Sephardic community should have no hesitation to following in the footsteps of the two Sephardic halachic authorities of the previous generation.[6]

Indeed, the prenuptial agreement should be part of every couple's wedding, especially Sephardic couples. After all, the genesis of the prenuptial agreement was in the Sephardic community!

6. It is important to note that both Rav Ovadia and Rav Messas toiled for many years as *dayanim* in prominent *batei din*. They are both extremely well-versed in both the Halacha and actual practice of *get* administration, which lends extra credibility to their support of the BDA/RCA agreement.

Chapter 85

Sephardic *Gittin* Standards

Are there differences between a Sephardic *get* and an Ashkenazic *get*? If so, are they significant?

The short answer is that there are differences. In fact, Rav Ovadia Yosef insisted that a *get* be conducted in accordance with Sephardic custom for a separating Sephardic couple. He took this matter so seriously that he even resigned from the Petah Tikva Bet Din when his Ashkenazic colleagues refused to conduct a *get* in accordance with Sephardic custom for a Sephardic couple (as related in *Teshuvot Yabia Omer* 10: *Even HaEzer* 34:6). Rav Ovadia returned to his seat on the court only after his colleagues relented.

Indeed, in Tammuz 5753 (July 1993), when Rav Ovadia certified me as *get* administrator (*mesader gittin*), he issued a stern warning that I oversee *gittin* for Sephardic Jews in accordance with Sephardic practice.[1] Rav Ovadia's firm tone still resounds in my ear.

The differences between Sephardic and Ashkenazic *gittin*, however, are relatively minor; the core process remains the same. Many of the differences relate to style of transliteration of foreign names into Hebrew

---

1. Many rabbinic courts in the United States administer an Ashkenazic *get* for a Sephardic couple if the *mesader haget* is Ashkenazic. Rav Moshe Feinstein is cited as advocating this practice, as is Rav Moshe Steinberg, the founding *Av Bet Din* of the Beth Din of America.

characters (as all of the person's names are mentioned in a *get*, no matter the language from which the name stems). For example, Sephardim use a *vav* to signify a *kamatz* (such that the name Boris would be written בוריס), whereas Ashkenazic Jews use an *alef* (באריס).

Other differences concern the shape of the letters written in the *get*. Ashkenazic Jews follow the specifications of the *Bet Yosef*, whereas Sephardic Jews follow those of the Ari z"l. Some of the letters, such as the *ayin* and *tzadi*, are written differently according to these two approaches. Rav Ovadia, however, notes (*Teshuvot Yabia Omer* 2: *Yoreh De'ah* 20:7; 4: *Even HaEzer* 12:8) that both of these scripts enjoy halachic validity, and thus *b'diavad* (post facto), either script is acceptable to both groups.

Finally, the text of the Sephardic *get* differs slightly from the Ashkenazic *get*. For example, the word "*peturin*" in the phrase "*get peturin*" (Targum Onkelos' translation of the Torah's phrase "*sefer keritut*," meaning "document of termination") is written פיטורין in a Sephardic *get*, whereas the initial *yud* is omitted in an Ashkenazic *get* (פטורין; see *Shulḥan Aruch, Even HaEzer* 126:12; *Pitḥei Teshuva* ad loc. 22).[2]

FOUR RULINGS OF RAV SHLOMO AMAR WITH REGARD TO SEPHARDIC *GITTIN*

During Rav Shlomo Amar's visit to Congregation Shaarei Orah on Shabbat Naḥamu 5777, I posed four questions regarding *get* administration for a Sephardic couple. Each of these issues is debated among *get* administrators throughout the world.

TRANSLITERATION OF "CH"

One issue regards the transliteration of the English phonic sound Ch, such as in the name Charlie.

The goal in general is to transliterate a foreign name as coherently as possible into Hebrew characters. This poses a significant challenge when dealing with sounds that do not exist in Hebrew (as traditionally spoken by Ashkenazim), such as the J or Th sounds. *Posekim* have attempted to transliterate these sounds into the closest Hebrew equivalents (see *Get Pashut* 129:142, citing the Ra'anah).

---

2. For a full comparison of Ashkenazic and Sephardic *gittin*, contrast the pictures of both versions that appear in the *Encyclopedia Tamudit* (5:568).

Regarding the English J sound, as in Joe, Ashkenazic *posekim* debate as to whether to use a *daled-zayin* (Rav Yosef Eliyahu Henkin, *Kitvei HaRav Henkin*, p. 229; *Teshuvot Igrot Moshe, Even HaEzer* 1:132) or *daled-zayin-shin* (*Teshuvot Melamed L'Ho'il* 3:41; *Teshuvot Yabia Omer* 4: *Even HaEzer* 13; *Teshuvot Minḥat Yitzḥak* 1:103; and *Get Mesudar*, p. 215, regarding James). This debate has not been resolved, and as a result, variation exists even regarding the transliteration of cities and rivers in *gittin*.[3] Sephardim, however, transliterate a J sound with a *gimmel* and a slash (what Israelis refer to as a "*pesik*" or "*chupchik*").

Regarding the English letters Ch, the standard practice among Ashkenazim is to use *tet-shin*. In the case of a Sephardic *get*, however, a fierce debate rages as to how to transliterate the Ch sound, as classic Sephardic *posekim* did not deal with this issue (at least in writing). It is reported that Rav Ovadia Yosef ruled that the common Israeli practice to write a *tzadi* with a *chupchik* should be followed (e.g. צ׳ארלי).[4]

Others object to this, since a *tzadi* with a *chupchik* is not part of our *mesora* of the Hebrew alphabet. They therefore rule that a *tet-shin* should be used for a Sephardic *get* to signify a Ch sound (טשארלי). The advocates of the *tzadi* with a *chupchik*, in turn, object that Sephardic rabbis never use two letters to express one sound.

I asked Rav Amar his opinion on the matter, and he firmly agreed with Rav Ovadia that a *tzadi* with a *chupchick* is appropriate. He cited with a smile the venerable Rav Meir Mazouz, who once proclaimed that if he saw a *get* written for a Sephardic couple with the English Ch sound transliterated as *tet-shin*, he would tear the *get*, since it is invalid!

TRANSLITERATING A CITY AND ITS RIVERS

The locale in a *get* is identified by the waters upon which it rests (*Shulḥan Aruch, Even HaEzer* 128:4). For example, Teaneck, New Jersey is identified in a *get* as "Teaneck, the city on the Hackensack River and the Overpeck Creek." Edison is referred to as "Edison, the city on the Raritan River and on well waters." As noted above, transliteration of foreign names differs

3. See the discussions regarding writing Los Angeles, Jacksonville, Lakewood (Lake Carasaljo), and Rochester (Genesee River) in Rav Mendel Senderovic's *Ha-Aretz L'Areha*.
4. This is apparent from *Teshuvot Yabia Omer* 11: *Even HaEzer* 93:44.

between Sephardic and Ashkenazic *gittin*. Thus, the question arises whether the transliteration established and practiced for many years with regard to cities such as Teaneck and Edison, which follows the Ashkenazic tradition,[5] should be maintained even in a Sephardic *get*.

Many *mesadrei gittin* follow the *Teshuvot Panim Me'irot* (2:19, cited without any dissent by the *Pitḥei Teshuva, Even HaEzer* 128:14), who rules that the original transliteration should be followed.[6] However, many other *mesadrei gittin* do not follow this practice, as it is reported that Rav Ovadia felt that the Sephardic transliteration should be used. Indeed, in his *HaAretz L'Areha*, Rav Mendel Senderovic presents both the Ashkenazic and Sephardic traditions for writing New York, Montreal, and Buenos Aires in a *get*.

Rav Amar told me that he wholeheartedly agrees with Rav Ovadia's view. He even approved the Sephardic manner in which our *bet din* transliterates Teaneck in a *get*.[7]

WHO IS A SEPHARDIC JEW?

On many occasions, I have administered a *get* for a husband who is of Sephardic origin but has thoroughly assimilated into Ashkenazic practice. These men pray regularly in Ashkenazic synagogues and observe Halacha entirely according to Ashkenazic practice. They even refrain from eating

---

5. טינעק מתא דיתבא על נהר העקענסעק ועל נהר אווערפעק קריק.
6. In London, for example, even the Ashkenazic rabbinic courts spell the word London in a *get* in accordance with the Sephardic tradition (לונדון), since this was the original manner in which *gittin* were written in this city (see *Pitḥei Teshuva, Even HaEzer* 128:10). Rav Shmuel Khoshkerman told me, however, that the *Panim Me'irot* and custom in London reflects the Ashkenazic tradition, which does not necessarily have to be adopted by Sephardic Jews. Moreover, it is potentially problematic for the *get* to be inconsistent regarding transliterations and spellings (see *Pitḥei Teshuva, Even HaEzer* 126:46). Therefore, it might be problematic to spell the cities and its rivers in accordance with Ashkenazic style and the rest of the *get* in accordance with Sephardic style.

   Rav Mendel Senderovic suggests a compromise—that a Sephardic version of the city's name be created only when that city has a significant Sephardic community, such as Brooklyn and Montreal. At the very least, Rav Senderovic told me, we must exercise great care when establishing a new version of how to write *gittin* in a particular city.
7. מתא טיניק דיתבא על נהר היקינסיק ועל נהר אווירפיק קריק.

kitniyot on Pesaḥ. Should we administer a Sephardic or Ashkenazic *get* in such circumstances?[8]

This question appears to hinge on the dispute between Rav Yosef Shalom Eliashiv (*Kovetz Teshuvot* 1:12) and Rav Ovadia as to whether one may change one's practice from Sephardic to Ashkenazic or vice versa. Rav Eliashiv rules that one may maintain the practices with which he was raised, whereas Rav Ovadia maintains that one may not.[9] Rav Amar follows Rav

8. A *bet din* would also need to determine if a litigant is Sephardic in the case of resolution of certain monetary disputes. Sephardic *posekim* (*Birkei Yosef, Ḥoshen Mishpat* 25:27; *Teshuvot Rav Pa'alim* 2:3; *Teshuvot Yabia Omer* 6: *Ḥoshen Mishpat* 2; and *Teshuvot Ohr L'Tzion* 2:11) state that Sephardic Jews must follow *Maran* Rav Yosef Karo regarding all laws, especially in regard to monetary laws. According to Rav Ovadia, a Sephardic litigant may not say, "*Kim li*" ("I follow") opinions that disagree with those of Rav Karo. Examples of cases in which Rav Karo disagrees with the Rama regarding monetary issues include whether one is responsible if he caused damage in a situation entirely beyond his control (*ones gamur*; see *Shulḥan Aruch, Ḥoshen Mishpat* 378:1; *Shach, Ḥoshen Mishpat* 378:1); if one who permits an item to be placed on his property is responsible for it if he does not explicitly accept upon himself the responsibility of watching the item (see *Shulḥan Aruch, Ḥoshen Mishpat* 398:5); and if a *shomer aveda* (guardian over a lost item) is regarded as a *shomer ḥinam* or *shomer sachar* (unpaid or paid watchman; see *Shulḥan Aruch, Ḥoshen Mishpat* 267:16).
9. In his *teshuva*, Rav Eliashiv permits a Sephardic Jew who was raised by his father to follow Ashkenazic practices to remain with the Ashkenazic practices, since he has joined an Ashkenazic community. Rav Ovadia disagrees.

   Rav Amar related to me that he was approached by a young man whose father is an Iraqi Jew and mother is a Yemenite Jew. The young man was raised in the Yemenite neighborhood of his maternal grandparents and was taught to read the Torah in accordance with Yemenite tradition. The young man then asked Rav Amar as to whether he may continue to follow the traditions of his mother's family or if he must revert to the practices of his father's family. Rav Amar was unsure as to the answer, and posed the question to Rav Ovadia, who replied that the young man must revert to his father's family's practice, despite the fact that he was raised in a different tradition. Rav Amar concluded from Rav Ovadia's ruling that a Sephardic Jew remains a Sephardic Jew and must follow Sephardic practices even if he has integrated into another community.

   Rav David Banon told me about a young man whose Sephardic mother was strictly observant and whose Ashkenazic father was not at all observant. The mother raised the young man to observe Sephardic practice, and the father was respectful and cooperative with the mother. When the young man got married, Rav Banon wrote the *ketuba* and conducted the wedding ceremony in accordance with Sephardic practice. Perhaps Rav Ovadia would concede that someone raised in such circumstances is regarded as a Sephardic Jew.

Ovadia's ruling and rules that one remains a Sephardic Jew despite his complete abandonment of Sephardic practice and community.[10] Thus, he rules that even in such a circumstance, a Sephardic *get* should be written.

This issue remains subject to a difference of opinion among contemporary *get* administrators. Rav Mendel Senderovic told me that he would write an Ashkenazic *get* in such circumstances; Rav Shmuel Khoshkerman told me he would write a Sephardic *get*.

GITTIN FOR YEMENITE JEWS

Finally, Rav Amar told me that the standard practice in the Israeli Rabbinate Rabbinic courts is to administer *gittin* for a Yemenite couple in accordance with standard Sephardic practice (which for the most part adheres to the rulings of Rav Yosef Karo set forth in the *Shulḥan Aruch*), instead of trying to replicate the original Yemenite practice.[11] Rav Asher Ehrentreu of Israel's Rabbinic Court Administration and Rav Tzvi Ben Yaakov, head of the Tel Aviv Bet Din, both confirmed that this is the accepted practice. Rav Ben Yaakov notes that there are a number of Yemenite *dayanim* in the Israel Rabbinic Court system, and they all administer *gittin* for Yemenite couples in accordance with standard Sephardic practice.[12]

---

10. Rav Shlomo Zalman Auerbach (*Halichot Shlomo, Tefilla* 5:37) similarly argues that one's ancestors' customs are accepted for perpetuity. Therefore, he rules that a *ba'al teshuva* should follow the practices of his ancestors, not his teachers. Rav Ben Tzion Abba Sha'ul (introduction to *Teshuvot Ohr L'Tzion* 2:17–18) agrees.
11. The Rambam holds special weight in the Yemenite tradition. The Rambam's text for a *get* (*Hilchot Gerushin* 4:12) differs significantly from that which is presented in the *Shulḥan Aruch*. For example, the Rambam's text includes the place of residence for the husband and wife, whereas the *Shulḥan Aruch*'s text does not. Another example is that the *Shulḥan Aruch* records the practice that the *get* is twelve lines long, whereas the Rambam does not.
12. As noted by Rav Zecharia Ben-Shlomo (*Orot HaHalacha*, pp. 1216–1218), different Yemenite Jews maintain different traditions as to whom they regard as their ultimate halachic authority. Some incline more to the Rambam, others more to the *Shulḥan Aruch*, and yet others to a mixture of the two. Accordingly, it makes most sense to administer *gittin* for Yemenite Jews based on the *Shulḥan Aruch*, since determining to which group of Yemenites the husband belongs would likely to add a layer of significant difficulty. Moreover, Rav Ovadia (*Teshuvot Yeḥaveh Da'at* 1:27) believes that once Yemenite Jews arrived in Israel, they must adhere to the rulings of Rav Yosef Karo, the *Mara D'Atra* (halachic authority) of Eretz Yisrael. Although many

CONCLUSION

Despite the variety of differences between the Sephardic and Ashkenazic *gittin*, the differences are subtle and nuanced. The fundamentals remain the same.

The implications of this are profound. It bears witness to the punctilious preservation of the *mesora* (tradition) by both Sephardic and Ashkenazic Jews. Despite a millennium of vast geographic separation between the two groups, when the communities reunited in the past seventy years, we have found that we have remained in essence the same! The legacy that prior generations have bequeathed us must be preserved by our generation for the future. Just as our forbearers steadfastly hewed to the *mesora*, so must we.

Perhaps even more significant, the fact that the Sephardic and Ashkenazic *gittin* are nearly identical means that an Ashkenazic *get* is acceptable for a Sephardic Jew and vice versa. This, in turn, is what permits Sephardic and Ashkenazic Jews' to marry one another. Had either group deviated from the *mesora*, our *gittin* would be invalid according to the others' standards, and each would have regarded the other as illegitimate, God forbid. The fact that we have remained steadfastly loyal to the *mesora* has maintained us as a nation.

Although Sephardim and Ashkenazim do indeed vary slightly in their respective practices, in the bigger picture, these differences amount only to small variations on a much larger and grander theme. We remain *am eḥad*, one nation, following *Hashem* and His holy Torah, which binds us and maintains us as a nation, unified in our commitment to our Creator.

---

vociferously disagree with this view, it is possible that this approach was adopted regarding *gittin*.

Avelut

Chapter 86

Hilchot Avelut: Differences Between Sephardic and Ashkenazic Practice

Sephardic and Ashkenazic practices regarding *Hilchot Avelut* (laws of mourning) are mostly identical, but we can identify at least twelve significant differences.[1]

1) The observance of mourning practices between death and burial (*aninut*) is the subject of a dispute between the Rambam and Ramban. The Rama (*Yoreh De'ah* 341:5) rules in accordance with Ramban that the prohibitions of *avelut* (such as showering) begin at death. Ashkenazic practice follows the Rama. It is not clear how the *Shulḥan Aruch* rules on this matter, however, and there is therefore division among Sephardic Jews regarding this issue. Rav Ovadia Yosef (*Ḥazon Ovadia* 1:153) writes

1. The references to Rav Ovadia in this chapter are from his authoritative and masterful three volume work *Ḥazon Ovadia* on *Hilchot Avelut*, which he wrote towards the end of his life. Moroccan *minhagim* cited in this chapter are based on the information presented by Rav Mordechai Lebhar in *Magen Avot*.

that the practice is to be strict. However, Egyptian and Moroccan Jews follow the lenient view of the Rambam.[2]

2) Sephardic Jews follow the lenient view of the *Shulḥan Aruch* (*Yoreh De'ah* 390:5) and permit female mourners to cut their hair after *shiva*, whereas Ashkenazic Jews follow the stricter ruling of the Rama.
3) The Rama (*Yoreh De'ah* 385:3) rules strictly regarding sending *mishlo'aḥ manot* to an *avel*, even with regard to an *avel* within the twelve-month mourning period for a parent. This constitutes the accepted Ashkenazic practice. The position of the *Shulḥan Aruch* is not clear regarding this matter, and once again there is a split of practices among Sephardim. Moroccan Jews adopt the strict ruling of the Rama. However, Rav Ovadia (*Ḥazon Ovadia* 2:252) believes that Sephardic Jews may be lenient regarding this matter.
4) The Rama (*Yoreh De'ah* 376:4) records the well-known Ashkenazic custom to recite *Kaddish* for only eleven months. The *mishna* (*Eduyot* 2:10) notes that *resha'im* suffer in *Gehinnom* for twelve months; Ashkenazim thus refrain from reciting *Kaddish* in the last month of *avelut* so as not to impugn their relatives as being *resha'im*. The *Ben Ish Ḥai* (year 1, *Parashat Vayeḥi* 14) and Rav Ovadia (*Ḥazon Ovadia* 1:336), by contrast, record the practice to recite *Kaddish* for eleven months, stop for a week, and then resume the *Kaddish* until the end of the twelve months. Moroccan Jews follow the Rama, with the exception of reciting the *Kaddish* on the Shabbat preceding the *azkara* (*yahrtzeit*) of the deceased.
5) The Rama (*Yoreh De'ah* 401:6) records the accepted Ashkenazic practice to refrain from saying the *Tziduk HaDin* following burial on days on which *Taḥanun* is not recited. Rav Mordechai Eliyahu (*Siddur Kol Eliyahu*) notes that Sephardic Jews have varied practices regarding this matter and that everyone should follow the practice of their specific Sephardic group. Rav Ovadia (*Ḥazon Ovadia* 1:91) writes that the prevailing Sephardic opinion is to follow the Rama regarding this issue; this is also the Moroccan practice.
6) The question of when to observe an *azkara/yahrtzeit* in a leap year for someone who died in Adar of a non-leap year is the subject of a dispute between the *Shulḥan Aruch* and the Rama (*Oraḥ Ḥayim* 568:7). Sephardic

---

2. The authoritative work on Egyptian customs, *Nehar Mitzrayim* (*Aninut* 14), notes that the ancient custom in Egypt is to follow the lenient view of the Rambam in this regard.

Jews follow the *Shulḥan Aruch*'s ruling to observe the *azkara* during the second Adar, whereas and Ashkenazic Jews follow the ruling of the Rama to observe the *yahrtzeit* in the first Adar.

7) The *Shulhan Aruch* and Rama (*Yoreh De'ah* 393:4) dispute whether an *avel* should change his seat in the *bet kenesset* even on Shabbat. Rav Ovadia (*Ḥazon Ovadia* 3:87) rules in accordance with the *Shulḥan Aruch* that on Shabbat he should sit in his regular seat. Ashkenazim, however, follow the Rama and change seats even on Shabbat. Moroccan Jews maintain a separate section in the synagogue for mourners for both Shabbat and weekday *tefillot*. However, on Yom Tov, mourners return to their usual seats.
8) Sephardic practice is to identify the *niftar* (deceased) by their mother's name in the *hashkava* memorial prayer, according to Rav Ovadia (*Ḥazon Ovadia* 1:368), whereas the Ashkenazic practice is to mention the father's name. The Moroccan custom is to identify a deceased male by his father's name and a deceased female by her mother's name.
9) Sephardic Jews typically serve food at the *bet avel* to enable visitors to recite each of the *berachot* to elevate the *neshama* of the *niftar*.
10) Sephardic mourners are comforted with the words "*Min haShemayim tenaḥamu*" (Rambam, *Hilchot Avel* 13:2). Ashkenazic Jews say, "*HaMakom yenaḥem etchem b'toch she'ar avelei Tzion V'Yerushalayim*" (*Perisha, Yoreh De'ah* 393:30).
11) Ashkenazic Jews do not recite *Birkat Kohanim* in a *bet avel* (*Mishna Berura* 121:6; *Aruch HaShulḥan, Oraḥ Ḥayim* 121:3). However, Rav Ovadia (*Ḥazon Ovadia* 3:8) insists that *Birkat Kohanim* should be recited in the *bet avel*. The Moroccan custom is to omit *Birkat Kohanim* in a *bet avel*.
12) Sephardic Jews recite the special formula for *Birkat HaMazon* in a *bet avel* even if the *avel* has eaten alone (as ruled in *Shulḥan Aruch, Yoreh De'ah* 379). However, the prevalent Ashkenazic custom is to omit this *beracha* version if ten men did not eat together at that occasion (*Gesher HaḤayim* 20:2).[3]

CONCLUSION

There are a relatively small number of other variations between Sephardic and Ashkenazic practice regarding *avelut*, but for the most part, the *halachot* are identical. After all, we are all *am eḥad* – one nation.

3. The *Aruch HaShulḥan* (*Yoreh De'ah* 379:3), however, decries this practice.

Monetary Matters

Chapter 87

Sephardic and Ashkenazic *Prozbol*

When the conclusion of the *shemitta* year is near, we turn our attention to the *halachot* of *shemitat kesafim*. The Torah commands that at the conclusion of *shemitta*, all loans are forfeited; any money due to a lender is no longer considered owed. The *mishna* (*Shevi'it* 10:3) records that Hillel the Elder devised the *prozbol* document to facilitate collection of loans even after the conclusion of the *shemitta* year, as he noted that people were refusing to extend loans at this time for fear that they would not be repaid, in violation of the Torah's explicit order against this (*Devarim* 15:9).

The method of creating the *prozbol* differs, however, among Sephardic and Ashkenazic Jews. This is an important point to bear in mind, as it may have practical ramifications.

THE EFFECTIVENESS OF THE *PROZBOL*

The *gemara* (*Gittin* 36a) asks how Hillel abrogated a Torah law through the creation of the *prozbol* document, whereby the *halachot* of *shemittat kesafim* are avoided entirely. Abaye responds that Hillel was able to do this because *shemitta* observance today is only a Rabbinic obligation. Indeed, the Rambam (*Hilchot Shemitta V'Yovel* 9:16) writes that when *shemittat kesafim* will again be a Torah obligation, a *prozbol* will no longer be effective.

Rava, however, maintains that a *prozbol* can be effective even when *shemittat kesafim* is a Torah obligation. He asserts that a *prozbol* is effective because of *bet din*'s ability to declare someone's possessions ownerless (*hefker bet din hefker*). Hence, although on a Torah level the borrower does not owe money, the Torah authorizes *Ḥazal* to transfer the value of the loan from the borrower to the lender. The Ra'avad (*Hilchot Shemittah V'Yovel*, ad loc.) rules in accordance with this understanding of the view of Rava. (*Tosafot, Gittin* 36a, s.v. *mi ikka*, understands Rava's view very differently.)

THE MECHANICS OF A *PROZBOL*

According to Rashi (*Makkot* 3b, s.v. *hamoser shetarotav*; see *Tosafot* ad loc., s.v. *hamoser shetarotav*), the mechanism of the *prozbol* is that the lender transfers authority to the *bet din* to collect his loans. The prohibition to demand the loan after *shemitta* applies only to an individual, but not to a *bet din*. The lender does not violate the prohibition to collect his loans after *shemitta* has passed, because fundamentally *bet din* collects the loan; the lender acts as an agent of the *bet din* to demand payment of the loans.

There are two ways to execute a *prozbol* (see *Shulḥan Aruch, Ḥoshen Mishpat* 67:21; *Aruch HaShulḥan, Ḥoshen Mishpat* 67:10; and Rav Ovadia Yosef, *Teshuvot Yeḥaveh Da'at* 2:63). One option is for the lender to appear before a *bet din* and declare that he submits all of his loans to the *bet din* before him. A second alternative is for the lender to appear before two individuals and inform them that they are witnesses to the submission of his loans to a particular *bet din*. The named *bet din* need not be present in order to execute a *prozbol* in this manner.

The *Shulḥan Aruch* and Rama (*Ḥoshen Mishpat* 67:18) disagree regarding the necessary composition of a *bet din* for the purpose of a *prozbol*. The *Shulḥan Aruch* requires that it be a *bet din* of eminent stature whose members are experts in Halacha in general and the laws regarding *prozbol* in particular and whose expertise is recognized by the local community. The Rama, however, rules that any *bet din* is acceptable for writing a *prozbol*. Accordingly, Ashkenazim often assemble an ad hoc *bet din* of three observant adult Jewish males to execute a *prozbol*.

Rav Ovadia Yosef (*op. cit.*) writes that it is proper for Sephardic lenders to execute a *prozbol* before witnesses that he submits his loans to a *bet din ḥashuv* (of eminent stature). It is far easier to find a *bet din ḥashuv* to mention in the *prozbol* than to actually assemble an eminent *bet din* before whom to execute a *prozbol.*

CONCLUSION

Sephardic Jews should be sure to execute the *prozbol* in a manner that transfers the right to collect the loan to a *bet din ḥashuv*. The following is a sample document issued by the Rabbinical Council of America in 2015 regarding how to execute a *prozbol* that satisfies Sephardic standards:

PROZBOL FORM BEFORE WITNESSES FOR SUBMISSION TO BETH DIN OF AMERICA

In the presence of the undersigned two witnesses, there appeared before us ________________________________, who declared before us as follows: "Be my witnesses that I am submitting all of the debts owed to me to the Beth Din of America in New York, comprised of the following judges (*dayanim*): Rabbi Gedalia Dov Schwartz, Rabbi Mordechai Willig, and Rabbi Yonah Reiss, so that I may therefore collect these debts at any time that I desire." IN WITNESS WHEREOF, we hereby affix our signatures this ______________ day of _______________, 5775, here in ________________________________.

Signed: ___________________________

Signed: ___________________________

Chapter 88

Gambling: The Stricter Sephardic Approach

I once asked Rav Yosef Dov Soloveitchik if it is permissible to go to a casino for a single visit. Rav Soloveitchik replied succinctly, "It's a bad habit. Don't do it!" Rav Mordechai Willig encouraged me to publicize Rav Soloveitchik's statement. Indeed, similar sentiments are expressed by the *Mishna Berura* (670, *Bi'ur Halacha*, s.v. *v'nohagim*), the *Aruch HaShulḥan* (*Oraḥ Ḥayim* 670:9), Rav Moshe Feinstein (*Teshuvot Igrot Moshe, Oraḥ Ḥayim* 4:35), Rav Yehuda Amital (in a discussion with this author), Rav Aharon Lichtenstein (in a discussion with this author), Rav Hershel Schachter (in a lecture delivered at Yeshiva University), and Rav Mordechai Willig (in a speech delivered at a National Conference of Synagogue Youth convention).

We will explore the basis for this attitude in the Talmud, *Rishonim*, and *Shulḥan Aruch*. As we shall see, Sephardic Jews adopt an even stricter approach towards gambling.

THE DISQUALIFIED DICE-PLAYER

The main Talmudic discussion of gambling appears in *Sanhedrin* (24b–25a). The *mishna* there lists different types of men who are disqualified from serving as witnesses, including a dice-player (*mesaḥek b'kubiya*).

The *gemara* cites two explanations for this disqualification. Rami Bar Ḥama believes that one's winnings in dice-playing constitute theft, as the losing party does not willingly give his money to the winner. This is a situation of *asmachta,* a case in which someone accepts a disproportionately large financial responsibility under the assumption that he will never have to pay it. Rashi (s.v. *asmachta*) explains that Rami Bar Ḥama considers gambling to be a case of *asmachta* because each gambler agrees to pay, should he lose, only due to the mistaken belief that he will win. Hence, when he hands the money to the winner, he does so unwillingly.

The *gemara* records that Rav Sheshet, on the other hand, does not view the losing gambler's payment as an *asmachta*. According to Rav Sheshet, the *mishna* disqualifies only a gambler who has no other profession, because he fails to engage in any constructive activity ("*eno osek b'yishuvo shel olam*"). The Rambam (*Hilchot Gezela VaAveda* 6:11) explains that a person should involve himself in learning and other activities that contribute positively to society, whereas even permissible forms of gambling have no socially redeeming value.

VIEWS OF THE *RISHONIM*

The Rambam (*Hilchot Gezela VaAveda* 6:10–11) rules that even in circumstances where gambling would not constitute theft, it is prohibited because it is a sheer waste of time; man should spend his time productively acquiring wisdom and developing the world.

The Rambam appears to contradict himself in *Hilchot Edut* (10:4), where he implies that even gambling which constitutes theft involves no technical prohibition. It is also unclear how his opinion fits into the *gemara* quoted above.

Rashi, Rabbenu Tam, and the Ri debate why Rav Sheshet maintains that gambling does not constitute *asmachta*. Rashi (*Sanhedrin* 24b, s.v. *kol ki hai gavna*) explains that when one plays dice, he does not have any control over whether he will win or lose, for rolling dice successfully does not depend on skill. Hence, if one agrees to pay in the event that he loses, he does so wholeheartedly, knowing that he might lose. Situations of *asmachta,* in contrast, arise when a person is certain that he will fulfill his promise and thus avoid paying the penalty.

For example, the *mishna* (*Bava Batra* 168a) discusses the case of a person who promises his creditor that, as a penalty, he will pay more money than he owes if he does not repay his loan by a certain date. He agrees to pay the extra money only because he is certain that he will be able to pay the creditor by the due date. Therefore, if the borrower defaults, the penalty is considered an *asmachta*; he did not expect to actually pay the penalty. The gambler, on the other hand, understands that he might lose his money. According to Rav Sheshet, he therefore consents to his loss, making the gambling payment a permissible transaction.

The Ri fundamentally agrees with Rashi's explanation of Rav Sheshet's view, but he adds a number of points to provide a full account of the parameters of *asmachta*. He outlines three basic categories of valid conditional agreements. The first category is when one makes an agreement whose terms are reasonable (*lo gazim*) and one is fully in control of the situation (*b'yado*). This conditional agreement is valid and does not constitute *asmachta*. The classic example of this category is a sharecropper who agrees to compensate the owner of a field if he fails to work the field according to their agreement (*Bava Metzia* 104a). The payment is not a penalty; rather, it constitutes appropriate compensation to the owner of the field for the lost profits. In addition, the sharecropper himself chooses whether he will work the field.

The second category described by the Ri is accepting a debt without seriously believing that one will ever have to pay it, such as when one agrees to pay an exaggerated penalty should he fail to do something. For example, if a sharecropper agreed to pay the owner of the field an exorbitant sum as a penalty for failing to work the field, the agreement is an *asmachta*, because the sharecropper undoubtedly never expected to pay such a great sum (*Bava Metzia* 104b). He agreed to the financial penalty only inasmuch as he believed that he would work the field properly and never need to pay it. Accordingly, the penalty constitutes an *asmachta* and is not legally binding.

The Ri considers playing dice to be a third category. Winning and losing are totally random, so the players recognize that they might lose and consciously agree to pay the required sum. No one is under the false impression that his superior skills give him a better chance of winning. Since each competitor knows in advance that he may reasonably need to pay this sum, playing dice is not an *asmachta* according to Rav Sheshet.

Rabbenu Tam offers a different explanation. He suggests that playing dice would be an *asmachta* if it were a unilateral agreement. However, playing dice involves a bilateral agreement, whereby one agrees to pay when he loses games because he wants the ability to collect when he wins. Rabbenu Tam believes that *asmachta* invalidates an agreement only if the person commits himself to pay without receiving any potential profit in return, such as in the aforementioned case concerning defaulting on a loan.

THE *SHULḤAN ARUCH* AND COMMENTARIES

The Rama (*Ḥoshen Mishpat* 207:13) cites the theories of both the Ri and Rabbenu Tam to explain why playing dice is not an *asmachta*. Elsewhere (*Ḥoshen Mishpat* 370:3), the Rama does not forbid occasional gambling, as the Halacha accepts the opinion of Rav Sheshet.

Rav Yosef Karo, however, rules in accordance with the view of the Rambam that dice playing constitutes theft on a Rabbinic level, asserting that the agreement between the two parties involved is an *asmachta*.

Accordingly, Sephardic Jews may not even gamble occasionally, since for them the rulings of Rav Yosef Karo constitute the halachic norm. Indeed, Rav Ovadia Yosef (*Teshuvot Yabia Omer* 7: *Ḥoshen Mishpat* 6) rules that a Sephardic Jew may not buy lottery tickets.

Even the Rama limits the permissibility of gambling occasionally to those games in which the winner is determined entirely at random, such that the players are aware that they may certainly lose. In order to engage in such an activity, one must ascertain that the game does not constitute an *asmachta* in any way. This task is far from simple, since crucial distinctions between valid and invalid agreements are very subtle. Rav Aharon Lichtenstein (cited in *Daf Kesher* 1, pp. 83–85) notes that sport-betting pools, for example, appear to be prohibited even for Ashkenazic Jews. In that form of gambling, each participant believes that his superior understanding of sports will help him bet on the right teams, so he does not expect to pay for losing.

Moreover, the Rama (*Ḥoshen Mishpat* 207:13) cites the opinion of Rabbenu Tam that gambling is permitted only when the prize money is placed on a table owned by both parties (see *Bi'ur HaGra, Ḥoshen Mishpat* 207:37). Most cases of gambling do not fulfill this requirement, as they usually take place in the home of a single player or in a casino. There is therefore significant reason for Ashkenazic Jews to be stringent as well.

RAFFLES AND LOTTERIES

A possible exception to the halachic problems with gambling is a lottery conducted to raise funds for a charity. Rav Yosef Adler reports that Rav Yosef

Dov Soloveitchik permitted purchasing a lottery ticket if the purpose of the lottery is to raise money for a charity, because the rule of *asmachta* does not apply to charitable contributions (*Shulḥan Aruch, Yoreh De'ah* 258:10). *Asmachta* occurs only when someone does not intend to truly obligate himself. The losers of a charity lottery fundraiser, however, feel comfortable relinquishing their money, knowing that it will be used for a positive purpose.

Rav Aharon Lichtenstein (*op. cit.*) offers a different reason to permit lotteries and raffles, explaining that one who purchases a ticket buys a right to compete in the lottery. At the time of this purchase, the buyer consents fully to the sale. Should the buyer regret the sale after he loses the lottery, it is too late to undo the sale. Undoing such a sale would be the equivalent of one who purchases a stock demanding to abrogate the sale after a subsequent stock market crash.

As noted above, Rav Ovadia Yosef prohibits purchasing lottery and soccer-pool tickets.[1] Nevertheless, Rav Ovadia cites the *Ben Ish Ḥai* (*Teshuvot Rav Pe'alim* 2: *Ḥoshen Mishpat* 30) as permitting raffles in which the prize is an object, as the winner does not directly take the money of the other participants.

Common practice in the observant community is to conduct raffles as fundraisers for charitable organizations.

MORAL CONSIDERATIONS

The Rivash (432) describes gambling as "disgusting, abominable, and repulsive," noting its terrible effect on society even according to those who do not technically define it as theft. Rav Ovadia Yosef (*op. cit.*) adds to the Rivash's comments:

> Also, regarding the lottery, there are many people who buy many tickets, [spending] almost their entire salary, thinking that one number may win, and in the end… they lose all their money and property.

1. Rav Ovadia adds that even Ashkenazic Jews should not purchase tickets in Israeli soccer-pools ("Toto"), as these tickets support soccer games played on Shabbat. We have already noted that according to Rav Aharon Lichtenstein, these pools may constitute an *asmachta*, as their participants believe that their superior understanding of soccer enables them to bet correctly.

Due to moral objections, the authorities cited at the beginning of this chapter similarly condemn engaging even in "recreational gambling," in addition to the potential problems of theft. In 1996, Rav Mordechai Willig instructed a convention of the National Conference of Synagogue Youth to refrain from all forms of gambling (including horse racing, football pools, and rotisserie leagues), due to the aforementioned rulings of the Rambam. Although many Ashkenazic authorities disagree with the Rambam's claim that gambling with a Jew constitutes theft, no one would question the truth of the Rambam's statement that gambling, even when there is no theft involved, is a sheer waste of time, the antithesis of wisdom, and contributes nothing positive to the world. Rav Willig cited many of the catastrophic results of habitual gambling, repeatedly decrying gambling and its results as "*ḥurbano shel olam*," destroying society.

Rav Hershel Schachter (Yeshiva University lecture, 5748) objects even to lotteries commonly conducted at weddings to determine which guest will keep the table centerpiece, based on a law in the *Shulḥan Aruch* (*Oraḥ Ḥayim* 322:6) prohibiting casting lots to determine which child in a family will receive the largest portion of food. Rav Schachter maintains that this ruling reflects a general prohibition against activities that involve gambling.

The *Mishna Berura* and *Aruch HaShulḥan* (cited at the beginning of this chapter) strongly discourage playing cards on Ḥanukka. It is highly unusual for the *Aruch HaShulḥan* to strongly condemn a practice of the observant community, but he does so regarding the practice of gambling. Perhaps he reacted so harshly because he served as the rabbi of a city (Novaradok, in pre-World War I Lithuania), where he may have seen the devastating effects that gambling has on individuals, their families, and society as a whole.

Modern day *Aḥaronim* have emphasized the ills of gambling. Rav Moshe Feinstein refers to card-playing and bingo as despicable activities ("*devarim mecho'arim*"), and Rav Aharon Lichtenstein commented to this author that casinos and gambling halls are "symbols of decadence in society." Rav Yehuda Amital said that these activities reflect people's drive for unhealthy forms of excitement. As Rav Soloveitchik put it so succinctly, "It is a bad habit. Don't do it!"

CONCLUSION

The Torah exhorts (*Vayikra* 19:2), "*Kedoshim tih'yu*," "Be holy." Many great rabbis have declared that gambling is incompatible with the Jewish People's goal of being a holy people.[2] Both Sephardic and Ashkenazic Jews should remember the words of the *Mishna Berura* regarding gambling: "*Hashomer nafsho yirḥak mizeh*" ("He who values his soul will stay away from it").

In addition to these moral considerations, one's quality of life will be dramatically upgraded by spending his non-working hours engaged in spiritually and psychologically enriching activities and spurning morally corrosive pursuits such as gambling. Finally, some halachic decisors do not regard winnings from gambling as a legitimate acquisition. One who regrettably gambled and won some cash must consult with his Rav as to whether he is required to return the winnings to the original owner.

2. Rav David Bassous (*Jewish Law Meets Modern Challenges*, vol. 1, p. 40) adds a very important point, noting that according to the Ramban's definition of holiness (in his commentary to *Vayikra* 19:2), "gambling definitely falls into the category of unseemly activities with which we, as a holy nation, should have nothing to do."

Hilchot Nidda

Chapter 89

Differences Between Sephardic and Ashkenazic Practices

Hilchot Nidda is an exceptionally sensitive and delicate topic, since these laws pertain to the most intimate aspects of our lives. Thus, it is a topic best discussed in private with a trusted Torah guide.

On the other hand, it is an area of Halacha regarding which there remains an extraordinary wide range of acceptable practices. Consensus approaches have not emerged regarding many classic disputes in this area. Thus, different halachic guides offer very different halachic guidance regarding *Hilchot Nidda*.

In addition, as in all other areas of Halacha, there are slight differences between the practices of Sephardic and Ashkenazic Jews in the context of *Hilchot Nidda*. Moreover, there are different approaches taken by the various Sephardic *posekim* regarding *Hilchot Nidda*. The approach adopted by Rav Ovadia Yosef in his magisterial three-volume work *Taharat HaBayit*, for example, differs from the approach articulated by Rav Mordechai Eliyahu in his highly regarded and oft-used guide *Darchei Tahara*. We must also take into account Moroccan and Yemenite approaches, which differ from that of both Rav Ovadia and Rav Eliyahu.

Thus, it is important to present an introduction to these differences in order to help couples choose the most appropriate guides for *taharat hamishpaḥa*.

RAV OVADIA YOSEF'S *TAHARAT HABAYIT*

Rav Yosef's *Taharat HaBayit* is an indispensable treasure-trove of halachic discussions regarding *Hilchot Nidda*. It presents an extraordinarily wide range of issues in full depth and breadth. In general, it presents a lenient approach to *Hilchot Nidda* that is suitable for the entire Jewish community and not limited to the spiritual elite. How is an Ashkenazic Jew to utilize this magnificent *sefer*?

An answer may be found by consulting Rav Zvi Sobolofsky's masterpiece on *Hilchot Nidda*, entitled *The Laws and Concepts of Niddah*. Rav Sobolofsky often quotes Rav Ovadia and often states that all Jews have a right to rely on his rulings regarding many specific issues. This is a practical way to discern outlier positions that lie beyond the consensus opinion and should not be followed. It also helps the reader to discern which of Rav Ovadia's rulings are unique to Sephardic Jews and are not appropriate for Ashkenazic Jews.

SIX SIGNIFICANT DIFFERENCES BETWEEN RAV YOSEF KARO AND THE RAMA

The following is a presentation of six significant differences between Sephardic and Ashkenazic *posekim* regarding *Hilchot Nidda*. While this is not an exhaustive list, it covers the disputes that are most common and well-known.

1) Most famous is the Ashkenazic *ḥumra* (stringency) to wait five days to begin the *shiva nekiyim* (seven clean days) due to concern for *poletet* (Rama, *Yoreh De'ah* 196:11). *Maran* Rav Yosef Karo clearly does not subscribe to this *ḥumra*, ruling that four days suffice to begin the *shiva nekiyim*. While Ashkenazic Jews undoubtedly must adhere to the Rama's *ḥumra* under normal circumstances, Rav Ovadia Yosef (*Taharat HaBayit* 13:55–62) insists that Sephardic Jews may follow the ruling of *Maran* Rav Yosef Karo.

However, it is important to note that not all Sephardic Jews agree with this approach. Rav Mordechai Eliyahu (*Darchei Tahara* 138) and Rav Shalom Messas (*Teshuvot Tevu'ot Shemesh, Yoreh De'ah* 105) argue that Sephardic Jews have accepted the *ḥumra* of the Rama in conventional circumstances.

2) Another *ḥumra* presented by the Rama (*Yoreh De'ah* 196:10) is that a *teliya* (attribution to a *tahor* source) is not permitted during the first three days of the *shiva nekiyim*. Both Rav Ovadia (*Taharat HaBayit* 13:49) and Rav Eliyahu (*Darchei Tahara* 138) rule that Sephardic Jews have not adopted this stringency.
3) In the area of *harḥakot*, there are a number of disputes between the *Shulḥan Aruch* and the Rama. The Rama (*Yoreh De'ah* 195:2) includes throwing an item in the *harḥaka* of *hoshata* (passing). Rav Ovadia essentially permits this for Sephardic Jews (*Taharat HaBayit* 12:6), but Rav Eliyahu does not permit this even for Sephardic Jews (*Darchei Tahara* 42).
4) The *harḥaka* of the *sefina hamitnadnedet* (rocking boat) is cited only by the Rama (*Yoreh De'ah* 195:5). Rav Ovadia (*Taharat HaBayit* 12:39) rules that Sephardim have not accepted this *ḥumra*.
5) According to Rav Ovadia (*Taharat HaBayit* 12:30), drinking leftover drinks of the husband or wife is forbidden according to *Maran* Rav Yosef Karo, whereas leftover foods are permitted. Only the Rama prohibits leftover food (*Yoreh De'ah* 195:3–4). Rav Eliyahu forbids leftover food for Sephardim as well.
6) Finally, there is well known dispute between *Maran* Rav Yosef Karo and the Rama as to whether the *beracha* should be recited before or after the *tevila* (*Yoreh De'ah* 200). *Maran* rules that it should be recited beforehand, whereas the Rama rules that it is recited after the *tevila*. Rav Ovadia, as is his wont, rules forcefully in accordance with *Maran* Rav Karo (*Taharat HaBayit* 15:1–2). Rav Eliyahu (*Darchei Tahara* 172) and Rav Ben Tzion Abba Sha'ul (cited in Rav Mordechai Lebhar, *Magen Avot, Yoreh De'ah* 200) disagree, arguing that the Sephardic practice has emerged in accordance with the view of the Rama. Indeed, the great classic Sephardic *posekim* the *Ḥida* (*Shiyurei Beracha* 200), *Ben Ish Ḥai* (year 2, *Parashat Shemini* 19), and the *Ḥesed LaAlafim* (*Yoreh De'ah* 200) all record the Sephardic practice to follow the Rama in this regard.

CONCLUSION

Couples must exercise good judgment in choosing their halachic guides regarding *Hilchot Nidda*. A wide variety of approaches are presented by a diverse range of experts.[1] Even among Sephardic *posekim*, differences persist. There is no monolithic Sephardic approach to *Hilchot Nidda*.

1. It is also significant to note that Rav Ovadia (*Taharat HaBayit* 2:452; *Halichot Olam* 4:209; *Yalkut Yosef, Oraḥ Ḥayim* 326:12) prefers that Sephardic women immerse shortly after *shekia* on Friday evenings. This is contrast to Ashkenazic practice, which does not permit immersion until after *tzet hakochavim* even on Friday evenings (*Shach, Yoreh De'ah* 197:6).

Sephardic Jewry

Chapter 90

Why are all Eastern Jews Referred to as Sephardic?

"Sepharad" is the word Jews use to refer to Spain. Why, then, are eastern (Mizraḥi) Jews, such as those whose families lived in Persia and Iraq, referred to Sephardic Jews? These Jews never lived in Spain! Referring to them as Sephardic appears to be inappropriate. Moreover, in centuries past, many eastern Jews who did not originate from Spain and lived in Arab lands were called Musta'arabim. Why are they now known as Sephardic Jews? Why is the term Musta'arabim no longer used?

RAV OVADIA YOSEF'S EXPLANATION

Rav Yehuda Azoulay relates:

> When meeting King Juan Carlos of Spain, Ḥacham Ovadia explained to the king why Sephardic Jewry goes by the word "Sephardim," which means "Spanish." Although [many] Sephardic Jews hail from Middle Eastern and North African countries, they are known as

> "Sephardim" because they received their guidance from the Rambam, a Spanish native.[1]

We may add to this explanation that Sephardic Jews are guided by Rav Yosef Karo, who was also a native of Spain.

THE GREAT RABBIS OF SPAIN

I would suggest an addition to Rav Ovadia's explanation based on the content of Rav Yosef Bitton's magnificent work, *Forgotten Giants: Sephardic Rabbis Before and After the Expulsion from Spain*. This slim volume offers brief descriptions of twenty-six great but almost all lesser-known rabbis of Spanish-Jewish origin who lived during the fifteenth, sixteenth, and seventeenth centuries. I suggest that the enormous impact of these rabbis on shaping the Halacha practiced by *Edot HaMizraḥ* (eastern communities) is yet another reason that Mizraḥim are commonly called Sephardim.

The first section of Rav Bitton's book describes rabbis who were born in Spain and lived most of their lives in Spain immediately before the Expulsion. The second section describes great Spanish rabbis who were born in Spain but were expelled from Spain at a young age and resettled elsewhere. The final section describes a group of great rabbis born to Jewish refugees from Spain who were born outside of Spain after the Expulsion.

The common denominator of all of these rabbis was that each lived, to some extent or another, a life that included severe disruption and suffering. Yet, despite the severe handicaps they experienced, their literary productivity and legacies are stunningly magnificent!

RAV ḤASDAI CRESCAS AND RAV DAVID BEN ZIMRA

The year 1391 was the beginning of the end of the rich Jewish life in Spain. In that year, Catholic leaders incited their community to engage in vicious pogroms against Jews in Spain that murdered tens of thousands of Jews and forcibly converted many others.

The great Rav Ḥasdai Crescas was not spared this onslaught, despite his special standing in the royal court of Spain as well as in the

1. *Maran: The Life and Scholarship of Hacham Ovadia Yosef*, pp. 387–388). This story is also related by Rav Ovadia's grandson, Rav Yaakov Sasson, at http://halachayomit.co.il/en/default.aspx?HalachaID=3965.

Jewish community. His only son was tragically murdered by Catholic extremists when he refused to convert. Yet despite this terrible loss and Rav Crescas' great efforts to secure permission from the royal family to rebuild Spanish Jewry and to help those forced to convert to move to North Africa, where they could return to Jewish observance, Rav Crescas still found time to make a very significant contribution to Torah scholarship.

All this activity was in addition to raising prominent *talmidim*, such as Rav Yosef Ibn Habib, the author of the authoritative *Nimukei Yosef* commentary to the Rif, and Rav Yosef Albo, the author of the *Sefer HaIkkarim*. Despite all of these enormous demands on his time, Rav Ḥasdai Crescas authored a lasting philosophical masterpiece entitled *Ohr Hashem*, which is studied until this very day.

Rav Crescas is most famous for his arguments with the Rambam about two matters. First, he argues that the introduction to the *Aseret HaDibrot* (Ten Commandments), "*Anochi Hashem Elokecha asher hotzeticha me'Eretz Mitzrayim*," should not be counted as a *mitzva*. He argues that *emuna* is a prerequisite to all other *mitzvot* but cannot be categorized as a *mitzva*. Moreover, Rav Crescas argues, *mitzvot* involve matters regarding which one has a choice. Belief cannot constitute a *mitzva*, since the belief in the existence of *Hashem* is obvious, and hence not subject to choice. Rav Crescas also famously minimizes belief in free will, standing in stark contrast to the Rambam in this regard.

Of course, *Ohr Hashem* discusses far more than these two topics. These are just two examples regarding which students of Jewish philosophy pay considerable attention to Rav Ḥasdai Crescas' views until this day. What makes this work so remarkable was that the author had both the time and presence of mind to author such a work for the ages despite living under such severe strain.

Rav David ben Zimra, known as the Radbaz, was born in Spain in 1479 and was forced to leave Spain with his family in 1492. They resettled in Eretz Yisrael.

The trauma experienced by the Jewish expellees from Spain, such as the Radbaz and his family, was profound. The Catholic Church forbade Jews to leave Spain with gold and silver, and Jews were left with no choice other than to sell their property for next to nothing. Homes were sold for as little as a donkey on which to leave Spain.

The impoverished Jewish refugees were extremely vulnerable at sea due to the danger of sea travel, pirates out to murder them, and slave traders who wished to sell them into slavery. Moreover, the trauma did not end when arriving at their new country. The difficulty of adjusting to an often hostile new society when the refugees had little or no resources is unfathomable.

Despite this horrific experience, the Radbaz flourished in his new country, learning with great rabbis in his new community of Tzfat and emerging as a great Torah scholar who was appointed as *Ḥacham Bashi* (chief rabbi) of the Egyptian Jewish community. While serving with distinction in this role for over forty years, the Radbaz published more than three thousand responsa that have had immeasurable impact on Mizraḥi (and all other) Jews. For example, there is hardly a *teshuva* authored by Rav Ovadia Yosef that does not quote the Radbaz! Moreover, he made time to compose these three thousand *teshuvot* while he was raising great *talmidim*, such as Rav Yitzhak Luria (the great Ari z"l), Rav Betzalel Asheknazy (author of the *Shita Mekubetzet*), and the Maharikash (Rav Yaakov Castro).

OTHER GREAT SPANISH RABBIS FROM THE PRE- AND POST-EXPULSION ERA

Other examples abound. The Mahram Alashkar, who was born in 1466 and suffered terrible tribulations during his voyage from Spain to North Africa in 1492, is an excellent example. The Maharam Alashkar eventually resettled in Jerusalem and was one of the shapers of Minhag Yerushalayim, the practices of Sephardic Jewish residents of Jerusalem.

Rav Yaakov Berav was born in Spain in 1474 and was expelled from Spain in 1492. He eventually made his way to Tzfat, where he mentored the great Rav Yosef Karo and authored authoritative *teshuvot* that are frequently cited to this day. Another Spanish Jewish refugee, Rav Yaakov Ibn Ḥabiv, wrote the classic work *En Yaakov* on the aggadic portions of the Talmud. The Tashbetz (Rav Shimon Duran) was forced to leave Spain during the violence of 1391, resettling in Algeria. Rav Duran published more than eight hundred *teshuvot*, which are cited until this very day.

Finally, the Maharashdam (Rav Shmuel De Medina) published nearly one thousand *teshuvot*, despite his heavy burden as the leader of the very large community of refugees from Portugal and Spain in Salonica, Greece.

Of course, we have not yet mentioned the extraordinary contribution made by Rav Yosef Karo's *Shulḥan Aruch*. As he writes in his introduction to the *Shulḥan Aruch*, the aftermath of the Spanish Inquisition left Jewish communities in halachic turmoil. Rav Karo, a refugee from Spain of 1492, sought and succeeded in stabilizing the halachic practice of Jews through the publication of the *Shulḥan Aruch*. This is clearly the most lasting and impactful of all the contributions of the Spanish rabbis of that era.

CONCLUSION

The accomplishments of the Spanish rabbis of the Expulsion era are truly remarkable. In fact, they reflect the phenomenon described in the Torah, "The more they tried to harm them, the greater they became" (*Shemot* 1:12). These great rabbis succeeded in taking all of the hideous negative energy unleashed upon them by the Catholic Inquisition and transforming it into extraordinary Torah productivity that bequeathed a lasting legacy for all generations.

Jews marching to the gas chambers during the Holocaust famously chanted, "We will outlive them" – referring, of course, to the Nazis – and indeed, we have outlived them. Similarly, the Jewish expellees from Spain have certainly outlived the leaders of the Inquisition. The Inquisition and its evil leaders are long gone and forgotten. By contrast, the works of the Spanish rabbis of the Expulsion era dramatically transformed Mizraḥi Judaism and are lovingly studied by hundreds of thousands of Jews until today.

I suggest that Mizraḥi Jews refer to themselves as Sephardic not only due to the influence of the Rambam and Rav Yosef Karo, who were born in Spain, but because of the totality of the influence of the great Spanish rabbis, especially those of the Expulsion era, whose writings made an extraordinary impact on the practice of eastern Jews.

Moroccan Jews

Chapter 91

Navigating the World of Moroccan Halacha

Serving as the rabbi of a heterogeneous Sephardic *kehilla* such as Congregation Shaarei Orah, the Sephardic Congregation of Teaneck, is a most challenging task. Not only must one be thoroughly familiar with the Minhag Yerushalayim-based approach of Rav Ovadia Yosef and his sons (which serves as the official guide for our *kehilla*), but one must also be familiar with the practices of other Sephardic communities and halachic authorities in order to properly respond to questions posed by individual members. Among the most challenging tasks that I have faced in this capacity is learning how to swim in the sea of Moroccan *minhagim* and *p'sak Halacha*.

DARKÉ ABOTENOU

The Moroccan approach varies significantly from the approach articulated by Rav Ovadia. Moreover, there are a myriad of varieties of approaches and styles within Moroccan sub-communities. However, the challenge of tracking Moroccan practice has become dramatically easier with the recent publication of the two volumes of *Darké Abotenou*.

Darké Abotenou was co-authored by Ariel Picillo and Dr. Adam Ohayon. These two lay authors were guided mainly by Rav Mordechai Lebhar of Los Angeles, an emerging leader in the Sephardic rabbinate, and the authors' rabbi, Rav Amram Assayag of Toronto.

The formidable task of cataloging Moroccan halachic practice is eloquently described by Jerusalem Sephardic Chief Rabbi Rav Shlomo Amar in his letter of approbation to *Darké Abotenou*:

> It should be known that the customs of Morocco are numerous and diverse. It is [a community consisting of] hundreds of cities and villages, each one different from the other. What was the custom in Fes was not so in Marrakech, and both of these are different from Meknes and Sefrou, and these are different from Rabat and Salé! We still have not even spoken about the great city of Casablanca and the hundreds of villages in the Atlas Mountains, as well as the great and important cities of Mogador and Agadir. [All of] these are further different from the Spanish region of Morocco – Tangier, Tetuoan, etc.

Despite these many differences, Rav Lebhar writes that the dean of the second half of the twentieth-century Moroccan rabbinate, Rav Shalom Messas, insists that the majority of Moroccan practices are the same. Mr. Picilo and Dr. Ohayon do a magnificent job of delineating practices regarding which a Moroccan consensus has emerged and issues where differences persist. The authors specifically note which communities observe the varied approaches.

We will discuss two specific examples. The first is a consensus custom, whereas there is divergence in practice among Moroccan Jews regarding the second.

YIGDAL BEFORE *BARUCH SHE'AMAR* ON SHABBAT

It is the practice of all Moroccan Jews to recite *Yigdal* before *Baruch She'Amar* on Shabbat and Yom Tov. The reason for this practice is that *Yigdal* summarizes the Rambam's thirteen principles of faith, and the word "*baruch*" appears thirteen times in *Baruch She'Amar*.

L'HADLIK NER ḤANUKKA OR *L'HADLIK NER SHEL ḤANUKKA*

Minhag Yerushalayim follows the ruling of the *Shulḥan Aruch* (*Oraḥ Ḥayim* 676:1) that the text of the first *beracha* recited before Ḥanukka lighting is *"l'hadlik ner Ḥanukka."*[1] This stands in contrast to the Ashkenazic and Yemenite practice to follow the ruling of the Rambam (*Hilchot Ḥanukka* 3:4) and recite *"l'hadlik ner shel Ḥanukka."* The *Ḥida* (*Birkei Yosef, Oraḥ Ḥayim* 676) explains that the lights of Shabbat are described as *"shel Shabbat"* ("of Shabbat",) since we may benefit from them. The Ḥanukka lights, by contrast, may not be utilized for one's own benefit, and thus cannot be described as *"shel Ḥanukka."*

What is the Moroccan practice? The authors of *Darké Abotenou* begin by noting that some Moroccan *Rabbanim* and communities say, *"l'hadlik ner Ḥanukka,"* as in Minhag Yerushalayim. This is endorsed by two great Moroccan authorities, Rav Amram Assayag and Rav Baruch Toledano. However, *Darké Abotenou* records, "it is likely that the original custom of Morocco was to say *l'hadlik ner shel Ḥanukka.*" This approach is recommended by Rav Yosef Messas, in accordance with the text that appears in the Talmud Bavli (*Shabbat* 23a) and many *Rishonim,* including the Rif, Rashi, and the Rambam. Rav Refael Ohayon is recorded as confirming that this is the *minhag* of the Jews of Marrakech.

CONCLUSION

Darké Abotenou is as enthralling as it is invaluable. Dozens upon dozens of issues are clearly presented with all of the nuances and varieties in Moroccan customs and traditions. Its introduction sets forth the basic principles and traditions of Moroccan *p'sak Halacha.* I could hardly put down this long-awaited *sefer.*

For those who wish to delve further into Moroccan *minhagim,* the voluminous *Magen Avot* by Rav Mordechai Lebhar is an absolute must. The venerated twentieth-century work *Nahagu HaAm* by Rav David Ovadya is also a highly authoritative source on Moroccan *minhagim.*

---

1. This is also the practice of Ḥassidic Jews.

Chapter 92

Three Secrets of Moroccan *P'sak Halacha*

The gates shuttering the world of Moroccan Halacha have been opened wide with the recent publication of *Darké Abotenou: The Laws and Customs of the Jews of Morocco* and Rav Mordechai Lebhar's *Magen Avot,* as we discussed in the previous chapter. The introduction to *Darké Abotenou* sheds light on an otherwise enigmatic enterprise – the inner workings of Moroccan Halacha. There are three key points that create the distinctive Moroccan approach to *p'sak Halacha.*

SECRET #1: THE INFLUENCE OF THE ROSH

How and why did Rabbeinu Asher, the "Rosh," who was born and raised in Germany, exercise a major influence on Moroccan Jewry? The Rosh was forced to flee from persecution in Germany, and he then settled in Spain, where he served as the leader of the community and was enormously influential. When the Jews were banished from Spain in 1492, many of the *megorashim* (refugees) moved to Morocco. The *megorashim* exerted an enormous influence in their adopted land, especially in Fes and northern (Spanish) Morocco.

The *megorashim* brought with them their affinity for the approach of the Rosh. In fact, a mantra of many Moroccan *posekim* is that wherever the

Rosh goes, we go (a play on the Hebrew word "*rosh*," which means "head"). Thus, although Moroccan Jews in general follow the rulings of *Maran* Rav Yosef Karo like other Sephardic Jews, they occasionally follow the Rosh.

Most famously, Moroccan Jews follow the Rosh's ruling (*Berachot* 2:5) that the *beracha* for full *Hallel* is "*l'gmor et HaHallel*," while the *beracha* for *Ḥatzi Hallel* is "*l'kro et HaHallel*." This stands in contrast to the ruling of the *Shulḥan Aruch* (*Oraḥ Ḥayim* 422:2), which rules that no *beracha* is recited on *Ḥatzi Hallel*.[1]

SECRET #2: FOLLOW THE RAMA WHEN THE *SHULḤAN ARUCH* IS UNCLEAR OR SILENT

Darké Abotenou records that Moroccan rabbis will follow the Rama in a case in which *Maran* Rav Yosef Karo is unclear or silent. Rav Ovadia most decidedly does not adhere to this rule. There are numerous examples of this phenomenon that account for significant differences between Rav Ovadia/Yerushalmi practices on the one hand and Moroccan practice on the other.

The following are two prominent examples. On a Motza'ei Shabbat preceding a week during which a Yom Tov falls, Moroccans omit *V'YeHi No'am*, whereas those who follow Minhag Yerushalayim do not. The *Shulḥan Aruch* does not address this issue, but this rule is recorded in the Rama (*Oraḥ Ḥayim* 295:1).[2]

Similarly, the Rama (*Oraḥ Ḥayim* 621:6) mentions the practice of mentioning the names of the deceased on Yom Kippur (serving as the basis for the Ashkenazic practice of *Yizkor*), while the *Shulḥan Aruch* is silent regarding this matter. Thus, Moroccan Jews mention the *neshamot* in a ceremony known as the *Hashkava Kelalit*, whereas Minhag Yerushalayim has nothing of this sort.

Darké Abotenou makes a critical clarification at this point. The similarity between some Moroccan and Ashkenazic practices leads some

1. Turkish Jews also follow the Rosh regarding the *beracha* on *Hallel*. This is not surprising, since the *megorashim* from Spain also emerged as the dominant community in Turkey after the Spanish expulsion. Indeed, many Turkish Jews retain Spanish names (such as Galanti and Varon) that memorialize their Spanish origins.
2. Moroccan practice differs somewhat from that of the Rama, as they omit *V'Yehi No'am*, but begin with the final *pasuk* of *Mizmor* 91. Minhag Yerushalayim in this instance is based on kabbalistic considerations (as presented in the *Birkei Yosef, Oraḥ Ḥayim* 295:1 and the *Ben Ish Ḥai*, year 2, *Parashat Vayetzei* 6). This is an example of how in many instances Moroccan practices do not follow kabbalistic considerations.

to wrongly conclude that Moroccan Jews were influenced by Ashkenazim in their midst. This unfounded rumor stemmed from the very strong and influential presence of Lubavitch *sheluḥim* in Morocco beginning in the 1950s. (Morocco was the first country outside North America to which the Lubavitcher Rebbe sent *sheluḥim*).

In response to this claim, *Darké Abotenou* cites a fiery letter sent by the Bet Din of Casablanca, headed by the venerable Rav Shalom Messas, to the Ḥabad emissaries in Morocco, warning them that although they are most welcome and encouraged in their outreach work, they dare not tamper with the local community's *minhagim*. *Darké Abotenou* also cites a letter from the eminent nineteenth-century authority Rav Yosef Berdugo, who wrote to the great Rav Yaakov Berdugo: "We should not use proofs for [our] customs from Ashkenazic sources, because we do not follow the custom of Ashkenazim whatsoever."

The similarity between Moroccan and Ashkenazic custom is not at all due to the influence of Ḥabad. Rather, the similarity emerges from the impact of the Rosh and the reliance on the Rama in cases in which Rav Karo is silent. The claim that Moroccan practices have been adulterated is unfounded and should not be repeated.

SECRET #3: WELL-BASED PRACTICES OF AN ANCIENT COMMUNITY WITH MANY GREAT RABBIS

On Shabbat Naḥamu 5777, we had the privilege of hosting Rav Shlomo Amar at Congregation Shaarei Orah. I had the pleasure of sitting next to Rav Amar at the Friday night meal during this incredible Shabbat, and I was shocked to see Rav Amar nibble on some olives and salad after *Kiddush* but before *netilat yadayim*. This seemed to create a *hefsek* (unwarranted interruption) between *Kiddush* and the meal. It also creates a question regarding recitation of a *beracha aḥrona*, as well as unnecessary *berachot*!

However, upon studying *Darké Abotenou*, I learned that this is an ancient Moroccan practice that began in order to help ensure the required daily 100 *berachot* are recited on Shabbat. *Darké Abotenou* offers a compelling defense for this practice, including the argument that all Jews make a similar interruption between *Kiddush* and the meal at the Pesaḥ *seder*.[3]

3. In general, the *Mishna Berura* (273:12) adopts a narrow and strict approach to the rule of "*en Kiddush ela b'makom seuda*" (*Kiddush* must be recited at the place of the

The Moroccan Jewish community is an ancient one, dating to the exile subsequent to the destruction of *Bayit Rishon*. In addition, the community has been blessed with great *Rabbanim*, including the Rif, Ri Migash, and the Ohr HaḤayim, as well as myriads of Torah luminaries throughout the generations. In fact, Morocco is one of the few places on earth where there has been uninterrupted Torah learning for at least the past two thousand years! Thus, venerated Moroccan customs approved by its great Torah authorities deserve enormous respect.[4]

In fact, many unique Moroccan customs predate the composition of the *Shulḥan Aruch*. Rav Karo specifically notes in his introduction to the *Shulḥan Aruch* that his intention is not to uproot already established community practices.

CONCLUSION

The *Rishonim* coined the phrase, "*Minhag Yisrael Torah hi*," the customs of the Jewish People constitute Torah. On a simple level, this phrase summons us to regard *minhagim* as a legitimate component of Torah. Rav Yosef Dov Soloveitchik adds that this phrase also teaches that the customs of our people need to be studied and explained like any other portion of the Torah. *Darké Abotenou* performs this task magnificently, helping all Jews appreciate the rich legacy of a great Jewish community with a rich past and bright future even now that almost all of the community no longer resides in Morocco.

---

meal), requiring a tight linkage between *Kiddush* and the meal. The *Aruch HaShulḥan* (*Oraḥ Ḥayim* 273:1) adopts an approach that is not as demanding in connecting *Kiddush* and the meal. The Moroccan *minhag* is obviously much more in harmony with the *Aruch HaShulḥan*'s approach to the principle.

4. Indeed, the deep respect Rav Shalom Messas shows for ancient Moroccan *minhagim* is a recurring theme in his writings.

Yemenite Jews

Chapter 93

Four Distinct Elements of Yemenite Practice

The most cogent way to describe Yemenite (Temani) Jews and their halachic practice is "very distinctive." Their pronunciation of Hebrew,[1] appearance,[2] and halachic rulings mark them as a unique segment of *Am Yisrael*. Indeed, it can certainly be said that the Jewish People is composed not only of Ashkenazic and Sephardic branches, but rather of Ashkenazic, Sephardic, and Yemenite branches.

There are four elements of Yemenite practice that give it its unique flavor.

ELEMENT #1: A VERY CONSERVATIVE BENT

Temani Halacha is the most conservative of all of the streams of our people; they adhere closely to the original practice recorded in the Talmud and

1. For example, Ashkenazic Jews recite *Borei Peri HaGofen*, Sephardic Jews say *Borei Peri HaGefen*, and most Yemenite Jews pronounce *Borei Peri HaJofan*.
2. There is ample DNA evidence that demonstrates that Ashkenazic, Sephardic, and Yemenite Jews stem from the same genetic background and geographic origin. For more on this topic, see: http://www.cohen-levi.org/jewish_genes_and_genealogy/jewish_genes_-_dna_evidence.htm.

Rishonim. Temanim are virtually the only Jews who still read the Targum Onkelos during Torah reading (as per *Megilla* 23b). In addition, unlike other Jews who have a *ba'al keri'a* read the Torah on behalf of those who receive an *aliya* at the public Torah reading (a practice already noted by *Tosafot*, *Megilla* 21b, s.v. *tanna*), Yemenite Jews preserve the original custom for the *oleh* to read the portion himself.

Other examples are the Yemenite practice to eat meat during the Nine Days until the *se'uda hamafseket*, the pre-fast meal, as is the original practice recorded in the *mishna* and *gemara* (*Ta'anit* 26b and 30a). Many Yemenites do not perform the ritual of *Tashlich*, as it does appear in the Talmud, Rambam, or *Shulḥan Aruch*.[3] On Rosh Hashana, many Yemenites sound only forty *kolot* (shofar blasts), the original practice in the time of the Talmud (as described by the Rambam, *Hilchot Shofar* 3:10), as opposed to the 100 *kolot* sounded by other Jews. Yemenite Jews are the only Jews who still practice *atifat harosh* (covering the head with a *tallit*) and *ḥalitzat katef* (exposing the shoulder) during *shiva*, as is the original practice presented in the *gemara* (*Mo'ed Katan* 22b).

The most famous example of Yemenite halachic conservatism relates to *Ḥerem D'Rabbenu Gershom*, which prohibited marrying more than one wife. Whether de facto or de jure, Temanim did not accept the practice to refrain from marrying more than one wife. Until their arrival in Eretz Yisrael, they continued the original practice to marry more than one wife.[4]

ELEMENT #2: MAINTAINING TRADITIONS

There is a distinct advantage to the ultra-conservative bent of Yemenite Jews. As a result of their extraordinarily strong inclination to preserve the past, they have succeeded in preserving many of our traditions (*mesora*) that have been lost by most other Jews over the centuries.

Rashi (*Vayikra* 11:22) already notes the loss of the tradition as to how to distinguish between kosher and non-kosher grasshoppers. Temani Jews have kept this tradition alive. The same applies to the processes of *nikur*

3. As noted by Rav Zecharia Ben-Shlomo, *Orot HaHalacha*, p. 819.
4. Although today even Temanim refrain from marrying more than one wife, in case of a woman's *get* recalcitrance, a recognized and competent *bet din* has considerable flexibility in relieving a Yemenite male from his predicament. Yemenite Jews neither accepted the *Ḥerem D'Rabbenu Gershom*, nor do they incorporate into their *ketubot* a solemn oath to refrain from marrying more than one wife, as other Sephardim did.

ḥelev and *gid hanasheh* (removing forbidden fats and sinews from slaughtered animals). Rav Eliezer Melamed explains:

> The accepted custom in Israel today goes according to *nikur Yerushalmi,* i.e. to be very stringent and to perform *nikur* on everything that is close and similar to *ḥelev* and the branches of the *gid hanasheh* and its fats, to the point that approximately 13–25% of the weight of the hind flesh is lost. Only the immigrants from two communities, Yemen and Morocco, meticulously guarded the tradition of *nikur,* according to which only about 5% of the weight of the hind flesh is lost.[5]

Similarly, although many Sephardic Jews maintained a tradition to bake soft *matzot,* the Temanim are the most renowned for their fidelity to this practice.

ELEMENT #3: ALLEGIANCE TO THE RAMBAM

As is well-known, Yemenite Jews had a very close relationship with the Rambam. The Rambam's grandson, Rav David HaNagid, reports that Yemenite Jews posed more questions to the Rambam than any other group of Jews. This special bond is maintained to this day, although to varying degrees, as we will discuss in our next chapter.

Temanim follow rulings of the Rambam that most other Jews do not accept. One example is the practice to recite a *beracha* upon entering a *sukka* even if one is not going to eat in the *sukka* (as per *Hilchot Sukka* 6:12). Another is allowing reheating of liquids (such as soup) on Shabbat that were cooked before Shabbat. Many Temanim follow the Rambam's ruling (*Hilchot Shabbat* 22:8) that the rule of "*en bishul aḥar bishul*" applies even to liquids.[6]

Most famously, Temanim respond "*Halleluya*" to each section of *Hallel,* for a total of no less than 123 times, in accordance with the Rambam's ruling (*Hilchot Ḥanukka* 3:12). Temanim similarly follow the Rambam's

5. http://www.israelnationalnews.com/Articles/Article.aspx/23093.
6. As noted in Chapter 33, Rav Melamed writes that it is permissible for all Jews to consume soup (even when it is hot) when served at a home of a Yemenite Jew who follows his ancestral practice. The *Yalkut Yosef* (*Oraḥ Ḥayim* 253:11) similarly permits food cooked in accordance with legitimate opinions even when the one eating the food does not usually follow that lenient approach.

requirement (*Hilchot Ma'achalot Assurot* 6:10) that meat be boiled (*ḥalita*) after salting to seal in any remaining blood. The *Shulḥan Aruch* (*Yoreh De'ah* 69:19), by contrast, does not require *ḥalita*.

Interestingly, many Yemenite Jews recite a *Borei Peri HaJofan* on all four cups of wine at the *seder*, in accordance with the ruling of the Rambam (*Hilchot Ḥametz U'Matza* 8:5, 10). This stands in sharp contrast to Sephardic Jews, who follow the *Shulḥan Aruch*'s ruling to recite *Borei Peri HaGefen* only on the first and third *kosot* (*Shulḥan Aruch, Oraḥ Ḥayim* 474:1, 480:1).

The custom accepted by the *Shulḥan Aruch* (*Oraḥ Ḥayim* 46:1) is to recite all the *Birkot HaShaḥar* at once, so as not to forget one of them. However, the original enactment of *Ḥazal* was for the *Birkot HaShaḥar* to accompany the process of arising in the morning and for everything to be blessed adjacent to its benefit (*Berachot* 60b). This is how the Rambam (*Hilchot Tefilla* 7:9) ruled in practice – but it is only in the Yemenite community that some still follow this custom to this day.

ELEMENT #4: UNIQUE PRACTICES

Yemenites maintain some unique practices, many of which are well-known. Whereas the Ashkenazic and Sefardic *shofar* is made from the horn of a domestic ram, a Yemenite *shofar* is made from the horn of an African kudu and has an elongated and curvy body. Interestingly, Yemenite Jews developed the practice to use this type of *shofar* in light of the preference to use the horn of a ram in order to invoke the memory of *akedat Yitzḥak* (see *Rosh Hashana* 16a).

The Yemenite *etrog* is also well known as a classic example of a type of *etrog* with a highly respected *mesora* that ensures it was not grafted with a lemon. The Temani *etrog* is distinguished by its lack of pulp. Yemenite Jews typically use a very large *Etrog*, somewhat reminiscent of the story recorded in the *gemara* (*Sukka* 36b) about the extraordinarily large *etrog* that Rabbi Akiva brought to his *bet kenesset*.[7]

It is also well-known that many Yemenites tie their *tzitzit* in a manner consistent with that which is set forth in the Rambam (*Hilchot Tzitzit* 1:6).

---

7. Yemenite *etrogim* were the *etrogim* of choice of Rav Ben Tzion Abba Sha'ul. For a review of the range of *etrogim* with a distinguished pedigree, see Rav Mordechai Lebhar's essay at https://theshc.org/an-etrog-or-a-lemon-2/.

Less well known is the Yemenite practice to eat roasted meat at the *seder*. The *mishna* (*Pesaḥim* 53a) records the differing communal practices as to whether roasted meat is consumed on the first night of Pesaḥ. The potential concern is the appearance that one is partaking of the *Korban Pesaḥ* (which was roasted) outside of the *Bet HaMikdash*. The *Mishna Berura* (476:1), *Aruch HaShulḥan* (*Oraḥ Ḥayim* 476:1), and Rav Ovadia Yosef (*Teshuvot Yeḥaveh Da'at* 3:27) all record that the *Aḥaronim* agree that the custom is to refrain from roasted meat on the night of Pesaḥ. The Yemenite community is the only Jewish community that still consumes roasted meat on the *seder* night!

CONCLUSION

One's knowledge of Jewish practice is not complete without awareness of Yemenite practices. When noting Jewish practices, one should be cognizant to note Ashkenazic, Sephardic, and Yemenite practices. Although outside of Israel Yemenite congregations are relatively few in number, in Israel their presence is keenly felt. Most Israeli communities boast not only Ashkenazic and Sephardic *batei kenesset*, but a Yemenite one as well. Our investment in discovering Yemenite practice is well worth the effort, as only when including Yemenite practice is the picture of Jewish practice complete.

Chapter 94

A Brief Sketch of Yemenite Halachic History

As we noted in the previous chapter, one cannot appreciate the full spectrum of halachic practice unless one takes in account the practices of Yemenite Jews. However, one can understand Yemenite Halacha only if one learns the basics of its history.

GEONIC PERIOD

The Jewish community in Yemen was extremely ancient and extremely geographically distant from other Jewish communities. Nevertheless, a key aspect of Yemenite (Temani) Jewish life is that Yemenite Jews – in contrast with other Jewish communities located at the outskirts of the Exile, such as Ethiopian Jewry – maintained contact with Jews worldwide throughout their many centuries in Yemen. Accordingly, the Jews in Yemen were aware of and fully observed Ḥanukka and Purim and were fully aware and practices that presented in the Mishna and Gemara.

There is evidence to this already dating to the time of the *Ge'onim*. The *Sha'arei Teshuva* (99), a collection of Geonic response, records that the *Ge'onim* in Babylon received inquiries regarding observance of Halacha from Jews all over the world, including Teman (Yemen) and Spain. The *Teshuvot*

HaGeonim (386 [Harkavy ed.]) specifically mentions the financial donations made by the Yemenite Jewish communities to the *yeshivot* in Babylon in exchange for providing halachic support.

This means that despite geographic distance, the Jews of Yemen made a great and successful effort to remain full-fledged members of the Jewish halachic mainstream. This explains why no halachic authority has ever questioned the Jewish status of the Jews of Yemen.

THE RAMBAM

The peak of Yemenite interaction with Jews outside its adopted land is their loving connection with the Rambam. The Rambam records in his famous *Iggeret Teman* how Jewish travelers reported regarding the very warm welcome they received when they visited Yemen. The travelers further reported that the Jews of Yemen were learned in Torah, fully observant of all the *mitzvot*, and thoroughly committed to both the Written and Oral Law.

In *Iggeret Teman*, the Rambam offered much needed encouragement to the Jews of Yemen, who were being persecuted by their Islamic rulers and were coping with a Jew claiming to be the *Mashiaḥ*. The Rambam in his letter showed Yemenite Jewry how Islam is false and that the Jew claiming to be the Messiah was false as well. The Rambam struck the perfect balance between encouragement and realistic appraisal of the Jews' situation. In doing so, the Rambam won the wholehearted devotion of the Jews of Yemen.

The Rambam wrote many halachic responsa to the Jews of Yemen. In fact, the Rambam's grandson, Rav David HaNagid, reports that the Rambam received more questions from the Jews of Yemen than from any other community.

The Ramban (letter 2 in *Kitvei HaRamban* [Chavel ed.]) records how the Rambam even used his political connections to relieve the Jews of Yemen from terribly burdensome taxes. The Jews of Yemen, continues the Ramban, loved the Rambam so much that they famously added a line to the *Kaddish* praying for his welfare during his lifetime: *"B'hayei d'Rabbana Moshe ben Maimon."*

Needless to say, the Jews of Yemen unreservedly embraced the Rambam as their halachic authority at this point.

THE MAWZA EXILE

The Jews of Yemen struggled, but they maintained Jewish life blessed with stability and success – until catastrophe struck. The Exile of Mawza

(1679–1680) was an extremely traumatic event for the Jews of Yemen, as Jews living in nearly all cities and towns in Yemen were banished by decree of the king, Iman al-Mahdi Ahmad, and sent to Mawza, a dry and barren region of the country.

Galut Mawza, as it is referred to by Yemenite Jews, caused a severe disruption in Jewish life. Approximately half of the Jews of Yemen died as a result of this horrific experience, including many of its great *Rabbanim* and leaders. The Jews' homes were confiscated by their Arab neighbors, Jewish manuscripts were lost, and the community had to rebuild itself nearly from scratch both materially and spiritually. *Galut Mawza* led to a serious disruption in the Torah traditions of the Yemenite community, and in the following decades Yemenite Jews endeavored to restore its equilibrium.

THE *SHETIL ZETIM* VS. THE MAHARITZ

Soon after the return from exile, the community produced two of its greatest halachic leaders, Rav David Mishrequi, the author of the *Shetilei Zetim* and the *Ravid HaZahav,* and Rav David's student Rav Yiḥyeh Tzalaḥ, known as the Maharitz. The Maharitz authored very important responsa and commentaries and is regarded as the primary halachic authority for Yemenite Jews.

The *Shetilei Zetim* and the Maharitz had a fundamental disagreement regarding the primary halachic authority of Yemenite Jews. The *Shetilei Zetim* felt that since Jews worldwide had accepted the authority of Rav Yosef Karo and the *Shulḥan Aruch,* Yemenite Jews should follow suit and remain in the halachic mainstream. The Maharitz, however, argued for maintaining traditional Yemenite customs and fidelity to the Rambam's rulings.

BALADI AND SHAMI

Neither the *Shetilei Zetim* nor the Maharitz were rigid in their respective approaches. The Maharitz was willing to accept some new customs accepted by the worldwide Jewish mainstream, and the *Shetilei Zetim* sometimes advocated for retaining some specific traditional Yemenite practices. However, the essential difference between their approaches led to a famous split among Yemenite Jews. Baladi Jews follow the Maharitz, whereas the Shami faction follows in the footsteps of the *Shetilei Zetim.*

Interestingly, even Shami Jews preserve many original Yemenite customs, such as eating meat until the *se'uda hamafseket* on the eve of Tisha B'Av and boiling meat after salting. The Baladi Jews similarly follow some practices set forth in the *Shulḥan Aruch* (*Oraḥ Ḥayim* 581:1), such as reciting *Seliḥot* all forty days from Rosh Ḥodesh Elul until Yom Kippur, despite the fact that this runs counter to the Rambam (*Hilchot Teshuva* 3:4), who describes *Seliḥot* as being recited only during the *Aseret Yemei Teshuva.*

A classic difference between the groups is that Baladi do not recite a *beracha* on *Hallel* on the night of Pesaḥ in the *bet keneset,* since the Rambam makes no mention of this *Hallel.* Shami, however, do recite a *beracha,* in accordance with the ruling of the *Shulḥan Aruch* (*Oraḥ Ḥayim* 587:4).

Similarly, Baladi recite a *Borei Peri HaJofan* on all four cups of wine at the *seder,* in accordance with the ruling of the Rambam (*Hilchot Ḥametz U'Matza* 8:5, 10), whereas Shami follow the *Shulḥan Aruch*'s ruling to recite a *beracha* only on the first and third *kosot* (*Shulḥan Aruch, Oraḥ Ḥayim* 474:1, 480:1).

Most famously, the Baladi *siddur* (*Tiklal*) follows the traditional Yemenite liturgy, which is heavily influenced by the Rambam, whereas the Shami group uses a *siddur* that incorporates the teachings of the Ari z"l and approximates the *siddurim* used by many Sephardic Jews.

Notably, the fact that there are different groups among Yemenite Jews does not create a source of conflict, as each group respects and often visits the synagogues of the other group. Indeed, the late twentieth-century leader of the Yemenite Jewish community in Israel, Rav Yosef Sabari, made an effort to try to blend the Baladi and Shami *minhagim* and create a united Yemenite practice.

RAV OVADIA YOSEF VS. RAV RATZABI

Further debate emerged in the twentieth-century upon the blessed return of Yemenite Jews to Eretz Yisrael. Rav Ovadia Yosef (*Teshuvot Yeḥaveh Da'at* 1:27) argues that now that they are in Eretz Yisrael, Yemenites should follow the rulings of the *Shulḥan Aruch.*[1] For example, the Yemenite practice is to follow the Rambam (*Hilchot Berachot* 11:3; *Hilchot Shabbat* 5), who makes no mention of lighting candles on Yom Tov; they therefore do not recite a *beracha* on the lighting of Yom Tov candles (Rav Yiḥyeh Tzalaḥ, *Teshuvot Pe'ulot Tzadik* 3:270). Rav Ovadia argues that in Israel, Yemenites should follow the *Shulḥan Aruch*'s ruling (*Oraḥ Ḥayim* 263:5, 514:11) to recite a *beracha* before lighting Yom Tov candles.

---

1. For further discussion of this debate, see Chapter 93, dedicated to this topic below.

The leading Yemenite sage Rav Yitzḥak Ratzabi, in his work *Ner Yom Tov*, strongly argues with Rav Ovadia concerning this specific point, as well as his overall agenda to convince Yemenite Jews to abandon their practices in favor of the rulings of Rav Yosef Karo.

Another example is the Yemenite practice to follow the Rambam (*Hilchot Ta'aniot* 5:7), who forbids eating meat only for the meal immediately preceding Tisha B'Av (*se'uda hamafseket*), in accordance with the *mishna* and *gemara* (*Ta'anit* 26b). Once again, Rav Ovadia (*Ḥazon Ovadia, Arba Ta'aniot*, p. 170) insists that Yemenites accept the ruling of Maran Rav Yosef Karo in this context.

Rav Zecharia Ben-Shlomo (*Orot HaHalacha*, p. 752) notes, however, that the Yemenite community has not accepted this ruling and continues to eat meat until the *se'uda hamafeseket* on Erev Tisha B'Av.

CONCLUSION

Yemenite *minhagim* are incredibly rich and fascinating. They add the final touches to the full picture of Jewish practice. Yemenite Jews tenaciously maintained their practices in face of enormous pressure throughout the centuries. Fortunately, this precious component of our people has been preserved, and with *Hashem*'s help, Temanim remain a vibrant community whose practices add a special flavor and dimension to the complete halachic spectrum.

Chapter 95

A Yemenite *Sefer Torah*

A congregant at a Sephardic congregation posed a poignant question: A Yemenite *Sefer Torah* had been donated to his Sephardic *kehilla,* and the congregant heard that a Yemenite *Sefer Torah* differs from the *sifrei Torah* of other Jews. He wondered whether these differences rendered the Torah invalid for use by those who are not part of the Yemenite Jewish community.

SEPHARDIC JEWS USING AN ASHKENAZIC *SEFER TORAH* (AND VICE VERSA)

There is a near consensus of halachic opinion that Sephardic Jews and Ashkenazic Jews fulfill their obligation if they hear Torah reading from each other's Torah scrolls. The *Kaf HaḤayim* (*Oraḥ Ḥayim* 143:34) already records in the early twentieth-century that the practice had emerged in Jerusalem that Sephardim and Ashkenazim receive *aliyot* and recite *berachot* on each other's *sifrei Torah.*[1]

This is because the only difference between the Torah scrolls is the different manner in which certain letters, such as the *tzadi* and *shin,* are

1. Of course, all agree that each community should acquire a Torah written in accordance with its traditions for their respective *batei kenesset.* However, if no Torah written in accordance with its community's tradition is available, a *sefer Torah* of the differing community may be used.

written. The *Kaf HaḤayim* explains that these differences are insufficient to disqualify a *sefer Torah* for the other *edah* (community). Indeed, the Ari z"l wrote that all the formations of the letters, according to both traditions, have deep and profound meaning, and we apply here the rule of "*elu va'elu divrei Elokim ḥayim*" (they both represent the authentic teaching of *Hashem*).[2]

A wide variety of *posekim* subscribe to this opinion, including Rav Ovadia Yosef (*Teshuvot Yeḥaveh Da'at* 2:3; *Yalkut Yosef, Oraḥ Ḥayim* 685:12), Rav Zvi Pesaḥ Frank (*Teshuvot Har Zvi, Oraḥ Ḥayim* 132), and Rav Yitzḥak Weisz (*Teshuvot Minḥat Yitzḥak* 4:27:1). Rav Weisz' responsum is particularly noteworthy in that he cites an oral communication from the *Ḥazon Ish* agreeing with this assertion, despite the *Ḥazon Ish*'s reservations regarding how Sephardic Jews (and those Ashkenazim who follow Nusaḥ Sefard) write the letter *tzadi*.

SEPHARDIC AND ASHKENAZIC JEWS USING A YEMENITE TORAH SCROLL

The *Kaf HaḤayim* (*Oraḥ Ḥayim* 143:34), however, rules that a Yemenite *sefer Torah* is not acceptable for either Sephardic or Ashkenazic Jews, as there are substantial differences between the Yemenite scroll and the other *sifrei Torah*. One well-known difference is the text of *Bereishit* 9:29. Yemenite Torah scrolls have, "*Vayehiyu kol yemei Noaḥ*," whereas other *sifrei Torah* state, "*V'yehi kol yemei Noaḥ*." Another difference relates to the spelling of

2. However, Sephardic men do not fulfill the *mitzva* of *tefillin* if they use *tefillin* written in accordance with Ashkenazic tradition (*Teshuvot Yeḥaveh Da'at* 4:3). This is not due to the different styles of writing certain letters, but rather to the fact that Rav Yosef Karo rules (*Shulḥan Aruch, Oraḥ Ḥayim* 32:36) that an empty space the length of nine letters is left between the third and fourth paragraphs, whereas according to the *Taz* (*Oraḥ Ḥayim* 32:26), empty space is left both at the end of the third paragraph and at the beginning of the fourth paragraph. In the view of Rav Yosef Karo, leaving additional empty space beyond what is required invalidates the *tefillin*. Thus, *tefillin* prepared in accordance with the view of the *Taz* are invalid according to *Maran* Rav Karo. Ashkenazim, by and large, prepare *tefillin* following the *Taz*'s opinion, and these *tefillin* are thus invalid for Sephardim, who follow the rulings of the *Shulḥan Aruch*.

Rav Ben Tzion Abba Sha'ul (*Teshuvot Ohr L'Tzion* 2:3:7) concurs with Rav Ovadia's ruling. However, he adds that if Ashkenazic *tefillin* are the only *tefillin* available to a Sephardic man, they should be worn, but the *beracha* omitted.

the word "*daka*" (*Devarim* 23:2). The Yemenite tradition is to write an *alef* as the last letter, whereas the other traditions write it with a *heh*.[3]

However, Rav Ovadia Yosef (*Teshuvot Yeḥaveh Da'at* 6:56) disagrees with the *Kaf HaḤayim* and endorses the use of Yemenite *sifrei Torah* by all Jews. He notes that there are only two differences in the lettering of the Yemenite Torah scroll, and there has been considerable dispute recorded in classic and authoritative sources (such as the *Minḥat Shai*) regarding the spelling of these two words. There is ample support for both the Yemenite tradition and the tradition of the rest of *Am Yisrael*. Thus, Rav Ovadia concludes that it is acceptable for all Jews to use a Yemenite *sefer Torah*.

Rav Ovadia adds eye-opening statements from Rabbenu Avraham ben HaRambam (*Teshuvot* 91) and the Meiri (*Kiddushin* 30a). Both of these *Rishonim* assert that there is no certain and definitive Torah scroll, such that one could possibly disqualify a Torah written in accordance with a different tradition. A Torah scroll is considered invalid only if no Jewish community maintains a tradition to write such a *sefer Torah*.

Indeed, Rav Ovadia Yosef points us to a remarkable note of Rabbi Akiva Eiger (*Shabbat* 55b), who records more than a dozen instances in which the spelling of words in the Torah scroll differs slightly from the manner in which the Talmud cites the word from the *pasuk*. This convincingly and irrefutably corroborates the point made by Rabbenu Avraham ben HaRambam and the Meiri.

Accordingly, no community has the ability to claim that its Torah is definitely correct and the others are invalid. In all of the areas of the slight and highly nuanced differences between the Yemenite *sifrei Torah* and the other Torah scrolls, there are considerable sources that support both the Yemenite tradition on the one hand and the Sephardic and Ashkenazic traditions on the other.

CONCLUSION

We should note that according to the *Kaf HaḤayim*, those who are not Ḥabad Ḥassidim cannot use a Ḥabad *sefer Torah*, since Ḥabad *sifrei Torah*

---

3. See https://en.wikipedia.org/wiki/Torah_scroll_(Yemenite) for a comprehensive listing of the other more minor differences between a Yemenite Torah scroll and Ashkenazic and Sephardic *sifrei Torah*.

also spell "*daka*" with an *alef* at the end, as in the Yemenite *sifrei Torah*.[4] The fact that so many Jews who do not follow Ḥabad practice recite *berachot* on Ḥabad *sifrei Torah* demonstrate that the ruling of the *Kaf HaḤayim* has been rejected in practice in favor of the ruling of Rav Ovadia.

Thus, I told the gentleman who inquired about the *sefer Torah* that it is undoubtedly acceptable for all Jews to use a Yemenite *sefer Torah*, despite the small number of very minor differences between the scrolls. Rav Ḥayim David HaLevy supports this position as well (*Teshuvot Aseh Lecha Rav* 8:44, *She'ilot U'Teshuvot Ketzarot* section).

Nevertheless, Rav Shmuel Khoshkerman informed me that the general custom *l'chatḥila* is to try to avoid using a Yemenite *sefer Torah*. Indeed, Rav Yitzḥak Yosef (*En Yitzḥak, Kelalei HaHora'a* 15) writes that it is preferable for non-Yemenite Jews to avoid using a Yemenite *sefer Torah*.

4. This follows the ruling of the first Lubavitcher Rebbe, Rav Shneur Zalman of Liadi. Interestingly, both the Leningrad Codex and Aleppo Codex, two very ancient and authoritative Torah codexes, present the word "*daka*" with an *alef* at the end of the word, in accordance with the Yemenite and Ḥabad scrolls.

Chapter 96

Must Moroccan and Yemenite Jews Abandon their Ancestral Practices in Israel?

Rav Ovadia Yosef famously calls upon all Sephardic Jews to abandon the unique practices imported to Israel from their exile communities in favor of adopting the practices of Rav Yosef Karo. Rav Ovadia claims that Rav Karo is the *Mara D'Atra*, halachic authority, of the Land of Israel. Thus, Rav Ovadia argues, Rav Karo's rulings override practices observed while living in exile communities.

Rav Ovadia addressed this assertion to all Sephardic communities, particularly to Moroccan and Yemenite communities, whose practices vary considerably from those promulgated by Rav Ovadia and his sons. Not surprisingly, Rav Ovadia's approach to this issue has been greeted with a mixed reception, and many Sephardic Jews in Israel do maintain their communities' distinctive practices.

THE MOROCCAN RESPONSE

Darké Abotenou, the recently published compendium and analysis of the customs of the Jews of Morocco that we described in Chapter 91, presents a cogent rebuttal of Rav Ovadia's approach. The authors note that Moroccan Jews do adhere to the rulings of Rav Yosef Karo, apart from certain exceptional circumstances. They further note that even Rav Ovadia does not always adhere to the rulings of Rav Yosef Karo. In fact, there are five examples where Moroccan Jews adhere to Rav Karo's ruling when Rav Ovadia does not!

Regarding *brit mila*, Moroccan Jews follow Rav Karo's ruling to recite the *beracha* between the initial cut and *peri'a* (the second part of *mila*), whereas Rav Ovadia rules that the *beracha* is recited before the cut begins.[1] Rav Ovadia rules that *Hoshanot* should not be recited on the Shabbat of Sukkot, whereas Moroccan Jews (as well as Syrian and Turkish Jews) follow Rav Karo's ruling and do recite *Hoshanot*.[2] Moroccan Jews do not don *tefillin* in the morning of Tisha B'Av, following the *Shulḥan Aruch*'s ruling, unlike Rav Ovadia, who encourages doing so. Rav Ovadia rules that the *ḥazan* should prompt the *Kohanim* with the first word of *Birkat Kohanim*, "*Yevarechecha*," whereas Moroccan Jews follow Rav Karo's ruling to refrain from doing so. Finally, Moroccan Jews follow Rav Karo's ruling to recite *Anenu* even during the *Arvit* of fast days, unlike Rav Ovadia, who rules that it is recited only at *Shaḥarit* and *Minḥa*.[3]

Accordingly, the venerable Moroccan sage Rav Shalom Messas, who loved and profoundly revered Rav Ovadia, respectfully but pointedly rejects Rav Ovadia's insistence that Moroccan Jews abandon their unique practices once they have come to Israel.

Rav Messas argues that just as Rav Ovadia's follows his traditions as to when it is appropriate to deviate from Rav Karo's rulings, Moroccan Jews are entitled to adhere to their traditions as to when they do not adhere to Rav Karo's rulings. In addition, Rav Yosef Karo himself wrote (*Teshuvot Avkat Rochel* 212) that any community that comes to Eretz Yisrael and establishes its own *bet kenesset* is obligated to maintain its prior customs.

---

1. See our discussion of this topic in Chapter 28.
2. The *Shulḥan Aruch* (*Oraḥ Ḥayim* 660:3) records that the custom is to recite *Hoshanot* on Shabbat *Ḥol HaMo'ed* Sukkot, whereas Rav Ovadia (*Teshuvot Yeḥaveh Da'at* 2:75) endorses that Minhag Yerushalayim (as noted by the *Ḥida, Birkei Yosef, Oraḥ Ḥayim* 660:3) to omit the *Hoshanot* on Shabbat *Ḥol HaMo'ed*.
3. We discuss these issues at length in Chapters 17, 65, and 67.

Moreover, there is ample precedent for Rav Messas's rejection of Rav Ovadia's approach. *Darké Abotenou* (*Darké Abotenou* 75) records:

> Ribi Refael Elazar HaLevy ibn Tobu, author of *Pekudat Elazar*, came from Morocco to Jerusalem in the early nineteenth century and established a *bet kenesset* that followed Moroccan customs. He writes (*Pekudat Elazar* 51:9) that a certain Ribi Moshe Nehemias suggested that they change the custom to that of Jerusalem, but in the end Ribi Refael Elazar HaLevy ibn Tobu ruled to continue the ancient Moroccan custom, since Jerusalem is a city of many established communities and customs. When the Yemenites came to Israel [in the early twentieth-century], the same discussion took place involving Ribi Avraham Hayim Nadoff. He writes that they kept their customs even though many advised them to change them.

As noted in Chapter 94, the leading Yemenite sage Rav Yitzḥak Ratzabi strongly argues with Rav Ovadia concerning his overall agenda to convince Yemenite Jews to abandon their practices in favor of the rulings of Rav Yosef Karo.

CONCLUSION

Rav Shalom's rebuttal of Rav Ovadia's ruling is most convincing. In fact, Rav Mordechai Eliyahu and Rav Yosef Shalom Elyashiv support Rav Shalom's ruling. In practice, many Moroccan Jews in Israel maintain their distinctive practices, though many have adopted the rulings of Rav Ovadia and Rav Yitzḥak Yosef. The same may be said of the Yemenite community, as we have seen.

Rav Shmuel Koshkerman reports that the accepted practice in Sephardic and Yemenite communities is that ancestral practices may be maintained even when they reach Eretz Yisrael and even when they run counter to the ruling of Rav Yosef Karo.

Tributes

Chapter 97

Rav Ovadia Yosef: In a Class by Himself

The post-World War II generations have been blessed with many great Torah scholars, such as my teacher Rav Yosef Dov Soloveitchik, Rav Moshe Feinstein, the Lubavitcher Rebbe, and Rav Shlomo Zalman Auerbach, to name but a few. The impact of these great *Rabbanim* might be measured by the attendance at their funerals, which ranged from 100,000 to 300,000 people. The attendance of an estimated one million people at the October 2013 funeral of Rav Ovadia Yosef is an indication of the enormous impact that Rav Ovadia had on the Jewish People.

The reaction to the death of Rav Ovadia may be compared to the weeping of all the Jewish People in response to the death of Aharon (Rashi, *Bemidbar* 20:29). Indeed, the fact that a moment of silence was observed at Israeli soccer games held soon after Rav Ovadia's death demonstrates the profound impact Rav Ovadia had even upon those far from the world of the *bet midrash* and *yeshiva*.

In this chapter, I seek to accomplish a difficult goal – to properly assess the greatness of Rav Ovadia. This *hesped* (eulogy) was originally delivered at Congregation Shaarei Orah, the Sephardic Congregation of Teaneck, where I have the privilege to serve as Rav of the *kehilla*, on the

Shabbat that followed Rav Ovadia's passing. I used the style of the *Dayenu* song we recite at our *sedarim* to provide perspective on Rav Ovadia's multi-faceted extraordinary talents and contributions.

FACET #1: EXTRAORDINARY MEMORY AND KNOWLEDGE

Had Rav Ovadia been famous only for his phenomenal memory and knowledge, that alone would suffice to regard him as a *gadol hador*. It is said that Rav Ovadia could complete the sentence of every line in every *sefer* in his voluminous home library. Every page of the dozens of *sefarim* he composed is replete with references to the full range of Torah sources, from the well-known to the most obscure. By way of example, more than five hundred sources appear in his twenty-three page long *teshuva* addressing the use of hot water from a *dud shemesh* (solar water heater) on Shabbat (*Teshuvot Yabia Omer* 4: *Oraḥ Ḥayim* 34)! Each *teshuva* written by Rav Ovadia constitutes a virtual encyclopedia on the topic he addresses.

The following two stories depict his incomparable memory. The Vatican library contains rare manuscripts of the writings of various *Rishonim* that its curators do not permit Jewish scholars to copy. The Rashba's commentary on *Masechet Eruvin* was available at the Vatican, but scholars were only permitted to read it; they were forbidden to photocopy it. The solution was to send Rav Ovadia, who, after reading the Rashba on *Eruvin*, committed the entire commentary to memory. Upon his return to Israel, Rav Ovadia rewrote the Rashba's commentary word for word from memory, which is how we have access to the Rashba to *Masechet Eruvin* today.

At one of Rav Ovadia's *shiurim* in the early 1980s, a skeptical attendee noted each of the sixty-four sources Rav Ovadia cited to support a ruling he had issued. He found it difficult to believe that each of these sources existed. The skeptic proceeded to engage in exhaustive research to investigate the accuracy of each of the sources cited. He found that sixty-three of the sources were accurate, but he thought he had caught Rav Ovadia in an error regarding the sixty-fourth source. He approached Rav Ovadia and told him that he searched throughout Israel for the sixty-fourth source and concluded it did not exist. Rav Yosef explained that he saw the source in a *sefer* he found in a *shteibel* (home synagogue) located in the Borough Park section of Brooklyn, New York.

FACET #2: EXTRAORDINARY *POSEK*

Had Rav Ovadia simply served as a *posek* for routine halachic matters regarding the issues that are addressed in the *Oraḥ Ḥayim* and *Yoreh De'ah* sections of the *Shulḥan Aruch*, it would be sufficient to classify him as a *gadol hador*. Rav Ovadia's *teshuvot* are not mere encyclopedic lists of opinions. He did not come to halachic conclusions simply by adding up the number of authorities who supported a particular approach and then ruling in accordance with the majority. Rav Ovadia addresses each and every issue, exercising skilled and sound halachic and practical judgment that in most cases is just as helpful to Ashkenazic *posekim* as it is to Sephardic *posekim*.[1]

Rav Ovadia often unabashedly supported the lenient approach to many issues, citing the *gemara*'s phrase, "*ko'aḥ d'hetera adif*" (*Betza* 2b; Rashi ad loc., s.v. *d'hetera*). The power of the lenient approach in Halacha is greater, since one must thoroughly master a topic before issuing a lenient ruling.

The most outstanding example of Rav Ovadia adopting a lenient approach is found in his *Sefer Taharat HaBayit*, a comprehensive presentation of *Hilchot Nidda*. The three premier late-twentieth century *sefarim* on this topic are the *Badei HaShulḥan* (written by Rav Feivel Cohen of Brooklyn, New York), the *Shiurei Shevet HaLevy* (the rulings of Rav Shmuel Wosner of Bnei Brak, Israel), and Rav Ovadia's *Taharat HaBayit*. The first two *sefarim* often adopt a stringent approach. *Taharat HaBayit*, on the other hand, is quite lenient regarding many issues. Rav Ovadia felt he needed to compose a work that was appropriate for the entire Jewish People. Indeed, the lives of both Sephardic and Ashkenazic Jews are enhanced by Rav Ovadia's reasonable approach. Had Rav Ovadia not published this work, there would have been a serious void in the Jewish community.

Rav Ovadia did not always adopt the lenient approach, however. In fact, there were certain strict rulings that Rav Ovadia vigorously encouraged, such as wearing the *tefillin* of both Rashi and Rabbenu Tam (*Yalkut Yosef, Kitzur Shulḥan Aruch* 31:3).[2] He also strongly encouraged waiting to end Shabbat until 72 minutes after sunset, in accordance with Rabbenu

1. *Shemirat Shabbat K'Hilchata* extensively quotes from Rav Ovadia, and Rav Hershel Schachter and Rav Mordechai Willig regularly cite Rav Ovadia in their rulings.
2. I heard Rav Ovadia tell a popular audience that their attendance at his *shiur* constitutes evidence that they are on a significantly high spiritual level, such that they should wear Rabbenu Tam's *tefillin* as well as those of Rashi. See our discussion of this topic in Chapter 14.

Tam's strict opinion (see, for example, *Yalkut Yosef, Oraḥ Ḥayim* 624:5), and he insisted that Sephardim eat only meat defined as *glatt* by the highest standards, *ḥalak bet Yosef* (*Teshuvot Yeḥaveh Da'at* 3:56).[3] It is also well-known that Rav Ovadia forbade women from wearing wigs to cover their hair (*Teshuvot Yabia Omer* 5: *Even HaEzer* 5).[4]

Nonetheless, on balance, Rav Ovadia preferred presenting the lenient approach as a viable option so that halachic observance would be practical and accessible for all Jews, not only the halachic elite.

Of course, Rav Ovadia's rulings are of monumental importance for Sephardic Jews. Prior to Rav Ovadia's emergence as a major authority, many Sephardic Jews regarded the *Ben Ish Ḥai* as their primary halachic authority. However, the *Ben Ish Ḥai* was renowned for basing many of his rulings on *Kabbala* and for ruling strictly in many areas of Halacha. Rav Ovadia created a sea change for Sephardic Jews by creating a more lenient halachic option for those for whom the strict approach is not a viable option. Rav Ovadia's *Yalkut Yosef* and *Taharat HaBayit* have created a new option for many Sephardic Jews, opening the door for a much wider circle of observance.

Moreover, the *Yalkut Yosef* (together with Rav David Yosef's *Halacha Berura*) addresses an extraordinary wide range of halachic issues. Although the *Ben Ish Ḥai* is a work of extraordinary importance, it is a one-volume work. The many volumes of *Yalkut Yosef* and *Halacha Berura* allow a Sephardic Jew to obtain straightforward guidance regarding tens of thousands of halachic issues, including the myriad of issues raised by the dramatic technological, social, and political changes of the twentieth and twenty-first centuries.

Finally, it is important to take note that even in his elder years, Rav Ovadia's extraordinary abilities and talents did not wane. That which is said in regard to Moshe Rabbenu, that even towards the end of his life "*lo chahata eno v'lo nas leḥo*," his strength and freshness did not diminish (*Devarim* 34:7), can be wholeheartedly applied to Rav Ovadia's activities as a *posek*.

For example, in the eleventh volume of *Yabia Omer* (*Ḥoshen Mishpat* 20) there appears a cogent *teshuva* written only two years before Rav Ovadia's

3. See our discussion of this topic in Chapter 72.
4. It should be noted that there are major Sephardic *posekim* who disagree with this ruling, including Rav Ovadia Hadaya (*Teshuvot Yaskil Avdi* 7: *Even HaEzer* 16) and Rav Shalom Messas (*Teshuvot Tevu'ot Shamesh, Even HaEzer* 137).

death endorsing the idea of severance pay for fired workers in Israel. In the same volume appear other *teshuvot* written even closer to his death, which very competently deal with matters of the highest importance. For example, Rav Ovadia permits a man to marry a divorcee even though his completely non-observant grandfather informed him that he is a *Kohen*. Rav Ovadia discounts the testimony regarding *Kohen*-status of someone whose family members never attended a *bet kenesset* for five generations (*Even HaEzer* 26). Finally, in a *teshuva* written only a little over than a year before his death, Rav Ovadia writes at length endorsing the *kashrut* of a *get* that seemed to have contained a significant error (*Even HaEzer* 78).

Moreover, in 2010–2011, at the age of ninety, Rav Ovadia composed a masterful and highly authoritative three-volume work, *Ḥazon Ovadia* on *Hilchot Avelut*. What is most impressive is that Rav Ovadia kept current and continued to master the many new *sefarim* that had been introduced during his elder years, including the *Pitḥei Ḥoshen, Halichot Shlomo,* and *Teshuvot Shema Shlomo.*

FACET #3: EXTRAORDINARY *DAYAN*

The area of Halacha in which Rav Ovadia found his most extraordinary greatness is in the area of *dayanut*, in dealing with extremely sensitive matters of personal status. In 1945, at age twenty-five, Rav Ovadia was appointed a *dayan* by the great Sephardic Chief Rabbi Rav Ben Tzion Ḥai Uziel, his first rabbinic position. Rav Ovadia excelled in adjudicating the most delicate cases of *agunot* (women unable to remarry due to uncertainty as to whether their husbands remain alive) and *mamzerut* (ineligibility to marry due to conception from an illicit circumstance).

Rav Ovadia exhibited utmost care, concern, and compassion in this capacity, issuing thousands of creative approaches to permit potential *agunot* and *mamzerim* to marry. Rav Eli Mansour, a leading Sephardic Rav from Brooklyn, New York, stated that of the nine thousand *agunot* that Rav Ovadia ruled were free to remarry, not one of their husbands ever reappeared, corroborating the proper judgment exercised by Rav Ovadia.[5]

Rav Yonah Reiss, presently the *Av Bet Din* of the Chicago Rabbinical Council, recounts that in 2005, he was struggling to find a halachic basis on

5. Rav Mansour stated this at the *hesped* he delivered for Rav Ovadia at Congregation Shaarei Orah in November 2013.

which to rule that a certain individual was not a *mamzer*. After exhaustive research and consultation, Rav Reiss was about to give up. The night after he lost hope, he had a dream in which Rav Ovadia appeared to him and told him not to worry; if he would write down his arguments in favor of declaring the individual to be legitimate, Rav Ovadia would take care of the situation. When Rav Reiss woke up, he resolved to submit his arguments to Rav Ovadia. Sure enough, within a short time, he received a lengthy reply from Rav Ovadia's son-in-law, *Dayan* Rav Ezra bar Shalom, agreeing with the conclusion that the individual was not a *mamzer*, together with a concurrence in writing from Rav Ovadia himself.[6]

Rav Ovadia's greatest hour as a *dayan* occurred in the wake of the 1973 Yom Kippur War, when nearly one thousand wives of married soldiers required halachic verification that their husbands had perished in the war in order for them to remarry. For months, Rav Ovadia focused only on these situations and found halachic permission for each one of these women to remarry. (Rav Ovadia presents the halachic basis at great length in *Teshuvot Yabia Omer* 6: *Even HaEzer* 3.)

In an example of extraordinary heroism, Rav Ovadia delayed emergency heart surgery that his physician ordered he undergo immediately in order to devote a few hours to complete the *teshuva* he was writing to permit an *aguna* to remarry. Rav Ovadia feared that if he died on the operating table, the woman would not find a Rav who would permit her to remarry.

The ruling of Rav Ovadia that had the greatest impact was the ruling he issued as Sephardic Chief Rabbi of the State of Israel that Ethiopian Jews are Jewish, following the rulings of the Radbaz and his student the Maharikash. More than 80,000 Ethiopian Jews were rescued by the State of Israel as a direct result of Rav Ovadia's ruling. In *Teshuvot Yabia Omer* 8: *Even HaEzer* 11), Rav Ovadia vigorously and persuasively articulates his assertion that the rulings of the Radbaz and Maharikash affirming the Jewish identity of Ethiopian Jews invalidate anthropologists' arguments that the Ethiopian Jews are not truly Jewish. Rav Yosef cogently and forcefully defends his ruling against the dissenting opinions of halachic giants, such as Rav Yitzḥak Herzog, Rav Moshe Feinstein, and Rav Eliezer Waldenberg.[7]

6. Rav Reiss records this correspondence in his work *Kanfe Yonah* (21).

7. This issue is discussed at length in Chapter 83.

In his eulogy for Rav Ovadia, Rav Shlomo Aviner related the following poignant anecdote:

> One day in our yeshiva, a student told me that he had gotten engaged. "Mazel Tov! I am happy to hear!" I said. "There is one problem, however," he added. "She is Ethiopian, and I am a *Kohen*." [Some authorities rule that Ethiopians must go through a *giyur l'ḥumra*, a conversion for the sake of stringency, since some question the Ethiopians' Jewish status, and a *Kohen* may not marry a convert.] "Why did you get yourself involved in a complication like that?" I asked. "I didn't think about it," he replied. "I appreciate her and I love her. I didn't notice her color." I sent him to a few different great Rabbis, whose opinions I knew, but they feared putting their rulings in writing. I then turned to *Maran* HaRav Ovadia Yosef. The next day, I received a letter permitting him to marry. "Take it," I said to him, "it is a piece of paper worth a billion dollars."[8]

FACET #4: CONNECTING WITH THE MASSES OF *AM YISRAEL*

Every truly great *gadol b'Yisrael* is not only successful in his discourse with Torah scholars, but is distinguished for his ability to relate to the wide masses of the Jewish People. The *Ben Ish Ḥai* and the *Ḥafetz Ḥayim* commanded the awe and respect of their Rabbinic collegues as well as the broader Jewish community, who flocked to hear their lectures. In the United States, the Lubavitcher Rebbe and Rav Yosef Dov Soloveitchik attracted both the greatest scholars as well as thousands of ordinary Jews to their speeches.

The rousing *haskamot* (Rabbinic endorsements) of the first two volumes of *Teshuvot Yabia Omer* from Jerusalem's greatest *posekim* in 1954–1955, Rav Zvi Pesaḥ Frank, Rav Yitzḥak Herzog, Rav Dov Ber Weidenfeld (author of *Teshuvot Dovev Mesharim*), Rav Shlomo Zalman Auerbach, and Rav Yosef Shalom Eliashiv, testify as one hundred witnesses to the great respect to which Rav Ovadia was held by the greatest of his older and contemporary Rabbinic colleagues. The fact that nearly a million Jews attended Rav Ovadia's funeral stands in awesome testimony of the ability of Rav Ovadia to connect with the masses of Jews. His radio broadcasts and his Motza'ei

8. http://www.ravaviner.com/2013/10/ha-gaon-ha-rav-ovadiah-yosef-ztzl.html.

Shabbat *shiurim*, which were televised via closed circuit television worldwide, attracted thousands of devotees. I recall as a Yeshiva student in Israel in 1981–1983 very much enjoying listening to Rav Ovadia's radio broadcasts on Friday afternoon. I, together with tens of thousands of listeners, was enthralled with his clear presentation and captivating charismatic manner.

Rav Ovadia was able to move vast audiences to reach closer to *Hashem* and His holy Torah. Tens of thousands of people would throng to hear Rav Ovadia deliver words of inspiration before *Seliḥot* recited a few days before Yom Kippur at the Kotel. He was able to deeply move audiences of thousands at motivational assemblies devoted to bringing Jews back to their Torah roots. Rav Ovadia knew how to connect with his audiences and brought warmth and a sense of humor that drew his audiences close to him – and, more importantly, to Torah allegiance. He took every opportunity that time and his health permitted to speak throughout Israel, and often throughout the world, to bring his special words of inspiration and spiritual uplift to as many Jews as possible.

Rav Ovadia was also extraordinarily successful in reaching the masses of Jews through his writings. In the 1980s, Rav Ovadia created a new genre of halachic writing with his *Teshuvot Yeḥaveh Da'at*. These were simplified *teshuvot* from which many people, ranging from extraordinary scholar to the average laymen, could learn. Rav Ovadia writes in an engaging, elegant, and concise manner, and the amount of substance he covers in a relatively short space is extraordinary. A prime example is found in *Teshuvot Yeḥaveh Da'at* 1:75, where in only a few pages Rav Ovadia analyzes and summarizes the great volume of halachic literature that addresses the question of whether to first recite *Havdala* or light Ḥanukka candles on the Motza'ei Shabbat of Ḥanukka.

Rav Ovadia helped his son Rav Yitzḥak compose the *Yalkut Yosef*, a true game-changer in the Sephardic community. These multiple and lengthy volumes codify Halacha for routine Jewish life and are summarized in two volumes of a version of the *Kitzur Shulḥan Aruch*. The *Yalkut Yosef* has become a standard work in Sephardic synagogues and homes, as it renders halachic practice in contemporary life accessible to all. Anyone with even just a basic knowledge of Hebrew can easily access these volumes for quick guidance for most halachic issues that a Jew will confront during his lifetime. Finally, Rav Ovadia, with help from his sons, produced Sephardic *siddurim* that provide clear and concise halachic guidance for Sephardic Jews.

Thus, through his countless public lectures and dozens of *sefarim*, Rav Ovadia was able to connect with hundreds of thousands of Jews.

FACET #5: RESTORING THE PRESTIGE OF SEPHARDIC JEWRY

The twentieth century was a time of great upheaval for most of Sephardic Jewry. Sephardim who had been living continuously in Arab countries for many centuries found themselves uprooted by wanton Arab violence in the wake of the 1947 United Nations' decision to partition Eretz Yisrael into Jewish and Arab states. Upon arrival in Israel and elsewhere, Sephardic Jews unfortunately found that their age-old and venerated halachic practices and customs were often not accorded proper respect.

Rav Ovadia led a movement "*l'haḥzir atara l'yoshena,*" to restore the crown of the majestic Sephardic tradition to its original prestige. Three examples in his *Teshuvot Yabia Omer* illustrate this monumental effort.

In *Yabia Omer* 6: *Oraḥ Ḥayim* 10 (a *teshuva* written in 1970), Rav Ovadia responds to a question regarding the *nusaḥ* of prayer at a Yeshiva High School in Afula. More than ninety percent of the students were Sephardic, yet the *tefilla* at the school was conducted utilizing Nusaḥ Sephard (the *nusaḥ* commonly used by Ḥassidic Jews, which is primarily the Ashkenazic text with some Sephardic practices incorporated). The argument was made that this *nusaḥ* prepares the students for service in Tzahal and learning in Yeshivot Bnei Akiva, where the *tefilla* was (in those years) conducted using a similar *nusaḥ* designed to accommodate the mix of Sephardic and Ashkenazic Jews in these venues.[9]

Rav Ovadia forcefully responded that since the overwhelming majority of the students in the Afula Yeshiva High School hailed from Sephardic families, proper Sephardic *siddurim* should be used and Sephardic customs observed. He writes that it is the responsibility of administrators and teachers *l'haḥzir atara l'yoshena,* to teach Sephardic students to take pride in their Sephardic heritage and observe Sephardic practices and customs.

9. Interestingly, today the practice in many or even most of the Yeshivot Bnei Akiva, Yeshivot Hesder, and the Israeli Army is to alternate Sephardic and Ashkenazic *tefilla,* depending on whether an Ashkenazic or Sepahrdic Jew is serving as the *shaliaḥ tzibur* (prayer leader). This practice is attributed to Rav Yehuda Amital, the founding Rosh Yeshiva of Yeshivat Har Etzion, Israel's largest Yeshivat Hesder.

Teshuvot Yabia Omer 10: *Even HaEzer* 34:6 (a *teshuva* from 1957) records a heartrending story of a woman scheduled to remarry whose first *get* was not recognized by the Bet Din of Petah Tikva. The *get* was conducted in Baghdad, Iraq before the woman made *aliya* to Eretz Yisrael. The *Av Bet Din* of Petah Tikvah, the venerable Rav Reuven Katz, was unwell and unable to attend the *bet din* session, and another *dayan*, who was not Sephardic, sat with Rav Ovadia on the *bet din* that day. The *dayan* argued that the woman's *get* was invalid due to improper transliteration of the husband's name, Victor. Rav Ovadia argued vociferously for the *kashrut* of the *get*, since it was transliterated properly according to Sephardic tradition. The *bet din* was deadlocked, and the non-Sephardic *dayan* ordered the woman to postpone her marriage. The woman cried in desperation, since her wedding was scheduled for that very day! Rav Ovadia vigorously defended the validity of the *get* and even resigned from the *bet din* in protest of his colleague's intransigence.

When Rav Katz recovered and returned to the *bet din*, he sustained Rav Ovadia's ruling and arranged for the marriage to take place as soon as possible. He also apologized to both the woman and Rav Ovadia and convinced him to return to the *bet din*. Rav Ovadia concludes his *teshuva*: "This incident is carved in my heart all these years since then until now,[10] and a wise individual should listen and derive a lesson."

On a personal note, when I met Rav Ovadia in 1993 to receive his authorization to administer *gittin*, he urged me in the strongest terms to administer *gittin* for Sephardim in accordance with Sephardic practice and to master the rules of transliterating Arabic, Persian, and other names in accordance with Sephardic standards, as set forth in *sefarim* such as the *Shem Ḥadash*.[11]

A final example may be found in *Teshuvot Yabia Omer* 6: *Even HaEzer* 14. In 1950, the Sephardic and Ashkenazic Chief Rabbis, Rav Ben Tzion Ḥai Uziel and Rav Yitzḥak Herzog, made a number of *takanot* (enactments) to unify the Jewish People. These included the acceptance of *Ḥerem D'Rabbenu Gershom* forbidding polygamy and an agreement that all Jews would eschew *yibum* in all circumstances and opt for *ḥalitza* instead, in accordance with Ashkenazic practice.[12]

---

10. The tenth volume of *Yabia Omer* was published in 2004.
11. For further discussion, see Chapter 85 on Sephardic *gittin*.
12. See the view of Rabbenu Tam presented in *Tosafot*, *Yevamot* 39b, s.v. *Amar Rav*; Rama, *Even HaEzer* 165:1.

Rav Ovadia noted, however, that Sephardic Jews have accepted the rulings of the Rambam (*Hilchot Yibum V'Ḥalitza* 1:2) and *Shulḥan Aruch* (*Even HaEzer* 165:1) that *yibum* is preferred and to be encouraged. In 1951, at the age of 31, Rav Ovadia courageously upheld Sephardic tradition and ruled that the *takana* of the Chief Rabbis was invalid![13] He argued that we are forbidden to abandon our traditional customs and practices.

Rav Ovadia did not make this ruling in a vacuum; he issued it acting as a *dayan* on the Bet Din of Petah Tikva in an actual case. The Sephardic Chief Rabbi of Jerusalem, Rav Shalom Messas, supported Rav Ovadia's bold ruling and followed it in practice in actual *bet din* situations (*Teshuvot Shemesh U'Magen* 1: *Even HaEzer* 8). Rav Eli Mansour notes that the approach of Rav Ovadia and Rav Messas has emerged as the accepted view by Israel's Chief Rabbinate.[14] Indeed, Rav Mordechai Lebhar (*Magen Avot, Even HaEzer* 165) writes that the universal practice among Sephardic Jews both in Israel and outside Israel is to perform *yibum.*[15]

In addition to restoring Sephardic practice to its original glory, Rav Ovadia also revived the use of dozens of *sefarim* of great Sephardic *Aḥaronim* that had tragically become neglected and forgotten. The works of the great eighteenth-century Algerian *posek* Rav Yehuda Ayash, the great eighteenth-century Turkish authority Rav David Pardo, the great nineteenth-century Turkish *posek* Rav Ḥayim Palagi, and the great nineteenth-century Tunisian *posek* Rav Yitzḥak Tayeb are among the many *posekim* and *sefarim* whom Rav Ovadia restored to their original glory

---

13. The full text of Rav Herzog and Rav Uziel's *takana* appears in Rav Herzog's *Teshuvot Hechal Yitzḥak* 1: *Even HaEzer* 5 (p. 51 in the 1960 ed.). It begins by noting that the *takana* was adopted by a unanimous decision at the national convention of the members of the Israeli Rabbinate, and it concludes by imposing a *ḥerem* (communal ban) on anyone who violates it. Nonetheless, the young Rav Ovadia Yosef was not deterred by the ominous threat of *ḥerem,* and instead championed Sephardic tradition, defying the ban both in theory and in practice.

    Despite Rav Ovadia's strong criticism of Rav Uziel's agreement with Rav Herzog regarding *yibum,* Rav Ovadia had great love and respect for both Rav Uziel and Rav Herzog. Rav Ovadia became quite upset at a Rav who did not extend proper respect to Rav Uziel (see the *Halacha Yomit* for October 19, 2018). In his *teshuvot,* Rav Yosef frequently cites both Rav Uziel and Rav Herzog with reverence.
14. Rav Mansour mentioned this in a talk he delivered at the Orthodox Union Day of Torah at Citi Field in April 2018, available at https://www.ou.org/torahny.
15. This refers only to a case in which the brother is not already married.

and now are firmly entrenched on the radar of the once again flourishing world of Sephardic *posekim*.

FACET #6: UNIFYING SEPHARDIC PRACTICE

Yet another major contribution would have been sufficient for us to consider Rav Ovadia the most accomplished Rav during the past half-century. Sephardic Jews hail from a wide variety of countries and maintain a dizzying array of customs. Yemenite Jews, for example, maintain practices that differ significantly from those of Sephardic Jews, and they themselves include major sub-groups (Baladi and Shami). The first generation of immigrants to Israel and elsewhere was able to maintain their specific *minhagim*, since immigrants tend to cluster and reside among those who emigrated from the same region. However, in subsequent generations, people no longer live in such groups. Thus, it is not uncommon to find in one community Sephardim who hail from a wide variety of countries. For example, Congregation Shaarei Orah, the Sephardic Congregation of Teaneck, includes Sephardic families who come from thirteen countries – Algeria, Azerbaijan, Egypt, Greece, Iran, Iraq, Italy, Lebanon, Morocco, Syria, Tunisia, Turkey, and Yemen. Moreover, marriages between the various groups are exceedingly common, *baruch Hashem*.

In such communities, which Sephardic customs should be followed? How can a compromise be forged between the myriad of Sephardic customs? Rav Ovadia came to the rescue with a halachic approach, presenting in *Yalkut Yosef* and in the *siddurim* published under his influence unified customs suitable for all Sephardic Jews. These practices accentuate Minhag Yerushalayim and the rulings of Rav Yosef Karo, the author of the *Shulḥan Aruch*. Rav Ovadia often writes that Rav Karo is the *Mara D'Atra*, the halachic authority for Eretz Yisrael, and ultimately for all Sephardic Jewry. Hundreds of pan-Sephardic *kehillot* in Israel and outside of Israel, such as Congregation Shaarei Orah, rally around the *Yalkut Yosef* and Rav Ovadia's *siddurim* to create a coherent and unified Sephardic custom suitable and appropriate for all Sephardic Jews.

FACET #7: EDUCATING JEWISH CHILDREN

We conclude with what is undoubtedly the most controversial aspect of Rav Ovadia's accomplishments – his political activities. Many *Rabbanim* would argue that *Rabbanim* should stay far removed from politics, since almost by definition politics is divisive and controversial. It is therefore important to understand why Rav Ovadia, in the last thirty years of his life, was not only a leading Rav, *posek*, and *dayan*, but also a significant political leader in Israel as the figurehead of the Shas political party.

Rav Shlomo Aviner, in his aforementioned eulogy for Rav Ovadia, presented a poignant quote from Rav Ovadia that succinctly explains his choice to enter politics in 1984, after completing his ten-year tenure as Sephardic Chief Rabbi of the State of Israel. He cited Rav Ovadia as saying that he could not sleep at night, as he worried about how he could reach ten thousand more Jewish children who would not be reading *keriat Shema*.

Rav Ovadia was a great man who had great ambitions and plans for the Jewish People, especially Sephardic Jewry. He understood that the only manner in which he would be able to make a profound and lasting impact on the education of Jewish children in Israel was by becoming a powerful part of the Israeli government. Rav Ovadia understood that the Israeli government has more influence over Jewish children than all other organizations combined. He realized that if he became an influential part of the Israeli government, his impact could be extraordinary.

Rav Ovadia also recognized that he lived in a time of spiritual crisis and opportunity. The transition into the modern era was a difficult one for many Jews in both the Ashkenazic and Sephardic communities. Tragically, many left Torah observance and ultimately lost their Jewish identity entirely in the course of a few generations. However, in most cases, the Sephardic Jews who stop observing Torah nonetheless remain "traditional." For example, they honor the holidays, light candles and recite *Kiddush* every Friday night, and observe a basic level of *kashrut*, at least at home. Moreover, they retain belief in the fundamentals of Torah belief and respect for Rabbis and Torah.

It is relatively easy to shepherd traditional and believing Sephardim towards Torah belief due to this residual observance and belief. Rav Ovadia knew very well, however, that this style of Jewish observance has a limited "shelf life." Such residual practices and beliefs are difficult to transmit to succeeding generations, and the allegiance to Torah becomes diluted as the generations pass. Thus, Rav Ovadia knew he had a limited window of opportunity to reach out to the masses of traditional Sephardic Jews and *l'haḥzir atara l'yoshena,* to restore full observance and allegiance to a Torah way of life. If he did not act when he did, tens of thousands of families would most likely lose any semblance of Jewish observance for eternity.

Rav Ovadia's political success facilitated the creation of the El HaMa'ayan Sephardic school system. The school day was made extra long to provide parents, especially poor parents, supervision for their children while they were at work. El HaMa'ayan schools also provided quality meals to the children during the longer school hours, making the schools even more attractive to traditional Sephardic Jews, especially to the poor.

This teaching of *keriat Shema* and providing food to tens of thousands of Jewish children could have been accomplished only by the Israeli government and only by those who had major clout in the Israeli government. Rav Ovadia's involvement in politics facilitated teaching Torah and feeding tens of thousands of poor Jews. For this alone, Rav Ovadia deserves to be regarded as a man of extraordinary accomplishments.

It is important to remember that politics anywhere is a very rough and tumble sort of enterprise, and in Israel it is even more so (as anyone who has watched the Kenesset in action has observed). Thus, the words of an Israeli politician will often be expressed sharply and will not be well-received by many. Accordingly, even if we do not agree with everything Rav Ovadia uttered in his role as the leader of a political party, we must understand that Rav Yosef did so in the pursuit of ensuring that as many Jewish children as possible would be adequately fed and taught to read the *Shema*.

However we evaluate his political activity, I am certain that Rav Ovadia's intentions were directed purely and entirely to *Hashem*. My student, Rav Ezra Frazer, reports that when the Orthodox Union decided to open Israeli branches of its NCSY youth outreach program, its leaders met with Rav Ovadia. Rav Ovadia was convinced of the sincerity and Torah fidelity of the program's leaders and said, "I have seventeen members of Kenesset at your service to help further your programs!" Rav Ovadia viewed his political involvement as focused on furthering Torah observance, even through organizations whose style and character differed significantly from Shas schools and programs.

Rav Ovadia had tremendous respect for Rabbanim whose approaches differed from his own. In his writings, Rav Ovadia refers to Religious Zionist *posekim*, such as Rav Kook and Rav Herzog, as "HaRav HaGaon."[16] Rav

16. Similarly, Rav Ovadia refers to Rav Eliashiv as "*yedidenu*," our friend (see, for example, *Teshuvot Yabia Omer* 10: *Even HaEzer* 14), even though the styles of these two eminent Torah scholars differed quite significantly.

Ovadia regularly visited Yeshivot Hesder and Yeshivot Bnei Akiva to deliver *shiurim*; he visited Yeshiva University a number of times and showed deep respect for my teachers, Rav Yosef Dov Soloveitchik and Rav Hershel Schachter. Rav Ovadia endorsed in writing the Rabbinical Council of America's prenuptial agreement, as well as a permission to remarry issued by the Beth Din of America to an *aguna* from the terrorist attack on the World Trade Center (*Teshuvot Yabia Omer* 10: *Even HaEzer* 18).[17] On a personal note, Rav Ovadia's 1993 endorsement of my credentials as a *mesader gittin* (Jewish Divorce Administrator) is a signature, to paraphrase Rav Aviner, worth a billion dollars to both me and the people I have served.

Rav Ovadia's political involvement was intended purely to advance the cause of Torah in a manner that is unparalleled in scope and reach. Thus, I firmly believe that when judged objectively, we can say that had Rav Ovadia only served as the political leader of Shas, he would be considered a great man.

CONCLUSION

Fortunately, Rav Ovadia did not leave us without great leaders to follow in his path, although no one can completely fill his shoes. Among his most outstanding *talmidim* are his son Rav Yitzḥak (the current Sephardic Chief Rabbi of the State of Israel), his son Rav David, Rav Pinḥas Zabihi, Rav Shmuel Pinḥasi, and Rav Shlomo Amar.[18]

Rav Ovadia's wide-ranging Torah accomplishments are in a class by themselves. Looking at events in the Jewish community over the past fifty years, Rav Ovadia's multi-faceted and far-reaching achievements are truly remarkable.

The giant of Torah has fallen, but we are left an unparalleled legacy of greatness that will inspire our and future generations to devote ourselves to excellence in Torah study, activity, and living. We thank *Hashem* for having

17. Rav Ovadia consented to have this *teshuva* translated into English and included in a publication of the Beth Din of America.

18. Rav Ahron Soloveichik stated at the funeral of his brother, Rav Yosef Dov Soloveitchik, that Rav Yosef Dov and his father Rav Moshe rank among the great father-son learning pairs in Jewish history. These include, according to Rav Ahron, Rabbi Shimon Bar Yoḥai and his son Rabbi Elazar, and Rabbi Akiva Eiger and his son Rav Shlomo Eiger. We now may add Rav Ovadia and *yibadel l'ḥayim arukim* his sons, Rav Yitzḥak and Rav David.

sent Rav Ovadia at the perfect time – a time of extraordinary spiritual challenge and crisis – and for giving him the remarkable talents that facilitated his rescue of the spiritual life of hundreds of thousands of Jews worldwide.

Chapter 98

Rav Shalom Messas: The Most Under-Appreciated *Posek* of the Generation

The greatest halachic authority of Moroccan Jewry in recent times was the universally respected and consulted Sephardic Rav of Yerushalayim, Rav Shalom Messas. Rav Shalom is regarded by many as the second-greatest Sephardic *posek* of the prior generation, after Rav Ovadia Yosef.

Rav Shalom was born in 1909 to a family with a long line of first rank Torah scholars, in the city of Meknes, which was renowned for its great Torah scholarship and piety. In 1978, Rav Ovadia, then Chief Rabbi of Israel, asked Rav Shalom to come to the holy city of Yerushalayim and serve as its Sephardic Chief Rabbi, a position in which he served with distinction and acclaim for 26 years, until his passing. When he departed for Eretz Yisrael, Rav Messas was escorted to the airport by Morocco's King Hassan himself, who requested that the rabbi bless him one last time before his departure.

During his tenure as Rav of Yerushalayim, Rav Shalom wrote many *teshuvot* to the great *posekim* of his generation, such as Rav Ovadia, Rav Yosef Shalom Elyashiv, Rav Eliezer Waldenberg, and others.

Rav Ovadia held Rav Shalom in the highest of esteem,[1] even asking Rav Shalom to compose a *haskama* (letter of approbation) to the tenth volume of *Teshuvot Yabia Omer*. Rav Ovadia often cites Rav Shalom as his support in issuing bold halachic decisions regarding matters of personal status, such as *mamzerut* and *aguna* (see, for example, *Teshuvot Yabia Omer* 9: *Even HaEzer* 5, 13). Rav Shalom, in turn, cites Rav Ovadia in support of his bold decisions regarding matters of personal status (see, for example, *Teshuvot Shemesh U'Magen, Even HaEzer* 3:18). Although he had many halachic disputes with Rav Ovadia, they admired each other greatly, as is evident from the countless times that they quote each other in their respective voluminous halachic works.

Rav Messas would not hold back from answering any of his critics, and he would often write back and forth five or six times to those who questioned his rulings, even if they were younger scholars. Rav David Yosef, son of Rav Ovadia, related that he once wanted to argue a matter of Halacha with Rav Shalom and received a warning from his father: "When you argue with Rav Messas, make sure to review your claims ten times!"

Alain Amar of Congregation Shaarei Orah is very close with the Messas family. Alain told me that when Rav Ovadia paid a *shiva* visit to the Messas family upon Rav Shalom's passing, Rav Ovadia told them that whenever he wrote his *teshuvot*, he wrote very cautiously, knowing that Rav Shalom would catch any lapse in rigor and judgment.

WIDENING THE CIRCLE OF RECOGNITION

Anyone who studies Rav Messas' *Teshuvot Tevu'ot Shemesh* and *Teshuvot Shemesh U'Magen* recognizes his greatness. This is similarly apparent to readers of this volume, who have seen our frequent quoting of his brilliant and compelling argumentation. Rav Messas is clearly and undoubtedly in the same class as the *Tzitz Eliezer*, Rav Ovadia, Rav Shlomo Zalman Auerbach, and Rav Yosef Shalom Eliashiv.

---

1. Rav Shmuel Khoshkerman reports that he once asked Rav Ovadia Yosef as to whether Sephardic Jews may rely on the ruling of Rav Moshe Feinstein presented in *Teshuvot Igrot Moshe, Even HaEzer* 1:139. Rav Ovadia, in turn, advised Rav Khoshkerman to pose the question to Rav Messas, who replied that it is permissible for a competent and recognized *bet din* to do so.

Why, then, have many, if not most, Ashkenazic *posekim* – especially those who do not have the merit of residing in Israel – never even heard of him? Rav Messas' lack of recognition in wider circles is reflected in the sad fact that his *teshuvot* do not even appear on the Bar Ilan Responsa website!

I shared this concern with the respected Rav David Bueganim, a prominent Rosh Kollel in Bnei Brak who visited Congregation Shaarei Orah a few years ago. He explained that Rav Messas arrived in Israel at the relatively advanced age of 69. He was preoccupied with *bet din* matters during his years in Eretz Yisrael and did not have the time to devote to traveling to various *yeshivot* so that *talmidim* would become familiar with him. Thus, *dayanim* and many Sephardic *Rabbanim* gained an appreciation for this great man, but outside of those circles, he remained mostly unknown.

Rav Shalom Messas passed away on Shabbat HaGadol 5763 (2003) at the age of 94. Tens of thousands of people flocked from all over Eretz Yisrael and abroad to attend his *levaya,* and he was buried in Har HaMenuḥot in Yerushalayim.

Rav Shalom's *kever* is located in the vicinity of the graves of my wife's grandparents, Hillel and Malca Tokayer *a"h.* Although I did not have the wisdom to visit Rav Messas during his lifetime, I visit his *kever* each time I travel to Israel, asking him to serve as a *melitz yosher* (advocate before *Hashem*) on my family's behalf and that I be successful with both my work as a *mesader get* and as the Rav of Shaarei Orah.

CONCLUSION

Rav Messas' many *sefarim* serve as an enlightening resource to many Torah scholars across the globe, and North African Jewish communities have held on to precious and ancient *minhagim* in accordance with his rulings.[2] We hope that a wider circle of Torah scholars and *posekim* become more aware of his writings and incorporate them in their learning and *piskei Halacha.*

2. Rav Messas frequently and vigorously defends Moroccan *minhagim.* He writes (*Teshuvot Shemesh U'Magen* 3: *Oraḥ Ḥayim* 27): "In my works *Tevu'ot Shemesh* and *Shemesh U'Magen,* I have written with the aim of bolstering our *minhagim* in many areas." He concludes, "All this I have written to strengthen my teachings… not to degrade our *minhagim* even in the slightest."

Chapter 99

Rav Mordechai Eliyahu: A Major Twentieth-Century Sephardic *Posek*

Many Jews outside the Sephardic orbit think that three individuals constitute the corpus of Sephardic Halacha: the Rambam, Rav Yosef Karo, and Rav Ovadia Yosef. Of course, the Rambam was far from the lone Sephardic great *Rishon*, and Rav Yosef Karo is joined by a phalanx of great Sephardic *Aḥaronim*, such as the *Peri Ḥadash* and the *Ḥida*. Rav Ovadia Yosef, in turn, was far from the only great Sephardic *posek* of the second half of the twentieth century. In this chapter, we introduce another twentieth century Sephardic "superstar," Rav Mordechai Eliyahu.

THREE DISTINCTIONS FROM RAV OVADIA

Rav Eliyahu, who served as Israel's Sephardic Chief Rabbi from 1983–1993, adopted a very different style from that of Rav Ovadia Yosef. We can point to three significant differences.

Rav Ovadia did not emphasize *Kabbala*, and his rulings famously differed quite often from those of the great nineteenth-century authority the *Ben Ish Ḥai*, Rav Yosef Ḥayim of Baghdad, who incorporated a great deal of kabbalistic thought and practice in his rulings. Rav Ovadia even composed a multi-volume work entitled *Halichot Olam* in which he defends his deviations from the *Ben Ish Ḥai*'s rulings.

By contrast, Rav Eliyahu retained a fierce loyalty to the rulings and approach of the *Ben Ish Ḥai*. For example, Rav Eliyahu's edition of the *siddur*, *Kol Eliyahu*, and his *sefer Darchei Tahara* are replete with references to the *Ben Ish Ḥai*. This is hardly surprising, considering that Rav Eliyahu's father and grandfather were close to the *Ben Ish Ḥai*, and Rav Eliyahu's wife Mazal was the *Ben Ish Ḥai*'s great-niece. One can fairly assert that Rav Eliyahu presented a contemporary version of the *Ben Ish Ḥai*'s rulings, which are noted by its infusion of kabbalistic influence and an orientation to accommodate a broad base of opinions.

Rav Eliezer Melamed describes Rav Mordechai Eliyahu's approach to Halacha:

> Rav Yosef Ḥayim of Baghdad was unique in that he merged and incorporated all the significant opinions in his halachic rulings. The base of his rulings was the *Bet Yosef* and *Shulḥan Aruch*. However, in addition he considered the other great *posekim*, both Ashkenazic and Sephardic. Rav Eliyahu remarked that at times the *Ben Ish Ḥai* followed the [Ashkenazic] *Magen Avraham* and the *Shulḥan Aruch HaRav*.
>
> Rav Eliyahu continued in this path. He would remark that it is not our role to discover lenient approaches and follow them. Rather, we should find the path to satisfy the consensus opinion, and only in case of pressing need (*sha'at hadeḥak*) rely on the lenient opinions.[1]

This stands in stark contrast to Rav Ovadia Yosef, whose halachic rulings are renowned for their lenient orientation. This difference in orientation is specifically pronounced with regards to *taharat hamishpaḥa* (laws of family purity). Rav Ovadia's three-volume work on this area of Halacha, entitled *Taharat HaBayit*, adopts a far more lenient approach than Rav Eliyahu's *Darchei Tahara*.

A third difference relates to the attitude towards the State of Israel specifically and modernity in general. While Rav Ovadia certainly adopted a positive approach to Medinat Yisrael, Rav Eliyahu was more of an ardent Zionist.

1. https://www.yeshiva.org.il/midrash/14089.

He thus captured the loyalty of Israel's "Ḥaredi Le'umi" (scrupulously observant Zionist) community. He served as a soldier in Israel's War of Independence, enthusiastically embraced Jewish settlement of Yehuda and Shomron, and often visited soldiers in the Israel Defense Forces to offer encouragement.

With regard to modernity, one example highlights a difference between Rav Eliyahu and other great *Rabbanim*. Rav Eliyahu wrote (*Teḥumin,* vol. 3, p. 244) that under current circumstances, religiously observant judges can make a positive contribution to the Israeli civil court system.[2] This is quite a contrast with the stance of Rav Shalom Messas (*Teshuvot Shemesh U'Magen* 3: *Even HaEzer* 44), who invalidated a wedding because one of the witnesses served as a judge in the Israeli civil court system. Although the witness was a practicing Orthodox Jew, Rav Messas claims that anyone who serves as a judge in civil court is considered a thief, because he forces people to pay money even when the Halacha does not necessarily require the payment.

Rav Yisrael Rozen, in his dedication of *Teḥumin* vol. 31 in memory of Rav Eliyahu, writes:

> At Machon Tzomet, we have stored numerous rulings of Rav Eliyahu regarding security in settlements and the Israel Defense Forces on Shabbat, as well as other government and communal service providers, such as hospitals, fire departments, and allied sectors. All of these rulings were thoughtful and effective.[3]

THREE SPECIFIC AREAS OF DISAGREEMENT

Three disputes regarding *tefilla* bring to life the difference in approach between Rav Mordechai Eliyahu and Rav Ovadia in terms of conflicting fidelity to the *Ben Ish Ḥai* and the *Bet Yosef.*

ONE WHO OMITS *HAMELECH HAMISHPAT*

Rav Ovadia (*Teshuvot Yeḥaveh Da'at* 1:57) famously rules that a Sephardic Jew who omits "*haMelech hamishphat*" during the *Aseret Yemei Teshuva*

2. Rav Eliyahu writes that the same applies to observant Jews serving as journalists working in a predominantly secular framework.
3. Rav Rozen was the long serving head of Machon Tzomet, which works to forge a working connection between Torah, the State of Israel, and contemporary Israeli society.

must repeat his *Amida*, in accordance with the ruling of the *Shulḥan Aruch* (*Oraḥ Ḥayim* 582:2). Rav Mordechai Eliyahu (*Siddur Kol Eliyahu; Teshuvot Ma'amar Mordechai, Aseret Yemei Teshuva* 19), on the other hand, rules that one should follow the ruling of the *Ben Ish Ḥai* (year 1, *Parashat Nitzavim* 19).[4]

SHE'ASA LI KOL TZORKI ON TISHA B'AV AND YOM KIPPUR

Rav Ovadia for many years ruled that one should not recite the *beracha* of *She'asa Li Kol Tzorki* on Tisha B'Av and Yom Kippur. Since this *beracha* is an expression of thanks for shoes (*Berachot* 60b), this *beracha* would appear to be inappropriate for Tisha B'Av and Yom Kippur, when we are forbidden to wear leather shoes. However, later in life, in his *Ḥazon Ovadia* (*Yamim Nora'im*, p. 320), Rav Ovadia disagreed with the *Ben Ish Ḥai* and ruled that a person should indeed make the *beracha* of *She'asa Li Kol Tzorki* even on Tisha B'Av and Yom Kippur.[5]

Among Rav Ovadia's explanations are that since there are Jews who legitimately wear shoes on Tisha B'Av (for example, a pregnant woman or the elderly), all Jews may say *She'asa Li Kol Tzorki* on Tisha B'Av and Yom Kippur. Most important for Rav Ovadia, Rav Yosef Karo does not distinguish between Tisha B'Av and Yom Kippur and all other days with regard to this *beracha*. Thus, *She'asa Li Kol Tzorki* should be said even on these two days.

Rav Mordechai Eliyahu (*Siddur Kol Eliyahu*) remains loyal to the ruling of the *Ben Ish Ḥai* (year 1, *Parashat Vayeshev* 9) that we should follow the Ari z"l, who urged that *She'asa Li Kol Tzorki* should not be recited on Tisha B'Av and Yom Kippur.[6]

---

4. This issue is discussed at length in Chapter 45.
5. I heard Rav Yitzḥak Yosef explain that in his earlier years, Rav Ovadia would apply the principle of *saba"l* (*safek berachot l'hakel*, omitting a *beracha* in case of doubt) in regard to this issue. However, in later years Rav Ovadia was more confident and felt we should undoubtedly follow the straightforward meaning of the *Shulḥan Aruch* and not concern ourselves with the *Kabbala*-influenced rulings of the Ari z"l in this context.
6. Interestingly, the Moroccan *siddurim* indicate agreement with Rav Ovadia regarding this issue. In general, Moroccan *posekim* are less influenced by kabbalistic concerns in their halachic rulings than other Sephardic decisors.

RECITING THE *AMIDA* AUDIBLY

Finally, Rav Eliyahu and Rav Ovadia disagree as to which is the proper way to recite the *Amida* – silently or audibly. The *Shulḥan Aruch* (*Oraḥ Ḥayim* 101:2) rules that when praying the *Amida,* one must move his lips and enunciate the words; thinking the words in one's mind does not fulfill the obligation. This is indicated in the verse describing the prayer of Ḥannah, mother of the *navi* Shmuel: "Only her lips were moving..." (*Shmuel I* 1:13). This view of the *Shulḥan Aruch* is shared by all authorities.

There is, however, disagreement among the authorities as to how loudly the *Amida* should be recited. The *Shulḥan Aruch* rules that one should recite the *Amida* softly enough that those standing near him will not hear his prayer, but loudly enough to allow him to hear his own prayer. Among the Kabbalists, however, we find a different tradition in this regard. The *Ben Ish Ḥai* (year 1, *Parashat Mishpatim* 3) cites from the *Zohar* that while one must enunciate the words of *tefilla,* they should not be audible even to the extent that the one praying hears the words. The *Ben Ish Ḥai* cites from the Ari z"l's student, Rav Ḥayim Vital, that if one's prayer is even slightly audible, the "*ḥitzonim*" (harmful spiritual forces) are capable of disrupting the prayer's efficacy and preventing it from reaching its destination.[7]

Nonetheless, the *Ben Ish Ḥai,* in his work *Od Yosef Ḥai* (*Parashat Mishpatim* 3), rules that the *halacha* on this issue depends on the individual's ability to properly pronounce the words and concentrate on his prayer. One who feels that he can accurately enunciate the words and pray with concentration when reciting the *Amida* inaudibly should do so, in accordance with the approach of the *Zohar* and Rav Ḥayim Vital. If, however, one suspects that he might swallow his words or experience difficulty concentrating unless he recites the *Amida* audibly, he should follow the *Shulḥan Aruch*'s ruling and pray the *Amida* loudly enough to hear his words.

Rav Mordechai Eliyahu (*Siddur Kol Eliyahu*) rules in accordance with the *Ben Ish Ḥai.* By contrast, Rav Ovadia Yosef (*Halichot Olam* 1:157; *Yalkut Yosef, Oraḥ Ḥayim* 101:2:1) writes that the *halacha* follows the position of the *Shulḥan Aruch,* that the *Amida* should be recited audibly. Of course, those who recite the *Amida* audibly must ensure to recite it softly enough

7. The *Ba'er Hetev* (*Oraḥ Ḥayim* 101:3) writes that the practice of the Ari z"l was to pray very low during the week; only on Shabbat did he raise his voice a bit.

that only they – and nobody else in the synagogue – can hear their prayer, in keeping with the example set by Ḥannah.

CONCLUSION

Rav Mordechai Eliyahu unfortunately does not get much attention, even among Sephardic Jews in the United States. However, his influence in certain circles in Israel, especially in the Ḥaredi Le'umi community, is profound.[8] While his halachic style may not suit every individual or every Sephardic community, his voice must be considered in rendering decisions, especially for the Sephardic community.

Far from detracting from the greatness of Rav Ovadia, considering Rav Eliyahu's opinions actually enhances Rav Ovadia's influence. A great musician, *l'havdil,* is enhanced when teamed with other great musicians. The symphony of Sephardic Halacha is similarly upgraded by including the entire cast of great players in the orchestra.

8. Rav Eliyahu's influence in the area of *taharat hamishpaḥa* is especially strong due to the flourishing of Machon Pu'ah, which assists couples experiencing fertility challenges. Machon Pu'ah is led by Rav Menahem Burstein, a leading student of Rav Eliyahu.

Most interestingly, Rav Eliyahu's influence extends to both Ashkenazic and Sephardic members of the Religious Zionist community in Israel.

Chapter 100

Rav Ben Tzion Abba Sha'ul: The Quintessential Sephardic *Rosh Yeshiva*

A review of contemporary Sephardic Halacha is not complete without discussing the great Rav Ben Tzion Abba Sha'ul. Of the great Sephardic *posekim* of the second half of the twentieth century, he may be regarded as the quintessential Sephardic *Rosh Yeshiva*.

In contrast to his peers, the three great Sephardic *posekim* of his time – Rav Ovadia Yosef, Rav Shalom Messas, and Rav Mordechai Eliyahu – Rav Ben Tzion did not serve as a longtime member of an established *bet din*. Rather, Rav Ben Tzion entered the iconic Sephardic Yeshiva Porat Yosef (located in Jerusalem's Old City) at the tender age of eleven and never left until the day he left this world at the age of seventy-four. Unlike his peers, he never served in an official rabbinic capacity. Rather, he died as the *Rosh Yeshiva* of Yeshivat Porat Yosef, and this is what characterized him and established his specific niche in the world of Sephardic Halacha.

Not surprisingly, the Sephardic Ḥaredi community has a special affinity for Rav Ben Tzion's rulings. For example, the Lakewood Yeshiva trained

Rav Eli Mansour, a leader in the Syrian Jewish community of Brooklyn, New York, very frequently cites and follows the rulings of Rav Ben Tzion.[1]

A STRICTER APPROACH IN HALACHA

In general, Rav Ben Tzion adopted a more strict (and, one might say, less pragmatic) approach to Halacha than his peers, as would typify one who spent his entire life in the *yeshiva*. A case in point is the stance Rav Ben Tzion adopts towards the *Heter Mechira*.

The *Heter Mechira* refers to the highly controversial sale of Israeli farmland to sidestep the restrictions of the *shemitta* year. While Rav Ovadia Yosef (*Teshuvot Yabia Omer* 10: *Yoreh De'ah* 37–43) vigorously defends the validity of the *Heter Mechira*,[2] Rav Ben Tzion does not accept its validity (introduction to *Teshuvot Ohr L'Tzion, Hilchot Shevi'it*). Although Rav Ovadia notes that the Sephardic tradition of the past hundred years has been to uphold the validity of the *Heter Mechira*, Rav Ben Tzion was very much influenced by the *Ḥazon Ish*,[3] who strongly rejected the *Heter Mechira*.

Another example is Rav Ben Tzion's firm insistence that males must wear a hat in addition to a *kippa* during *Birkat HaMazon* (*Teshuvot Ohr L'Tzion* 2:13:3). This contrasts with Rav Ovadia Yosef and Rav Yitzḥak Yosef, who believe that while it is preferable to do so, strictly speaking, it is not necessary.

A BALANCED APPROACH

However, Rav Ben Tzion did not always adopt the strict stance to halachic issues. In fact, Rav Shmuel Khoshkerman reports that Rav Ben Tzion did not fully subscribe to Rav Ovadia's prohibition of a wig (*sheịtel*) for married women (see *Teshuvot Yabia Omer* 5: *Even HaEzer* 5).[4]

---

1. Rav Ben Tzion made a number of highly memorable and well-received visits to the Syrian communities of Brooklyn, New York and Deal, New Jersey, whose impact remains until today. For a vivid description of these visits see http://communitym.com/article.asp?article_id=102378.
2. Rav Ovadia does rule that it is preferable to be strict about this matter.
3. Another example of this influence is the fact that Rav Ben Tzion follows the *Ḥazon Ish*'s ruling regarding a larger *shiur*, despite the fact that this deviates from Sephardic tradition (introduction to *Teshuvot Ohr L'Tzion*, vol. 2).
4. Rav Ben Tzion seems to permit wearing a wig in *Teshuvot Ohr L'Tzion* 1:11. However, there is considerable discussion regarding his precise view on this topic.

Moreover, Rav Ben Tzion does not subscribe to the dominant approach in the Ashkenazic Ḥaredi community that the current generation must adopt a stricter approach than was done in prior generations. For example, while it is accepted in Ashkenazic circles to adopt a strict approach to folding clothes and a *tallit* on Shabbat, Rav Ben Tzion sanctions following the accepted Sephardic practice to adopt the lenient approach to this matter (*Teshuvot Ohr L'Zion* 2:24:3–4).[5]

Another difference between Rav Ben Tzion and Ashkenazic Ḥaredim relates to the relationship to non-observant Jews. For Sephardic Jews, family connections are overwhelmingly important, and even Ḥaredi Sephardic Jews maintain warm connections with non-observant relatives (and vice versa).[6] Thus, it is not surprising that Rav Ben Tzion permits giving an *aliya* to a non-observant relative at a family *simḥa* (*Teshuvot Ohr L'Tzion* 2:9:8), which would be anathema at an Ashkenazic Ḥaredi event.

RICH DISAGREEMENTS WITH RAV OVADIA

Rav Ben Tzion disagreed with Rav Ovadia on a wide variety of topics. These disagreements serve as a springboard for rich halachic analysis. One locus of the disagreements is *Teshuvot Yabia Omer* 9: *Oraḥ Ḥayim* 108, where Rav Ovadia devotes no less than 42 pages to explain at length 195 (!) disagreements with Rav Ben Tzion on a wide variety of issues.

On a personal note, Rav Ben Tzion was a classmate of both Rav Ovadia and Rav Mordechai Eliyahu and maintained a warm relationship with both of his great peers throughout his lifetime.

Rav Shalom Messas also vigorously disputed Rav Ovadia's stringent approach to wigs (*Teshuvot Tevu'ot Shemesh, Even HaEzer* 137; *Teshuvot Shemesh U'Magen* 1: *Oraḥ Ḥayim* 42:5; 2: *Even HaEzer* 15–16; 3: *Oraḥ Ḥayim* 3:32:7; 3: *Even HaEzer* 47:2, 39; 4: *Even HaEzer* 93). It seems that much of the Sephardic community has not, in fact, accepted the ruling of Rav Ovadia. However, Rav Shlomo Amar told me that although those who are lenient have authorities upon whom to rely, he believes it is proper to follow Rav Ovadia's ruling regarding this matter.

5. For further discussion, see *Teshuvot Yeḥaveh Da'at* 2:40.
6. At a family *simḥa*, I noticed Rav David Bouganim, a respected Sephardic Rosh Kollel in Bnei Brak, having a warm and heartfelt conversation with his not fully observant teenaged niece. The Sephardic niece, in turn, harbors enormous respect for her uncle. She remarked to me, "What a cool uncle I have!" regarding Rav Bouganim.

CONCLUSION

A thoughtful student once remarked that Moshe Rabbenu's humility convinces him of the authenticity of the Torah. It is fair to compare Rav Ben Tzion Abba Sha'ul to Moshe Rabbenu in this regard. Rav Ben Tzion's humility was stunning. For example, Rav Ben Tzion never pushed to advance to the role of *Rosh Yeshiva* of Porat Yosef, and even declined the position when it was offered to him, while his teacher, Rav Yehuda Tzadka, remained alive. In addition, he declined to publish his *sefarim* until he became seriously ill.[7] Rav Ben Tzion's humility convinces me of his authenticity as a true *gadol* (great Torah leader).

Rav Ben Tzion's dignified endurance of his long years of illness bears witness as well to his tremendous and authentic devotion to *Hashem*, Torah, and his many students, who continue to make a major and ongoing contribution to the Torah world. The Sephardic community takes enormous pride in Rav Ben Tzion, who rightfully takes his place astride the great Sephardic *posekim* of his time, Rav Ovadia Yosef, Rav Shalom Messas, and Rav Mordechai Eliyahu.

PERSONAL REMINISCENCES OF RAV BEN ZION BY MRS. LOREE COHEN OF ENGLEWOOD, NEW JERSEY

Rav Abba Sha'ul and his family and my husband Elie's family lived in the Beit Yisrael neighborhood along Reḥov Shmuel HaNavi in Yerushalayim. Life was precarious in this neighborhood prior to the Six Day War, as it straddled the border with Jordan. This neighborhood is where so many of the great rabbis of that generation were raised, such as Rav Ovadia Yosef, Rav Baruch Ben Ḥayim of Brooklyn, Rav Tzadka, and others. Today, the Mir Yeshiva flourishes in this neighborhood. Tradition has it that this neighborhood is built over the area where the ashes of *korbanot* from the *Bet HaMikdash* were buried.

Rav Abba Sha'ul's father and my father-in-law, Binyamin, along with a few others, formed Kehillat Ohel Raḥel, which is still led by the Abba Sha'ul family. This is where Rav Abba Sha'ul delivered his weekly *derasha* on Shabbat for many years. This is also where my brother-in-law, *Ḥazan* Yaacov Cohen, learned the *tefilla* that he brought to the Sephardic *kehilla* of Englewood.

---

7. As noted in the introduction to *Teshuvot Ohr L'Tzion*, vol. 1.

The families were very close. When my husband Elie was born, Rav Abba Sha'ul told Elie's father that since his uncle Elazar had no children, the baby should be named for him – and that is why Elie is named Elazar! Over the years, we would visit Rav Abba Sha'ul whenever we traveled to Israel. On two occasions when Rav Abba Sha'ul came to America, we had the privilege of hosting him at our house in Englewood, together with his wife, son, and his oldest grandson. I remember that on one occasion, in around 1980, I took them shopping to Alexander's Department Store, which was then located in Paramus. I remember how he wanted his wife Hadas to buy a few dresses (including a sweater dress, so that she would be warm). I remember the extreme *kavod* (honor) that he showed to her.

Rav Abba Sha'ul was so humble that he did not want people to stand for him. When he would attend the *bet kenesset,* he would wait to enter until everyone was already standing. He never sought honor; he desired only to study Torah.

My son Ben and daughter Kiki had the great honor to spend Shabbat with Rav Abba Sha'ul at his Jerusalem home, but this occurred after he had already suffered a stroke and was unable to speak. Ben and Rav Abba Sha'ul's grandson, Benzion, took Rav Abba Sha'ul down the steps in a wheelchair to get to the *tefilla.*

We remain in touch with many members of the Abba Sha'ul family until today. When my son Isaac studied in Israel for the year, one of his teachers was the nephew of Rav Abba Sha'ul. Our connection with the Abba Sha'ul family is one of the most special memories of our family!

Chapter 101

Rav Ḥaim David HaLevy: The Sephardic Chief Rabbi of Tel Aviv

Rav Ḥaim David HaLevy served with distinction as the Chief Rabbi of Tel Aviv from 1973–1998, succeeding Rav Ovadia Yosef in that position.[1] He composed volumes of very accessible *teshuvot* entitled *Aseh Lecha Rav,* in which he responded to an astonishing range of questions for an equally astonishing range of ordinary Israelis.[2] He composed *Kitzur Shulḥan Aruch Mekor Ḥayim,* a one-volume digest of Halacha providing practical conclusions only, which served as the standard text for teaching Halacha at Religious Zionist schools in Israel for decades.[3] Rav HaLevy

1. I had the honor and pleasure of personally meeting Rav HaLevy at the Tel Aviv Bet Din in July 1993 while training to be a *mesader gittin* (Jewish Divorce Administrator). I was struck by Rav HaLevy's regal and dignified bearing on the one hand and his kind manner on the other.
2. These volumes stemmed from Rav HaLevy's popular Israeli radio program by the same name.
3. Rav HaLevy also composed a five-volume *Mekor Ḥayim* with explanations of his rulings.

is also noted for devoting much attention in writing to the relationship between Medinat Yisrael and Halacha.

Despite all of this, mention the name of Rav Ḥaim David HaLevy to even knowledgeable Sephardic Jews, and many will say they never heard of him!

ONE OF THE PORAT YOSEF STARS OF THE 1930–1940S

Four great Sephardic luminaries emerged from iconic Sephardic *yeshiva* Porat Yosef (located in the Old City of Jerusalem) in in the 1930s and 1940s: Rav Ovadia Yosef, Rav Mordechai Eliyahu, Rav Ben Tzion Abba Sha'ul, and Rav Ḥaim David HaLevy.

However, unlike the other three scholars, who were profoundly influenced by Porat Yosef's *Rosh Yeshiva*, the great Rav Ezra Attia, Rav HaLevy was deeply influenced by Porat Yosef's *Nasi* (president), Rav Ben Tzion Ḥai Uziel, who also served as Rishon L'Tzion, the Sephardic Chief Rabbi of Israel. The special connection between these two great *Rabbanim* may have been due to their shared Turkish Jewish background. Rav HaLevy was particularly influenced by Rav Uziel's enthusiasm for Religious Zionism and his pragmatic approach to Halacha. He even became Rav Uziel's assistant for a significant amount of time.

TESHUVOT ASEH LECHA RAV

Teshuvot Aseh Lecha Rav belongs in the home of every Jew. Here is a sampling of some of the topics of the questions posed to Rav HaLevy by Israelis of all religious backgrounds that he addresses in the first volume of this wonderful work: Extravagant weddings and bar mitzvahs, transcendental meditation, the Yom Kippur War as *Milḥemet Gog U'Magog,*[4] and Palestinian or Jordanian rule in Yehuda V'Shomron. These are examples of issues not typically dealt with in more conventional works of halachic responsa.

Of course, Rav HaLevy also responds to many conventional questions, such as if it is permissible to visit a church or mosque, if a religious male Israeli army medic may administer an injection to a female soldier, and the like. Most important to Rav HaLevy was to provide Torah guidance to Israelis of all backgrounds, in a manner and language that speaks to a very

4. This disastrous war, described in *Yeḥezekel* 38, will usher in the Messianic age.

wide audience.[5] It was, in my opinion, providential for him to serve as Chief Rabbi of Tel Aviv. Residents of this diverse city were and still are most in need of the religious leadership style offered by Rav HaLevy.

BOLDNESS IN HALACHA

Rav HaLevy's bold approach to Halacha is succinctly expressed in an essay printed in *Teḥumin* (vol. 8, p. 367). Rav HaLevy speaks about the need for halachic creativity within the bounds of tradition. He makes a dramatic assertion: "Whoever is bonded to the written Halacha of the prior generations is a 'halachic Karaite.'[6] He is attached to the written letter and rejects the oral law."

Since Rav HaLevy's comment can be misconstrued, I share the example he provides in this essay – youths interacting with non-Jewish counterparts about intellectual and social concerns. While Rav HaLevy is not comfortable with such meetings between religious and secular youths, he feels that Jews have something to learn from the outside world and may be exposed to the thought of others outside our nation. However, he insisted on strict gender separation during these meetings.[7]

TWO FAMOUS RULINGS

The two rulings for which Rav HaLevy is most well known are his rulings regarding smoking and the recitation of *Naḥem* on Tisha B'Av.

Rav HaLevy is regarded as the first *posek* of note to formally and officially declare that smoking is forbidden according to the Halacha (*Teshuvot Aseh Lecha Rav* 2:1, 3:18, and 9:28–29). Rav HaLevy labels smoking as "slow suicide." He notes:

5. A noteworthy example is Rav HaLevy's ruling (*Teshuvot Aseh Lecha Rav* 3:16) permitting giving an *aliya* (among the usual seven *aliyot*) to someone who clearly drove to the *bet kenesset* on Shabbat. Rav HaLevy explains that although strictly speaking such an individual should at most receive only an added *aliya* to the required seven *aliyot* of Shabbat, in our times we must seek ways to draw non-observant Jews closer to observance. Many Sephardic and Ashkenazic *batei kenesset* follow this approach.
6. Karaites are Jews who believe exclusively in the authority of the Written Torah but reject the authority of the Oral Law.
7. The insistence of separation of the genders is a recurring theme in Rav HaLevy's writings. See, for example, *Teshuvot Aseh Lecha Rav* 1:73.

> In enlightened countries, smoking is banned in public places, commercial advertisements of smoking are banned, and manufacturers of cigarettes are compelled to print health warnings on every pack of cigarettes. Should we, whose holy Torah is a *Torat ḥayim* (a life-giving Torah), lag behind?

Rav HaLevy (*Teshuvot Aseh Lecha Rav* 6:58, 7:65) addresses the question as to whether one must honor his father's request to purchase cigarettes for him. Normally, Halacha requires one to fulfill a parent's request for service (*Kiddushin* 31b). On the other hand, one is not required to follow a parent's order to violate Halacha (*Bava Metzia* 32a). Rav HaLevy rules that one should not give his father cigarettes if he requests them. Rather, he should politely and gently explain to his father (in accordance with *Shulḥan Aruch, Yoreh De'ah* 240:11) that smoking is very dangerous and that the Torah obligates us to preserve our bodies.

Rav HaLevy's ruling regarding smoking, issued in the 1970s, was quite bold, in light of the fact that so many Rabbis and Torah scholars at that time (sadly) smoked. Nonetheless, Rav HaLevy set the bar, and by the 2000s, nearly every rabbi of major stature has declared smoking to be forbidden.[8]

Another famous ruling issued by Rav HaLevy is his stance regarding modern day recital of *Naḥem,* the prayer for the rebuilding of Jerusalem and the *Bet HaMikdash* added to the *Amida* on Tisha B'Av.[9] In this special *beracha,* we describe Yerushalayim as "the mournful, destroyed city, degraded, desolate without inhabitants." After our recapture and reunification of Jerusalem in 1967, the question arose as to whether the language of *Naḥem* needs to be adjusted to fit the new reality.

Rav HaLevy felt that while it was too soon to change the prayer, it is dishonest to say in our *tefillot* to *Hashem* that Jerusalem is in a state of destruction and denigration. After all, the *gemara* (*Yoma* 69b) teaches that we cannot be dishonest in our prayers to *Hashem*! Therefore, he advocated adding the word "*shehayeta,*" "that was," before the words of destruction,

---

8. See my *Gray Matter,* vol. 3, pp. 15–27.
9. While Ashkenzic Jews recite *Naḥem* only at *Minḥa,* many Sephardic Jews recite this prayer during each of the *tefillot* on Tisha B'Av. We discuss this topic at length in Chapter 66.

indicating that the city had been destroyed, but no longer is (*Teshuvot Aseh Lecha Rav* 1:14, 2:36–39, 7:35).

Indeed, the reality of Yerushalayim seems to accord with this approach. More than a half a million Jews currently reside in Yerushalayim, many or even most of them are observant, and tens of thousands of them are devoted to full-time Torah study. The Jewish Quarter of Yerushalayim is pulsating with Jewish life. The synagogues destroyed by Arabs during the years of Jordanian occupation between 1948 and 1967 have almost all been restored, with even more glory than before. The Kotel HaMa'aravi has more than ten million visitors per year. Even though more than fifty years have passed since the Kotel has been restored to Jewish control, the Jewish attachment to the Kotel grows in intensity as each year passes, as the number of visitors continues to soar. As Rav HaLevy argues, how can we describe Yerushalayim as destroyed and desolate in the current condition?

Although Rav HaLevy's position on this issue was accepted within certain portions of the Religious Zionist community, it has not been accepted by most Jews. Most Sephardic congregations do not implement Rav HaLevy's recommendation and continue to recite the traditional text without emendation. At Congregation Shaarei Orah, for example, we do not accept Rav HaLevy's ruling on this matter.[10]

CONCLUSION

I asked a young Sephardic Rav if he ever heard of Rav Ḥaim David HaLevy. His answer was, "Yes – I think he wrote *Teshuvot Aseh Lecha Rav*." In other words, Rav HaLevy was barely on his radar. It is time to change this unfortunate state of affairs. I recommend that *Rabbanim* and learned laymen incorporate *Teshuvot Aseh Lecha Rav* in their learning and teaching. We may not necessarily follow each one of Rav HaLevy's rulings, but his is an important late twentieth-century halachic voice that we should not and cannot continue to ignore.

10. See my essay archived at https://www.koltorah.org/halachah/reciting-nacheim-on-tishah-beav-in-2014-by-rabbi-chaim-jachter, where I present at length why both Rav Yosef Dov Soloveitchik (cited in *Nefesh HaRav*, p. 79) and Rav Ovadia Yosef (*Teshuvot Yeḥaveh Da'at* 1:43) roundly rejected Rav HaLevy's proposals.

Epilogue

Four Common Questions about Sephardic and Ashkenazic Jews

As a conclusion of our exploration of the differences between Ashkenazic and Sephardic practice, we will address four frequently posed questions about the differences between the two Jewish groups.

QUESTION #1 - WHY ALL THESE DIFFERENCES?

Many ask why there are so many differences between Sephardic and Ashkenazic practice. I respond that the differences should not be as surprising as compared to that which is shared. While at first there seem to be many differences, to the keen observer the differences are vastly outnumbered by that which is common between the groups. I would estimate that 90–95 percent of the practices are the same. Certainly the core is identical. The differences are limited, for the most part, to style and nuance.

I am fond of retelling a conversation I had with Congregation Shaarei Orah member Dr. Binyamin Benson (formerly Binyaminzadha), who arrived in Teaneck, New Jersey in 2000 after arriving in the United States from Iran. I asked him in 2002 how long it took him to adjust to the Ashkenazic *tefilla* at the school he attended (Torah Academy of Bergen County). He answered, "One week."

One week? After Binyamin's family lived in Persia/Iran for millennia, thousands of miles from Ashkenazic Jews, it took only a week for him to adjust to Ashkenazic *tefilla*?!

This reminded me of the summer of 1984, when I spent two months in a special program helping Jews in the poor section of Tel Aviv known as the HaTikvah Quarter. I often prayed during that summer at the Yemenite *bet kenesset* located next door to the house our group rented. It also took me only a short while to adjust to the Yemenite *tefilla,* even though I had never been exposed to such services before.

The fact that after thousands of years and thousands of miles of separation we find it easy to learn each other's *minhagim* is a grand testament to each community's preservation of the *mesora* (tradition) of our people. While each group certainly has its own unique flavor and style, we have all successfully preserved the core of Torah.

Our loyal adherence to the *mesora* has preserved *Am Yisrael* as a nation. The fact that Sephardic and Ashkenazic Jews share a common Torah is what unites us as a people. It is the reason why Ashkenazic and Sephardic Jews marry each other with great frequency, *baruch Hashem*. Rav Sa'adia Gaon was certainly correct when he declared, "*En umatenu uma ela b'Torah*" (the Torah is what forms us into a nation) (*Emunot VeDe'ot* 3:7).

This, in turn, imposes a solemn responsibility upon our shoulders. There is a well-known story about Ḥoni HaMa'agel, who saw an old man planting a carob tree (*Ta'anit* 23b). Carob trees take seventy years to bear fruit. Why, then, was this old man bothering to plant the tree? The man responded: "I found ready grown carob trees in the world; as my forefathers planted these for me, so I too plant these for my children."

Similarly, just as our ancestors preserved the *mesora* for us, it is our solemn obligation and responsibility to preserve our tradition for future generations.

QUESTION #2: WHO DECIDED TO MAKE THE BREAK BETWEEN SEPHARDIC AND ASHKENAZIC JEWS?

The division into Sephardic and Ashkenazic Jews was not a matter of choice, but rather resulted from the difficult circumstances of the *galut* (exile), which compelled Jews to scatter throughout the world. The Jews that resettled in lands on the Mediterranean Sea and the Middle East became known as Sephardic Jews; Ashkenazic Jews were those who moved to France and Germany.

The slight nuanced differences emerged mostly due to the slight differences between the *batei midrash* (houses of study) in the different lands. Rashi and the *Ba'alei HaTosafot* had great impact on Ashkenazic practice, while the Rif and Rambam exerted profound influence over Sephardic practice.

But all the while, *Rabbanim* were in contact with each other and learned each other's Torah works. The Rambam was familiar with the practices of Jews in Ashkenazic lands (see, for example, *Hilchot Issurei Bi'ah* 11:6–7), and the *Ba'alei HaTosafot* cite the Rambam (see *Tosafot, Berachot* 44a, s.v. *al ha'etz*).

Most famously, of course, the Jewish People share one code of law, the *Shulḥan Aruch*. While Ashkenazic Jews generally follow the Rama and Sephardic Jews generally follow the rulings of Rav Yosef Karo, we both share that one book as the authoritative work on Jewish practice. Thus, despite the many years of exile and many miles separating us, Torah leaders made heroic and successful efforts to unite us as one people.

QUESTION #3: IS THERE A SOURCE IN THE TORAH FOR VARIATIONS IN PRACTICE?

I once heard Rav Yosef Dov Soloveitchik share that he had been bothered by this question for many years. He responded that an answer may be found in the Ramban's comment to *Devarim* 16:18, which indicates that each *shevet* needs its own supreme *bet din*. The Ramban explains that each supreme *bet din* of each *shevet* is authorized to issue enactments for its *shevet*, in accordance with its specific needs.

Clearly, then, some practices varied among the *shevatim;* practice among the different tribes was not be uniform. We see from this, Rav Soloveitchik explains, that the Torah allows for some degree of variety in practice among the different groups of Jews. Rav Soloveitchik concluded that just as there were small differences in practice among the different *shevatim*, so too there are small differences among the different communities that exist today, such as Sephardic and Ashkenazic Jews.

QUESTION #4: WILL THE DIFFERENCES BETWEEN SEPHARDIC AND ASHKENAZIC JEWS REMAIN IN MESSIANIC TIMES?

This is quite a challenging question. On the one hand, the *navi Yeḥezkel* (ch. 37, the *haftara* for *Parashat Vayigash*) envisions a time of a united *Am*

Yisrael, all together under one king (37:22). However, this may refer only to political unity.

At the very end of *Sefer Yeḥezkel,* however, the *navi* describes a vision of Yerushalayim at the time of the rebuilt third *Bet HaMikdash,* when Jerusalem will be blessed with twelve gates. Each of these twelve gates is designated as corresponding to one of the twelve *shevatim.* In other words, the division into twelve tribes will persist into the age of *Mashiaḥ.*

If the division into *shevatim* persists, that means that the divisions of the various groups within our people, which correspond to the different *shevatim,* will also persist into the Messianic era.

Of course, during the times of *Mashiaḥ,* brotherhood and love will prevail among our people. The different divisions of our nation will live in harmony and respect with one another. Differences need not be a source of tension if each group harbors respect and affection for the other groups.

CONCLUSION

Our division into Sephardic and Ashkenazic Jewry should not be seen as an unwanted relic and legacy of the many years of the exile. Rather, it is a healthy expression of the legitimate variety within our nation. As long as Sephardic and Ashkenazic Jews maintain a commitment of reverence and esteem for each other, the divisions will not serve as a source of tension, but rather part and parcel of a truly Messianic vision for our people.

We hope that this book plays an important role in the realization of this magnificent vision.

Appendix A

Comments by Rabbi Mordechai Lebhar on *Bridging Traditions* which accompanied Rabbi Lebhar's Michtav Beracha

אמרתי להעיר הערות קצרות כפי מסת הפנאי יען שענינים אלו חביבים הם עלי במיוחד, וארשום מקצת מהרהורי הדברים בבחינת תן לחכם, ועוד חזון למועד.

א) **מש"כ לגבי ברכת המינים**, הגם שכתבנו במגן אבות (או"ח ס' ק) שהורה לנו מרן הגריש"א זצ"ל דהגם שרוב ככל הראשונים גורסים "זדים" מכ"מ מאחר שהחיד"א כתב לומר מינים, הכי יש לנהוג. הן עתה ראיתי בהג' לרבי רפאל אבן צור זצ"ל (הוצאת אהבת שלום-מקבציאל) שגם חיזק לומר מינים. ברם, נתגלה לאחרונה, שכל מקורו של החיד"א מסידור הר"ש ויטאל, והרי בסידורו העתיק גם גרס זדים! וכן נתגלה אצל סידורי האריז"ל ועוד מקורות, נמצא שמלבד החמדת ימים, אין כמעט מקור לברכת המינים. וכמו ששינו מזדים למינים, כי יש לצדד שיש לחזור ולשנות לזדים. מאחר שנתגלה כמה וכמה מקורות לזה.

ברם, מאידך יש לטעון שא"כ אכן כן, יש לנו לשנות לפתיחת הברכה "למשומדים" שכן הגירסא האמיתית וכבר מטא משמיה דהגר"ח מבריסק

זצ"ל שיש לשנות, אל"כ יש חשש משנה ממטבע, וע"כ ממה שלא שינו הו"ל "כקודשו הטעות," (כענ"ז השיב מרן הגרש"א זצ"ל בענין אחר ודו"ק). ואולי עדיף לחתום כדברי הסידור האר"י שממנו ציין החיד"א "מינים וזדים" כדי לצאת לכו"ע, ואין זה חותם בשנים. חדא כעין מה שחותמים על המחיה ועל הכלכלה שהכל ענין אחד. ואין לטעון שזה כנגד מנהג, שהרי קשה לקבוע מנהגים בנוסחאות התפלה כמו שכתבתי בשרשים בספר מגן אבות (יו"ד), וגם אין בזה נוסח ברור מאחר שבסידורים כתוב זדים בסוגריים ויש שאמרו אותו כן, ואולי ע"י שאומר מינים וזדים אינו נחשב כמשנה המסורה שסו"ס מזכיר מינים בחתימה.

ברם, ירא אני לשלוח יד במה שכבר קיבלו רבותינו לשנות. ועדיין נבוך אני בזה.

ב) **מש"כ לגבי שיר של יום:** ע' מה שכתבנו במגן אבות שמנהגנו במערב הפנימי שבימים מיוחדים שאומרים מזמור מיוחד, רק אומרים המזמור ותו לא. וכבר האריך בזה בספר חקרי לב (או"ח ס'לב).

ג) **מש"כ לגבי תפילין דר"ת** מסתברא שבזמנינו שכבר רבים לובשים תפילין דר"ת מכמה סיבות. יש שקיבלו עליהם הוראות הגר"ע יוסף זצ"ל, ורבים מהם אפ' אינם ת"ח לובשים, א"כ תו לא שייך יוהרא. וכן שמעתי ממרן הגריש"א זצ"ל וע' במגן אבות (או"ח ס' לד).

ד) מש"כ לגבי מצה בזמנינו לספרדים. הארכתי בתשובה שבזמנינו מסתבר לברך על מצה המוציא, והא לך לשון החיד"א וז"ל במח"ב (ס' קנח) שכתב לדחות טעמו השני של הבית דוד "והטעם האחר, דהיה פת בחג הפסח יש לדחות **דאימא תמיד נעשה על דעת כיסנין** ובפסח קובע סעודה ומברך המוציא וברהמ"ז כדין פהב"ב דכשקובע עליו דינו כפת גמור וכו.' ,הד" דמפורש שמצה נעשית ע"ד כיסנין. ואינ"ז המציאות בזמננו אלא במציות קטנות, אבל במצה רגילה, הרי זה תחליף לפת לרובא דעלמא. וגם הגר"ג בן משה שליט"א כתב לי כן.

ה) **מש"כ לענין חלה מתוקה** הארכתי במקום אחר שבזמנינו יש לברך על חלה מתוקה המוציא ובפרט בצירוף דברי המג"א, ובפרט בשבת שקובע כדברי הזרע אמת, וגם פעמים רבות אוכל כשיעור פת לפי חשבון כזית לפי

החזו״א. ואכ״מ אמנם שו״ר שכן דעת הרבה פוסקים ספרדים לברך המוציא בלחמניות מתוקות. בשו״ת והשיב משה ח״ב ס׳ יט לרבי משה מלכה זצ״ל כתב וז״ל אשר לאותם האוכלים לחמניות מתוקות באולמות הרי דינם מפורש בשו״ע או״ח ס׳ קסח ס״ו שאם קובעים עליהם סעודה צריכים נט״י והמוציא ואפילו לאכלן עם בשר ודגים. וכ״כ רבי משה לוי בספרו ברכת ה׳ חלק ב עמוד קפח וכ״כ בשו״ת שערי ציון בוארון ח״א ס׳ ה ושם כתב שכן דעת הרה״ג שלמה עמאר שליט״א. עיי״ש. [דלא כפי שהבאתם משמו]. ושכן דעת הרב יצחק ירנן ח״ו ס׳ י, וכן שמעתי מהג״ר יעקב בנאים שליט״א שכן מורה ובא.

ו) **מש״כ לגבי עניית ברוך הוא וברוך שמו**, יש לציין שלפני שהסתפק הדבר שמואל אם לענות בהוב״ש לא מצאנו בפוסקים שכתבו להמנע מזה, ופשטות לשון הטור והשו״ע שעל כל ברכה וברכה שאתה שומע לענות... משמע דעל כל ברכה צריך לענות.

ברם, דא עקא שענין זה של עניית בהוב״ש נהיה כ״כ מזולזל בעיני העם שאפ׳ על ברכות שכו״ע אינם יוצאים ידי חובתם אינם עונים בהוב״ש מחמת הרגלם שלא לענות.

וכפי שהבאתם ידוע שהגר״י אבוחצירא זיע״א חרה אפו בענין זה, ופעמים רבות חיכה כדקה (!) עד שיענו בהוב״ש על ברכותיו (וע׳ בדברי האביר יעקב בספר שערי תשובה ס׳ כג בענין גודל חשיבות עניית בהוב״ש ותבין מהיכן נובע קפידא זו).

וגם ידענא מעשה שהיה שהגר״ש משאש זצ״ל הוזמן לברך על כוס של מילה בישיבה של ספרדים בעלי תשובה מפורסם, וכשהמתין אחרי שהזכיר שם ה,׳ כדי שיענו בהוב״ש (שהרי בזה כו״ע אינו מוציא אותם ידי חובתם). אין קול ואין עונה, וחרה אפו עד מתי ה׳ ששומעים שמו הקדוש ולא עונים. אתמהה.

אשר ע״כ ברור שהרוצה לנקוט כדברי החיד״א שהעונה אפי׳ על ברכות שיצא יד״ח אין מוחין בידו, רשאי אע״פ שאין זה מנהגו, מאחר שהענין בזמנינו נחלש בעו״ה, גם בברכות שלא יוצאים יד״ח. ודי בהערה זו.

ז) **מש"כ לגבי ברכת להכניסו**. תימה להורות כנגד השו"ע למי שאין לו מנהג. ולענ"ד ברור שמי שאין לו מנהג בזה שינהג כעיקר דברי מר"ן שאין לנו אלא דבריו.

ח) **מש"כ לגבי ברכה על הדלקת נר שבת**, יש לציין שלא מצאנו אצל הספרדים מנהג לברך לפני הדלקת נרות (מלבד הרב גדולת אלישע שהביא שני מנהגים בבגדד), ורק המאמר מרדכי כתב מדיליה לברך לפני כהרמב"ם אבל מנהג ספרדים ואשכנזים מדורי דורות לחוש לשיטת הבה"ג ולהדליק ואח"כ לברך ואדרבה, אם בירכה לפני ההדלקה הערה"ש מתבטא שהרי זה "כברכה לבטלה" לומר על הדלקת נר שבת ושוב להדליק, רק מרן הגרע"י ביבי"א (ח"ט ס' כד) בהערה שם בעוצם גדלותו כתב שגדול הדור רשאי לשנות מנהגים, אבל ברור שהמנהג הקדום היה לברך אחרי ההדלקה.

ט) **מש"כ לגבי עמידה בעשרת הדברות** יש לציין שגם אחרי שיצא הרמב"ם נגד המנהג, אעפ"כ המשכו קהילות רבות לעמוד בעשרת הדברות, ועיני ראו ולא זר היראת שמים המרובה שהקהילות קיבלו כשעמדו בעשרת הדברות, ויש לשקול בפלס לפני שמבטלים מנהג כמה יראת שמים מפסידים מזה, ובפרט שבזמנינו לא שייך טענות מינים הללו כמו שבזמן הרמב"ם.

י) **לענין אמירת עננו בערבית של צום** מה שכתבתם שלא ראינו קהילות נוהגים כן, בזמנינו, קהילות רבות החזירו העטרה ליושנה, והתחילו שוב לנהוג כדעת מר"ן ולהכריז בערבית של צום לומר עננו. וכהמנהג הקדום, ומה שקהילות רבות של יוצאי מרוקו לא אומרים אותו, אין זה אלא מהרגל וחוסר ידיעה.

יא) **אנו נוהגים כדעת מר"ן לומר הפטרת שובה בצום גדליה**. וכמנהגים רבים שיוצאי המערב הפנימי נוהגים כמר"ן דלא כפי שנוהגים רבים מעדות המזרח דלא כמר"ן בזה.

יב) **גם בתפילין בשחרית ת"ב** נוהגים כדעת מר"ן שלא ללבוש תפילין דר"ת דלא כפי שנוהגים רבים מבני עדות המזרח דלא כמר"ן בזה אלא כמנהג בית אל (אע"פ שאינם עתה בירושלים ותימה הוא).

יג) **לגבי חלק ב"י**, אם הבשר לפנינו, ואינו יודע אם גם הכשר זה מפרישים דוקא חלק ב"י מבשר רגיל, הוי כנאבדה הראיה, ודעת מר"ן שנאבדה

הראיה שרי. וכן שמעתי מהגר״ש מילר שליט״א, וכן פסק בשו״ת יבי״א (ח״ה יו״ד ס׳ ג) שבבשר לפנינו מותר לאכול. ועובדא ידענא שגם הוא נהג כן כשהבשר לפנינו שאכל ממנו.

יד) **לגבי חדש בחו״ל**, יש גם לציין שהכל תלוי באיזה מוצרים ויש לחשוש יותר לחלות, פסטה, פיצה וכל דבר רק שמכיל יותר גלוטן וגם תלוי בזמן העונה קרוב לפסח, ושקשה לברר טפי יש להקל, ועי״ש בתשובותי.

טו) **לגבי שבע ברכות שלא בבית החתן**, עי׳ היטב במגן אבות (שם) שכן עולה גם מדברי מר״ן עצמו.

טז) **לגבי ההסכם טרום נשואין**. הגם שבמרוקו תיקנו הרבנים הסכם טרום נשואין וכ״ש הסכם כזה היו מסכימים, והגר״ש משאש זצ״ל גם הצדיק תקנתם, מכ״מ כתבתי באריכות לכם במקו״א שאינ״ז לכו״ע (שם) ושחידושו של התורת גיטין מבוסס על אמירתו ולא כוונתו, וכל שלא תלה הדברים בגט אלא בדבר אחר זה גט מעושה. וכבר העיר בחזו״א אבה״ע ס׳ צט ס״ק ו ,ועוד טענות ואכ״מ. ובענינים חמורים כהנ״ל אם אפשר לתקן הסכם שילכו לבי״ד מסויים ותו לא, עדיף טפי.

יז) **לגבי מנהג מרוקו בברכה על חצי הלל**, יש לציין שמרן בב״י (פ׳ תכה) מציין לדברי המגיד משנה שמנהג ספרד לברך על חצי הלל כדעת הרי״ף, ולא בלבד אלא מסתבר שגם בא״י לא שינה ממנהגו בספרד לברך על הלל שהרי בשו״ת ב״י כותב בכמה מקומות שלא שינה ממנהגים שהיה נוהג בספרד. וכן נהגו הרבה קהילות ספרד לברך על חצי הלל בר״ח. וגם מר״ן רק כותב שנהגו המסתוערבים בא״י שלא לברך על הלל בר״ח אך אינו מכריע כן.

יח) ע׳ בסו״ס מגן אבות (או״ח) יותר מט״ו מקומות שנוהגים כמר״ן דלא כעדות המזרח, והוא מחמת שנהגו כמנהגי ספרד הקדום, והיו במערב הראשונים בקבלת פסקי מר״ן ביותר עז וביותר שאת.

כעת העמד הקנה עומד על מקומו, ויה״ר שהקב״ה יערה ממרום הרבה ברכה למחבר ולכל עדתו ולכל עם ישראל אמן!

בברכת התורה

מרדכי לבהר